NINTH EDITION

MOTOR LEARNING AND CONTROL

Concepts and Applications

RICHARD A. MAGILL

New York University

The McGraw·Hill Companies

MOTOR LEARNING AND CONTROL, NINTH EDITION
International Edition 2011

10 09 08 07 06 05 04 03 02 01
20 15 14 13 12 11 10
CTF ANL

Photo credits: Page 1: Brand X Pictures/Jupiterimages; **17 (left):** David Madison/Digital Vision/Getty Images; **17 (right):** © Royalty-Free/Corbis; **33:** Courtesy of the Author; **82:** © Steven Mason/Photodisc/Getty Images; **102:** Royalty-Free/Corbis; **125:** Courtesy of Dr. Paul Milgram, Translucent Technologies, Inc., Toronto, Canada; **142 (left):** © Stockbyte/PunchStock; **142 (right):** © Jules Frazier/Photodisc/Getty Images; **152:** © Jules Frazier/Photodisc/Getty Images; **176:** Ryan McVay/Getty Images; **188:** © Kim Steele/Getty images; **200:** © Royalty-Free/Corbis; **207:** © Ryan McVay/Getty Images; **229:** © Karl Weatherly/Getty images; **256:** © Karl Weatherly/Getty Images; **266:** © Royalty-Free/Corbis; **278:** © D.Berry/Photolink/Getty Images; **293:** © Photodisc/Getty Images; **301:** Courtesy of Stephen A. Wallace; **320:** © Brand X Pictures/PunchStock; **342:** © PhotoLink/Getty Images; **374:** © Royalty-Free/Corbis; **404:** © Ryan McVay/Getty Images; **410:** © mylife photos/Alamy; **419:** Courtesy of Mobility Research, LLC, Tempe, AZ; **429:** © Royalty Free/Corbis

When ordering this title, use ISBN 978-007-128940-5 or MHID 007-128940-2

Printed in Singapore

www.mhhe.com

Detailed Contents

UNIT THREE   Attention and Memory   193

UNIT FOUR   Introduction to Motor Skill Learning   247

References can now be found on the book's Online
Learning Center, www.mhhe.com/magill9e.

Preface

This ninth edition of *Motor Control and Learning* extends and updates the major revisions in the previous edition. The many changes in that edition included new chapters, restructured chapters, and new pedagogical features. Based on the insightful comments of people who use this book in their classes and from the reviewers of that edition, those changes were well received. As a result of that reception this new edition focuses on maintaining the chapter structure of the previous edition, while extending and updating the discussion of topics that continue to generate new research as well as interest by practitioners.

This new edition continues features of preceding editions that have distinguished this book from other motor learning and control textbooks. The two most distinctive features continued in the ninth edition are its overall approach to the study of motor learning and control, and the organization of the implementation of that approach. Beginning with the first edition of this book the overall approach has been the presentation of motor learning and control "concepts" to identify the common theme of each chapter. The concepts are generalized statements and conclusions synthesized from collections of research findings. Within each chapter, the organization scheme is designed to first present the concept, then establish the meaningful real-world application of the concept, and then discuss specific topics and issues associated with the concept. Within these discussions are summaries of research evidence, on which we base our present knowledge

of each topic and issue, as well as the implications of this knowledge for practitioners.

Also continued in this edition is the goal of providing an introductory study of motor learning and control for students who aspire to become practitioners in various professions. As in previous editions the achievement of this goal involves the inclusion of research examples that demonstrate the evidence-based foundation for the motor control and learning concepts. It is important to note that the research examples are just that—examples; the intent of the discussion of research about a specific topic, therefore, is not to present an extensive review of the research literature or to investigate the various controversial views that may exist on a topic.

NEW TO THIS EDITION

Enhanced Discussions of the Neural Bases for Motor Control and Learning Concepts

In the previous edition a new chapter (chapter 4) was included that presented an introductory discussion of the neuromotor basis of motor learning and control. This chapter complements the behavioral orientation of the book for the increasing number of students in introductory courses on motor learning and control who plan to go into professions in which this information is essential. In the present edition this neural basis has been extended to be part of the discussions of many of the concepts in the book. These additions are intended to extend those discussions to accommodate students' interests in the study of the neurological aspects of motor learning and control while maintaining the book's behavioral orientation.

New Research

The study of motor learning and control continues to expand throughout the world. This expansion has produced an abundance of new research published since the previous edition. An important goal of this book is to provide research evidence to support the various concepts and applications, so it is essential to regularly update the research to maintain the book's relevance. As in previous editions, each chapter of the ninth edition includes updated research in the text, the *A Closer Look* boxes, and in the *Related Readings* sections. As in previous editions, the intent is to present examples of research studies that provide empirical support for the concepts discussed rather than to provide exhaustive reviews of the available research.

NEW OR EXPANDED TOPICS IN SPECIFIC CHAPTERS

Chapter 1: The Classification of Motor Skills

- Additional discussion of Gentile's motor skills taxonomy to enhance the descriptions of each of the components of the taxonomy

Chapter 2: The Measurement of Motor Performance

- Added a figure to illustrate fractionated reaction time (RT)
- Added two measurement techniques (MEG and TMS) to the section on Brain Activity Measures
- Added "A Closer Look" box to describe a quantitative coordination index for swimming strokes, which includes recommendations for swimmers and coaches

Chapter 3: Motor Abilities

- Added a section devoted to "balance" to the discussion of "Abilities as Individual-Difference Variables"; related the term "balance" to "postural stability"; and elaborated on the distinction between static and dynamic balance
- Added to the discussion of balance a discussion of the Berg Balance Scale (BBS) as an example of the application of the relative independence of static and dynamic balance
- Added "A Closer Look" box to describe a research study that assessed the relationship between falls among the elderly and balance
- Revised the discussion of the relationship between motor abilities and motor skill performance

Chapter 4: Neuromotor Basis for Motor Control

- Updated and expanded "A Closer Look" box discussion of Brain-Computer Interfaces
- Added "A Closer Look" box with an example of research describing brain regions activated when playing a piece of piano music

Chapter 5: Motor Control Theories

- Included a statement explaining why this chapter topic precedes the presentation of specific topics about motor control and learning
- Elaborated on the discussion of the closed-loop control system diagram (figure 5.3) to identify an important limitation of the diagram
- Revised the section discussing "nonlinear changes in movement behavior" to simplify and make it more relevant to real-world motor skills
- Added real-world motor skills examples to the discussion of "attractors"
- Revised the section discussing "coordinative structures" to simplify, provide more examples of real-world motor skills, and enhance application to motor skill performance

Chapter 6: Sensory Components of Motor Control

- Changed chapter title to better describe chapter content and keep it in context of other chapter titles

- Deleted detailed discussion of animal deafferentation studies; summarized them in brief paragraph
- Included information about vision-related issues in motor control and learning to be discussed more specifically in later chapters—to overcome concerns expressed by some reviewers about certain motor control topics not included in this chapter
- Added "A Closer Look" box ("Vision and Proprioception in Gymnastics") to highlight and summarize from previous edition text content about use of vision in gymnastics
- Enhanced discussion about functional roles of rods and cones in motor control in section "The Neural Components of the Eye"
- Enhanced motor control related discussion about monocular vision versus binocular vision

Chapter 7: Performance and Motor Control Characteristics of Functional Skills

- Added a discussion on how vision and movement interact in speed-accuracy skills to section on "The role of visual information in the speed-accuracy trade-off"
- Updated "A Closer Look" box on the use of constraint-induced movement therapy (CIMT)
- Added to discussion of Bimanual Coordination Skills a discussion of why it is more difficult to perform asymmetric than symmetric bimanual skills
- Added a physical rehabilitation application of rhythmic coordination characteristics of gait to section on Head Stability and Locomotion
- Added a discussion of how batting involves perception–action coupling to section on Vision and Baseball Batting

Chapter 8: Action Preparation

- Revised section on Postural Preparation to discuss "anticipatory postural adjustments" more specifically
- Revised and expanded section on "End-state comfort control" to enhance its application to

real-world situations and its significance for understanding preparation for grasping

Chapter 9: Attention as a Limited Capacity Resource

- Added to "A Closer Look" box on "Attention and cell phone use while driving" containing new evidence comparing conversations on cell phones with conversations with passengers
- Moved section on the "action effect hypothesis" from chapter 14 in the eighth edition to section in chapter 9 on "Focusing attention on movements versus movement effects"
- Expanded section on "Focusing attention on movements versus movement effects" to discuss hypothesis on why external focus leads to better learning and performance
- Added section on neural components of "automaticity"
- Changed title of section "Visual Search and Action Preparation" in the eighth edition to "Visual Search and Motor Skill Performance" to reflect broader scope of topics discussed in this section
- Added "A Closer Look" box discussing the "Quiet Eye" in visual search as it relates to performing motor skills

Chapter 10: Memory Components, Forgetting, and Strategies

- Added reference for a discussion on the debate concerning the neural structure of memory
- Updated discussion of the working memory to reflect changes in views since the eighth edition
- Added information concerning brain locations of the components of working memory

Chapter 11: Defining and Assessing Learning

- Related term "adaptability" to "generalizability" to reflect its use in broader contexts

Chapter 13: Transfer of Learning

- Changed title of section "Instructional Methods" in the eighth edition to "Instructional and

Training Methods" to better reflect content and apply to broader contexts

- Added to examples described in section "Instructional and Training Methods"
- Added discussion of fMRI research in section on bilateral transfer explanations to include neural basis of bilateral transfer
- Revised the "motor control explanation" in the section "Why Does Bilateral Transfer Occur?" to add the dynamic pattern theory's answer to this question

Chapter 14: Demonstration and Verbal Instructions

- Added new section "The Neural Basis for Observational Learning: Mirror Neurons in the Brain"
- Added "A Closer Look" box on "Clinical applications of a mirror neuron system"

Chapter 15: The Effect of Augmented Feedback on Skill Learning

- Expanded discussion in "A Closer Look" box of "Augmented Feedback as Motivation"

Chapter 16: Practice Variability and Specificity

- Added to section "Performance errors benefit learning" (p. 370, 8e) examples of evidence from physical rehabilitation research
- Clarified some points that have caused some confusion about the contextual interference effect
- Added a discussion of the relevance of the "challenge point hypothesis" to section on "What are the limits of the contextual interference effect?"
- Updated discussion of explanations for the contextual interference effect to reflect current views

Chapter 18: Whole and Part Practice

- Expanded the discussion of the use of the body weight support (BWS) system to direct

students to a recently published review of research concerning the effectiveness of the use of this system

- Expanded the discussion of the use of auditory cues for gait therapy for Parkinson's disease patients to better reflect the research about this issue
- Expanded and updated the discussion of virtual reality (VR) training in the "Simplification" section

Chapter 19: Mental Practice

- Added discussion of benefits for speed training to section on "mental practice benefits for power training" (changed section title to add "and speed")
- Added information about fMRI based research to section on "brain activity hypothesis"
- Expanded discussion of imagery ability tests to acknowledge availability of more tests than MIQ and to direct students to a published review of these tests

SUCCESSFUL FEATURES

Motor Learning and Control: Concepts and Applications offers the following features from the previous editions that have helped enhance student learning.

Concepts

Each chapter begins with a concept statement to present a principle or conclusion that describes the focus of the chapter. The goal of these statements is to provide students with a guide for understanding the chapter content, which provides the various pieces of information that led to the concept statement.

Applications

Following the concept statement, the applications section describes in practical terms the relevance of the chapter concept and content to everyday experiences and professional practice.

Application Problem to Solve

This feature, which follows the application section at the beginning of each chapter, presents a specific application problem for students to work on as they engage in reading the discussion section of the chapter.

Discussion

This section presents the specific information from which the concept statement was derived. It includes the key topics and issues relevant to the chapter concept along with summaries and examples of research that provide evidence to support the various points presented in the chapter.

A Closer Look Boxes

Each chapter contains several boxes. The title for each box indicates its content. These boxes typically serve one of several purposes: to provide more detail about a research study than is provided in the text; to describe situation(s) that apply a point in the discussion to a professional practice situation; or to describe a relevant issue that allows the student to explore a topic beyond the limits of the text.

Summary

Each chapter concludes with a summary that presents the main ideas addressed in the discussion section. Using this tool, the student can return easily to a topic in the chapter for clarification or study.

Points for the Practitioner

This feature describes how the chapter topic relates to the practice or performance setting. It encourages students to think about how they will use this information in practical ways.

Related Readings

For students who want to know more about a particular topic, this list at the end of each chapter offers carefully selected research journal articles, books, and book chapters for further exploration.

Internet Resources

A list of Web sites is presented at the end of each chapter that invites students to explore topics of special interest.

Study Questions

A set of questions appears at the end of each chapter to encourage students to review and analyze the chapter content.

Specific Application Problem as a Study Question

The final study question presents an application problem to solve as a culminating experience for the student to use the information presented in the chapter. This problem differs from the one located at the beginning of the chapter by describing a situation students might experience in their future professional experience.

Definition Boxes

Key terms, which are highlighted in the text in boldface type, are defined in corresponding boxes for easy reference. Other important terms in the text appear in italics for emphasis.

Lab Links

The previous three editions included, as part of McGraw-Hill's Online Learning Center for this book, a laboratory manual of laboratory experiences for most chapters. These experiences are available for this edition as well. In the ninth edition these laboratory experiences are identified by "Lab Links" boxes in the margins.

Glossary

At the end of the book, all the key terms defined in the definition boxes are included in a comprehensive glossary. This glossary is useful as a quick reference and a helpful review to prepare for examinations.

Name Index

In addition to the regular subject index, this book features a name index, which identifies and locates all the names referred to in the book. Included in this list are the names of important people who have been or are leaders in the field of motor learning and control.

SUPPLEMENTS

Online Learning Center
www.mhhe.com/magill9e
The Online Learning Center for *Motor Learning and Control* includes all the main supplements for the text. Instructors have access to the following:

- **Instructor's Manual** This manual includes key concepts, lecture outlines, suggested activities, and readings.
- **Test Bank** The electronic Test Bank (Microsoft Word files) has been expanded for this edition and includes multiple choice and true-false questions.
- **PowerPoint slides** A comprehensive set of PowerPoint lecture slides for your course completes this package of tools. The Power-Point presentations, ready to use in class, were prepared by the author. The slides correspond to the content in each chapter of *Motor Learning and Control,* making it easier for you to teach and ensuring that your students will be able to follow your lectures point by point. You can modify the presentation as much as you like to meet the needs of your course.
- **Lab Manual** The online Lab Manual to accompany *Motor Learning and Control* is an interactive tool that helps students put their knowledge about motor skills into practice in various professional settings as well as in everyday life. The Lab Links boxes in the text direct students to chapter-related experiments presented in the Lab Manual. Sample topics include tapping tasks and Fitts' law, catching a ball when the hands can be seen versus not seen, movement complexity, remembering movements, and the characteristics of novices and experts in performing the same skill.

In addition, links to professional resources are included for instructors.

For students, the Online Learning Center offers the interactive Lab Manual, practice quizzes, glossary, and career information.

ACKNOWLEDGEMENTS

The creation of a new edition of a textbook requires the support of colleagues, friends, and loved ones. In particular I want to acknowledge the support I received from the Steinhardt School of Culture, Education, and Human Development, New York University. I moved to NYU in 2007 after many years at Louisiana State University. At NYU I have been wonderfully supported by Dean Mary Brabeck and several departments in Steinhardt, each of which I want to acknowledge and thank for their continued support: Department of Music and Performing Arts Professions (Larry Ferrara, Director), Department of Applied Psychology (Jacqueline Mattis, Chair), and Department of Physical Therapy (Wen Ling, Chair). Without the excellent support of these individuals this ninth edition would not have been possible. I also want to acknowledge colleagues throughout the world who have told or sent me their ideas and suggestions concerning ways to make the book work better for them in the classes they teach. I greatly appreciate their interest in assisting my efforts to develop this new edition. On a more personal level, I want to again acknowledge and thank my wife, Susan Koff, for her support, encouragement, suggestions, and patience. I once again dedicate this edition to her.

A new edition of a book would not be possible without the effort and encouragement of the developmental and production editors at McGraw-Hill. I thank them both for their direction, suggestions, and patience. Finally, as I have in each of the previous editions, I thank the many undergraduate and graduate students who have been in my motor learning classes. Few of them will ever know how much I have learned from them and how they have influenced much of the content of this book.

The publisher's reviewers made especially helpful comments and suggestions to guide my revision of the previous edition of this textbook. I greatly appreciate these contributions from the following reviewers: David Anderson, San Francisco State University; Stephen Juaire, Winona State University; Bob Martin, Delaware State University; Duane Millslagle, University of Minnesota–Duluth; Nick Murray, East Carolina University; and Marcio Oliveira, University of Maryland–College Park.

Richard A. Magill
New York City, New York

 This text is available as an eTextbook from CourseSmart, a new way for faculty to find and review eTextbooks. It's also a great option for students who are interested in accessing their course materials digitally and saving money. CourseSmart offers thousands of the most commonly adopted textbooks across hundreds of courses from a wide variety of higher education publishers. It is the only place for faculty to review and compare the full text of a textbook online, providing immediate access without the environmental impact of requesting a print exam copy. At CourseSmart, students can save up to 50 percent of the cost of a print book, reduce their impact on the environment, and gain access to powerful Web tools for learning including full text search, notes and highlighting, and email tools for sharing noted for sharing notes between classmates. For further details contact your sales representative or go to www.coursesmart.com.

To My Lovely Wife
Susan Ruth Koff

UNIT ONE

Introduction to Motor Skills and Abilities

CHAPTER 1

The Classification of Motor Skills

Concept: Motor skills can be classified into general categories.

After completing this chapter, you will be able to

■ Define and distinguish the terms *actions* and *movements,* and give examples of each

■ Describe the one common motor skill characteristic for each of three motor skill classification systems, the two categories of skills in each system, and examples of motor skills in each category of each system

■ Describe the two dimensions used to classify skills in the Gentile taxonomy of motor skills and the classification characteristic included within each dimension

■ Discuss ways to use the Gentile taxonomy of motor skills in physical rehabilitation or physical education and sport contexts

APPLICATION

When people run, walk with an artificial limb, throw a baseball, hit a tennis ball, play the piano, dance, or operate a wood lathe, they are engaged in the performance of a type of human behavior called *motor skills.* In this book, the focus is on helping you understand how people learn, and how you can help people learn, motor skills such as these.

As you engage in this study, you will find it useful to draw general conclusions to apply what you learn to a broad range of motor skills, rather than making many specific statements about many skills. The starting point for doing this is the classification of motor skills into broad categories that emphasize the similarities rather than the differences among skills.

For example, the skill of maneuvering a wheelchair through a crowded hallway and that of hitting a pitched baseball seem quite distinct. However, both skills have one characteristic in common that influences the learning and performance of them. People must perform both skills in an "open" environment.

This means that to perform the skill successfully, a person must adapt certain aspects of his or her movements to changing characteristics in the performance environment. For the wheelchair skill, this means that the person must be able to maneuver successfully through a crowded hallway in which people are walking in various directions and speeds. For hitting a baseball, the changing environment involves the ball itself as it moves toward the person. For both of these skills, performance success requires the performer to adapt quickly and accurately to changing conditions. When we view them in terms of this common characteristic, we can see that these two seemingly diverse skills are related.

Application Problem to Solve Identify five motor skills that you can perform, either those that you do routinely or those you do for recreation, fitness, or sports, and classify each into one of the categories in each of the motor skill classification systems you will study in this chapter; indicate why each skill would be classified this way.

DISCUSSION

To begin our study of motor learning and motor control, we will describe how researchers and professionals use these two terms to delineate areas of research and professional application. Both areas of study share a focus on the performance of **motor skills,** which we define as *activities or tasks that require voluntary head, body, and/or limb movement to achieve a specific purpose or goal.* Researchers study motor skills in many ways. Two are especially relevant to discussions in this book: *motor learning* and *motor control;* a third (known as *motor development)* is commonly related to these two areas of study, but it is not a focus of this book.

The study of **motor learning** emphasizes the acquisition of motor skills, the performance enhancement of learned or highly experienced motor skills, or the reacquisition of skills that are difficult to perform or cannot be performed because of injury, disease, and the like. Of interest are the *behavioral and/or neurological changes* that occur as a person learns a motor skill and the variables that influence those changes. An example of a question that a motor learning researcher would seek to answer is, Does the type of feedback an instructor gives to a person learning (or relearning) a motor skill influence how quickly and how well the skill will be learned?

In the study of **motor control,** the question of interest is how our neuromuscular system functions to activate and coordinate the muscles and limbs involved in the performance of a motor skill. Researchers may investigate this question while a person is learning a new skill or performing a well-learned or highly experienced skill. An example of a question that a motor control researcher would seek to answer is, Are the movements of the arms and legs coordinated in similar or distinct ways when a per-son walks or runs at various speeds?

A related area of study, known as **motor development,** concerns issues related to either or both motor learning and control, but is primarily interested in the relationship between these issues and human development from infancy to old age. An example of a question that a motor development researcher would seek to answer is, How do the elderly compare with young adults in terms of how quickly they can decide what they need to do to avoid a collision with another person while walking in a crowded hallway?

In their investigations researchers in these areas of study assume that motor skill performance is influenced by the (1) motor skill, (2) performance environment, and (3) physical and cognitive characteristics of the person performing the skill (see figure 1.1). Researchers use this assumption to investigate questions about learning, control, and development from *behavioral and/or neurophysiological levels of study.*[1] At the *behavioral level,* researchers investigate questions by observing and analyzing human behavior as it is affected by characteristics of any or a combination of these influences. Researchers may observe people performing motor skills in laboratory, clinical, or natural settings. To answer the research questions described in the preceding paragraphs, researchers could engage in either the behavioral or

[1]You will sometimes see the term *level of analysis* rather than *level of study.* We will consider these phrases to be synonymous and interchangeable.

---

motor skills   activities or tasks that require voluntary head, body, and/or limb movement to achieve a goal.

motor learning   the study of the acquisition of motor skills, the performance enhancement of learned or highly experienced motor skills, or the reacquisition of skills that are difficult to perform or cannot be performed because of injury, disease, and the like. Of interest are the behavioral and/or neurological changes that occur as a person learns a motor skill and the variables that influence those changes.

motor control   the study of how our neuromuscular system functions to activate and coordinate the muscles and limbs involved in the performance of a motor skill. Researchers may investigate this question while a person is learning a new skill or performing a well-learned or highly experienced skill.

motor development   the study of human development from infancy to old age with specific interest in issues related to either motor learning or motor control.

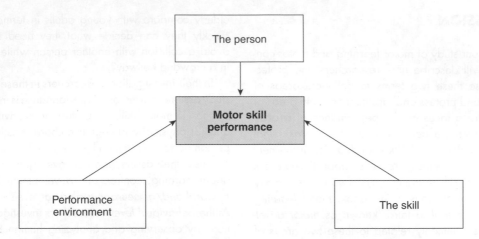

FIGURE 1.1   Three influences on how we perform a motor skill. To understand the learning and control of motor skills, it is important to recognize that the performance of any motor skill is influenced by characteristics of the skill itself, the person performing the skill, and the environment in which the skill is performed.

neurophysiological level of study. As you will read in chapter 2, researchers, as well as practitioners, use a variety of performance measures to quantitatively or qualitatively evaluate a person's performance of a skill. Researchers who study motor learning, control, and development will often use their observations of behavior (i.e., motor skill performance) to infer neurophysiological mechanisms that are responsible for the behavior. For investigations at a neurophysiological level of study, researchers directly or indirectly observe central and peripheral nervous system components as they interact with muscles involved in performing a motor skill.

The focus of this textbook is on motor learning and control without reference to developmental concerns, although developmental relevance is considered in a few instances. Also, while you will be introduced to some neurophysiological aspects of motor learning and control, a behavioral level of study dominates the textbook's approach. In addition, you will see evidence for and examples of how the three influences on motor skill performance, as described in the previous paragraph, form the basis for our understanding of the learning and control of motor skills.

To establish a foundation on which to build your study of motor learning and control, it is essential to have a good understanding of motor skills, which

are the focus of both areas of study and are an important component of the three general influences on motor skill performance depicted in figure 1.1. To help you develop your understanding of motor skills, the remainder of this chapter will address two important points. First, we will consider what distinguishes motor skills from other skills and define some other commonly used terms related to the term *motor skill*. Second, we will discuss four different approaches to classifying motor skills into categories that identify common characteristics of various skills.

The benefit of classifying skills is that it can provide you with an appropriate basis for establishing generalizations, or principles, about how we perform and learn motor skills. These generalizations will enable you in turn to understand theories about skill performance and learning. Additionally, they help establish guidelines for instructors, coaches, and therapists who must develop effective strategies that will enhance motor skill learning and rehabilitation.

SKILLS, ACTIONS, AND MOVEMENTS

Several terms in the motor learning and control literature are related to the term *motor skills*. These are *skills*, *actions*, and *movements*. Each term is used in a specific way you should understand and use correctly.

Skills and Actions

The term **skill** is a commonly used word that in this text denotes an activity or *task that has a specific purpose or goal to achieve.* For example, we commonly say that "multiplication is a fundamental skill of mathematics" or "playing the piano is a skill that takes practice." Of these two examples, the skill of piano playing includes a *motor skill* because it requires voluntary limb movement to achieve its goal, which is to play the piano. Looked at this way, the skill of piano playing involves the goal of striking the correct keys in the proper sequence and at the appropriate time, and it requires finger and hand movement to achieve that goal.

It is important to point out that multiplication, which was used in the previous paragraph as an example of a skill, is commonly referred to as a *cognitive skill.* This means that the skill requires cognitive (i.e., mental) activity, which includes decision making, problem solving, remembering, and the like. It differs from a motor skill in that it does *not* require head, body, and/or limb movement to achieve its goal. Although a person could use a motor skill such as handwriting or pressing the keys on a calculator or computer to carry out the multiplication task, movement activities such as these are not required. In contrast, the skill of piano playing involves cognitive activities, but requires hand and finger movements.

In the motor learning and control research literature, a term that has become increasingly common is the term **actions.** For our purposes, we will use this term synonymously and interchangeably with the term *motor skills.*

Characteristics of skills and actions. Several characteristics are common to motor skills. First, there is *a goal to achieve.* This means that motor skills have a purpose. Sometimes you will see the term *action goal* used to refer to the goal of a motor skill. Second, the types of motor skills of interest in this text are *performed voluntarily;* in other words, we are not considering reflexes as skills.

Although an eye blink may have a purpose and involve movement, it occurs involuntarily and is therefore not a skill in the sense in which we are using the term. Third, a motor skill *requires head, body, and/or limb movement* to accomplish the goal of the task. This characteristic is especially important because it is the basis for distinguishing motor skills from other types of human skills.

One additional characteristic identifies the types of motor skills of interest in this text: they *need to be learned, or relearned,* in order for a person to achieve the goal of the skill. In our example, piano playing clearly must be learned. But consider a skill like walking. Although walking may seem to be something that humans do "naturally," it must be learned by the infant who is attempting to move in his or her environment by this new and exciting means of locomotion. And walking is a skill some people may need to relearn. Examples are people who have had strokes, or hip or knee joint replacements, as well as people who must learn to walk with artificial legs.

Movements

In the motor learning and control research literature, the term **movements** indicates *behavioral characteristics of the head, body, and/or a specific limb or combination of limbs.* This means that movements are the component parts of motor skills. A variety of head, body, and limb movement characteristics can occur that enable a person to walk successfully. For example, our arms and legs move in different and distinct ways when we walk on a concrete sidewalk and when we walk on an icy

---

skill   (a) an activity or task that has a specific purpose or goal to achieve; (b) an indicator of quality of performance.

actions   see *motor skills.*

movements   behavioral characteristics of specific limbs or a combination of limbs that are component parts of an action or motor skill.

A CLOSER LOOK

Examples of Skills/Actions, Goals, and Movements

The following examples illustrate how a skill or action can have various goals, which would require movements that differ according to the action goal. For each of the goals within a skill/action, consider different movements that could be used to allow a person to achieve the goal while carrying out the same skill/action.

Skills/Actions	Goal
1. Walking	a. To walk from the front of an empty room to the back of the room
	b. To walk from one store to another store in a crowded mall
	c. To walk on a treadmill
2. Throwing	a. To accurately throw a small round ball at a target on the wall
	b. To throw a small round ball as far as possible
	c. To throw a beach ball to a friend to catch
3. Reaching and grasping an object	a. To pick up a full coffee mug from a table and drink from it
	b. To pick up a bowl of soup to move it from one location on a table to another location on the table
	c. To pick up a can of juice and shake it
4. Sit to stand	a. To stand up from sitting on a wooden chair
	b. To stand up from sitting on a seat in a bus
	c. To stand up from sitting on the side of a bed

sidewalk—or on a sandy beach. However, although the actual movements may differ, the motor skill we perform in each of these different situations is walking.

The important point here is that a variety of movements can accomplish the same action goal. For example, if a person's goal when walking up a set of stairs is to get to the top of the stairs, he or she can achieve this goal by using a variety of different movements. A person can take one step at a time very slowly, or take each step very quickly, or take two steps at a time, and so on. In each situation, the action goal is the same but the movements the person uses to achieve the goal are different. Similarly, if a person's action goal is to throw a ball so that it hits a target—which might be a person who would catch it—the goal can be achieved with several different movement characteristics. For example, the person could throw the ball overhand, sidearm, or underhand. All would achieve the action goal but would use very different movement characteristics.

Why Distinguish Movements from Skills

There are three reasons why it is important and useful to consider movements as distinct from motor skills. First, *people learn actions especially when they begin to learn or relearn motor skills.* Although people must produce movements to perform a motor skill, different people may move in different ways to achieve the same action goal. For example, how many professional golfers swing a golf club exactly alike? All golfers must learn to hit a golf ball with a golf club, but each person will likely have some unique movement characteristics.

Second, *people adapt movement characteristics to achieve a common action goal.* Why do golfers have different swing characteristics, yet achieve the same action goal? People differ in physical features that limit the movement characteristics they can produce to perform a skill. This physical feature limitation is an especially critical concern to take into account when working with people in fitness or physical rehabilitation settings.

Although there may be a "preferred" way for people to walk, certain sensory or motor impairments may not allow a person to walk in that way. But this person can make movement modifications, or even add a physical assistance device such as a cane, and still be able to successfully walk. Even though the gait pattern may look different from the nondisabled pattern, the person can successfully achieve the action goal.

Third, as you will see in chapter 2, *people evaluate motor skill performance and movements with different types of measures.* We typically evaluate motor skill performance in terms of measures that relate to its outcome, such as the distance a person walked, the length of time it took a person to run a certain distance, or the number of points a basketball shot was worth. Movements, on the other hand, are evaluated by measures that relate to specific characteristics of body, head, limb, and/or muscle activity, such as kinematic, kinetic, and electromyographic (EMG) measures. (These measures of movement characteristics will be defined and discussed in chapter 2.)

ONE-DIMENSION CLASSIFICATION SYSTEMS

We can classify motor skills by determining which skill characteristics are similar to those of other skills. The most prevalent approach has been to categorize skills according to one common characteristic. This common characteristic is divided into two categories, which represent extreme ends of a continuum rather than dichotomous categories (as illustrated in figure 1.2). This continuum approach allows a skill to be classified in terms of which category the skill characteristic is more like, rather than requiring that the characteristic fit one category exclusively.

Consider an analogy. The concepts "hot" and "cold" represent two categories of temperatures. Although we typically consider them as distinct categories, we also can view hot and cold as words describing opposite ends of a temperature continuum, because there are degrees of hot or cold that do not fit exclusively into one or the other category. By considering hot and cold as anchor points on a continuum, we can maintain the category distinctions, while at the same time we can more accurately classify various temperature levels that do not fit into only one or the other category.

We will consider three motor skill classification systems that use the one-dimension approach to categorize skills. These classification systems are summarized in figure 1.2.

Size of Primary Musculature Required

One characteristic that distinguishes categories of motor skills is the size of the primary muscle groups required to perform the skill. Skills like walking and hopping do not require as prime movers muscle groups of the same size as those used for skills like piano playing and eating with chopsticks. By distinguishing skills based on the size of the muscle groups required to perform the skills, researchers have established a motor skill classification system in which there are two categories, known as gross and fine motor skills.

To achieve the goals of **gross motor skills,** people need to use *large musculature.* These skills need less movement precision than fine motor skills do. We commonly see skills such as the so-called *fundamental motor skills*—walking, jumping, throwing, leaping, etc.—classified as gross motor skills.

Fine motor skills fall at the other end of this classification continuum. Fine motor skills require greater control of the *small muscles,* especially those involved in hand-eye coordination, and require a high degree of precision in hand and finger movement. Handwriting, typing, drawing, sewing, and fastening a button are examples of motor skills that

---

gross motor skill   a motor skill that requires the use of large musculature to achieve the goal of the skill.

fine motor skill   a motor skill that requires control of small muscles to achieve the goal of the skill; typically involves eye-hand coordination and requires a high degree of precision of hand and finger movement.

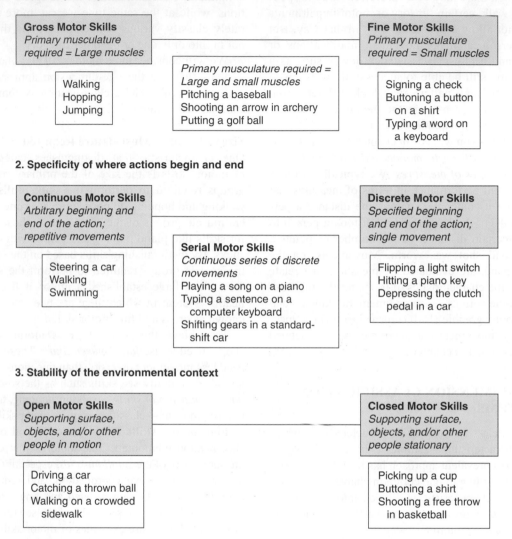

1. Size of primary musculature required

Gross Motor Skills
Primary musculature required = Large muscles

Walking
Hopping
Jumping

Primary musculature required = Large and small muscles
Pitching a baseball
Shooting an arrow in archery
Putting a golf ball

Fine Motor Skills
Primary musculature required = Small muscles

Signing a check
Buttoning a button on a shirt
Typing a word on a keyboard

2. Specificity of where actions begin and end

Continuous Motor Skills
Arbitrary beginning and end of the action; repetitive movements

Steering a car
Walking
Swimming

Serial Motor Skills
Continuous series of discrete movements
Playing a song on a piano
Typing a sentence on a computer keyboard
Shifting gears in a standard-shift car

Discrete Motor Skills
Specified beginning and end of the action; single movement

Flipping a light switch
Hitting a piano key
Depressing the clutch pedal in a car

3. Stability of the environmental context

Open Motor Skills
Supporting surface, objects, and/or other people in motion

Driving a car
Catching a thrown ball
Walking on a crowded sidewalk

Closed Motor Skills
Supporting surface, objects, and/or other people stationary

Picking up a cup
Buttoning a shirt
Shooting a free throw in basketball

FIGURE 1.2   Three one-dimension motor skill classification systems. Each is illustrated as a continuum of the two skill classification categories for the dimension on which the system is based. Also shown are some examples of motor skills for each of the two categories. For the first two classification systems, skills are also shown that best fit on the continuum between the two categories.

are on the fine motor skill end of the continuum in the muscle size classification system. Note that although large muscles may be involved in performing a fine motor skill, the small muscles are the primary muscles involved in achieving the goal of the skill.

We can see the benefit of using a continuum for this skill classification system when we consider motor skills that involve both large and small muscles as the primary muscles required to achieve the action goal. We cannot categorize these types of skills as gross or fine, but, as shown in figure 1.2, these skills would be located along the continuum between these two categories. For example, to shoot an arrow at a target in archery requires the precision in hand and finger control of fine motor skills and the involvement of the larger arm and shoulder muscles that characterizes gross motor skills. Although many fine motor skills may also involve the arm and shoulder muscles (e.g., the three examples in figure 1.2), these do not constitute the primary musculature required. A person could achieve the action goals of these skills with the arms restricted in such a way that he or she would have to use hand and finger movements only.

The use of the gross/fine distinction for motor skills is popular in a number of settings. In education settings, special education and adapted physical education curricula and tests commonly distinguish skills on this basis. We also find this classification system in rehabilitation environments. Physical therapists typically work with patients who need to rehabilitate gross motor skills such as walking, whereas occupational therapists more commonly deal with patients who need to learn fine motor skills. People who are involved in early childhood development also find the gross/fine categorization useful and have developed tests of motor development along the gross/fine dimension. Also, industrial and military aptitude tests commonly use the gross and fine motor skill distinction.

The Specificity of Where Movements of a Skill Begin and End

Another way to classify motor skills is on the basis of how specific the beginning and end locations are for the movements of a skill. If a skill requires a specified beginning and end location, we categorize the skill as a **discrete motor skill.** Discrete skills include flipping a light switch, depressing the clutch of an automobile, and hitting a piano key. Each of these skills involves a specified place in the environment to begin and end movement. Also, as the examples suggest, discrete skills typically are simple, one-movement skills.

At the opposite end of this classification system continuum fall **continuous motor skills,** which are skills with arbitrary beginning and end locations. In addition, continuous skills usually contain repetitive movements. We can classify skills such as steering an automobile, tracking a moving cursor on a computer monitor with a joystick, swimming, and walking as continuous skills. Although some continuous skills, such as walking and swimming, may have distinct movement beginning locations, the end location is arbitrary, and the movements are repetitive.

Sometimes a skill requires a series or sequence of discrete movements, such as shifting gears in a standard shift car, or playing a piece on a piano. We refer to these types of skills as **serial motor skills,** although sometimes they are called *sequential motor skills.* As figure 1.2 indicates, these skills include the repetitive movements characteristic of continuous skills and the specified beginning and end points of each movement that characterize discrete skills. As a result, it is best to locate serial motor skills on the continuum between the continuous and discrete skills categories. The gear shifting example is a good illustration. To shift gears in a car, the driver must perform a sequence of discrete movements. To shift from second to third gear, the driver performs a sequence of seven discrete movements. First he or she lifts a foot off the accelerator, then depresses the clutch with the other foot, then moves the gear shift forward to neutral, then to the right, then forward again to third gear, then releases the clutch, and finally depresses the accelerator.

This classification system has been especially prevalent in the motor control research literature. Researchers have found, for example, that certain phenomena about how we control movement are applicable to discrete skills but not to continuous skills and vice versa. The distinction between

---

discrete motor skill   a motor skill with clearly defined movement beginning and end points, usually requiring a simple movement.

continuous motor skill   a motor skill with arbitrary movement beginning and end points. These skills usually involve repetitive movements.

serial motor skill   a motor skill involving a series of discrete skills.

discrete and continuous skills is especially popular in the research literature of those who view motor skill performance from the perspectives of human engineering and human factors.

The Stability of the Environmental Context

One classification system has its roots in industrial as well as educational and rehabilitation settings. Researchers base this system on the stability of the environmental context in which the skill is performed (see Gentile, 2000). For this classification system, the term **environmental context** refers to the specific physical location where a skill is performed. It consists of *three features:* The *supporting surface* on which the person performs the skill, *objects involved* in performing the skill, and *other people* involved in the performance situation. For example, if a person is hitting a ball, the relevant feature of the environmental context is the ball. For the skill of walking, the relevant environmental context features are the surface on which the person must walk, the presence or absence of an object, and/or other people. And if other people are present, what is their activity? For example, walking while carrying luggage on a moving walkway on which some people are standing and others are walking is a much different, and more difficult, environmental context than is walking in a hallway with no other people.

In this classification scheme, the term *stability* refers to whether the relevant environmental context features are *stationary* (i.e., stable) or *in motion* (i.e., not stable). When the supporting surface, object, or other people involved in the performance of a skill are stationary, the skill is a **closed motor skill.** For these skills, *the relevant environmental context features are stationary, which means they do not change locations during the performance of a skill.* For example, picking up a cup from a table while you are sitting on a chair is a closed motor skill; the chair (i.e., supporting surface) and the cup (i.e., object) do not move between the time you decide to pick up the cup and the moment you pick it up. Walking in a room full of furniture is also a closed motor skill, because nothing in the environmental context moves or changes location while you are walking. Other examples of closed

motor skills are shooting an arrow at a stationary target, buttoning a shirt, climbing a flight of stairs, and hitting a ball off a tee.

An important feature of closed motor skills is that the performer initiates the movements involved in performing the skill when he or she is ready to do so. Because of this timing of movement initiation characteristic, some motor learning and control researchers refer to these types of skills as *self-paced.*

Conversely, an **open motor skill** is *a skill that a person performs in an environment in which supporting surfaces, objects, and/or other people, are in motion while the person performs the skill.* To perform this type of skill successfully, the performer must act according to the movement of a supporting surface, object, and/or other people. Because performers of open skills must time the initiation of their movement with an external feature in the environment, some motor learning and control researchers refer to these types of skills as *externally paced.*

Some examples of open motor skills that involve the performer's supporting surface in motion include driving a car and stepping onto a moving escalator; skills that involve objects in motion include striking a moving ball and catching a thrown ball; and skills that involve other people in motion include walking on a sidewalk crowded with people walking and running a distance race with other runners.

Notice that we have classified the skill of walking as *both an open and a closed skill.* This example illustrates that to classify a skill as open or closed, it is necessary to determine whether or not there are objects or other people in the environmental context and, when there are objects or other people, whether they are stationary or in motion. Also taken into consideration for this distinction is whether the supporting surface on which a person walks is stationary or in motion. This means that when walking occurs in a hallway with no objects or other people, walking is a closed skill. Walking is also a closed skill if objects and/or other people are in the hallway, but stationary. However, if the objects and/or other people are in motion, walking becomes an open skill. Similarly, walking is an open skill when a person walks on a treadmill, which means the supporting surface is in motion. We can make the same distinction for several other motor skills. For example, hitting a ball from a tee is a closed skill, whereas hitting a pitched ball is an open skill. And, throwing a ball is a closed skill when throwing to a stationary person, but an open skill when throwing to a person who is moving.

Consider how closed and open skills differ in terms of the performance demands placed on the person. A person can initiate his or her movements at will when performing a closed skill. In addition, the person does not need to adjust the movements to changing conditions while the performance is in progress. For example, to climb a set of stairs, a person can initiate his or her first step at will. However, quite the opposite is the case when someone performs open skills. To perform an open skill successfully, a person must time the initiation of movement to conform to the movement of the supporting surface, other people, and/or object involved in the action. If, for example, the person must step onto a moving escalator, the timing of when the first step can be initiated must conform to the speed and position of the escalator. And for many open skills, changes can occur while an action is in progress that will require the person to make movement adjustments to conform to these environmental changes. For example, the spin of a tennis ball will influence the direction and height of its bounce, which may require the tennis player to adjust his or her planned movements to return a serve after the ball hits the ground.

The open/closed classification system has achieved a large degree of popularity in instructional methodology contexts and increasing popularity in rehabilitation contexts. A likely reason for this is that the closed and open skill categories relate so generally and easily to the types of motor skills involved in these settings. Skills in each of these categories follow common principles of instruction that instructors and therapists can readily apply to specific situations. The closed and open distinction between motor skills also has become increasingly common in the motor learning research literature,

undoubtedly because of its simplicity and its ability to accommodate both complex "real-world" skills and laboratory skills.

GENTILE'S TWO-DIMENSIONS TAXONOMY

A problem with the one-dimension basis for the classification of motor skills is that it does not always capture the complexity of many skills that a practitioner must take into account when making decisions about instruction, practice routines, or therapy regimens. To overcome this limitation, Gentile (2000) broadened the one-dimension approach by considering two general characteristics of all skills: (1) the *environmental context* in which the person performs the skill and (2) the *function of the action* characterizing the skill. She then subdivided these two characteristics to create an expansive taxonomy that yields sixteen skill categories, depicted in table 1.1. A **taxonomy** is a classification system that is organized according to relationships among the component characteristics of whatever is being classified. For example, taxonomies have been developed in biology to provide systematic classification systems for plants and animals.

---

environmental context   the supporting surface, objects, and/or other people involved in the environment in which a skill is performed.

closed motor skill   a motor skill performed in a stationary environment where the performer determines when to begin the action.

open motor skill   a motor skill that involves a nonstable, unpredictable environment where an object or environmental context is in motion and determines when to begin the action.

taxonomy   a classification system organized according to relationships among the component characteristics of the group of items or objects being classified.

TABLE 1.1 Gentile's Taxonomy of Motor Skills

Environmental ⬇ Context	Action Function			
	Body Stability		Body Transport	
	No Object Manipulation	Object Manipulation	No Object Manipulation	Object Manipulation
Stationary Regulatory Conditions and No Intertrial Variability	**1A** Body stability No object Stationary regulatory conditions No intertrial variability • *Standing alone in a room* • *Practicing a basketball free-throw shot without a ball*	**1B** Body stability Object Stationary regulatory conditions No intertrial variability • *Brushing teeth standing alone at a sink each day of the week* • *Shooting basketball free-throws*	**1C** Body transport No object Stationary regulatory conditions No intertrial variability • *Climbing stairs* • *Running through a basketball play several times without a ball*	**1D** Body transport Object Stationary regulatory conditions No intertrial variability • *Climbing stairs while holding a book* • *Running through a basketball play several times with a ball*
Stationary Regulatory Conditions and Intertrial Variability	**2A** Body stability No object Stationary regulatory conditions Intertrial variability • *Standing on different surfaces* • *Swinging a baseball bat at different ball locations without a bat or ball*	**2B** Body stability Object Stationary regulatory conditions Intertrial variability • *Washing dishes while standing at a sink* • *Putting golf balls from various locations on a putting green*	**2C** Body transport No object Stationary regulatory conditions Intertrial variability • *Walking on different surfaces* • *Running through several basketball plays without a ball*	**2D** Body transport Object Stationary regulatory conditions Intertrial variability • *Walking on different surfaces while carrying a bag of groceries* • *Running through several basketball plays with a ball*
In-Motion Regulatory Conditions and No Intertrial Variability	**3A** Body stability No object Regulatory conditions in motion No intertrial variability • *Walking on a treadmill at a constant speed* • *Passing basketballs to a moving player running the same pattern several times, without a ball*	**3B** Body stability Object Regulatory conditions in motion No intertrial variability • *Walking on a treadmill at a constant speed while reading a book* • *Catching a series of softballs thrown at the same speed by a pitching machine*	**3C** Body transport No object Regulatory conditions in motion No intertrial variability • *Standing on a moving escalator at a constant speed* • *Running through a basketball play without a ball but with moving defenders*	**3D** Body transport Object Regulatory conditions in motion No intertrial variability • *Standing on a moving escalator while holding a cup of water* • *Running through a basketball play with a ball and moving defenders*
In-Motion Regulatory Conditions and Intertrial Variability	**4A** Body stability No object Regulatory conditions in motion Intertrial variability • *Walking on a treadmill at different speeds* • *Passing basketballs to a moving player running different patterns, without a ball*	**4B** Body stability Object Regulatory conditions in motion Intertrial variability • *Walking on a treadmill at different speeds while reading a book* • *Catching softballs thrown at various speeds by a pitching machine*	**4C** Body transport No object Regulatory conditions in motion Intertrial variability • *Walking in a crowded mall* • *Practicing several soccer plays without a ball but with defenders*	**4D** Body transport Object Regulatory conditions in motion Intertrial variability • *Walking in a crowded mall carrying a baby* • *Practicing several soccer plays with a ball and defenders*

Note: (1) The number/letter labels for each skill category were not included in Gentile's original presentation of the taxonomy, but are included here to provide an easy reference to each skill category. The numbers 1–4 represent the four environmental context subdimensions; the letters A–D represent the four action function subdimensions. (2) The two examples of skills for each of the categories include an example of a daily activity skill and one of a sport/physical education skill.

Gentile's taxonomy presents a similar approach to the classification of motor skills.

In addition to providing a classification system for motor skills, Gentile originally proposed this taxonomy as a functional guide for physical therapists to assist them in assessing patients' movement problems and selecting functionally appropriate activities for these patients. However, *the taxonomy is not limited to the physical therapy context.* It provides an excellent basis for understanding the performer demands for a wide variety of motor skills. Everyone who is involved in teaching or training motor skills can benefit from the use of this taxonomy. It is an excellent means of becoming aware of the characteristics that make skills distinct from, as well as related to, other skills. It demonstrates that small changes in certain characteristics of a motor skill can result in a considerable increase in the demands placed on a person to perform the skill. And it is an excellent guide for establishing practice or training routines.

Because the taxonomy is complex, the specific parts of it will be described and discussed in the following sections before discussing the taxonomy as a whole. The two dimensions are discussed separately along with the specific characteristics of each dimension. Use table 1.1 as the basis for identifying these dimensions and their sub-categories.

Environmental Context

The first dimension of Gentile's taxonomy can be seen in the first column of table 1.1. This dimension is the *environmental context* in which a person performs a skill. Two characteristics are involved in this dimension. We see these in the category labels in the first column in table 1.1.

Regulatory conditions. The first environmental characteristic concerns regulatory conditions. This is the term Gentile used to describe the "relevant environmental context features," which we discussed previously in this chapter in the section concerning the motor skills classification scheme based on the stability of the environmental context. The term **regulatory conditions** refers to *those features of the environmental context that*

specify the movements a person must implement to successfully perform a skill. Recall from our earlier discussion about open and closed motor skills that the environmental context features include the supporting surface on which the person performs the skill and any objects or other people that may be involved. It is important to note that regulatory conditions do not refer to characteristics of a person's movements but only to characteristics in the environmental context in which a skill is performed.

Consider, for example, the regulatory conditions involved in walking from one location to another. The surface on which the person walks is a regulatory condition that determines the movement characteristics the person must use to achieve the action goal on that surface. The surface may be soft or hard, rough or smooth, flat or inclined, among other possible characteristics. To walk on a sandy beach, you would very likely move your body, legs, and feet differently from the way you would walk on a concrete sidewalk. Similarly, you would use different movements as you walked on a flat surface compared to a steep incline. Objects and other people may also be regulatory conditions in the walking environmental context. For example, how would your walking movements differ if a child's tricycle were in the pathway from a situation in which no object was there? And how would your walking movements compare when another person walked beside you, behind you, or in front of you?

We can see additional examples of regulatory conditions in the environmental context when a person must manipulate an object. If a person's action goal is to throw a ball to another person, or to catch a ball thrown by another person, important regulatory conditions relate to certain characteristics of the ball, such as size, shape, and weight.

---

regulatory conditions   characteristics of the environmental context that determine (i.e., "regulate") the movement characteristics needed to perform an action.

Examples of Stationary and In-Motion Regulatory Conditions

Stationary Environmental Context

Spatial features of the environment control spatial movement characteristics of an action; the *timing* of the initiation of an action is controlled by the performer.

e.g. picking up a cup
    walking up a flight of stairs
    hitting a ball from a tee
    throwing a dart at a target

In-Motion Environmental Context

Spatial and timing features of the environment control spatial movement characteristics and timing of the initiation of an action.

e.g. stepping onto an escalator
    standing in a moving bus
    hitting a pitched ball
    running on a treadmill

For example, throwing a baseball and throwing a basketball would require distinctly different arm, hand, and finger movements to achieve the throwing action goal. Similarly, a person could catch a tennis ball with one hand, but may need to use two hands to catch a beach ball.

In Gentile's taxonomy, an important distinction for differentiating motor skills is whether the regulatory conditions are *stationary* or *in motion.* Sometimes the regulatory conditions are stationary; this is the case when you walk on a sidewalk or hit a ball off a tee. Sometimes the regulatory conditions are in motion; this occurs when you must step onto an escalator or hit a pitched ball. It is important to note that in this part of Gentile's taxonomy, you can see the application of the closed and open motor skills categories. Skills for which the regulatory conditions are stationary are closed skills, whereas those for which they are in motion are open skills. However, Gentile maintained that this closed/open distinction is too limiting to capture the wide range of skills that people perform every day. Because of this limitation, she added another environmental context characteristic.

Intertrial variability. The second environmental characteristic in the taxonomy is **intertrial variability,** which refers to *whether the regulatory conditions during performance are the same or different from one attempt to perform the skill to another.* We can distinguish motor skills according

to whether intertrial variability is *absent* or *present.* For example, when a person walks through an uncluttered room several times, intertrial variability is absent, because the regulatory conditions do not change each time the person walks across the room. On the other hand, intertrial variability is present when someone walks through a room several times in which various objects are located in different places each time, because each walk through requires the person to walk with different movements to avoid colliding with the objects.

Relating the two environmental context characteristics. One way to illustrate the relationship between the two environmental context characteristics is to use a 2 × 2 diagram, with regulatory conditions either stationary or in motion on one dimension and intertrial variability either present or absent on the other. As you can see in table 1.2, this arrangement creates four distinct motor skill categories.

These four categories are the same as those in table 1.1 in the first column under the heading Environmental Context. Gentile (2000) presented the 2 × 2 array as a preliminary way of presenting the complete taxonomy. The addition of the two intertrial variability categories provides a more realistic way of understanding closed and open skills. For example, shooting free throws in basketball and hitting golf balls during a round of golf

TABLE 1.2 Taxonomy of Motor Skills Based on the Environmental Context Dimension of Gentile's Two-Dimensions Taxonomy

	No Intertrial Variability	Intertrial Variability
Stationary Regulatory Conditions	Closed skills with no intertrial variability • *Free throws in basketball* • *Walking in an uncluttered hallway*	Closed skills with intertrial variability • *Golf shots during a round of golf* • *Taking several drinks of water from the same glass*
In-Motion Regulatory Conditions	Open skills with no intertrial variability • *Hitting tennis balls projected at the same speed from a ball machine* • *Walking on a treadmill at a constant speed*	Open skills with intertrial variability • *Hitting tennis balls during a rally in a game* • *Walking in a hallway crowded with moving people*

Note: This 2 × 2 taxonomy extends the one-dimension classification of open and closed skills by adding the characteristic of intertrial variability.

are both closed skills. But shooting free throws in a game involves no intertrial variability because the regulatory conditions remain the same for each shot, even though the situations in which they are performed may differ. In contrast, hitting golf balls during a round of golf involves regulatory conditions that differ for each shot. Thus, the performance demands of the round of golf require greater amounts of shot-to-shot preparation than shooting a free throw because the golfer cannot plan to repeat the same movements from one shot to the next. Similarly, the regulatory conditions for open skills may remain the same from one performance of the skill to the next. An example is hitting a series of tennis balls projected at the same speed by a ball machine. In contrast, during a tennis match, regulatory conditions change for every shot. Table 1.2 presents a taxonomy of motor skill based on the environmental context dimension of Gentile's two-dimensions taxonomy.

The Function of the Action

The *function of the action* is the second dimension on which the taxonomy is based. This dimension is presented in the top row of table 1.1. We can determine the function of an action by deciding whether or not performing a skill involves moving the body from one location to another, and whether or not the skill involves holding or using an object. Gentile viewed these characteristics as parts of two action functions: body orientation and manipulation.

In the taxonomy *body orientation* refers to the *changing or maintaining of body location.* Two body orientation characteristics are important for classifying motor skills. *Body stability* refers to skills that involve no change in body location during the performance of the skill, such as standing, drinking from a cup, and shooting an arrow in archery. For skills that require the body to move from one place to another, the orientation is *body transport.* Skills such as walking, running, and swimming

intertrial variability   an environmental characteristic in Gentile's taxonomy of motor skills. The term refers to whether the regulatory conditions associated with the performance of a skill in one situation or for one trial are present or absent in the next situation or trial.

A CLOSER LOOK

A Practical Application of the Closed/Open Motor Skills Continuum to Organizing Instruction for Teaching Open Skills

Those who teach motor skills can apply the environmental context dimension of Gentile's taxonomy to the teaching of open skills by changing the 2 × 2 diagram in table 1.2 to the continuum in figure 1.3 to develop a logical progression from completely closed to completely open skills from these components. Consider the following example of a practice sequence when the performance goal of a person is to hit a baseball thrown by a pitcher under game conditions.

1. Practice begins with a closed version of the open skill; the instructor or coach keeps the regulatory conditions "stationary" and has intertrial variability "absent."
   ➡ the learner bats the ball from a batting tee at the same height on each practice attempt
2. Next, the instructor or coach keeps the regulatory conditions "stationary" but has intertrial variability "present."
   ➡ the learner bats the ball from a batting tee, but from different heights on each practice attempt

3. Next, practice proceeds to an open version of the skill; the instructor or coach has the regulatory conditions "in motion" but intertrial variability "absent."
   ➡ a pitching machine that can keep the speed and location of each pitch constant puts the ball in motion
4. Finally, the instructor or coach has the learner practice the completely open skill itself; the regulatory conditions are "in motion" and intertrial variability is "present."
   ➡ a live pitcher pitches the ball using different speeds and locations on each practice attempt

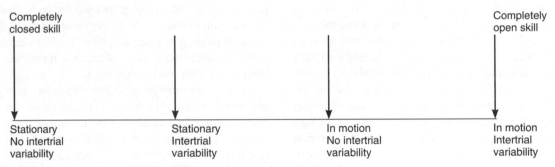

FIGURE 1.3   A skill category continuum for open and closed motor skills. The four subdimensions of the environmental context dimension of Gentile's taxonomy of motor skills on a continuum from the most closed to most open skills.

Note: For research evidence supporting the effectiveness of this progression for helping people learn an open skill, see Hautala and Conn (1993).

involve body transport. It is important to note that *body transport includes active and passive changes of body locations.* This means that both walking, which involves the active changing of body location, and standing in a moving bus, which involves the passive changing of body location, involve body transport.

The second type of action function concerns *object manipulation.* In the taxonomy, the term *manipulation refers to maintaining or changing the position of an object,* such as a ball, a tool, or another person. Another way to think about the meaning of this term would be in reference to *holding or using* an object. Skills that require object

LAB LINKS

Lab 1 in the Online Learning Center Lab Manual for chapter 1 provides an opportunity for you to become more familiar with Gentile's taxonomy of motor skills by applying it to sports skills or to motor skills we experience in the everyday world.

manipulation are more difficult to perform than skills that involve no object manipulation because the person must do two things at once. First, the person must manipulate the object correctly, and second, he or she must adjust body posture to accommodate for the imbalance created by the object.

The Sixteen Skill Categories

The interaction of the four environmental context characteristics and the four action function characteristics creates sixteen skill categories. Table 1.1 shows the critical characteristics of these sixteen categories, along with two examples of skills in each category. Gentile specified that each skill category poses different demands on the performer in terms of the characteristics and number of variables the performer needs to physically control and pay attention to in order to achieve the action goals. Skills that demand the least of the performer are the simplest; those that demand the most are the most complex. Accordingly, the *skill categories in table 1.1 are organized in terms of increasing complexity,* beginning at the top leftmost category with the simplest skills and progressing to the most complex skills in the bottom rightmost category.

The taxonomy specifies that any motor skill must be considered in terms of the environmental context in which it is performed and the functional role it plays when performed. As a result, these two dimensions form the basis for creating sixteen categories of motor skills. The *environmental context dimension* includes the regulatory conditions to which the performer of a skill must conform, and whether these conditions change from one performance attempt to the next. The *action function dimension* establishes that all motor skills are performed to serve a specific purpose, or function. The action function may require the maintaining or changing of the performer's body location and/or the maintaining or changing of the position of objects.

Shooting a basketball free throw and hitting a golf ball are closed motor skills. But, in a basketball game, the regulatory conditions do not change from one shot to the next; in a round of golf, they change from one shot to the next.

A CLOSER LOOK

Examples of Using the Gentile Taxonomy to Evaluate Movement Capabilities and Limitations

Physical Therapy

An evaluation of the static and dynamic standing posture capabilities and limitations of a neurologic or orthopedic patient could follow the sequence of taxonomy categories by progressing across the top row of categories. The patient

1. stands without assistance (category 1A)
2. stands without assistance while holding a book (category 1B)
3. walks without assistance a specified distance in an uncluttered walkway (category 1C)
4. walks without assistance a specified distance in an uncluttered walkway while holding a book (category 1D)

Further assessments could then include standing and walking activities that would follow the progression of skill requirements in the three other rows of skill categories in the taxonomy.

Physical Education

An evaluation of a student's ball-catching capabilities and limitations could use the following sequence of taxonomy categories. The student

1. catches a ball thrown from the same distance at the same speed for several trials (category 3B)
2. catches a ball thrown from various distances at the same speed for several trials (category 4B)
3. catches a ball while running along a line parallel to the thrower for several trials. The ball should be thrown the same distance and at the same speed in each trial, and the student should run at the same speed in each trial (category 3D)
4. catches a ball while running along a line parallel to the thrower for several trials. The ball should be thrown the same distance but at various heights, and the student should run at the same speed in each trial (category 4D).

For both the physical therapy and physical education examples, the performance evaluation steps provide a basis for determining a person's capabilities and limitations by systematically increasing the degree of complexity of the skill. For example, if the physical therapy patient can perform steps one and two but not three, the therapist knows that the patient is capable of static posture without and with holding an object, but has limitations when performing dynamic posture skills. Similarly, if the physical education student can perform steps one and two but not three, the teacher knows the student is capable of catching a ball while standing but has limitations when trying to catch a ball while running. Based on these evaluations, the therapist or teacher can then develop a systematic plan of activities to help the patient or student increase his or her capabilities in the performance of these skills. Note that the examples given here involve two motor skills related to two professions. If you are, or will be, involved in a different profession, develop a sequence of steps similar to those described here but that are specific to a skill you currently teach or would teach.

Practical Application of the Taxonomy

Gentile proposed that the taxonomy has practical value for practitioners. First, it can be a useful guide for *evaluation of movement capabilities and limitations.* The practitioner can determine deficiencies by systematically altering environmental contexts and/or action functions to identify skill performance characteristics that pose difficulty for an individual. For example, a physical therapist could evaluate a neurological patient for static and dynamic standing posture capabilities. The assessment could follow the taxonomy by beginning with the simplest skill situation (category 1A) and then systematically progress to include more complex skill requirements of categories 1B, 1C, and 1D. Similarly, a physical education teacher could use the taxonomy to evaluate a student's ball-catching capabilities and limitations. Because this skill involves in-motion regulatory conditions and the manipulation of an object, the evaluation would include only those taxonomy categories that involve these characteristics (i.e., categories

3B, 3D, 4B, and 4D). And to evaluate the simpler skills before the more complex skills, the teacher should begin with the body stability action function categories (3B and 4B), and then progress to those involving body transport (3D and 4D). By identifying the specific characteristics limiting performance, the therapist or teacher can determine what he or she needs to do to help the person improve his or her performance capabilities.

Second, after the practitioner assesses performance problems, the taxonomy becomes a valuable tool for systematically *selecting a progression of functionally appropriate activities* to help the person overcome his or her deficits and increase his or her skill performance capabilities. This is an important feature of the taxonomy, because it emphasizes the complementary part of the rehabilitation or skill training process. To assess skill deficits is important, but the effectiveness of any rehabilitation or training protocol depends on the implementation of appropriate activities to achieve functional goals for the patient or student. In the activity selection process, the therapist or teacher begins selecting activities related to the taxonomy category in which the person is not capable at first of handling the demands of the skill. Then, the professional can develop a program of rehabilitation or instruction by systematically increasing the complexity of the skills included in the program.

A third practical use of the taxonomy is as a means of *charting the individual progress* of patients or students as they work to attain their rehabilitation or physical activity performance goals. Gentile emphasized the benefit of using the taxonomy to create a "profile of competencies" that can aid the therapist or teacher in the assessment of the effectiveness of the rehabilitation or instructional program he or she developed for the patient or student. Because the taxonomy follows a simple-to-complex progression of skills, it provides an objective basis for determining progress in overcoming skill performance deficits and increasing skill performance capabilities. When used in this way, the taxonomy provides an effective way for the therapist or teacher to establish a record that can satisfy demands for accountability of his or her time and effectiveness.

SUMMARY

- Researchers and professionals use the terms *motor learning* and *motor control* to describe related areas of research and professional application that emphasize specific interests concerning the performing of motor skills. The study of *motor learning* emphasizes the acquisition of motor skills, the enhancement of performance of learned or highly experienced motor skills, and the reacquisition of skills that are difficult to perform or cannot be performed because of injury, disease, and so on. The study of *motor control* emphasizes how the neuromuscular system functions to activate and coordinate the muscles and limbs involved in the performance of motor skills. A related area of study is known as *motor development,* which emphasizes either or both motor learning and control issues but from the perspective of the relationship to human development from infancy to old age.

- *Motor skills* are activities or tasks that require voluntary head, body, and/or limb movement to achieve a specific purpose or goal. Motor skills are commonly distinguished from *cognitive skills,* which are activities or tasks that require mental (i.e., cognitive) activity, such as decision making, problem solving, remembering, and the like. People may use a motor skill to perform a cognitive skill (e.g., using a calculator to solve an addition problem), and they may use a cognitive skill while performing a motor skill (e.g., reading music while playing a piano).

- *Motor skills* and *actions* are similar terms that refer to goal-directed activities that involve voluntary head, body, and/or limb movements. The term *movements* refers to the behavioral characteristics of the head, body, and/or specific limb or combination of limbs that serve as components of actions and motor skills.

- Motor skills can be classified according to common characteristics. One-dimension classification systems place skills into categories based on one common characteristic; two-dimension classification systems place skills into categories based on two common characteristics.

- Three one-dimension classification systems distinguish skills on the basis of (a) the size of the primary musculature required to perform the skill, classifying skills as gross or fine; (b) the specificity of where movements of the skill begin, classifying skills as continuous or discrete; and (c) the stability of the environmental context in which the skill is performed, classifying skills as open or closed.

- Gentile's taxonomy of motor skills is a two-dimension classification system that describes sixteen categories of skills that are created from characteristics associated with the dimensions: the environmental context in which the skill is performed and the function of the action. The taxonomy provides a means of understanding the factors that influence motor skill complexity and the unique requirements placed on a person when he or she performs skills of different complexity. The taxonomy can serve as (1) a useful guide for the evaluation of movement capabilities and limitations, (2) a valuable tool for selecting a progression of functionally appropriate activities to help a person overcome his or her skill performance deficits and increase performance capabilities, and (3) a means of charting the individual progress of physical rehabilitation patients and students as they work to attain specific physical activity performance goals.

POINTS FOR THE PRACTITIONER

- The distinction between actions and movements indicates that you should evaluate a learner's achievement of the action goal of a skill as well as the associated movements. For many motor skills

it is possible for different people to achieve the action goal of a skill by using different movements.

- Understanding the bases for categorizing motor skills can help you determine how different motor skills place different demands on people to learn and perform them. As a result, you can establish teaching and learning conditions that are appropriate for the person or people with whom you work.

- Evaluation of motor skill capabilities and limitations should follow systematic guidelines. The use of a taxonomy of motor skills, such as the one proposed by Gentile, provides a systematic guide that can be used for this purpose.

- After you determine a person's specific motor skill performance deficits and limitations, you can use the Gentile taxonomy of motor skills to plan a progression of appropriate activities to help the person overcome these deficits and limitations as well as improve his or her performance capabilities.

RELATED READINGS

Dawes, J. (2008). Creating open agility drills. *Strength and Conditioning Journal, 30,* 54–55.

Ebben, W.P., Davies, J.A., & Clewien, R.W. (2008). Effect of the degree of hill slope on acute downhill running velocity and acceleration. *Journal of Strength and Conditioning Research, 22,* 898–902.

Kincaid, A. E., Duncan, S., Scott, S. A. (2002). Assessments of fine motor skill in musicians and nonmusicians: Differences in timing versus sequence accuracy in a bimanual fingering task. *Perceptual and Motor Skills, 95,* 245–257.

Maraj, B., Allard, F., & Elliott, D. (1998). The effect of non-regulatory stimuli on the triple-jump approach run. *Research Quarterly for Exercise and Sport, 69,* 129–135.

Mathie, M. J., Celler, B. G., Lovell, N. H., & Coster, A. C. F. (2004).Classification of basic daily movements using a tri-axial accelerometer. *Medical & Biological Engineering & Computing, 42,* 679–687.

Ulrich, B. D., & Reeve, T. G. (2005). Studies in motor behavior: 75 years of research in motor development, learning, and control. *Research Quarterly for Exercise and Sport, 76 (Supplement to No. 2),* S62–S70.

Wulf, G., & Shea, C. H. (2002). Principles derived from the study of simple skills do not generalize to complex skills. *Psychonomic Bulletin & Review, 9,* 185–211. [Note especially the first two sections, pp. 185–187.]

INTERNET RESOURCES

• A book about the design of computer games includes a chapter that presents how the distinction between cognitive and motor skills forms the basis for a taxonomy of computer games. An electronic version of the book (by Chris Crawford) was prepared by Professor Sue Peabody of Washington State University, Vancouver, Washington, where the Web site is maintained. To find the taxonomy chapter, go to http://www.vancouver.wsu.edu/ and type a search for Peabody. Follow the links to the book *The Art of Computer Game Design* and find chapter 3.

• Web sites devoted to providing instructional materials for coaches of sports teams can be valuable resources for finding suggestions about evaluation of motor skill capabilities and limitations, finding instructional strategies for skills, identifying the relationships among the skills of the sport and ways to develop progressions of activities to help develop more complex skills, and so on. An excellent example of this type of Web site is at http://www.webball.com, which is devoted to baseball coaching.

STUDY QUESTIONS

1. Discuss how the terms *actions* and *movements* are related to motor skills. Give an example that illustrates this relationship.

2. What are three reasons for distinguishing between actions and movements?

3. Describe the one dimension that distinguishes the two categories in each of the following skill classification schemes, and give three examples of motor skills for each category: (a) gross vs. fine motor skills; (b) discrete vs. continuous motor skills; (c) closed vs. open motor skills.

4. (a) What are the two dimensions used to classify skills in the Gentile taxonomy? (b) Describe the four classification characteristics included under each of these two dimensions.

5. (a) What does the term *regulatory conditions* refer to in Gentile's skill classification system? (b) Why are regulatory conditions important to consider when categorizing skills?

6. What does the term *intertrial variability* mean in Gentile's skill classification system? How does this term provide an additional characteristic for distinguishing open and closed motor skills? Give two examples of motor skills for each of the four categories of skills that are created by this added distinction.

7. Discuss how you would implement the three practical uses Gentile described for her taxonomy of motor skills.

Specific Application Problem:
(a) You are working in your chosen profession. Describe an open skill with intertrial variability that people you work with would perform.

(b) Describe a sequence of three preliminary skills that you would have people practice to provide them with experiences that would increase their chances for performing the open skill you described in part (a).

(c) Provide a rationale for the sequence of three preliminary skills.

(d) Discuss how you would determine which of the three preliminary skills a person should begin practicing.

(e) Discuss how you would determine the amount of practice that a person should devote to each of the preliminary skills that the person should practice.

CHAPTER 2

The Measurement of Motor Performance

Concept: The measurement of motor performance is critical to understanding motor learning.

After completing this chapter, you will be able to

■ Describe the differences between and give examples of performance outcome measures and performance production measures

■ Describe the differences among simple, choice, and discrimination RT situations

■ Describe three measures for measuring performance outcome accuracy for skills that require discrete spatial and/or temporal accuracy in one and two dimensions and for continuous skills that require spatial and temporal accuracy

■ Define three kinematic measures of motion and describe one way to calculate each measure for a specific movement

■ Describe ways that EMG can be used to provide information about human movement

■ Describe several techniques for measuring brain activity during the performance of a motor skill

■ Describe how angle-angle diagrams provide useful information about the coordination characteristics of limbs or limb segments

■ Describe two methods of quantifying the measurement of coordination during the performance of a motor skill

APPLICATION

Suppose that you are a physical educator teaching your students a tennis serve. What characteristic of performance will you measure to assess students' progress? Consider a few possibilities. You could count the number of serves that land in and out of the proper service court. Or you could mark the service court in some way so that the "better" serves, in terms of where they land, are scored higher than others. Or you could develop a measure that is concerned with the students' serving form.

Now imagine that you are a physical therapist helping a stroke patient learning to walk again. How will you measure your patient's progress to determine if what you are doing is beneficial to his or her rehabilitation? You have several possible walking characteristics to choose from. For example, you could count the number of steps made or the distance walked on each walking attempt; these measures could give you some general indicators of progress. If you wanted to know more about some specific walking-related characteristics, you could measure the balance and postural stability of the person as he or she walked. Or you could assess the biomechanical progress the person was making by analyzing the kinematic characteristics of the movements of the legs, trunk, and arms. Each of these measurements can be valuable and will tell you something different about the person's walking performance.

In both of these performance assessment situations, your important concern as an educator or therapist is using a performance measure, or measures, to make as assessment. As a first step in addressing this problem, you must determine which aspects of performance you should measure to make a valid performance assessment. Then, you must determine how to measure those aspects of performance. The following discussion will help you to know how to accomplish this two-step measurement process by describing several different motor skill performance measures. Throughout this text, we will refer to the various measures introduced in this section, especially as researchers use these measures to investigate various concepts.

> **Application Problem to Solve**   Select a motor skill that you might help someone learn or relearn in your future profession. Which aspects of the person's performance of this skill should you measure to validly assess his or her performance capabilities and limitations? Describe the types of measures you would use to assess these aspects of the person's performance, and describe how these measures would help you determine what you would do to help this person.

DISCUSSION

There are a variety of ways to measure motor skill performance. A useful way to organize the many types of motor performance measures is by creating two categories related to different levels of performance observation. We will call the first category **performance outcome measures.** Included in

this category are measures that *indicate the outcome or result of performing a motor skill.* For example, measures of how far a person walked, how fast a person ran a certain distance, and how many degrees a person flexed his or her knee all are based on the outcome of the person's performance.

Notice that performance outcome measures do not tell us anything about the movements of the limbs, head, or body that led to the observed outcome. Nor do these measures provide any information about the activity of the various muscles involved in each action. To know something about these types of characteristics, we must use measures in the category called **performance production measures.** These measures *relate to performance characteristics that produced the outcome.* As a result, they can tell us such things as how the nervous system is functioning, how the muscular system is operating, and how the limbs or joints are acting before, during, or after a person performs a skill.

Although additional categories of performance measures could exist, these two represent the motor skill performance measures found in this text. Table 2.1 presents examples of these two categories of measures. For the remainder of this discussion, we will discuss several of the more common performance measures found in the motor learning and control research literature.

---

performance outcome measures   a category of motor skill performance measures that indicates the outcome or result of performing a motor skill (e.g., how far a person walked, how fast a person ran a certain distance, or how many degrees a person flexed a knee).

performance production measures   a category of motor skill performance measures that indicates the performance of specific aspects of the motor control system during the performance of an action (e.g., limb kinematics, force, EEG, EMG, etc.).

TABLE 2.1   Two Categories of Motor Skill Performance Measures

Category	Examples of Measures or Measurement Device	Performance Examples
1. Performance outcome measures	Time to complete a task, e.g., sec, min, hr	Amount of time to run a mile or type a word
	Reaction time (RT), e.g., sec, msec	Time between starter's gun and beginning of movement
	Amount of error in performing criterion movement, e.g., AE, CE, VE	Number of cm away from the target in reproducing a criterion limb position
	Number or percentage of errors	Number of free throws missed
	Number of successful attempts	Number of times the beanbag hit the target
	Time on/off target	Number of seconds cursor in contact with target during a computer tracking task
	Time on/off balance	Number of seconds stood in stork stance
	Distance	Height of vertical jump
	Trials or repetitions to completion	Number of trials or repetitions it took until all responses correct
2. Performance production measures	Displacement	Distance limb traveled while moving a cursor on a computer monitor to a target
	Velocity	Speed limb moved while moving a cursor on a computer monitor to a target
	Acceleration	Acceleration/deceleration pattern while moving a cursor on a computer monitor to a target
	Joint angle	Angle of each joint of arm at impact in hitting ball
	Joint torque	Net joint torque of the knee joint at takeoff on a vertical jump
	Electromyography (EMG)	Time at which the biceps initially fired during a rapid flexion movement
	Electroencephalogram (EEG)	Brain wave pattern while shooting an arrow in archery
	Positron-emitting topography (PET)	Brain areas active while typing on a computer keyboard
	Functional magnetic resonance imaging (fMRI)	Brain areas active while finger tapping to a metronome

REACTION TIME

The common measure indicating how long it takes a person to prepare and initiate a movement is **reaction time (RT).** Figure 2.1 shows that RT is the interval of time between the onset of a signal (stimulus) that indicates the required movement and the *initiation* of the movement. Note that RT does not include any movement related to a specific action, but only the time *before* movement begins.

The stimulus (or "go") signal is the indication to act. In laboratory or clinical settings, the signal can take one of a variety of forms, such as a light,

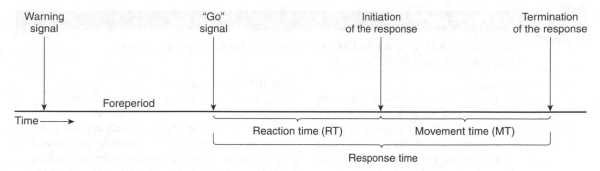

FIGURE 2.1   The events and time intervals related to the typical measurement of reaction time (RT) and movement time (MT).

a buzzer, a shock, a word on a screen, or a spoken word or sound. As such, the signal can relate to any sensory system—vision, hearing, or touch. The person can be required to perform any type of movement. For example, the person might be required to lift a finger off a telegraph key, depress a keyboard key, speak a word, kick a board, or walk a step. Finally, to assess optimal RT, some type of warning signal should be given prior to the stimulus signal.

The Use of RT as a Performance Measure

Reaction time has a long history as a popular measure of human motor skill performance. Although RT can be used as a performance measure to assess how quickly a person can initiate a required movement, researchers and practitioners also use it as a basis for inferring other characteristics related to performing a motor skill. The most common is to identify the environmental context information a person may use while preparing to produce a required action, which will be the topic of discussion in chapter 8. For example, if one performance situation results in a longer RT than another situation, the researcher can determine what may have led to the different RT lengths, which then can tell us something about influences on the amount of time it takes us to prepare an action. In chapter 8 you will study several ways that researchers use RT as a performance measure to investigate how we prepare to perform a motor skill and the factors that influence this preparation.

Another use of RT is to assess the capabilities of a person to anticipate a required action and determine when to initiate it. In a sport situation, a basketball coach may want to know how long it takes a point guard to recognize that the defender's actions indicate the guard should pass the ball rather than shoot it. When used in this way, RT provides information about decision making. Thus, in addition to indicating how fast a person responds to a signal, RT also provides a window for examining how a person interacts with the performance environment while preparing to produce a required action.

Relating RT to Movement Time and Response Time

In any situation in which a person must move in response to a signal, two additional performance measures can be assessed. You saw these measures in figure 2.1 as movement time (MT) and response time. **Movement time (MT)** begins when RT ends.

---

reaction time (RT)   the interval of time between the onset of a signal (stimulus) and the initiation of a response (e.g., the amount of time between the "go" signal for a swimming sprint race start and the beginning of the feet moving off the starting block).

movement time (MT)   the interval of time between the initiation of a movement and the completion of the movement.

A CLOSER LOOK

Examples of the Use of RT and MT to Assess Skill Performance Problems in Decision-Making Situations

Sport Skill Example

An offensive lineman in football must perform his assignment as quickly as possible after the center snaps the ball. If the lineman is consistently slow in carrying out his assignment, the problem could be that he is not giving enough attention to the ball snap, he is not sure about his assignment, or he moves too slowly when carrying out his assignment. The first two problems relate to RT (the time between the ball snap and the beginning of foot movement); the third relates to MT (the time between the beginning of foot movement and the completion of the assignment). By assessing both RT and MT in an actual situation, the coach could become more aware of the reason for the lineman's problem and begin working on helping the lineman improve that specific part of the problem.

Car Driving Example

Suppose you are helping a student in a driving simulator to reduce the amount of time he or she requires to stop the car when an object suddenly appears in the street. Separating RT and MT would let you know if the slow stopping time is related to a decision-making or a movement speed problem. If RT (the time between the appearance of the object and the person's foot release from the accelerator) increases across various situations, but MT (the time between the foot release from the accelerator and foot contact with the brake pedal) is constant, you know that the problem is primarily related to attention or decision making. But if RT remains relatively constant whereas MT changes across various situations, you know the problem is movement related. In either case, by measuring both RT and MT you can more specifically help the person to improve his or her performance in these situations.

It is the interval of time between the initiation and the completion of an action. **Response time** is the total time interval, involving both RT and MT.

An important characteristic of RT and MT is that they are relatively *independent* measures. This means that RT does not predict MT or vice versa. The independence of RT and MT as performance measures indicates that if one person in a group of people has the fastest RT in a performance situation, that person may not have the fastest MT in the group. Thus, RT and MT measure different aspects of human performance. You will learn more about the independence of these two performance measures in chapter 3.

Types of RT Situations

Figure 2.2 depicts three of the most common types of RT situations. For illustration purposes, this figure shows a light as the stimulus signal and lifting a finger from a computer keyboard key as the required movement. However, the three types of RT situations discussed here do not need to be limited to these characteristics.

When a situation involves only one signal and requires only one action in response, the RT situation is known as **simple RT.** In the example presented in figure 2.2, the person must lift a finger from the keyboard key when a light comes on. Another type of RT situation is **choice RT,** where there is more than one signal to which the person must respond, and each signal has a specified response. The example in figure 2.2 indicates that the person must respond to the red light by lifting the index finger from a keyboard key, to the blue light by lifting the middle finger from a different key, and to the green light by lifting the ring finger from a third key. The third type of RT situation is **discrimination RT,** where there is also more than one signal, but only one response. In the figure 2.2 example, the person is required to lift his or her finger from the telegraph key only when the red light comes on. If the blue or green light is illuminated, the person should make no response.

Although these examples of simple, choice, and discrimination RT situations refer to laboratory conditions, these different types of RT situations also

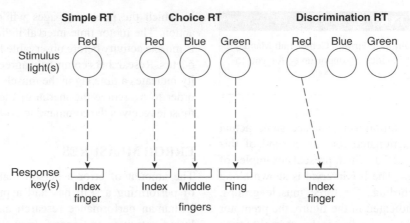

FIGURE 2.2   Three different types of reaction time (RT) test situations: simple RT, choice RT, and discrimination RT.

exist in everyday life and in sport environments. For example, a sprinter in track is involved in a *simple RT situation* when he or she starts a race. He or she hears a verbal warning signal from the starter, then hears the gun sound, which is the signal to begin to run. *Choice RT situations* are more common in everyday activities, such as when driving a car you come to an intersection with a traffic signal, which has three possible signals, each of which requires a different movement. If the light is red, you must depress the brake pedal and come to a complete stop. If the light is yellow, you need to prepare to stop. And if the signal is green, you can continue to keep the accelerator pedal depressed to move through the intersection. Joggers experience *discrimination RT situations* when they find something in their path that indicates they need to step over it, such as a tree root or a curb. There are many different stimuli in the jogger's environment, but only those with specific, distinct features will specify to the jogger to step up and over an object. Thus the jogger engages in this specific action only when the environmental stimuli have these features.

RT Interval Components

Through the use of electromyography (EMG), which will be discussed later in this chapter, to measure the beginning of muscle activity in an RT situation, a researcher can *fractionate* RT into two component parts. The EMG recording will indicate

the time at which the muscle shows increased activity after the stimulus signal has occurred. However, there is a period of time between the onset of the stimulus signal and the beginning of the muscle activity. This "quiet" interval of time is the first component part of RT and is called the *premotor time*. The second component is the period of time from the increase in muscle activity until the actual beginning of observable limb movement. This RT component is called the *motor time*. You can see an illustration of how RT is fractionated in

response time   the time interval involving both reaction time and movement time; that is, the time from the onset of a signal (stimulus) to the completion of a response.

simple RT   the reaction time when the situation involves only one signal (stimulus) that requires only one response.

choice RT   the reaction time when the situation involves more than one signal and each signal requires its own specified response.

discrimination RT   the reaction time when the situation involves more than one signal but only one response, which is to only one of the signals; the other signals require no response.

LAB LINKS

Lab 2 in the Online Learning Center Lab Manual
for chapter 2 provides an opportunity for you to
measure and compare RT and MT.

figure 2.3. In addition you can see some actual
examples of fractionated RTs at the end of this
chapter in figure 2.10, which presents examples of
EMG recordings. The RT interval is shown along
with EMG recordings for three muscle groups.
Although not indicated in the figure, the premotor
time for each EMG recording is the interval of time
prior to the beginning of muscle activity; the motor
time is the remainder of the RT interval in which
muscle activity is recorded.

As you will see in chapter 8, by fractionating the
RT interval into two parts, researchers interested in
understanding the action preparation process are able
to obtain more specific insights into what occurs as
a person prepares to move. Most researchers agree
that the premotor time is a measure of the receipt
and transmission of information from the environment, through the nervous system, to the muscle
itself. This time interval seems to be an indicator of
perceptual and cognitive decision-making activity

in which the person engages while preparing an
action. The motor time interval indicates that there
is muscle activity before observable limb movement
occurs. Researchers commonly agree that this activity indicates a time lag in the muscle that it needs in
order to overcome the inertia of the limb after the
muscle receives the command to contract.

ERROR MEASURES

The amount of error a person makes as a result
of performing a skill has had a prominent place
in human performance research and in everyday
living activities and sport. *Accuracy* can involve
either spatial accuracy, temporal accuracy, or
both. *Spatial accuracy* refers to situations involving space dimensions, such as distance. *Temporal
accuracy* refers to situations involving time dimensions. For both types of accuracy situations error
measures allow us to evaluate performance for
skills for which accuracy is the action goal. Skills
as diverse as reaching to grasp a cup, throwing a
dart at a target, walking along a prescribed path,
and driving a car on a street require people to perform actions that demand spatial and/or temporal
accuracy. To assess performance outcome for these
types of skills, the amount of error a person makes

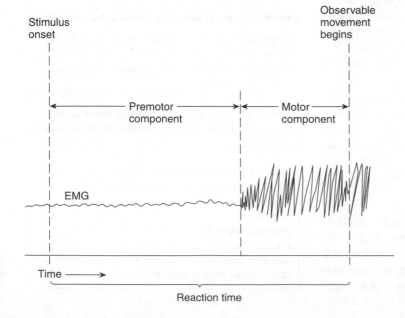

FIGURE 2.3 Schematization of fractionated reaction time indicating the relationship between the EMG signal activity and
the premotor and motor components of the
RT interval.

in relation to the goal is an important and meaningful performance measure.

Error measures not only provide indicators of performance accuracy but certain types of error measures also tell us about possible causes of performance problems. This is especially true if performance is assessed for more than one repetition. For a series of repetitions (typical in a sport skill instruction or a rehabilitation setting), the instructor or therapist can determine whether the observed movement inaccuracy is due to problems associated with *consistency* or to those associated with *bias.* These important measures provide the practitioner with a basis for selecting the appropriate intervention to help the person overcome the inaccuracy. *Consistency problems* indicate a lack in acquiring the basic movement pattern needed to perform the skill, whereas *bias problems* indicate that the person has acquired the movement pattern but is having difficulties adapting to the specific demands of the performance situation. We will discuss the measurement of these characteristics, along with some motor skill performance examples, in the following section.

Assessing Error for One-Dimension Movement Goals

When a person must move a limb a specified amount in one dimension, as when a patient attempts to achieve a certain knee extension, the resulting spatial error will be a certain distance short of or past the goal. Similarly, if a pitcher in baseball is attempting to throw the ball at a certain rate of speed, the resulting temporal error will be either too slow or too fast in relation to the goal. Measuring the amount of error in these situations simply involves subtracting the achieved performance value (e.g., 15 cm, 5°, 20 sec) from the target or goal amount.

We can calculate at least *three error measures* to assess the general accuracy characteristics of performance over repeated performances, and to infer possible causes of the accuracy problems. To obtain a general indicator of how successfully the goal was achieved, we calculate **absolute error (AE).** AE is *the absolute difference between the actual performance on each repetition and the goal.* For multiple-repetition situations, summing these differences and dividing by the number of repetitions will give you

the average absolute error for the repetitions. AE provides useful information about the *magnitude of error* a person has made on a repetition or over a series of repetitions. This score gives you *a general index of accuracy* for the session for this person. But evaluating performance solely on the basis of AE hides important information about the source of the inaccurate performance. To obtain this information, we need two additional error measures.

One reason a person's performance may be inaccurate is that the person has a tendency to overshoot or to undershoot the goal, which is referred to as *performance bias.* To obtain this information, we must calculate **constant error (CE),** which is the signed $(+/-)$ deviation from the goal. When calculated over a series of repetitions, CE provides a meaningful *index of the person's tendency to be directionally biased* when performing the skill. Calculating CE involves making the same calculations used to determine AE, except that the algebraic signs are used for each repetition's performance.

Another reason for performance inaccuracy for a series of repetitions is *performance consistency* (or, conversely, variability), which is measured by calculating **variable error (VE).** To determine this consistency index, calculate the *standard deviation of the person's CE scores for the series of repetitions.*

Assessing Error for Two-Dimension Movement Goals

When the outcome of performing a skill requires accuracy in the vertical and horizontal directions, the person assessing error must make modifications

---

absolute error (AE)   the unsigned deviation from the target or criterion, representing amount of error. A measure of the magnitude of an error without regard to the direction of the deviation.

constant error (CE)   the signed $(+/-)$ deviation from the target or criterion; it represents amount and direction of error and serves as a measure of performance bias.

variable error (VE)   an error score representing the variability (or conversely, the consistency) of performance.

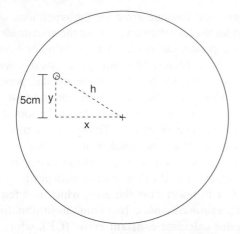

FIGURE 2.4   An example of measuring radial error (RE) to assess performance accuracy. The performance situation involves a person throwing a dart at a circular target. The goal of the throw is to hit the center of the target (represented by the +). The throw hit the location indicated by the O. RE is the hypotenuse (h) of the right-angle triangle formed by the intersection of the X-axis and Y-axis. The following example of X-axis and Y-axis distances associated with this location demonstrates the calculation of RE for this throw.

X-axis distance = 10 cm → 10^2 =   100
Y-axis distance = 5 cm → 5^2 =   25
                            Sum =   125
                            RE = $\sqrt{125}$ = 11.2 cm

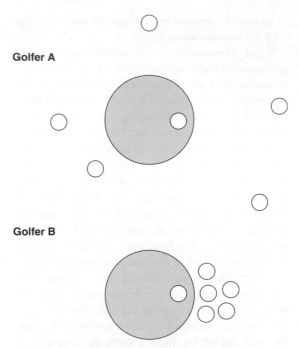

FIGURE 2.5   A golf putting example of a qualitative assessment of two-dimension performance outcome error. Golfers A and B putt six balls at a hole on the putting green. The grouping of the six putts by Golfer A shows a high degree of performance variability, while Golfer B shows a strong performance bias (i.e., tendency) for putting to the right of the hole.

to the one-dimension assessment method. The general accuracy measure for the two-dimension situation is called *radial error (RE),* which is similar to AE in the one-dimension case. To calculate RE for one repetition, calculate the hypotenuse of the right-angle triangle formed by the intersection of the X-axis (extended horizontally from the center of the target) and the Y-axis (extended vertically from the center of the location of the performance result). This calculation involves the following steps:

• Measure the length of the error in the horizontal direction (i.e., X-axis); square this value.
• Measure the length of the error in the vertical direction (i.e., Y-axis); square this value.
• Add the squared X-axis and Y-axis error values; take the square root of the total.

An example of the calculation of RE is shown in figure 2.4. To determine the average RE for a series

of repetitions, simply calculate the mean of the total RE for the series.

Performance bias and consistency are more difficult to assess for the two-dimension case than in one dimension, because the algebraic signs + and − have little meaning for the two-dimension case. Hancock, Butler, and Fischman (1995) presented a detailed description of calculating measures of bias and consistency in the two-dimension situation. Rather than go into the details of this calculation, which is commonly used only in motor learning and control research, we will consider a general approach to the problem here. For a series of repetitions, a researcher or practitioner can obtain a *qualitative assessment of bias and consistency* by looking at the actual grouping of the locations. For example, if two golfers each putt six balls at a hole on a practice green, from the same location, and the results are as shown in figure 2.5, a quick assessment

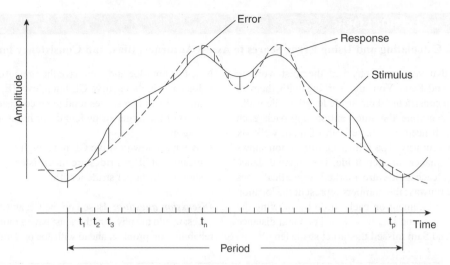

FIGURE 2.6   The difference between the subject's response and the stimulus at each specified time interval is used to calculate one root-mean-squared error (RMSE) score. [From Franks, I. M. et al. (1982). The generation of movement patterns during the acquisition of a pursuit tracking task. *Human Movement Science, 1,* 251–272. Copyright © 1982 Elsevier/North-Holland, Amsterdam, The Netherlands. Reprinted by permission.]

of the grouping of each golfer's putts reveals that the golfers have specific but different problems to overcome to improve their putting performance. Although both golfers holed one putt, Golfer A scattered the other five balls around the hole, which indicates a movement *consistency problem,* while Golfer B grouped the other five balls to the right of the hole, which indicates a movement *bias problem.* As for the one-dimension situation, the practical benefit of assessing these characteristics is that the strategies used to improve performance would differ for the bias and the consistency cases.

Assessing Error for Continuous Skills
The error measures described in the preceding two sections are based on accuracy goals for discrete skills. Some continuous motor skills also require accuracy. For example, when a person must walk along a specified pathway, performance assessment can include measuring how well the person stayed on the pathway. Or if a person is in a car simulator and must steer the car along the road as projected on a screen, a measure of performance can be based on how well the person kept the car

on the road. Error measures for these types of skills must be different from those used to assess discrete skill performance.

A commonly used error score for continuous skills is the **root-mean-squared error (RMSE),** which you can think of as AE for a continuous task. To understand how this error measure is determined and used, consider the following example taken from performing a continuous skill known as *pursuit tracking.* To perform this skill, subjects move a joystick, steering wheel, or lever to make an object, such as a cursor, follow a specified pathway. The criterion pathway can be described kinematically as a displacement curve. Figure 2.6 provides an example.

root-mean-squared error (RMSE)   an error measure used for continuous skills to indicate the amount of error between the performance curve produced and the criterion performance curve for a specific amount of time during which performance is sampled.

A CLOSER LOOK

Calculating and Using Error Scores to Assess Accuracy, Bias, and Consistency for Gait

Suppose that you are a physical therapist working with Joe and Sam. You are working with them to maintain a consistent 50 cm stride length while walking. To determine the intervention approach each of them will need, you have both of them walk six strides on a runway. The following illustration shows their performance for each stride. The 50 cm distance targets for each stride are marked as vertical lines across the runway; the numbers represent the location of the foot placement on each stride by showing the direction ($+$ = too far; $-$ = too short) and distance (cm) Joe and Sam missed the target stride length.

Note that both Joe and Sam have the *same AE,* but that
- Joe has a high negative CE but a low VE, which means that his 6 strides tend to be consistently short of the target stride length for his stride lengths.
- Sam has a low positive CE but a high VE, which means that his 6 strides are inconsistently long and short of the target stride length.

Discussion question: Based on the CE and VE differences, would the physical therapist have a more difficult rehabilitation problem ahead with Joe or Sam? Why?

Sam		$+15$ -12			$+10$ -12		$+12$	$+5$
Joe	-15	-12	-10		-12		-12 -5	

$$\text{Avg. AE} = \sum |x_i - T| / k$$

Where

x = score for repetition i
T = target score
k = number of repetitions

$$\text{Avg. CE} = \sum (x_i - T) / k$$

$$\text{VE} = \sqrt{\sum (x_i - \text{Avg. CE})^2 / k}$$

Calculating the average AE, average CE, and VE:

	AE	AE	CE	CE
Stride No.	Joe	Sam	Joe	Sam
1	15	15	-15	15
2	12	12	-12	-12
3	10	10	-10	10
4	12	12	-12	-12
5	12	12	-12	12
6	5	5	-5	5
Total	66	66	-66	18
Avg	11	11	-11	3
VE			3.3	12.1

The displacement curve represents the subject's tracking performance. To determine how accurately the subject tracked the criterion pathway, we would calculate an RMSE score.

Calculate RMSE by determining the amount of error between the displacement curve produced by the subject's tracking performance and the displacement curve of the criterion pathway (see figure 2.6). The actual calculation of RMSE is complex and requires a computer program that can sample and

record the subject's movement in relation to the criterion pathway at specified points of time, such as 100 times each second (100 Hz; note that 1 Hz = 1 time/sec). At each of the 100 sampling points, the difference between the criterion pathway location and the subject's movement location is calculated. This means that for the 100 Hz example, there are 100 error scores each second. If the criterion pattern were 5 sec, there would be 500 error scores for the repetition. The computer then derives one score, RMSE, from these by calculating an average error score for the total pathway.

KINEMATIC MEASURES

Kinematic measures, traditionally associated with biomechanics, have become important descriptors of performance in research on motor learning and control. The term **kinematics** refers to the description of motion without regard to force or mass. Three of the most common of such descriptors refer to an object's changes in spatial position, its speed, and its changes in speed. The terms used to refer to these kinematic characteristics are *displacement, velocity,* and *acceleration.*

Kinematic measures are performance production measures that are based on recording the movement of specific body segments while a person is performing a skill. A typical procedure is first to mark the joints associated with the body segments of interest in a distinctive way with tape, a marking pen, special light-reflecting balls, or light-emitting diodes (LEDs). The researcher then records the person's performance of the skill on videotape or by using special cameras. Computer software developed to calculate kinematic measures then analyzes the recordings. This approach is used in commercially available movement analysis systems.

Another way to obtain kinematic measures is to record the person's movement of an object, which was the case for the pursuit tracking task described earlier and depicted in figure 2.6. Here, a computer samples (i.e., detects at a specified rate per second) and records the movements of the tracking device. In this example, a horizontal lever on a tabletop was the movement device. A potentiometer attached to the axle of the lever provided movement-related information that the computer sampled. Similar samplings of movement can be taken from the movement of a joystick, a mouse, or a rollerball.

Displacement

The first kinematic measure of interest is **displacement,** which is *the spatial position of a limb or joint during the time period of the movement.* Displacement describes changes in spatial locations

This participant in a research study has reflective markers attached to various joints and body and head locations for kinematic movements analysis purposes.

as a person carries out a movement. We calculate displacement by using a movement analysis system to identify where the movement device or marked joint is in space (in terms of its X-Y coordinate in two-dimensional analysis or its X-Y-Z coordinate in three-dimensional analysis) at a given time. The system then determines the location of that joint for the next sampled time. The analysis system samples

---

kinematics   the description of motion without regard to force or mass; it includes displacement, velocity, and acceleration.

displacement   a kinematic measure describing changes in the spatial positions of a limb or joint during the time course of the movement.

these spatial positions at specific rates, which vary according to the analysis system used. For example, a common videotape sampling rate is 60 Hz, which means the spatial position is detected and recorded 60 times each second. Faster sampling rates are possible, depending on the analysis system used. Thus, the spatial location of a movement device or limb can be plotted for each sampled time as a displacement curve.

Velocity

The second kinematic measure of interest is **velocity,** which is a time-based derivative of displacement. *Velocity,* which we typically call speed in everyday terms, refers to *the rate of change in an object position with respect to time.* That is, how rapidly did this change in position occur and in what direction was this change (faster or slower than its previous rate)? Movement analysis systems derive velocity from displacement by dividing it by time. That is, divide a change in spatial position (between time 1 and time 2) by the change in time (from time 1 to time 2). Velocity is always presented on a graph as a position-by-time curve (see figure 2.7, in which the velocity curve is based on the same movement as the displacement curve). We refer to velocity in terms of an amount of distance per an amount of time. The example in figure 2.7 shows velocity as the number of degrees per second. As the slope of this curve steepens, it represents increasing velocity, whereas negative velocity is represented by a slope that goes downward. Zero velocity is indicated by no change in positive or negative position of the curve.

Acceleration

The third kinematic measure is **acceleration,** which describes *change in velocity during movement.* We derive acceleration from velocity by dividing change in velocity by change in time. We also depict acceleration curves as a function of time, as you can see in the acceleration graph in figure 2.7, which is based on the displacement and velocity graphs also in that figure. The acceleration curve depicts the speeding up and slowing down of the movements as the subject moves. Rapid acceleration means that a velocity change occurred quickly.

Linear and Angular Motion

In kinematic descriptions of movement, the measures of displacement, velocity, and acceleration can refer to either linear or angular motion. The distinction between these types of motion is important to understand and is a critical distinction in the analysis of movement. *Linear motion* refers to motion in a straight line and involves all the body or object moving the same distance over the same amount of time. *Angular motion,* which is sometimes called *rotary motion,* refers to motion that occurs about an axis of rotation and involves specific body segments as they rotate about joints, which are the axes of rotation for body segment movement. For example, if you want to describe the kinematics of walking, linear motion descriptions are appropriate for movement from one location to another, because the whole body is moving linearly. However, if you want to describe the foot movement characteristics during walking, angular motion descriptions are more appropriate because the foot rotates about the ankle joint during walking.

A common way researchers describe angular motion is by measuring the motion of a limb segment as it rotates about a joint while a movement is occurring. Two examples are shown in figure 2.8. The top part of this figure shows an angle-angle diagram for a skilled runner. According to Enoka (2008), because we move by rotating body segments about each other, *angle-angle diagrams* provide an insightful means of examining movement by looking at the relationship between two joints during a movement. The angle-angle diagram usually plots the angle between two adjacent body segments against the angle of one body segment.

In figure 2.8, the angular displacement of the knee joint is compared to that of the thigh during the four discrete events of a running stride: takeoff, opposite footstrike, opposite foot takeoff, and opposite footstrike. Note that this angle-angle diagram produces a heart-shaped pattern, which is the classic knee-thigh relationship pattern during gait. The bottom part of the figure shows similar diagrams for three persons who had amputation below the knee and were wearing an artificial limb. What is noticeable here is that the amputees do not flex the knee joint at the beginning of the stance as the

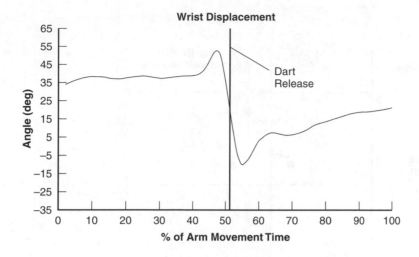

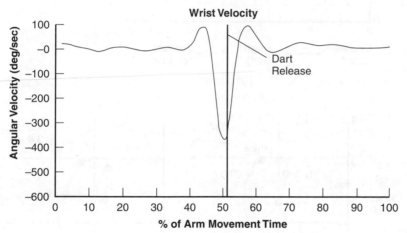

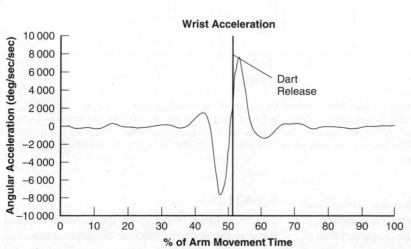

FIGURE 2.7 Recordings of displacement, velocity, and acceleration of the wrist joint during the performance of a dart throw. The X-axis in each graph is the percentage of the total movement time of the arm movement for the dart throw. The vertical line in each graph indicates the release of the dart, which occurred at approximately 51% of the total movement time of the arm movement. [Data from one participant in an experiment that was part of Jeansonne, J. J. (2003). *The effect of environmental context on performance outcomes and movement coordination changes during learning of complex motor skill.* Ph.D. dissertation, Louisiana State University.]

Skilled runner

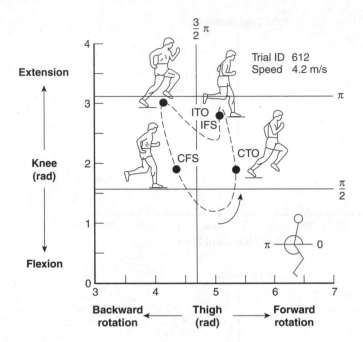

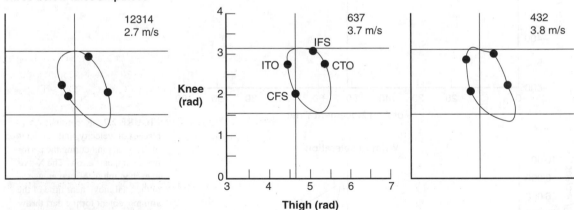

Three below-knee amputees

FIGURE 2.8   Angle-angle diagrams showing knee-thigh relationships during running by a skilled runner (top) and three below-knee amputees (bottom). The abbreviations indicate ipsilateral (left) footstrike (IFS), ipsilateral takeoff (ITO), contralateral (right) footstrike (CFS), and contralateral takeoff (CTO), which are the four components of a running stride. [From Enoka, R. M., et al. (1978). Below knee amputee running gait. *American Journal of Physical Medicine and Rehabilitation, 61,* 70–78. Copyright © 1978 Williams & Wilkins Company, Baltimore, Maryland. Reprinted by permission.]

skilled runner does. These examples demonstrate that an important benefit of kinematic measures is that they allow us to describe the characteristics of critical components of a skill during movement.

KINETICS

The term **kinetics** refers to the consideration of force in the study of motion. Whereas *kinematics* refers to descriptors of motion without concern for

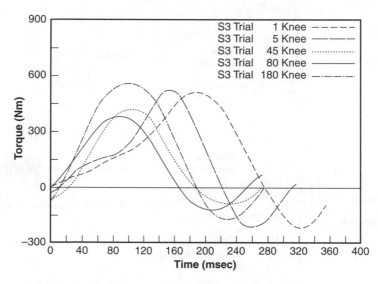

FIGURE 2.9   Results of an experiment by Sanders and Allen showing knee torques for one subject during contact with a surface after the subject drop-jumped from a platform and immediately initiated a vertical jump for maximum height. Each line on the graph represents performance for the trial noted in the key on the graph. [Reprinted from Sanders, R. H., & Allen, J. B. (1993). *Human Movement Science, 12,* pp. 299–326, with kind permission of Elsevier Science-NL, Sara Burgerharstraat 25, 1055 KV Amsterdam, The Netherlands.]

the cause of that motion, *kinetics refers to force as a cause of motion.* In other words, as Susan Hall (2003) stated in her textbook on biomechanics, "a force can be thought of as a push or pull acting on a body" (p. 63). Human movements can involve both external and internal sources of force. For example, gravity and air resistance are external forces that influence running and walking; water resistance is an external force that influences swimming movements. Muscles provide the basis for internal forces by pushing and pulling on joints of the body.

One way to see the importance of the role of force in our understanding of human movement is to note that all three of *Newton's laws of motion* refer to the role of force. In his first law, force is presented as necessary to start, change, or stop motion. His second law indicates that force influences the rate of change in the momentum of an object. And his third law presents force as being involved in the action and reaction that occurs in the interaction between two objects.

An important force-related characteristic of human movement is that human motion involves rotation of body segments around their joint axes. The effect of a force on this rotation is called *joint torque,* or rotary force (see figure 2.9 for an example of how to graphically present joint torque). Because of the many different types of force and their influence on human

---

velocity   a kinematic measure describing the rate of change of an object's position with respect to time. It is derived by dividing displacement by time (e.g., m/sec, km/hr).

acceleration   a kinematic measure that describes change in velocity during movement; we derive it from velocity by dividing change in velocity by change in time.

kinetics   the study of the role of force as a cause of motion.

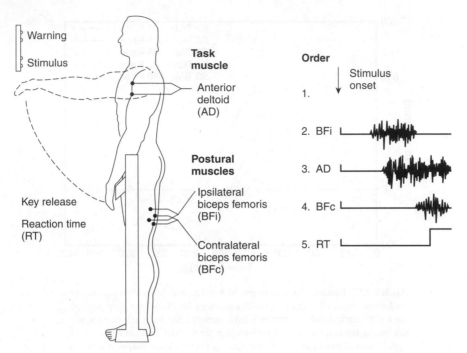

FIGURE 2.10   Using EMG recordings to measure a movement response. The figure on the left shows the reaction-time apparatus and where each electrode was placed to record the EMG for each muscle group of interest. The figures on the right show the EMG recordings for each of the three muscle groups and the reaction-time interval for the response. [From Lee, Wynne. (1980). *Journal of Motor Behavior, 12,* 187. Reprinted by permission of the author.]

movement, researchers studying motor skill learning and control are increasingly including the measurement of forces as part of their research.

Researchers can measure certain forces directly using devices such as force plates, force transducers, and strain gauges. They use force plates to measure ground reaction forces, which are involved in the interaction between an object, such as a person, and the ground. Force plates are popular force measurement devices in laboratories and clinics in which locomotion research and rehabilitation take place. Researchers use force transducers and strain gauges to measure force that is muscle produced; these are popular in laboratory and clinical settings to determine the magnitude of force generated while a subject is performing limb movement tasks.

Newton's second law of motion allows us to measure force indirectly by taking into account the relationship of force to velocity or acceleration and

to the mass of the object: *force = mass × acceleration*. Because of this, we can calculate force without needing to use mechanical and electronic force measurement instruments, if acceleration can be assessed from a kinematic analysis of the movement.

EMG

Movement involves electrical activity in the muscles, which can be measured by **EMG (electromyography).** Researchers commonly accomplish this by either attaching surface electrodes to the skin over muscles or inserting fine wire electrodes into a specific muscle. These electrodes detect muscle electrical activity, which then can be recorded by a computer or polygraph recorder. Figure 2.10 shows some EMG recordings of electrical activity in the ipsilateral biceps femoris (BFi) and contralateral biceps femoris (BFc) of the legs and the anterior deltoid (AD) of the shoulder girdle for a task that required the person to move his or her arm, on a signal, from the reaction-time key to a position directly in front of the shoulder. The EMG signals presented for these muscles show when electrical activity began in the muscles; we can identify this activity by the increase in the frequency and height of the traces for each muscle. The actual beginning of movement off the RT key is designated in the diagram by the vertical line at the end of the RT recording (line 5 of figure 2.10).

Researchers use EMG information in a variety of ways. One that is most relevant to motor learning and control issues is the use of EMG recordings to indicate when a muscle begins and ends activation. Muscle activation begins when the EMG recording increases in frequency and height compared to when the muscle is not active. When EMG recordings include several muscles involved in the same movement, researchers can gain insight into the process of movement coordination by observing the sequence of muscle activation patterns. For example, in figure 2.10, the first muscle to show activation after the signal to move the arm was the ipsilateral biceps femoris (Bfi), which is a leg muscle on the same side of the body as the arm that moved; next in sequence was the anterior deltoid (AD), which moves the arm for the type of movement in the experiment. This activation sequence tells the researcher that more than arm muscle activity is involved for the simple arm movement performed in the experiment. The researcher would interpret the sequence of muscle activity as indicating that the body prepares itself for an arm movement like this one by first activating leg muscles responsible for stabilizing body posture.

BRAIN ACTIVITY MEASURES

With the increase in the availability of technology to study brain activity, an increasing number of motor learning and control researchers are investigating the relationship between brain activity and the performance of motor skills. Rather than rely on behavioral measures from which they must infer brain activity, these researchers use various techniques to measure brain activity itself. Most of these techniques have been adapted from hospital and clinical settings where they are used for diagnostic purposes. For researchers who study motor learning and control from a neurophysiological level, these techniques provide a window into brain activity as a person performs a motor skill. In the following sections, we will briefly discuss some of the more prominent brain activity measurement techniques that are used by motor learning and control researchers and that you will see referred to in other chapters of this book.

EEG

Like skeletal and cardiac muscle, the brain produces electrical activity, which can be measured by **EEG (electroencephalography).** Neurologists commonly use EEG to assess brain disorders. Researchers use this same noninvasive and painless procedure, which is similar to recording surface EMG for skeletal muscle. EEG recording involves the placement of several surface electrodes on a person's scalp; each electrode is placed to detect electrical activity in specific areas on the surface of the brain's cortex. Typically, electrodes are placed on standard locations on the scalp at specific brain sites. The number of electrodes can vary according to the needs of the researcher or equipment limitations. In their review of the use of EEG for skilled motor performance research, Hatfield, Haufler, Hung, and Spaulding (2004) indicated that four to sixteen electrodes are typically used. The sites for electrode placement are categorized by brain

---

EMG (electromyography)   a measurement technique that records the electrical activity of a muscle or group of muscles. It indicates the muscle activity.

EEG (electroencephalography)   the recording of brain activity by the detection of electrical activity in specific areas on the surface of the cortex by several surface electrodes placed on a person's scalp. Brain activity is recorded as *waves,* which are identified on the basis of the speed of the rhythmic activity.

cortex lobe location, with each site designated by a letter for the lobe (frontal [F], temporal [T], central [C], parietal [P], and occipital [O]) and a number for the hemisphere location (the even numbers 2, 4, 6 and 8 indicate right hemisphere sites; the odd numbers 1, 3, 5 and 7 indicate left hemisphere locations). Note that although there is no "central" lobe in the brain, a central location is designated for identification purposes. The electrodes can be individually placed on the scalp or, as is more common in research settings, contained in an elastic cap, or bonnet, in their appropriate locations.

The electrical activity detected by EEG electrode pairs is transmitted by wires to amplifiers and recording devices. Because brain activity is rhythmic, the EEG recordings relate to specific rhythms, which are commonly called *waves*. Four waves can be identified according to the speed of the rhythmic activity. The fastest rhythms are the *beta waves,* which occur when an area of the cortex is active; next are *alpha waves,* which occur during quiet, awake states; *theta waves* are the next to slowest and occur during some sleep states; the slowest are *delta waves,* which are characteristic of deep sleep. In general, mental activity generates the fast beta waves, while nondreaming sleep and coma produce slow theta waves.

In the study of motor skill performance, researchers have used EEG to investigate several issues (see Hatfield & Hillman, 2001, and Hatfield et al., 2004, for reviews of this research literature). The most popular has been to describe brain cortex excitability characteristics of skilled athletes in sport such as rifle sharpshooting (e.g., Deeny, Hillman, Janelle, & Hatfield, 2003), pistol shooting (Loze, Collins, & Holmes, 2001), dart throwing (Radlo, Sternberg, Singer, Barba, & Melnikov, 2002), golf (Crews & Landers, 1993), and archery (Landers et al., 1991). Less popular has been the use of EEG to study the learning of motor skills (e.g., Etnier, Whitwer, Landers, Petruzello, & Salazar, 1996; Landers et al., 1994).

PET

One of the limitations of EEG as a technique for assessing brain activity is that it is limited to activity in the brain cortex surface and does not show the anatomical structures that are active in specific brain regions. The development of *neuroimaging techniques,* which provide clear and precise images of activity in specific brain regions, overcame this limitation and presented exciting opportunities for researchers to gain a better understanding of the relationship between observable motor skill performance and brain activity. *Positron emission topography (PET)* was the first of these techniques. Developed in the 1970s, PET scans show blood flow or metabolic activity in the brain and provide a window into all areas of the brain. The technique involves the injection into the bloodstream, or the inhalation, of a radioactive solution in which atoms emit positively charged electrons (i.e., positrons). Interaction of the positrons with electrons in the blood produces photons of electromagnetic radiation. The locations of these positron-emitting atoms can then be found by a scanner in which detectors pick up the photons' locations in the brain (see Bear, Connors, & Paradiso, 2001, for further details). Computer programs then analyze levels of activity of the photons in brain neurons. Increased activity "lights up" the brain area; the computer programs capture and produce images of these active brain areas. When the "lighted up" brain areas are color enhanced according to a color spectrum, the researcher can determine the amount of activity in each area.

Motor learning and control researchers who use PET imaging engage a person in the performance of a motor skill that can be performed in the PET scanner, which surrounds only the head but requires the person to be lying on his or her back throughout the scanning procedure. As the person performs specific aspects of the skill, the PET scan detects the activated brain regions. Although PET remains popular as a neuroimaging technique for researchers interested in the neural substrates of cognitive and motor activities, its use for this type of research has diminished in recent years. The primary reason has been the development of improved technology, which can provide greater image resolution, is more cost-effective, and does not require injection of a radioactive isotope into the bloodstream.

fMRI

A common diagnostic technique used in many hospitals and clinics is *magnetic resonance imaging (MRI)*. The MRI machine, or scanner, contains a magnetic field that realigns the body's hydrogen atoms, which become the basis for creating extraordinarily clear two- and three-dimensional images of body tissue. The MRI can produce an image of any part of the body from any direction (i.e., plane) in "slices" that are a few millimeters thick. In addition to imaging body tissue, the MRI can also assess changes in blood flow by detecting blood oxygenation characteristics. To study brain function, researchers take advantage of the blood flow detection capability of the MRI by using **fMRI** *(functional magnetic resonance imaging)*. The term *functional* is important because researchers use this technique to observe brain function (i.e., activity) while a person performs a task. When a part of the brain is active, more blood is directed to that area. The fMRI detects blood flow changes and can provide colored images that show active brain areas at a specified time, and it can provide quantitative results by computing BOLD (blood oxygenation level dependent) amplitudes, which researchers use to determine active areas of the brain. When researchers report their use of fMRI, they typically describe the specific brain areas from which the slices were taken and the size and direction of the slices. An important aspect of the use of fMRI for motor control and learning experiments is that, as with the constraints imposed by the PET scanner, researchers need to engage participants in tasks that can be performed within the physical confines and restrictions of the MRI machine. Although the use of fMRI is relatively new for research in motor control and learning, we find an increasing number of studies reporting its use. You will see some examples in various chapters throughout this book.

MEG

One of the most recent technological advances in brain activity assessment is *MEG (magnetoencephalography)*. The assessment is a variation of the EEG (notice the "encephalography" similarity). While the EEG assesses electrical activity in the brain, the MEG assesses magnetic fields created by neuronal activity in the brain. One of MEG's advantages for researchers is that it provides a direct measure of brain function; this differs from other brain measures such as fMRI and PET that are secondary measures because brain activity is assessed on the basis of brain metabolism. MEG provides very high temporal resolution, which makes it especially useful for the identification of damaged brain tissue; this is critical for both diagnosis and surgical purposes, as well as for observing brain activity during the performance of cognitive and motor activities. The recording system for MEG involves the use of sensors that detect magnetic fields in the brain that result from neuronal activity. The spatial distributions of these fields are analyzed and used to determine the location of the activity. Researchers commonly combine results from MEG with those from EEG and MRI. The addition of the MEG results provides more accurate localization of the active brain structures associated with the activity in which the subject is engaged.

TMS

A method of assessing brain activity that is targeted directly at determining motor activity is **TMS (transcranial magnetic stimulation).** Different

---

fMRI   (functional magnetic resonance imaging) a brain-scanning technique that assesses changes in blood flow by detecting blood oxygenation characteristics while a person is performing a skill or activity in the MRI scanner. It provides clear images of active brain areas at a specified time and can provide quantitative information about the levels of brain region activity

TMS   (transcranial magnetic stimulation) a non-invasive method of assessing brain activity that involves a short burst (referred to as a pulse) of a field of magnetic waves is directed at a specific area of the cortex. This pulse of magnetic activity temporarily disrupts the normal activity in that area of the brain, which allows researchers to observe a subject's behavior when that area of the brain is not functioning.

from the types of brain activity measures that involve a scan of the brain and the recording of electrical, magnetic, or bloodflow activity of the brain, TMS excites or inhibits activity in the cortex of the brain which causes a temporary disruption of the normal activity in that area of the brain. As a result, the function of specific brain areas is inferred on the basis of how a person behaves when a brain area is not functioning normally. TMS involves the external placement of a coil on a person's skull at a brain cortex location of interest. From this coil a short burst (referred to as a pulse) of a field of magnetic waves is directed at that area of the cortex. Because this pulse of magnetic activity disrupts brain activity in a specific area, researchers often use TMS to verify the function of a brain region based on the predicted function derived from brain activity measures such as fMRI or PET. Researchers interested in determining the neurological basis for motor control and learning have found TMS to be a useful technique for their research. You will see examples of the use of this technique in various chapters of this book.

MEASURING COORDINATION

One of the more exciting phenomena of recent motor learning and control research is the investigation of movement-related coordination. One reason for this is methodologically based. Prior to the advent of computer-based technology for movement analysis, kinematic measurement of movement was an expensive, labor-intensive, and time-consuming process involving frame-by-frame analysis of slow-motion film. With the development of the computer-based movement analysis systems, there has been a dramatic increase in research involving complex skills, which allows for the assessment of coordination.

A measurement issue concerns how best to assess coordination. Although researchers have developed several methods for quantifying coordination characteristics, we will consider only two as examples of the ways it is possible to measure coordination. Common to all these methods is analyzing the movement of limbs and limb segments

in specific time (i.e., temporal) and space (i.e., spatial) patterns while a person performs a motor skill. One of the ways to observe these patterns is to create graphic angle-angle plots of the movements of joints associated with limb segments, such as the knee and thigh joints depicted in figure 2.8. However, a measurement issue has developed concerning angle-angle diagrams. We discuss this issue next.

Quantitative Assessment of Angle-Angle Diagrams

As researchers gained the capability to analyze complex movements, they tended to report only the qualitative kinematic descriptions of limb segment relationships. However, to make inferences about coordination from these descriptions researchers needed to provide quantitative assessments of them. Although researchers have proposed various techniques, the cross-correlation technique has gained general acceptance.

Cross-correlation technique. The angle-angle diagrams that describe coordination patterns for two joints lend themselves to correlational analysis because researchers are interested in the relationship between the two joints at specific points in time. Because movement analysis of the joints provides many data points to compare (recall the discussion earlier in the chapter concerning kinematic measures), it is possible to correlate each data point (an X-Y spatial position at a specific point in time: i.e., the time when the movement analysis software sampled the joint's position in space) of one joint with each data point on the other joint. To do this type of correlation requires a statistical procedure known as cross-correlation, which is required when the relationship of interest occurs across a period of time. Rather than describe the details of computing a cross-correlation, it will suffice to say it results in a correlation coefficient that is interpreted as the extent to which the two joints follow similar movement patterns. (For more information about the cross-correlation technique see Mullineaux, Bartlett, & Bennett, 2001, and Li & Caldwell, 1999.)

A CLOSER LOOK

An Index of Coordination for Swimming Strokes

Chollet and his colleagues in France developed a quantitative assessment of the coordination of swimming strokes, which they described as having practical value for assessing and improving swimming stroke performance by elite swimmers (Chollet, Chalies, & Chatard, 2000).

The Index of Coordination (IdC)

The researchers derived the IdC from video-based motion analysis of elite swimmers' performance. Four cameras (one underwater, one on a trolley above water at the side of the pool, one providing a frontal underwater view, and one above the pool tracking the swimmer's head) provided the data needed to calculate the IdC.

Backstroke Coordination and Swimming Speed

An excellent example of how a quantitative assessment of coordination can be used in a sport context was presented in an experiment involving elite swimmers performing the backstroke. Chollet, Seifert, and Carter (2008) calculated an IdC for arm movements for various swim speeds for each swimmer. The IdC was calculated from right and left arm position data during six phases of a stroke: 1. Entry and catch of the hand in the water; 2. Pull; 3. Push; 4. Hand lag time; 5. Clearing; 6. Recovery. The durations of the pull and push phases were summed to establish a propulsive phase; the sum of the durations of the other four phases was considered to be the non-propulsive phases.

Calculation of the IdC:

IdC = (time at the beginning of the propulsion in the first right arm stroke and the end of propulsion in the first left arm stroke) − (time at the beginning of the propulsion in the second right arm stroke and the end of propulsion in the first right arm stroke)

The experiment involved 14 international-standard male swimmers performing the backstroke at four different speeds. The IdC analysis results showed that the swimmers maintained a standard arm stroke coordination mode regardless of speed.

Recommendations for swimmers and coaches: Based on the results of their quantitative coordination assessment the researchers presented three recommendations for enhancing swimming performance: Swimmers should

1. Minimize the clearing phase . . . and the hand's lag time at the thigh . . . by increasing the hand speed in this specific phase. . .
2. Modify their hand sweep from a "two-peak" to a "three-peak stroke pattern" with a partly propulsive clearing phase . . .
3. Compensate the loss of speed in the clearing phase . . . by increasing the distance per stroke.

In addition the authors claimed that the IdC can be "used by coaches to assess mistakes in backstroke coordination, particularly regarding the hand's lag time at the thigh." (p. 681)

Relative Phase as a Coordination Measure

Many motor skills involve movements that are cyclic. This means that they repeat a movement pattern for a certain amount of time, such as walking or running (the step-cycle in gait in figure 2.8 is an example of a cyclic movement). These types of skills are especially interesting because they provide a quantifiable means of measuring coordination. This is accomplished by calculating the relative phase between two limb segments or limbs during one cycle, or part of a cycle, of the skill. A *phase* of a cyclic movement refers to a specific point on the cycle. Because any point on the cycle involves both a spatial position of a limb or limb segment and a point in time, the movements of the limb or limb segment can be described by a displacement-velocity graph that portrays the relationship between the spatial and temporal characteristics of the movements. This graph, which is called a *phase plot* (or *phase portrait*), presents the limb or limb segment's angular displacement on one axis and its angular velocity on the other axis. When a cyclic movement is graphed in this way, the result is a graph like the one in figure 2.11,

a. Normalized angular velocity

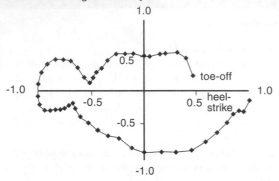

b. Normalized angular position

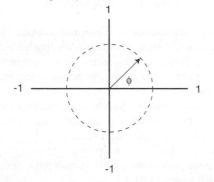

FIGURE 2.11   (a) A phase plot of the movement of a leg segment during the stance portion of one step cycle during running. (b) An example of the derivation of a phase angle from the phase plot shown above in panel (a). [Adapted from Hamill, J., van Emmerik, R. E. A., Heiderscheidt, B. C., & Li, L. (1999). A dynamical systems approach to lower extremity running injuries. *Clinical Biomechanics, 14,* 297–308.]

a specific point on the phase plot. The resulting angle is the *phase angle* for that point in time of the movement. One way that researchers use phase angles to assess movement coordination is by comparing the phase angles of two limb segments, or limbs, at a specific point in time. This comparison establishes the **relative phase,** which is calculated by subtracting the phase angle for one limb segment or limb from the phase angle of the other limb segment or limb. Relative phase can range from 0 (or 360 degrees), which indicates an *in-phase relationship* between the limb segments or limbs, to 180 degrees, which indicates an *antiphase* (or *out-of-phase*) *relationship*. The interpretation of relative phase as an index of coordination is that a high degree of coordination between the two joints or limbs is associated with a relative phase that remains consistent for several cycles of the movement.

In addition to using relative phase as an index of coordination between limb segments, researchers commonly use it to describe the relationship between two arms or two legs, or between one arm and one leg. For example, if you hold your arms in front of you and move them side to side so that each moves in the same horizontal direction (i.e., both move right and left simultaneously), the phase relationship between them is 0 (or 360) degrees. If both move simultaneously toward the midline of your body, the phase relationship between them is 180 degrees. If a 0- or 180-degree relative phase between the two arms is maintained for several repetitions, or cycles,

which is based on the movement of a leg segment during the stance portion of a step cycle (from the heel strike of one foot to the toe-off of the same foot). The data points on the phase plot are the X-Y coordinates sampled at specific times in the movement analysis (e.g., if the sampling rate is 100 Hz, there will be 100 X-Y coordinate data points). The calculation of a movement's phase is complex and will not be described here. But you can see how a phase angle is derived from a phase plot by looking at the bottom panel of figure 2.11. Here a line is drawn from the origin of the X-Y coordinate to

> **relative phase**   an index of the coordination between two limb segments or limbs during the performance of a cyclic movement. It is based on calculating the phase angles for each limb segment or limb at a specific point in time and then subtracting one phase angle from the other. Relative phase ranges from 0 (or 360 degrees), which indicates an in-phase relationship between the limb segments or limbs, to 180 degrees, which indicates an antiphase (or out-of-phase) relationship.

of moving the arms, then the conclusion is that they are strongly coordinated, or "tightly coupled" as some researchers describe the coordination relationship. You can see an example of this use of relative phase as a coordination measure in figure 5.6 in chapter 5 and figure 11.4 in chapter 11.

The relative phase measurement described in the preceding paragraphs is referred to as *continuous relative phase,* because it presents the relative phase of a cyclic movement throughout the movement's cycle. Another type of relative phase measurement, known as *point estimate relative phase,* refers to only one point in the movement cycle. As indicators of coordination, the point-estimate relative phase is a more general indicator. The continuous relative phase provides a more detailed analysis of coordination.

SUMMARY

An essential element in understanding motor learning is the measurement of motor performance. All concepts presented in this text are based on research in which researchers observed and measured motor performance. Measuring motor performance is essential for the assessment of motor deficiencies, as well as for the evaluation of performance by students or patients as they progress through practice and therapy regimes. In this chapter, we focused on different ways to measure motor performance, along with the ways we can use these measurements in motor learning research and applied settings.

The performance measurement issues and examples discussed in this chapter were these:

• Two categories of performance measures: performance outcome measures (which measure the result of the performance of a movement activity) and performance production measures (which measure movement-related characteristics that produce the performance outcome of a movement activity).

• Performance outcome measure examples: reaction time (RT), movement time (MT), and three measures of performance outcome error (AE, CE, and VE) for one- and two-dimension movement goals.

• Performance production measure examples: three kinematic measures (displacement, velocity, and acceleration), joint torque as a kinetic measure, and EMG. Also included were five measures of brain activity: EEG, PET scans, fMRI, MEG, and TMS.

• Concerns about the qualitative and quantitative measurement of movement coordination, including the cross-correlation technique and the use of relative phase.

POINTS FOR THE PRACTITIONER

• The measurement of motor skill performance is important for providing a quantitative basis for the assessment of performance capabilities and limitations, the locus of the source of performance limitations, and evidence of skill improvement resulting from your intervention strategies.

• You can measure the outcome of motor skill performance and/or the movement and neurological basis for the outcome. Select the types of measures based on the performance-related information you need to address your goals for the person or people with whom you are working.

• Reaction time can be a useful measure to provide information about a person's readiness to perform a skill in a specific situation.

• Error measures can provide information about the types of movement problems a person needs to correct to achieve the action goal of a skill.

• Kinematic, kinetic, EMG, brain activity, and coordination measures can help assess a person's movement-related problems when performing a skill. In addition to needing the appropriate technology to determine these measures, you need to ensure that the measures are interpreted correctly.

RELATED READINGS

Boyd, L. A., Vidoni, E. D., & Daly, J. J. (2007). Answering the call: The influence of neuroimaging and electrophysiological evidence on rehabilitation. *Physical Therapy, 87,* 684–703.

Cacioppo, J. T., Bernston, G. G., & Nusbaum, H. C. (2008). Neuroimaging as a new tool in the toolbox of psychological science. *Current Directions in Psychological Science, 17,* 62–67.

Hallett, M. (2000). Transcranial magnetic stimulation and the human brain. *Nature, 406,* 147–150.

Kimberley, T. J., & Lewis, S. M. (2007). Neuroimaging techniques. *Physical Therapy, 87,* 670–683.

Mah, C. D., Hulliger, M., Lee, R. G., & Marchand, A. R. (1994). Quantitative analysis of human movement synergies: Constructive pattern analysis for gait. *Journal of Motor Behavior, 26,* 83–102.

Soderberg, G. L., & Knutson, L. M. (2000). A guide for use and interpretation of kinesiologic electromyographic data. *Physical Therapy, 80,* 485–498.

Van Emmerik, R. E. A., Rosenstein, M. T., McDermott, W. J., & Hamill, J. (2004). A nonlinear dynamics approach to human movement. *Journal of Applied Biomechanics, 20,* 396–420.

Waldert, S., Preissl, H., Demandt, E., Braun, C., Birbaumer, N., Aertsen, A., & Mehring, C. (2008). Handmovement direction decoded from MEG and EEG. *Journal of Neuroscience, 28,* 1000–1008.

Wascher, E., & Wolber, M. (2004). Attentional and intentional cueing in a Simon task: An EEG-based approach. *Psychological Research, 68,* 18–30.

INTERNET RESOURCES

- To try an interesting version of a simple reaction time (RT) test, go to http://www.bbc.co.uk/science/. In the Search box type Sheep Dash. Then click on the link that includes "Sheep Dash" in the title.

- See if your RT is fast enough to hit a baseball that is traveling at a speed of 95 mph at http://www.exploratorium.edu/baseball/. Then click on Fastball Reaction Time.

- For detailed information about how to use EMG and examples of a variety of applications of the use of EMG, go to http://www.delsys.com/. Click on Knowledge Center. Then click on Tutorials and Technical Notes, which will take you to a page of several tutorials on the use of EMG.

- For detailed information about various techniques used to scan the brain, go to a Web site provided by the Public Broadcasting System (PBS) at http://www.pbs.org/. In the Search box, type "brain scanning." Then click on any link.

- To see brain scan images from various neuroimaging devices, do a Google search on "brain scans." One of the links is "Image results for brain scans" which will provide numerous examples of brain scan images.

- To watch a short video of the use of MEG go to http://www.sciencedaily.com/ specify a search for MEG, then click on the Videos link to find a video and article about the use of MEG to pinpoint the source of an epilepsy seizure in the brain.

STUDY QUESTIONS

1. (a) Describe the differences between performance outcome measures and performance production measures. (b) Give three examples for each of these measures of motor performance.

2. (a) Describe how simple RT, choice RT, and discrimination RT situations differ. (b) What does it mean to fractionate RT? (c) How does MT differ from RT?

3. What different information can be obtained about a person's performance by calculating AE, CE, and VE when performance accuracy is the movement goal?

4. How would you determine the type of problem a golfer needs to correct based on the results of a series of missed putts?

5. How can performance error be determined for a continuous skill such as steering a car on a road?

6. Describe three kinematic measures of movement and explain what each measure tells us about the movement.

7. What do the terms *linear motion* and *angular motion* mean when used in reference to descriptions of movement? When would you use each of these types of analysis if you were measuring a person's walking performance?

8. What is meant by the term *kinetics* as it is related to measuring human movement?

9. What information about a movement can be obtained by using EMG?

10. Describe three techniques commonly used to measure brain activity during the performance of a motor skill. What are the limitations of each technique in terms of the types of motor skills that could be used?

11. Briefly describe two techniques that can be used to tell us something about the coordination characteristics of two limbs or two limb segments.

Specific Application Problem:
Describe a situation in which you are working with people to help them improve their performance of a motor skill. Your supervisor has asked you to respond to several questions before you begin this work:

(a) What are some performance outcome measures that you could use to assess their performance?

(b) What would be the advantages and disadvantages of each?

(c) Which outcome measures would you use and why?

(d) Since you have the appropriate technology available, what kinematic measures would help you assess their performance?

(e) How would the information the kinematic measures provide help you in assessing their performance of the skill?

CHAPTER 3

Motor Abilities

Concept: A variety of abilities underlie motor skill learning and performance success.

After completing this chapter, you will be able to

- Define the term *ability* and distinguish it from the term *skill*
- Explain the difference between the general motor ability hypothesis and the specificity of motor abilities hypothesis
- Name and describe several motor ability categories and explain how researchers have identified the various motor ability categories
- Describe how motor abilities relate to motor skill performance

APPLICATION

Some people perform many different physical activities very well. Why is this the case? Are they born with some special "motor ability" that enables them to be successful at all they do? Have they had an abundance of good training and practice in a wide variety of activities? Are they really good at everything, or only at certain activities?

Also, people differ in how quickly and successfully they learn motor skills. If you observe a physical activity class for beginners, you will see various degrees of success and failure during the first few days. For example, in a beginning golf class, when the students first start to hit the ball, some will spend an inordinate amount of time simply trying to make contact with the ball. But some will be at the other extreme, able to hit the ball rather well. The remainder of the class usually will be distributed somewhere along the continuum of success between these two extremes. We can observe parallel differences in other physical activity situations, such as dance classes, driving instruction classes, and physical therapy sessions.

The understanding of the role played by motor abilities in the learning and performance of motor skills can help explain some of the differences we observe

in how well people perform skills. The benefit of this understanding for practitioners is that it can provide the basis for carrying out specific aspects of their work, such as interpreting skill performance assessments, developing effective methods to help people overcome performance deficits, acquire new skills, and enhance performance of well-learned skills.

Application Problem to Solve Select a motor skill that you perform for recreational or sports purposes. Other than for reasons related to the quality and amount of instruction or coaching and practice, why do some people perform this skill at a higher level than you and some perform it at a lower level?

DISCUSSION

In chapters 1 and 2, you were introduced to motor skills and the measurement of motor skill performance. Now, you will be introduced to a type of personal characteristic known as *ability*, which influences the way people perform and learn motor skills.

ABILITY AND MOTOR ABILITY

One of the difficulties in studying the concept of ability as it relates to motor skill performance is that the term *ability* is used in so many different ways. For example, physical and occupational therapists refer to "functional ability"; a baseball coach might refer to a player's "running ability"; educators often refer to students' "cognitive ability" or "intellectual ability." The list of examples could go on, but these few examples illustrate the problem. As a result, it is important to specify the precise manner in which the term will be used.

For this discussion, the term *ability* will be used according to its meaning in the area of psychology that involves the study of *individual differences*. People who study individual differences are concerned with the identification and measurement of abilities that characterize and differentiate individuals. Individual-difference psychologists also investigate the relationship between abilities and the performance and learning of skills. In this context, the term **ability** means *a general trait or capacity of the individual that is a relatively enduring characteristic which serves as a determinant of a person's achievement potential for the performance of specific skills.* When the term **motor ability** is used in this context, it refers to *an ability that is specifically related to the performance of a motor skill.* It is important to note that some researchers and practitioners use terms such as "psychomotor ability" and "perceptual motor ability" to refer to what we will call motor ability.[1]

The identification of specific motor abilities is not an easy task. As a result, few researchers have ventured into this area of study. However, those who have undertaken this challenge have provided us with useful information that helps us have a better understanding of an important factor related to determining why people differ in achievement levels of motor skill performance.

[1]Although the terms *motor ability, psychomotor ability,* and *perceptual-motor ability* can have specific meanings, they are sufficiently similar, for purposes of this book, to use the term *motor ability* to refer to all three terms.

Abilities as Individual-Difference Variables

The individual differences we observe in the amount of success that people achieve in the performance of a motor skill depends in large part on the degree to which the person has the motor abilities that are important for the performance of that skill. For example, people with differing levels of the motor abilities important for playing tennis will have differing *achievement potentials* in tennis. This example indicates that various motor abilities underlie the performance of a complex motor skill such as tennis and that people have different levels of these abilities. It also indicates that if two people have the same training experiences and amount of practice, but differ in their levels of the motor abilities important for playing tennis, the one with the higher levels of the appropriate abilities has the potential to perform at a higher level. Although researchers generally agree with this view, they debated for many years, especially in the 1950s and 1960s, how motor abilities relate to one another within the same person.

General versus specific motor abilities. In the debate about the relationship of motor abilities, one viewpoint holds that motor abilities are *highly related* to each other. The opposite view is that they are *relatively independent* of one another. This debate is not commonly pursued in the current research literature. However, an understanding of the different points of view will help you apply the concept of motor abilities to motor skill performance achievement.

The **general motor ability hypothesis** maintains that although many different motor abilities

---

ability   a general trait or capacity of an individual that is a determinant of a person's achievement potential for the performance of specific skills.

motor ability   an ability that is specifically related to the performance of a motor skill.

general motor ability hypothesis   a hypothesis that maintains that the many different motor abilities that exist in an individual are highly related and can be characterized in terms of a singular, global motor ability.

can be identified within an individual, they are highly related and can be characterized in terms of a singular, global motor ability. It holds that the level of that ability in an individual influences the ultimate success that person can expect in performing any motor skill. This viewpoint has been in existence since the early part of the last century (e.g., Brace, 1927; McCloy, 1934), having been developed as the motor ability analogue to the then popular cognitive ability concept of a general intelligence (IQ). The hypothesis predicts that if a person is highly skilled in one motor skill, then he or she would be expected to be or become highly skilled in all motor skills. The reasoning behind this prediction is that there is *one* general motor ability. In fact, one proponent of this view developed a motor ability test battery that he proposed could be used to classify students into one of five homogeneous motor ability subgroups for purposes of teaching and engaging in physical activities (Barrow, 1957).

But contrary to the expectations of proponents of the general motor ability hypothesis, very little research evidence supports this viewpoint. One suspects that the basis for the continued existence of this hypothesis is its intuitive appeal. Tests of general motor ability are convenient, appealing to those who seek an easy explanation for why certain people are successful or unsuccessful at performing motor skills. The fact that these tests are poor predictors of specific motor skill performance has not diminished the appeal of the general motor ability hypothesis.

The alternative perspective, for which there has been substantial support, is the **specificity of motor abilities hypothesis.** Franklin Henry is generally credited with deriving the specificity hypothesis to explain results from his research that the general motor ability hypothesis could not explain. This specificity view states that individuals have many motor abilities, and these abilities are relatively *independent.* This means, for example, that if a person exhibited a high degree of balancing ability, we could not predict how well that person would do on a test of reaction time.

Support for the specificity hypothesis has come from experiments that were reported primarily in the 1960s. These experiments were based on the common assumption that if motor abilities are specific and independent, then the relationship between any two abilities will be very low. Thus, in the simplest of cases, the relationship would be very low between abilities such as balance and reaction time, or between reaction time and speed of movement, or between static and dynamic balance.

The research evidence that provided most of the initial support for the specificity hypothesis, and became an impetus for further research, came from Franklin Henry's laboratory at the University of California, Berkeley. This research was based on the premise that motor abilities are relatively independent. Henry and his colleagues reasoned that they could demonstrate this independence rather simply by investigating the relationship between reaction time and arm movement speed. Recall from the discussion in chapter 2 that reaction time is the amount of time to see, hear, or feel a stimulus (i.e., a "go" signal) and then initiate the required movement; movement time is the amount of time from the initiation of the movement to its completion. The common result from many experiments from Henry's laboratory (e.g., Henry, 1961a, 1961b) was that reaction time and movement speed are uncorrelated, which means that each is an independent motor ability.

Balance and Timing Abilities

Although researchers now generally accept the specificity of motor abilities hypothesis, some have raised questions about the generality of certain specific motor abilities. That is, do certain motor abilities represent one ability, or are there several variations of these abilities, each of which is task specific and relatively independent of the other(s)? Two examples of these motor abilities, which are especially relevant to our discussions in this book, are balance and timing.

Balance. When used in reference to motor skill performance, the term balance refers to *postural stability* (see Shumway-Cook & Wollacott, 2006), which involves maintaining equilibrium while stationary or while moving. In other words, balance concerns our capability to stand, sit, or move without falling. Although sometimes regarded as a single motor ability, balance should be viewed as comprised of at least two types: static and dynamic. *Static balance* is the maintenance of equilibrium while stationary, such as while standing, sitting, or kneeling. *Dynamic balance,* on the other hand, is the maintenance of equilibrium while in motion, such as while walking or running. Static balance is sometimes considered to be a simpler variation of dynamic balance. This viewpoint is seen, for example, when rehabilitation protocols specify that a person should develop static postural balance capabilities before engaging in activities requiring dynamic postural balance, such as walking. However, research evidence consistently indicates that static and dynamic balance are relatively independent motor abilities. For example, Rose et al. (2002) reported that fourteen of twenty-three children with gait disorders related to cerebral palsy showed normal standing balance characteristics.

Research evidence also indicates that several relatively independent variations of static and dynamic balance exist. Drowatzky and Zuccato (1967) reported an excellent example of this research many years ago. In this experiment, participants performed six different balancing tasks that generally have been regarded as measures of either static or dynamic balancing ability. The results of the correlations among all the tests (table 3.1) showed that the highest correlation (.31) was between two dynamic balance tests, the sideward leap and the Bass stepping stone test. The highest correlation between a static and dynamic balance test was .26 (between the stork stand and sideward leap). Most of the correlations ranged between .12 and .19. A more recent study by Tsiglis, Zachopoulou, and Mavridis (2001) supported the Drowatsky and Zucatto results for various types of dynamic balance. The highest correlation between two of three different types of dynamic balance tests was .22. The two other correlations between the tests were .05 and .13.

LAB LINKS

Lab 3 in the Online Learning Center Lab Manual for chapter 3 provides an opportunity for you to experience several different types of balance tests and compare your results to the predictions of the general motor ability and specificity of motor abilities hypotheses.

On the basis of results such as these, it would be difficult to conclude that only one test could be considered a valid measure of balancing ability. At the most basic level, we need to consider static balance and dynamic balance as two independent types of balance ability. The application of the relative independence of static and dynamic balance to professional practice can be seen in several of the balance tests commonly used in physical rehabilitation contexts. For example, the Berg Balance Scale (BBS), which is one of the most commonly used balance tests, involves fourteen types of static and dynamic tests of balance. Research evidence has shown that the BBS is a useful assessment tool in a variety of contexts, such as determining the risk of falling by the elderly and evaluating treatment effects for post-stroke patients (see Blum & Korner-Bitensky, 2008). Many other balance tests have been developed that also include the use of multiple static and dynamic activities. Research has shown that these tests are for use with specific populations and for specific purposes (e.g., Cattaneo, Jonsdottir, & Repetti, 2007; Haines, et al. 2007; Rose, Lucchese, & Wiersma, 2006). The important conclusion to draw from the research on balance tests is that *balance is a multi-dimensional ability* that is specific to the task or skill in which balance is involved,

specificity of motor abilities hypothesis
a hypothesis that maintains that the many motor abilities in an individual are relatively independent.

TABLE 3.1   Results from the Experiment by Drowatzky and Zuccato (1967) Showing the Correlations among Six Different Tests of Static and Dynamic Balance

| Test | Static Balance Tests | | | Dynamic Balance Tests | | |
| | 1 | 2 | 3 | 4 | 5 | 6 |
	Stork Stand[a]	Diver's Stand[b]	Bass Stick Stand[c]	Sideward Leap[d]	Bass Stepping Stone Test[e]	Balance Beam Test[f]
1	—	.14	−.12	.26	.20	.03
2		—	−.12	−.03	−.07	−.14
3			—	−.04	.22	−.19
4				—	.31	.19
5					—	.18
6						—

[a]*Stork stand*—Person stands for as long as possible on the foot of the dominant leg while placing the other foot on the inside of the supporting knee and the hands on the hips.

[b]*Diver's stand*—Person stands erect with both feet together, arms extended in front. When ready he or she rises onto the balls of the feet, closes his or her eyes, and maintains this position for as long as possible.

[c]*Bass stick test*—Person stands for as long as possible, up to 60 sec, with the ball of the foot of the dominant leg crosswise on a 1 in. wide × 1 in. high × 12 in. long stick; the other foot must be off the floor.

[d]*Sideward leap*—Person stands on the left foot, leaps sideward to the right to a mark on the floor (distance = person's leg length), leans forward to push small object off a mark (18 in. in front of landing mark), then holds balance for 5 sec.

[e]*Bass stepping stone test*—Person stands on the right foot on the starting mark, then leaps to a series of targets located in front of the person, alternating left and right feet. At each target, the person maintains balance for as long as possible, up to 5 sec.

[f]*Balance beam test*—On a balance beam (4 in. wide, 4.5 in. off the floor, 10 ft long) person walks, with hands on hips, heel to toe for 10 steps or until falls; if falls, gets back on beam, continues walking; stops walking at 10 steps or second fall.

Source: From Drowatzky, J. N. & Zuccato, F. C. (1967). Interrelationships between selected measures of static and dynamic balance. *Research Quarterly for Exercise and Sport, 38,* 509–510. Copyright © 1967 American Alliance for Health, Physical Education, Recreation, and Dance. Reprinted by permission.

with static and dynamic balance viewed as general categories of types of balance.

Timing. As a motor ability, timing is an important component of the performance of many motor skills. For some skills we need to precisely time our movement initiation with the movement of an external object, such as hitting a moving baseball or starting a sprint in track. This type of timing is commonly referred to as *external,* or *anticipation, timing.* For other skills, we time our movements according to our knowledge of time, which occurs when we walk or jog at a desired pace or when a dancer performs without music but must maintain a specific

rhythm and tempo. This type of timing is known as *internal timing.* In the study of individual differences, researchers have held different views about internal timing as a motor ability. One view proposes that timing is controlled by a common timing process, much like an internal clock, that provides the musculature with the rhythmic information needed to produce the continuous timing requirements of a skill (e.g., Ivry & Hazeltine, 1995). An alternate view argues that the precise rhythmic timing we observe for the skills described as examples of internal timing results from task-specific characteristics related to the interaction between the person and the performance environment.

One of the ways researchers have tested views about the control of internal timing is to follow the approach used to test the specificity of motor abilities hypothesis that we discussed earlier. If an "internal clock" controls timing, we would expect a general ability for timing, and therefore people should perform similarly across a variety of tasks that require timing. On the other hand, if timing is task specific, performance on one type of task should not predict how well we would perform on a different task. These two possibilities were first tested in a series of experiments by Robertson and her colleagues (Robertson et al., 1999). Included in these experiments was a comparison of the performance of two tasks that included the same timing requirement, a series of 800 msec simple movements. One task required participants to repetitively tap an index finger on a tabletop at a speed of 800 msec per tap; the other required repetitive circle drawing at 800 msec per circle. Participants were initially provided a metronome as a guide so they could become familiar with the 800 msec rate of movement. Then the metronome stopped, and participants continued to tap or draw circles as a test of their timing ability. The results showed a low correlation between the two tasks, which indicated that performance on either of the two tasks did not predict how well participants would perform on the other task. Additional research by Zelaznik and his colleagues has shown similar results for repetitive movements performed at the participants' preferred rate of speed (e.g., Zelaznik, Spencer, & Doffin, 2000).

Looking at correlational results is not the only way to determine whether timing is a general or task-specific ability. Spencer and Zelaznik (2003) compared timing accuracy for several tasks that required a common timing of several simple movements. If timing is a general ability, we would expect timing accuracy to be similar across these tasks. But, as figure 3.1 shows, the participants varied greatly in how accurately they could time a 500 msec (i.e., 0.5 sec) movement for repetitive finger tapping, line drawing (horizontal and vertical lines of the same length), and circle drawing.

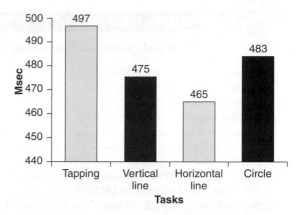

FIGURE 3.1 Results of the experiment by Spencer and Zelaznik (2003) showing the accuracy for timing 500 msec movements when performing tasks that required repetitive finger tapping, drawing vertical and horizontal lines of the same length, and drawing a circle. [Data from Spencer, R. M. C., & Zelaznik, H. N. (2003). Weber (slope) analyses of timing variability in tapping and drawing tasks. *Journal of Motor Behavior, 35,* 371–381.]

Although they very accurately timed their finger tapping, their timing accuracy for the other tasks was notably poorer.

A considerable amount of evidence now exists to support the conclusion that although people are capable of precise timing when performing motor skills, timing ability is specific to the requirements of the skill being performed rather than a general timing ability.

The "All-Around Athlete"

You have undoubtedly read about professional athletes who could have become a professional in several sports. Or perhaps you know people who seem to be "good at" a lot of different physical activities. If motor abilities are numerous and independent, then how can we explain these people whom we often hear referred to as an "all-around athlete," the person who is very proficient at a variety of physical activities? According to the specificity view, abilities fall somewhere along a range containing low, average, and high amounts within individuals. Because people differ in a way that is consistent with a normal distribution scale, we would expect that some people have a large number of abilities at an average

A CLOSER LOOK

The Relationship between Falls among the Elderly and Balance

A common problem for the elderly is falling. Both clinicians and researchers have determined that among the many reasons for why the elderly fall, difficulty maintaining balance is one of the primary causes. Thus it is not surprising that the assessment of balance is important for identifying people who may be more at risk for falling than others. At the forefront of developing falls prevention programs is the Center for Successful Aging at California State University at Fullerton (http://hdcs.fullerton.edu/csa/). A publication in 2006 by a group from this center (Rose, Lucchese, & Wiersma, 2006) discussed the development of a balance test the center developed and has successfully used as part of its programs. The following is a summary of some of the information they reported concerning the incidence of falling among the elderly and the test they developed. One of the noteworthy features of the test is that it is based on a multidimensional view of balance, which has been emphasized in this chapter.

Falling Incidence Among the Elderly
- 35% of people over 65 years old fall at least once a year

- 20–30% of these falls result in injuries that affect mobility and independence

The Fullerton Advanced Balance Scale (FAB)
Although many tests are available to assess a person's risk of falling, the Center for Successful Aging determined that a new test was needed to overcome specific problems associated with available tests. The result was the development of a multidimensional test designed to "identify balance problems of varying severity in functionally independent older adults and also evaluate more of the system(s) (e.g., sensory, musculoskeletal, neuromuscular) that might be contributing to balance problems" (p. 1478). The FAB consists of 10 items that require approximately 10 to 12 min to administer. Table 3.2 summarizes the items and the primary physiological systems or mechanisms each item assesses. A complete description of the test items, the scoring for each item, and the psychometric evaluations of the test are presented in the article.

---

level, and other people have a majority of abilities at either the high or the low end of the scale.

According to the specificity hypothesis, the person who excels in a large number of physical activities has high levels of a large number of abilities. We would expect that a person would do very well in those activities for which the underlying abilities required for successful performance matched the abilities for which the person was at the high end of the scale.

In actual fact, the true all-around athlete is a rare individual. Typically, when a person shows high performance levels in a variety of physical activities, a close inspection of those activities reveals they involve many foundational motor abilities in common. We would expect a person exhibiting high levels for a variety of abilities to do well in activities for which those abilities were foundational to performance. However, we would expect average performance if this person engaged in activities for

which those abilities were less important, activities based on other abilities, of which the person possessed only average levels.

Identifying Motor Abilities
As a general trait or capacity, an ability is a relatively enduring attribute of an individual. Researchers who study individual differences assume that we can describe the skills involved in complex motor activities in terms of the abilities that underlie their performance. For example, the ability called spatial visualization is related to the performance of such diverse tasks as aerial navigation, blueprint reading, and dentistry. An important step in understanding how abilities and skill performance are related is identifying abilities and matching them with the skills involved.

When researchers and practitioners identify specific motor abilities, they usually refer to the work of Edwin Fleishman (see Fleishman &

A CLOSER LOOK *(Continued)*

The Relationship between Falls among the Elderly and Balance

TABLE 3.2   Test Items and Primary Physiological Systems or Mechanisms Evaluated by Each Item

Test Item	Systems and/or Mechanisms Evaluated
1. Stand with feet together and eyes closed	Sensory systems and strategies (somatosensation, vision), internal representations, musculoskeletal components, neuromuscular synergies
2. Reaching forward to object	Sensory systems (vision), neuromuscular response synergies, musculoskeletal components, anticipatory mechanisms
3. Turn in full circle	Sensory systems and strategies (vestibular, vision), neuromuscular synergies, musculoskeletal components
4. Step up and over	Sensory systems and strategies (vision, somatosensation), anticipatory and adaptive mechanisms, neuromuscular synergies, musculoskeletal system
5. Tandem walk	Sensory systems and strategies (vision, somatosensation), neuromuscular synergies, musculoskeletal components
6. Stand on one leg	Sensory systems (vision), anticipatory and adaptive mechanisms, musculoskeletal components
7. Stand on foam with eyes closed	Sensory systems and strategies (vestibular), internal representations, neuromuscular synergies, musculoskeletal components
8. Two-footed jump	Neuromuscular synergies, musculoskeletal components, anticipatory and adaptive mechanisms
9. Walk with head turns	Sensory systems and strategies (vestibular, vision), neuromuscular synergies, adaptive mechanisms
10. Reactive postural control	Neuromuscular synergies, adaptive mechanisms, musculoskeletal system

Adapted from Table 1, p. 1480 in Rose, D.J., Lucchese, N., & Wiersma, L.D. (2006). Development of a multidimensional balance scale for use with functionally independent older adults. *Archives of Physical Medicine and Rehabilitation, 87,* 1478–1485.

Quaintance, 1984, for a description of this work). His pioneering research, which was carried out for four decades beginning in the 1950s, continues to influence our understanding and study of motor abilities and how they relate to motor skill performance. Perhaps the most significant achievement of Fleishman's work was the development of a taxonomy of abilities that includes a taxonomy of motor abilities.

A taxonomy of motor abilities. From the results of extensive batteries of perceptual motor tests given

to many people, Fleishman developed a "taxonomy of human perceptual motor abilities" (Fleishman, 1972; Fleishman & Quaintance, 1984). The goal of the taxonomy was "to define the fewest independent ability categories which might be most useful and meaningful in describing performance in the widest variety of tasks" (Fleishman, 1967, p. 352). The taxonomy included two broad categories of human abilities in the perceptual motor and physical domains: *perceptual motor abilities and physical proficiency abilities.* Table 3.3 presents and

TABLE 3.3   Perceptual Motor Ability Categories Identified by Fleishman (1972) as a Result of
Numerous Research Studies

Ability Category	Definition	Ability Category Test and Related Motor Skill Example
Multilimb coordination	Ability to coordinate movements of a number of limbs simultaneously	*Complex coordinator task:* Person simultaneously controls two levers, one with each hand, and two pedals, one with each foot, in response to signals *Skill example:* Playing the piano or organ, where both hands and feet are involved
Control precision	Ability to make rapid and precise movement adjustments of control devices involving single arm-hand or leg movements; adjustments are made to visual stimuli	*Rotary pursuit task:* Person keeps a hand-held stylus in contact with a small disk embedded in a phonograph-like turntable as it rotates at 60 rpm *Skill example:* Operating a joy stick in a computer video game
Response orientation	Ability to make a rapid selection of controls to be moved or the direction to move them in	*Visual discrimination tasks, e.g., choice reaction time task:* Person responds as quickly as possible when one of several visual signals illuminates *Skill example:* Soccer player with the ball responding to defensive player's movements by dribbling past the player, passing, or making a shot at the goal
Reaction time	Ability to respond rapidly to a signal when it appears	*Visual or auditory simple reaction time task:* Person responds as quickly as possible to a visual (e.g., a light) or auditory (e.g., a buzzer) signal *Skill example:* Start of a sprint in swimming
Speed of arm movement	Ability to rapidly make a gross, discrete arm movement where accuracy is minimized	*Two-plate reciprocal tapping task:* Person moves a handheld stylus back and forth between two metal plates, 25 cm apart, as rapidly as possible for 10 sec *Skill example:* Throwing a ball for speed rather than for accuracy
Rate control	Ability to time continuous anticipatory movement adjustments in response to speed and/or direction changes of a continuously moving target or object	*Pursuit tracking task:* Person moves a computer mouse to move a cursor on a computer monitor to maintain contact with a target cursor that changes in speed and direction *Skill example:* Driving a car on a highway
Manual dexterity	Ability to make skillful arm-hand movements to manipulate fairly large objects under speeded conditions	*Minnesota Manual Dexterity task:* Person picks up with one hand and turns over as quickly as possible a series of wooden pegs in holes *Skill example:* Dribbling and maintaining control of a basketball while running
Finger dexterity	Ability to make skillful, controlled manipulations of tiny objects involving primarily the fingers	*Purdue Pegboard task:* Person picks up and assembles small peg, washer, and collar units and inserts them into small holes *Skill example:* Buttoning a shirt

TABLE 3.3   (*Continued*)

Ability Category	Definition	Ability Category Test and Related Motor Skill Example
Arm-hand steadiness	Ability to make precise arm-hand positioning movements where strength and speed are minimized; includes maintaining arm-hand steadiness during arm movement or in a static arm position	*Track tracing task:* Person moves a handheld stylus through a trough in a board without touching the sides of the trough; and *Hand-steadiness task:* Person holds a stylus in a small hole without touching the sides of the hole *Skill example:* Applying eyeliner
Wrist, finger speed	Ability to make rapid and repetitive movements with the hand and fingers, and/or rotary wrist movements when accuracy is not critical	*Tapping task:* Person holds a pencil and taps its point as many times as possible in a large circle for a specified amount of time *Skill example:* Handwriting for speed
Aiming	Ability to rapidly and accurately move the hand to a small target	*Manual aiming task:* Person holds a pencil and rapidly makes a dot in a series of very small circles *Skill example:* A drummer rapidly moving a stick from a snare drum to a small cymbal

Note: The ability labels, definitions, and tests are as Fleishman presented them in two reports on his work (Fleishman, 1972, p. 1019f; Fleishman & Quintance, 1984, p. 164f).

defines the eleven perceptual motor ability categories Fleishman proposed. Note that table 3.3 also includes an example of one of the tests he used to assess each ability and an example of a motor skill whose performance would be associated with the ability category.

In addition to perceptual motor abilities, Fleishman also identified nine abilities that he designated as *physical proficiency abilities.* These abilities differ from the perceptual motor abilities in that they are more generally related to gross motor skill performance, which most people would consider as physical fitness abilities. The physical proficiency abilities identified by Fleishman are as follows: (1) *static strength,* the maximum force that a person can exert against external objects; (2) *dynamic strength,* the muscular endurance used in exerting force repeatedly; (3) *explosive strength,* the ability to mobilize energy effectively for bursts of muscular

effort; (4) *trunk strength,* the strength of the trunk muscles; (5) *extent flexibility,* the ability to flex or stretch the trunk and back muscles; (6) *dynamic flexibility,* the ability to make repeated, rapid trunk-flexing movements; (7) *gross body coordination,* the ability to coordinate the action of several parts of the body while the body is in motion; (8) *gross body equilibrium,* the ability to maintain balance without visual cues; and (9) *stamina,* the capacity to sustain maximum effort requiring cardiovascular effort.

We should not consider Fleishman's lists to be exhaustive inventories of all the abilities related to motor skill performance, because Fleishman wanted to identify the smallest number of abilities that would describe the tasks performed in the test battery. Although he used hundreds of tasks to identify those abilities, the inclusion of additional types of tasks besides those Fleishman used could lead to the identification of other motor abilities.

The Relationship between Perceptual Motor Abilities and Handwriting Speed: Implications for Occupational Therapists' Interventions

Slow handwriting speed can affect children's school performance by preventing them from completing handwritten work that must meet time constraints. To investigate factors that are associated with slow handwriting, Tseng and Chow (2000) administered three perceptual or motor abilities tests and a vigilance test to 7- to 11-year-old Chinese schoolchildren who hand wrote slow or normal speed.

Handwriting speed: The amount of time required for the children to copy in pencil a previously studied text (speed = the number of Chinese characters written per minute)

The abilities tests measured:
- arm movement speed and hand dexterity
- nonmotor visual perception (including discrimination, sequential memory, figure closure, etc.)
- visual-motor integration (which required the copying in sequence of a set of geometric forms)
- focusing and maintaining attention over time

Results: The following abilities were predictors of slow handwriting:
- arm speed and hand dexterity
- focusing and maintaining attention
- visual memory
- visual-motor integration
- visual sequential memory

Authors' conclusion: These results suggest that "intervention for slow handwriting should focus on facilitating visual processing, including memory and visual-motor integration, rather than the fine motor training so often emphasized in occupational therapy programs" (p. 87).

For example, Fleishman did not include the following abilities in his two lists:

- *Static balance*—The ability to maintain postural stability on a stable surface or when not engaging in locomotor activities (e.g., standing on the floor while reading a book)
- *Dynamic balance*—The ability to maintain postural stability on a moving surface or when engaging in locomotor activities (e.g., walking on a sidewalk)
- *Visual acuity*—The ability to see clearly and precisely (e.g., reading a street sign)
- *Visual tracking*—The ability to visually follow a moving object (e.g., watching the flight of a ball that is thrown to you to catch)
- *Eye-hand or eye-foot coordination*—The ability to perform skills requiring vision and the precise use of the hands (e.g., correctly typing a sentence on a keyboard) or feet (e.g., kicking a penalty kick in soccer)

An important assumption of this view of human abilities is that all individuals possess these motor abilities. Another is that because it is possible to measure these motor abilities, it is also possible to determine a quantified measure of the level of each ability in a person. People differ in the amount of each ability they possess. Their motor abilities indicate limits that influence a person's potential for achievement in motor skill performance.

Relating Motor Abilities to Motor Skill Performance

Figure 3.2 illustrates the view that motor abilities are underlying, foundational components of motor skill performance. This figure shows how we can analyze complex motor skills by a process known as *task analysis* in order to identify the abilities that underlie any motor skill. For example, to serve a tennis ball successfully, a player must perform certain components of that skill properly.

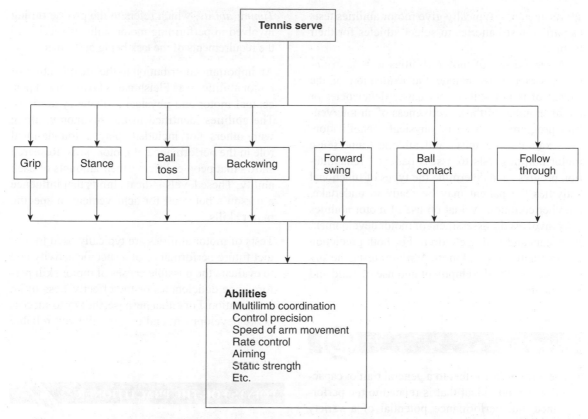

FIGURE 3.2 A task analysis for the tennis serve indicating the component parts of the serve and some examples of perceptual motor abilities underlying performance of the serve.

Figure 3.2 identifies these components, which are the first level of analysis of the tennis serve, in the middle tier of the diagram. Identification of these components helps us identify more readily the underlying motor abilities that are involved in the successful performance of this task. The bottom tier of the diagram presents these abilities. Based on Fleishman's lists, they include such abilities as multilimb coordination, control precision, speed of arm movement, rate control, aiming, and static strength. You undoubtedly could add others. However, these few examples should serve to illustrate the foundational role perceptual motor and physical proficiency abilities play in the performance of motor skills.

Uses for tests of motor abilities. Because of the foundational role played by motor abilities in the performance of motor skills, tests of motor abilities are used for a variety of purposes. We will consider two of the most common. One use is the *prediction* of future performance of a motor skill or physical activity. Tests used for this purpose are sometimes called aptitude tests. For example, the military and industry use tests of motor abilities in their batteries of tests to select people to train for or work in specific jobs (e.g., Chan, 2005). Medical and dental schools often include motor abilities tests in their selection of students for specialist training or admission into specific programs. And professional sports teams, and national and international sports agencies, typically give motor abilities tests as part of test batteries to select athletes for their teams.

A second use of motor abilities tests is *evaluation,* which may include the evaluation of the causes of motor skill performance deficiencies or the assessment of the effectiveness of an intervention program, such as in physical rehabilitation. For example, therapists and athletic trainers use motor abilities tests to assess patients' rehabilitation progress and determine the types of functional activities the patient may be ready to undertake. Another common evaluation use of motor abilities tests involves the assessment of motor development in infants and young children. For both prediction and evaluation uses of motor abilities tests, the key to success is the development and use of valid and reliable tests.

SUMMARY

- The term *ability* refers to a general trait or capacity of the individual that is related to the performance and performance potential of a variety of skills or tasks. A variety of motor abilities underlie the performance of a motor skill; people have different amounts, or quantities, of these abilities.

- Historically researchers have proposed two hypotheses to describe how the various motor abilities relate to one another. The *general motor ability hypothesis* states that the abilities are highly related; the *specificity hypothesis* argues that the abilities are relatively independent of one another. Research evidence has consistently supported the specificity hypothesis.

- There has been some debate among those who hold the specificity hypothesis concerning the generality of certain specific motor abilities, such as balance and timing. Research indicates that *balance* consists of static and dynamic balance as two relatively independent motor abilities and that several relatively independent variations of each exist.

Timing ability, which refers to the precise timing involved in performing motor skills, is specific to the requirements of the task being performed.

- An important contribution to the identification of motor abilities was Fleishman's taxonomy of perceptual motor and physical proficiency abilities. The abilities identified in this taxonomy, along with others not included, play a foundational role in the performance of motor skills. Research shows that people differ in their amounts of each ability. These levels indicate limits that influence a person's potential for achievement in specific motor skills.

- Tests of motor abilities are typically used to predict future performance of a specific activity and to evaluate the possible causes of motor skill performance deficiencies or the effectiveness of an intervention. For either purpose, the key to success is the development and use of valid and reliable tests.

POINTS FOR THE PRACTITIONER

- Because of the specificity of motor abilities, students should not be classified according to motor ability categories that indicate amounts of motor ability.

- The identification and assessment of specific motor abilities can provide you insight into possible reasons for a person's difficulty performing or learning a motor skill. For example, a physical education student may have difficulty catching a thrown ball because of a poorly developed ability to visually track a moving object.

- Because certain motor abilities underlie the successful performance of various motor skills, you can develop physical activities to improve performance in a variety of skills that involve the same foundational motor ability. For example, various activities that require hand-eye coordination can serve as a unit of instruction in physical education.

• Evaluation of motor skill performance deficits should be skill specific. For example, the assessment of balance problems should be specific to the type of balance required by a skill of interest. Similarly, the assessment of locomotor movement problems should be specific to the types of gait of interest.

RELATED READINGS

Ackerman, P. L., & Cianciolo, A. T. (1999). Psychomotor abilities via touch-panel testing: Measurement innovations, construct, and criterion validity. *Human Performance, 12,* 231–273.

Campbell, L. S. K., & Catano, V. M. (2004). Using measures of specific abilities to predict training performance in Canadian forces operator occupations. *Military Psychology, 16,* 183–201.

Hoffman, J. R., Kahana, A., Chapnik, L., Shamiss, A., & Davidson, B. (1999). The relationship of physical fitness on pilot candidate selection in the Israel Air Force. *Aviation, Space, and Environmental Medicine, 70,* 131–134.

Johnston, P. J. (2002). Psychomotor abilities tests as predictors of training performance. *Canadian Journal of Behavioural Science, 34,* 75–83.

Kanbur, N. O., Duzgun, L., Derman, O., & Baltaci, G. (2005). Do sexual maturation stages affect flexibility in adolescent boys aged 14 years? *Journal of Sports Medicine and Physical Fitness, 45,* 53–57.

Kohmura, Y., Aoki, K., Yoshigi, H., Sakuraba, K., & Yanagiya, T. (2008). Development of a baseball-specific battery of tests and a testing protocol for college baseball players. *Journal of Strength and Conditioning Research, 22,* 1051–1058.

Kritz, M. F., & Cronin, J. (2008). Static posture assessment screen of athletes: Benefits and considerations. *Strength and Conditioning Journal, 30,* 18–27.

Schijven, M. P., Jakimowicz, J. J., & Carter, F. J. (2004). How to select aspirant laparoscopic surgical trainees: Establishing concurrent validity comparing Xitact LS500 index performance scores with standardized psychomotor scores. *Journal of Surgical Research, 121,* 112–119.

Tseng, M. H., & Cermak, S. A. (1993). The influence of ergonomic factors and perceptual-motor abilities on handwriting performance. *American Journal of Occupational Therapy, 47,* 919–926.

Vescovi, J. D., & McGuigan, M. R. (2008). Relationships between sprinting, agility, and jump ability in female athletes. *Journal of Sports Sciences, 26,* 97–107.

INTERNET RESOURCES

• To read a detailed autobiography of Edwin Fleishman, the developer of the taxonomy of motor abilities discussed in this chapter, go to http://www.siop.org/Presidents/fleishman.aspx.

• Many motor ability tests are available commercially. To learn more about some of the tests and companies that provide them, here are the Web sites for a few of these companies and the tests they sell (note that these companies sell more than tests of motor ability):

Go to http://www.creativeorgdesign.com/. Click on Test categories to open a menu of a variety of tests related to abilities and aptitudes

Go to http://www.rehaboutlet.com/. Go to Evaluation and Testing

Go to http://www.lafayetteinstrument.com/.

• To see an example of the use and comparison of a battery of cognitive, perceptual, and motor ability tests for personnel selection, and read a report presented at the 2004 Conference of the International Personnel Management Assessment Council (IPMAAC) that compares two tests designed to predict training and job performance for various military jobs at http://www.ipmaac.org/conf04/morath.pdf.

STUDY QUESTIONS

1. (a) How do people who study individual differences define the term *abilities?* (b) Distinguish the meaning of *abilities* from that of the term *skill.*

2. (a) What is the difference between the general motor ability hypothesis and the specificity of motor abilities hypothesis? (b) Give an example of research evidence indicating which of these hypotheses is more valid.

3. How is balance an example of a motor ability that includes at least two types of relatively independent variations?

4. How can a specificity view of motor abilities explain how a person can be very successful at performing a lot of different motor skills?

5. (a) Name and describe five perceptual motor abilities identified by Fleishman. (b) What other motor abilities can you identify?

6. Describe how the assessment of motor abilities can be used in a battery of tests designed to identify people who would be good candidates for jobs or professions that require specific motor skills.

Specific Application Problem:
(a) You are working in your chosen profession. Describe a motor skill that a person you are working with is having difficulty performing.
(b) Describe how you would determine whether the reason for the difficulty is related to a motor ability problem or to some other reason, such as lack of practice, poor instruction, and the like.

UNIT TWO

Introduction to Motor Control

CHAPTER 4

Neuromotor Basis for Motor Control

Concept: The neuromotor system forms the foundation for the control of movement.

After completing this chapter you will be able to

- Describe the general structure of a neuron and the types and functions of neurons
- Identify and describe the structural components of the brain that are most directly involved in control of movement and describe their primary functions
- Identify and describe the neural pathways that make up the ascending and descending tracts
- Describe a motor unit, the recruitment of motor units, and their relationship to the control of movement
- Describe the basic components of a conceptual hierarchical model that describes the CNS structures and their functions in the control of movement

APPLICATION

When you are reading at your desk and want to write a few notes about what you are reading, you must undertake a sequence of coordinated movements to accomplish your goal. You must first pick up your pen and then position your head, body, arm, hand, and fingers so that you can use the pen. Then you must initiate the movements required to write the words you want to put on the paper. Although this example may seem to describe a relatively simple task that you can do very easily and quickly, have you ever thought about what is happening in your nervous system to allow you to carry out this sequence of events? As simple as the individual movements may be, a rather complex array of neural activity is associated with planning and performing the task. For example, your decision to pick up the pen was a cognitive activity,

but what happened in the nervous system to change this cognitive act into a motor act? To answer this question, we need to consider two important issues in the study of motor control. One concerns the neurophysiologic basis of the neural activity associated with this sequence of events. The other is the more theoretical issue of how the cognitive intention to perform an action becomes a sequence of movements that enables a person to achieve the intended action goal. We will consider the first of these issues in this chapter by looking at the central nervous system in terms of its structure and function as related to the performance of motor skills. We will briefly consider the second issue from a neurological perspective but then address it in more detail in chapter 5, where we discuss theories of motor control.

You may be asking why understanding this process is necessary for someone who wants to pursue a professional career that essentially entails helping people learn or relearn motor skills or improve their performance of skills. The answer is that a basic understanding of the physiology underlying the control of voluntary movement establishes a more comprehensive appreciation and awareness of the capabilities and limitations of the people with whom a practitioner works. The person who plans to enter a profession where physical rehabilitation is the focus needs this knowledge for the assessment of physical dysfunctions and limitations as well as for the development of appropriate rehabilitation interventions.

Application Problem to Solve   Describe a motor skill that you perform or might help people learn. Describe the parts of the central nervous system involved in the performance of this skill.

DISCUSSION

Our study of the structure and function of the neuromotor system will focus on the parts of the central nervous system (CNS) that are involved in the control of voluntary, coordinated movement. It is important to note that the peripheral nervous system's sensory components are not included here but will be considered in chapter 6 in discussions concerning the role of the tactile, proprioception, and visual sensory systems in motor control. In addition, it is important to point out that the study of the neuromotor system in this chapter and in chapter 6 are intended to be basic introductions, or reviews (for some students), rather than in-depth studies.

THE NEURON

The basic component of the nervous system is the nerve cell, which is called a **neuron.** Neurons in the nervous system number in the billions. These functional units, which vary in size from 4 to 100

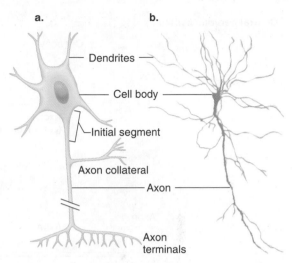

FIGURE 4.1   (a) An illustration of a neuron (the break in the axon indicates that axons may extend for long distances). (b) A neuron as observed through a microscope. [From Widmaier, E. P., Raff, H., & Strang, K. T. (2006). *Vander's human physiology: The mechanisms of body function* (10th ed.), p. 152. New York: McGraw-Hill.]

microns, provide the means for receiving and sending information through the entire nervous system. Although there are several types of neurons, most share a similar general three-part structure: the cell body and two processes, which are called dendrites, and the axon (see figure 4.1).

General Structure of Neurons
The *cell body* contains the all-important nucleus, which regulates the homeostasis of the neuron. **Dendrites** are extensions from the cell body and are primarily responsible for receiving information from other neurons. A neuron may have none

---

neuron   a nerve cell; the basic component of the nervous system.

dendrites   extensions from a neuron's cell body that receive neural impulses from other neurons; a neuron may have none or as many as thousands of dendrites.

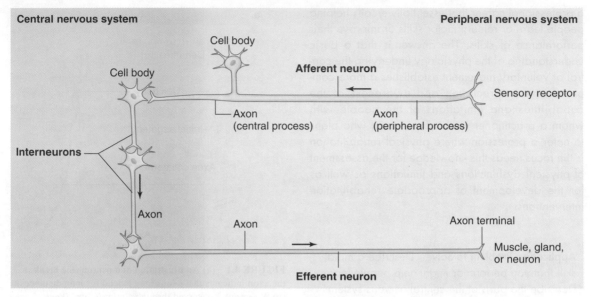

FIGURE 4.2   Three types of neurons. The arrows indicate the direction of transmission of neural activity. [From Widmaier, E. P., Raff, H., & Strang, K. T. (2006). *Vander's human physiology: The mechanisms of body function* (10th ed.), p. 155. New York: McGraw-Hill.]

or as many as thousands of dendrites. The **axon,** which is also called a nerve fiber, is responsible for sending information from the neuron. Unlike dendrites, there is only one axon per neuron, although most axons have many branches, which are known as *collaterals.* The ends of the axons, called axon terminals, provide a signal transmission relay station for neurotransmitters, which are the chemical signals passed on to other neurons or to muscles, in the specific case of movement control. Many axons are covered by layers of *myelin,* which is a cellular membrane that speeds up the transmission of neural signals along the axon. The passing on of neural signals from one neuron to another occurs at a *synapse,* which is the junction between the axon of a neuron and another neuron.

Types and Functions of Neurons

The most convenient way to classify neurons is according to their function in terms of sending and receiving information (i.e., neural impulses) to, from, and within the central nervous system (CNS),

which consists of the brain and spinal cord. There are three functional classes (see figure 4.2 for illustrations of examples of types of neurons). **Sensory neurons** (also called *afferent neurons*) send neural impulses to the CNS, while **motor neurons** (also called *efferent neurons*) send neural impulses from the CNS to skeletal muscle fibers. **Interneurons** function within the CNS. Estimates of the quantity of each type of neuron in the body indicate that for each sensory neuron, there are ten motor neurons and 200,000 interneurons (Widmaier, Raff, & Strang, 2006).

Sensory neurons. In their role of receiving information from various sensory receptors in the body, sensory neurons function much like transducers in electronics in that they receive a neural signal and then convert it to an electrical signal that can be transmitted along the neural pathways and received by the CNS. The unique structural characteristic of sensory neurons is that they are unipolar; that is, they have no dendrites and only one axon. The cell body and most of the axon of sensory neurons are in the peripheral nervous system, with only the central process of the axon entering the CNS.

Motor neurons. Two types of motor neurons influence the control of movement. *Alpha motor neurons* are found predominantly in the spinal cord. Sometimes referred to as motor horn cells, they emanate from the horn of the spinal cord and have many branching dendrites and long branching axons that connect directly with the skeletal muscle fibers. *Gamma motor neurons* supply a portion of the skeletal muscle called intrafusal fibers, which will be discussed in more detail in chapter 6.

Interneurons. These specialized neurons originate and terminate in the brain or spinal cord. They function as connections between axons descending from the brain, and they synapse on motor neurons and axons from sensory nerves and the spinal nerves ascending to the brain.

THE CENTRAL NERVOUS SYSTEM

The central nervous system (CNS) functions as the "command center" for human behavior, although there are varying views about the precise nature of the commands it issues (in chapter 5 we will discuss two of these views as they relate to motor control). This incredibly complex system, which comprises the brain and spinal cord, forms the center of activity for the integration and organization of the sensory and motor information in the control of movement. Rather than present a complete anatomical and physiological picture of the components of the CNS, we will concentrate on those portions most directly related to the motor control associated with learning and performing the types of motor skills that are the focus of this book, as discussed in chapter 1.

The Brain

The structural components of the brain that are most directly involved in control of movement are the cerebrum, diencephalon, cerebellum, and brainstem. The cerebrum and diencephalon are sometimes referred to as the forebrain. The locations of

these components, their subcomponents, and other notable components are illustrated in figure 4.3.

The cerebrum. The **cerebrum** consists of two halves, known as the right and left *cerebral hemispheres,* which are connected by a sheet of nerve fibers known as the corpus callosum. Both hemispheres are covered by what is commonly pictured in photographs as an undulating, wrinkly, gray-colored surface called the **cerebral cortex.** This covering is a thin tissue of nerve cell bodies called *gray matter.* The gray matter is about 2–5 mm thick and, if unfolded, would cover about 20 sq ft. The folding results in ridges (each ridge is called a *gyrus*) and grooves (each groove is called a *sulcus*). Cortical neurons are either *pyramidal cells* (based on the shape of the cell body), which are the primary cells

---

axons   (also called nerve fibers) extensions from a neuron's cell body that transmit neural impulses to other neurons, structures in the CNS, or muscles; a neuron has only one axon, although most axons branch into many branches.

sensory neurons   (also called afferent neurons) nerve cells that send neural impulses to the CNS.

motor neurons   (also called efferent neurons) nerve cells that send neural impulses from the CNS to skeletal muscle fibers.

interneurons   specialized nerve cells that originate and terminate in the brain or spinal cord; they function between axons descending from the brain and synapse on motor neurons, and between the axons from sensory nerves and the spinal nerves ascending to the brain.

cerebrum   a brain structure in the forebrain that consists of two halves, known as the right and left cerebral hemispheres.

cerebral cortex   the undulating, wrinkly, gray-colored surface of the cerebrum; it is a thin tissue of nerve cell bodies (about 2–5 mm thick) called gray matter.

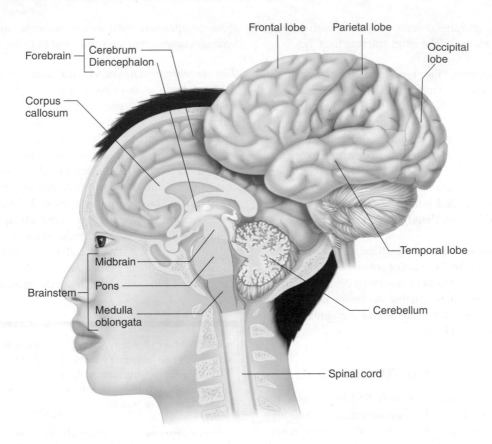

FIGURE 4.3   The major divisions of the brain and the surface of the cerebral cortex with its four lobes. [From Widmaier, E. P., Raff, H., & Strang, K. T. (2006). *Vander's human physiology: The mechanisms of body function* (10th ed.), p. 192. New York: McGraw-Hill.]

for sending neural signals from the cortex to other parts of the CNS, or *nonpyramidal cells.* Underneath the cortex is an inner layer of myelinated nerve fibers called the *white matter.*

The cortex of each hemisphere consists of four lobes that are named according to the skull bones nearest them. The *frontal lobe,* which is the area anterior to the central sulcus and the lateral fissure, contains brain areas that are vital to the control of voluntary movement. The *parietal lobe,* which is the area just posterior to the central fissure and superior to the lateral fissure, is a key brain center for the control of perception of sensory information. The most posterior lobe of the cortex is the *occipital lobe,* which contains areas important in visual perception. Finally, the *temporal lobe,* which is located just below the lateral fissure, plays important roles in memory, abstract thought, and judgment.

Several cortex areas are involved in sensory functions. As you can see in figure 4.4, the **sensory cortex** areas are located posterior to the central sulcus. Specific types of sensory information are transmitted via the sensory nerves to the area of the cortex that receives that type of information. Note in figure 4.4 that sensory-specific areas exist for vision, taste, speech, and body (for example, the somatic sensory area receives pain, temperature, and pressure sensory information). Also note in

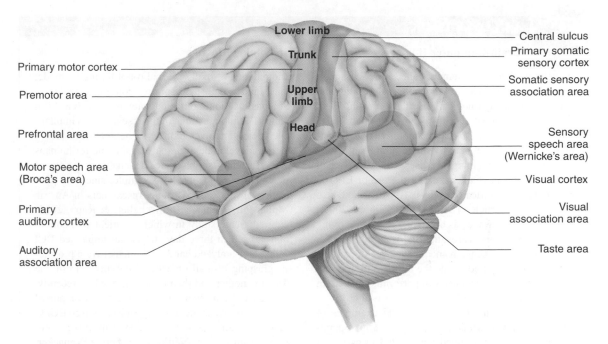

Lower limb

Trunk

Upper limb

Head

Central sulcus

Primary somatic sensory cortex

Somatic sensory association area

Sensory speech area (Wernicke's area)

Visual cortex

Visual association area

Taste area

Primary motor cortex

Premotor area

Prefrontal area

Motor speech area (Broca's area)

Primary auditory cortex

Auditory association area

FIGURE 4.4   Functional regions of the cerebral cortex. [From Seeley, R. R., Stephens, T. D., & Tate, P. (2005). *Essentials of anatomy and physiology,* 5th ed., p. 222. New York: McGraw-Hill.]

figure 4.4 the proximity of the sensory and motor areas of the cortex. This proximity is the basis for these areas sometimes being referred to as the *sensorimotor cortex.*

Additional areas of the cortex that are important to note are the *association areas,* which lie adjacent to each specific sensory area in the parietal, temporal, and occipital lobes. The term *association* is used to describe these areas because it is there where the brain "associates," or connects together, information from the several different sensory cortex areas. This connecting together involves the integration of various types of sensory information as well as the sensory information from various parts of the body. In addition, the association areas connect with other cortex areas in ways that allow for the interaction between perceptual and higher-order cognitive functions, such as would occur in a choice reaction time situation where each choice alternative has a different probability of being the correct choice (see Platt & Glimcher, 1999, for an example of research showing parietal cortex involvement in this type of

choice situation). Because of the activity that occurs in the association areas of the cortex, some neuroscientists consider these areas as the location for the transition between the perception of sensory information and the resulting action.

Four cortex areas are especially involved in the control of movement (figure 4.4 shows these and other areas related to the control of movement as well as specific sensory functions). One area, the **primary motor cortex,** which is located in the

---

sensory cortex   cerebral cortex area located posterior to the central sulcus; it includes several specific regions that receive sensory information transmitted via the sensory nerves specific to that type of information.

primary motor cortex   a cerebral cortex area located in the frontal lobe just anterior to the central sulcus; it contains motor neurons that send axons to specific skeletal muscles throughout the body.

A CLOSER LOOK

Brain-Computer Interfaces: Movement by Imagining Moving

A technological advancement called brain-computer interfaces (BCI) has exciting potential for helping people whose neurological disorders prevent them from physical movement to regain the capability to move. This computer-based technology takes advantage of the electrical activity in the brain that results from actively imagining the act of moving (recall the discussion in chapter 2 about the use of EEG to record brain electrical activity). As described in a "News Focus" article in *Science* (Wickelgren, 2003), BCIs read brain waves as a person imagines moving a body part. In some cases, the BCI is part of an EEG skull cap. More recent advances have developed BCIs that can be implanted inside the brain. With training the BCI can provide a means of performing in certain functional activities.

The *Science* article reports several examples of success stories in which patients with various paralysis problems were trained with a BCI to carry out a variety of movement activities, including typing, manipulating a small wheeled robot through a model house, and moving a cursor on a computer monitor to hit icons that communicated statements such as "I'm hungry." Although much of the research with implantable devices involves monkeys, the goal of researchers is to develop devices that are suitable for humans and sufficiently sophisticated to enable a variety of functional movements. For example, since the publication of the *Science* article, researchers in Austria (Muller-Putz, Scherer, Pfurtscheller, & Rupp, 2005) reported a case study in which a patient was able to train himself in three days to use an implanted BCI so that his paralyzed hand could maneuver a prosthesis, grasping a small object and moving it from one place to another and then releasing it. More recently, researchers from several European countries reported success with two subjects using an EEG-based BCI to drive a real and a simulated wheelchair along a prescribed path (Galán, Nuttin, Lew, Ferrez, Vanacker, Philips, & Milán, 2008).

---

frontal lobe just anterior to the central sulcus, contains motor neurons that send axons to specific skeletal muscles throughout the body. This area of the brain is especially critical for movement initiation and the coordination of movements for fine motor skills, such as the finger movements required to type on a keyboard or play a piano. The motor cortex is also involved in the control and learning of postural coordination (see Ioffe, Ustinova, Chernikova, & Kulikov, 2006; Petersen, Rosenberg, Petersen, & Nielsen, 2009). The second area, anterior to the primary motor cortex is the **premotor area,** which controls the organization of movements before they are initiated and rhythmic coordination during movement, thus enabling the transitioning between movements for a skill that involves sequential movement, such as keyboard typing or piano playing. Research has also shown the importance of the premotor cortex in the performance benefit derived from the observation of actions performed by another person (Buccino et al. 2001). Third, the **supplementary motor area (SMA),** which is

located on the medial surface of the frontal lobe adjacent to portions of the primary motor cortex, plays an essential role in the control of sequential movements (see Parsons, Harrington, & Rao, 2005) and in the preparation and organization of movement, especially in the anterior portion known as the pre-SMA (see Cunnington, Windischberger, & Moser, 2005). Finally, the **parietal lobe** has emerged in recent years as an important cortical area involved in the control of voluntary movement (Fogassi & Luppino, 2005; Gottlieb, 2006). For example, the parietal lobe plays a significant role in the control of visual and auditory selective attention (Gottlieb, 2007; Shomstein & Yantis, 2007), visually tracking a moving target (Hutton & Weekes, 2007) and grasping (Rice, Tunik, & Grafton, 2006; Rice, Tunik, Cross, & Grafton, 2007). Based on an impressive amount of research demonstrating its role in the control of perceptual and motor activities such as these, there is general agreement that the parietal lobe is especially important in the integration of movement preparation and execution processes by interacting with the premotor cortex, primary motor cortex, and SMA before and during movement (Wheaton, Nolte, Bohlhalter, Fridman, & Hallett, 2005).

An important *subcortical component* for the control of movement is the **basal ganglia** (also known as the *basal nuclei*), which are buried within the cerebral hemispheres and consist of four large nuclei: the *caudate nucleus,* the *putamen,* the *substantia nigra,* and the *globus pallidus.* The basal ganglia receive neural information from the cerebral cortex and the brainstem. Motor neural information from the basal ganglia goes primarily to the brainstem. A loop of information flow, which is important for motor control, involves the nuclei of the basal ganglia, thalamus, and motor cortex.

The basal ganglia play critical roles in the control of movement, especially in the planning and initiation of movement, the control of antagonist muscles during movement, and the control of force (see Pope, Wing, Praamstra, & Miall, 2005). Much of our knowledge of the role of the basal ganglia in motor control comes from research involving people with Parkinson's disease and cerebral palsy, both of which are basal ganglia disorders (see Ioffe et al. 2006), and strokes affecting the basal ganglia (see Boyd & Winstein, 2004). For instance, in **Parkinson's disease,** several neural activities associated with the basal ganglia are negatively influenced, with decreased neural information going into the basal ganglia, unbalanced neural facilitation and inhibition interactions, and lower than normal interactions with the motor cortex. Several movement difficulties result from these problems, including bradykinesia (slow movements), akinesia (reduced amount of movement), tremor, and muscular rigidity. People with Parkinson's disease often have difficulty standing from a sitting position, initiating walking, and writing with a pen. The basal ganglia dysfunction associated with this disease results primarily from the lack of dopamine, which is a neurotransmitter important for normal basal ganglia function. Dopamine is produced by neurons of the *substantia nigra;* Parkinson's disease causes these neurons to degenerate, which reduces the production of dopamine.

The diencephalon. The second component of the forebrain is the **diencephalon,** which lies between the cerebrum and the brainstem. It contains two groups of nuclei, the thalamus and hypothalamus. The *thalamus* serves an important function as a relay station, receiving and integrating most of the sensory neural inputs from the spinal cord and brainstem and then passing them through to the cerebral cortex. The thalamus plays an important role in the control of attention, mood, and the perception of pain. The hypothalamus lies just under the thalamus and is the most critical brain center for the control of the endocrine system and the regulation of body homeostasis, including temperature, hunger, thirst, and physiological responses to stress.

---

premotor area   a cerebral cortex area located in the frontal lobe just anterior to the primary motor cortex.

supplementary motor area (SMA)   a cerebral cortex area located on the medial surface of the frontal lobe adjacent to portions of the primary motor cortex.

parietal lobe   an area of the cerebral cortex that plays an important role in the control of voluntary movement, such as the integration of movement preparation and execution processes by interacting with the premotor cortex, primary motor cortex, and SMA before and during movement.

basal ganglia   (also known as the basal nuclei) a subcortical collection of nuclei (caudate nucleus, substantia nigra, putamen, and globus pallidus) buried within the cerebral hemispheres; they play an important role in the planning and initiation of movement and the control of antagonist muscles during movement.

Parkinson's disease   a basal ganglia disorder caused by the lack of production of the neurotransmitter dopamine by the substantia nigra; the disease is characterized by slow movements (bradykinesia), a reduced amount of movement (akinesia), tremor, and muscular rigidity.

diencephalon   a component of the forebrain located between the cerebrum and the brainstem; it contains the thalamus and hypothalamus.

Cerebellum. Located behind the cerebral hemispheres and attached to the brainstem, the **cerebellum** has several distinct parts. The cerebellar cortex covers the cerebellum and, like the cerebral cortex, is divided into two hemispheres. Under the cortex lies white matter in which are embedded the deep cerebellar nuclei: the red nucleus and the oculomotor nucleus.

Sensory neural pathways into the cerebellum arise from three principal regions: the spinal cord, the cerebral cortex, and the brainstem. The motor neural pathways from the cerebellum connect to the spinal cord via the red nucleus and the descending reticular formation. Output also goes to the motor cortex by way of the central lateral nuclei of the thalamus, a neural pathway known as the cerebello-thalamo-cortico (CTC) pathway. Finally, there is output to the oculomotor nuclei, which are involved in the control of eye movements.

The cerebellum plays a key role in the execution of smooth and accurate movements. Damage to the cerebellum typically results in clumsy movement. In its role in the control of movement, the cerebellum functions as a type of movement error detection and correction system as it receives a copy of signals about an intended movement sent from the motor cortex to the muscles (often referred to as an *efference copy*) and compares the motor information with the sensory information it receives from sensory nerves that connect to the cerebellum. This comparison functions in a way that signals to the muscles any needed adjustments to movements already in progress, thus assuring achievement of the intended movement's goal. The cerebellum is also active in the control of other movement activities such as those requiring eye-hand coordination (see Miall & Jenkinson, 2005), movement timing (see Spencer, Ivry, & Zelaznik, 2005; Molinari, Leggio, & Thaut, 2007), and posture control (see Ioffe et al., 2006). In addition, the cerebellum is very much involved in the learning of motor skills as it interacts with areas of the cerebral cortex (see Ioffe et al, 2006).

Brainstem. Located directly under the cerebral hemispheres and connected to the spinal cord, the **brainstem** contains three main areas that are significantly involved in motor control. The *pons,* which is located at the top of the brainstem, acts as a bridge between the cerebral cortex and cerebellum. Various neural pathways either pass through the pons from the cortex on their way to the spinal cord or terminate as they come from the cortex. The pons appears to be involved in the control of body functions such as chewing, swallowing, salivating, and breathing. It may also play a role in the control of balance.

The second area, the *medulla* (also called the *medulla oblongata*), is like an extension of the spinal cord and serves as a regulatory agent for various internal physiologic processes, such as respiration, in which it interacts with the pons, and heartbeat. In terms of voluntary movement, the medulla functions as a site where the corticospinal tracts of the sensory and motor neural pathways cross over the body midline and merge on their way to the cerebellum and cerebral cortex.

The third area of the brainstem involved in motor control is the *reticular formation.* This composite of nuclei and nerve fibers is a vital link in the chain of neural structures that lie between the sensory receptors throughout the body and the motor control centers of the cerebellum and cerebral cortex. Its primary role in the control of movement is as an integrator of sensory and motor neural impulses. The reticular formation appears to have access to all sensory information and can exert direct influence on the CNS to modify activity of the CNS either by inhibiting or increasing that activity, which in turn influences skeletal muscle activity.

The limbic system. An important group of brain structures form what is known as the **limbic system.** It consists of parts of the frontal and temporal lobes of the cerebral cortex, the thalamus and hypothalamus, and the nerve fibers that interconnect these parts and other CNS structures. This system plays important roles in the learning of motor skills as well as in the control of emotions and several visceral behaviors.

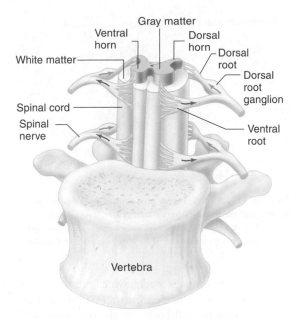

Gray matter

Ventral horn

Dorsal horn

White matter

Dorsal root

Dorsal root ganglion

Spinal cord

Spinal nerve

Ventral root

Vertebra

FIGURE 4.5   The structure of the spinal cord and its placement in a vertebra. The arrows indicate the direction of transmission of neural activity. [From Widmaier, E. P., Raff, H. & Strang, K. T. (2006). *Vander's human physiology: The mechanisms of body function* (10th ed.), p. 196. New York: McGraw-Hill.]

The Spinal Cord

The traditional view of the spinal cord is that it is like a telephone cable that simply relays messages to and from the brain. However, we now know that the spinal cord is much more than that. It is a complex system that interacts with a variety of systems and is critically involved in motor control processes.

Spinal cord composition. The two major portions of the spinal cord are the *gray matter* and the *white matter.* The gray matter is the butterfly- or H-shaped central portion of the cord (note figure 4.5). It consists primarily of cell bodies and axons of neurons that reside in the spinal cord. Two pairs of "horns" protrude from the gray matter; both of which are vital to motor control. The posterior pair of horns, known as the *dorsal horns,* contains cells involved in the transmission of sensory information. Sensory neurons from the various sensory receptors in the musculature synapse on dorsal horn neurons. The anterior pair of horns, known as the *ventral horns,*

contains alpha motor neuron cell bodies whose axons terminate on skeletal muscles.

In addition to alpha motor neurons and sensory neurons, the spinal cord also contains *interneurons.* Located primarily in the ventral horn, these interneurons are called *Renshaw cells.* Many of the nerve fibers that descend from the brain terminate on interneurons rather than on motor neurons. These interneurons can influence the neural activity of alpha motor neurons by inhibiting the amount of activity, sometimes turning off the activity so that the neurons can fire again in a short period of time.

Sensory neural pathways. Several sensory neural pathways, called **ascending tracts,** pass through the spinal cord and brainstem to connect with the various sensory areas of the cerebral cortex and cerebellum. These tracts contain sequences of two or three neurons, the first of which synapses in the spinal cord with neurons from sensory receptors in the body. Most of these tracts are specialized to carry

---

cerebellum   a brain structure located behind the cerebral hemispheres and attached to the brainstem; it is covered by the cerebellar cortex and is divided into two hemispheres; it plays a key role in the execution of smooth and accurate movements.

brainstem   a brain structure located directly under the cerebral hemispheres and connected to the spinal cord; it contains three areas that are significantly involved in motor control: the pons, medulla, and reticular formation.

limbic system   A group of brain structures consisting of parts of the frontal and temporal lobes of the cerebral cortex, the thalamus and hypothalamus, and the nerve fibers that interconnect these parts and other CNS structures; it is involved in the learning of motor skills.

ascending tracts   sensory neural pathways in the spinal cord and brainstem that connect with the various sensory areas of the cerebral cortex and cerebellum.

neural signals from certain types of sensory receptors, such as those specific to proprioception, touch, pain, and the like. Two ascending tracts to the sensory cortex are involved in the transmission of sensory information important for the control of voluntary movement: the *dorsal column,* which transmits proprioception, touch, and pressure information, and the *anterolateral system,* which transmits pain and temperature information as well as some touch and pressure information. Before reaching the cerebral cortex, these tracts enter the thalamus where they synapse with another sensory neuron to continue to the cortex. Several ascending tracts, called the *spinocerebellar tracts,* transmit proprioception information to the cerebellum. Two of these tracts originate in the arms and neck, and two originate in the trunk and legs. The ascending tracts cross at the brainstem from one side of the body to the other, which means that sensory information from one side of the body is received in the opposite side of the brain.

Motor neural pathways. The several sets of motor pathways (called **descending tracts**) that descend from the brain through the spinal cord can be collectively classified as *pyramidal tracts* and the *extrapyramidal tracts.* Although these tracts are anatomically distinct, they are not functionally independent because both function together in the control of movement (see Beatty, 2001). The *pyramidal tract* (also called the *corticospinal tract*) arises from various parts of the cerebral cortex with axons projecting to the spinal cord. This tract's name results from the pyramid shape of the tract's collection of nerve fibers as it travels from the cortex to the spinal cord. Approximately 60 percent of the pyramidal tract fibers arise from the primary motor cortex (Beatty, 2001). Most of the fibers of this tract cross over to the opposite side of the body at the medulla in the brainstem (referred to as *decussation*) and continue down the lateral column of the spinal cord. The pyramidal tract transmits information that is primarily involved in the control of movements associated with the performance of fine motor skills. Because of the pyramidal tract crossover in the brainstem, the muscles on each side of the body are controlled by the opposite cerebral hemisphere.

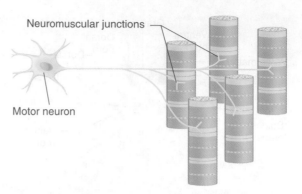

FIGURE 4.6   A single motor unit consisting of one motor neuron and the muscle fibers it innervates. [From Widmaier, E. P., Raff, H. & Strang, K. T. (2006). *Vander's human physiology: The mechanisms of body function* (10th ed.), p. 290. New York: McGraw-Hill.]

The *extrapyramidal tracts,* which are sometimes referred to as *brainstem pathways* (Widmaier et al., 2006), have their cell bodies in the brainstem with axons descending into the spinal cord. Different from the pyramidal tract fibers, most of the extrapyramidal tract fibers do not cross over to the opposite side of the body. The neural pathways of these tracts are involved in postural control as well as in the facilitation and inhibition of muscles involved in the flexion and extension of hands and fingers.

The Motor Unit

The ultimate end of the transmission of motor neural information is the motor unit (figure 4.6). The concept of the motor unit was first introduced at the beginning of the twentieth century by Sherrington (1906). Defined as the alpha motor neuron and all the muscle fibers it innervates, the **motor unit** serves as the functional unit of motor control for the innervation of the muscles involved in a movement (figure 4.6). Some researchers estimate that in the spinal cord there may be as many as 200,000 motor neurons with their dependent motor units. The connection between an alpha motor neuron and skeletal muscle fibers occurs at the neuromuscular junction, which is located near the middle of muscle fibers. This special type of synapse allows nerve impulses to be transmitted from the nerve fiber to the muscle fibers so that the appropriate muscle contraction can occur.

A CLOSER LOOK

Playing a Piece of Music on a Piano Activates Different Brain Regions

One of the ways to identify the complex nature of brain activity during the performance of a motor skill, as well as the involvement of specific brain regions to process specific aspects of the performance, is to observe brain activity while a person performs a skill. An excellent demonstration of this complexity and specificity of brain activity was reported by Bengtsson and Ullén (2006), researchers at the Karolinska Institute in Sweden. Their research was based on the premise that the performance of a piece of music on a piano involves two distinct processes:

• The identification of and movement to spatial locations of the piano keys as specified by the notes on the written music (referred to as the *melodic* component of the written music).
• The identification and performance of specific timing features of the notes on the written music (referred to as the *rhythmic* component of the written music).

Using fMRI, the researchers scanned 11 professional concert pianists while they played visually displayed musical scores with their right hands on a modified keyboard that could be used in the MRI scanner. Each score required 32 key presses. The results showed that during the performances of the scores, the melodic and rhythmic components were processed by the following distinct brain regions (note that some of the brain regions are not specifically identified in the discussion in this chapter):

Melodic Component
• Medial occipital lobe
• Superior temporal lobe
• Rostral cingulated cortex
• Putamen
• Cerebellum

Rhythmic Component
• Lateral occipital lobe
• Inferior temporal lobe
• Left supramarginal gyrus
• Left inferior and ventral frontal gyri
• Caudate nucleus
• Cerebellum

The number of muscle fibers served by one alpha motor neuron axon varies greatly. In general, muscles involved in the control of fine movements, such as the muscles of the eye and larynx, have the smallest number of muscle fibers for each motor unit, which in some cases is one per fiber. On the other hand, large skeletal muscles, such as those involved in the control of posture and gross motor skills, have the largest number of muscle fibers per motor unit, with as many as 700 muscle fibers innervated by one motor unit. When an alpha motor neuron activates (i.e., it "fires"), all the muscle fibers to which it connects contract.

Motor unit recruitment. The number of muscle fibers active at any one time influences the amount of force the muscle can exert. This variation of force is controlled by the number of motor units active in the muscle. To increase the amount of force exerted by a muscle, a process known as recruitment occurs in which the number of motor neurons activated increases. The recruitment of motor units follows

---

descending tracts   motor neural pathways that descend from the brain through the spinal cord.

motor unit   the alpha motor neuron and all the muscle fibers it innervates; it serves as the functional unit of motor control for the innervation of the muscles involved in a movement.

motor unit recruitment   the process of increasing the number of motor units needed to increase the number of muscle fibers active at any one time and thereby increase the amount of force the muscle can exert.

a specific procedure that involves motor neuron size, which refers to the diameter of the neuron's cell body. The process of recruitment begins with the smallest, and therefore the weakest, motor units and systematically progresses to the largest, which are the most powerful motor units.

THE NEURAL CONTROL OF VOLUNTARY MOVEMENT

Performing a motor skill typically begins with a cognitively derived intent that is based on the dictates of the situation or needs of the person. If the person needs to go to a room that is up a flight of stairs, the situation and personal needs require that the person walk up the stairs. The movement implementation of this intent requires numerous neurophysiologic events that involve the cooperative interaction of many CNS structures in addition to sensory-peceptual system components and the peripheral nervous system. This interaction occurs both hierarchically and in parallel, as conceptually illustrated in figure 4.7 and table 4.1. Although the organizational diagram in the figure presents a hierarchical model of structures, many of the functions of the structures described in the table are carried out in parallel, which means they occur at the same time rather than as a sequence of events. One of the notable features of the figure is its depiction of the wide distribution of brain structures involved from the initial intent to perform a skill until the neural innervation of the muscles associated with producing the movements needed to perform the skill. Clearly, a complex array of neural activities underlies the performance of seemingly simple behavioral activities.

In an essay addressing the issue of the neural correlates of coordinated movement, Carson and Kelso (2004) emphasized the importance of not limiting our understanding of the involvement of brain structures in the control of movement to different types of movements. They argue that we should also understand the interactions between regions of the CNS and the muscles in terms of the cognitive intent of the movement. That is, different CNS patterns of activity can occur when the same movement

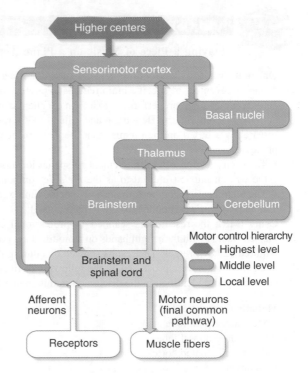

FIGURE 4.7   The diagram shows a conceptual hierarchical organization of the neural systems controlling voluntary movement. Table 4.1 describes the function of each of the three levels of the hierarchy and the specific neural structures in each level. [From Widmaier, E. P., Raff, H., & Strang, K. T. (2006). *Vander's human physiology: The mechanisms of body function* (10th ed.), p. 325. New York: McGraw-Hill.]

pattern is used to achieve two different action goals. Their example involves a simple flexion movement of the index finger. The two different action goals are to have the peak amount of flexion coincide with the beat (synchronization) or occur off the beat (syncopation) of an auditory metronome. Carson and Kelso describe research evidence of different neural activity in the cerebral cortex for the synchronization and syncopation tasks. When the participants' intent was to perform the synchronization task, activation of the contralateral sensorimotor cortex, SMA, and ipsilateral cerebellum occurred. In contrast, when their intent was to perform the syncopation task, additional brain areas activated, including the premotor, prefrontal, and temporal association areas, along with the basal ganglia.

TABLE 4.1   Conceptual Motor Control Hierarchy for Voluntary Movements

I. Higher centers
   a. Function: forms complex plans according to individual's intention and communicates with the middle level via "command neurons."
   b. Structures: areas involved with memory and emotions, supplementary motor area, and association cortex. All these structures receive and correlate input from many other brain structures.

II. The middle level
   a. Function: converts plans received from the highest level to a number of smaller motor programs, which determine the pattern of neural activation required to perform the movement. These programs are broken down into subprograms that determine the movements of individual joints. The programs and subprograms are transmitted through descending pathways to the lowest control level.
   b. Structures: sensorimotor cortex, cerebellum, parts of basal neclei, some brainstem nuclei.

III. The lowest level (the local level)
   a. Function: specifies tension of particular muscles and angle of specific joints at specific times necessary to carry out the programs and subprograms transmitted from the middle control levels.
   b. Structures: levels of brainstem or spinal cord from which motor neurons exit.

Source: Widmaier, E. P., Raff, H., & Strang, K. T. (2006). *Vander's human physiology: The mechanisms of body function* (10th ed.), New York: McGraw-Hill (Table 10-1, p. 325).

SUMMARY

- The neuron is the basic component of the nervous system. There are three types of neurons in the nervous system: sensory neurons, which transmit neural information along neural pathways to the CNS; motor neurons, which transmit neural information to the muscles; and interneurons, which interact in the spinal cord with both sensory and motor neurons.

- The structural components of the brain that are most directly involved in control of movement are the cerebrum, diencephalon, cerebellum, and brainstem.

- The cerebrum consists of the right and left cerebral hemispheres, which are covered by the cerebral cortex. The cortex of each hemisphere consists of four lobes: the frontal lobe, parietal lobe, occipital lobe, and temporal lobe.

- The sensory areas of the cerebral cortex receive specific types of sensory information from the sensory nerves. Sensory-specific areas of the cortex exist for vision, taste, speech, and body.

- The association areas of the cerebral cortex integrate various types of sensory information as well as the sensory information from various parts of the body. These areas also interconnect with other cortex areas to enable the interaction between perceptual and higher-order cognitive functions.

- Four cerebral cortex areas are especially involved in the control of movement:

  ▸ Primary motor cortex, which is especially critical for movement initiation and the coordination of movements for fine motor skills and posture.

  ▸ Premotor area, which is involved in the organization of movements before they are initiated and the control of rhythmic coordination during movement; it plays an important role in the observation of actions performed by another person.

▶ Supplementary motor area (SMA), which plays an essential role in the control of sequential movements and in the preparation and organization of movement.

▶ Parietal lobe, which is involved in the integration of movement preparation and execution processes by interacting with the premotor cortex, primary motor cortex, and SMA before and during movement.

• The basal ganglia are an important subcortical component for the control of movement. They consist of the caudate nucleus, the putamen, the substantia nigra, and the globus pallidus. The basal ganglia play critical roles in the planning and initiation of movement, the control of antagonist muscles during movement, and the control of force.

• The diencephalon contains the thalamus and hypothalamus. The thalamus receives and integrates most of the sensory neural inputs from the spinal cord and brainstem and then passes them through to the cerebral cortex. The hypothalamus is the most critical brain center for the control of the endocrine system and the regulation of body homeostasis.

• The cerebellum receives sensory neural pathways and is the beginning location for several motor neural pathways. It plays a key role in the execution of smooth and accurate movements; it also functions as a type of movement error detection and correction system; and it is an important site for the control of movement activities requiring eye-hand coordination, movement timing, and posture control.

• The brainstem, which is connected to the spinal cord, contains three main areas that are significantly involved in motor control: the pons, medulla (also called the medulla oblongata), and reticular formation. Each area functions in specific ways that influence the control of voluntary movement.

• The spinal cord is a complex system that interacts with a variety of systems and is critically involved

in motor control processes. It consists primarily of cell bodies and axons of neurons that reside in the spinal cord.

• Several sensory neural pathways, called ascending tracts, carry neural signals from the various types of sensory receptors through the spinal cord and brainstem to connect with the sensory areas of the cerebral cortex and cerebellum. The dorsal column and the anterolateral system are two ascending tracts to the sensory cortex. The spinocerebellar tracts are ascending tracts to the cerebellum.

• Several sets of motor pathways, called descending tracts, transmit motor neural information from the brain through the spinal cord. The pyramidal tract (also called the corticospinal tract) begins in various parts of the cerebral cortex and projects to the spinal cord. The extrapyramidal tracts (also called the brainstem pathways) have their cell bodies in the brainstem with axons descending into the spinal cord.

• The motor unit, which is the ultimate end of the transmission of motor neural information, is made up of the alpha motor neuron and all the muscle fibers it innervates. It serves as the functional unit of motor control for the innervation of the muscles involved in a movement. The amount of force generated by a muscle is controlled by the number of motor units active in the muscle. To increase the amount of force exerted by a muscle, a process known as the recruitment of motor units increases the number of motor neurons activated.

• The neural control underlying the performance of a motor skill is a complex process that begins with a cognitively derived intent to perform the skill. The implementation of the movements required to achieve the goal of the intended action requires numerous neurophysiologic events that involve the cooperative interaction of many CNS structures. The structural interactions can be conceptualized hierarchically with the intent located in the higher centers of the cortex; the planning and organization of the required movements occurring in middle centers of the brain, including the sensorimotor cortex, diencephalons, cerebellum, and brainstem; and finally the execution of the movement plan involving the brainstem, spinal cord, muscle fibers, and sensory receptors.

POINTS FOR THE PRACTITIONER

- Because the intent of an action is a critical part of the planning, organization, and execution of it, be certain that the person or people you are working with have a clear understanding of what they are supposed to do when you give them instructions related to performing a skill.

- If you are working with a person who has a neurological dysfunction, be sure that you know the location of the damage in the nervous system so that you are aware of the person's capabilities and limitations in terms of planning, organizing, and executing movements.

- If you are working with a person who is taking medication to help overcome the limitations imposed by a neurological dysfunction, check with the person to make sure he or she has taken the most recent dose of the medication before beginning a rehabilitation session.

RELATED READINGS

Edgerton, V. R., Tillakaratne, N. J. K., Bigbee, A. J., de Leon, R. D., & Roy, R. R. (2004). Plasticity of the spinal neural circuitry after injury. *Annual Review of Neuroscience, 28,* 145–167.

Fritz, S. L., Chiu, Y. P., Malcolm, M. P., Patterson, T. S., & Light, K. E. (2005). Feasibility of electromyography-triggered neuromuscular stimulation as an adjunct to constraint-induced movement therapy. *Physical Therapy, 85,* 428–442.

Grabb, P. A. (2000). A neurosurgeon's view of sports-related injuries of the nervous system. *The Neurologist, 6,* 288–297.

Hagmann, P., Cammoun, L, Gigandet, X., Meuli, R., Honey, C. J. et al. (2008). Mapping the structural core of human cerebral cortex. *PLoS Biology,* 6(7): e159. doi 10.1371/journal.pbio. 0060159 [an online open access journal].

Maki, B. E., & McIlroy, W. E. (2007). Cognitive demands and cortical control of human balance-recovery reactions. *Journal of Neural Transmission, 114,* 1279–1296.

Matthews, P. B. C. (2004). Historical analysis of the neural control of movement from the bedrock of animal experimentation to human studies. *Journal of Applied Physiology, 96,* 1478–1485.

Poldrack, R. A., & Wagner, A. D. (2008). The interface between neuroscience and psychological science. *Current Directions in Psychological Science, 17,* 61.

Seger, C. A. (2006). The basal ganglia in human learning. *Neuroscientist, 12,* 285–290.

Shadmehr, R., & Krackauer, J. W. (2008). A computational neuroanatomy for motor control. *Experimental Brain Research, 185,* 359–381.

Tunik, E., Rice, N. J., Hamilton, A., & Grafton, S. T. (2007). Beyond grasping: Representation of action in human anterior intraparietal sulcus. *NeuroImage, 36,* 777–786.

°INTERNET RESOURCES

- To access information about brain anatomy, brain diseases, and brain imaging techniques, go to the Whole Brain Atlas Web site sponsored by Harvard Medical School at http://www.med.harvard.edu/AANLIB/home.htm.

- To visit the Web site of a national organization devoted to the study and treatment of brain injury go to http://www.biausa.org/. On this site you will find several options to learn more about brain injuries, their behavioral effects, and treatments.

- To visit a Web site produced by the BBC that includes a wide range of information concerning the human nervous system, go to http://www.bbc.co.uk/science/humanbody/. In the Search box, type "nervous system." This will take you to a list of links related to the nervous system. Included is an "interactive body" that allows you to specify, drag, and drop parts of the nervous system into their correct anatomical locations.

- To visit a Web site created by the Rush University Medical Center that presents descriptions and discussions about many different nervous system diseases and disorders, including Parkinson's disease, stroke, muscular dystrophy, multiple sclerosis, and the like, go to http://www.rush.edu/rumc. In the search box type "nervous system disorders." This will take you to a page of links, the first of which will take you to the "Nervous Systems Disorders Homepage"

- If you are interested in seeing brain scan images as well as knowing more about various brain scan techniques, do a Google search on "brain scans." One of the links is "Image results for brain scans." If you open this link, you will find numerous examples of brain scan images from various brain scanning techniques.

- To see examples of people performing various tasks using a brain-computer interface, go to http://www.youtube.com/ and type "brain-computer interface" in the search box.

- To see a demonstration of a brain-actuated wheelchair, which is a wheelchair that can be driven by a brain-computer interface that recognizes the intent of the wheelchair operator, go to http://thefutureofthings.com/pod/7237/brain-actuated-wheelchair.html/.

STUDY QUESTIONS

1. (a) Describe the general structure of a neuron, the function of each component, and the three different types of neurons and their functions. (b) How does the structure of a sensory neuron differ from the structure of the other two types of neurons?

2. Identify by name and location the four parts of the brain that are the most actively involved in the control of voluntary movement.

3. Identify by name and location the areas of the cerebral cortex that are most actively involved in the control of voluntary movement, and describe the role each area plays in motor control.

4. Describe the location of the cerebellum and discuss its roles in motor control.

5. Describe the disease known as Parkinson's disease and identify the brain basis for it.

6. Describe the structural characteristics of the spinal cord and their functions in the control of voluntary movement.

7. Distinguish between the ascending and descending tracts of the CNS and describe their functions in the control of voluntary movement.

8. Describe a motor unit and its function in the control of voluntary movement. Discuss how the motor unit is involved in the generation of muscular force.

9. Discuss the three-part hierarchical organization that characterizes the neural control of voluntary movement.

Specific Application Problem:
Describe a motor skill that you perform and describe the performance effects that would result from an injury to or neurological dysfunction of one of the parts of the central nervous system.

CHAPTER 5

Motor Control Theories

Concept: Theories about how we control coordinated movement differ in terms of the roles of central and environmental features of a control system.

After completing this chapter, you will be able to

- Discuss the relevance of motor control theory for the practitioner
- Define the term *coordination* as it relates to the performance of motor skills
- Describe the *degrees of freedom problem* as it relates to the study of human motor control
- Compare and contrast an open-loop control system and a closed-loop control system
- Describe a primary difference between a motor program–based theory of motor control and a dynamic pattern theory of motor control
- Define a generalized motor program and describe an invariant feature and a parameter proposed to characterize this program
- Define the following terms associated with a dynamic pattern theory of motor control: order and control parameters, self-organization, coordinative structures, and perception-action coupling
- Discuss how a motor program–based theory and a dynamic pattern theory each explain the basis for the relative-time characteristics of human walking and running

APPLICATION

To successfully perform the wide variety of motor skills we use in everyday life, we must coordinate various muscles and joints to function together. These muscle and joint combinations differ for many skills. Some skills, such as hitting a serve in tennis or getting out of a chair and into a wheelchair, require us to coordinate muscles and joints of the trunk and limbs. Other skills involve coordination of the arms, hands, and fingers; examples are reaching to pick up a pencil, playing the guitar, and typing on a keyboard. Other skills require us to coordinate our two arms or legs in such a way that each one does something

different at the same time, such as when we hold a jar with one hand and screw open the top with the other or kick a ball with one leg while the other is firmly on the ground. For still other skills, where only one arm and hand are involved, we must coordinate only a few muscles and joints. We do this when we manipulate a computer joystick or a car's gearshift.

Motor skill performance has other important general characteristics in addition to body and limb coordination. For example, we perform some skills with relatively slow movements; think of how we position a bow before releasing an arrow or pick up a cup to take a drink from it. Other skills, such as throwing a ball or jumping from a bench to the floor, require fast, ballistic movements. Some motor skills, such as writing a numeral or buttoning a shirt, have few component parts; other skills, such as performing a dance routine or playing the piano, have many parts and therefore are very complex.

Also, we can produce remarkably accurate and consistent movement patterns from one performance attempt to another. We are capable of performing well-learned skills with a remarkable degree of success in a variety of situations, even though we have never before been in similar situations. For example, a skilled tennis player will have to use a forehand stroke in many different situations in matches. The many different characteristics in any situation, such as the ball's flight pattern, speed, spin, bounce, and location on the court, as well as the opponent's position, the wind and sun conditions, and so on, provide little chance that any two situations can be exactly alike. Yet a skilled player can hit the ball successfully.

These examples of the variety of motor skills we can perform indicate the many different ways we must coordinate various parts of our body in order to achieve the action goals of these skills. Underlying this amazing capability we have to perform such a variety of motor skills in so many different situations and contexts is an active nervous system. How does the nervous system function to enable us to carry out the movements required for the vast array of action goals we need to achieve on a daily basis? Answering this question is at the heart of the topic we discuss in this chapter.

Application Problem to Solve   Select a motor skill that you perform well for recreational or sports purposes. As you study this chapter, address each of the following points: (1) Consider the coordination demands of this skill by describing the degrees of freedom the skill requires at the joint level. (2) How do you adapt the way you perform this skill to different characteristics you might encounter in the environmental context (recall what is included here from our discussion in chapter 1)? Describe some of those environmental context characteristics and indicate how you adapt to them in terms of the movement adjustments you make. Consider whether the adjustments involve some modifications to the movement coordination pattern you use to perform the skill or involve a change in the movement coordination pattern you use.

Walking down a crowded flight of stairs is a good example of an action that requires a person to adapt his or her pattern of head, body, and limb movements to the characteristics of the stairs and the other people on the stairs.

DISCUSSION

Before we discuss some theories of how the nervous system controls coordinated movement, we will consider the importance of understanding the basic components of motor control theory. Then, we will clarify a few terms, to provide a foundation for understanding those theories.

THEORY AND PROFESSIONAL PRACTICE

Students who are preparing for professions in which their primary responsibilities involve motor skill instruction often question the need to study motor control theory. This type of questioning often comes from those who believe their preparation needs to involve only "practical" information that will help them carry out their day-to-day responsibilities in the workplace. Unfortunately, this view is often the result of a lack of understanding of the relevance of theory to professional practice. In this section, we will discuss what a theory is and the relevance of motor control theory for practitioners. One of the goals of this section is to establish why the discussion of motor control theory is presented in this book before the discussion of specific topics related to motor control and learning.

What Is a Theory?

If we base our understanding of the term *theory* on how it is commonly used in everyday language, we come away with the view that a theory has little relevance to reality. But this view is short-sighted and misleading. In science, a theory helps us understand phenomena and explains the reasons why these phenomena exist or behave as they do. Stephen Hawking (1996), the world-renowned physicist at Cambridge University in England, states that a good theory should satisfy "two requirements. It must accurately describe a large class of observations . . . and it must make definite predictions about the results of future observations" (p. 15). In Hawking's domain of physics, theories are developed to help us understand various aspects of the physical universe in which we live. They do this by providing us with explanations of observable physical events, such as identifying the variables that make a rolling ball eventually stop rolling. By identifying these variables, we can then predict how far a ball will roll given specific characteristics of these variables.

In the behavioral sciences, which include the study of human motor control and learning, theories focus on explaining human behavior. When the human behavior of interest is the performance and learning of motor skills, we look to theories to provide us with explanations about why people perform skills as they do, which means identifying the variables that account for the performance characteristics we observe. For example, we know from our observations of people performing skills that a person can perform the same skill in a variety of different situations. A skilled basketball player can shoot a one-hand jump shot from a variety of locations on the floor and in a variety of game-related situations. A good theory of motor control will explain why this capability is possible. Similarly, if a rehabilitation therapist uses a specific intervention to treat an injury, a good theory of motor control will explain why this intervention is effective.

The Relevance of Motor Control Theory for the Practitioner

A benefit of a basic understanding of motor control theory is that it provides the practitioner with a base of support on which he or she can develop effective skill instruction and practice environments. Figure 5.1 illustrates the connection between theory and practice by indicating some of the many applications that will be enhanced when a practitioner has knowledge about the variables that influence motor skill performance. To use one of the examples given at the end of the preceding section, if we know *why* people can adapt to a variety of situations when they perform a motor skill, we can use this knowledge to develop practice conditions that we can confidently predict will facilitate this adaptation capability. Consider a different example. Suppose you need to help a person reacquire the capability to walk. Knowledge about the motor control mechanisms that underlie human locomotion and the environmental variables that affect it will allow you to develop more appropriate assessment and intervention strategies, because they will be based on variables that influence locomotion.

MOTOR CONTROL THEORY

In the earlier section titled "What is a theory?" you read that a good theory should describe and provide explanations for a large class of observable events. In light of this requirement, what should a good theory

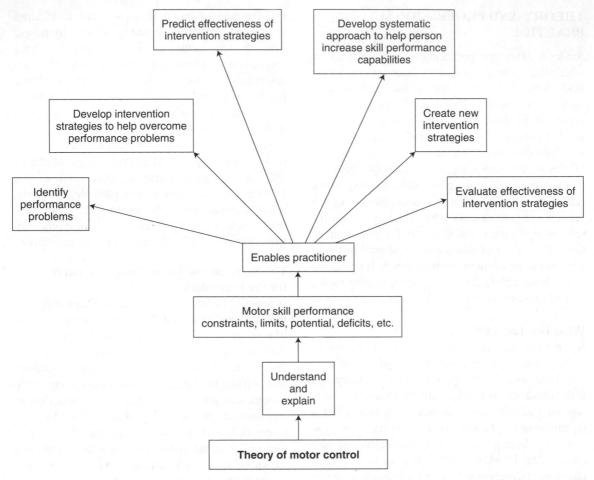

FIGURE 5.1   Motor control theory provides a foundation on which practitioners can base many tasks and responsibilities.

of motor control describe and explain? Researchers generally acknowledge that it should describe and explain how the nervous system produces coordinated movement such that we are able to successfully perform a variety of motor skills in a variety of environmental contexts. In many respects, the attempt to understand how we produce coordinated movement is similar to wanting to know how a watch, which also involves the precise coordination of many components, keeps time.

The following sections discuss two essential issues important to a theory of motor control: the meaning of the term *coordination* as it applies to motor skill performance, and the "degrees of freedom

problem." Although researchers have proposed additional issues that a theory of motor control should address,[1] these two will provide a sufficient foundation on which to base your introduction to the two prominent motor control theories discussed in this chapter.

It is important to note that the theories described here address motor control from a predominantly *behavioral level*. As you saw in chapter 1, this means

[1]For broader and more in-depth discussions of issues that are relevant for a theory of motor control, see books devoted to motor control issues, e.g., Kelso (1995), Rosenbaum (1991), Rothwell (1995) and Shumway-Cook and Woollacott (2006).

that they focus on explaining observed behavior without attempting to specify neural-level features of the control process (for examples of neural models of motor control, see Bullock & Grossberg, 1991; Grossberg & Paine, 2000; Wolpert & Ghahramani, 2000). An important goal of behaviorally based motor control theories is to propose laws and principles that govern coordinated human motor behavior. A neural-level theory would be expected to describe neural mechanisms or neural mechanism interactions that explain how the nervous system is involved in these behavioral principles (for example, see Willingham, 1998).

Coordination

An important characteristic of all motor control theories is that they include explanations of how we control coordination. Therefore, it is essential that we establish an understanding of the meaning of the term coordination as it applies to the performance of motor skills. The performance of a motor skill involves a person's organization of the activation of muscles in such a way that the goal of an action can be accomplished. It is this organizational feature that is at the heart of the definition of the term *coordination*. For the purposes of this textbook, we will use as a general definition one provided by Turvey (1990): **coordination** is the patterning of head, body, and limb movements relative to the patterning of environmental objects and events.

This definition contains two parts. Each is important to consider further. First, note that the definition specifies that coordination involves *patterns of head, body, and/or limb movements.* Although a common colloquial use of the term *coordination* relates it to a characteristic of skilled performance, it should not be limited to this use. When used in reference to a movement pattern associated with the performance of a skill, coordination refers to the organizational relationship of movement characteristics of the head, body, and limb involved in the performance, *regardless of the skill level of the performer.* This means that when we consider the assessment of movement characteristics of the performance of a skill, it is necessary to consider coordination as referring to the relationship among the head, body,

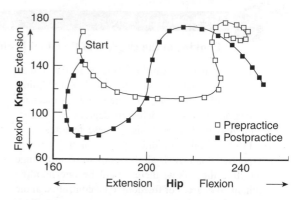

FIGURE 5.2 Angle-angle diagram from an experiment by Anderson and Sidaway showing coordination changes resulting from practice for the hip and knee relationship while performing a soccer kick. [Reprinted with permission from *Research Quarterly for Exercise and Sport,* Vol. 65, pp. 93–99, Copyright © 1994 American Association for Health, Physical Education, Recreation, and Dance, 1900 Association Drive, Reston, VA 20191.]

and/or limbs *at a specific point in time* during the skill performance.

As you saw in chapter 2, a common way to portray movement patterns is to represent graphically in an angle-angle diagram the relationship between the displacement patterns of limbs as they move while performing the skill. An example of this type of representation can be seen in figure 5.2, where the coordination of the knee and hip joint angles during a soccer kick is shown.

The second part of the definition states that the pattern of head, limb, and body motion is *relative to the pattern of environmental objects and events.* This is important because it establishes the need to consider movement coordination in relation to the context in which the skill is performed. The characteristics of the environmental context constrain the head, body, and limbs to act in certain ways so that the goal of the action can be achieved.

For example, to walk along a pathway, people must adapt their head, body, and limb movement patterns to the characteristics of the pathway. If,

---

coordination   the patterning of head, body, and/or limb motions relative to the patterning of environmental objects and events.

A CLOSER LOOK

Looking at the Degrees of Freedom Problem at the Level of Muscles and Joints

We know that there are 792 muscles in the human body that can act to make the one hundred joints behave in different ways. And each joint has mechanical characteristics that define its degrees of freedom for movement. On the basis of these features, Turvey (1990) put the coordination control problem into perspective this way. If all the joints were only hinge joints like the elbow, there would be one hundred mechanical degrees of freedom to be controlled at the joint level. But if two specific characteristics, such as position and velocity, needed to be defined for these joints to carry out a specific act, the degrees of freedom would increase to two hundred.

Consider the following examples. If you were seated at a table and decided to pick up a drinking glass in front of you on the table, the number of degrees of freedom involved just in terms of the number of joints (this does not take into account the number of ways each joint can move) would be the

shoulder joint (1), elbow joint (1), wrist joint (1), and all the finger (3 joints × 4 fingers = 12 joints) and thumb (3) joints. The total number of joints that need to be controlled for this simple action is 18. Now suppose that the drinking glass in front of you is very large and requires two hands to pick it up. The nervous system must now control at least double the number of degrees of freedom compared to the one-hand situation. In both cases, you probably would not have any difficulty coordinating the joints of one or two limbs to achieve the action goal. But, if we consider these tasks from the level of neuromuscular control where the many degrees of freedom must be controlled to operate in very specific ways, the simple task of picking up a drinking glass becomes a very complex one. Yet, the nervous system handles this complex operation. Theories of motor control need to be able to explain how the nervous system does this.

---

for example, a person is walking on a sidewalk and encounters a tree branch lying across it, he or she must use a new pattern of movements in order to step over the branch. The characteristics of the tree branch will dictate the characteristics of the movement pattern. If it is small, the person may simply need to adjust the length of a walking stride and take a large step; if it is a large branch, he or she may have to stop walking and climb over it.

The Degrees of Freedom Problem

Because coordination involves head, body, and limb movement patterns, an important question in the study of motor control is this: *How does the nervous system control the many muscles and joints involved in producing a complex movement pattern?* To answer this question, we must consider an important problem that was first posed by Nicolai Bernstein, a noted Russian physiologist whose work, produced from the 1930s to the 1950s, did not become known to the Western world until 1967.

His work continues to influence research and theory related to motor control. Bernstein proposed that to perform a well-coordinated movement, the nervous system had to solve what he termed the "degrees of freedom problem."

The **degrees of freedom** of any system reflect the number of independent elements or components of the system. Each element is "free" to vary in specific ways, as in the case of the elbow joint, which can vary (i.e., move) in two ways: flexion and extension. The **degrees of freedom problem** arises when a complex system needs to be organized to produce a specific result. The control problem is as follows: How can an effective yet efficient control system be designed so that a complex system, having many degrees of freedom, is constrained to act in a particular way?

Consider the following example of the degrees of freedom control problem in a complex mechanical system. A helicopter is designed so that it can fly up or down, to the left or the right, forward or backward, and so on, and at a variety of speeds. The

A CLOSER LOOK

Bernstein's Demonstration of the Degrees of Freedom Problem

Nicolai Bernstein's classic book *The Co-ordination and Regulation of Movement* (published in English in 1967) was a compilation of several of his publications. In the chapter titled "Some emergent problems in the regulation of motor acts" (originally published in Russian in 1957), Bernstein discussed the degrees of freedom problem that the motor control system must overcome in order to produce well-coordinated movement. In this discussion (p. 126f), he provided the following example to demonstrate the problem (which he said was "very useful for demonstrations in auditoriums").

> Fasten the handle end of a ski-stick in front of the buckle of a subject's belt. Attach a weight of 1–2 kg to the far end and on the right and left sides of the wheel [at the end of the stick] attach a length of rubber tubing long enough to allow the ends to be held in the

subject's left and right hands. Instruct the subject . . . to stand before a vertical board on which a large circle, square or other simple figure has been drawn, and to try, manipulating the ski-stick only by pulling on the rubber tubing, to follow the contours of the figure with the point of the ski-stick. The stick here represents one segment of an extremity with two degrees of freedom; the tubing is analogous to two antagonistic muscles introducing a further two degrees of freedom into the system. This experiment . . . makes clear to all who attempt it just how difficult and complicated it is to control systems which require the co-ordination of four degrees of freedom, even when under the control of a human being in full possession of his full complement of receptors, but without motor practice with the task, who has been dealing with his bone-muscle motor apparatus from the first weeks of his life.

helicopter designer must enable the pilot to control many different features so that the helicopter can do all these things. And the designer must help the pilot do so as simply as possible. If the pilot had to control one switch or lever for each component needed to make the helicopter fly a certain way, the pilot's job would be overwhelming. Therefore, the designer reduces the complexity of the task by providing control sticks and pedals that the pilot can control simultaneously with his or her hands and feet. Each stick or pedal controls several functions at once.

When the nervous system must control the human body so that it performs a complex motor skill, such as hitting a baseball, it faces a degrees of freedom control problem similar to that involving the helicopter. The determination of the actual number of degrees of freedom that must be controlled in coordinated human movement depends on which level of control we are considering. At a very basic level, we might consider motor units as the elements that must be controlled. At another level, we could consider joints as the element of

interest. Regardless of the control level considered, it becomes evident that for any motor skill, the control problem involved in enabling a person to perform that skill is an enormous one. However, as you will see in chapter 12, when a person practices a skill and progresses from a beginner to a skilled performer, the motor control system solves the degrees of freedom problem in ways that are evident from the changes we can observe in specific coordination characteristics.

degrees of freedom   the number of independent elements or components in a control system and the number of ways each component can act.

degrees of freedom problem   a control problem that occurs in the designing of a complex system that must produce a specific result; the design problem involves determining how to constrain the system's many degrees of freedom so that it can produce the specific result.

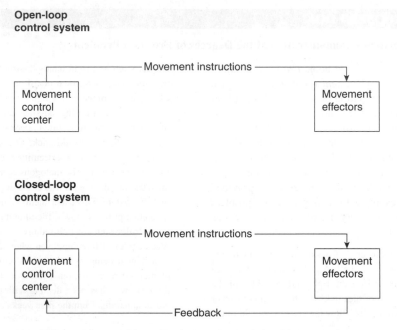

FIGURE 5.3   Diagrams illustrating the open-loop and closed-loop control systems for movement control.

OPEN-LOOP AND CLOSED-LOOP CONTROL SYSTEMS

Most theories of motor control incorporate two basic systems of control. These two systems, called **open-loop** and **closed-loop control systems,** are based on mechanical engineering models of control. Rather than provide exact descriptions of the control processes in complex human movement, these two models are general descriptions of different ways the central and peripheral nervous systems initiate and control action. These models serve as useful guides that illustrate some of the basic components involved in that process.

Figure 5.3 presents diagrams illustrating simple open-loop and closed-loop control systems. These are the typical diagrams you would see in any general presentation of these types of control systems. Notice that each of these systems has a *control center.* The control center is sometimes referred to as an *executive.* An important part of its role is to generate and issue movement instructions to the *effectors,* which, in the human, are the muscles of the limbs, body, and/or head involved in producing the desired movement. Both control systems also contain *movement instructions* that come from the control center and go to the effectors.

Differences between the Systems

These systems differ in two ways. First, a closed-loop control system involves **feedback,** whereas an open-loop system does not. In human movement, the feedback is *afferent* information sent by the various sensory receptors to the control center. The purpose of this feedback is to update the control center about the correctness of the movement while it is in progress.

In terms of the involvement of feedback in human movement control, figure 5.3 is somewhat misleading. The diagram indicates that the "effectors" that enable the head, body, and limbs to move are the only source of feedback. But in complex human movement, feedback can come also from several other sources, such as visual and auditory receptors.

The second important difference between open- and closed-loop control systems relates to the *movement instructions* issued by the control center. In

A CLOSER LOOK

Mechanical and Human Motor Skill Examples of Open-Loop and Closed-Loop Control Systems

Open-Loop Control
Mechanical example
- **Videocassette recorder.** It can operate as an open-loop control system by being programmed to tape television programs on specified dates and at specified times. The VCR will turn on and off at the specified times. (Note that it will turn off at the specified time even if the program being taped continues past that time.)

Human motor skill example
- **Throwing a dart at a dartboard.** When the person initiates the throw, the arm movement and dart release occur as specified by movement instructions developed before the initiation of the arm movement.

Closed-Loop Control
Mechanical example
- **Thermostat in a house.** It controls the air-conditioning and heating systems in a house. The desired room temperature is set on the thermostat. This setting becomes a reference against which actual room temperatures are compared. The room temperature serves as the feedback to the thermostat to indicate when to turn the air-conditioning or heating system on or off.

Human motor skill example
- **Driving a car.** When a person drives a car on a street or highway, he or she must keep the car within a specified lane. To do this the driver uses visual and proprioceptive feedback to control the steering wheel to make the needed adjustments to keep the car from going outside the lane boundaries.

the open-loop system, because feedback is not used in the control of the ongoing movement, the instructions contain all the information necessary for the effectors to carry out the planned movement. Although feedback is produced and available, it is not used to control the ongoing movement. This may be so because feedback is not needed, or because there is not enough time to use feedback to effectively control the movement after it is initiated.

In the closed-loop system, the movement instructions are quite different. First, the control center issues an initial instruction to the effectors that is sufficient only to initiate the movement. The actual execution and completion of the movement depend on feedback information that reaches the control center. The feedback provides information about the status of the movement, which serves to enable the control center to do one of several things: allow the movement to continue as initially instructed, provide additional instructions to continue the movement in progress, or correct a movement error. It is important to note that one of the drawbacks of the classic diagram of the closed-loop system, as

shown in figure 5.3, is that it depicts the movement effectors as the only source for feedback. However, in the actual performance of skills in which the closed-loop control system operates, there are several other sources of sensory feedback, such as the visual and auditory systems. These sources of feedback will be discussed in chapter 6.

---

open-loop control system   a control system in which all the information needed to initiate and carry out an action as planned is contained in the initial instructions to the effectors.

closed-loop control system   a system of control in which during the course of an action, feedback is compared against a standard or reference to enable an action to be carried out as planned.

feedback   information from the sensory system that indicates the status of a movement to the central nervous system; in a closed-loop control system, feedback is used to make corrections to an ongoing movement.

A CLOSER LOOK

The Evolution of the Motor Program Concept

- Early Greek philosophers such as *Plato* talked about a person's creation of an "image" of an act preceding the action itself.
- *William James* (1890) alluded to Plato when he stated that to perform an action, a person must first form a clear "image" of that action.
- *Karl Lashley* (1917) is regarded as the first person to use the actual term *motor program*. He initially viewed motor programs as "intention[s] to act," but later described them as "generalized schemata of action which determine the sequence of specific acts" (Lashley, 1951, p. 122). He proposed that these schemata were organized to provide central control of movement patterns.
- *Sir Frederick Bartlett* (1932) implied that a motor program exists when he used the term *schema* to describe internal representations and organizations of movements.
- *Miller, Galanter, and Pribram* (1960) proposed the notion of a "Plan," which was "essentially the same as a program for a computer" (p. 16), and was responsible for controlling the sequence of events of an action.
- *Franklin Henry* (Henry & Rogers, 1960) gave the motor program concept a needed conceptual and empirical boost. He hypothesized that the "neural pattern for a specific and well-coordinated motor act is controlled by a stored program that is used to direct the neuromotor details of its performance" (p. 449). Henry's concept of the motor program was also that of a computer program. He proposed that when initiated, the program controls the exact movement details, with essentially no modifications possible during the execution of the movement.
- *Stephen Keele* (1968) offered a view similar to Henry's by defining the motor program as "a set of muscle commands that are structured before a movement sequence begins, and that allow . . . the entire sequence to be carried out uninfluenced by peripheral feedback" (p. 387).
- *Richard Schmidt* (1975) proposed that the motor program is not specific muscle commands, but is an abstract memory-based representation of a class of actions, with each class defined by invariant features. Because of these characteristics he called his version the "generalized" motor program.

TWO THEORIES OF MOTOR CONTROL

We can classify theories of how the nervous system controls coordinated movement in terms of the relative importance given to movement instructions specified by central components of the control system and by the environment. Theories that give prominence to movement instructions specified by the central nervous system in the control process have in common some form of memory representation, such as a motor program, that provides the basis for organizing, initiating, and carrying out intended actions. We will discuss a motor program–based theory as an example of this type of theory. In contrast, other theories give more influence to movement instructions specified by the environment and to the dynamic interaction of this information with the body, limbs, and nervous

system. We will discuss the dynamic pattern theory as an example of this type of theory.

Motor Program–Based Theory

At the heart of central control–oriented theories is the **motor program,** a memory-based construct that controls coordinated movement. Various theoretical viewpoints attribute different degrees of control to the motor program. Undoubtedly, the view that best characterizes present-day thinking about the motor program comes from the work of Richard Schmidt (1988, 2003; Schmidt & Lee, 2005). In his "schema theory," Schmidt (1975) proposed that a serious problem with previous views was that they limited the motor program to controlling specific movements or sequences of movements. To overcome this limitation, Schmidt hypothesized the **generalized motor program (GMP)** as a mechanism that could

A CLOSER LOOK

Defining the Motor Program: A Memory Representation versus a Plan of Action Prepared Just Prior to Moving

A problem that has arisen over the years has led to difficulties in understanding what the motor program is and how it functions. The problem is that the term *motor program* has been used to describe different functional constructs. In some discussions, the motor program refers to the memory representation of a movement or action. The generalized motor program (GMP) construct in Schmidt's schema theory is a good example. The theoretical arguments about the memory-representation type of motor program focus

on which characteristics of a movement or action are stored in memory as a part of the motor program. We use the term this way in the present chapter.

The other use of the term *motor program* refers to what is constructed or prepared just prior to movement initiation, but following an intention to act. This use of the term, sometimes referred to as *motor programming,* is the focus of chapter 8, although we do make some reference to this preparation aspect of motor program–based control in the present chapter.

---

account for the adaptive and flexible qualities of human coordinated-movement behavior.

Schmidt's generalized motor program. Schmidt proposed that a GMP controls a *class of actions,* rather than specific movements or sequences. He defined a class of actions as a set of different actions having a common but unique set of features. For Schmidt, these features, which he called **invariant features,** are the "signature" of a GMP and form the basis of what is stored in memory. These movement-related features form the basis of what Schmidt (2003) referred to as *the fundamental pattern of the class of actions.* These features remain consistent from one performance of an action to another. In order for a person to produce a specific action to meet the demands of a performance situation, the person must retrieve the appropriate program from memory and then add movement-specific **parameters.** These are movement-related features of the performances of an action that can be varied from one performance to another.

An analogy that can help you understand the distinction between invariant features and parameters of a GMP is the distinction between rhythm and tempo in music and dance. A piece of music has a *rhythmic structure* that is specified by the time signature, or meter, which is indicated on the written music score, such as 3/4 or 4/4. The first

number (which would be the top number on the music score) indicates the number of beats with equal proportions of time intervals per measure of music. This number establishes the music's rhythmic structure. The second, or bottom, number specifies which type of note receives one beat, which in the case of the two examples would be the quarter note—that is, the $\frac{1}{4}$ note. For the 3/4 meter there are three beats with equal proportions of time intervals in every measure (i.e., the equivalent of three

---

motor program   a memory representation that stores information needed to perform an action.

generalized motor program (GMP)   the memory representation of a class of actions that share common invariant characteristics; it provides the basis for controlling a specific action within the class of actions.

invariant features   a unique set of characteristics that defines a GMP and does not vary from one performance of the action to another.

parameters   features of the GMP that can be varied from one performance of a skill to another; the features of a skill that must be added to the invariant features of a GMP before a person can perform a skill to meet the specific movement demands of a situation.

quarter notes in each measure); for the 4/4 there are four beats to every measure. In dance, a waltz for example, has a 3/4 meter, which gives it its familiar 1-2-3 sequence of steps. *Tempo* refers to the speed at which the music is performed. The same rhythmic structure can be played slowly or fast. You can try this by clapping your hands with one clap for each beat. Try a consistent series of three claps with equal proportions of time intervals between claps, which establishes the rhythmic structure of your clapping. Then clap the same way but faster. Notice that the rhythmic structure doesn't change even though you increase the speed of the clapping. In this analogy, rhythm in music is analogous to an invariant feature of the GMP; tempo is analogous to a parameter.

Invariant features and parameters. Although many possible characteristics could be invariant features of the GMP, one that Schmidt (2003) considered to be the most likely is the **relative time** (which is analogous to rhythm in music) of the components of the skill. Another, is the order, or sequence, of the components. The term *relative* in *relative time* indicates that what is invariant are the percentages, or proportions, of the overall duration, or movement time of the components of a skill.

Figure 5.4 presents an illustration of how to interpret the concept of invariant relative time. Suppose you move the index finger of your hand as quickly as possible to press five keys on a keyboard in sequence. Now, suppose that the four components of this task (the time intervals between the keys: keys 1-2, 2-3, 3-4, 4-5) yield the following movement time (MT) proportions: component 1 takes up 30 percent of the total MT (component % = component MT/total MT); component 2, 20 percent; component 3, 40 percent; and component 4, 10 percent. If the performance of this skill under typical conditions has an overall duration of 10 sec [represented in part (a) of the figure], then regardless of how much you speed up or slow down this overall duration, the actual amount of movement time for each component changes proportionately. In figure 5.4, parts (b) and (c) represent this proportional component change for speeding up the skill

[part (b)] and slowing it down [part (c)]. Thus, if you typically perform this skill in 10 sec, then the amount of time you spend performing each component is 3, 2, 4, and 1 sec respectively. If you performed the skill twice as fast, in 5 sec, then each component would change proportionately to be 1.5, 1, 2, and 0.5 sec respectively. If you slowed down your overall movement time to 15 sec, then each component would change to 4.5, 3, 6, and 1.5 sec respectively.

Although motor program theory proposes that the invariant features of a GMP are rather fixed from one performance of a skill to another, it also holds that there are other features, called *parameters,* that can be varied. Examples include the *overall duration* and the *muscles* used to perform the skill. Skilled performers can easily change these from one performance situation to another, readily adapting them to the specific requirements of each situation.

The following two examples illustrate the relationship between invariant features and parameters. One relates to figure 5.4, which, as just discussed, portrays relative time as an invariant feature. This figure also illustrates the parameter of *overall duration.* The normal, faster, and slower speeds in the figure show that a person can change the overall amount of time taken to move without altering the relative time structure of the components of the movement. This type of situation occurs, for example, when a person walks faster or slower than his or her typical speed.

The second example concerns *muscles* as parameters. Research evidence shows that whether you sign your name with a pen held in your preferred hand, in the opposite hand, between your toes, or with your teeth, the two signatures have distinct invariant spatial as well as relative time features (see Wright, 1990 for an excellent review of this research). These results suggest that you can change the muscles involved in writing your signature without altering the invariant features represented in the generalized motor program. Interestingly, Rijntjes et al. (1999) provided neurological evidence for muscles as a movement parameter related to the signing of one's name by comparing brain regions

a. Normal speed (10 sec)

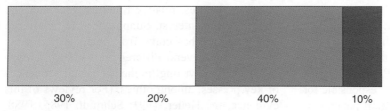

30%   20%   40%   10%

b. Faster (5 sec)

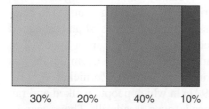

30%   20%   40%   10%

c. Slower (15 sec)

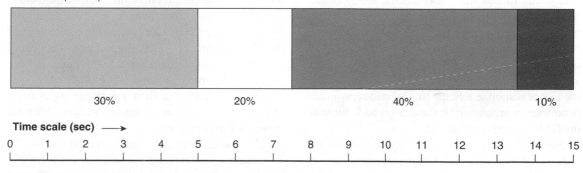

30%   20%   40%   10%

Time scale (sec) ⟶

0   1   2   3   4   5   6   7   8   9   10   11   12   13   14   15

FIGURE 5.4   An illustration of invariant relative time for a hypothetical four-component motor skill when it is performed normally at a 10 sec duration (a), speeded up to a 5 sec duration (b), and slowed down to a 15 sec duration (c).

activated by people signing their name with the finger of the preferred hand and with the big toe. Additional evidence and examples of muscles as parameters will be discussed in chapter 13, when we consider the topic of bilateral transfer.

Schmidt's schema theory. A formalized theory of how the GMP operates to control coordinated movement is Schmidt's schema theory (Schmidt, 1975, 1988, 2003). A **schema** is a rule or set of rules that serves to provide the basis for a decision. It is developed by abstracting important pieces of information from related experiences and combining

them into a type of rule. For example, your concept of *dog* is the result of seeing many different types of dogs and developing a set of rules that will allow

> **relative time**   the proportion, or percentage, of the total amount of time required by each component of a skill during the performance of that skill.
>
> **schema**   a rule or set of rules that serves to provide the basis for a decision; in Schmidt's schema theory, an abstract representation of rules governing movement.

you to identify correctly as a "dog" an animal you have never seen before.

Schmidt used the schema concept to describe two control components involved in the learning and control of skills. Both are characterized as based on abstract rules. The first is the *GMP,* which, as just described, is the control mechanism responsible for controlling the movement coordination patterns of classes of actions, such as throwing, kicking, walking, and running. The second component is the *motor response schema,* which is responsible for providing the specific rules governing the performance of a skill in a given situation. Thus, the motor response schema provides parameters to the GMP.

The schema theory provides an explanation for how well a person can *adapt* to new situations or environmental contexts. People can successfully perform a skill requiring movements that have not been made in that same way before. For example, when you walk in a crowded mall or return a tennis serve, characteristics of the situation change in ways that you have not previously experienced. It is possible to perform the skill successfully in these situations because the person can use the rules from the motor response schema to generate appropriate parameter characteristics; the person adds these to the GMP to perform the skill.

Schmidt's schema theory claims to *solve the degrees of freedom problem* in movement coordination through an executive control operation that organizes motor programs and schemas. An important emphasis in this approach is the abstract, or general, nature of what is stored in the control center. The GMP and motor response schema work together to provide the specific movement characteristics needed to initiate an action in a given situation. The action initiation is an open-loop control process. However, once movement is initiated, feedback can influence its course if there is sufficient time to process the feedback and alter the movement in progress.

Testing the invariant relative-time feature. Researchers have attempted to provide empirical support for motor program–based control by investigating Schmidt's claim that a generalized motor program controls a class of actions defined by specific invariant features. Of the proposed invariant features, relative time has generated the most research interest. Support for the invariance of this feature has come from many experiments investigating several different skills, such as typing, gait, handwriting, prehension, and sequences of key presses, among others. (For reviews of this evidence, see Heuer, 1991; Schmidt, 1985, 1988, 2003; Shea & Wulf, 2005.)

Researchers typically have investigated relative time invariance by observing changes in relative time across a range of values of an associated parameter, such as overall duration or speed. The most commonly cited research example in this regard is a study by Shapiro, Zernicke, Gregor, and Diestel (1981) in which people walked and ran at different speeds on a treadmill. The researchers were interested in the percentages of the total step cycle time (i.e., relative time) that would characterize the four components, or phases, of the step cycle at each treadmill speed (i.e., the overall duration parameter). Their hypothesis was that if relative time is invariant for the generalized motor program involved in controlling walking and/or running gait patterns, then the percentages for a specific gait component should remain constant across the different speeds.

The results were consistent with the hypothesis of relative time invariance (see figure 5.5). As gait sped up or slowed down (at least up to 6 km/hr and beyond 8 km/hr), the percentage of time accounted for by each step cycle component remained essentially the same for different speeds. The differences between the relative time characteristics of walking and running are especially notable in the pie charts in the (b) section of figure 5.5. The pie charts show the relative time percentages for the average of the walking speeds and the running speeds for each of the four step cycle phases. Because the relative time percentages differed between walking and running, the authors concluded that two *different* motor programs control walking and running gaits. Within each gait pattern, the overall duration (i.e., speed) parameter could be increased or slowed down while the relative timing among the components of the step cycle was maintained.

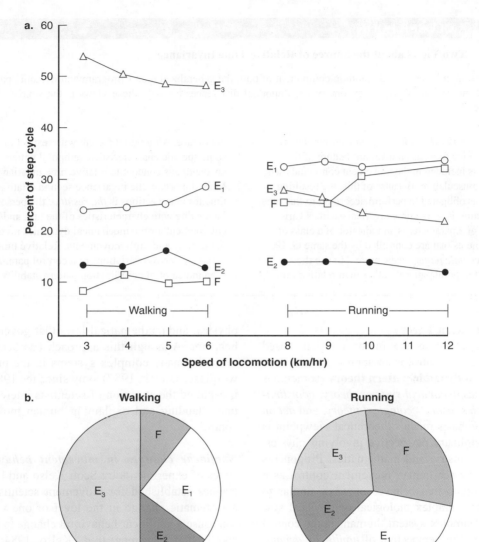

FIGURE 5.5   Results of the experiment by Shapiro et al. (a) The relative time percentage of total step cycle time for each of the four step cycle phases (Phillipson step cycle) at different speeds of walking and running. F = Flexion phase (from toeoff to beginning of knee extension); E_1 = Extension phase 1 (from beginning of knee extension to heelstrike); E_2 = Extension phase 2 (from heelstrike to maximum knee-angle flexion); E_3 = Extension phase 3 (from maximum knee-angle flexion to toeoff). (b) The average (of the four speeds) relative time percentages of total step cycle time for each of the four step cycle phases for walking and running. [From Shapiro, D. C., et al. (1981). Evidence for generalized motor programs using gait pattern analysis. *Journal of Motor Behavior, 13,* 33–47. Copyright © 1981 Heldref Publication, Inc. Washington, DC. Reprinted by permission.]

Two Views about the Source of Relative Time Invariance

Relative time invariance is a common component of both the generalized motor program and dynamic pattern views of motor control. However, one of the important differences between these views is the source of the invariance.

- The *generalized motor program view* emphasizes that relative time, as an invariant feature of the GMP, is included in the movement commands sent to the musculature. Because of this, the resulting action is obligated to perform according to this time constraint. Relative time invariance across variations of a parameter is an indicator of a class of movements that are controlled by the same GMP.
- The *dynamic pattern view* prefers to use the term "temporal pattern" rather than relative time

invariance. Although different with respect to some specific characteristics, temporal pattern is an analogous concept to relative time invariance. More important, the invariance seen in relative time for many actions is *the result of* the person interacting with characteristics of the task and/or environment, or the mechanical dynamics involved in the body and limb movements. Relative time invariance across variations of a control parameter is an indicator of coordination pattern stability.

Dynamic Pattern Theory

In sharp contrast to the motor program–based theory of motor control is an approach commonly referred to as **dynamic pattern theory** (sometimes referred to as *dynamical systems theory, coordination dynamics theory, ecological theory,* and *action theory*). The basis for this theoretical viewpoint is a multidisciplinary perspective involving physics, biology, chemistry, and mathematics. Proponents of this theory see human movement control as a complex system that behaves in ways similar to those of any complex biological or physical system. As a complex system, human motor control is seen from the perspective of *nonlinear dynamics;* this means that behavioral changes over time do not follow a continuous, linear progression, but make sudden abrupt changes. For example, in the physical world, when the temperature of water is increased gradually, there is a specific temperature (100° C) at which the water boils, its behavior abruptly changes. This type of change represents a **nonlinear behavior.**

Those who study dynamic pattern theory are particularly interested in how a system changes over time from one stable state to another because of the influence of a particular variable. In addition, they are interested in identifying

physical and mathematical laws that govern such behavior. Although this approach has been used to model many complex systems in the physical world (see Gleick, 1987), only since the 1980s has it captured the attention of scientists interested in understanding and explaining human movement control.

Nonlinear changes in movement behavior. A series of experiments by Scott Kelso and his colleagues established for movement scientists that a systematic change in the level of one variable can cause a nonlinear behavioral change in human coordinated movement (e.g., Kelso, 1984; Kelso & Scholz, 1985). In these experiments participants began moving their right and left index fingers at a specified rate of speed in one stable coordination state, or pattern, described as an *antiphase* relationship (sometimes referred to as an *out-of-phase* relationship). This means that the muscle groups controlling the right and left fingers were operating simultaneously but in opposite ways: when the right finger was flexed, the left finger was extended, similar to the motion of windshield wipers in many vehicles. Quantitatively, the fingers were 180° out of phase with each other throughout the movement cycle. The participants systematically increased the speed of their finger movements by keeping their finger speed consistent with that of a metronome controlled by the experimenters. The result was that at a specific speed the finger movements spontaneously shifted to a second stable coordination state, or pattern, described as an *in-phase* relationship between the two fingers, where both were flexed or extended at the same time (i.e., 0 or 360° in phase with each other).

You can experience this spontaneous, nonlinear, coordination change yourself by making two fists with your hands and putting them on your desk or tabletop so that the little finger side of your fist rests on the desktop. Extend your two index fingers so that they face forward. Then begin to move them side-to-side (keep them parallel to the desktop) in the same way that was done in the Kelso experiment.

The shift to the in-phase coordination state occurred during the *transition* between the stable antiphase and in-phase states. The transition was a mixture of both antiphase and in-phase coordination patterns. But at slower speeds, only an antiphase pattern occurred, whereas at faster speeds, only in-phase pattern occurred. Thus, a linear increase in movement speed led to a nonlinear change in the fundamental coordinaion pattern of movement between the two index fingers.

When viewed from the perspective of coordination patterns, these experiments established that distinct coordination patterns can *spontaneously* develop as a function of a change in one specific variable; which in this case was movement speed. In the finger-movement task used in the Kelso experiments, the antiphase and in-phase finger-movement relationships represent stable coordination patterns. The importance of these experiments is that they provided an initial step in the investigation of coordination changes that can occur without resorting to a mechanism such as a motor program to specify movement characteristics for each coordination pattern.

These spontaneous coordination pattern changes are not limited to laboratory tasks. They also have been found for motor skills involved in sports and daily activities. For example, front-crawl strokes in swimming exhibit spontaneous arm-coordination pattern changes at a specific swimming speed (Seifert, Chollet, & Bardy, 2004). Another example is the change from a walking to a running coordination pattern that spontaneously occurs at a specific speed. The experiment by Shapiro et al. (1981), which was discussed earlier in this chapter, was an early demonstration of this spontaneous gait pattern change. Since that experiment, the walk-to-run and, conversely, the run-to-walk gait changes that occur as a function of speed have been demonstrated numerous times and have become the basis for an increasing amount of research (e.g., Diedrich & Warren, 1995, 1998; Wagenaar & van Emmerik, 1994). We will discuss this spontaneous gait change phenomenon in more detail in chapter 7

Stability and Attractors

At the heart of the dynamic pattern view is the concept of **stability.** In dynamic terms, stability refers to the behavioral steady state of a system. It is important to note that this use of this term is different from the concept of invariance. As used here, stability incorporates the notion of variability

---

dynamic pattern theory   an approach to describing and explaining the control of coordinated movement that emphasizes the role of information in the environment and the dynamic properties of the body and limbs; it is also known as the dynamical systems theory.

nonlinear behavior   a behavior that changes in abrupt, nonlinear ways in response to systematic linear increases in the value of a specific variable (e.g., the change from smooth to turbulent water flow in a tube at a specific increase in water velocity; the change from a walking to a running gait at a specific increase in gait velocity).

stability   a behavioral steady state of a system that represents a preferred behavioral state and incorporates the notion of invariance by noting that a stable system will spontaneously return to a stable state after it is slightly perturbed.

A CLOSER LOOK

Spontaneous Coordination Pattern Changes due to Speed in the Front-Crawl Strokes of Elite Swimmers

A change in the arm coordination pattern of the front crawl stroke in swimming is a sports skill example of the type of spontaneous coordination pattern development originally reported by Kelso (1984) for the finger movement task. In an experiment in France by Seifert, Chollet, and Bardy (2004), fourteen elite male sprint swimmers performed eight swim trials at a specified distance. The trials began at a speed that was similar to the pace for a 3,000 m distance. On succeeding trials swimmers were required to increase their speed by a specified amount, which was based on paces that would be used for 1,500, 800, 400, 200, 100, and 50 m; the eighth trial was at the swimmers' maximum speed. Arm coordination was quantified for each trial. The analysis of arm coordination revealed *two distinct coordination patterns:* a *catch-up pattern,* in which there was a lag time between the propulsive phases of each arm, and a *relative opposition pattern,* in which the propulsive phase of one arm ended when the propulsive phase of the other arm began. Analysis of the arm strokes showed that all the swimmers used a catch-up pattern during the first trial. But as they increased their swimming speeds on successive trials, there was a critical speed at which they all began to use a relative opposition pattern for their arm strokes.

by noting that when a system is slightly perturbed, it will return spontaneously to a stable state.

By observing characteristics of a stable state, scientists can gain understanding of the variables that influence a system to behave as it does. For example, in the reciprocal rhythmic finger movements in the Kelso experiment just described, the researchers observed behavioral stability when the fingers were in antiphase and in-phase relationships with each other. These two stable states indicate two coordinated movement patterns. Between these states, as finger speed increased, a *phase transition* occurred during which instability characterized the behavioral patterns. The instability continued until finger speed reached a point at which a new stable state spontaneously occurred.

The stable behavioral steady states of systems are known as **attractors** (or *attractor states*). In terms of human coordinated movement, attractors are *preferred behavioral states,* such as the in-phase and antiphase states for rhythmic finger movements in the Kelso experiment. Attractors represent stable regions of operation around which behavior typically occurs when a system is allowed to operate in its preferred manner.

For example, when people locomote at a speed of 3 mi/hr (i.e., 4.8 km/hr), the arms and legs are "attracted to" a coordination relationship that produces a walking gait. This gait pattern represents the preferred behavioral state for engaging in a locomotion action at this particular speed. But when people locomote at a speed of 10 mi/hr (16 km/hr), the walking gait is not the preferred locomotion state. At this speed, most people run, which, as you saw in figure 5.5, involves a coordination pattern that is different from a walking gait pattern.

Another example of attractors is postural coordination patterns. According to Bardy and his colleagues (e.g., Bardy, Ouiller, Lagarde, & Stoffregen, 2007) there are two stable patterns of postural coordination, as determined by the relationship between the movements of the hips (i.e., the joints that influence trunk movement) and ankles: an in-phase and antiphase patterns. These two patterns are analogous to the rhythmic finger-movement patterns described earlier, which means that the hips and ankles both exhibit flexion in the in-phase pattern, but one joint extends while the other flexes during the antiphase pattern. Each of these patterns characterize standing postural control coordination in situations in which a person is trying to maintain standing balance on a non-stable surface, as would occur when you are standing in a moving bus. From a dynamical pattern theory perspective, the transition from one coordination pattern to the other (in response to the movement of the bus) occurs automatically and spontaneously because the in-phase and antiphase modes of the postural coordination components (the hips and ankles) establish the "preferred" pattern.

Finally, attractor states are not only stable states characterized by minimal behavioral variability, but also optimally *energy-efficient* states. This means that when a person is moving at a preferred rate or using a preferred coordination pattern, that person uses less energy than he or she would if moving at a nonpreferred rate.

Order and Control Parameters
Proponents of the dynamic pattern view place a priority on developing formal nonlinear equations of motion that specify the stability and loss of stability of movement coordination patterns in addition to changes that result from learning and development. To develop these equations, scientists must identify the variables responsible for and associated with coordination. Primary among these variables are **order parameters** (sometimes the term *collective variables* is used). These are functionally specific and abstract variables that define the overall behavior of a system. The order parameters enable a coordinated pattern of movement that can be reproduced and distinguished from other patterns.

Because *order parameters define a movement pattern,* it is essential to identify specific types. The most prominent of the order parameters identified by researchers is *relative phase* for rhythmic movements. Relative phase, which we briefly discussed in chapter 2, refers to a quantified value that represents the movement relationship between two movement segments. For the rhythmic finger-movement task in the Kelso (1984) experiment, the relative phase for the in-phase movement relationship was 360° (which is the same as 0°); the relative phase for the antiphase movement relationship was 180°. These two relative phases were determined by establishing that the maximum adduction of a finger had a phase value of 360° (i.e., 0°), and the maximum abduction had a phase value of 180°. On the basis of a common starting point, the relative phase was then calculated as the difference between the phase values of the two fingers at any point during the movement.

To apply the description from chapter 2 of the calculation of relative phase to this rhythmic finger-movement task, consider the following. For the in-phase movement, both fingers had a common starting point of maximum adduction (i.e., 360°). The fingers then moved together to a maximum abduction position (180°) and then returned to the initial maximum adduction position. At any time during the fingers' movement, they had a relative phase of 360°, indicating that both fingers are at the same abduction position. The opposite holds for the antiphase pattern. At any point, the one finger is abducting the same amount as the other is adducting, which means the two fingers have a relative phase of 180°.

Another way to consider this phase relationship is from the perspective of the amount of simultaneous adduction and/or abduction movement. When moving in-phase with each other, both fingers abduct or adduct the same amount at the same time; when moving antiphase, both fingers move the same amount simultaneously, but one is adducting while the other is abducting.

The **control parameter** represents the variable that when increased or decreased will influence

---

attractors the stable behavioral steady states of systems. In terms of human coordinated movement, attractors characterize preferred behavioral states, such as the in-phase and antiphase states for rhythmic bimanual finger movements.

order parameters functionally specific variables that define the overall behavior of a system; they enable a coordinated pattern of movement to be reproduced and distinguished from other patterns (e.g., relative phase); known also as collective variables.

control parameters coordinated movement control variables (e.g., tempo, or speed, and force) that freely change according to the characteristics of an action situation. According to the dynamic pattern view of motor control when a control parameter is systematically varied (e.g., speed is increased from slow to fast), an order parameter may remain stable or change its stable state characteristic at a certain level of change of the control parameter.

the stability and character of the order parameter. For example, in the Kelso experiment, movement frequency (i.e., speed) was the control parameter. As the movement frequency was systematically increased by the metronome, the phase relationship between the two fingers underwent distinct changes. The in-phase relationship was maintained through several frequencies, but then began to destabilize as frequency continued to increase during which neither an in-phase nor an antiphase relationship was detectable during a period of increasing frequencies, which is known as a *phase transition*. However, as the frequency continued to increase, there was a critical frequency at which the new antiphase relationship emerged and became stable.

From an experimental point of view, the control parameter is important to identify because it becomes the variable to manipulate in order to assess the stability of the order parameter, which in turn provides the basis for determining attractor states for patterns of limb movement. From an applied perspective, the control parameter can be the basis for assessing the stability of a coordination pattern and may provide insights into a person's coordination characteristics that might not otherwise be observed.

An example of a situation in which a practitioner could vary the control parameter was reported in a study by van Emmerik and Wagenaar (1996). They demonstrated that Parkinson's disease patients had more difficulty than healthy age-matched control participants in adapting a specific coordination pattern while walking to gradually increasing speeds (i.e., the control parameter) on a treadmill. In this study, the relative phase (i.e., the order parameter) of interest was based on the relationship between the arm and leg swings while walking. The researchers concluded from their results that the assessment of the stability of the phase relationship for the arm and leg swings at various walking speeds provides a sensitive technique to diagnose and detect early stages of Parkinson's disease.

Self-organization. An important element of the dynamic pattern perspective is the concept of **self-organization.** This means that when certain conditions characterize a situation, a specific stable pattern of behavior emerges. Many examples of self-organization exist within the physical world that illustrate applications of this concept to the human movement domain. For example, there is no hurricane program in the universe, but hurricanes commonly occur. However, they occur only when certain wind and water temperature conditions exist. When these variables achieve certain characteristics, a hurricane will self-organize in an identifiable pattern that distinguishes it from a tropical depression or any other weather system.

When applied to human movement coordination, the concept of self-organization means that when certain conditions characterize a situation, a specific pattern of limb movement emerges. Thus, rather than being specified by a motor program, the coordinated pattern of movement self-organizes within the framework of the characteristics of environmental conditions and limb dynamics. For example, in the bimanual finger-movement task performed in the Kelso experiments, the in-phase coordination pattern self-organized as a function of the movement speed (i.e., the control parameter). This same type of self-organization is seen for the walk-to-run, or run-to-walk, gait transitions that occur as gait speed increases or decreases and for the arm coordination change that occurs as swim speed increases (see, for example, Seifert, Chollet, & Bardy, 2004).

Coordinative Structures; Muscle Synergies
Another important aspect of the dynamic pattern view relates to the unit of behavior that is controlled. Proponents of the view assert that skilled action results when a person's nervous system constrains *functionally specific collections of muscles and joints* to act cooperatively, so that the person can achieve an action goal according to the dictates of the situation. An individual may develop these performance synergies, called **coordinative structures,** through practice or experience, or they may exist naturally.

One example of a coordinative structure is the muscles and joints (the degrees of freedom to be controlled) involved in the action of reaching and grasping an object. The groups of muscles and joints that must act together to enable a person

A CLOSER LOOK

Evidence for Relative Time in Brain Activity and Coordinated Movement

In an excellent discussion comparing and contrasting the motor programming and dynamic pattern views of motor control, Kelso (1997) addressed various issues related to relative time, which is a key variable common to both views. One of the issues that motor control researchers have struggled with over the years is determining the relationship between brain activity and observable performance characteristics associated with movement. A possible breakthrough in this struggle appears possible through the use of functional brain imaging technology, which enables researchers to observe brain activity while a person engages in performing a motor skill.

Below are two key findings from research by Kelso and his colleagues in which they used this technology to investigate the issue of relative time. In these experiments, participants performed bimanual coordination skills to produce either in-phase or out-of-phase (antiphase) movement coordination patterns to a signal that specified movement speed, which was systematically increased (see figure 5.6).

• At low speeds, relative time remained stable (i.e., invariant) across a range of speeds for both in- and out-of-phase coordination patterns.

• Spontaneous transitions from out-of-phase to in-phase coordination patterns occurred (i.e., a new coordination pattern self-organized) at a critical movement speed.

The results indicated that for relative time, the brain produced essentially the same pattern of activity as was observed at the movement level during the performance of a motor skill. Kelso stated that an important implication of these results for the motor control theory controversy is that the dynamic pattern view predicts these results, whereas the motor programming view does not.

---

to successfully reach and grasp an object are "converted" through practice into a task-specific ensemble.

An analogy here may help. The term "task-specific ensemble" can be thought of as analogous to singing groups, commonly called "ensembles," in which many individuals sing specific parts of a specific song; all the individual singers work together cooperatively (i.e., synergistically) to achieve a specific goal. Similarly, coordinative structures are ensembles of muscles and joints that work cooperatively to allow a person to achieve a specific action goal, such as grasping an object.

For the motor control system the existence of coordinative structures reduces the degrees of freedom that the system must control. Rather than having to control the many degrees of freedom represented by the many muscles and joints involved in performing an action, the motor control system can control one ensemble of muscles and joints. For the reach-and-grasp action the activation of the coordinative structure begins when a person has the intention to reach and grasp a cup and the

environmental conditions specify that this action should occur. Then, in accordance with the characteristics of the limb and of the environmental constraints, the coordinative structure self-organizes to carry out the action.

An important behavioral benefit of coordinative structures is that they allow a person to achieve an action goal even when a muscle or joint that is

---

self-organization   the emergence of a specific stable pattern of behavior due to certain conditions characterizing a situation rather than to a specific control mechanism organizing the behavior; for example, in the physical world hurricanes self-organize when certain wind and water temperature conditions exist.

coordinative structures   functionally specific collections of muscles and joints that are constrained by the nervous system to act cooperatively to produce an action; sometimes referred to as muscle, or motor, synergies.

The coordination characteristics of hitting a tennis serve provide a good example of a coordinative structure that is acquired as a result of extensive practice.

a part of the structure is not able to function normally. For example, if you have a cast on your leg that keeps your knee from bending, you are able to walk up or down the stairs. This is possible because some of the muscles in the ensemble of muscles and joints (i.e., the coordinative structure) associated with walking up and down the stairs will activate in a way that compensates for the lack of involvement by muscles that can't normally function because of the cast. Consider this compensatory activity as similar to what occurs in sports teams when one of the players is not able to perform at his or her best, but the team performs well because players "step up" and perform at a higher level than they typically perform.

Coordinative structures can be intrinsic or developed through practice. *Intrinsic coordinative structures* are involved in actions such as walking, running, and bimanual coordination. When we perform these actions, the muscles and joints of the limbs involved have a natural tendency to demonstrate interlimb coordination patterns that have characterized our performance of them since early in life. For example, when performing a skill involving bimanual coordination, which requires the simultaneous use of both arms and hands, both infants (see, for example, Corbetta & Thelen, 1996) and adults (see Kelso, Southard, & Goodman, 1979, for instance) typically demonstrate a similar natural tendency to move the arms and hands in synchrony—that is, simultaneously both spatially and temporally. This means that when people first learn to perform a tennis serve, which requires each arm to simultaneously move in different ways, their initial tendency is to move their arms in the same way at the same time.

In contrast, *coordinative structures developed through practice* become new combinations of muscles and joints that act together to produce a coordination pattern that will allow the achievement of an action goal. The tennis serve just described is a good example of the development of a new coordinative structure as a result of extensive practice. Another example was described by Seifert, Chollet, and Allard (2004) for swimmers. As front crawl swimmers achieved elite status, they began to demonstrate a stroke speed and length relationship with breathing frequency that allowed them to adapt to race situation demands more successfully than less skilled swimmers.

For the learning of certain skills, the intrinsic coordinative structures can lead to initial performance difficulties, as in the case of learning a tennis serve. However, after overcoming these initial difficulties, the person's performance of the skill will benefit from the newly developed coordinative structure, because it will allow him or her to achieve an action goal even though some slight perturbation occurs during the action. For example, if a tennis player is serving, and during the serve a gust of wind makes the ball deviate from its intended path, the player can quickly and easily adjust the movements involved in his or her serving action and achieve a successful serve. Similarly, if a person is jogging on a sidewalk and must step over a curb, the jogger can quickly and easily adjust movement characteristics of his or her gait pattern to avoid tripping while maintaining the jogging coordination pattern.

Perception and action coupling. Proponents of the dynamic pattern view emphasize the interaction of the performer and the physical environment in which the skill is performed. From a motor control perspective, this interaction involves perception and movement variables that must be taken into account in any attempt to explain the mechanisms involved in the control of open motor skills, which, as discussed in chapter 1, involve a person or object in motion. The dynamic pattern theory proposes that this interaction, which is referred to as **perception-action coupling,** is an essential element in accounting for skillful performance of open skills. The perception part of the interaction detects and uses critical invariant information in the environment (e.g., the amount of time until the object contacts the person, or vice versa); the action part involves the setting and regulating of movement control features that enable the person to achieve the action goal (e.g., kinematic and kinetic components of movements).[2]

An example of a perceptual variable involved in this type of coupling process is known by the Greek letter *tau* (τ), which is related to the time-to-contact between an object and a person's eye. (We will discuss *tau* further in chapters 6 and 8.) Researchers have demonstrated that *tau* guides actions such as steering a car, catching a ball, hitting a ball, jumping from a platform, and performing the long jump. As a person gains experience, the perceptual variable couples with the dynamics of movement so that a distinct coordination pattern can be reproduced as needed.

Some additional examples of perception-action coupling include the coordination pattern people use to get on or over an obstacle, climb stairs, and go through a doorway. Researchers have found that obstacles in a person's pathway, stairs, and door openings specify size-related information that a person perceives in terms of an invariant relationship between an object's size and her or his own leg length (in the case of obstacles and stairs) or body size (in the case of door openings). Thus the person will step or climb over the obstacle on the basis of this perceived relationship, choose one of various stair-climbing options, and walk through a doorway sideways or face-forward depending on this perceived relationship between the environmental feature and his or her own body size–related feature.

THE PRESENT STATE OF THE CONTROL THEORY ISSUE

The motor program–based theory and the dynamic pattern theory are the predominant behavioral theories currently addressing how the nervous system produces coordinated movement. Debate and research continue as scientists attempt to answer this important theory question. A benefit of the debate

---

[2]For an excellent discussion of perception-action coupling and its application to sport skill performance, see Buekers, Montagne, and Laurent, 1999.

---

perception-action coupling   the spatial and temporal coordination of vision and the hands or feet that enables people to perform eye-hand and eye-foot coordination skills; that is, the coordination of the visual perception of the object and the limb movement required to achieve the action goal.

An Example of How Motor Program Theory and Dynamic Pattern Theory Differ in Explaining the Motor Control of a Behavior: The Walk-to-Run Gait Change

People spontaneously change from a walk to a run gait pattern at a certain speed of locomotion. Although individuals vary in terms of the actual speed at which this change occurs, the shift appears to be common to all people. The motor program and dynamic pattern theories differ in their explanations of why this coordination change occurs.

- **Motor Program Theory** The relative time structure of a coordination pattern distinguishes one generalized motor program from another. Because walking and running gaits are characterized by different relative time structures, they are controlled by different generalized motor programs. The walk-to-run gait pattern change occurs at a certain speed because the person chooses to change from the program that controls walking to the program that controls running.
- **Dynamic Pattern Theory** Interlimb and body coordination patterns self-organize as a function of specific control parameter values and environmental conditions. For walking and running gait patterns, speed is a critical control parameter. The walk-to-run gait transition involves a competition between two attractors. At slow speeds, the primary attractor state is a walking coordination pattern. But as walking speed increases, there is a certain range of speeds at which this attractor state loses stability, which means

that for this range of speeds, the walking pattern undergoes some change as a running coordination pattern self-organizes and eventually becomes the stable attractor state for gait at a certain speed.

Interpreting the Shapiro et al. (1981) Experiment Results (Figure 5.5)

Motor program theory. Gait is controlled by one generalized motor program when walking gait is observed (3–6 km/hr) and by a different generalized motor program when the running gait is observed (8–12 km/hr).

Dynamic pattern theory. The walking and running gaits represent two attractor states that remain stable within the speed ranges of 3–6 km/hr and 10–12 km/hr. But for gait speeds of 7–9 km/hr, the order parameter becomes unstable during a transition period in which a new gait pattern (running) self-organizes and becomes stable for a certain range of speeds.

---

between proponents of these theories is that critical issues have become clarified and future directions more evident. We now know, for example, that a theory of control cannot focus exclusively on the movement information that is specified by the central nervous system. Theorists also must take task and environmental characteristics into account. As Newell (1986) rightly stated, the optimal pattern of coordination is determined by the interaction among constraints specified by the person, the environment, and the task.

Opinions vary in terms of the resolution of the motor control theory debate. For example, some researchers foresee a compromise between the two theories, which would lead to the development of a hybrid theory that incorporates the strengths of each theory (e.g., see Abernethy & Sparrow,

1992; Walter, 1998). Some research evidence that suggests the potential for some compromise was reported by Amazeen (2002). In a series of experiments, she demonstrated that the application of specific aspects of a dynamic pattern theory to the generalized motor program theory could account for performance characteristics associated with the acquisition of rhythmic bimanual coordination skills that the generalized motor program theory alone could not. However, she left open the possibility that her results could be interpreted as support for only the dynamic pattern theory.

Others argue that a hybrid theory is unlikely. For example, Abernethy and Sparrow (1992) speculated that a compromise theory would not emerge because the two theories represent two vastly different approaches to explaining the control of coordinated

LAB LINKS

Lab 5 in the Online Learning Center Lab Manual provides you the opportunity to experience the spontaneous, nonlinear change in gait coordination that occurs with increases in gait speed.

movement. They reasoned that because of this difference, the history of science would predict that one will eventually become the predominant theory. Kelso (1997) expressed a similar view, but was more specific in his projections. He argued that because many aspects of the motor program view can be subsumed within the dynamic pattern theory, especially those related to invariant features and control parameters, and because the dynamic pattern theory can explain and predict more of the behavioral features of coordinated movement, the dynamic pattern theory will eventually become the predominant theory. However, at this point in time, that predominance has yet to be established.

SUMMARY

- Motor control theory, like any theory, provides an explanation for why observable phenomena or behavior exist or behave as they do. It also provides the practitioner with a base of support on which to develop effective motor skill instruction and practice environments.

- The term *coordination* refers to the patterning of head, body, and/or limb movements in relation to the patterning of environmental objects and events. When the term *coordination* is used in reference to the movement patterns associated with the performance of a skill, it refers to the relationship among head, body, and/or limbs at a specific point in time during the skill performance.

- For a person to learn to produce a well-coordinated movement that achieves an intended action goal, the motor control system must solve the degrees of freedom problem, which concerns constraining the many degrees of freedom that characterize muscles, joints, and the like. A theory of motor control should provide an explanation of how the motor control system solves this problem.

- Theories of motor control typically incorporate features of open-loop and closed-loop control systems. Both involve a control center, movement instructions, and effectors. The closed-loop system also includes feedback as part of the system. In an open-loop system, the control center sends the effectors all the movement instructions they need to perform a skill from beginning to end. In contrast, the control center in a closed-loop system sends movement instructions to the effectors that enable them to initiate the performance of a skill; feedback from the effectors and other sources provides the control center with the information needed to give the effectors the instructions to continue and end the movement.

- Motor control theories can be distinguished in terms of the relative importance given to the movement instructions specified by central components of the control system or by the environment. Theories that give prominence to instructions from the control center have in common some form of stored memory representation, such as a motor program, that provides the movement instructions to the effectors. In contrast, theories that give prominence to movement instructions specified by the environment emphasize the dynamic interaction of this information with the body, limbs, and nervous system.

- Schmidt's schema theory is the most popular representative of motor program–based theories. It proposes that a generalized motor program (GMP) serves as the central, memory-based mechanism for the control of motor skill performance. The GMP is an abstract representation of a class of movements that is stored in memory and retrieved when a skill involving that class of movements is to be performed. Stored in the GMP are invariant features of the movement class, such as the order of movement events and the relative time of the movement components. When a specific action is to be performed, specific parameter values must be added to the GMP; these include the overall duration of the movement and the muscles that will be used.

- The dynamic pattern theory takes issue with the importance motor program theories give to memory-based representations for the control of motor skills. The dynamic pattern theory proposes that factors such as environmental invariants and limb dynamics can account for much of the control ascribed to the motor program. The theory views coordinated movement as following rules associated with nonlinear dynamics. The theory incorporates dynamic features such as attractor states, which are preferred, stable patterns that define specific coordination patterns; order parameters, such as relative phase, that functionally define attractor states; and control parameters, such as speed or frequency, that influence the stability and instability of attractor states. Coordinated movement self-organizes as coordinative structures according to the characteristics of the interactions among the person, the environment, and the skill to be performed.

- At present, there are strong proponents of both the motor program and the dynamic pattern theories of motor control. Opinions vary in terms of how the current theory debate will be resolved.

POINTS FOR THE PRACTITIONER

- Theories are more than abstract ideas. Good theories provide a foundation on which you should build effective instruction and practice condition environments; good theories also provide a base for creating instruction and practice condition alternatives when those that were planned are not successful.

- People will develop their own strategies to control the number of degrees of freedom involved in the coordination of the limbs, trunk, and/or head when they first try to perform a skill. You should be aware of these strategies and determine whether they need to be changed with practice in order for the learner to improve performance beyond an initial level.

- The relative time invariance of a GMP and the changeable characteristic of the overall duration

parameter indicate that when teaching a skill in which a specific rhythm must be performed at a fast speed, the rhythm feature of the skill should be taught first at a slow speed. When the rhythmic pattern has been learned, then the speed of performing the skill can be increased.

- You can assess movement problems and capabilities for functional skills by testing performance characteristics across skill and environment characteristics that can be systematically modified, such as speed or distance, and observing movement changes that accompany these modifications.

- Coordination characteristics observed in people with movement disorders may be optimal because of the constraints imposed on the motor control system by the pathological condition and the environmental conditions in which a skill is performed. As a result, attempts to make adjustments to the coordination characteristics may not be fruitful or desirable.

RELATED READINGS

Barton, S. (1994). Chaos, self-organization, and psychology. *American Psychologist, 49,* 5–14.

Bongaardt, R., & Meijer, O. G. (2000). Bernstein's theory of movement behavior: Historical development and contemporary relevance. *Journal of Motor Behavior, 32,* 57–71.

Cauraugh, J., Light, K., Kim, S., Thigpen, M., & Behrman, A. (2000). Chronic motor dysfunction after stroke: Recovering wrist and finger extention by electromyography-triggered neuromuscular stimulation. *Stroke, 31,* 1360–1364.

Chow, J.Y., Davids, K., Button, C., Shuttleworth, R., & Araújo, D. (2007). The role of nonlinear pedagogy in physical education. *Review of Educational Research, 77,* 251–278.

Clark, J. E. (1995). On becoming skillful: Patterns and constraints. *Research Quarterly for Exercise and Sport, 66,* 173–183.

Davids, K., Renshaw, I., & Glazier, P. (2005). Movement models from sports reveal fundamental insights into coordination processes. *Exercise and Sports Sciences Reviews, 33,* 36–42.

Krishnamoorthy, V., Latash, M. L., Scholz, J. P., & Zatsiorsky, V. M. (2003). Muscle synergies during shifts of the center of pressure by standing persons. *Experimental Brain Research, 152,* 281–292.

Schwerin, S., Dewald, J. P. A., Haztl, M., Jovanovich, S., Nickeas, M., & MacKinnon, C. (2008). Ipsilateral versus Contralateral cortical motor projections to a shoulder adductor in chronic hemiparetic stroke: Implications for the expression of arm synergies. *Experimental Brain Research, 185,* 500–519.

Van Emmerik, R. E. A., Rosenstein, M. T., McDermott, W. J., & Hamill, J. (2004). A nonlinear dynamics approach to human movement. *Journal of Applied Biomechanics, 20,* 396–420.

Wallace, S. A. (1996). Dynamic pattern perspective of rhythmic movement: An introduction. In H. N. Zelaznik (Ed.), *Advances in motor learning and control* (pp. 155–194). Champaign, IL: Human Kinetics.

INTERNET RESOURCES

- To gain more insight into the basis for the dynamic pattern theory, read a review of Kelso's influential book Dynamic Patterns. Go to

  http://www-users.cs.york.ac.uk/~susan/

  Click on the link: book reviews

  Click on the link: all reviews

  Click on the letter K

  Click on the link: J. A. Scott Kelso *Dynamic Patterns*

- In 1983 Schmidt's 1975 article in the research journal *Psychological Review,* in which he first presented his schema theory, was cited as a "Citation Classic," indicating that researchers had cited his article in their own research many more times than is the norm for a research journal article. You can read Schmidt's comments about why and how he developed the theory at

  http://www.garfield.library.upenn.edu/

  Click on the link: Citation Classic Commentaries

  Click on the "S" in the alphabet list

  Scroll down to Schmidt, RA and click on the link

STUDY QUESTIONS

1. (a) Describe two characteristics of a good theory in science. (b) How can a good theory in a behavioral science like motor control and learning be useful to a practitioner?

2. Define the term coordination and describe how a limb movement displacement graph can portray a coordinated movement pattern.

3. What is the *degrees of freedom problem* as it relates to the study of human motor control and learning?

4. Describe the similarities and the differences between a closed-loop control system and an open-loop control system. For each system, describe a motor skill that could be characterized as having that type of control system.

5. Define a generalized motor program and describe one invariant feature and two parameters proposed to characterize this program.

6. Describe an example of nonlinear changes in human coordinated movement.

7. Define and give an example of the following key terms used in the dynamic pattern theory of motor control: (a) stability; (b) attractors; (c) order parameters; (d) control parameters; (e) coordinative structures; (f) self-organization.

8. Discuss how relative-time characteristics of human walking and running gaits are explained by (a) motor program–based theory and (b) dynamic pattern theory.

Specific Application Problem:
(a) You are working in your chosen profession. Describe a *motor skill* that people with whom you work would need to improve their performance capabilities.
(b) Describe how you would apply concepts from a motor program–based theory and the dynamic pattern theory to help you identify the performance problems a person currently has and would need to improve.

CHAPTER 6

Sensory Components of Motor Control

Concept: Touch, proprioception, and vision are important sensory components of motor control.

After completing this chapter, you will be able to

- Describe the sensory receptors in the skin that provide tactile sensory information to the central nervous system
- Discuss several movement-related characteristics influenced by tactile sensory feedback
- Describe various types of sensory receptors that provide proprioception information to the central nervous system
- Describe several procedures researchers use to investigate the role of proprioception in motor control
- Discuss several movement-related characteristics influenced by feedback from the proprioceptors
- Describe key anatomical components of the eye and neural pathways for vision
- Describe several procedures researchers use to investigate the role of vision in motor control
- Discuss motor control issues related to the use of binocular and monocular vision, central and peripheral vision, the perception-action coupling of vision and movement, vision-based movement corrections, and the optical variable *tau*.

APPLICATION

When you reach for a glass of water to drink from it, the tactile (i.e., touch), proprioceptive, and visual sensory systems come into play as you carry out the action. Vision helps you locate the glass and grasp it with your hand and fingers. Touch and proprioception help you lift the glass, move it toward your mouth, and not have the glass slip out of your hand. Without the sensory information provided by these key sensory systems, you would have considerably more difficulty carrying out relatively simple tasks like

drinking from a glass. You accomplish other everyday skills, such as putting your door key into the keyhole, maneuvering around people as you walk in a hallway, and driving your car with ease, because of the information that touch, proprioception, and vision provide your motor control system. Similarly, sport activities also require and benefit from the roles played by these same sensory systems. For example, to catch a ball, you must see where the ball is, time its arrival to your hand, position your hand in space, and then close your fingers around the ball when it is in your hand.

In all of these skill performance situations, practitioners can benefit from an understanding of the tactile, proprioception, and visual sensory systems in terms of their anatomical and physiological basis, how they influence the control of movement, and the limits they place on human motor skill performance. In the following discussion, we will consider each of these three sensory systems by addressing their anatomical and physiological basis and their relevance to the control of coordinated movement. The intent is to help practitioners establish a foundation on which they can build effective strategies to facilitate skill learning or rehabilitation for the people with whom they work.

> **Application Problem to Solve** When you reach for and grasp a glass of water, how do you know how far to reach, how much force to use to grasp the glass, and how to keep the glass from slipping out of your hand as you bring it to your mouth to drink from it? When you walk across campus, how do you not trip over a curb when you cross a street or bump into someone who is walking in front of you or in the opposite direction toward you?

DISCUSSION

A key feature of any theory of motor control is the role played by sensory information in controlling action. Of our various senses, touch, proprioception, and vision contribute to the motor control of skills in significant ways. In the study of human sensory physiology, touch and proprioception are included as senses in the *somatic* sensory system, whereas vision is the sense associated with the visual sensory system. In the following sections, we will look specifically at these three senses by describing their neural bases and the roles each plays in the control of human movement.

Before beginning the discussion of these sensory systems, it is important to point out that the limiting of this chapter to these three senses should not be interpreted as suggesting that they are the only senses involved in motor control. We know from the research literature, (e.g., Huber, Stathopoulos, & Sussman, 2004) that auditory sensory information

is especially important for speech production; and anecdotal evidence from skilled athletes describes the importance of auditory information for influencing their behavior, such as determining the ball flight characteristics of a batted ball in baseball and a serve or ground stroke in tennis. In addition, research (e.g., Guerraz & Day, 2005) has shown the important role of the vestibular system of the inner ear in the control of balance and possibly arm-trunk coordination during trunk-assisted reaching movements (Mars, Archambault, & Feldman, 2003), although both also involve the tactile, proprioception, and vision sensory systems. However, for purposes of this chapter, which is to introduce you to the involvement of the sensory systems in motor control, we will limit our discussion to touch, proprioception, and vision.

TOUCH AND MOTOR CONTROL

Consider the variety of ways in which we involve our sense of touch when we perform motor skills. Skills that require us to manipulate an object (e.g., holding a fork, typing a text message, picking up a ball) or person (e.g., wrestling, boxing, tae kwon do) and to interact with natural features in our environment, such as walking barefoot on the beach, include the detection of specific characteristics of the object, person, or environment through tactile sensory receptors in our skin that are part of our somatic sensory system. But how is this sensory information used to help us perform these skills? To answer this question, we will first consider the neural basis for the detection of this type of sensory information and then describe what research has shown as some of the movement characteristics of motor skill performance that are influenced by tactile sensory information.

Neural Basis of Touch

When we touch something, mechanoreceptors in the skin activate to provide the CNS with information related to pain, temperature, and movement. These receptors, which are illustrated in figure 6.1, are located just below the skin surface in the dermis portion of the skin. As mechanoreceptors,

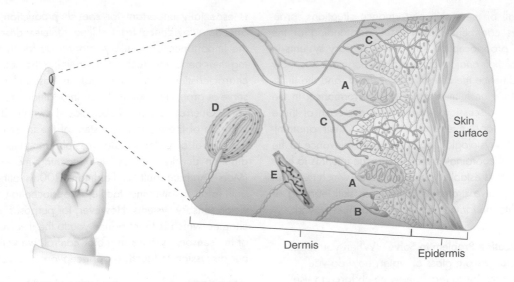

A – Tactile (Meissner's) corpuscle (light touch)
B – Tactile (Merkle's) corpuscles (touch)
C – Free nerve ending (pain)

D – Lamellated (Pacinian) corpuscle
(vibration and deep pressure)
E – Ruffini corpuscle (warmth)

FIGURE 6.1   Skin receptors involved in tactile sensation. (Note that the figure is not drawn to scale; for example, Pacinian corpuscles are actually four to five times larger than Meissner's corpuscles.) [From Widmaier, E. P., Raff, H., & Strang, K.T. (2006). *Vander's human physiology: The mechanisms of body function* (10th ed.). New York: McGraw-Hill.]

these sensory receptors detect skin stretch and joint movement. The greatest concentration of these receptors is in the fingertips.

The Role of Tactile Sensory Information in Motor Control

Researchers generally agree that touch plays an important role in the performance of a variety of types of motor skills and motor control processes. We will briefly consider four movement-related characteristics influenced by tactile sensory information the CNS receives from touch. A predominant characteristic is *movement accuracy,* which decreases when tactile information is not available, especially at the fingertips. Research has demonstrated this effect for several skills and movements including pointing movements (Rao & Gordon, 2001), reaching and grasping (Gentilucci, Toni, Daprati, & Gangitano, 1997), typing on a keyboard (Gordon & Soechting, 1995; Rabin & Gordon, 2004), maintaining a precision grip (Fisher, Galea, Brown, & Lemon, 2002),

rhythmically tapping a finger to an auditory stimulus (Pollok, Müller, Ascherleben, Schnitzler, & Prinz, 2004), and playing a sequence of notes on a piano (Goebl & Palmer, 2008). In most of these studies, the researchers anesthetized the fingertips so that tactile afferent information would not be available, which provided the opportunity to compare movement accuracy to performance with no anesthesia. A different approach to determining the role of tactile afferent information in motor control is to add touch to the performance of an activity. For example, in the experiment by Rao and Gordon (2001), participants increased their pointing accuracy when they reproduced a pointing movement to a target they had touched compared to when they moved their arm to the target location without touching it.

Movement consistency is another movement characteristic influenced by tactile feedback. Experiments by Gordon and colleagues (e.g., Gordon & Soechting, 1995; Rabin & Gordon, 2004) demonstrated this effect for keyboard typing by comparing typing

A CLOSER LOOK

Typing without Tactile Sensory Feedback

In an experiment designed to investigate the importance of tactile sensory feedback for the control of movement, Rabin and Gordon (2004) had twelve skilled typists (all could type more than 50 words per minute) type on a personal computer keyboard lists of sentences that were placed in front of them. They could see the computer monitor but not their hands as they typed. They were instructed not to correct errors. The typists typed the sentences before and during anesthesia of the right index finger. The sentences were short and consisted of letters typed by the left hand except for one letter (*y, u, h, n, m*), which is typed by the right index finger (e.g., "we wash*ed*"). Also included in the sentences were words that required the right index finger to type all the letters (e.g., *yummy*).

The anesthesia: A mixture of long-acting 2 percent lidocaine and short-acting 2 percent marcaine was injected near the median nerve on either side of the distal interphalangeal joint of the right index finger.

Results

Typing accuracy: Without the right index finger anesthetized, the typists made 3.5 percent of the keypress errors with their right index finger. But, with the right finger anesthetized, the percentage increased to 16.5 percent. Almost all of these errors (90 percent) were "aim" errors, i.e., missing the key. No other fingers on either hand showed an increase in errors with the right finger anesthetized.

Finger kinematics: With anesthesia, finger trajectories from a preceding key to the target key were similar to what they were before anesthesia, although there was greater trial-to-trial variability with anesthesia.

performance before and after anesthetizing a finger. They showed that without tactile sensory feedback from the finger, not only did typing accuracy decrease, as described above, but movement consistency from one trial to another also decreased. Third, *movement force adjustments* while holding and using an object also depend on tactile feedback. For example, when you grasp a cup and lift it from a table to drink from it, you need to regulate the amount of grip force as you move the cup to your mouth and properly position the cup to drink from it. Evidence for the role played by tactile sensory feedback in adjusting grip forces during movement has been reported in several studies (e.g., Gysin, Kaminski, & Gordon, 2003; Nowak & Hermsdorfer, 2003). These researchers have shown that the sensory feedback from the grasping fingertips intermittently updates the movement command center in the CNS (as illustrated in the closed-loop control system in figure 5.3 in chapter 5) to adjust grip forces as necessary. Finally, Rao and Gordon (2001) concluded that tactile feedback could be used to improve the use of proprioceptive feedback to *estimate movement distance* when the beginning and end of a pointing movement involved touching a surface.

PROPRIOCEPTION AND MOTOR CONTROL

Proprioception refers to our sensation and perception of limb, trunk, and head position and movement.[1] Although it is often overlooked as one of

---

[1]*Kinesthesis* is a term that is related to the term *proprioception*. There has been considerable debate about the distinction between them. Sometimes they are used to refer to specific types of sensory information; in other cases they are used synonymously. For the purposes of this book, the term *proprioception* is used to refer to sensory information about body and limb position and movement that is transmitted to the CNS from the proprioceptors.

---

proprioception   the perception of limb, body, and head movement characteristics; afferent neural pathways send to the central nervous system proprioceptive information about characteristics such as limb movement direction, location in space, and velocity.

our basic senses, proprioception is sensory information transmitted to the central nervous system about such movement characteristics as direction, location in space, velocity, and muscle activation. In closed-loop models of movement control, proprioceptive feedback plays a significant role, whereas in open-loop models, central commands control movement without involving proprioceptive feedback. Questions about whether we can control movements without proprioceptive feedback, and what role proprioceptive feedback plays in the control of coordinated movement, have intrigued movement scientists for many years (see Willingham, 1998, p. 574f for a brief historical review).

Researchers have taken a variety of experimental approaches to determine the role of proprioception in controlling coordinated movement. We discuss a few of these to introduce you to the current thinking about this issue. However, before considering proprioception's role in motor control, we will take a brief look at the neural basis of proprioception.

The Neural Basis of Proprioception

The CNS receives proprioceptive information from afferent neural pathways that begin in **proprioceptors,** which are sensory neurons located in the muscles, tendons, ligaments, and joints. These neurons pick up information about body and limb position and changes in position. There are several types of proprioceptors, each of which detects specific characteristics of body and limb position and movement.

Muscle spindles. Proprioceptors called **muscle spindles** lie within the fibers of most skeletal muscles. As illustrated in figure 6.2, they are specialized muscle fibers that contain a capsule with both sensory receptors and muscle fibers, known as intrafusal muscle fibers. Spindles lie in parallel with extrafusal muscle fibers and are attached directly to the muscle sheath. Type Ia axons, which conduct nerve impulses very rapidly, are the primary sensory receptors in the muscle spindle. These axons wrap around the middle region of intrafusal muscle fibers and detect *changes in muscle length and velocity.* As mechanoreceptors, the sensory receptors of the

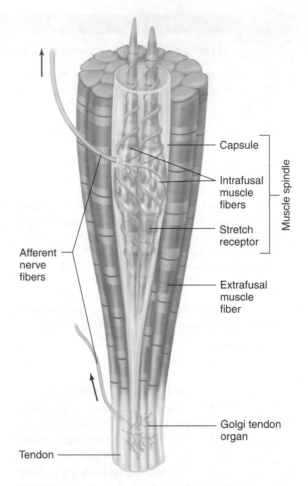

FIGURE 6.2   A muscle spindle and Golgi tendon organ. (Note that the figure is not drawn to scale; for illustration purposes, the muscle spindle is exaggerated in size compared to the extrafusal muscle fibers.) [From Widmaier, E. P., Raff, H., & Strang, K. T. (2006). *Vander's human physiology: The mechanisms of body function* (10th ed.). New York: McGraw-Hill.] Adapted from Elias, H., Pauly, J. E., & Burns, E. R. (1978), *Histology and human microanatomy* (4th ed.) New York: Wiley.

muscle spindles respond to changes in muscle length which cause a mechanical deformation of the receptors and result in a nerve impulse. Within the muscle spindle are stretch receptors that detect the amount of stretch as well as the speed of the stretch. When a muscle stretches, the nerve impulse rate from the muscle spindle increases; when the muscle shortens, the rate reduces. According to Macefield (2005) the muscle-length detection capability of muscle spindles allows them to detect changes in joint angle in one axis, which provide the basis for the muscle spindles distributed throughout the muscles that act on a joint to provide feedback about complex patterns of muscle-length changes.

The nerve impulses from the muscle spindle travel along afferent nerve fibers to the dorsal root of the spinal cord. In the spinal cord, these afferent fibers divide into branches that allow the nerve impulses to do any of several things, depending on the movement situation. If the movement is a simple reflex movement, such as a knee jerk, the impulse follows a branch that synapses with an alpha motor neuron in the ventral horn of the spinal cord that activates the agonist muscle to produce the reflex movement. Another branch synapses with inhibitory interneurons that inhibit activity of antagonistic muscles. A third branch synapses with motor neurons that activate synergistic muscles associated with the intended movement. The fourth branch continues up the spinal cord to the brainstem where it synapses with interneurons to connect with areas of the brain responsible for motor control.

In the control of voluntary movement the muscle spindle serves as a feedback mechanism. For many years, researchers gave the muscle spindles a minor role in providing feedback about limb position and movement. However, since the early 1970s, this view has changed dramatically as research has demonstrated through experiments involving muscle vibration and fatigue that the muscle spindles are the *most important source* of proprioceptive information to the CNS about the *limb movement characteristics of position, direction, and velocity, as well as a sense of effort* (for a brief overview of this history, see Albert, Ribot-Ciscar, Fiocchi, Bergenheim, & Roll, 2005; Collins, Refshauge, Todd, & Gandevia, 2005; Winter, Allen, & Proske, 2005). The CNS uses the limb movement feedback in the control of a discrete movement that must stop at a specific location in space and in the control of ongoing movements to ensure the spatial and temporal accuracy of the movements. In addition some researchers (e.g., Albert et al., 2005) contend that the feedback from muscle spindles also assists the CNS in movement planning.

Golgi-tendon organs (GTO). As illustrated in figure 6.2 the **Golgi-tendon organs (GTO)** are located in the skeletal muscle near the insertion of the tendons into the muscle. The GTO consist of type Ib sensory axons that detect *changes in muscle tension, or force;* they are poor detectors of changes in muscle length. These sensory receptors respond to any tension created by the contracting muscle to which it is attached. The axons of the GTO enter the dorsal horn of the spinal cord and synapse on interneurons in the ventral horn, where the interneurons synapse with alpha motor neurons that can cause inhibition of the contracting muscle and related synergistic muscles and that can stimulate the motor neurons of antagonistic muscles.

Joint receptors. Several types of proprioceptors are located in the joint capsule and ligaments; together these are referred to as **joint receptors.** The specific identity of these receptors is an issue of some debate among neuroscientists (e.g., Collins, Refshauge, Todd, & Gandevia, 2005). However, there is agreement that some are the *Ruffini endings, Pacinian corpuscles,* and *Golgi-like* receptors

---

proprioceptors   sensory neurons located in the muscles, tendons, ligaments, and joints. These neurons pick up information about body and limb position and changes in position.

muscle spindles   a type of proprioceptor consisting of specialized muscle fibers that lie within the fibers of most skeletal muscles; they detect changes in muscle length.

Golgi-tendon organs (GTO)   a type of proprioceptor located in the skeletal muscle near the insertion of the tendons into the muscle; they detect changes in muscle tension, or force.

joint receptors   a collection of various types of proprioceptors located in the joint capsule and ligaments; they detect changes in joint movement at the extreme limits of movement and position.

(Macefield, 2005). Not all joints contain the same types of receptors. As a result, it is common to see researchers refer to "joint receptors" as a collective term rather than specify the individual receptors within the joint. As mechanoreceptors, the joint receptors respond to changes in force and rotation applied to the joint and to changes in joint movement angle, especially at the extreme limits of angular movement or joint positions.

Investigating the Role of Proprioception in Motor Control

Proprioception is an important source of feedback. When performance of an action is under closed-loop control, proprioceptive information allows us to make movement corrections as we move. When an action is under open-loop control, as in a rapid, ballistic movement, proprioceptive feedback is available, but we cannot make movement corrections as we move because of time limitations.

Researchers have used several techniques to investigate the role of proprioception in the control of movement. We will consider three techniques in this discussion. Two of the techniques involve the observation of movement after **deafferentation** in some way. This means that the proprioceptive afferent pathways to the CNS are not available. The third involves the observation of movement while a tendon of a muscle involved in the control of a movement is vibrated, which distorts the proprioceptive feedback that is normally received from the muscle and tendon proprioceptors.

Deafferentation Techniques

Surgical deafferentation. One method used to investigate the role of proprioception in the control of movement involves the observation of movement of animals or humans following surgical deafferentation, which means that the afferent neural pathways associated with the movements of interest have been surgically severed or removed. Several studies have been reported in which a surgical deafferentation procedure was used with monkeys. For example, two of the most well-known sets of experiments involving animals were reported in the 1960s and 1970s by Taub and Berman (1963,

1968) and Bizzi and his colleagues (e.g., Bizzi & Polit, 1979; Polit & Bizzi, 1978). These studies involved observing monkeys performing either typical activities, such as grooming and climbing, or newly learned movements, such as pointing to a light without vision of the arm and hand, before and after surgical deafferentation. Results showed that although the deafferented monkeys could still perform the skills, the degree of movement precision was notably less than it had been with proprioceptive feedback available.

Surgically deafferenting human subjects for experimental purposes is not possible, for obvious reasons. However, some people are surgically deafferented because of certain trauma- or disease-related problems. For example, rheumatoid arthritis patients who have had finger *joint replacement* surgery have no joint receptors available. The most commonly cited example of using this approach to the study of proprioception is an experiment done many years ago by Kelso, Holt, and Flatt (1980). On each trial, participants moved their fingers to a criterion finger position or a criterion distance, returned their fingers to a new starting point, and then attempted to reproduce the criterion position or distance. Results indicated that the patients had little difficulty in accurately reproducing the criterion finger *position* from a starting point that was different from the original starting point. However, they did have problems reproducing the movement *distance* from these new starting points.

Deafferentation due to sensory neuropathy. The observation of movement characteristics of people who have a sensory neuropathy (also called a peripheral neuropathy) involving a limb provides a nonsurgical technique for investigating deafferented humans. For these people, peripheral afferent nerves in various parts of the body are not functioning properly. In some cases, the efferent motor pathways are intact.

To demonstrate how this type of deafferentation has helped identify some of the roles proprioception plays in motor control, we will consider a few examples of experiments that have compared participants with and without sensory neuropathy performing a variety of tasks. One of the early studies

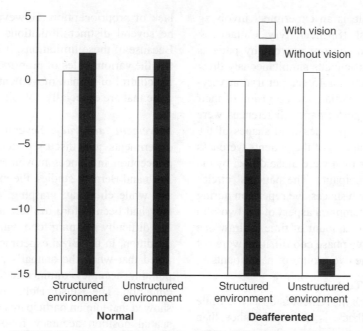

FIGURE 6.3 Results of the experiment by Blouin et al. showing the amount of error during the reproduction of an arm position for normal and deafferented subjects with vision of the environment available (structured) or not available (unstructured), and vision of the moving arm available or not. [Source: Data from Blouin, J., et al. (1993). Reference systems for coding spatial information in normal subjects and a deafferented patient. *Experimental Brain Research, 93,* 324–331, Springer-Verlag, New York, NY.]

reporting the use of this research strategy was an experiment by Blouin et al. (1993). They compared a sensory neuropathy patient with normal participants on a pointing task involving an arm moving a pointer. On some trials, participants could see the task environment, whereas on other trials, they performed without this visual information available. Results, shown in figure 6.3, were that with vision, the patient performed as accurately as the normal participants. However, without vision of either the environment or the arm while moving, the deafferented patient consistently undershot the target. Thus, without visual feedback, the deafferented patient was not able to reproduce movement accurately to a specific location in space.

More recently, additional research has confirmed and extended the Blouin et al. (1993) results. For example, in one study (Messier, Adamovich, Berkinblit, Tunik, & Poizner, 2003) a sensory neuropathy patient (identified as C. F.) and five neurologically normal adults were asked to make reaching movements without vision to remembered targets in front of them in a smooth, continuous motion. C. F. made large limb movement spatial errors and did not produce smooth and simultaneous movements at the shoulder and elbow joints at slow, preferred, and fast speeds during movement.

deafferentation a procedure that researchers use to make proprioceptive feedback unavailable (through surgically severing or removing afferent neural pathways involved in the movement); it also can result from injury, surgery, or disease to afferent neural pathways involved in proprioception.

The third example is an experiment involving a more complex task (Spencer, Ivry, Cattaert, & Semjen, 2005). Two sensory neuropathy patients and three control participants simultaneously drew circles with each hand for 15 sec per trial at varying speeds with full, partial, and no vision of their hands. The notable performance differences were that the sizes (i.e., amplitudes) and shapes of the circles drawn by each arm of the patients were less similar to each other than were those drawn by the non-neuropathy participants. The patients' circles tended to drift on each successive repetition during a trial. Notably, the temporal aspect of the two-arm coordination (i.e., the amount of time to draw one circle) and the relative phase coordination were not different between the two groups of participants.

Tendon Vibration Technique

A procedure in which movement is observed while proprioceptive feedback is distorted rather than removed involves the high-speed vibration of a tendon connected to a muscle that is an agonist in the movement of interest. This vibration distorts muscle spindle firing patterns, which leads to a distortion of proprioceptive feedback. Examples of the use of this technique can be found in several experiments reported by Verschueren. For example, one experiment (Verschueren, Swinnen, Cordo, & Dounskaia, 1999a) applied vibration to the tendons of the biceps and/or anterior deltoids of the preferred arm of blindfolded participants as they simultaneously drew circles with each arm. The results (see figure 6.4) showed that the vibration influenced the spatial characteristics of the circles drawn by the vibrated arm, but not for the nonvibrated, nonpreferred arm. In addition, the vibration of the preferred arm influenced the relative phase relationship between the two arms during the circle drawing.

The Role of Proprioception in Motor Control

The research examples we just considered show that people *can* carry out certain limb movements in the absence of proprioceptive feedback. Most notably, as demonstrated in the experiment by Spencer et al. (2005), the *timing synchrony between limbs* that characterizes the performance of bimanual coordination movements is not influenced by the lack of proprioception. However, there appear to be several distinct limitations to this capability. Because of these limitations, it is possible to identify the various roles of proprioceptive feedback in the control of human movement. We will consider three that are especially notable.

Movement accuracy. Several results from the experiments just discussed demonstrate that proprioception influences movement accuracy. In the Taub and Berman studies, the monkeys were clumsier while climbing, grasping, and grooming than they had been before deafferentation. In fact, they had difficulty grasping food with their hands in this condition. In the Bizzi experiments, the researchers noted that when the animal's posture was altered, pointing accuracy diminished in the deafferented condition. The Kelso, Holt, and Flatt experiment showed that human participants could maintain only spatial position accuracy following joint capsule replacement; distance movements were severely disrupted. And the experiments involving sensory neuropathy patients were consistent in demonstrating that the lack of proprioception resulted in large spatial errors. In addition, the experiment by Spencer and colleagues extended the evidence for movement accuracy problems without proprioception to include repetitive bimanual coordination movements.

The influence of proprioception on movement accuracy appears to be due to the specific kinematic and kinetic feedback provided by the proprioceptors to the CNS. Feedback about limb displacement provides the basis for spatial position corrections, which enable the limb to achieve spatial accuracy by a continuous updating of limb position to the CNS, which in turn can send movement commands that will modify the position accordingly, provided that the movement occurs for a sufficient amount of time to allow movement corrections to occur. In addition, proprioceptors provide feedback about limb velocity and force, which influence movement distance accuracy.

Onset of motor commands. Proprioceptive feedback also influences the *timing of the onset of motor commands*. An experiment by Bard and colleagues (1992) provides a good example of evidence for this

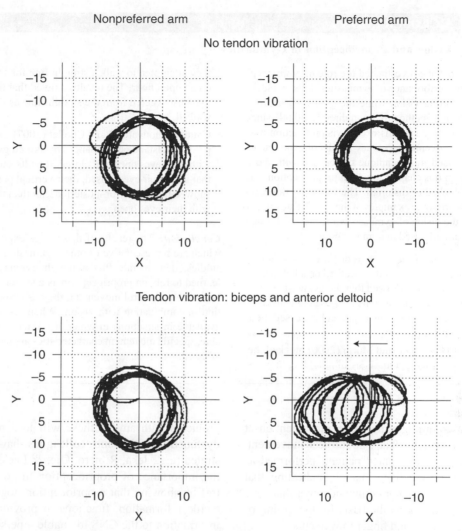

FIGURE 6.4   Results from the experiment by Verschueren et al. showing the effects of vibrating the tendons attached to the biceps and anterior deltoid of the preferred arm during bimanual circle drawing with no vision of the arms. The top row shows one participant's drawings during one trial when no tendon vibration was applied. The bottom row shows the drawings by the same participant during one trial with tendon vibration. [Adapted from Figure 1A–D, p. 185, of Verschueren, Swinnen, Cordo, & Dounskaia (1999). *Experimental Brain Research, 127,* 182–192, Copyright © 1999 Springer-Verlag, New York, NY.]

role. They compared movements of normal participants with a patient deafferented due to a sensory neuropathy. The participants were asked to simultaneously extend an index finger and raise the heel of the ipsilateral foot. When they performed this task in reaction to an auditory signal, both the normal and the deafferented participants performed similarly by initiating the finger extension first. We would expect this if a common central motor command were sent to each effector. Because of the difference in distance of efferent neural pathways to the finger and heel, finger movement would occur first. Conversely, when asked to do the task at their own pace, the normal participants raised the heel first; this suggests

A CLOSER LOOK

Vision and Proprioception in Gymnastics

Researchers have investigated the role of proprioception for the performance of gymnastics skills by blocking or distorting vision while the gymnast performs. Although this method is an indirect method, since all other sensory systems except vision function normally, the movement accuracy results of experiments that have used this technique correspond with those described in this chapter in which proprioception was directly blocked or distorted. The following three experiments are some examples of the use of distorting or blocking the vision of gymnasts while they performed skills commonly used in gymnastics events.

- Robertson and Elliott (1996) distorted the vision of skilled gymnasts as they walked on a balance beam. The results showed that the gymnasts increased the number of steps they used to walk as fast as possible along the beam and increased their movement form errors.
- Danion, Boyadjian, and Marin (2000) blocked the vision of skilled gymnasts by blindfolding them as

they attempted to walk a straight line for 15 m on an open floor. The results showed that the gymnasts veered from the straight line as they walked.
- Gautier, Thouvarecq, and Chollet (2007) compared handstand performances by skilled gymnasts with their eyes open and closed. Results showed that with their eyes closed, their vertical posture showed more anterior–posterior lean than they had with their eyes open.

Conclusion: The results of these three experiments, which are representative of other gymnastics specific studies, demonstrate that although gymnasts have learned to rely on proprioception as a source of feedback to help control movement, they use proprioception in combination with vision. When vision is not available in situations in which it normally is available, specific movement characteristics are negatively affected.

that they based timing of the finger movement onset on proprioceptive feedback about heel movement. In contrast, the deafferented patients performed as they had in the reactive situation, indicating that they used a central motor command rather than proprioceptive feedback as the basis for the timing of the onset of the heel and finger movements.

Coordination control. Finally, proprioception plays an important role in various aspects of the *coordination of body and limb segments.* Two coordination characteristics influenced by proprioceptive feedback will serve to demonstrate this role.

First, *postural control* requires proprioceptive feedback. Although a considerable amount of research evidence shows that postural control is a function of many interacting variables, such as vision, the musculoskeletal system, activity of the cerebellum and basal ganglia, cognitive processes, the tactile sensory system, and proprioception,

problems with any of these will lead to postural dysfunction. Jeka and colleagues have demonstrated (e.g., Jeka, Ribiero, Oie, & Lackner, 1998) the importance of proprioception in postural control by showing that proprioception, together with tactile information, functions to provide essential information to the CNS to enable a person to control upright stance posture in body sway situations. Additional evidence of the role of proprioception in postural control was provided by Barbieri et al. (2008) in an experiment in which they used the tendon vibration technique. The vibration of the Achilles tendon induced a three degree backward tilt of the participants' vertical posture.

The second coordination characteristic involves the *spatial-temporal coupling between limbs and limb segments.* Results of the experiment by Messier et al. (2003), which we described earlier, showed that a sensory neuropathy patient demonstrated problems with coordinating the multijoint movements

The "Rubber Hand Illusion": An Example of Vision Overriding Proprioception and Tactile Senses

A neuroimaging study reported in *Science* by Ehrsson (2004) and his colleagues in England provided evidence of the brain activity that underlies a perceptual illusion known as the "rubber hand illusion," which was first described by Botvinick and Cohen (1998) in the journal *Nature*. This illusion relates to our feeling of ownership of our limbs, which we use to distinguish our limbs from other objects. The illusion also presents a procedure that is different from the "moving room" procedure of Lee and Aronson (1974) to establish the predominant place we give vision with respect to our other senses, especially proprioception and tactile sensation.

The Illusion
A person sits at a table while looking at a realistic life-size rubber hand on the tabletop. The person's own hand is out of view, either placed under the table or covered by a screen. The experimenter uses two small paintbrushes to simultaneously brush the person's hand and the rubber hand. An important part of creating the illusion is to synchronize the timing of the brushings. After several repeated brushings of

the two hands, the person experiences the illusion that he or she can feel the brush strokes on the rubber hand as if it were his or her own. In fact, subjects have often spontaneously reported that the rubber hand feels like it is their own hand. Thus the pairing of the visual observation of the brushing of the rubber hand with the tactile sensation of the brushing of the real hand results in a perception that the visually observed rubber hand is part of the person. Interestingly, Botvinick and Cohen (1998) showed that part of the illusion involves a distortion of proprioceptive information when a moving of the rubber hand's position gets reported by the person as a moving of his or her own hand.

Brain Activity during the Illusion
In their experiment Ehrsson and colleagues (2004) used fMRI to assess brain activity during the illusion experience. The results showed activation in the *prefrontal cortex,* which suggests that the mechanism underlying the feeling of limb ownership resides in this area of the brain, although other research has indicated the importance of the *parietal lobe* as well.

---

involved in reaching to a target in front of him. For between-limb movement coordination, the study by Verschueren et al. (1999a), which we considered earlier, showed the importance of proprioceptive feedback for the spatial and temporal coupling between the arms when we perform bimanual coordination tasks. And in another study by this same researcher and colleagues (Verschueren et al. 1999b), they demonstrated that proprioception influences the coupling between two limb segments of the same limb, such as the upper arm and forearm. Also, Spencer et al. (2005) demonstrated similar bimanual coordination problems for a sensory neuropathy patient, especially in terms of the control of spatial coordination and consistency between movements for a repetitive series of movements.

VISION AND MOTOR CONTROL

Our own personal experiences as well as research evidence tells us that of all our sensory systems, we tend to use and trust vision the most. For example, when you first learned to type or play the piano, you undoubtedly felt that if you could not see your fingers hit each key, you could not perform accurately. Beginning dancers and stroke patients learning to walk have a similar problem. They often act as if they cannot perform the activity if they cannot watch their feet.

These anecdotal experiences illustrate our tendency to give vision a predominant role when we perform motor skills. Research evidence also supports this phenomenon. The best example is a classic experiment by Lee and Aronson (1974) that is often referred to as the "moving room" experiment. Participants stood in a room in which the walls could move up or down, as well as forward or backward. However, the floor was stationary and did not move. In this sensory conflict situation, the participants' vision indicated they were moving, but their proprioceptors indicated they were not. The researchers observed the participants' postural responses to the movement of the walls. When the walls moved, children and adults made posture correction adjustments that were in keeping with trying to maintain their standing balance when the walls and floor were moving. But because the floor did not move, their proprioceptors were not signaling that their bodies were losing stability. Only their visual systems detected any loss of balance. It is important to note that similar "moving room" effects on postural control have been reported more recently by Stoffregen, Hove, Schmit, and Bardy (2006).

The moving room experiments demonstrate the special priority we assign to vision in our daily activities. In those experiments, when the proprioceptors and vision provided conflicting information to the central nervous system, people gave attention to vision while ignoring the proprioceptors. The result was that they initiated unnecessary postural adjustments.

In the following sections we will discuss the role of vision in motor control in several ways. First, we will consider the neurophysiology of vision as it relates to motor control. We will then discuss some of the methods researchers use to investigate the role of vision in motor control. And finally we will look into several motor control issues that provide us with a general understanding of the many roles vision plays in the control of coordinated movement.

It is important to note that this discussion is not intended to be a detailed description of the anatomy and physiology of the components of the visual system, but rather a general introduction to establish a basic understanding of the system. It is also important to point out that we will revisit the role of vision in the learning and control of motor skills in many other chapters of this book. For example, in chapter 7 vision is discussed in terms of its role in the control

of specific skills; in chapter 8 it is considered in its role in the preparation of movement; and in chapter 9 vision is an important part of the discussion about attention, as it relates to the selection of environmental context information that is essential for action goal achievement. In addition, chapter 12 includes a discussion on vision as it relates to the stages of learning, and chapter 14 discusses the role of vision in the use of demonstration.

The Neurophysiology of Vision

Vision is the result of the sensory receptors of the eyes receiving and transmitting wavelengths of light to the visual cortex of the brain by way of sensory neurons known as the optic nerve. In a section about the eye in their neuroscience book, Bear, Connors, and Paradiso (2001) state, "the eye acts like a camera, forming crisp, clear images of the world. . . . Like a quality 35-mm camera, the eye automatically adjusts to differences in illumination and automatically focuses itself on objects of interest. The eye has some additional features not yet available on cameras, such as the ability to track moving objects (by eye movement) and the ability to keep its transparent surfaces clean (by tears and blinking)" (p. 281).

Basic anatomy of the eye. As illustrated in figure 6.5, the human eye is a fluid-filled ball with distinct components. The **cornea** is the most anterior component. It is a clear surface that allows light to enter the eye and serves as an important part of the eye's optical system. Because it does not have blood vessels, it can be surgically removed with relative ease and, if necessary, a donated cornea can be transplanted. Behind the cornea are the pupil, iris, and lens. The **pupil** is the opening that lets light into the eye. Its diameter increases and decreases according to the amount of light detected by the eye. You have undoubtedly experienced this when you looked into a mirror and watched the pupil of your eye get larger and smaller depending on the amount of light in the room or shining in your eye. This diameter change is controlled by the two smooth muscle fibers shown in figure 6.5 that are attached to the iris (the *ciliary muscle* and *zonular fibers*). The **iris** surrounds the pupil and provides

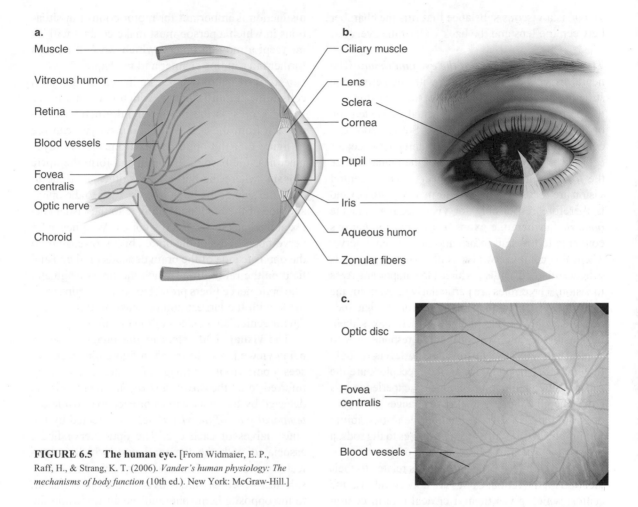

a.

Muscle

Vitreous humor

Retina

Blood vessels

Fovea
centralis

Optic nerve

Choroid

b.

Ciliary muscle

Lens

Sclera

Cornea

Pupil

Iris

Aqueous humor

Zonular fibers

c.

Optic disc

Fovea
centralis

Blood vessels

FIGURE 6.5   The human eye. [From Widmaier, E. P.,
Raff, H., & Strang, K. T. (2006). *Vander's human physiology: The
mechanisms of body function* (10th ed.). New York: McGraw-Hill.]

the eye its color. The **lens,** which sits just behind
the iris, is a transparent structure that is responsible
for allowing the eye to focus at various distances.
The lens is held in place by the zonular fibers. The
sclera, which makes up 80 percent of the eye, surrounds these structures. The anterior portion of
this firm white capsule forms what we commonly
call the "white" of the eye. The sclera functions
to help maintain the shape of the eye and protect
the eye's inner structure. It also is an attachment
site for the extrinsic eye muscles responsible for
eye movement. The eye contains two chambers of
fluid: *aqueous humor* is a clear fluid that fills the
chamber between the cornea and lens, and *vitreous*

cornea   a clear surface that covers the front of the
eye; it serves as an important part of the eye's optical
system.

pupil   the opening in the eye that lets in light; its
diameter increases and decreases according to the
amount of light detected by the eye.

iris   the eye structure that surrounds the pupil and
provides the eye its color.

lens   the transparent eye structure that sits just behind
the iris; it allows the eye to focus at various distances.

humor is a viscous substance that fills the chamber between the lens and the back wall of the eye.

The neural components of the eye and vision. The neural aspects of vision begin with the **retina,** the structure that lines the back wall of the eye. Although it is part of the eye, the retina is actually an extension of the brain (Widmaier, Raff, & Strang, 2006). It contains various types of neurons and photoreceptor cells. The primary components of the retina include the *fovea centralis,* where objects seen in central vision are focused (hence the term *foveal vision*) and is therefore responsible for visual acuity, and the *optic disk,* where the axons of the retina's neurons converge to transmit information to the optic nerve. The retina contains two types of photoreceptor cells called **rods** and **cones,** which play important roles in vision. Three roles are particularly relevant for the performance of motor skills. One role is that rods respond to low levels of light (which makes them responsible for night vision); cones respond only to bright light. Because of the specific levels of light to which they respond, these photoreceptors are the cause of the "temporary blindness" experience you have when the lighting in a room changes from very bright to dark. In such a situation the responsibility for light detection shifts from the cones to the rods, a process that requires a brief amount of time.

A second role for rods and cones relates to their location on the retina. Cones are concentrated at the center, which gives them a critical role in central vision and visual acuity. Rods are located more on the retina periphery and, therefore, are important for peripheral vision. Third, cones play a critical role in color vision.

The retina receives light waves from the cornea and lens, where the waves are *refracted*—that is, bent—in such a way that an observed image is turned upside down and reversed right to left on the retina. Image size and distance from the eye are determined by the size of the angle the light waves from the image form when they pass through the cornea; there is more bending for bigger and closer images to create larger images on the retina, and less bending for smaller and more distant images to create smaller images on the retina. This distinction is important for motor control in situations in which a person must make contact with or intercept a moving object, which we will discuss further later in this chapter and in chapter 7.

Axons of neurons in the retina called ganglion cells form the **optic nerve,** which is cranial nerve II and serves as the means of information transmission from the eye to the brain. As you can see in figure 6.6, the optic nerves from the two eyes meet near the base of the brain and form the **optic chiasm,** where the nerve fibers either continue to the same side of the brain or cross over to the opposite side of the brain and continue to the visual cortex at the back of the brain's cortex. Whether optic nerve fibers cross at the optic chiasm or change to the opposite side of the brain depends on the visual field on the retina from which the fibers originate. The optic nerve fibers project to several brain structures, with the largest number passing through the lateral geniculate nucleus of the thalamus.

The **visual field** refers to the image or scene being viewed. As illustrated in figure 6.6, each eye sees a portion of the image or scene. One portion, referred to as the *nasal part of the visual field,* is detected by the inner halves of each eye, while the *temporal part of the visual field* is detected by the outer halves of each eye. The optic nerve fibers associated with the temporal part, which is projected through the lens and cornea to the interior side of the retinas, cross over at the optic chiasm to the opposite hemisphere of the cortex while the optic nerve fibers associated with the nasal part pass through the optic chiasm to remain in the same cortex hemisphere. The visual cortex of the brain unites these images in a way that allows us to see three-dimensional images. As we will discuss later in this chapter, this *binocular vision*—that is, seeing with both eyes—is the basis for our depth perception as we observe the world around us.

INVESTIGATING THE ROLE OF VISION IN MOTOR CONTROL

Researchers use a variety of techniques to study the role of vision in motor control. The most direct technique involves the recording of eye movements as a

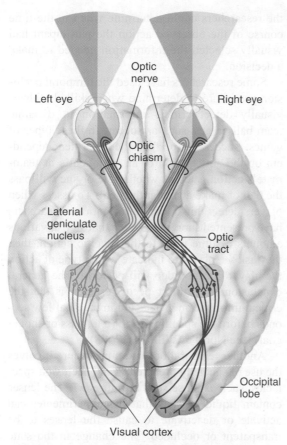

Optic
nerve

Left eye   Right eye

Optic
chiasm

Laterial
geniculate
nucleus

Optic
tract

Occipital
lobe

Visual cortex

FIGURE 6.6   The neural pathways for vision. [From Widmaier, E. P., Raff, H., & Strang, K. T. (2006). *Vander's human physiology: The mechanisms of body function* (10th ed.). New York: McGraw-Hill.]

person performs a skill. Other techniques provide indirect ways to determine how a person uses vision during the performance of a skill. We will briefly discuss these techniques in the following sections.

Eye Movement Recording

The recording of a person's eye movements requires the use of specialized equipment that tracks the movement of the eyes and records where the eyes are "looking" at a particular time. A researcher can record the displacement of *foveal vision* for a specific time interval, as well as the place and the length of time the person fixates his or her gaze while tracking. One way researchers use this technique is

to have the participant observe a film simulation of a performance situation and then make a response. The movement of the eye is then plotted on the film scene to determine the spatial location of the participant's eye movements (displacement), along with his or her gaze fixation characteristics related to observing the serving action. A more difficult way to use this procedure is to record eye movements while a person is actually performing a skill in the performance setting. (For a more detailed discussion about the use of eye-movement recordings, see Reimer & Sodhi, 2006).

An experiment by Williams, Ward, Knowles, and Smeeton (2002) provides a good example of the use of eye-movement recordings to investigate the use of vision in the performance of a motor skill. The experiment compared skilled and less skilled tennis players as they viewed and responded to action sequences that would occur

retina   the eye structure that lines the back wall of the eye; as an extension of the brain it contains the neuroreceptors that transmit visual information to the brain.

rods   one of two types of photoreceptors in the retina; they detect low levels of light and are important for peripheral vision.

cones   one of two types of photoreceptors in the retina; they detect bright light and play critical roles in central vision, visual acuity, and color vision.

optic nerve   cranial nerve II; it serves as the means of information transmission from the retina to the brain.

optic chiasm   the place near the base of the brain where the optic nerve fibers meet and either continue to the same side or cross over to the opposite side of the brain.

visual field   the image or scene being viewed; it typically extends approximately 200 degrees horizontally and 160 degrees vertically.

in a tennis match. The players observed videos of near-life-size images of opponents as a means of simulating play during a match. A player's view was of an opponent positioned midcourt on the other side of the net. The videos presented opponents hitting forehand and backhand shots during match play situations toward the players' left court, right court, center forecourt, and center backcourt. The players, who each wore an eye-movement recording device, were asked to respond to each shot as they would in an actual tennis match, which is to respond as quickly and accurately as possible. The results showed that the skilled players spent more time viewing the opponent's trunk-hip and head-shoulder areas than did the less-skilled players, while the less-skilled players spent more time than the skilled players viewing the opponent's racquet.

Temporal Occlusion Procedure
This procedure allows an investigation of the amount of time a person requires to visually detect the environmental context information he or she uses to perform a skill. This procedure is especially useful for skill performance situations in which choices among several movement alternatives must be made, which includes situations such as returning a serve in racquet sports, deciding whether to (and when to) dribble, pass, or shoot in basketball, or deciding when to walk across a busy street.

The experimenter determines the time periods of interest as they relate to the skill performed and then has the film or video stop at these predetermined time points during the action. The observer is then required to make a response as quickly as possible. An excellent example of the use of this procedure is in an experiment by Abernethy and Russell (1987), in which badminton players watched film sequences of a player making different shots. When the film stopped, participants marked their predictions of the landing positions of the shuttle. The film stopped at different times prior to, during, and after shuttle contact. By noting the relationship between the accuracy of a participant's predicted shuttle landing location and the moment he or she made the decision,

the researchers could determine when in the time course of the observed action the participant had visually selected the information needed to make a decision.

Some researchers have used the temporal occlusion procedure to determine when skilled athletes visually detect critical information in dynamic team ball games, such as soccer. In these types of games, successful performance is often dependent on the anticipation of an opponent's or teammate's action, such as whether he or she will pass the ball or make a shot at the goal. To assess when players detect this critical information, researchers have presented short video clips that stop at various amounts of time prior to the specific action; then they ask the player to indicate which type of action the player on the video will perform. The general conclusion from this type of research is that the critical information is detected in the final few seconds before the specific action (e.g., pass or shot at goal) (see North & Williams, 2008).

Another temporal occlusion procedure involves the use of specially prepared visual occlusion spectacles, such as those seen in figure 6.7. The lenses contain liquid crystals that the experimenter can activate or deactivate to cause the lenses to be transparent or occluded. The change in the state of the lenses occurs very quickly (1 to 5 msec). A benefit of the lenses is that they change the visual condition almost instantaneously without the eyes requiring the typical amount of time to adapt to changes between light and dark conditions. The visual occlusion lenses provide an advantage over the procedure of stopping a video or film by allowing researchers to have research participants perform skills in their typical environmental context.

A question that arises from the use of the temporal occlusion technique in laboratory environments is this: Are the results obtained from this procedure consistent with the way people use vision when performing the same skills in real-world environments? Two experiments by Farrow, Abernethy, and Jackson (2005) addressed this question using novice and skilled tennis players. Results indicated that the laboratory-based temporal occlusion technique generalizes very well to real-world environments.

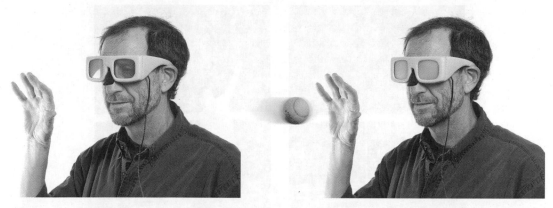

FIGURE 6.7   The PLATO (Portable Liquid-Crystal Apparatus for Tachistoscopic Occlusion) visual occlusion spectacles in use to study the role of vision in ball catching; here the person can see the ball until it is near his hand and then his vision is occluded. The lenses are constructed with specially designed liquid crystal cells, which are powered by an electrical field applied across each lens. The lenses can change almost instantaneously from transparent to translucent (approximately 3–5 msec), which prevents the wearer from perceiving visual information, and from translucent to transparent (approximately 1 msec). [Courtesy of Dr. Paul Milgram, Translucent Technologies, Inc., Toronto, Canada (http: home.ca.inter.net/~milgram/plato.html); photograph by Avner Levona.]

Event Occlusion Procedure

To identify the specific visual information a person uses to make the required response, researchers use the *event occlusion procedure*. Parts of each frame of film or video are masked so that the observer cannot see selected parts of the action. Figure 6.8 presents an example of this procedure, taken from the second part of the Abernethy and Russell (1987) study. In their experiment, participants predicted the landing location of the shuttle when they could not see the arm and racquet, racquet, head, or legs of the person hitting the shuttle. The logic of this approach is that if the person performs worse without being able to see a specific feature of the opponent's action, then that feature includes the visual information the person uses to determine the location of the shot.

THE ROLE OF VISION IN MOTOR CONTROL

Vision plays many roles in the control of coordinated movement. We will consider some of these roles in the following sections by discussing them in the context of several issues that researchers have investigated. We will further explore the role of vision in motor control in chapter 7 by discussing

its involvement in the control of specific motor skills, such as prehension, locomotion, and catching and striking objects.

Monocular versus Binocular Vision

One of the questions researchers have investigated concerning the role of vision in motor control relates to *the use of monocular (i.e., one eye) compared to binocular (i.e., two eyes) vision* to perform motor skills. Research evidence (e.g., Goodale & Servos, 1996; Coull et al., 2000; Servos, 2000) has shown that the motor control system operates more effectively and efficiently when it receives visual information from *both* eyes. Although people can reach and pick up objects when the use of only one eye is available, the accuracy and efficiency of the movement decrease as the distance to the object increases. Experiments (e.g., Coull et al., 2000) that have shown this influence of distance provide support for the view that binocular vision is important for *depth perception*.

The monocular vision problem appears to be due to movement preparation and execution problems. Without binocular vision during movement preparation, people consistently underestimate the distance to objects and the size of the objects. These

FIGURE 6.8   An example of the event occlusion procedure: Examples of what subjects saw in the Abernethy and Russell experiment when they watched a film of a badminton serve where various parts of the serving action were masked and could not be seen. Note that in these frames, the occluded parts (i.e., "events") of the server are (top row left to right): arm and racquet, racquet, (bottom row left to right): legs, head, a no-event control frame. [*Source:* Abernethy, B. & Russell, D. G. (1987). Expert-novice differences in an applied selective attention task. *Journal of Sport Psychology, 9,* 326–345.]

underestimates are not corrected during the movement itself, which indicates the need for binocular vision to provide important limb movement error-correction information. Research investigations of these problems have shown errors in movement kinematics during the movement (e.g., Bingham, 2005; Jackson, Newport, & Shaw, 2002) and movement end-point accuracy (e.g., Heath, Neely, & Krigolson, 2008). Interestingly, when people are not permitted to use binocular vision and must reach for and grasp an object using monocular vision, they will

move their heads in a manner that enables them to obtain more accurate information about the size of an object and the distance to it (see Marotta, Kruyer, & Goodale, 1998).

Binocular vision also provides better movement control than monocular vision for other motor skills, such as locomotion and intercepting moving objects. For example, research evidence shows that when a person is walking along a pathway and must step over an obstacle, binocular vision is important for the detection of the three-dimensional characteristics of the environment needed to initiate and step over the obstacle (Patla, Niechwiej, Racco, & Goodale, 2002). This information enables the person to move the stepping leg accurately to clear the obstacle while stepping over it. Here again we see evidence for the importance of binocular vision for visual depth perception.

Finally, binocular vision also provides important information to help us intercept moving objects. An example of research evidence supporting this role for binocular vision was reported in an experiment in which participants used monocular or binocular vision to hit a moving object (Scott, van der Kamp, Savelsbergh, Oudejans, & Davids, 2004). Results showed that the participants using monocular vision missed the object more frequently, indicating that binocular vision provides important information to guide interceptive actions in skills such as hitting a moving ball.

Central and Peripheral Vision
Another question of interest relates to the *roles of central and peripheral vision* in the control of movement. **Central vision,** which is sometimes called *foveal* vision, detects information only in the middle 2 to 5 degrees of the visual field. **Peripheral vision,** on the other hand, detects information in the visual field outside these limits. For most people, the visual field extends approximately 200 degrees horizontally and 160 degrees vertically. The current understanding is that each makes specific contributions. To demonstrate how central and peripheral vision each provide distinct information for motor control, we will consider research related to two types of motor skills related to everyday living: reaching and grasping an object, and locomotion.

First, imagine yourself sitting at a table with the intent to pick up a cup sitting on the table. In this situation, as you prepare to move, central vision fixates on the cup to obtain information on its size, shape, and distance from your present position. As you begin to reach for the cup your moving hand is seen by peripheral vision, which will provide online feedback to guide the reaching and grasping of the cup. As your hand nears the cup, central vision becomes critical again for providing information needed to actually grasp the cup.

There is an abundance of research evidence to support the roles of central and peripheral vision in the prehension task situation just described. For example, an experiment by Sivak and MacKenzie (1990) showed that when participants could use only central vision to reach and grasp an object, the organization and control of the movement to the object was affected, but not the grasping of the object. When the researchers blocked the participants' use of central vision, which meant they could use only peripheral vision for reaching and grasping an object, problems occurred with both the transport and grasp phases.

---

central vision   the middle 2 to 5 degrees of the visual field; it is sometimes called *foveal* vision.

peripheral vision   the visual field outside the 2 to 5 degrees of central vision.

The results of the Sivak and MacKenzie experiment match those reported in other research by showing the distinct roles played by central and peripheral vision in the control of limb movements, especially those involved in manual aiming and prehension (see Jeannerod & Marteniuk, 1992, for a review of this research).

Central and peripheral vision also play different roles in locomotion. For example, research has shown that when we walk along a pathway, central vision provides information that guides us so that we can stay on the pathway, whereas peripheral vision is important to provide and update our knowledge about the spatial features of the walking environment, such as pathway dropoffs or bumps (Turano, Yu, Hao, & Hicks, 2005). The information received through peripheral vision during locomotion is particularly important to help people maintain their action goal without being affected by pathway problems, such as obstacles, other people, or irregular steps on a stairway.

Peripheral vision detects visual cues in the environment by assessing **optical flow** patterns. Optical flow refers to the pattern of rays of light that strike the retina of the eye from all parts of the environment. The word "flow" is significant because it indicates the dynamic nature of this visually detected information. As we move in an environment, or when something in our environment moves, our visual system detects and interprets invariant patterns of light rays that are specific to and emanate from objects and features in that environment. As a result, vision's use of optical flow allows us to locomote through an environment and helps us to achieve action goals. (For an excellent review of research concerning optical flow and an experiment involving the use of optical flow, see Konczak, 1994.)

Two visual systems for motor control. The distinctive behavioral roles for central and peripheral vision, along with supporting neurophysiological evidence, have led some researchers to propose that the visual system is actually two anatomical systems that operate in parallel (see Brown, Halpert, & Goodale, 2005, for a more detailed discussion of the two vision systems). Paillard (1980),

for example, proposed that a *kinetic* visual channel was responsible for processing visual information in peripheral vision. This channel would process high-speed movement information and control limb movement direction. To process visual information in central vision and for slow-speed movements, Paillard proposed a *static* visual channel.[2] Other researchers have proposed similar two-channel visual systems but have given them different names. Some examples include the *vision-for-perception* system, which would be responsible for recognizing and describing what a person is seeing, and the *vision-for-action* system which would be responsible for perceptually guided movements (Goodale & Milner, 1992; Brown, Halpert, & Goodale, 2005); another is the *focal* vision system, which is responsible for the detection of static objects by central vision, and the *ambient* vision system, which detects objects and movement around us, involving peripheral vision (Trevarthen, 1968).

When described in anatomical terms, the two visual systems have been referred to as the *ventral stream,* which is used for fine analysis of the visual scene into form, color, and features—in other words, what a person is seeing—and the *dorsal stream,* which is responsible for the spatial characteristics of what is seen as well as for guiding movement (e.g., Reed, Klatzky, & Halgren, 2005; Cameron, Franks, Enns, & Chua, 2007). As this designation of the two systems suggests, the neural pathways of the two systems are anatomically distinct. To use the Goodale and Milner terms for the two systems, the vision-for-perception system processes visual information via a cortical pathway leading from the primary visual cortex to the temporal lobe, whereas the vision-for-action system routes information from the primary visual cortex to the posterior parietal cortex (Brown, Halpert, & Goodale, 2005; Reed et al., 2005).

One important characteristic of the two systems relates to our conscious awareness of the information detected by each system. We are generally

---

[2]For a review of research that has tested Paillard's two visual systems model, and two experiments that support and extend this model, see Proteau, Bolvin, Linossier, and Abahnini (2000).

consciously aware of information detected by the visual system related to central vision, but not of that detected by the system related to peripheral vision.

Perception-Action Coupling:
The Coordination of Vision and Movement

When you play a video game on your computer and you must move the mouse quickly and precisely so that the object you control on the screen hits a target, or when you want to quickly unlock the door to your residence, your eyes and hand work together in a coordinated way to allow you to carry out these actions. Similarly, when you want to kick a moving ball or stop it with your foot, your eyes and feet coordinate so that you can successfully carry out the intended action. The spatial and temporal coordination of vision and the hands or feet in these types of skill performance situations is known as **perception-action coupling.** This means that the visual perception of the object and the limb movement required to achieve the action goal are "coupled," or coordinated, in a way that enables people to perform eye-hand and eye-foot coordination skills.

One of the ways researchers have determined this coordination characteristic is by pairing the eye-movement recording technique, which we discussed in the preceding section, with the motion analysis technique discussed in chapter 2. Although perception-action coupling can involve movements of the hands or feet, research has almost exclusively investigated the coupling of vision and hand movements. But similar effects have been reported for eye-foot coordination skills.

For eye movement analysis, the characteristic of interest is the *point of gaze,* which is the specific location in the environment on which central (i.e., foveal) vision is fixated at any particular moment. For example to assess the coordination of vision and hand movement to a target, researchers calculate the relationship between the timing and/or location of the termination of the point of gaze with the timing and/or location of the hand movement. If the point of gaze and hand movement are temporally or spatially coupled, the point of gaze should be at a specific location at a consistent proportion of the total movement time and/or distance of the hand movement.

A good example of research evidence that demonstrates the coupling between vision and hand movement is an experiment by Helsen, Elliott, Starkes, and Ricker (1998). Participants moved their index fingers 40 cm to the right from a starting location in front of them to a 1 cm by 2 cm target as fast as possible. Both point of gaze and hand movements tended to undershoot the target and then made one or more corrections to hit the target. The analysis of eye and finger movements showed that the participants typically initiated eye movements approximately 70 msec *before* they began to move their hands from the start location. The initial eye movement moved the point of gaze very close to the target (about 95 percent of the total distance), after which they made a second eye movement to correct the undershooting of the first. The point of gaze typically arrived at the target 450 msec *before* the finger, which would allow for inflight hand movement corrections based on visual feedback. The researchers found evidence for *temporal coupling* between the eye movements and hand movements because the completion of the initial eye movement coincided with the timing of the peak acceleration and velocity of the hand movement. Evidence for *spatial coupling* was shown by the point of gaze consistently terminating on the target when the hand movement was at 50 percent of the total movement distance.

Since that experiment, the same researchers (Helsen, Elliott, Starkes, & Ricker, 2000) showed that the initiation of elbow and shoulder movements is also coupled in time with eye and finger movement initiation. The sequence of events was that the eyes moved first, followed by the shoulder, then the elbow, and finally the finger. On every trial for every participant, the point of gaze was on the target long before the hand arrived at the target. Similar coupling effects have been demonstrated for vision and feet during locomotion. For example, researchers have shown that people with vision gaze control

---

optical flow   the patterns of rays of light that strike the retina of the eye that emanate from and are specific to objects and features in the environment.

deficits exhibit foot lift and stepping problems during stair climbing (DiFabio, Zampieri, & Tuite, 2008). Thus, the results of these experiments, and others like them support the importance of vision for picking up critical spatial information to initiate and guide limb movements to a target and to provide spatial and temporal feedback to ensure the accurate arrival of the limb at the target.

The Amount of Time Needed to Make Vision-Based Movement Corrections

An important factor that influences the role of vision in motor control is the amount of time available to use visual feedback to make movement corrections while the movement is in progress. Recall from our discussion in chapter 5 of the closed-loop motor control system that feedback can be used to make movement corrections only when the person has sufficient time to detect a movement error and modify the movement. This means there is a minimum total movement time requirement in order for the performer to be able to use visual feedback to correct movement errors prior to the completion of the movement.

The important question here is: *What is the minimum amount of time required for movement corrections* to be carried out on the basis of visual feedback? Researchers have been attempting to answer this question for more than 100 years, beginning with research by Woodworth in 1899. The most vigorous effort to investigate this question occurred in the latter part of the twentieth century, beginning with an influential experiment by Keele and Posner in 1968. Unfortunately, all this research effort has not provided us with a precise answer to the question (see Carlton, 1992; and Elliott, Helsen, & Chua, 2001, for excellent reviews of this research). Part of the problem is that different experimental procedures have resulted in a variety of time estimates for the processing of visual feedback.

The most common experimental procedure has been to have people perform manual aiming movements with different goal movement times. On some trials, the lights would go out just as the person began to move, whereas on other trials the lights remained on. The logic to this procedure was that if visual feedback were necessary, aiming accuracy would decrease with the lights out because the person could not see the target and therefore would not be able to use visual feedback. When participants did not know when the lights would be on or off, the amount of time to process visual feedback was estimated to be between 190 and 260 msec. However, later experiments used the same lights-on-or-off technique, but participants knew when they would perform under each condition (e.g., Zelaznik, Hawkins, & Kisselburgh, 1983; Elliott & Allard, 1985). This advance knowledge indicated that visual feedback could be used in less than 100 msec.

Other experimental procedures have led researchers to conclude that visual feedback can be processed in amounts of time that are faster or slower than those estimated by the lights-on-or-off procedure. These have included such procedures as distorting the visual information by having people wear prism glasses (e.g., Smith & Bowen, 1980, estimated the time to be about 150 msec); moving the target location after the person initiated a movement to a target (e.g., Brenner & Smeets, 1997, estimated the time to be about 110 msec); and preventing visual feedback for portions of the distance to the target (e.g., Spijkers & Lochner, 1994, estimated the time to be about 135 msec).

Although it is not possible to establish an exact minimum amount of time required to use visual feedback to enable movement corrections, it appears that an estimate of a range from *100 to 160 msec* is reasonable to capture movement correction limits for most motor skills. However, it is important to note that the minimum amount of time could be faster in situations where the person is anticipating the need to make a movement correction.

Application to real-world motor skill performance. How does the question concerning the minimum amount of time needed to make a movement correction relate to the performance of motor skills in real-world situations? Knowing this time limitation for human performance becomes especially

The Use of Looming in Television and Movies: An Illustration of Our Use of *Tau*

In their review of the issues related to determining the visual information people use to time the approach of an oncoming object, Abernethy and Burgess-Limerick (1992) stated that if a *tau*-based method for picking up time to contact is viable, "observers must first and foremost be sensitive to information provided by optical expansion or 'looming'" (p. 366). They went on to describe several research studies supporting this prediction. Although these studies are important to establish scientific support for *tau,* we can find evidence of our sensitivity to looming from a common everyday experience.

Have you ever watched a television program or movie and experienced the illusion of an object flying out of the screen directly at you? Because television and movies are two-dimensional media, creators of visual effects implement the concept of looming to create the three-dimensional quality of an object moving from

far away and then acting as if it were flying out of the screen directly at the viewer. This illusion is created by making the object appear small on the screen and then having it nonlinearly expand in size (i.e., slowly at first and then rapidly). This change in the rate of expansion creates the optical illusion that the object will fly out of the screen and hit you. Undoubtedly you have observed this looming illusion, and have actually responded to it by moving your head to avoid the object hitting you. What is especially interesting about this behavioral reaction is that it occurs even though you know it is not possible for the object to physically fly out of the screen and hit you. The important point here is that the object made no distance and velocity changes; only size changed. It is this size-based change, and its nonlinear rate of expansion, that is the basis for *tau* providing a means for people to time the approach of an oncoming object.

---

relevant when we try to evaluate performance associated with sports skills and activities of daily living. For example, whether or not a person will have time to adjust his or her initial hand movement to catch a ball will depend on the amount of time available to catch the ball. If the ball speed is too fast or the distance the ball travels is too short to allow any movement modification, success at catching the ball will depend on the initial hand position. Similarly, if a person is stair climbing at a pace that is too fast to allow foot-position adjustments while the foot is in flight, the risk of falling increases.

Time to Contact: The Optical Variable Tau

In situations in which a person moves toward an object to make contact with it, or the object moves toward the person, such as when a person is catching or hitting a thrown ball, vision plays an important role in specifying *when* to initiate the action and make contact with the object. The important visual information in these situations is the *time to contact,* which is the amount

of time remaining until the object contacts the person (or vice versa) from a specific distance (see Bootsma & Peper, 1992). Time to contact is specified according to the relative rate of change of the size of the image of the object on the retina of the eye. As the person approaches the object, or vice versa, the object produces an increasingly larger retinal image. When this image attains a certain critical size, it triggers the action required by the situation.

In the early 1970s, David Lee (1974) provided evidence that time to contact is specified by an optical variable, which he termed *tau* (τ). He also showed that *tau* can be quantified mathematically by relating object size, the distance of the object from the person, and the angle subtended at the person by the object size and distance. In mathematical terms, *tau* is the inverse of the relative rate of change of the visual angle subtended by the moving object, given the speed of approach of the object is constant.

The motor control benefit of the *tau* variable is its predictive function, which allows action initiation and object contact to occur "automatically" at a specific time to contact regardless of the speed of the object or person. When driving a car, for example, the driver's initiation and amount of braking action to avoid collision with another car is not dependent on the driver's cognitive knowledge of the distance to and velocity of the other car. Rather, by specifying the time to contact at any distance and velocity, the rate of change of the size of the retinal image of the other car provides the information needed by the driver to determine the type of braking, or deceleration, required by the situation. We will consider *tau* and its relation to specific motor skills in chapter 7.

SUMMARY

- Touch, proprioception, and vision are important sources of feedback involved in movement control.

- Touch provides the tactile sensory information that is important for the control of movement. Mechanoreceptors in the skin are the sensory receptors that provide this information by detecting skin stretch and joint movement. Research has shown that tactile feedback is important in motor control for influencing movement-related characteristics such as movement accuracy, movement consistency, and force adjustments for ongoing movements for and assisting proprioception in the estimation of movement distance.

- Proprioception information is detected by proprioceptors located in the muscles, tendons, ligaments, and joint capsules. The muscle spindles are the most important receptors for providing the CNS with feedback about limb position, direction, and velocity. The Golgi-tendon organs detect changes in muscle force. The joint receptors provide feedback about joint movement when the angular movement or joint positions are at their extreme limits.

- To investigate the role of proprioception in motor control, researchers use several experimental techniques that remove or distort proprioceptive feedback. The results of this research have established that proprioceptive feedback influences several motor control functions, including movement accuracy, the timing of the onset of motor commands, and various aspects of the coordination of body and limb segments, such as postural control, the spatial-temporal coupling between limbs and limb segments, and adaptation to movement situations that require the use of nonpreferred coordination patterns.

- We tend to use and trust vision more than our other senses for information to control movement. Vision's dominant role as a source of sensory information is commonly observed in situations in which vision and proprioception provide conflicting information about characteristics of our movement, a phenomenon that was demonstrated in the "moving room experiment."

- Vision results from sensory receptors in the eyes that receive wavelengths of light through structures such as the cornea, pupil, lens, and retina and transmit the information that reaches the retina to the visual cortex in the brain by way of the optic nerve.

- To investigate the role of vision in motor control, researchers use several experimental techniques, such as eye-movement recording and the occlusion of temporal and event information in a scene.

- Research evidence has established that vision plays several important roles in motor control, such as providing depth perception for interacting with objects, other people, and our daily environment; providing information that enables us to identify objects, people, and other environmental context components; providing information that enables us to move through our environment; coordinating movements involved in eye-hand coordination activities; and making movement corrections as we move.

- Research evidence shows that the visual system is actually two anatomical and physiological systems. The vision-for-perception system allows us to recognize and describe what we see; the vision-for-action system allows us to move in our environment.

- In situations in which a person moves toward an object to make contact with it, or in which an object moves toward a person, the visual variable *tau* specifies the amount of time until contact. At a critical time-to-contact, the motor control system initiates the action required in the situation.

POINTS FOR THE PRACTITIONER

- Because touch, proprioception, and vision are important for enabling people to carry out their daily living and recreational activities, it is important to determine how deficits in any of these sensory systems may explain difficulties a person may have performing a specific activity. Movement accuracy and coordination problems may be the result of sensory-related problems.

- People will typically use vision to substitute for touch and/or proprioception when they begin learning a skill that requires them to rely on touch and/or proprioception for successful performance, such as watching their fingers hit keyboard keys when learning to keyboard or play the piano, watching their hands when learning to dribble a ball, or watching their feet when learning a dance routine.

- Make certain that a person's central vision (i.e., the point of gaze) is focused directly on an object that needs to be grasped or caught to ensure the successful achievement of the action goal.

- People can make movement corrections while performing a skill only when there is a sufficient amount of time to make the corrections. As a result, movement errors may be the result of movement or environmental context conditions that were too fast to allow a correction, even though the person knew he or she needed to make a movement adjustment. Examples include ball speed that is too fast to allow a correction of hand position to catch it or of bat or racquet position to hit it or a person moving too fast to correct a foot position or movement error when stepping over an obstacle in the pathway or on a stair step when ascending stairs.

RELATED READINGS

Berencsi, A., Ishihara, M., & Imanaka, K. (2005). The functional role of central and peripheral vision in the control of posture. *Human Movement Science, 24,* 689–709.

Brenner, E., & Smeets, J. B. J. (2003). Fast corrections of movements with a computer mouse. *Spatial Vision, 16,* 365–376.

Cardosa de Oliveira, S., & Barthelemy, S. (2005). Visual feedback reduces bimanual coupling of movement amplitudes, but not direction. *Experimental Brain Research, 162,* 78–88.

Ergen, E., & Ulkar, B. (2008). Proprioception and ankle injuries in soccer. *Clinics in Sports Medicine, 27,* 195–217.

Fajen, B. R., Riley, M. A., & Turvey, M. T. (2009). Information, affordances, and the control of action in sport. *International Journal of Sport Psychology, 40,* 79–107.

Glasauer, S., Schneider, E., Jahn, K., Strupp, M., & Brandt, T. (2005). How the eyes move the body. *Neurology, 65,* 1291–1293.

Hajnal, A., Fonseca, S., Harrison, S., Kinsella-Shaw, J., & Carello, C. (2007). Comparison of dynamic (effortful) touch by hand and foot. *Journal of Motor Behavior, 39,* 82–88.

Hecht, D., & Reiner, M. (2009). Sensory dominance in combinations of audio, visual and haptic stimuli. *Experimental Brain Research, 193,* 307–314.

Kanade, R. V., Van Deursen, R. W. M., Harding, K. G., & Price, P. E. (2008). Investigation of standing balance in patients with diabetic neuropathy at different stages of foot complications. *Clinical Biomechanics, 23,* 1183–1191.

Khan, M. A., Lawrence, G. P., Franks, I. M., & Buckolz, E. (2004). The utilization of visual feedback from peripheral and central vision in the control of direction. *Experimental Brain Research, 158,* 241–251.

Proffitt, D. R. (2006). Distance perception. *Current Directions in Psychological Science, 15,* 131–135.

Starkes, J., Helsen, W., & Elliot, D. (2002). A ménage a trois: The eye, the hand and on-line processing. *Journal of Sports Sciences, 20,* 217–224.

Weiler, H. T., Pap, G., & Awiszus, F. (2000). The role of joint afferents in sensory processing in osteoarthritic knees. *Rheumatology, 39,* 850–856.

INTERNET RESOURCES

- To visit a laboratory in which researchers are investigating several issues related to sensory information as it pertains to various human performance situations, including catching and hitting a ball, go to the home page of the Ishikawa Namiki Komuro Laboratory in Tokyo, Japan, at http://www.k2.t .u-tokyo.ac.jp. Note especially the "Sensor Fusion" link under Research.

- For a tutorial of the anatomy and physiology of the eye, as well as related topics on vision go to http://www.tedmontgomery.com/the_eye/index.html

- To view an exhibit titled "The Painter's Eye Movements," which is a multipage exhibit of the eye and hand movements of skilled artists as they paint and draw, go to http://prism.bham.ac.uk/~rcm/pem/index.htm. The site includes a brief description, with pictures, of eye-movement tracking equipment and how it is used with hand-movement analysis equipment to provide information about the coordination of eye and hand movements.

- To learn about "beep baseball," an adapted version of baseball for the visually impaired and the blind, go to the Web site of the National Beep Baseball Association at http://www.nbba.org. To watch video of beep baseball being played, go to http://espn.go.com/swf/eticket/beep/beep.html

- For an interesting Web site that includes information and activities related to several topics discussed in this chapter, go to http://www.exploratorium.edu/snacks/. Listed are the numerous topics included on this Web site, including proprioception and several topics related to the eye and vision.

STUDY QUESTIONS

1. Describe the sensory receptors located in the skin that provide tactile sensory information related to movement.

2. Discuss three movement-related characteristics influenced by tactile sensory information; indicate how we know each of them is influenced by tactile sensory information.

3. Describe three types of proprioceptors, where each is located, and the type of movement information each provides.

4. Discuss three methods researchers have used to investigate the role of proprioception in motor control and what the results of that research have told us about two roles of proprioception in the control of movement.

5. Describe the anatomical pathway the image of an object would take through the eye and visual neural system.

6. Discuss why binocular vision is superior to monocular vision for perceiving distance to objects and the size and shapes of objects.

7. (a) Discuss the differnt roles of central and peripheral vision in the control of movement, and explain how these roles indicate that there are two anatomical visual systems. (b) If you wanted to reach for a cup of water to take a drink from it, describe how the two visual systems would operate to allow you to do this task.

8. Describe the spatial and temporal relationships between your eyes and hand when you move the computer mouse so that the cursor points to an icon on the monitor.

9. Discuss why a volleyball player who jumps up at the net to block a spike is vulnerable to the offensive player successfully dinking the ball over his or her hands.

Specific Application Problem:
You have been asked by your supervisor to evaluate the performance of a recent knee replacement patient. What would you expect to be the movement capabilities and limitations of this person who now has no joint receptors in the knee?

Performance and Motor Control Characteristics of Functional Skills

Concept: Specific characteristics of the performance of various types of motor skills provide the basis for much of our understanding of motor control.

After completing this chapter, you will be able to

- Describe Fitts' law and explain how it relates to the speed-accuracy trade-off phenomenon
- Define the term *prehension;* describe a prehension example; discuss, from a motor control perspective, the relationship among the components of a prehension action; and discuss the role of vision in prehension
- Describe how handwriting provides a good example of the concept of motor equivalence and the influence of vision on handwriting
- Describe the difference between symmetric and asymmetric bimanual coordination, and discuss why asymmetric bimanual coordination is more difficult to maintain than symmetric
- Describe the rhythmic relationships associated with walking and running gait patterns, the role of maintaining head stability during locomotion, and the characteristics associated with gait transitions that occur at certain speeds of locomotion
- Describe how vision influences locomotion when the action goal is to contact an object or avoid contact with an object in the environment
- Describe the three movement phases of catching a moving object and the role vision plays in each phase and answer the question of whether it is important to be able to see one's hands throughout the flight of an object to catch it
- Discuss how vision influences the striking of a moving object and what that influence tells us about the control of this type of action

APPLICATION

Appropriate instruction and practice intervention procedures are important to develop to help people acquire or rehabilitate skills effectively and efficiently. As you saw in chapters 5 and 6, a basic understanding of motor control theory and the sensory processes involved in motor control form important parts of a

foundation on which to base the developme
procedures. Consider the following tw
a person were having difficulty re
and drinking from a cup, how
determine the reason for
develop an appropriate i
the person perform this typ
of the answer to these questi

135

concerned with the motor control of prehension. Or, suppose a beginning student in a tennis class is having problems learning to serve because he or she cannot coordinate the ball toss and racquet movement that must simultaneously occur to perform a successful serve. Motor control researchers have identified some distinct characteristics of bimanual coordination that provide teachers and coaches some insight into how to overcome the tennis serve problem.

These two examples illustrate situations in which an understanding of motor control processes and characteristics associated with specific motor skills can give you insights into helping people overcome performance problems in skill learning and rehabilitation contexts. We could consider many more examples, but these two should allow you to see how to apply an understanding of performance and motor control characteristics to working with people in their pursuit of learning or rehabilitating motor skills. In the chapter discussion, you will be introduced to specific performance and motor control characteristics associated with a variety of skills. Some of these are unique to a specific motor skill; others are common across several skills. If the skills you expect to help people in your future profession learn or rehabilitate are included, you can discover the specific performance and motor control characteristics you will need to take into account to facilitate their acquisition of these skills. If the skills you expect to help people learn or rehabilitate are not included, the information presented should provide you with a knowledge base from which you can make specific applications to those skills.

Application Problem to Solve Choose a motor skill that in your future profession you expect to help people learn or rehabilitate. What are the performance characteristics of this skill that will pose distinct difficulties for these people as they learn or rehabilitate the skill? What motor control characteristics should you take into account in the strategies and procedures you use to help these people learn or rehabilitate the skill?

DISCUSSION

The motor control theories discussed in chapter 5 and the roles of sensory information discussed in chapter 6 were derived from researchers' observations of people performing a variety of everyday and sport skills in many different situations. These observations have established that each type of skill involves distinct performance characteristics that are essential to consider in our understanding of motor control processes and to provide guidance for practitioners as they help people learn or rehabilitate skills. In the following sections, we will consider some of the more prominent types of motor skills researchers have investigated with these goals in mind. It is important to point out that in the discussion of these skills, we will limit the discussion of the sensory systems' involvement in motor control to the role of vision. Although, as you read in chapter 6, tactile and proprioceptive sensory information play roles in the motor control of functional skills, discussion of those roles is beyond the scope of this introductory book.

SPEED-ACCURACY SKILLS

Many motor skills require a person to perform with both speed and accuracy. For example, kicking a penalty kick in soccer, pitching a fastball for a strike in baseball and softball, playing a song on a piano at a fast tempo, and speed typing all require fast and accurate movement to achieve successful performance. Other motor skills require limb-movement accuracy but not speed. For example, many **manual aiming skills,** which involve hand movement to a target, require that the hand arrive at the target but at a speed that the performer determines. Such skills include putting a key into a keyhole, placing a pen in a penholder, typing on a computer keyboard, and threading a needle.

For both types of speed-accuracy skills, those that require fast and accurate movement and those that require accurate movement at an unspecified speed, we commonly observe a phenomenon known as the **speed-accuracy trade-off.** This means that the accuracy requirements of the movement will influence the movement speed so that an emphasis on accuracy will reduce speed, while an emphasis on speed will reduce accuracy. Thus, we typically "trade off" speed for accuracy, and vice versa. Consider how this trade-off would occur in the examples of the two types of skills described above. For a penalty kick in soccer, when a player tries to kick the ball at the fastest speed possible, the typical result is an inaccurate kick. Conversely, when the player emphasizes accuracy by trying to kick the ball to a small part of the goal, the result is often a ball kicked too slowly to get past the goalkeeper. For the example of putting a key in a keyhole, moving the key too quickly toward the keyhole typically results in missing the keyhole, whereas an emphasis on accuracy results in slower hand movement.

Fitts' Law

Research evidence demonstrating a speed-accuracy trade-off can be traced back to an 1899 publication by R. S. Woodworth, who was one of the pioneers in the study of motor control (see Elliott, Helsen, & Chua, 2001, for a review of Woodworth's experiments and influence on research). For the following half century, evidence for a speed-accuracy trade-off in motor skill performance had become so common that a mathematical law was developed to predict movement speed given specific accuracy characteristics. This law, which has become known as Fitts' law, was described by and based on the work of Paul Fitts (1954). It has become one of the most significant "laws" associated with human performance. In science, a *law* refers to a situation in which a result, or outcome, can be predicted when certain variables are involved.

Fitts' law predicts the movement time for a situation requiring both speed and accuracy in which a person must move to a target as quickly and accurately as possible. The variables that predict the performance outcome are the *distance* to move and the *target size*. According to Fitts' law, if we know the spatial dimensions of these two variables, we can predict the movement time required to hit the

target. In mathematical terms, Fitts' law describes this relationship as

$$MT = a + b \log_2(2D/W)$$

where

MT is movement time
a and *b* are constants
D is the distance moved
W is the target width, or size

That is, movement time will be equal to the $\log_2$ of two times the distance to move divided by the width of the target. As the target size becomes smaller or as the distance becomes longer, the movement speed will decrease in order to allow for an accurate movement. In other words, there is a speed-accuracy trade-off.

Fitts indicated that because of the lawful relationship between target size and movement distance, the equation $\log_2(2D/W)$ provides an **index of difficulty (ID)** for speed-accuracy skills. The

---

manual aiming skills   motor skills that involve arm, hand, and/or finger movement to a target; e.g., putting a key into a keyhole, threading a needle with thread, and typing on a computer keyboard.

speed-accuracy trade-off   a characteristic of motor skill performance in which the speed at which a skill is performed is influenced by movement accuracy demands; the trade-off is that increasing speed yields decreasing accuracy, and vice versa.

Fitts' law   a human performance law specifying the movement time for an aiming movement when the distance to move and the target size are known; it is quantified as MT = $a + b \log_2(2D/W)$, where *a* and *b* are constants and W = target width, and D = distance from the starting point to the target.

index of difficulty (ID)   according to Fitts' law, a quantitative measure of the difficulty of performing a skill involving both speed and accuracy requirements; it is calculated as the $\log_2(2D/W)$, where W = target width, and D = distance from the starting point to the target.

LAB LINKS

Lab 7a in the Online Learning Center Lab Manual for chapter 7 provides an opportunity for you to perform reciprocal tapping tasks with characteristics that will allow you to experience how Fitts' law describes the speed-accuracy trade-off.

index specifies that the higher the ID is, the more difficult the task will be. This is because more difficult tasks will require more movement time.

Figure 7.1a shows several examples of reciprocal tapping task dimensions that would characterize different IDs. Figure 7.1b shows approximate movement times for tasks with these, and other, IDs to illustrate the relationship between task difficulty (ID) and movement speed when people are instructed to move accurately—that is, hit the target.

Fitts' law applies to many skills. Fitts based his original calculation on a reciprocal tapping task in which participants made repetitive back-and-forth movements as fast as possible between two targets for a specified period of time. For this task, they were told to place an emphasis on accuracy.

Although Fitts' law was developed on the basis of performance on a laboratory task, it is important to note that the lawful speed-accuracy relationship also applies to a wide range of motor skill performance situations. For example, research shows that when people perform manual aiming tasks, such as throwing darts at a target, reaching or grasping containers of different sizes, playing a piano, moving pegs from one location to insert them into a hole, and moving a cursor on a screen to a target, their actions demonstrate movement time characteristics predicted by Fitts' law.

If we apply Fitts' law to the sport skills described earlier in this section, it should be possible to see the implications of this law for instruction and practice. For example, suppose a soccer player is asked to practice scoring a goal on a penalty kick by kicking the ball so that it travels as fast as possible to each of three different-sized areas in the goal. Fitts' law predicts that the highest speed will occur for the ball

kicked to the largest area. Conversely, the slowest speed will characterize the ball kicked to the smallest area. Later in this book (Unit VI), we will discuss the practice conditions that will help a person achieve both speed and accuracy in these types of situations.

Open- and closed-loop motor control processes related to the speed-accuracy trade-off. Researchers have proposed several hypotheses to explain the motor control processes related to the speed-accuracy trade-off. Most have elaborated on Woodworth's (1899) original hypothesis, which was that two motor control processes operate during the rapid limb movement to a target. One, which occurs initially and moves the limb into the vicinity of the target, is an *open-loop control* process where the initial movement's speed, direction, and accuracy are under CNS control. The second process involves *closed-loop control* in which visual feedback about the limb's relative position to that target is used to guide the "homing in" phase of the limb to ensure its accurate landing on the target. The hypotheses proposed since Woodworth's have focused on providing more detailed descriptions of the motor control activities involved in either the open- or closed-loop, or both, phases of the movement. However, all agree that, as we discussed in chapter 6, the amount of time available is the primary determinant of whether a person can make movement corrections as the limb nears the target. This means that if the movement speed is too fast during the initial open-loop phase, there will not be sufficient time for visual feedback to generate a movement adjustment as the limb nears the target.

The role of visual information in the speed-accuracy trade-off. When we consider the involvement of our sensory-perceptual systems in the performance of a speed-accuracy skill, such as putting a key into a keyhole, vision plays a predominant role in enabling successful performance. The specific role played by vision in speed-accuracy skills depends on the phase of the limb movement. Although the hypotheses described in the preceding section proposed two distinct movement phases for these skills, researchers generally

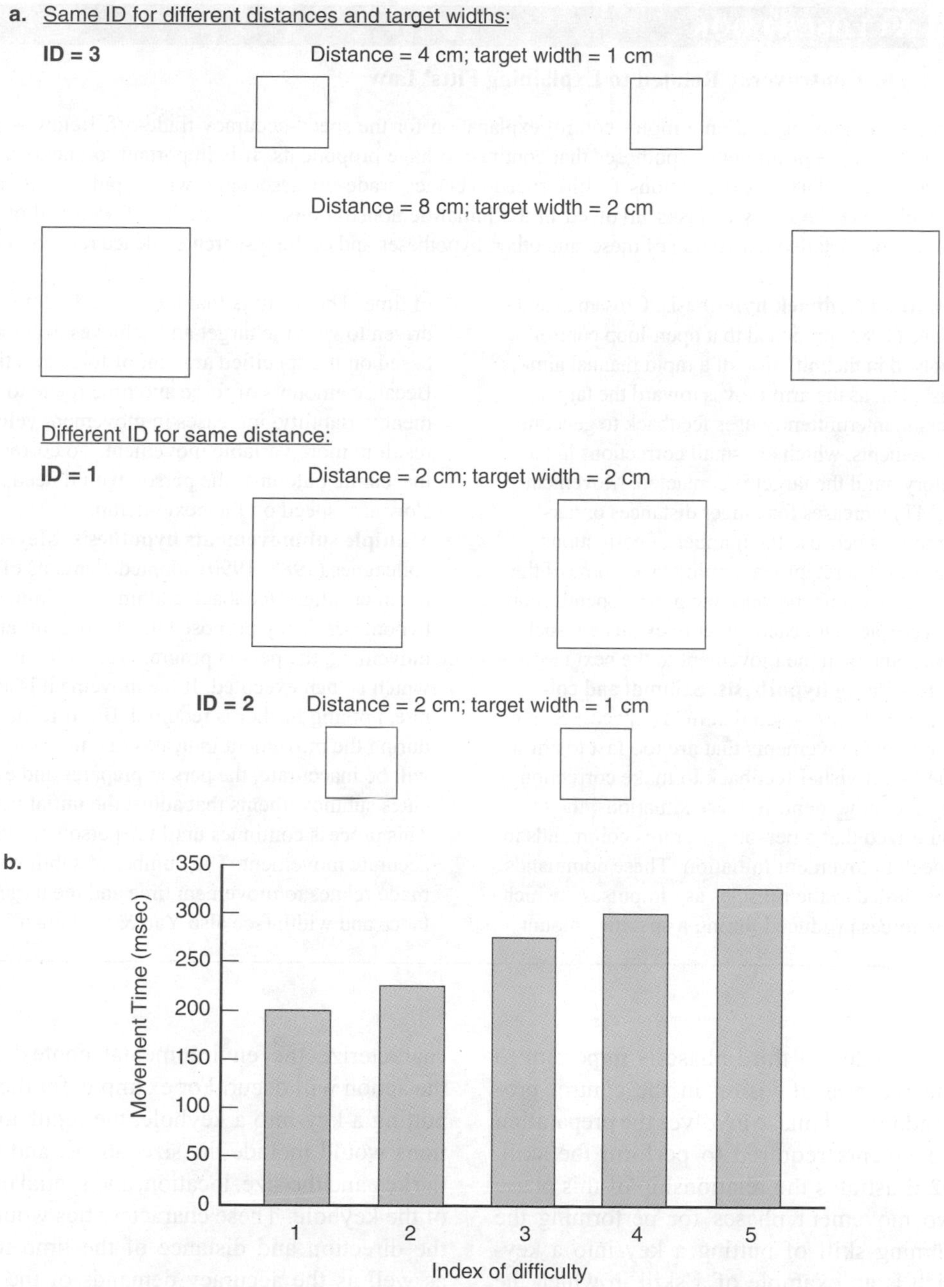

a. Same ID for different distances and target widths:

ID = 3 Distance = 4 cm; target width = 1 cm

Distance = 8 cm; target width = 2 cm

Different ID for same distance:

ID = 1 Distance = 2 cm; target width = 2 cm

ID = 2 Distance = 2 cm; target width = 1 cm

b.

FIGURE 7.1 (a) Examples of indexes of difficulty (ID) for reciprocal tapping tasks with different target size and/or distance characteristics. Task difficulty is indexed according to the ID such that the higher the ID is, the more difficult the task is. The ID is calculated according to the Fitts' law equation: ID = $\log_2$ (2 • Distance/Width) [Note that W is measured from the near edge of each target.] (b) Approximate movement times (in msec) for each tap of reciprocal tapping tasks of five different indexes of difficulty.

A CLOSER LOOK

The Controversy Related to Explaining Fitts' Law

Researchers have not agreed on a motor control explanation for the speed-accuracy trade-off. Below is a sampling of some of the prominent hypotheses that continue to have proponents. It is important to understand that these hypotheses relate to explanations for the speed-accuracy trade-off associated with rapid manual-aiming tasks, which were the types of tasks involved in the initial demonstrations of the trade-off. (See Elliott et al., 2001, for a more detailed discussion of these, and other, hypotheses and of the research evidence related to them.)

- **Intermittent feedback hypothesis.** Crossman and Goodeve (1983) proposed that open-loop control is involved in the initiation of a rapid manual aiming task. But as the arm moves toward the target, the person intermittently uses feedback to generate submovements, which are small corrections in the trajectory, until the target is contacted. Movement time (MT) increases for longer distances or narrower targets because the number of corrections increases. For a reciprocal aiming task, some of the MT increase occurs because the person spends more time in contact with each target to evaluate visual feedback and plan the movement to the next target.

- **Impulse-timing hypothesis.** Schmidt and colleagues (1979) proposed that many speed-accuracy tasks involve movements that are too fast to allow for the use of visual feedback to make corrections during the movement. In these situations, they hypothesized that a person programs commands in advance of movement initiation. These commands are forwarded to the muscles as "impulses," which are the forces produced during a specific amount

of time. The result is that the arm is forcefully driven toward the target and achieves accuracy based on the specified amount of force and time. Because amounts of force and time relate to movement variability, increases in movement velocity result in more variable movement. To correct an inaccurate outcome, the person would need to slow arm speed on the next attempt.

- **Multiple submovements hypothesis.** Meyer and colleagues (1988, 1990) adopted elements of both the intermittent-feedback and impulse-timing hypotheses. They proposed that before initiating movement, the person programs an initial impulse, which is then executed. If the movement is accurate, nothing further is required. But if feedback during the movement indicates that the movement will be inaccurate, the person prepares and executes submovements that adjust the initial velocity. This process continues until the person produces an accurate movement. The number of submovements made relates to movement time and the target distance and width (see also Yao & Fischman, 1999).

---

agree that including a third phase is important to understand the role of vision in the control process. This additional phase involves the preparation of the movements required to perform the skill. Figure 7.2 illustrates the relationship of this phase to the two movement phases for performing the manual aiming skill of putting a key into a keyhole, which is an example of a skill in which the speed-accuracy trade-off occurs.

The *first phase* is the *movement preparation phase,* which begins when the person makes the decision to perform the skill involving a speed-accuracy trade-off. In this phase, the person uses vision to determine the regulatory conditions that

characterize the environmental context in which the action will occur. For example, for the action of putting a key into a keyhole, the regulatory conditions would include the size, shape, and weight of the key and the size, location, and spatial orientation of the keyhole. These characteristics would specify the direction and distance of the limb movement as well as the accuracy demands of the situation. Together with other relevant information detected by the sensory system, such as the characteristics of the key that touch would provide, this sensory information would be transmitted to the CNS to prepare the specific movement characteristics to initiate and carry out the intended action.

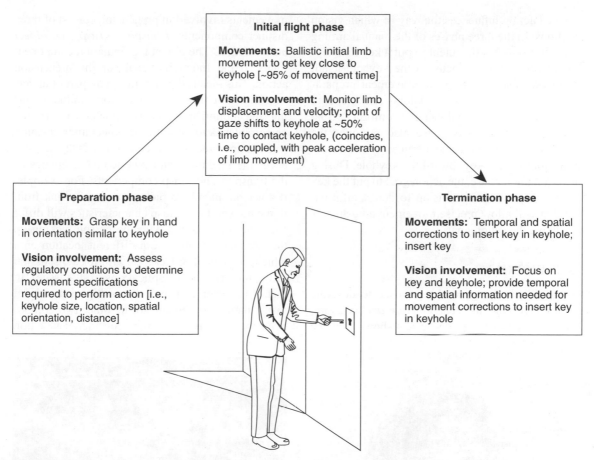

FIGURE 7.2 The three movement phases of putting a key in a keyhole in the lock on a door. In this figure, the use of vision is described to illustrate the role of an important source of sensory information in performing a manual aiming skill.

The *second phase,* which is the first movement phase in the hypotheses described in the preceding section, is commonly referred to as the *initial flight phase.* It includes the beginning of the limb movement in the direction of the target, which in our example is the keyhole. As you read in the preceding section, this movement is relatively fast (i.e., ballistic) and occurs without the influence of sensory feedback (i.e., open-loop control). Although vision plays a minor role in this phase, it acquires limb displacement and velocity information and acquires time-to-contact information that will be used later as the movement nears the target to make movement modifications. Researchers continue to debate the need

for vision of the moving limb during this phase (see Elliott, Helsen, & Chua, 2001, for a discussion of the research concerning this issue).

The third phase is the *termination phase.* It begins just before and ends when the target is hit, which in our example is when the key is inserted into the keyhole. Vision of the limb and target are important in this phase so that movement accuracy information can be transmitted to the CNS and any needed movement corrections can occur to allow the person to achieve the action goal of hitting the target.

One final point to consider here is the way in which *vision and movement interact* in skills involving a speed-accuracy tradeoff. Note that the intended action influences the way in which vision functions. In the three phases of the manual aiming task just discussed, the intent to put a key in a keyhole directs vision to focus on the keyhole itself, which establishes, during the movement preparation phase, the critical regulatory conditions to which the movements will need to conform. Visual information during this phase also provides the basis for the initial movement trajectory and velocity for moving the key toward the keyhole. During the termination phase, the action goal to put the key into the keyhole directs vision to detect information that will allow precise movement adjustments to achieve the action goal.

PREHENSION

Prehension is the general term used to describe actions involving the *reaching for and grasping of objects*. Research evidence has shown that the movements involved in prehension consist of three distinct components: *transport, grasp,* and *object manipulation*. The object manipulation component refers to the functional goal for the prehension action. This means that, an important part of understanding the control of prehension—unlike pointing and aiming movements—relates to what the person intends to do with the object after grasping it. The importance of this component is that it influences the kinematic and kinetic characteristics of the transport and grasp components. For example, if a person intends to pick up a cup to drink from it, the transport and grasp characteristics will differ from those associated with the person picking up the cup and moving it to a different location on a table (see Newell & Cesari, 1999, for a discussion of the motor control implications of this issue). In fact, it is because of the relationship of the object manipulation component to the other two components that prehension must be considered an action

To achieve the same object manipulation goal for a prehension action, people can use different movement characteristics to grasp the object.

A CLOSER LOOK

Using Constraint-Induced Movement Therapy to Improve Prehension and Other Upper Extremity Skills for Individuals with Hemiparesis

People with hemiparesis (i.e., partial paralysis on one side of the body) have difficulty using one arm, usually due to a stroke or other CNS disorder such as cerebral palsy. A physical rehabilitation intervention strategy that has been shown to be effective as a treatment of upper-limb impairment for individuals with hemiparesis is called *constraint-induced movement therapy* (CIMT). The goal of this therapy is to encourage the use of the impaired arm while discouraging the use of the unimpaired arm to perform tasks that the impaired arm should perform. It is common for people with hemiparesis to eventually not use the impaired arm at all, a condition known as learned disuse.

The therapy, which was first introduced by Edward Taub and colleagues (see Taub, Crago, & Uswatte, 1998, for a review of the research and theory on which CIMT is based), involves constraining the unimpaired arm with a splint, cast, or sling and forcing the use of the impaired arm. The majority of the evidence supporting the efficacy of this treatment has come from patients with stroke, although more recent applications have been reported for children with cerebral

palsy (CP) (see Gordon, Charles, & Wolf, 2005, for a brief review of this research).

The general protocol of CIMT: The therapy is an intensive procedure that requires the active participation of the patient and therapists for several hours a day for two weeks. Patients typically have their unimpaired hand restrained for 90 percent of their waking hours for fourteen consecutive days, during which they engage in six hours of intensive repetitive task practice and "shaping." Tasks include screwing and unscrewing bolts, picking up coins and moving them to specified locations, and so on. "Shaping" refers to practicing small parts of functional tasks and progressively increasing the complexity and difficulty of the parts until the actual functional task can be performed.

Effectiveness of CIMT: Numerous research studies have provided results that describe the effectiveness of CIMT, especially for improving and increasing the daily functional use of the impaired arm. (For a review of the history of the development of CIMT and research that has demonstrated its effectiveness, see Wolf, 2007).

---

that is different from the action of reaching and pointing to an object.

The Relationship of Prehension Components

From a motor control perspective, prehension involves the arm transporting the hand to an object as the hand forms the grip characteristics that are needed to grasp the object. A motor control question of interest here concerns the relationship between the *transport and grasp components.* Although initial attempts to answer this question proposed that these components were relatively independent (e.g., Jeannerod, 1981, 1984), more recent evidence has established that these *two components are temporally coupled and interact synergistically* (i.e., cooperatively) according to task demands. This means that although the reach and the grasp are two separate movement

components, they function in an interdependent manner.

The most compelling evidence demonstrating this coupled relationship has come from movement analyses of the fingers and thumb as the hand moves toward the object. For example, Jakobson and Goodale (1991) showed that the object's size and distance from the hand influenced the timing of when the distance between the fingers and thumb (i.e., grip aperture) reaches its maximum during the reach, as well as the velocity profile of the transport component. Interestingly, they, along with others (e.g., Chieffi & Gentilucci, 1993; Hu, Osu, Okada,

---

prehension   the action of reaching for and grasping an object that may be stationary or moving.

A CLOSER LOOK

Relating Fitts' Law to Drinking from a Mug

In the experiment by Latash and Jaric (2002) the researchers studied the control of coordination required to grasp, pick up, and sip from a mug, just as a person would do in everyday life. As part of this study, they developed a way to identify the index of difficulty (ID) that accounted for mug size and the amount of liquid in the mug. Instead of target size and distance, the accuracy characteristic of most tasks researchers have used to investigate Fitts' law, they considered the accuracy component of the task to be the transporting of the mug from a tabletop to the mouth without spilling its contents. Their logic was that a mug that is full to its rim requires more movement accuracy and is therefore a more difficult task than a mug that is less full. And, if consistent with Fitts' law, this task should require more movement time than transporting the mug that is less full.

Calculating the index of difficulty (ID): Four mugs of different diameters (10.0, 6.5, 3.2, and 8.5 cm) were filled with levels of water beginning from 0.5 to 1.0 cm from the rim to a small amount on the bottom. The researchers calculated the ID for each mug size and water level by determining the ratio of mug diameter to the distance of the water level from the mug rim—that is, *mug diameter/water level distance (in cm) from the rim*. For example, the mug with a diameter of 10 cm that was filled with water to 1 cm from the rim had an ID of 10 (i.e., 10/1 = 10); the

same mug filled to 6 cm from the rim had an ID of 1.67 (i.e., 10/6 = 1.67). The four mug sizes and water levels resulted in 16 IDs.

The relationship between ID and movement time (MT): When the participants' movement times (MT) (from initial mug movement to initial mouth-mug contact) were compared for the 16 IDs, the results were consistent with the Fitts' law prediction that movement times would be fastest for the lowest IDs and slowest for the highest IDs.

Relating the results to the control of the coordination of many degrees of freedom: On the basis of the relationship between ID and MT, as well as other movement-related measures (head angle, mug tilt angle, and head position), the researchers concluded that "ID could be viewed as a significant parameter that reflects task constraints within the natural movement of taking a sip from a mug" (p. 147). In terms of the nervous system's control of the coordination of hand, arm, and head movements required to perform this task (which represents the control of many degrees of freedom), this conclusion means that the ratio of the mug diameter to the distance of the contents from the rim directly influences the nervous system's spatial and temporal organization of the appropriate coordination elements to allow a person to drink from a mug without spilling its contents.

Goodale, & Kawato, 2005), found that regardless of object size and distance, hand closure occurred at approximately two-thirds of the total movement time duration of the action. More conclusive support for the temporal coupling of hand transport and grip aperture was provided by researchers who presented a mathematical model that can predict this temporal relationship for any hand transport duration (Hu et al., 2005). As is consistent with the research just described, this model shows that the maximum grip aperture occurs when the hand is approximately two-thirds through the total time duration of the reaching movement.

In addition, research evidence has shown that the kinematics of both the transport and grasp components are modified when the object is suddenly and unexpectedly moved during the transport phase (e.g., Gentilucci, Chieffi, Scarpa, & Castiello, 1992), and when an obstacle needs to be avoided to get to the object (e.g., Saling, Alberts, Stelmach, & Bloedel, 1998). These kinematic changes give additional support to the conclusion that there is a strong *temporal coupling* between the reach and grasp components of a prehension action. Thus, prehension serves as an additional example to those described in chapter 5 of how muscles and joints involved in a complex action cooperate synergistically as a *coordinative structure* to enable people to achieve an action goal in a variety of situations.

The Role of Vision in Prehension

Prehension actions are a type of speed-accuracy skill because accurate hand movement is required and the movement speed will be influenced by that accuracy demand. As a result, we should expect to find that vision is involved in prehension actions in ways that are similar to those we discussed in the preceding section on speed-accuracy skills. In fact, this is the case, with one exception. The exception involves the object manipulation component of prehension actions.

As with its role in the performance of the speed-accuracy skills we discussed previously, vision provides information for the performance of prehension actions prior to the initiation of movement by assessing the regulatory conditions of the environmental context, which includes the object itself and its surrounding context features. Together with the person's intended use of the object, the regulatory condition information is transmitted to the CNS, which then prepares "ballpark" estimates of the spatial and temporal movement characteristics for the transport and grasp components to use to reach and grasp the object. Vision next plays an essential role as the hand travels toward the object by detecting time-to-contact and arm movement information that will control the grasp aperture and other characteristics of the hand and finger movements required for grasping and manipulating the object. Visual feedback related to these movement characteristics will be used by the CNS to modify movements as needed to allow achievement of the prehension action goal. In fact, research has shown that grasp characteristics are negatively affected when a person cannot see the object during the initial portion of the transport phase (Fukui & Inui, 2006). Unlike the speed-accuracy skills we discussed earlier, vision monitors the grasp itself to supplement tactile and proprioceptive feedback to ensure that the grasp adjusts as needed during the grasping and using of the object.

As you read in chapter 6, the performance of prehension actions is enhanced with the use of binocular vision, especially in terms of the preparation of grip size and force (Jackson, Newport, & Shaw, 2002). In addition, research by Brown, Halpert, and Goodale (2005) has shown that because of the different roles of central and peripheral vision, especially as they relate to the two visual systems of vision-for-perception and vision-for-action, prehension skill performance is enhanced when the person looks directly at the object. This directing of the point-of-gaze at the object allows the two visual systems to optimally function during the prehension action, which enhances performance.

Prehension and Fitts' Law

One final point that is important to note with regard to the motor control aspects of prehension is that it demonstrates speed-accuracy trade-off characteristics. In fact, researchers have established that Fitts' law consistently applies to prehension for both laboratory tasks and activities of daily living. For example, in an experiment by Bootsma, Marteniuk, MacKenzie, and Zaal (1994), movement distance and object width influenced movement time during prehension in accordance with the predictions of Fitts' law. In addition, these object characteristics influenced the movement kinematics of the action. The relevance of the kinematic evidence is that it provides a way to explain why movement time increases as object width decreases. The kinematics showed that as objects decrease in size, the amount of time involved in the deceleration phase of the movement increases, suggesting that the increase in movement time associated with the smaller objects is due to the person reducing the speed of the limb as it approaches the object. This means that when a person reaches for a cup that has a small handle, not only will the transport and grasp kinematics differ from reaching for a cup with no handle, but the movement time will also be slower, because of the increased accuracy demands of grasping the small handle.

A different approach to relating prehension actions to Fitts' law was reported by Latash and Jaric (2002). They developed a way to identify an index of difficulty that would account for the size of a mug and the amount of liquid in it. They reasoned that reaching,

Prehension Situations Illustrate Motor Control Adaptability

An experiment by Steenbergen, Marteniuk, and Kalbfleisch (1995) provides a good illustration of how adaptable the motor control system is. We see this adaptability when people alter movements of a specific action to accommodate characteristics of the task situation. The authors asked the participants to reach and grasp with the right or left hand a Styrofoam cup that was either full or empty. Participants had to grasp the cup, located 30 cm in front of them, then place it on a round target 20 cm to the right or left. Movement analyses of the hand transport and grasp phases revealed interesting differences at the movement level depending on which hand a person used and whether the cup was full or empty. For example, during the transport phase, hand velocity was distinctly faster and peak velocity was earlier when the cup was empty. The grasp aperture time also varied according to the cup characteristic. Maximum grasp aperture occurred earlier in the transport phase for the full cup, a situation demanding more movement precision. In terms of coordination of the joints involved in the action, participants froze the degrees of freedom of the shoulder, elbow, and wrist joints during the prehension movements for both full and empty cups. However, when the cup was full, participants increased stabilization during the movement by making a trunk postural adjustment that moved the shoulder forward.

grasping, and drinking from a mug demands accuracy in a way that should influence arm movement speed as well as coordination of the limb segments involved, which means that Fitts' law should apply. But the accuracy component for this type of task is different from manual aiming tasks. Drinking from a mug, or any container, involves not only the size of the container or handle, but also how full it is. This is because the movement involved is transporting the container from its location to the person's mouth without spilling the contents. In their experiment, the researchers developed a ratio of mug size and water level that calculated an index of difficulty, which like Fitts' law, predicted movement times from initial mug movement to the drinker's mouth.

Implications for Practice

From an applied perspective, the motor control research evidence about prehension has important implications for the development of practice conditions to help people improve their prehension capabilities. Because of the cooperative relationship between the reach, grasp, and object manipulation components, it is essential that prehension practice or therapy strategies involve functional activities (e.g., Wu, Trombly, Lin, & Tickle-Degnen, 1998). In addition, because movement characteristics of reach and grasp components interact in various ways according to object characteristics, it is important that practice involve reaching, grasping, and manipulating a variety of object characteristics and manipulation goals. Finally, because of the interdependent relationship of the components of prehension, it would not be beneficial to separate the reach, grasp, and object manipulation goal so that a person could practice each component separately.

HANDWRITING

Investigation of the control mechanisms responsible for handwriting is a prominent theme in the study of motor control (see Bullock, 2004). Researchers generally agree that different control mechanisms are involved in controlling *what people write* (letters, words, numbers, etc.) and *how they write it* (the writing strokes producing the letters, words, etc., on the writing surface).

When we consider the act of handwriting from an anatomical perspective, we see that there is a great deal of individual variation in terms of limb segment involvement. But when researchers obtain handwriting samples from one person, they offer strong evidence for what Bernstein (1967) referred to as **motor equivalence.** That is, a person can

A CLOSER LOOK

A Handwriting Demonstration of Motor Equivalence

Write Your Signature

1. with a pen in your preferred hand.
2. with a pen in your nonpreferred hand.
3. with a pen held in your mouth by your teeth.
4. with your preferred hand on the chalkboard.

Compare the Spatial Characteristics of the Four Handwriting Samples

1. Describe the similarities you see.
2. Describe the differences you see.

Undoubtedly, specific elements of your signature remained constant regardless of which muscle groups were involved in the writing action. Your ability to engage various muscle groups to write your signature demonstrates how the act of handwriting illustrates the concept of motor equivalence. Variations of this demonstration have been reported by researchers since the 1940s (e.g., Lashley, 1942; Raibert, 1977).

---

adapt to the specific demands of the writing context and adjust size, force, direction, and even muscle involvement to accommodate those demands. The notable outcome is that there is a great degree of similarity in characteristics such as letter forms, writing slant, relative force for stroke production, and relative timing between strokes. People have little trouble varying characteristics such as movement time and writing size, among others.

The complexity of handwriting control makes it difficult to develop a simple control model describing the components of this process. A person can write his or her signature or a familiar phrase with the preferred hand, with the nonpreferred hand, with a foot, or by holding a pen in the mouth. This suggests that at least the spatial features of writing are represented in the memory system in an abstract form. Also, this motor equivalence capability suggests the involvement of coordinative structures in handwriting control.

Another interesting feature of the act of handwriting is that several control processes occur at the same time. To write a sentence, a person must use lexical and semantic cognitive processes, as well as motor control processes. Writing requires the person to retrieve words from memory. These words must have meanings that fit what the writer intends to convey. The written sentence requires specific grammatical construction. The words require a certain spelling, which involves the person's

movement of the limb to produce specific letters that are of an appropriate size and shape for what he or she is writing on. Further, the individual must hold the writing instrument with an appropriate amount of force to allow these letters to be formed. The capability of humans to carry out these various cognitive and motor elements in relatively short amounts of time demonstrates both the complexity and the elegance of the control processes underlying the act of handwriting.

Vision and Handwriting

A substantial amount of research evidence indicates that vision plays an important role in the control of handwriting actions. One of the best demonstrations of this role was provided by Smyth and Silvers (1987), who showed that a person who is asked to write with his or her eyes closed adds extra strokes to some letters, omits strokes from some letters, and duplicates some letters. And if visual feedback is delayed while a person is writing, that person makes many errors, including repeating and adding letters.

---

motor equivalence   the capability of the motor control system to enable a person to achieve an action goal in a variety of situations and conditions (e.g., writing your signature with either hand).

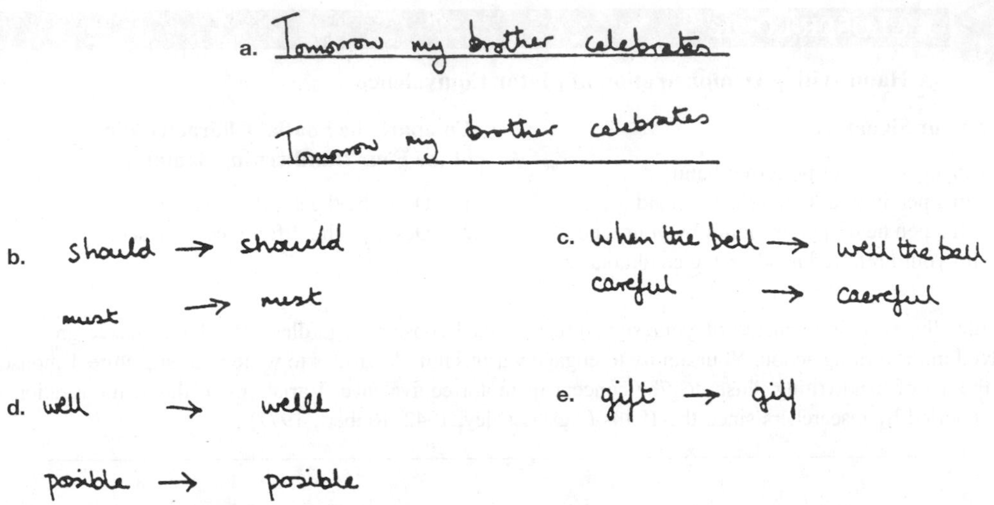

FIGURE 7.3   Handwriting examples from the experiment by Smyth and Silvers showing errors related to writing without vision available (bottom line in (a); right side of arrows in others) as compared to writing with vision available. (a) Shows errors as deviating from the horizontal; (b) shows errors as adding and deleting strokes; (c) shows adding and deleting of letters; (d) shows adding or deleting of repetitions of double letters; (e) shows reversing of letters. [Reprinted from Smyth, M. M., & Silvers, G. (1987). Functions of visions in the control of handwriting. *Acta Psychologica, 65,* 47–64. With kind permission of Elsevier Science-NL, Sara Burgerhartstraat 25, 1055 KV Amsterdam, The Netherlands.]

On the basis of their own research and that of others, Smyth and Silvers proposed that vision performs two distinct functions in the control of handwriting. One function is to help the writer *control the overall spatial arrangement of words on a horizontal line.* We see an example of this function in figure 7.3, where handwriting samples taken from people writing without vision available show distinct deviations from a horizontal line. The second function for vision is to help the writer *produce accurate handwriting patterns,* such as the appropriate strokes and letters required for the written material. Again, evidence of this is seen in figure 7.3. People who wrote without vision available added or omitted strokes, added extra letters, deleted letters, and reversed letters.

BIMANUAL COORDINATION SKILLS

In addition to unimanual coordination skills, people perform many motor skills that require the simultaneous performance of the two arms, i.e., **bimanual coordination.** Sometimes the two limbs do essentially the same thing (*symmetric bimanual coordination*);

this occurs when someone rows a boat or when a person in a wheelchair rolls the wheels of the chair in order to go straight forward or backward. But more interesting from a motor control perspective are *asymmetric bimanual coordination* situations in which each limb must do something different. For example, a guitar player holds strings with one hand to determine chords, while plucking or striking strings with the other hand to produce sound. A skilled drummer can produce one rhythm with one hand while producing another with the other hand. The serve in tennis requires the player to toss the ball into the air with one arm while moving the racquet with a very different movement pattern with the other. And unscrewing the cap from a jar requires each hand to perform different movements because one hand holds the jar.

Bimanual Coordination Preferences

An intriguing question about the performance of bimanual coordination skills is this: *Why is it more difficult to perform skills that require asymmetric than symmetric bimanual coordination?* For example, why is it difficult to rub your stomach with one hand while at the same time tapping the top of your head with the other hand? This task is clearly more difficult to perform (especially the first time you try it) than doing the same movements with each hand. The answer to this question is based on an important characteristic of the motor control system: its inherent preference for controlling limb movements; it prefers symmetry. For the two arms, this means that the two limbs *prefer* to do the same thing at the same time. This preference helps the performance of symmetric bimanual skills, but can lead to problems for asymmetric skills.

The earliest research to demonstrate the motor control system's preference to coordinate the two arms to move together involved the simultaneous performance of discrete movements. In what is now seen as a classic series of experiments, Kelso, Southard, and Goodman (1979) had people perform rapid aiming movements simultaneously with each arm to targets that had the same or different Fitts' index of difficulty (ID) values. Results showed a *temporal basis* for the coordination of the two arms as they moved with similar movement times not only to two targets with the same ID values, but also to two targets that had different ID values.

In the bimanual coordination task just described, the *more difficult* of the two aiming tasks influenced the performance of the arm doing the less difficult task. That is, the arm that was required to move a shorter distance (i.e., the less difficult task) slowed down in comparison to when it moved the same distance alone. Similar results have been shown when *task complexity* differences characterized the bimanual coordination task. For example, the task used in an experiment by Swinnen, Schmidt, Nicholson, and Shapiro (1990) required participants to rapidly move their arms in different spatial-temporal patterns. The task involved moving one arm in a simple one-direction arm-flexion movement while at the same time moving the other in a two-part flexion and extension movement. Both arms were to complete their movements in a movement time of 800 msec. At the beginning of practice, participants generally produced with each arm the similar movement patterns, which typically resembled the more complex two-part movement required by one arm.

Motor Control of Bimanual Coordination

Researchers are not certain how the motor control system is involved in the control of bimanual coordination. At present, we know that there is a synergistic coupling of the arms, which forms a natural coordinative structure that prefers to operate in spatial-temporal symmetry. And an in-phase relationship between the arms (i.e., both arms flexing and extending at the same time) appears to be the predominant symmetrical relationship. In addition, we know that with practice, a person can learn to uncouple (sometimes referred to as "dissociate") the two limbs and simultaneously move his or her arms asymmetrically. But, we do not yet understand the control mechanisms involved in this dissociation process. Some researchers (e.g., Verschueren et al., 1999a) report evidence that *proprioceptive feedback* is important in this process, while others (e.g., Mechsner, Kerzel, Knoblich, & Prinz, 2001) propose that *visual feedback* is the basis for performing the complex asymmetric bimanual coordination.

In terms of motor control theory perspectives on learning to uncouple the limbs, researchers have proposed distinctive views. Those who support the motor program theory argue for generalized motor program involvement, but there is disagreement about whether two new generalized motor programs develop so that each arm becomes controlled by a separate program or whether one generalized motor program develops in which each arm can perform somewhat independently. From a dynamic pattern theory perspective, the control issue is rather straightforward. The initial tendency for the arms to be spatially and temporally coupled represents an attractor state in which a specific relative phase relationship is the order parameter. But, with practice, the stable relationship becomes unstable as the new relationship becomes more stable and a new attractor state emerges.

---

bimanual coordination   a motor skill that requires the simultaneous use of the two arms; the skill may require the two arms to move with the same or different spatial and/or temporal characteristics.

LAB LINKS

Lab 7b in the Online Learning Center Lab Manual for chapter 7 provides an opportunity for you to perform symmetric and asymmetric bimanual coordination tasks that will allow you to experience the intrinsic coordination characteristic of symmetric bimanual coordination even though the achievement of the action goal of the skill requires asymmetric bimanual coordination.

Implications for Practice

Teachers, coaches, and therapists who are aware of bimanual coordination tendencies will recognize the need to give special attention to people who are learning skills that require the arms to perform different spatial-temporal movement patterns. The required unlinking of bimanual movements can be a difficult process for people. But, as both experience and research evidence (e.g., Lee, Swinnen, & Verschueren, 1995; Swinnen et al., 1990; Walter & Swinnen, 1994) tell us, people can achieve success in performing these types of skills when they receive appropriate instruction, feedback, and practice. We will consider some of the strategies practitioners can use to facilitate the learning of asymmetric bimanual coordination skills in Units V and VI.

LOCOMOTION

There is general agreement that at the nervous system level, *central pattern generators* (CPG) in the spinal cord are involved in the control of human locomotion, which you will sometimes see referred to as gait (see Zehr & Duysens, 2004; and Rossignol, Dubuc, & Gossard, 2006, for reviews of CPGs). These mechanisms provide the basis for stereotypic locomotive patterns such as walking and running. We can trace evidence for this spinal level of control to the work of the British Nobel laureate Sir Charles Sherrington and his colleagues at the end of the nineteenth and beginning of the twentieth centuries (e.g., Sherrington, 1906).

Using a procedure known as decerebration, which involves severing the spinal cord from the brain, Sherrington observed that decerebrated cats performed locomotor rhythmic muscular activity similar to that performed by intact animals. Later, Brown (1911) went a step further by additionally severing a cat's sensory pathways to the spinal cord; still, the cat showed rhythmic leg contractions appropriate for walking. More recent research (e.g., Grillner, 1981, 1985) has confirmed and extended these earlier observations (see Field-Fote, 2000, for an excellent overview of the spinal cord's role in the control of locomotion).

It is important to note that CPG is a term used to refer to a "functional network, generating the rhythm and shaping the pattern" of motor neuron activity (Zehr & Duysens, 2004, p. 348). For locomotion, the assumption is that we have at least one CPG per leg located in the spinal cord. Although research evidence supports a CPG-based control of human locomotion, there is also evidence that the CPG is not the sole basis for this control. Results from several studies have shown that proprioceptive feedback from muscle spindles and Golgi tendon organs can influence locomotor movement patterns (see Zehr & Duysens, 2004 for an excellent review of this research, as well as clinical implications). For example, Dietz, Müller, and Colombo (2002) mechanically induced paraplegic and tetraplegic patients to produce stepping movements on a treadmill and found evidence from EMG recordings that afferent feedback from the hip joints was an important part of the locomotor activity. A different approach involved using the tendon vibration technique that was described in chapter 6, with healthy participants (Verschueren, Swinnen, Desloovere, & Duysens, 2003). The researchers showed tendon vibration of specific leg muscles influenced EMG amplitude and muscle activity onset times for muscles involved in the swing and stance phases of walking.

The Rhythmic Structure of Locomotion

To understand how humans control the wide range of gait they are capable of, we must consider higher-level nervous system involvement, along with musculoskeletal dynamics and environmental interactions. The rhythmic structure of locomotor actions is an important characteristic that will serve to illustrate the roles of these various factors.

A CLOSER LOOK

Applying the Dynamic Pattern View of Gait Control to Physical Therapy Interventions

We can see the involvement in locomotor control of dynamic interactions between the person and the environment in the effectiveness of a therapy strategy that helps reestablish normal rhythmic gait. Based on the dynamic pattern control perspective, Wagenaar and van Emmerik (1994) recommended that therapists use various methods to help patients attain spontaneous production of the appropriate rhythmic structures for specific gait patterns by systematically altering gait speeds.

Wagenaar and Beek (1992) showed an example of the effectiveness of this procedure. They used a metronome to present rhythms to hemiplegic patients. When the authors systematically increased the rhythmic beat from 60 to 96 steps a minute, these patients improved the phase relationships of their arms and legs; this in turn positively influenced trunk rotation.

In the discussion in chapter 5 of the study by Shapiro et al. (1981), you saw that on the basis of an analysis of the four components of the Phillipson step cycle, walking and running each have a distinct rhythmic structure. In fact, this rhythmic characteristic is so common for walking and running gaits that mathematical models have been developed to describe their structures. Those who have developed these models view the leg movements in walking and running gaits as operating similar to a pendulum (see Wagenaar & van Emmerik, 1994; and Donker et al., 2001, for discussions about these models).

The rhythmic structure of gait patterns is not limited to leg movements. For example, when a person walks, distinct *rhythmic relationships exist between the movement of the arms and that of the legs,* and the specific character of this relationship relates to walking speed. Craik, Herman, and Finley (1976) first demonstrated this relationship by providing evidence that there are two arm-leg coordination patterns for walking: a 2:1 ratio (i.e., two arm swings to each leg stride) for very slow walking, and a 1:1 ratio for walking at speeds greater than 0.75 m/s (1.7 mi/hr, or 2.72 km/hr). Van Emmerik and Wagenaar (1996) reported that additional research has established that the transition from the 2:1 to the 1:1 arm-leg relationship occurs within the walking speed range of 0.2 to 1.2 m/s (0.5 to 2.7 mi/hr, or 0.3 to 4.32 km/hr). In addition to the arm-leg relationship, the pelvis and thorax also demonstrate a rhythmic relationship during walking. At lower speeds, they move in phase with each other, but out of phase at higher walking speeds.

What is the practical benefit of knowing about these various coordination characteristics of gait patterns? Van Emmerik and Wagenaar (1996) presented an excellent argument, along with research evidence, to support their view that knowing about these characteristics and using them as assessment techniques allow us to identify coordination problems in the trunk and extremities, especially for people with Parkinson's disease. For example, when walking at preferred speeds, Parkinson's patients show pelvis and thorax phase relationships that are exactly opposite those described in the previous paragraph for healthy people.

Another example of the clinical use of coordination characteristics of gait patterns was presented in a study of people who recently had experienced anterior cruciate ligament (ACL) replacement surgery (Kurz, Stergiou, Buzzi, & Georgoulis, 2005). The researchers calculated the relative phase (a coordination quantification technique that was discussed in chapter 2) for the foot-shank and shank-thigh leg segments. The results showed relative phase characteristics for the ACL-reconstructed knee that differed from the normal knee. These differences led the researchers to conclude that the analysis of the relative phase dynamics of the reconstructed knee would provide clinically important information for patient performance at various stages of rehabilitation.

Another application of understanding the rhythmic coordination characteristics of gait is the use of this understanding to develop training or therapy strategies practitioners can use to help people improve their gait. For example, results from an experiment reported by Ford, Wagenaar, and Newell (2007) showed that post-stroke patients improved several aspects of their gait following treadmill training, with a metronome set at specific rhythmic frequencies (which systematically increased and decreased while the treadmill was at a constant speed), and with instructions to move their arms and legs to the beat of the metronome. The improvements included gait cadence, stride length, arm–leg swing coordination, and the phase relationship of the pelvic–thoracic rotation.

Head Stability and Locomotion

When a person engages in locomotor activity, a goal of the motor control system is to *maintain head stability*. Researchers have demonstrated that head stability, as measured by the vertical orientation and minimal horizontal motion, is maintained during locomotor actions such as walking, walking in place, running in place, and hopping (for brief reviews of this research literature, see Cromwell, Newton, & Carlton, 2001; and Holt, Ratcliffe, & Jeng, 1999). In addition, researchers who have investigated the head stability characteristics of people walking at their preferred speed have found that the least amount of head movement in the vertical and anterior–posterior planes occurs at the preferred walking speed (e.g., Latt, Menz, Fung, & Lord, 2008).

Why is head stability so important to maintain during locomotion? The answer relates to the role the head plays. When we consider that the head contains the complex of sensory and motor nervous system components essential for us to navigate through an environment and maintain postural stability so that we don't fall, it becomes evident that head stability is important to maintain during locomotion. In addition, maintaining a stable head position during locomotion optimizes the use of vision in actions in which vision of an object while running is essential for achieving the action goal. For

Vision is used in various ways when we walk on a dirt road.

example, a baseball or tennis player must visually track the flight of the ball while running in order to catch or hit it. Finally, it is interesting in light of the importance of head stability during locomotion that researchers have found that children with cerebral palsy and adults with neurological impairment commonly adopt what could be considered "abnormal" postural and gait characteristics as strategies to enable them to maintain head stability while walking (e.g., Holt, Jeng, Ratcliffe, & Hamill, 1995; Holt, Ratcliffe, & Jeng, 1999).

Gait Transitions

Another important gait characteristic, which was briefly described in chapter 5, is the spontaneous change from a walking to a running gait (and vice versa) at certain speeds. Although these spontaneous gait transitions are common to all people, the speed at which transition occurs varies between individuals. Some people continue to walk at higher speeds than others, whereas some people continue to run at lower speeds than others. In addition, the walk-to-run transition typically occurs at higher speeds than the run-to-walk transition.

Why do spontaneous gait transitions occur? There is general agreement that the reason is not due to physical limitations. As a result, researchers have developed and tested several hypotheses (see Guerin & Bardy, 2008, for an overview of these hypotheses). The most prevalent of these has been that the transition occurs to minimize metabolic energy consumption (i.e., VO_2). Although researchers have provided evidence that supports this hypothesis, others have reported results that fail to support it (see Hreljac, 1993). At present, no single cause for gait transitions has been determined. Interestingly, Turvey et al. (1999), after reporting results that did not support their hypothesis based on the role of kinetic energy, expressed doubts that a single cause can be identified because of the nature of complex biological systems. Kao and Ringenbach (2004) found evidence that supported the Turvey et al. conclusion by demonstrating that multiple factors, which may be specific to individuals, underlie gait transitions. However, until further research is carried out, the identification of the reason(s) why people spontaneously change gaits at certain speeds remains a puzzle for researchers to solve.

Vision and Locomotion

In the preceding section, you saw that the control of locomotion depends on both proprioception and vision as sources of sensory information to augment and modify movement commands generated by the CNS. In this section we will look more specifically at the important roles that vision plays in two types of activities involving locomotion. As you will see, vision is more than a source of feedback; it also influences movement characteristics *before* action initiation.

Contacting objects. When you walk or run in your daily or sports activities, there are situations in which you must make contact with an object with one or both feet. For example, if you need to cross a street with a lot of puddles it is essential that your feet make contact with the dry areas among the puddles as you walk. In sports activities, baseball players must step on bases as they run, gymnasts performing the vault must contact the spring board with their feet at the end of the run-up, and long jumpers must step on the take-off board at the end of the run-up to the jumping area.

To discuss the motor control issues associated with making contact with objects with our feet during locomotor activity, we will use the long-jump situation as an example. It is an activity that many researchers have studied, with results that apply to other types of activities. To successfully perform the long jump, the athlete needs to make contact with the take-off board at maximum running speed. This run-up portion of the long jump can be thought of as similar to an aiming task; it requires the athlete to move a certain distance and then hit a target. The target is the take-off board, which is about 20 cm long (from front to back) and 1.2 m wide (from side to side). If any part of the athlete's foot extends beyond the back edge of the board (i.e., the edge nearer the landing pit), a foul is called and the jump does not count. On the other hand, if the tip of the foot strikes short of the board, the jump is that amount shorter because the jump distance is measured from the back edge of the board.

The motor control question related to the run-up is this: What does the athlete do during the run-up to hit the take-off board as accurately as possible? One possibility is that the athlete performs the same programmed step pattern during each run-up on each jump. This would mean that any error in hitting the take-off board would be due to an error in the programmed step pattern. However, research evidence has shown that this is *not* what the athlete does. Although each long jumper takes a number of steps during each run-up that is specific to him

A CLOSER LOOK

Gymnasts' Use of Vision While Walking on the Balance Beam

Shannon Robertson and her colleagues (e.g., Robertson, Collins, Elliott, & Starkes, 1994; Robertson & Elliott, 1996) have shown that skilled gymnasts use visual information as they perform their routines on a balance beam. In several studies, they involved gymnasts walking as fast as possible across a standard balance beam (5 m long × 10.5 cm wide). In the Robertson and Elliott (1996) experiment, nine female college varsity gymnasts performed the task with full vision, no vision, or distorted vision (goggles with a prism oriented vision to the left or right). Results for each condition were as follows:

	Amount of time to cross the beam	Number of times stepped off beam	Number of steps to cross beam	Number of form errors
Full Vision	3.0 sec	0.2	7	10
No Vision	4.0 sec	2.5	8	30
Distorted Vision	7.5 sec	8.4	9	42

The increase in form errors when the gymnasts had no vision or distorted vision was due primarily to deviations from an upright posture. These deviations resulted from the gymnasts' postural adjustments to maintain their balance as they walked.

or her, the step lengths of the last few steps vary across run-ups. Most scholars now agree that the reason for this is that the athletes use visual information that specifies the amount of time it will take to contact the take-off board. The motor control system uses this *time-to-contact* information, which is specified by the visual variable *tau* (τ), to make stride-length adjustments during the last few steps to correct for the distance error that has accumulated during the run-up. Without these adjustments, the athlete would either be short or long of the take-off board.

In what has become a classic experiment demonstrating this time-to-contact influence for a locomotor skill requiring object contact, Lee, Lishman, and Thomson (1982) filmed three highly skilled female long jumpers during their approaches to the take-off board. By analyzing stride-length changes as each athlete approached and contacted the take-off board for a series of six long jumps, the researchers observed several important gait pattern characteristics. We will examine these using the results from one of these athletes (an Olympic-level performer), presented in figure 7.4.

Initially, the athlete's stride length increased at a relatively constant rate for the first five to six strides; it then began to become similar for the next six strides. These strides were relatively consistent across the six jumps. Then, *on the final six strides,* something different occurred. The athlete made stride-length adjustments so that she could hit the board accurately. In fact, she made almost 50 percent of these adjustments on the last stride. The lower half of the figure shows why she had to make these adjustments. As the athlete ran down the track, small inconsistencies in each stride had a cumulative effect, so that when she was five strides from the board the error had risen to 37 cm. If she had not adjusted her stride lengths on the remaining strides, she would have missed hitting the take-off board by a long distance.

These stride-length characteristics led the authors to describe the long jump run-up as consisting of two phases: an *initial accelerative phase,* where an athlete produces stereotypic stride patterns, followed by a *zeroing-in phase,* where the athlete modifies stride patterns to eliminate accumulated error. They concluded that a long jumper

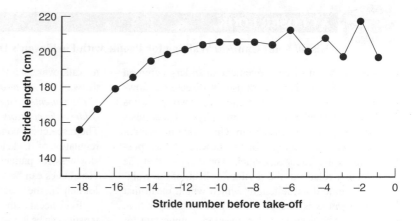

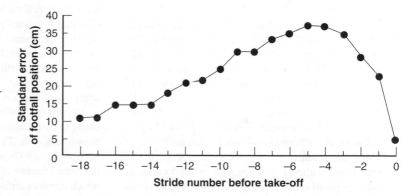

FIGURE 7.4 Redrawn from results of the experiment by Lee, Lishman, and Thomson showing the stride-length characteristics (top) and the standard errors for six long jumps by an Olympic-class female long jumper. [From Lee, D. N., Lishman, J. R., & Thomson, J. A. (1982). Regulation of gait in long jumping. *Journal of Experimental Psychology: Human Perception and Performance, 8,* 448–459. Copyright © 1982 The American Psychological Association. Adapted with permission.]

bases the correction process during the second phase on visual information obtained *in advance of* these strides. This means that the visual system picks up time-to-contact information from the board and directs the locomotor control system to make appropriate stride-length modifications for the strides remaining until contact with the take-off board.

It is worth noting that the use of visual time-to-contact information to regulate gait does not depend on the expertise of the person. Although the participants in the Lee and authors long jump study were highly skilled, novice long jumpers also have demonstrated similar stride-length adjustments consistent with the influence of *tau* (Berg, Wade, & Greer, 1994).

In the second phase of the run-up, the percentage of the total stride-length corrections made on each stride can be used as a way to demonstrate the *perception-action coupling* involved in the long jump run-up. If *tau* is the visual variable that influences the long jumper's performance during this phase of the run-up, we would expect to see evidence of a coupling between the visually detected time-to-contact and movement corrections. This coupling would be best demonstrated by a linear relationship between the percentage of the total adjustment and the number of strides remaining to hit the take-off board. Montagne et al. (2000) presented evidence of this relationship in a study involving long jumpers of various levels of expertise. As you can see in figure 7.5,

Visual Cues Can Aid Walking for People with Parkinson's Disease

One of the primary movement disorders common to people who have Parkinson's disease is slowness of gait (i.e., gait hypokinesia). Two questions have interested researchers and physical therapists concerning this gait problem. One, what movement characteristic accounts for the slowness? Two possibilities are cadence, which would mean that the difficulty relates to the rhythm, or beat, of the walking pace, and stride length, which would mean that the slowness is due to strides that are shorter than normal. The answer to this question is important for the second question: Is there a rehabilitation strategy that would help patients improve their control of walking gait speed?

To address these questions, Morris, Iansek, Matyas, and Summers (1994) compared walking gaits of Parkinson's patients with age-matched controls (60–85 years old) for instructions to walk along a 12 m walkway at "a comfortable pace" and at a "fast speed." *The results showed this:*

• *The Parkinson's patients walked more slowly than the control participants at both speeds, and had shorter stride lengths, but similar cadences.*

Then, the researchers provided visual cues to the Parkinson's patients by placing 50 cm by 5 cm laminated strips of cardboard on the walkway at intervals matching the mean stride lengths of the control participants for each speed. The patients were instructed to walk over each floor marker as they walked along the walkway. *The results showed this:*

• *The patients' velocity and stride lengths were similar to the controls for both speeds.*

The researchers concluded from their results that the regulation of stride length was the "key deficit" in gait slowness for patients with Parkinson's disease. And visual cues can be an effective rehabilitation strategy for helping these patients regulate gait speed.

Evidence that the improvement in these gait characteristics can be long-lasting was provided in a case study reported by Sidaway, Anderson, Danielson, Martin, and Smith (2006). The Parkinson's patient walked during a four-week training period with visual cues on the floor that were similar to those used in the Morris et al. (1994) experiment. At the end of the training period, the patient's stride length and gait speed improved. What was especially impressive, however, was that these improvements were maintained without the use of the visual cues one month after the training ended.

In light of these results for visual cues, it is interesting to note that several researchers (e.g., McIntosh, Brown, Rice, & Thaut, 1997; Baker, Rochester, & Nieuwboer, 2007) have provided evidence to show the effectiveness of rhythmic auditory stimulation, which involves embedding a tone at specific intervals in music to provide a stepping pace for Parkinson's patients. Walking speeds can be varied by using music of different tempos.

---

the percentage of the total amount of adjustment increased linearly for the final five strides from the take-off board. And, similar to what Lee, Leshman, and Thomson (1982) found for elite jumpers, approximately 40 percent of the total amount of adjustment occurred on the stride before the take-off board.

Researchers have found that other types of gait also involve adjustments during locomotion on the basis of visual time-to-contact information. Some examples are walking a given distance and stepping on the target with a specified foot (Laurent & Thomson, 1988); running and stepping on targets, as people do when crossing a creek on rocks (Warren, Young, & Lee, 1986); doing run-ups to the springboard and horse while performing the vault in women's gymnastics (Meeuwsen & Magill, 1987). In all of these activities, the persons adjust stride length on the basis of time-to-contact information as they near the targets.

Avoiding contact with objects. When you walk through a doorway, you want to avoid contact with the sides of the doorway. How do you successfully

A CLOSER LOOK

Avoiding Obstacles While Walking or Running

Research by James Cutting and his colleagues at Cornell University (e.g., Cutting, 1986; Vishton & Cutting, 1995) has shown that if a person is walking or running and wishes to maintain footspeed while avoiding an obstacle, three time periods are critical:

The Time Needed to

1. recognize that an object needs to be avoided;
2. adjust the footfall;
3. turn the foot to avoid the obstacle.

Of these three periods, the first is the most critical and takes up about 75 percent of the distance covered while the subject is approaching an object.

Implication for Clinical Rehabilitation and Sport
Because of the importance of early visual recognition of an object to be avoided, it is important to train people to actively visually search the environment in which they locomote. To avoid collision, a person must recognize objects sufficiently early to allow appropriate movement adjustments. Therefore, the therapist or coach who focuses training on only the movement-adjustment aspect of this task ignores the most critical component of object recognition.

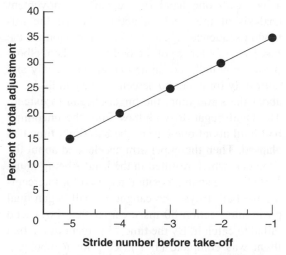

FIGURE 7.5 The percentage of the total amount of stride-length adjustments for the final five strides for the long-jumpers in the experiment by Montagne et al. [Modified Figure 3 from Montagne et al. (2000). A perception-action coupling type of control in long jumping. *Journal of Motor Behavior, 32,* 37–43.]

achieve the action goal of this locomotor activity? Research evidence indicates that vision provides the motor system with *body-scaled information* about the size of a specific body part in relation to the size of the doorway. A person decides how to orient his or her body to walk through an open doorway on the basis of visually perceived information related to the proportion of his or her shoulder width to the width of the door opening. More specifically, Warren and Whang (1987) reported that a doorway needs to be 1.3 times wider than the person's shoulder width for the person to determine that he or she can walk through it without having to turn his or her shoulders.

A different type of object avoidance situation occurs when we need to go safely over an obstacle in our pathway. People can employ a variety of avoidance strategies while walking or running to accomplish this goal. Patla and his colleagues have reported several studies in which they investigated the role vision plays in the strategy people select to go over an obstacle (e.g., Patla et al., 2002; Mohagheghi, Moraes, & Patla, 2004). Here again, vision provides predictive information that specifies to the motor control system the type of step-pattern alteration that will be needed to step over the object. The primary information is specified by the height, width, and shape of the object. In addition, predictions about how solid or fragile the object is are also important. For example, people will increase the height of their leading leg, which increases the amount of toe clearance, more for an obstacle perceived to be fragile than for an object perceived to be solid.

A CLOSER LOOK

Vision Provides Body-Scaled Information When We Climb Stairs

Stair climbing is a common, everyday activity. But, how do we know that the stairs we need to climb are actually climbable? That is, how do we know that we can use a typical forward-stepping movement to climb a set of stairs? Vision operates in this situation in a way that is similar to how it enables us to determine if we can walk through a doorway without having to turn our shoulders to avoid contact with the sides of the doorway. The visual system detects and uses body-scaled information that involves the *relationship between the stair/step height and the person's leg length.* Researchers (e.g., Warren, 1984) have shown that if the riser height is equal to or less than 88 percent of the person's leg length, the person will judge that stair step to be climbable by a normal, forward-stepping movement. If the proportion exceeds 88 percent, the person will use a different movement pattern to climb the stair steps, such as children often do when they sit on the step first, or lift a knee to put the lower leg on the step first.

CATCHING A MOVING OBJECT

In many ways, catching an object is like the prehension action discussed earlier. However, there are two important differences. First, catching involves intercepting a moving object; prehension typically involves a stationary object. Second, the grasp of the object in the catching action ends the action; prehension typically involves doing something with the grasped object. Although in some sport situations, such as baseball and softball, there are occasions in which a player must remove the ball from the glove after the catch and throw the ball, this situation is uniquely sport and situation specific and will not be included in this discussion of catching.

Three Phases of Catching an Object

To catch an object, the person must first move the arm and hand toward the oncoming object. Then, he or she must shape the hand to catch the object. Finally, the fingers must grasp the object.

Williams and McCririe (1988) provided research evidence demonstrating the phases of catching with their study of 11-year-old boys trying to catch a ball with one hand (figure 7.6). A movement analysis of the catching action showed the following sequence. There was no arm motion for the first 160 to 240 msec of the ball flight. Then, elbow flexion gradually began and continued slowly and uniformly for about 80 percent of the ball flight. At about the same time, the fingers began to extend. The hand began to withdraw from the oncoming ball until about one-half of the ball flight time had elapsed. Then the upper arm accelerated about the shoulder, which resulted in the hand's being transported to the spatial position required for intercepting the ball. Boys who caught the ball began final positioning action 80 msec earlier than boys who failed to catch it. By the time 75 percent of the ball flight was complete (113 msec prior to contact), each successful boy had his hand and fingers in a ready state for catching the ball.

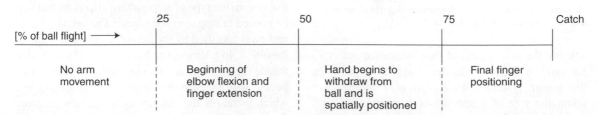

FIGURE 7.6 The arm, hand, and fingers movement characteristics involved in catching a ball in relation to the percentage of ball flight time. [Data from Williams & McCririe (1988). *Journal of Human Movement Studies, 14,* 241–247.]

These results indicate that vision provides advance information enabling the motor control system to *spatially and temporally set the arms, hands, and fingers before the ball arrives* so that the individual can catch the ball. It is especially noteworthy here that the person bases the grasping action on visual information obtained *before* the ball actually makes contact with the hand, rather than on feedback obtained after the ball has hit the hand. The extent of involvement of proprioception during pre–ball contact stages is not well understood. However, we know that proprioceptive and tactile feedback become involved after contact because the catcher needs to make adjustments to the grasp. Research evidence also shows that both central and peripheral vision operate when a person picks up information critical to catching an object.

Vision of the Object and Catching

Catching an object, such as a ball, is a complex perception-action skill that has challenged researchers in their efforts to understand how the visual and motor control systems interact. The results of these research efforts have identified several factors that influence successful catching which relate specifically to the visual observation of the object.

Amount of visual contact time. One factor is the amount of time of visual contact with the moving object. Research evidence indicates that constant visual contact is needed during two critical periods of time in the object's flight: the initial part of the flight and the period of time just prior to contact with the hand(s). How much time is required during each of these time periods has not been established, and undoubtedly depends on the situation.

Some researchers have reported evidence indicating that observation of the initial flight should continue until the ball reaches its zenith (Amazeen, Amazeen, Post, & Beek, 1999), although others have indicated that only the first 300 msec of flight are important (e.g., Whiting, Gill, & Stephenson, 1970). The important point here is that visual contact with the object is needed for an amount of time during its initial flight phase that is sufficient

LAB LINKS

Lab 7c in the Online Learning Center Lab Manual provides an opportunity for you to compare catching a ball when you can and when you cannot see your hands.

to obtain information to determine estimates of the direction and distance of the flight.

In terms of visual contact with the object during its final portion of flight, research evidence indicates that the time period between 200 and 300 msec before hand contact is critical for successful catching (Savelsbergh, Whiting, Pijpers, & van Santvoord, 1993), although the precise amount of time may depend on the specific characteristics of the situation, especially the length of time the object is in flight and its velocity (see Bennett, Davids, & Craig, 1999). The need to see the ball during the final portion of its flight is to obtain specific time-to-contact information for the final spatial positioning of the hand and fingers, and the timing of the closing of the fingers during the grasp of the object.

What about visual contact with the object in flight between these two time periods? Research by Elliott and his colleagues (e.g., Elliott, Zuberec, & Milgram, 1994) indicates that continuous visual contact with the ball during this period of time is *not* essential. The Elliott et al. (1994) study showed that people can catch a ball that has a flight time of 1 sec by *intermittently seeing brief "snapshots"* (approximately 20 msec) of the ball every 80 msec of its flight. Thus, people can use visual samples of ball flight characteristics to obtain the information they need to catch the ball. This capability to use intermittent visually detected information to catch an object helps us understand how an ice hockey goalie can catch a puck or a soccer goalkeeper can catch a ball even though he or she must visually track it through several pairs of legs on its way to the goal.

Tau and catching. Another important motor control question concerning vision of the object and catching is this: Does the motor control system use the visual variable *tau* to enable people to catch an object? Although there is considerable debate about the answer to this question (see Caljouw, van der Ramp, & Savelsbergh, 2004, for a more complete discussion of this issue), a significant amount of research evidence indicates that *tau* is involved in solving the time-to-contact problem when catching an object, although *tau* alone does not appear to be sufficient to explain vision's role in catching (Mazyn, Lenoir, Montagne, & Savelsbergh, 2004).

When an object moves directly toward a person, the angle created at the person's eyes by the top and bottom edges of the object increases in size in a nonlinear way as the object approaches the person. The nonlinearity refers to the perceived slowness of this angle increase when the ball is farther away from the person and the rapid increase in size as it gets close to the person. It is this rate of expansion of angular size, which is often referred to as *looming,* that the visual system uses to determine when collision of the object with the person will occur. For the action of catching, this optical expansion establishes *when* the appropriate movement characteristics for the arm, hand, and finger will be in place to catch the object. For objects that do not move directly toward the person but require the person to run to catch them, *tau* also provides the visual basis for timing the catch, although the mathematics for calculating *tau* are distinctly more complex.

Vision of the hands and catching. An important question related to catching is this: *Must a person be able to see his or her hands throughout the flight of a ball to successfully catch the ball?* In one of the first experiments investigating this question, Smyth and Marriott (1982) attached a screen to the participants so they could see the oncoming ball, but not their hands. When the participants were able to see their hands, they averaged 17.5 catches out of 20 balls thrown. However, when they could *not* see their hands, they were able to catch an average of 9.2 balls out of 20. More important, when they could *not* see their hands, participants typically made a hand-positioning error: they could not get their hands into the correct spatial position

to intercept the ball. But when they could see their hands, their typical errors involved grasping: they initiated too early the finger flexion they needed to grasp the ball.

Interesting as the Smyth and Marriott results may be, research since their work has shown that *experience* is an important factor influencing a person's catching success when he or she cannot see his or her hands. We might expect this, as Davids (1988) argued, because the effective use of peripheral vision is a function of age and experience. Because we use peripheral vision to see our hands as we try to catch an oncoming object, it is logical to expect that our need to see our hands to catch a ball will depend on our age and experience.

Fischman and Schneider (1985) provided empirical evidence that supports the influence of experience. Using the same experimental procedures as those of Smyth and Marriott, they included participants who had at least five years' experience in varsity baseball or softball. The results of this experiment (figure 7.7) showed that although the number of catches decreased when the people could not see their hands, the type of error did not depend on whether or not the participants could see their hands. However, for the inexperienced ball catchers, more positioning errors than grasp errors occurred when they could not see their hands.

Researchers now generally agree that both ball catching experience and skill level influence the need for a person to see his or her hands while catching a ball (see Bennett, Davids, & Craig, 1999). More-experienced and skilled catchers do not need to see their hands; less-experienced and low-skill catchers require vision of their hands. The reason for this difference appears to relate to a person's capability to use proprioceptive feedback to catch a moving object. The less-experienced, low-skilled person needs visual feedback to assist in the use of proprioceptive feedback to spatially position his or her arms and hands and to effectively grasp the object. In terms of helping people improve their catching skill, this relationship between experience and the need for vision of the hands suggests that beginners and less-skilled people should practice

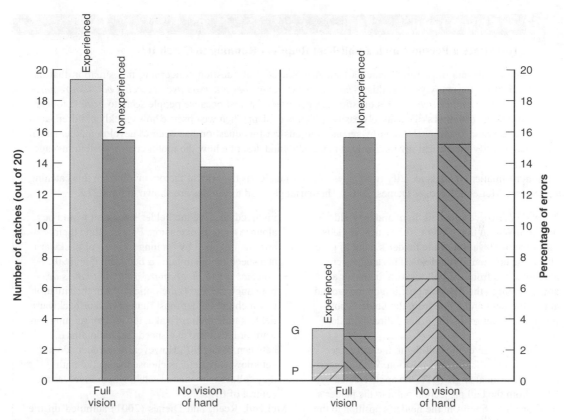

FIGURE 7.7   Results of the experiment by Fischman and Schneider showing the number of right-hand catches made (out of 20 chances) for experienced softball/baseball players and nonexperienced subjects and the percentage of errors made (based on 360 attempts) by each group that were classified as positioning (P) or grasp (G) errors when subjects either could or could not see their hands. [*Source:* Data from Fischman, M. G., & Schneider, T. (1985). Skill level, vision, and proprioception in simple one-hand catching. *Journal of Motor Behavior, 17,* 219–299.]

catching primarily in situations where they can see their hands throughout the ball flight, from the point where the ball leaves the thrower's hand until the ball is grasped.

STRIKING A MOVING OBJECT

Like the action of catching a moving object, striking a moving object involves the spatial and temporal interception of an object. And, as we discussed for catching, the motor control of this action involves the coordination of movements that is influenced by vision in specific ways. Two experiments investigating the striking of a moving

object illustrate how vision influences the control of this action.

Vision and Baseball Batting
The classic experiment related to the role of vision in baseball batting was performed many years ago by Hubbard and Seng (1954). Using cinematography techniques, they found that professional baseball players tracked the ball only to a point, at which time they made their swing. This point did not coincide with the point where the bat made contact with the ball. Each batter tended to synchronize the start of the step forward with the

A CLOSER LOOK

How Does a Person Catch a Ball That Requires Running to Catch It?

In many sports, players must run to catch a ball. A motor control question concerning this situation that has intrigued scientists for many years is this: *What control strategy does a person use to catch a ball that requires running some distance to catch it?* This question has generated interest because people seem to be able to learn to successfully perform this skill relatively easily, which is evident when we observe how quickly children learn this skill. The primary approach taken by scientists to answer this question has been to develop mathematical models that identify the critical favors involved in this skill and describe how the motor control system manages these factors.

The mathematical models identify two angles of two triangles as the critical factors involved in this catching situation (see McLeod, Reed, & Deines, 2001). These triangles and the angles are shown in figure 7.8.

- *Triangle 1* involves the ball flight and the fielder's position. Within this triangle, the critical angle is the angle of elevation of the fielder's point of gaze above the horizontal (angle α). This angle is created by a line from the ball location in the air at any moment to the fielder's position on the ground at that moment and a line from the fielder's position to the location on the ground directly under the ball.
- *Triangle 2* involves the ball flight, the ball projection point, and the fielder's position. Within this triangle, the critical angle (β) is the angle created by a line from the ball projection point to the fielder's position and a line from the fielder's position to the location on the ground directly under the ball.

Research based on this type of mathematical model has resulted in some general agreement with Chapman's (1968) original model for the catching situation in which the person must run straight forward or backward. However, there is no consensus among scientists for the situation in which the person must run to the side to catch the ball.

- *To catch a ball that requires running directly forward or backward,* angle α is the primary angle

involved because the fielder's position would be along A₂ and its extension. Fielders time their arrival at the ball by running forward or backward at a speed that maintains α between 0° and 90°.
- *To catch a ball that requires running to the side,* both angles α and β are critical. As in the situation in which the fielder must run forward or backward, fielders time their arrival at the ball by running forward or backward at a speed that maintains α between 0° and 90°. However, researchers do not yet know why fielders choose the spatial path they follow to make the catch, which involves the control of β.

McLeod, Reed, and Dienes (2001) summed up the status of our current knowledge about the issue of how people run to catch a ball by saying: "We understand how α is controlled but not β" (p. 1355). Regardless of how this issue is resolved, the important point in terms of the discussion in this chapter is the critical involvement of the visual system. And vision appears to be involved in a way that requires little conscious control of the movements that must be executed to enable a person to achieve the action goal.

---

release of the ball from the pitcher's hand. And, perhaps most important, the durations of the batters' swings were remarkably consistent from swing to swing, indicating that it was the initiation of the swing that batters adjusted according to the speed of the oncoming pitch. Interestingly, these findings agree precisely with expectations from a *tau*-based strategy for hitting. That is, the initiation of the batting action occurred at a critical time to contact.

Some of the findings of Hubbard and Seng have been either verified or extended in research reported since their study. For example, thirty years later, Bahill and LaRitz (1984) used more sophisticated technology to closely monitor eye and head movements of a major league baseball player and several college baseball players. The study was done in a laboratory situation that simulated players' responses to a high-and-outside fastball thrown

A CLOSER LOOK

"Watch the Ball All the Way to Your Bat!"

A common instruction coaches give when teaching hitting in baseball is to tell players, "Watch the ball all the way to your bat." In light of this, it is interesting to note that research (e.g., Bahill & LaRitz, 1984) indicates that batters probably never see the bat hit the ball. If they do, it is because they have jumped in their visual focus from some point in the ball flight to the bat contact point. They do not visually track the ball continuously all the way to bat contact because this is virtually a physical impossibility. Batters commonly track the ball to a certain point and then visually jump to a point where they predict the ball will be at bat contact.

It is worth noting that more-skilled batters watch the ball for a longer amount of time than less-skilled players. Beginners tend to have the bat swing initiation movement influence their head position and "pull" their head out of position to see the ball/bat contact area.

From an instruction point of view, these characteristics suggest that *it is worthwhile* to instruct a person, "Watch the ball all the way to your bat." Even though the person can't really do that, this instruction directs the person's visual attention so that the person tracks the ball for as long as physically possible and keeps his or her head in position to see the ball/bat contact area.

by a left-handed pitcher to a right-handed batter. The major league player visually tracked the ball longer than the college players did. The college players tracked the ball to a point about 9 ft in front of the plate, at which point their visual tracking began to fall behind the ball. The major league player kept up with the ball until it reached a point about 5.5 ft in front of the plate before falling behind in his tracking. Also, regardless of the

pitch speed, the major league player followed the same visual tracking pattern and was very consistent in every stance he took to prepare for the pitch. While tracking the ball, his head position changed less than one degree across all pitches but he never moved his body.

Batting also involves perception—action coupling, as demonstrated by research by Katsumata (2008). Two timing characteristics showed this coupling. First, as other researchers have reported, the timing of the initiation of stepping with the front foot and its associated weight shift was influenced by the speed of the pitch; stepping initiation began later for slow pitches than for fast pitches.

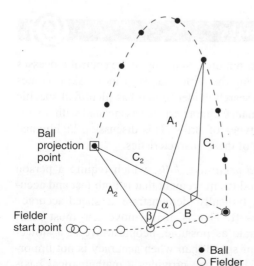

FIGURE 7.8 An illustration depicting the critical angles that McLeod, Reed, and Dienes propose the motor control system must manage so that a fielder can run and catch a ball. The filled circles represent the locations of the ball during its flight; the open circles represent the locations of the fielder who must run to catch the ball. The figure shows a ball hit to the fielder's right. To make the figure represent a ball hit along the line directly in front or behind the fielder, the lines that converge to form angles α and β (which are to the left of the final ball and fielder location) would converge to form these angles along line C_2 in front of or behind the final ball and fielder location. [*Source:* Modified Figure 1, p. 1348 in McLeod, P., Reed, N., & Dienes, Z. (2001). Toward a unified fielder theory: What we do not yet know about how people run to catch a ball. *Journal of Experimental Psychology: Human Perception and Performance, 27,* 1347–1355.]

General Vision Training Programs for Athletes: Do They Improve Sports Performance?

Bruce Abernethy and his colleagues at the University of Queensland in Australia have asserted for many years that although general vision training programs (e.g., Eyerobics) may help to improve certain basic vision functions, they do not improve sport-specific performance. Abernethy and Wood (2001) presented three lines of reasoning, all of which are supported by research evidence, as the basis for their position:

- Above-normal basic visual function (e.g., foveal and peripheral acuity, contrast sensitivity) does not favor elite athletes. A significant amount of research has shown that the visual advantage of elite athletes is sports-specific and perceptual in nature, i.e., the interpreting and use of visual information to specific sports activities.
- Although many commonly measured visual functions can improve with training and repetitive practice, many of the reported improvements occur for people with visual defects. And, the exercises used to train specific visual functions are commonly

procedures that are the same as, or similar to, the tests used to evaluate the functions.
- Experimental evidence is lacking to validate the effectiveness of general vision training programs for improving sports performance. In fact, in the experiment reported in this article, two visual training programs (Sports Vision and Eyerobics) led to performance improvements that were no better than reading about and watching televised tennis matches during the four-week training time, which consisted of four 20 min sessions each week.

Second, the coordination of the timing of the initiation of the batter's moving his front foot forward and the initiation of swinging the bat was consistent regardless of pitch speed. Thus the temporal coupling of these events establishes a well-developed coordinative structure for the action of batting a pitched baseball.

Vision and Table Tennis Striking

In a study of five top table tennis players in the Netherlands, Bootsma and van Wieringen (1990) showed from movement analysis results that the players could not rely completely on consistent movement production. Players seemed to compensate for differences in the initiation times of their swings in order to hit the ball as fast and as accurately as possible. For example, when time to contact was shorter at swing initiation, players compensated by applying more force during the stroke. And evidence suggests that some of these players were making very fine adjustments to their swings while they were moving. Thus, whereas visual information may trigger the initiation of the swing and provide information about

its essential characteristics, vision also provides information that the player can use to make compensatory adjustments to the initiated swing, although these are very slight in terms of time and space quantities.

SUMMARY

Much of our understanding of the control processes underlying the performance of motor skills comes from research evidence that has identified specific performance characteristics associated with a variety of types of skills. This discussion highlighted several of these characteristics.

- *Speed-accuracy skills,* which require a person to produce movement that is both fast and accurate, typically demonstrate a speed-accuracy trade-off. That is, if the movement must be as accurate as possible, people move at a slower rate of speed than when accuracy is not important. Fitts' law provides a mathematical basis for predicting this trade-off on the basis of the task's movement distance and target size characteristics.

▶ Fitts' law applies to a wide range of motor skill performance situations in daily living activities and sports skills.

▶ Both open- and closed-loop motor control processes operate when a person performs a speed-accuracy skill.

▶ The role of vision in the control of speed-accuracy skills depends on the phase of the limb movement.

• Performance of *prehension skills,* which involve the reaching for and grasping of objects, demonstrates the synergistic temporal coupling of movement components that allow a person to achieve an action goal in a variety of situations. The transport and grasp components function interdependently by adjusting certain movement kinematics to adapt to specific characteristics of the object to be grasped and the manipulation goal of the prehensive action. Unlike manual aiming, pointing, and reaching, prehension movement kinematics vary during both the transport and the grasp phases as a function of what the performer intends to do with the object after it is grasped.

▶ The role of vision in the control of prehension skills is similar to that of speed-accuracy skills except that visual feedback influences the grasp component according to the grasp and object manipulation requirements of the intended use of the object.

• *Handwriting* demonstrates an important motor control characteristic known as motor equivalence, which means that a person can achieve the same action goal in a variety of situations that require movement adaptations dictated by the environmental context or by task characteristics such as size, force, direction, and muscles involved. The movement adaptations result in remarkable similarities in handwriting characteristics such as letter forms and the relative time relationship between strokes, among others.

▶ Vision influences the control of the overall spatial arrangement of words on a horizontal line and the production of accurate handwriting patterns.

• *Bimanual coordination skills* require the simultaneous performance of the two arms. Some tasks require symmetric bimanual coordination (i.e., both arms perform in the same way at the same time); others require asymmetric bimanual coordination (i.e., each arm performs differently). An important motor control characteristic of these skills is the natural, or intrinsic, spatial and temporal coupling of the arms, which means that we have a preference to move the arms symmetrically. Personal experience and research evidence shows that people can learn to uncouple the arms to perform asymmetric bimanual coordination skills. At the present time, researchers have not determined the specific motor control mechanism that underlies the control of arms in this uncoupled, asymmetric state, especially in terms of the roles played by proprioceptive and visual feedback.

• The performance of *locomotion* actions, such as walking and running, is characterized by the rhythmic relationships that exist between step-cycle components, arm and leg movements, and the movement of the pelvis and thorax. Also, the maintenance of head stability is an important characteristic associated with locomotor activities. And a locomotion characteristic that has yet to be explained in terms of why it occurs is that spontaneous gait transitions (from walking to running, and running to walking) occur at certain gait speeds.

▶ At the nervous system level, central pattern generators (CPG) in the spinal cord provide the basis for the stereotypic locomotor movement patterns, although proprioceptive and visual feedback are also important for the control of locomotion.

▶ The rhythmic structure of locomotion can be observed for the temporal relationships between the two legs as well as between the legs and arms.

▶ The importance and role of vision in the control of locomotion are especially notable in locomotor activities that require the feet to contact an object after running a certain distance (e.g., long-jumping in track and field) and during walking or running (e.g., ascending and descending stairs) and the avoidance of contact with objects (e.g., walking in a crowded hallway).

• The *catching of moving objects* involves control processes similar to those for prehension actions except that catching involves intercepting a moving object and the grasping of the object ends the action. Catching involves three distinct movement phases: moving the arm and hand toward the oncoming object, shaping the hand to catch the object, and using the fingers and hand to grasp the object. The first two phases are typically completed by the time 75 percent of the object flight is complete.

▶ Vision is an important part of the control of catching by providing advance information to the CNS to enable the spatial and temporal presetting of the arms, hands, and fingers before object arrival. Both central and peripheral vision operate in distinct ways to enable a person to catch an oncoming object.

▶ Several factors related to vision influence the achievement of the action goal of catching a moving object. These include the amount of time of visual contact with the object, the portion of the object's flight during which visual contact occurs, and whether or not the hands can be seen during the object's flight.

• The involvement of vision in the control of striking a moving object relates to the influence of vision on the initiation of the striking movements and the compensatory adjustments to the initiated movements.

POINTS FOR THE PRACTITIONER

• When helping people initially learn speed-accuracy skills, you should emphasize achieving the accuracy goal more than the speed goal.

• The application of Fitts' law to practice or training contexts, especially in terms of the index of difficulty (ID), can provide a basis for creating easier and more difficult variations of a skill for people to practice.

• When helping people rehabilitate their prehension capabilities, provide functional prehension activities that include a wide range of object sizes, reach distances, grip configurations, and object uses.

• When helping people learn or rehabilitate their handwriting skill, emphasize that they need to look at what they are writing; monitor this aspect of handwriting performance for evaluation and correction purposes.

• When helping people learn or rehabilitate the performance of bimanual coordination skills, give special attention to the difficulty people may have with learning asymmetric bimanual coordination skills.

• When helping people learn or rehabilitate locomotor actions, monitor the rhythmic relationship between the arms and legs and include this aspect of gait performance for evaluation and correction purposes.

• When helping people learn or rehabilitate locomotor actions, emphasize the need to maintain head stability during locomotion; monitor head movement during locomotion to evaluate head stability in terms of vertical orientation and the amount of horizontal motion of the head.

• When helping people learn or rehabilitate locomotor actions, emphasize the need to maintain visual contact with an object that the person needs to step on or avoid contact with during locomotion; monitor this aspect of locomotion activity performance for evaluation and correction purposes.

• When helping people learn or rehabilitate skills involving the interception of moving objects, such as catching and striking balls or other objects, emphasize the need to maintain visual contact with the object for as long as possible before it begins its flight and during its flight.

RELATED READINGS

Bennett, K. M. B., Adler, C. H., Stelmach, G. E., & Castiello, U. (1993). A kinematic study of the reach to grasp movement in a subject with hemi-Parkinson's disease. *Neuropsychologia, 31,* 709–716.

Bonnard, M., & Pailhous, J. (1993). Intentionality in human gait control: Modifying the frequency-to-amplitude relationship. *Journal of Experimental Psychology: Human Perception and Performance, 19,* 429–443.

Bradshaw, E. J., & Sparrow, W. A. (2001). Effects of approach velocity and foot-target characteristics on the visual regulation of step length. *Human Movement Science, 20,* 401–426.

Cardosa de Oliveira, S., & Barthelemy, S. (2005). Visual feedback reduces bimanual coupling of movement amplitudes but not of directions. *Experimental Brain Research, 162,* 78–88.

Cutting, J. E., Vishton, P. M., & Braren, P. (1995). How to avoid collisions with stationary and with moving objects. *Psychological Review, 102,* 627–651.

Gowen, E., & Miall, R. C. (2006). Eye–hand interactions in tracing and drawing tasks. *Human Movement Science, 25,* 568–585.

Kelso, J. A. S., Fuchs, A., Lancaster, R., Holroyd, T., Cheyne, D., & Weinberg, H. (1998). Dynamic cortical activity in the human brain reveals motor equivalence. *Nature, 392,* 814–818.

Li, L. (2000). Stability landscapes of walking and running near gait transition speed. *Journal of Applied Biomechanics, 16,* 428–435.

Oliveira, F. T. P., & Ivry, R. B. (2008). The representation of action: Insights from bimanual coordination. *Current Directions in Psychological Science, 17,* 130–135.

Schieber, M. H., & Santello, M. (2004). Hand function: Peripheral and central constraints on performance. *Journal of Applied Physiology, 96,* 2293–2300.

Shaffer, D. M., Krauchunas, S. M., Eddy, M., & McBeath, M. K. (2004). How dogs navigate to catch Frisbees. *Psychological Science, 15,* 437–441.

van Vliet, P. M., & Sheridan, M. R. (2007). Coordination between reaching and grasping in patients with hemiparesis and healthy subjects. *Archives of Physical Medicine and Rehabilitation, 88,* 1325–1331.

Xu, D. L., Rosengren, K. S., & Carlton, L. G. (2004). Anticipatory postural adjustments for altering direction during walking. *Journal of Motor Behavior, 36,* 316–326.

Zago, M., McIntyre, J., Senot, P., & Lacquanti, F. (2009). Visuo-motor coordination and internal models for object interception. *Experimental Brain Research, 192,* 571–604.

Zatsiorsky, V. M., & Latash, M. L. (2008). Multifinger prehension: An overview. *Journal of Motor Behavior, 40,* 446–475.

INTERNET RESOURCES

- To participate in an online interactive demonstration of Fitts' law, go to http://www.tele-actor.net/fitts/.

- If you are interested in issues related to human–computer interactions you can see how Fitts' Law applies to interface design at http://particletree.com/features/visualizing-fittss-law/.

- To read an article that describes a power orthosis that allows over-ground training in gait rehabilitation, go to http://www-personal.umich.edu/~ferrisdp/Sawicki,2005.pdf.

- To read a discussion of bimanual coordination and some related neurophysiological research by Dr. Jörn Diedrichsen at the University of Wales Bangor, go to http://www.bangor.ac.uk/~pss412/res_bimancoord.htm.

- To see videos of pneumatically powered lower-limb exoskeletons being used to help people walk, go to the Web site of the Human Neuromechanics Lab at the University of Michigan, at http://www-personal.umich.edu/~ferrisdp/laboratory.html.

- For a discussion of how we catch a ball and how a ball-catching experiment in space with astronauts helped provide a part of the answer, go to http://science.nasa.gov/headlines/y2002/18mar_playingcatch.htm.

- See and learn about a three-finger robotic catcher that can catch balls traveling as fast as 300 km/hr (~180 mi/hr)—go to http://www.newscientist.com/ article.ns?id=dn7790.

- To see a computer vision controlled robot arm reach for, grasp, and place objects in a specific location, go to http://www.youtube.com/ and do a search for "vision controlled robot arm."

STUDY QUESTIONS

1. (a) Describe the speed-accuracy trade-off that occurs in the performance of many motor skills and give two motor skill performance examples (b) How is Fitts' law related to the speed-accuracy trade-off phenomenon?

2. (a) Describe a prehension situation and indicate the components of this situation. (b) Describe the movement characteristics involved in each component, and how they might change in different prehension situations. (c) Discuss what is meant by the term "temporal coupling" and how it relates to prehension actions.

3. (a) Discuss how the skill of handwriting can provide a good example of the meaning of the term *motor equivalence*. (b) Discuss how your handwriting would be affected if you cannot see what you are writing.

4. Discuss why the performance of a skill requiring asymmetric bimanual coordination is difficult when it is first attempted.

5. (a) What are two examples of the rhythmic structures involved in walking and running? (b) Describe how gait lends itself to the use of an identified order parameter and control parameter to be the basis for assessment of coordination problems.

6. Discuss why it is important to maintain head stability during locomotion.

7. (a) Describe a situation in which a person must contact an object, or objects, while running. (b) Discuss the influence of *tau* in this situation and how we know it influences the person's behavior as he or she performs this skill.

8. Discuss how it is possible for a person to catch a ball without seeing his or her hands make the catch.

9. Discuss the role of vision in the skill of hitting a baseball or softball and the implications of this role for teaching a person this skill.

Specific Application Problem:
You are working in your chosen profession. Describe a skill (related to one of those discussed in this chapter) that you may help people learn or improve their performance of. How would you take into account the specific motor control characteristics associated with this skill as you develop strategies to help the people you are working with?

Action Preparation

Concept: Performing voluntary, coordinated movement requires preparation of the motor control system.

After completing this chapter, you will be able to

■ Discuss why reaction time (RT) can be an index of preparation required to perform a motor skill

■ Explain how Hick's law describes the relationship between the number of alternatives in a choice-RT situation and RT

■ Describe various task and situation characteristics that influence action preparation

■ Describe various performer characteristics that influence action preparation

■ Discuss several motor control activities that occur during action preparation

APPLICATION

Many sport, recreation, fitness, and daily activities demonstrate our need to prepare the motor control system to carry out an intended action. For example, many sports events, such as running, swimming, and trap shooting, incorporate the importance of preparation into the rules of the activity by requiring an audible signal warning the competitors to get ready.

Certain performance characteristics of activities also provide evidence of the need to prepare for the action. For example, when you decide to pick up a glass of water for a drink, there is a slight delay between your decision and the intended action. In another example, if you are driving a car along a street and another car unexpectedly pulls out in front of you, there is a measurable time delay between the moment you see this and the moment you begin to move your foot off the accelerator and onto the brake pedal. In each of these very different activity scenarios, the initial movement of the intended action is preceded by an interval of time in which the

motor control system is prepared according to the demands and constraints of the situation.

Consider the preparation of action from a different perspective. Undoubtedly, at some time or other you have said, following a poor performance in an activity, I wasn't "ready." By saying this, you imply that if you had been "ready" you would have performed much better than you just have. Or, if you work with physical therapy patients, you undoubtedly have heard one tell the therapist, "Don't rush me. If I get out of this chair before I'm ready, I'll fall."

> **Application Problem to Solve** Describe a motor skill that you perform or that you teach other people to perform. Describe the motor control characteristics of this skill that you, or the people you teach, must prepare to perform the skill successfully. Are there situations in which there are fewer or more characteristics to prepare? What are these situations and how do they influence the need to prepare fewer or more motor control characteristics?

DISCUSSION

In chapters 5 through 7, we focused on factors influencing the control of the performance of a skill. Although there was occasional mention of the initiation of the action, we only touched on what is involved in the actual preparation of an intended action. In the present discussion, our interest is in what occurs between the intention to act and the initiation of movement to perform the action itself. In the motor control literature, researchers sometimes use the term *movement preparation* to designate this activity. However, in keeping with the distinction we made in chapter 1 between actions and movements, we will use the term **action preparation** when referring to this process.

In this context, *preparation* does not refer to the long-term preparation that occurs during the days prior to an event, but to *the specific preparation the motor control system makes just prior to initiating movement.* We will address two preparation issues here. First, how do different skill, performance-context, and personal factors influence the preparation process? Second, exactly what does the motor control system prepare that makes preparation such a critical part of the performance of any skill? But, before we discuss these issues, we will establish how we know that the motor control system needs to be prepared for action.

ACTION PREPARATION REQUIRES TIME

The principle that the motor control system needs preparation before it can initiate an action has its roots in research carried out in the middle of the nineteenth century by Donders (1868–1969), a Dutch physician. This principle is derived from an inference based on the effects of various factors on observed differences in the amount of time between the onset of a signal telling a person to begin performing a skill and the instant experimenters actually observe the beginning of movement. As you read in chapter 2, we call this interval of time *reaction time (RT)*. When considered in the context of action preparation, *RT is an index of*

preparation required to produce an action.[1] You may sometimes see this interval of time called a *response-delay* interval. By investigating the factors that increase or decrease this time interval and the mental activities that occur during this interval, we can gain some understanding of the action preparation processes our motor control system engages in to enable us to perform a skill.

One of the things that RT tells us is that preparing to produce voluntary movement takes time. Planned movement does not occur instantaneously. Certain actions and circumstances require more preparation than others. In the following sections, we discuss a variety of factors that influence the amount and type of preparation needed.

TASK AND SITUATION CHARACTERISTICS INFLUENCING PREPARATION

One set of factors that influence action preparation includes characteristics of both the task itself and the situation in which it must be performed.

The Number of Response Choices
An important characteristic of task and performance situations that influences preparation time is the number of response alternatives the performer has to choose from. *As the number of alternatives increases, the amount of time required to prepare the appropriate movement increases.* The easiest way to demonstrate this relationship is by looking at the choice-RT situation you were introduced to in chapter 2. RT increases according to the number of stimulus or response choices. The fastest RTs occur in simple-RT situations, which involve no choices because they have only one stimulus and one response. RT slows down when more than one stimulus and more than one response are possible, as in the choice-RT situation.

The relationship between the amount of RT increase and the number of response choices is

---

[1] When RT is used as an index of action preparation, it is often used to determine the amount of time required for "motor programming," which we described in chapter 5.

A CLOSER LOOK

A Historical Look at Donders' Use of Reaction Time to Study Action Preparation

The study of reaction time (RT) as an indicator of mental operations has a history that can be traced back to the middle of the nineteenth century. Scientists were becoming interested in determining the basic elements of thought. The investigation of RT provided a useful means of investigating this question because it represented the time interval between the detection of a stimulus and the initiation of a response to it. Dr. F. C. Donders, a Dutch physician, hypothesized that specific mental operations occur in a specific series of stages during the RT interval and was certain that he could identify each stage. He initiated research that was published in 1868 (Donders, 1868–1969) and continues to influence researchers today. To test his hypothesis, he set up three different "methods" for performing reaction-time tasks.

- *Simple reaction-time task* (Donders called this the *a* method): The participant pressed a telegraph-type key as soon as possible when a light illuminated.
- *Choice reaction-time task* (Donders called this the *b* method): The participant pressed a telegraph-type key as soon as possible with the right hand when the right light illuminated and with the left hand when the left light illuminated.
- *Discrimination reaction-time task* (Donders called this the *c* method): The participant pressed a telegraph-type key as soon as possible when a light of specified color illuminated, but not when any other light illuminated (e.g., respond to the red light, but not to the green light).

Donders reasoned that the RTs for the three tasks would be different because of the different "mental operations" involved in identifying the stimulus and selecting the appropriate response for each task. He developed the following subtraction method to determine the speed of each of the two mental operation stages:

- RT for the *c* task − RT for the *a* task = Amount of time for the *stimulus discrimination* stage
- RT for the *c* task − RT for the *b* task = Amount of time for the *response selection* stage

The simple-RT task provided the baseline RT because it involved only stimulus identification and the selection of one response, whereas the choice- and discrimination-reaction time tasks required the discrimination of different stimuli and the selection of one response from more than one possible response.

Unfortunately, few researchers followed Donders' lead with any degree of effort until after World War II, when in 1952 Hick reported his work concerning the systematic influence of the number of stimulus-response alternatives on RT (which is discussed in this chapter). Since that time, the study of reaction time as a means of understanding the action preparation process, which is now a part of the area of study referred to as *mental chronometry,* has generated a substantial amount of research (for a review of this research, see Meyer et al., 1988).

so stable that a law, known as Hick's law, was developed that predicts a person's RT when his or her simple RT and the number of choices are known. **Hick's law** (Hick, 1952), which is sometimes referred to as the Hick-Hyman law, states that RT will increase logarithmically as the number of stimulus-response choices increases. This means that when we calculate the logarithm of the number of choices in a choice-RT situation and plot the resulting RT on a graph, RT increases linearly as the number of choices increases. The equation that describes this law is Choice RT = k $[\log_2 (N + 1)]$, where k is a constant (which is simple RT in

most cases) and N equals the number of possible choices. Figure 8.1 illustrates the results of using

action preparation   the activity that occurs between the intention to perform an action and the initiation of that action; sometimes, the term *motor programming* is used to refer to this preparation activity.

Hick's law   a law of human performance stating that RT will increase logarithmically as the number of stimulus-response choices increases.

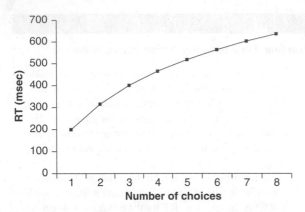

FIGURE 8.1   Predicted reaction times (RT), according to Hick's law, for one through eight choice-RT situations, based on a simple (i.e., one choice) RT of 200 msec.

Hick's equation to predict the choice RTs for one to eight choices, beginning with a simple RT of 200 msec (i.e., one choice; therefore the k in the equation = 200).

The important component of Hick's law is the $\log_2$ function, because it designates that the RT increase is due to the information transmitted by the possible choices, rather than to the actual number of choice alternatives. In information theory, *$\log_2$ specifies a bit of information.* A *bit,* short for *bi*nary digi*t,* is a yes/no (i.e., 1/0) choice between two alternatives. In a 1-bit decision, there are two alternatives; there are four alternatives in a 2-bit decision; a 3-bit decision involves eight choices; and so on. The number of bits indicates the smallest number of "yes/no" decisions needed to solve the problem created by the number of choices involved. For example, if eight choices were possible in a situation, a person would have to answer three yes/no questions to determine the correct choice. Thus, an eight-choice situation is a 3-bit decision situation. Accordingly, Hick's law not only correctly predicts that RT increases as the number of choice alternatives increases; it also predicts the specific size of increase to expect.

The Predictability of the Correct Response Choice

If a number of possible responses exist in a performance situation and one alternative is more predictable than the others, action preparation time will be shorter than it would if all the alternatives were equally likely. Research evidence has consistently shown that *RT decreases as the predictability of one of the possible choices increases.*

An experimental procedure, popularized in the early 1980s by Rosenbaum (1980, 1983), has been commonly used to investigate this relationship. In this procedure, known as the *precuing technique,* researchers provide participants with differing amounts of advance information about which movement must be made in a choice situation. In Rosenbaum's experiments, participants had to move a finger as quickly as possible to hit the signaled target key. There were three response dimensions, all of which involved a two-choice situation: the *arm* to move (left or right); the *direction* to move (away from or toward the body); and the *extent* of the movement (short or long). Prior to the signal to move, the participants could receive advance information (i.e., the precue) specifying the correct upcoming response for none, one, two, or all three of the dimensions. The results showed that as the number of precued dimensions increased, the RT decreased, with the fastest RT occurring when all three dimensions were precued. The benefit of the advance information was that participants would need to prepare only the remaining non-precued dimensions after the "go" signal.

An important finding about the effect of a precue on the time required to prepare an action is that the person must maintain his or her attention to the location of the advance information until the actual signal to move occurs. Eversheim & Bock (2002) showed in a series of experiments that when a

A CLOSER LOOK

Applying Hick's Law to a Sport Performance Situation

When a soccer player is dribbling the ball down the field and notices that a defender will soon confront him or her, the player has several choices in terms of what to do with the ball. One choice is to continue dribbling; a second is to pass to a teammate; and a third could be, depending on the player's location on the field, to make a shot at the goal. The player's decision depends on a variety of factors related to the other players on the field, which include the actions of the individual defender, the locations and actions of the defender's teammates, as well as the locations and actions of the teammates of the player with the ball. When considered in terms of Hick's law, all of these players are possible "stimulus" choices. If the player with the ball tried to take into account all of these players' locations and actions, he or she would need much more time to make a decision about what to do with the ball and prepare the action based on that decision than the situation would allow.

How does the player reduce the stimulus choices in order to reduce the decision and action preparation time? One way is for the player with the ball to look for the minimum number of specific characteristics related to the defenders and his or her own teammates that will provide the information needed to make a decision. As Hick's law indicates, the fewer characteristics the player needs to observe, the shorter the amount of time he or she needs to decide what to do with the ball and prepare the appropriate action.

person's attention was diverted by some other activity between the precue and the signal to move, the person lost the RT benefit of the advance information.

The Influence of the Probability of Precue Correctness

An interesting twist to the precuing situation occurs when the advance information may or may not be correct. The critical factor influencing preparation time in this situation is the *probability* of the advance information's correctness. For example, if a basketball player is defending one-on-one against a player with the ball and knows that the player must either shoot or pass the ball, the defensive player has a 50–50 chance of guessing what the offensive player will do and preparing an appropriate action. But, if the defensive player knows that when the offensive player is at that specific location on the court, he or she will pass the ball 80 percent of the time, the defensive player will in all likelihood begin to prepare to defend against the player passing the ball. In this situation, the advance information (i.e., the precue) provides the defensive player with an option that is better than 50–50. As a result, especially with only a 20 percent chance of making the wrong choice, the defensive player would probably *bias* his or her action preparation to defend against the player passing the ball.

What advantage would the defensive player gain by biasing his or her preparation in this way? Would it be possible that this preparation bias might be a disadvantage? The answer to these questions depends on whether the defensive player is correct or not in biasing his or her preparation. Research in laboratory settings provides evidence that shows the advantage-disadvantage that can occur in situations like this one. The best example is an experiment by Larish and Stelmach (1982), which, although published many years ago, has become the model approach to study this issue. Participants received advance information about whether the right hand or the left hand should hit the target. But this information was correct only 20 percent, 50 percent, or 80 percent of the time. The results (shown in figure 8.2) illustrate the **cost-benefit trade-off**

cost-benefit trade-off   the cost (in terms of slower RT), and benefit (in terms of faster RT) that occur as a result of biasing the preparation of an action in favor of one of several possible actions (as opposed to preparing as if each possible action were equally probable).

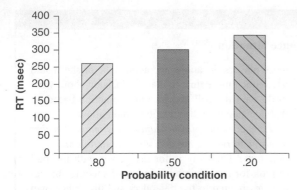

FIGURE 8.2   Results from the experiment by Larish and Stelmach showing the effects on RT of different probabilities of a precue's correctness. Notice the time advantage for the .80 probability condition compared to the time disadvantage for the .20 probability condition. [Adapted from Larish, D., & Stelmach, G. E. (1982). Preprogramming, programming, and reprogramming of aimed hand movements as a function of age. *Journal of Motor Behavior, 14,* 322–340. Copyright © 1982 Heldref Publications, Inc., Washington, DC. Reprinted by permission.]

associated with this situation. When there was a 50–50 chance (50 percent correct condition) of the precue's being correct, participants responded as if the task were a two-choice RT task. However, in the 80–20 condition, participants obviously biased their responses to move in the direction of the precued target. When they were correct, there was a benefit; their RTs were *faster* than if they had not biased their responses. However, when they were wrong (the 20 percent case), there was a cost: their RT was *slower* than it was in the 50–50 condition.

Stimulus-Response Compatibility

Another task characteristic that influences the movement preparation time is the physical relationship between the stimulus and response choices. The study of what is termed **stimulus-response compatibility** (S-R compatibility) has a long history that dates back to World War II (for a discussion of this history, see Proctor & Reeve, 1990, or Proctor, Vu, & Pick, 2005). This extensive study has shown consistently that *RT will be faster as the relationship between the stimulus characteristics and their required response becomes more*

compatible. Conversely, RT will be slower as this relationship becomes less compatible.

Spatial relationship effects. The spatial relationship between the stimulus and response devices is the most common way of considering stimulus-response compatibility. For example, suppose a person has to push one of three keys in response to the illumination of one of three lights. If the lights and keys are arranged horizontally with the key to be pushed located under the light indicating that response, then the situation is more compatible than if the lights are vertical and the buttons are horizontal. A more compatible relationship would lead to faster RTs (and fewer errors) than a less compatible situation.

The Stroop effect. A different type of S-R compatibility situation occurs when the appearance of the stimulus suggests one type of response, but the situation requires a different response. The best example of this is the **Stroop effect,** which is a phenomenon that occurs when a person must verbally respond to the ink color of a word that names a color. This phenomenon is named after J. R. Stroop who first reported it (Stroop, 1935). When the word name and ink color of the word are the same, RT is faster than if the word is a different color than its name. For example, if BLUE is the word, people will say "blue" faster when the ink color is blue than when the word name is RED but the ink color is blue. In terms of stimulus-response compatibility, a compatible situation exists when the ink color of a word is the same as the color it names and the person must say the ink color; but an incompatible situation exists when the word is written in a color that is different from the one it names and the person must say the ink color.

Why does S-R compatability affect RT? To account for the effect of stimulus-response compatibility on RT, Zelaznik and Franz (1990) presented evidence showing that when S-R compatibility is low, RT increases are due to *response selection* problems. On the other hand, when S-R

A CLOSER LOOK

A Stimulus-Response Compatibility Example in the Kitchen with Potential Serious Consequences

The article by Proctor, Vu, and Pick (2005) described the following example of how S-R compatibility is an important concern for the design of a kitchen appliance. The typical stovetop has four burners, usually arranged in a 2×2 layout of two in the front and two in the rear. However, the controls for these burners are organized in ways that vary in the degree of compatibility with the layout of the burners. The following examples illustrate two of these situations:

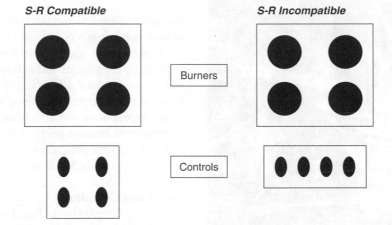

The selection of the correct controls is easy and fast for the high-S-R-compatible arrangement, but more difficult and slower for the S-R-incompatible arrangement. The potential for making a control selection error, with possible serious consequences, is much higher for the incompatible arrangement, especially in an emergency situation when a fast and accurate response is required.

compatibility is high, response selection processing is minimal, so that any RT changes reflect motor processes related to preparation of the selected response. Weeks and Proctor (1990) further developed this point by demonstrating that the specific response selection problem is due to translation problems involving the mapping of the stimulus locations to the response locations. Because this translation process requires time, RT increases.

Foreperiod Length Regularity

A part of the preparation process begins when a person detects a signal indicating that the signal to respond will occur shortly. The interval between this "warning" signal and the stimulus, or "go" signal,

stimulus-response compatibility   a characteristic of the spatial arrangement relationship between a stimulus and a response. This relationship includes the spatial arrangement of stimuli and the limb movements required to respond to them, and the physical characteristics or meaning of a stimulus and the type of response required. The degree of compatibility influences the amount of preparation time in a reaction time task involving stimulus and response choices.

Stroop effect   a type of stimulus-response compatibility situation in which a color's name and ink are the same or different. RT for saying the word is faster when both are the same color than when the word is a different ink color.

Several situation and performer characteristics discussed in this chapter influence a swimmer's preparation to start a race

LAB LINKS

Lab 8b in the Online Learning Center Lab Manual provides an opportunity for you to experience the influence of movement complexity on RT by participating in an experiment that is similar to the one by Henry and Rogers (1960).

is known as the **foreperiod.** In simple-RT situations, the regularity of the length of this interval influences RT. If the foreperiod is a constant length, that is, the same amount of time for every trial, RT will be shorter than the amount of time that typically characterizes simple RT.

We can attribute the shorter RT associated with constant foreperiods to *anticipation* by the performer. Because it is a simple-RT situation, the person knows before the warning signal what response will be required. And because every trial has the same foreperiod length, he or she knows when the go signal will occur after the warning signal. As a result, the person can prepare the required action in advance of the go signal, such that the actual initiation of it begins before the go signal.

The starts of sprint races in track or swimming illustrate the need to implement an understanding of the effect on RT of a constant foreperiod length. If

the starter of these races maintains a constant amount of time between his or her signal for the athletes to get ready and the gun or sound to start running or swimming, the athletes can anticipate the go signal and gain an unfair advantage over other athletes who did not anticipate the signal as accurately. We would expect some variation in the actual initiations of movement because people vary in terms of their capability to time the precise amounts of time typically involved in the RT foreperiods of sprint starts.

Movement Complexity
Movement complexity is based on the number of parts to a movement. Research evidence demonstrating the effect of movement complexity on RT was reported primarily in the 1960s through the early 1980s, beginning with the now classic experiment by Henry and Rogers (1960). They demonstrated that for a ballistic task, which requires both fast RT and fast movement, RT increases as a function of the number of component parts of the required action. Numerous other experiments have confirmed these findings since that time (e.g., Anson, 1982; Christina & Rose, 1985; Fischman, 1984). From a preparation-of-action perspective, these results indicate that the *complexity of the action to be performed influences the amount of time a person requires to prepare the motor control system.*

A question arose from these experiments related to whether, in fact, the key factor is the number of component parts involved in the action. Because the amount of time to perform the action and the number of component parts of the action are confounded when actions of different complexity are compared, it is possible that the amount of time required may be the cause of the RT increase. To

The Classic Experiment of Henry and Rogers (1960)

Henry and Rogers (1960) hypothesized that if people prepare movements in advance, a complex movement should take longer to prepare than a simple one. In addition, the increased preparation time should be reflected in changes in reaction time (RT). To test this hypothesis, they compared three different rapid-movement situations that varied in the complexity of the movement. The least complex movement required participants to release a telegraph key as quickly as possible after a gong (movement A). The movement at the next level of complexity (movement B) required participants to release the key at the gong and move the arm forward 30 cm as rapidly as possible to grasp a tennis ball hanging from a string. The most complex movement (movement C) required participants to release the key at the gong, reach forward and strike

the hanging tennis ball with the back of the hand, reverse direction and push a button, and then finally reverse direction again and grasp another tennis ball. Participants were to perform all of these movements as quickly as possible.

The results supported the hypothesis. The average RT for movement A was 165 msec; for movement B the average RT was 199 msec; and for movement C the average RT was 212 msec.

The researchers held that the cause of the increase in RT was the increase in the amount of movement-related information that had to be prepared. They proposed that the mechanism involved in this movement preparation was a motor program, similar to a computer program, that would control the details of the sequence of events required to perform the movement.

investigate which of these two factors influenced RT in the Henry and Rogers experiment, Christina and colleagues carried out a series of experiments that provided support for the Henry and Rogers conclusion that the number of component parts is the key in the RT increase (for a review of this research, see Christina, 1992).

Movement Accuracy

As the accuracy demands for a movement increase, the amount of preparation time required also increases. Researchers have nicely demonstrated this effect in comparisons of RTs for manual aiming tasks that differed according to the target sizes. For example, Sidaway, Sekiya, and Fairweather (1995) had people perform manual aiming tasks in which they had to hit two targets in sequence as quickly as possible. Two results showed the influence on preparation of the accuracy demands of the task. First, RT increased as target size decreased. Second, when the first target was a constant size, the dispersion of the location of hits on that target was related to the size of the second target. These results have been replicated by additional research (e.g., Fischman, Yao, & Reeve, 2000).

An important aspect of this research is that it extends our understanding of Fitts' law, which we discussed in chapter 7. Fitts' law concerns the increase in movement time associated with the accuracy demands of a movement, regardless of movement complexity. The research we have discussed here by Sidaway and others shows that the increase in accuracy demands also increases the amount of time needed to *prepare* to move. The need for additional time for action preparation in these situations is likely due to the additional preparation required for a person to constrain his or her limb to move within spatial constraints imposed by the smaller target.

The Repetition of a Movement

A well-known characteristic of human performance is that when the performance situation requires a person to repeat the same response on the next attempt, that person's RT for the next trial will

foreperiod   in a reaction time paradigm, the time interval between a warning signal and the go signal, or stimulus.

a. No-fake situations:

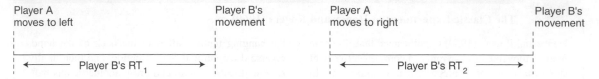

b. Fake situation:

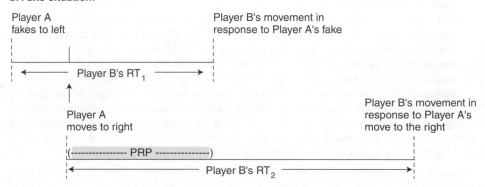

FIGURE 8.3   The psychological refractory period (PRP) illustrated in terms of the time advantage gained by an athlete for moving to the right when it follows a fake for moving to the left. (a) Player B's RT when Player A moves to the left (RT_1) or the right (RT_2), when neither is preceded by a fake in the opposite direction. (b) Player B's RT when Player A first fakes moving to the left but then moves to the right. In this situation, Player A gains extra time to carry out the move to the right because of the increased RT_2 for Player B, which results from the delay caused by the PRP.

be faster than it was for the previous attempt. As the number of trials increases, the influence of the repetitions on RT lessens. Again, as in other performance situations, the decrease in preparation time is due to a reduction in the response-selection process (see Campbell & Proctor, 1993).

The Time between Different Responses to Different Signals

There are some performance situations that require a person to respond to a signal with one action and then very quickly respond to another signal with a different action. For example, when a basketball player is confronted by a defensive player in a one-on-one situation, he or she might fake a move in one direction (the first signal) before moving in the opposite direction (the second signal). Each "signal" by the offensive player requires the defensive player to initiate a movement. In this situation,

RT will be slower for the defensive player's second movement than for his or her first.

The RT delay for the second movement is due to the **psychological refractory period (PRP),** which can be thought of as a delay period (the term *refractory* is synonymous with *delay*) during which a person cannot select the second movement until after he or she selects and initiates the first. As such, the *PRP reflects a distinct limitation in the action preparation process.*

Figure 8.3 illustrates the PRP using the basketball one-on-one situation described earlier. The player with the ball (Player A) fakes a move to the left but then quickly moves to the right. He or she gains extra time to carry out the move to the right because of the RT delay created by the PRP that results from Player B's initial reaction to the fake. The illustration shows that Player B's RT would be the same amount of time for Player A's move to the right if it had not been preceded by a fake move to the left. But the fake requires Player B to initiate a response to the fake before he or she can initiate a response to the move to the right.

The first evidence of the PRP was published in 1931 by Telford. Since that time, the delay has been demonstrated by numerous researchers and in a variety of settings (for a review of this research, see Lien & Proctor, 2002). Although researchers continue to seek an appropriate theoretical explanation for the PRP, there is general consensus that the delay in responding to the second stimulus is related to the *response selection* demands of the two S-R tasks that must be performed in rapid succession. The response to the second stimulus waits for the completion of the response to the first stimulus. In fact, the PRP can be eliminated if the second stimulus occurs after the response to the first stimulus. The theoretical issue concerns why the second response must wait until the completion of the first response. We will consider this issue in chapter 9.

PERFORMER CHARACTERISTICS INFLUENCING PREPARATION

In addition to task and situation characteristics, certain characteristics of the performer also influence the process of action preparation. We should think of these characteristics as situational, because they refer to the state of the person at the time a skill must be performed. It is important to note here that these performer characteristics typically influence not only the time needed to prepare a voluntary movement but also the quality of its performance.

Alertness of the Performer
An important principle of human performance is that the degree of alertness of the performer influences the time he or she takes to prepare a required action, as well as the quality of the action itself. In two types of performance situations, the role of alertness is especially critical. One type is the RT task, where a person does not have to wait for

any length of time beyond a few seconds, but must respond as quickly and as accurately as possible. The other type, involving the long-term maintenance of alertness, is the task for which fast and accurate responding is important, but the signals to which the person must respond occur infrequently and irregularly.

For RT tasks, a way to increase the likelihood that a person is optimally alert and prepared to respond appropriately is to provide some type of *warning signal* that indicates he or she must respond within the next few seconds. Researchers demonstrated the benefit of this warning signal more than a century ago, in the early days of human performance research. In fact, there was sufficient evidence accumulated in the first half of the 1900s to conclude that RT is significantly faster when a warning signal precedes the signal to respond than when there is no warning signal (Teichner, 1954).

An important point is that after the warning signal, there is an optimal length of time for the person to develop and maintain alertness while waiting for the go signal. If the go signal occurs too soon after the warning signal, or if the person must wait too long, RT will be longer than if the go signal occurs sometime between these two points in time. These performance effects indicate that people require a minimum amount of time to develop optimal alertness and that we can maintain that level of alertness for a limited amount of time.

As you can see in figure 8.4, there is an optimal time range during which the go signal should occur following the warning signal. The exact amounts of time to insert in this figure will depend on the skill and situation. However, for simple-RT situations, a reasonable rule of thumb is this: *the optimal foreperiod length should range between 1 and 4 sec.*

---

psychological refractory period (PRP)   a delay period during which a person seems to put planned action "on hold" while executing a previously initiated action.

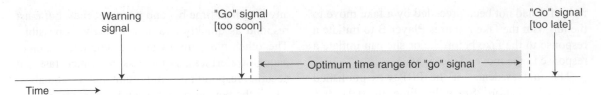

FIGURE 8.4   An illustration of the warning signal to "go" signal time relationship necessary to ensure optimal readiness to respond in a reaction time situation. The actual amounts of time for these events depend on the task and situation in which they are performed.

Vigilance. The long-term maintenance of alertness is known as **vigilance.** In vigilance situations, an individual must perform an appropriate action when he or she detects a signal to act. The problem is that *signals occur very infrequently and irregularly.* There are many vigilance situations in motor skill performance contexts. In sports, a situation involving vigilance occurs when a baseball outfielder must maintain alertness throughout an inning in the field despite having only one ball hit his or her way, out of the many pitches thrown. In industry, a worker who must detect and remove defective products from the assembly line will see many products move past him or her for long periods of time, but only a few will be defective. Similarly, driving a car or track along an uncrowded freeway is a vigilance task when a person drives for an extended time. Lifeguarding at a pool or beach can be a vigilance problem, because during a long shift on duty, situations requiring a response are very infrequent. Medical personnel often are required to work long hours and still be able to identify symptoms of health problems correctly and perform surgical techniques requiring precise motor control.

In each of these situations, RT increases as a function of the amount of time the person must maintain alertness to detect certain signals. Detection errors increase as well. Scientists first reported this phenomenon during World War II (see Mackworth, 1956). In experiments investigating the detection of signals simulating those observed on a radar screen, results showed that both the RT to a signal and the accuracy of detecting signals deteriorated markedly with each half hour during a two-hour work interval.

Although performance in vigilance situations deteriorates the longer a person needs to remain attentive to the possibility of needing to detect a signal and make a response, lack of sufficient sleep makes vigilance performance even worse. Research has consistently demonstrated that sleep deprivation (i.e., lack of sleep for extended periods of time), insufficient sleep (i.e., sleeping for fewer hours at night than needed), and sleep disruption negatively impact a person's performance in vigilance situations (see for example, Dinges et al. 1997; Drummond et al. 2005). There is general agreement that the best way to overcome sleep-related performance problems is to sleep. However, this option is not always possible, which has led researchers to investigate various stimulants as alternative ways to provide short-term enhancement of performance (e.g., Magill et al., 2003; Wesensten, Killgore, & Balkin, 2005).

Eason, Beardshall, and Jaffee (1965) nicely demonstrated that alertness deterioration contributes to the performance decrements associated with long-term vigilance. They provided physiological evidence consistent with decreases in vigilance performance over one-hour sessions. Skin conductance in participants decreased, indicating increased calming and drowsiness over the session. In addition, participants' neck tension steadily increased, as their nervous systems attempted to compensate by increasing muscle activity in the neck.

Attention Focused on the Signal versus the Movement

Many motor skills, such as sprints in track and swimming, require a person to move as fast as possible when the signal to move occurs. In these situations, there are two important components, the RT and the movement time (MT). To prepare to initiate his or her movement, the person can focus

A CLOSER LOOK

Vigilance Problems Resulting from Closed-Head Injury

Closed-head injury involves brain damage and often results from an auto accident or a fall. Numerous cognitive and motor problems can accompany this type of injury, depending on the area of the brain that is damaged. Included in the problems associated with closed-head injury is difficulty sustaining attention over a period of time in vigilance situations.

Loken et al. (1995) provided evidence for this difficulty by comparing patients with severe closed-head injuries to non-brain-injured people. All participants observed on a computer screen sets of two, four, or eight small blue circles (1.5 mm diameter). On some trials, one of the circles was solid blue (this occurred on only 60 percent of the 200 trials). When participants detected the solid blue circle, they were to

hit a specified keyboard key. The set of trials lasted 20 min, with only 2 to 5 sec between trials.

The authors pointed out that the following results were most noteworthy because they added to previous knowledge of vigilance problems related to closed-head injury. *In contrast to the non-brain-injured participants,* the patients showed that their:

1. **overall vigilance performance** was differentially affected by the complexity of the stimulus array on the computer screen (i.e., detection performance decreased as the set size of circles increased)
2. **detection time latency** (RT) increased as a function of the length of time engaged in performing the task (i.e., the amount of time taken to detect a solid blue circle increased linearly across the 200 trials)

---

on the signal itself (a *sensory set*) or on the movement required (a *motor set*). Research evidence, first provided by Franklin Henry (1960), indicates that which of the two components the performer consciously focuses attention on influences RT.

However, because Henry's results were based on the participants' opinions of what their sets were, Christina (1973) imposed on each participant either a sensory or a motor set to initiate a fast arm movement. The sensory-set group was told to focus attention on the sound of the go signal, a buzzer, but to move off the response key as fast as possible. The motor-set group was told to focus on moving as quickly as possible. Results showed that the sensory-set group had an RT 20 msec faster than that of the motor-set group. Interestingly, MT was not statistically different for the two groups. Thus, participants' focusing of attention on the signal and allowing the movement to happen naturally shortened the preparation time required and did not penalize movement speed, yielding a faster overall response time.

Jongsma, Elliott, and Lee (1987) replicated these laboratory results in a sport performance situation. They compared sensory and motor sets for a sprint

start in track. To measure RT, the authors embedded a pressure-sensitive switch in the rear-foot starting block. They measured MT as the time from the release of this switch until a photoelectric light beam was broken 1.5 meters from the starting line. Results showed that for both novices and experienced sprinters, RT was faster for the sensory-set condition.

WHAT OCCURS DURING PREPARATION?

On the basis of the discussion so far, you can see that the process of preparing an action is complex. It includes perceptual, cognitive, and motor components. One way to demonstrate that the preparation process includes these components is to divide an EMG recording of the RT interval into components by using a technique known as *fractionating RT,* which was introduced in chapter 2.

---

vigilance   maintaining attention in a performance situation in which stimuli requiring a response occur infrequently.

A Summary of Task and Performer Characteristics that Influence the Amount of Time Required to Prepare an Action

Characteristics that *Increase* Action Preparation Time

- An increase in the number of movement alternatives
- An increase in the unpredictability of the correct movement response alternative
- Following an expectation bias toward performing one of several movement alternatives, the required movement is not the one expected
- An increase in the degree of spatial incompatibility between environmental context features and their associated movements
- An increase in the irregularity of foreperiod lengths in an RT situation
- No previous experience (i.e., practice) performing the task in the required situation
- A decrease in performer alertness
- An attention focus on the movement rather than the "go" signal

Characteristics that *Decrease* Action Preparation Time

- A decrease in the number of movement alternatives
- An increase in the predictability of the correct movement response alternative
- Following an expectation bias toward performing one of several movement alternatives, the required movement is the one expected
- An increase in the degree of spatial compatibility between environmental context features and their associated movements
- An increase in the regularity of foreperiod lengths in an RT situation
- An increase in the amount of experience (i.e., practice) performing the task in the required situation
- An appropriate level of performer alertness
- An attention focus on the "go" signal rather than the movement

Evidence from Fractionating RT

As we described in chapter 2, to fractionate RT, the EMG recording taken from the agonist muscle involved in a movement is divided into two distinct components (see figure 2.3). The first is the *premotor* component (sometimes referred to as electromechanical delay). The EMG signal does not change much from what it was prior to the onset of the signal. However, shortly after the onset of the signal, the EMG signal shows a rapid increase in electrical activity. This indicates that the motor neurons are firing and the muscle is preparing to contract, even though no observable movement has yet occurred. In this period of time, the *motor* component is the increased EMG activity preceding the observable movement.

The premotor and motor components of RT represent two distinct activities that occur prior to observable movement and reflect different types of movement preparation processes. The premotor component includes the perceptual or cognitive processing of the stimulus information and preparing

the movement features of the required action. The motor component begins the actual motor output phase of a movement. During this time, the specific muscles involved in the action are firing and preparing to begin to produce observable movement.

By fractionating RT, we can gain insight into what occurs during the action preparation process. Researchers look at which of these RT components is influenced by the various factors we discussed earlier that influence RT. For example, Christina and Rose (1985) reported that the changes in RT due to increases in *response complexity* were reflected in increases in the premotor component. For a two-part arm movement, the premotor component increased an average of 19 msec over that for a one-part arm movement, whereas the motor component increased only 3 msec. Siegel (1986) found that RT increased linearly as *movement durations* increased from 150, through 300 and 600, to 1,200 msec, the length of the premotor component also increased linearly. The motor component, on the other hand, remained the same length until the response duration became 1,200 msec; then it showed a slight increase. Sheridan (1984) showed that the premotor component was also responsible for RT increases due to increases in *movement velocity*. However, Carlton, Carlton, and Newell (1987) found changes in both the premotor and motor components by altering *force-related characteristics* of the response. Similar changes in both premotor and motor components were reported by Davranche, Burle, Audiffren, and Hasbroucq (2005) in their investigation of the basis for the improvement in choice-RT performance that occurs while *performing a submaximal exercise*.

Postural Preparation

This postural preparation process is commonly referred to as *anticipatory postural adjustments*. The term "anticipatory" indicates that prior to the execution of an intended action or movement, there are additional muscles that activate, a process that occurs non-consciously. Researchers typically use EMG recordings to investigate these muscular activities. The demonstration of anticipatory postural adjustments presents further support for the complexity and sophistication of the motor control system. Although numerous experiments have been reported that provide evidence for the postural preparation activities that precede the initiation of an intended action, we will consider only a few examples. These examples include actions that involve simple and complex limb movements as well as whole-body movements. These research examples show us that all of the actions we perform, even those involving the simplest of movements, require a complex synergistic system of muscles to work together.

Weeks and Wallace (1992) asked people to perform an elbow-flexion aiming movement in the horizontal plane while standing in an erect posture. Participants learned to make this movement in three different velocities defined by criterion movement times. The authors made EMG recordings from various muscles of both legs and the responding arm. The results showed that a specific sequence of supporting postural events occurred. For each movement velocity, the muscles of the contralateral

and ipsilateral legs (biceps femoris and rectus femoris) activated *prior to* the onset of the arm agonist muscles (biceps brachii). And as the arm velocity increased, the onset of the anticipatory postural muscle activity occurred at an earlier time prior to arm agonist muscle activation. The authors also found different onset orders for the various postural muscles.

More recently, Bonnetblanc, Martin, and Teasdale (2004) found that for an arm-pointing movement at different-sized targets (5, 10, and 25 cm wide) while standing, leg muscles not only activated before the arm began to move (similar to what Weeks and Wallace found), but the amount of activation of specific muscles also varied according to the size of the target. For example, as target size decreased, EMG activity increased in the erector spinae but decreased in the tibialis anterior and the rectus femoris of the quadriceps. When considered in relation to Fitts' law, which we discussed in chapter 7, these results suggest that the relationship between movement time and movement accuracy demands has a basis in the preparation of the movements. In addition, these results provide evidence of muscle preparation differences associated with the relationship between RT and movement accuracy as reported by Sidaway and others, which we considered earlier in this chapter.

Postural preparation effects have also been shown for leg movements. For example, in a study by Mercer and Sahrmann (1999), people of three age groups (8–12, 25–35, and 65–73 yrs), who had no neuromuscular impairments, performed two types of stair-stepping movements: stepping onto a stair step with one foot (the "place task") and stepping onto a stair step with one foot and then putting the other foot on the step (the "step task"). The experimenters analyzed EMG recordings from four muscles of the stance leg (tibialis anterior, gastrocnemius-soleus, hamstring, and gluteus maximus) and two muscles of the moving leg (rectus femoris and gluteus maximus). When the experimenters analyzed the EMG results in terms of the onset (i.e., activation) times for each muscle for all participants, they found that the tibialis anterior (TA) of the stance leg was the first muscle to

A CLOSER LOOK

Anticipatory Postural Adjustments in Hemiparetic Stroke Patients Compared to Healthy Adults

Following a stroke, people commonly experience paralysis on one side of the body (i.e., hemiparesis). One of the motor control characteristics influenced by hemiparesis is the impairment of the anticipatory postural adjustments of the trunk and limbs prior to an intended movement of either a paretic (i.e., paralyzed) or nonparetic limb. A study by Dickstein, Shefi, Marcovitz, and Villa (2004) provided some insight into this problem by investigating the anticipatory postural adjustment characteristics of specific trunk muscles for arm and hip flexion movements.

Participants: 50 hemiparetic men and women (mean age = 72 yrs) who had experienced a stroke approximately one month prior to the study. The stroke in all patients involved the middle cerebral artery. Some had left hemiparesis and some had right hemiparesis.

In addition, 30 healthy men and women (mean age = 71 yrs) were involved as a healthy control group.

Tasks: Flexion (as fast as possible) of (1) *paretic arm* of the patients and left arm of the controls; (2) *nonparetic arm* of the patients and right arm of the controls; (3) *paretic hip* of the patients and left hip of the controls; (4) *nonparetic hip* of the patients and right hip of the controls

EMG recording: Posterior trunk (back muscles): bilateral lumbar erector spinae and latissimus dorsi muscles; *anterior trunk (abdominal muscles):* bilateral rectus abdominis and external oblique muscles; *arm flexors:* anterior deltoid and biceps brachii muscles; *hip flexors:* rectus femoris muscles

Results:

Task: *Paretic and left arm flexion*

Stroke patients & healthy controls	1. Activation of contralateral back muscles prior to ipsilateral back muscles 2. Activation of erector spinae muscles prior to arm flexor muscles
Stroke patients	Longer delay for onset of activation of ipsilateral back muscles

Task: *Nonparetic and right arm flexion*

Stroke patients & healthy controls	1. Activation of contralateral back muscles prior to ipsilateral back muscles 2. Activation of both back muscles prior to arm flexors
Stroke patients	Longer delay for onset of activation of ipsilateral erector spinae muscle

Task: *Paretic and left hip flexion*

Stroke patients & healthy controls	Concurrent activation of contralateral and ipsilateral abdominal muscles
Stroke patients	Longer delay for onset of activation of abdominal muscles

Task: *Nonparetic and right hip flexion*

Stroke patients & healthy controls	1. Concurrent activation of contralateral and ipsilateral rectus abdominis muscles 2. Activation of contralateral external oblique muscles prior to ipsilateral external oblique muscles
Stroke patients	Longer delay for onset of activation of abdominal muscle

Conclusions: The longer delay for the onset of back and abdominal muscles indicates that the anticipatory postural adjustment activity of these muscles is impaired in hemiparetic poststroke patients. The implication of these results for physical rehabilitation is that treatments should include the enhancement of activation levels of these trunk muscles on the paretic side of the body, with special consideration given to the latissimus dorsi, external oblique, and rectus abdominis muscles.

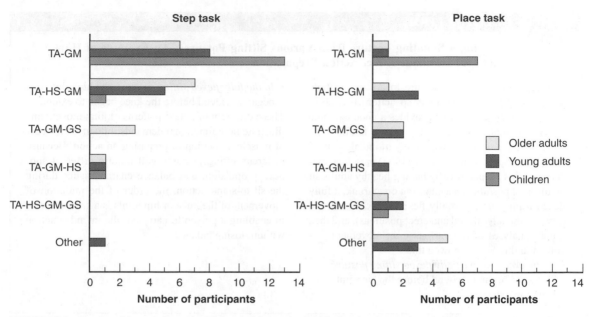

FIGURE 8.5   Results of the experiment by Mercer and Sahrmann (1999) showing the number of children, young adults, and older adults who exhibited specific "preferred" sequences of muscle activation for the stance leg for the place and step tasks. Each sequence indicates the order of activation for the muscles listed (TA = tibialis anterior, GM = gluteus maximus, HS = hamstring, GS = gastrocnemius-soleus). *Source:* Figure 4, p. 1149 in Mercer, V. S., & Sahrmann, S. A. (1999). Postural synergies associated with a stepping task. *Physical Therapy, 79,* 1142–1152.

activate. On average, it activated 215 msec *before* the initiation of movement by the opposite leg for the stepping task and 307 msec *before* movement initiation for the place tasks. This initial activation of the TA in the stance leg ensured postural stability when the opposite leg stepped forward. Another important result of this experiment is the variety of muscle activation sequences demonstrated by each participant and across the participants for each task. Figure 8.5 shows the specific muscle activation sequences exhibited for the two tasks and the number of participants in each age group who displayed each sequence on at least 75 percent of the trials (which the experimenters referred to as representative of a "preferred" sequence). These results demonstrate that no specific sequence of muscle activation characterized all or any one of the participants for either task.

Finally, would you expect anticipatory postural adjustments to precede a simple movement like

tapping your index finger on a tabletop while sitting in chair? Two researchers in Italy (Caronni & Cavallari, 2009) reported that prior to the activation of the prime mover muscles for this tapping activity (i.e., the flexor digitorum superficialis) several upper-limb and upper-back muscles activated in specific sequences that served to stabilize the upper limb during the finger tapping movements.

The sequences of muscle activation reported in these experiments demonstrate that the preparation of postural stability is an important part of action preparation. The experiments show that *postural preparation involves organizing a flexibly organized synergy* of muscles. This conclusion is important because movement scientists traditionally have assumed that postural muscle preparation is rigidly temporally organized. The advantage of the flexibly organized synergy is that anticipatory postural activity can occur according to the person's equilibrium needs for specific situations.

A CLOSER LOOK

Achieving a Standing Posture from Various Sitting Postures: An Example of How Functional Demands Affect Action Preparation

Changing from a sitting posture to a standing posture (referred to as a sit-to-stand action) is a common everyday activity that provides a good example of how the motor control system adapts to allow the same action to occur from a variety of initial postural positions. Shepherd and Gentile (1994) presented evidence of this adaptability by having healthy adults sit in different postures on a chair (an erect trunk, a fully flexed trunk, and a partially flexed trunk, i.e., flexed between the fully flexed and erect positions), and then stand. Analyses of the various joint movements involved in this action showed this:

• *In the erect and partially flexed sitting postures:* The knee began to extend before the hip joint began to extend.

• *In the fully flexed sitting posture:* the hip joint began to extend before the knee began to extend.

These different initiation patterns of joint movements illustrate how functional demands influence the order of muscle activation in preparing an action. Because different sitting postures will require different support, propulsion, and balance characteristics during the sit-to-stand action, the order of the initiation of movement of the knee or hip joints is a critical factor in enabling a person to carry out the intended action without losing balance.

Preparation of Limb Movement Characteristics

An essential part of the action preparation process is selecting and organizing the specific movement characteristics of the limbs to perform according to the dictates of task constraints and characteristics. Because an individual often can perform the same action using several different limbs or different segments of the same limb, he or she must specify and prepare the limb or limb segments to be involved in performing a given task.

One feature of limb movement a person must prepare is the *direction* or directions in which the limbs must move. For a very rapid movement, a person may prepare several different directions before initiating the movement. Another feature related to direction preparation is the *trajectory* the arm will follow during movement. For a task requiring a ballistic movement and spatial accuracy, an individual must prepare in advance, constraining the limb movement to meet the accuracy constraints of the task. In addition, as we discussed in chapter 7, a person catching a ball must prepare his or her hand and finger movements before the oncoming ball reaches him or her.

Preparation of Movements for Object Control

When the action to be performed involves manipulating an object, a part of the preparation process involves specifying certain movement features needed to control the object. The following are two of those features involved in this aspect of movement preparation.

Force control. An important movement feature prepared prior to manipulating an object is setting the amount of force required to lift or move the object. As an illustration of this type of preparation, think about situations in which you have looked at an object and, because of certain characteristics, judged it to be heavy. But when you began to lift it, you discovered it was light. Undoubtedly, you lifted the object much more quickly and higher in the air than you had intended. Why did you respond in this way? The reason is that because of certain observable characteristics of the object, such as a beverage can that looks unopened although it is actually empty, you anticipated that a certain amount of muscular force would be required to lift the object. This anticipated amount of force was used to prepare the musculature for the lifting action.

Correcting Handwriting Problems due to Grip and Pen Force

The results of the experiment by Wann and Nimmo-Smith (1991) showed that children with handwriting problems often have these problems because they use excessive pen pressure and grip the pen barrel with excessive force. They have not acquired the necessary association between the "feel" of the pen against the surface and the appropriate pen pressure to apply. The researchers speculated that adults who made the appropriate force adjustments had acquired this capability through experience, which had led to their nonconsciously learning the amount of pressure required based on sensations in the fingers holding the pen.

Teachers and therapists who work with children struggling with this type of problem can encourage an increasing sensitivity in the children to appropriate pen pressure. One way to do this is by providing handwriting experiences with a variety of writing surfaces. A teacher or therapist should monitor each child's grip force, with the goal of keeping it at the minimum amount of force needed to produce a visible trace on the writing surface.

Researchers have used this common everyday experience to provide evidence that the movement force characteristics are prepared in advance of the manipulation of objects. For example, Butler et al. (1993) showed that when men did not know the weight of a box that looked like it was filled with heavy objects, they performed with a jerking motion. Movement kinematics of these lifts showed that velocities at the shoulders and knees were much higher than the velocities when the men knew the actual weight of the box.

Another example of the preparation of force control can be seen in handwriting. To prepare to write with a pen, a person needs to specify the amount of grip force on the pen as well as the amount of pressure to apply on the writing surface. Research (e.g., Wann & Nimmo-Smith, 1991) has shown that experienced writers adjust the amount of pen pressure on the writing surface according to the characteristics of the surface to allow energy-efficient, continuous, fluent motion. In contrast, children with handwriting problems often grip the pen with excessive force and use excessive pen pressure on the writing surface.

End-state comfort control. When you reach to grasp an object that you plan to do something with, how do you position your hand to grasp the object? According to an increasing amount of research, we grasp objects based on what we plan to do with them. This means that when we grasp the object our hand position is based on the position that will feel the most comfortable to complete the action—do what we intended to do with the object. For example, if you want to pick up a cup that is upside down on a table so that you can fill the cup with water, you will probably pick up the cup with the grip that will be most comfortable when you place the cup upright in order to fill it, even if this grip feels rather awkward when you initially grasp the cup.

The typically spontaneous grasp position based on the final position of the hand when the object is used in its intended way is a phenomenon known as the end-state *comfort effect*. Stated simply, this effect is "the tendency to take hold of an object in an awkward posture to permit a more comfortable, or more easily controlled, final posture once the object is brought to its target position." (Zhang & Rosenbaum, 2008, p. 383). The significance of the end-state comfort effect is that it demonstrates an important feature of object control that is part of the action preparation process. This feature involves the planning of the final hand posture that will be the most comfortable or easiest to control. Several studies have reported support for this effect since it was first reported by Rosenbaum and Jorgenson (1992) (for reviews of this research, see Fischman, Stodden, & Lehman, 2003; Rosenbaum, D. A.,

Cohen R. G., Meulenbroek, R. G., & Vaughan J., 2006). Results from a series of experiments by Cohen and Rosenbaum (2004) indicate that the preparation of hand posture in this way demonstrates that the preparation process for prehension actions involves planning that is based on the generation of a new plan or the recall of an action that was successfully used in similar situations in the past.

Of the several hypotheses proposed to explain the end-state comfort effect, one that continues to gain support is the precision hypothesis (e.g., Rosenbaum, van Heutgen, & Caldwell, 1996; Short & Cauraugh, 1999). This explanation proposes that precision in limb positioning will be greater, and the movement will be faster, when a person's limb is in a comfortable position. Thus, to ensure a faster and more accurate final limb and object position, a person prepares movement characteristics according to the comfort of the final rather than the starting position of the limb. Although this strategy may require some awkward hand and arm postures when picking up an object, it enables the person to more effectively and efficiently achieve the object manipulation goal.

Preparation of Sequences of Movements
Playing the piano and typing on a keyboard are examples of skills that involve the sequencing of series of movements. Two types of research evidence indicate that short sequences of these movements are prepared in advance of the initial movement. One is the systematic increase in RT as movement complexity increases, which we discussed earlier in this chapter. The other type of evidence is the kinematic characteristics of hand movements during the performance of typing and piano playing (e.g., Engel, Flanders, & Soechting, 1997; Soechting & Flanders, 1992). For example, in the Engel, Flanders, and Soechting study, skilled pianists played short excerpts from three pieces written for the piano. In one piece, the first four notes were the same for the right hand. However, the fourth note in one phrase is typically played by a different finger from the fourth note of the other phrase. For one phrase, the sequence of finger movements for the same first four notes was: thumb—

Playing the piano is an example of a skill that involves the preparation of sequences of movements.

index finger—middle finger—ring finger; but for the other phrase it was: thumb—index finger—middle finger—thumb. To hit the fourth note with the thumb the pianists moved the thumb under the fingers and repositioned the hand between the third and fourth notes. Because of the consistency of the kinematics of the third and fourth note movements for several trials of playing these phrases, the researchers concluded that movements for each phrase were prepared in advance. If the hand and finger repositioning had not been prepared in advance of playing the previous three notes, the kinematics of the hand and finger positioning would have been somewhat variable across the several trials.

Rhythmicity Preparation
Many skills require that the component movements follow specific rhythmic patterns. We can see this characteristic in any of the various types of gait, performance of a dance sequence, shooting of a free throw in basketball, and so on. In some of these activities, the participant can take time before performing it to engage in some preperformance activities that are commonly referred to as rituals. Interestingly, rhythmic patterns also characterize

TABLE 8.1   Types of Behaviors Involved in Preperformance Rituals in Activities Investigated by Southard and Amos (1996)

Activity	Behaviors in Preperformance Rituals
Golf putt	1. Swinging the putter back and forth without contacting the ball 2. Pause; no movement for 1 sec or more 3. Moving the toes or either foot up and down 4. Swaying the body back and forth without swinging the putter 5. Lifting the putter vertically
Tennis serve	1. Bouncing the ball with the racquet or the hand not holding the racquet 2. Pause; no movement for 1 sec or more 3. Moving the racquet forward to a position in front of the body waist high 4. Moving the racquet back from the front of the body and then forward again 5. Moving the racquet to a ready position in order to initiate serving the ball
Basketball free throw	1. Bouncing the ball 2. Pause, no movement for 1 sec or more 3. Bending at the knees or waist 4. Moving the ball upward with the arms 5. Spinning the ball 6. Bringing the ball to an initial shooting position

Table based on text and table 1 (p. 290) in Southard, D., & Amos, B. (1996). Rhythmicity and preperformance ritual: Stabilizing a flexible system. *Research Quarterly for Exercise and Sport, 67,* 288–296.

preperformance rituals and appear to influence performance. Although this relationship has not been widely studied, the few research studies investigating it have consistently shown a positive correlation between the rhythm of the preperformance routine and the success of the performance itself (e.g., Jackson, 2003; Southard & Miracle, 1993; Southard & Amos, 1996; Wrisberg & Pein, 1992). In terms of the preparation of action, the preperformance rituals would appear to stabilize the motor control system and orient it to engaging in a rhythmic activity.

The Southard and Amos (1996) study will serve as a good example of how these researchers have determined that such a relationship exists. They video-recorded fifteen basketball free throws, golf putts, and tennis serves for experienced university men who had established rituals for each of these activities. Each video recording was analyzed to determine the preperformance behaviors each participant

used on each trial. The types of behaviors for each activity are listed in table 8.1. It is important to note that although each of the behaviors was observed, individual participants did not exhibit every behavior. The researchers also analyzed the total time to perform the ritual and the relative time for each behavior in the ritual, which was the percentage of time engaged in each behavior in the ritual. Results showed a moderately high .77 correlation between the relative time for the ritual behaviors and successful performance. This relationship suggests that the consistent relative timing of preperformance ritual behaviors may be an important part of the successful performance of closed motor skills that provide an opportunity for the performer to engage in preperformance rituals.

Mack (2001) provided additional evidence that the consistent performance of the components of a preperformance routine is more important than the total amount of time taken to perform the routine. Although he did not assess the relative time of the components of a routine, he compared the influence of altering a normal routine in terms of its duration and component activities. He found essentially no influence on the free-throw shooting performance of university basketball players when they had to double the amount of time they normally took for their pre-shot routine, but a decrease in performance when they had to include some new activities in their normal routine.

SUMMARY

To perform a motor skill, a person prepares the motor control system just prior to performing the skill.

- The preparation process requires time, which is commonly measured by reaction time (RT); the amount of time required depends on a variety of task, situation, and personal characteristics. When used in this way, RT is an index of the preparation time needed to perform a skill.

- *Task and situation characteristics* that influence the amount of time required to prepare an action include:
  - ▶ the number of movement response alternatives (i.e., choices) in the situation from which the performer must choose only one; Hick's law describes the relationship between RT and the number of choices.
  - ▶ the predictability of the correct movement response alternative when there are several from which to choose
  - ▶ the probability of precue correctness
  - ▶ the degree of stimulus-response compatibility
  - ▶ the regularity of the length of the RT foreperiod
  - ▶ movement complexity
  - ▶ movement accuracy demands
  - ▶ the amount of movement response repetition involved in a situation

  - ▶ the amount of time available between different movement responses; when the time between two responses is short, the psychological refractory period (PRP) will influence the initiation of the second response

- *Personal characteristics* that influence the amount of time required to prepare an action include:
  - ▶ the degree of the performer's alertness
  - ▶ attention focus on the signal to move or on the movement required at the signal

- The premotor and motor components of the RT interval, which can be identified by fractionating the interval on the basis of EMG recordings from the agonist muscles, provide insight into the extent to which various preparation activities involve perceptual, cognitive, or motor processes.

- Motor control activities that occur during action preparation include:
  - ▶ postural organization
  - ▶ limb movement characteristics
  - ▶ object control movements
  - ▶ sequencing of movements
  - ▶ movement rhythmicity

POINTS FOR THE PRACTITIONER

- In situations in which people must make a decision about which of several alternative actions to perform:
  - ▶ Provide specific cues for them to use to reduce the number of "stimulus choices" in the situation on which to base the decision.
  - ▶ When it is possible to do so, provide specific advance information about which action will most likely need to be performed.

- When designing performance environments in which people will need to perform different movements to different stimuli, design the spatial relationship between the locations of the stimuli and their associated movements to be as spatially compatible as possible.

- If a person must perform a skill that requires him or her to initiate movement as quickly as possible to a specific "go" command:
  - ▸ Provide a warning signal, such as "get ready," before the command.
  - ▸ Allow a brief amount of time between the warning and command signals, but don't make this interval of time so long that the person will not be optimally prepared to move on the command.

- To obtain a reliable indication of how quickly a person can initiate movement to a specific command, have the person perform several successive repetitions of the activity and make the interval of time between the "get ready" and "go" signals different for each repetition.

- The degree of accuracy required by a movement will influence the amount of time a person needs to initiate the movement. Encourage the person to focus his or her movement preparation on the accuracy demands imposed by the environmental context and not on the movements that will be performed.

- When teaching an athlete to fake movements to gain an advantage over an opponent, emphasize the need to perform the fake as convincingly as possible so that the opponent initiates movement in response to the fake and then to perform the intended movement as soon as possible.

- When working with people who will perform skills in vigilance situations, provide strategies for them to take breaks from a sustained and continued maintenance of attention in the situation in which they must perform. These strategies will differ according to the demands of the situation.

- When helping people rehabilitate functional skills or activities of daily living, give attention to the postural preparation requirements of the situation in which the skills or activities will be performed. The muscles involved in the postural preparation process are as critical to the success of performing an activity as are the muscles involved in performing the activity itself.

RELATED READINGS

Jiang, Y., Saxe, R., & Kanwisher, N. (2004). Functional magnetic resonance imaging provides new constraints on theories of the psychological refractory period. *Psychological Science, 15,* 390–396.

Kibele, A. (2006). Non-consciously controlled decision making for fast motor reactions in sports—A priming approach for motor responses to non-consciously perceived movement features. *Psychology of Sport and Exercise, 7,* 591–610.

Klapp, S. T. (1996). Reaction time analysis of central motor control. In H. N. Zelaznik (Ed.), *Advances in motor learning and control* (pp.13–35). Champaign, IL: Human Kinetics.

Mohagheghi, A. A., & Anson, J. G. (2002). Amplitude and target diameter in motor programming of discrete, rapid aimed movements: Fitts and Peterson (1964) and Klapp (1975) revisited. *Acta Psychologica, 109,* 113–136.

Musallam, S., Corneil, B. D., Greger, B., Scherberger, H., & Andersen, R. A. (2004). Cognitive control signals for neural prosthetics. *Science, 305,* 258–262.

Petersen, T. H., Rosenberg, K., Petersen, N. C., & Nielsen, J. B. (2009). Cortical involvement in anticipatory postural reactions in man. *Experimental Brain Research, 193,* 161–171.

Rosenbaum, D. A., Cohen, R. G., Jax, S. A., Weiss, D. J., & van der Wel, R. (2007). The problem of serial order in behavior: Lashley's legacy. *Human Movement Science, 26,* 525–554.

Sarlegna, F. R., & Sainburg, R. L. (2009). The roles of vision and proprioception in the planning of reaching movements. In D. Sternad (Ed.), *Progress in motor control* (pp. 317–335). Berlin: Springer.

Van Dongen, H. P. A., & Dinges, D. F. (2005). Sleep, circadian rhythms, and psychomotor vigilance. *Clinics in Sports Medicine, 24,* 237.

Williams, A. M., Ward, P., Knowles, J. M., & Smeeton, N. J. (2002). Anticipation skill in a real-world task: Measurement, training, and transfer in tennis. *Journal of Experimental Psychology: Applied, 8,* 259–270.

Wing, A. M., & Ledeman, S. J. (1998). Anticipating load torques produced by voluntary movements. *Journal of Experimental Psychology: Human Perception and Performance, 24,* 1571–1581.

Wright, D. L., Black, C., Park, J. H., & Shea, C. H. (2001). Planning and executing simple movements: Contributions of relative-time and overall-duration specification. *Journal of Motor Behavior, 33,* 273–285.

INTERNET RESOURCES

- To watch a video presentation of an application of Hick's Law to self-defense in close quarter combatives go to http://www.youtube.com and search Hick's law; click on link: Tony Blauer on Hick's Law.

- To read an extensive discussion about the benefits, use, and development of pre-performance routines for various sports and non-sports activities, go to http://www.flowinsports.com/readingspreperformanceroutines.

- To experience the Stroop effect, go to http://faculty.washington.edu/chudler/java/ready.html.

- To read a basketball coach's application of the psychological refractory period (PRP) to various situations in basketball, go to http://www.bbhighway.com/and type PRP in the search box.

STUDY QUESTIONS

1. Discuss how we can use reaction time (RT) as an index of the preparation required to perform a motor skill.

2. Discuss how Hick's law is relevant to helping us understand the characteristics of factors that influence motor control preparation.

3. What is the cost-benefit trade-off involved in biasing the preparation of an action in the expectation of making one of several possible responses? Give a motor skill performance example illustrating this trade-off.

4. (a) Describe the relationship between stimulus-response (S-R) compatibility and the time needed to prepare to perform the action required. (b) Describe two examples of S-R compatible and S-R incompatible situations that you might experience.

5. Describe the Stroop task and what performance of it tells us about what we do when we prepare to perform an action.

6. Describe two performer characteristics that can influence action preparation. Discuss how these characteristics can influence preparation.

7. Select a motor skill and describe two motor control features of that skill that a person prepares prior to the initiation of performance of the skill.

8. Discuss how a preperformance routine can involve rhythmicity preparation and why this type of action preparation benefits performance of the action.

Specific Application Problem:
You are working in your chosen profession. Describe how you would take into account in helping people learn or relearn skills
(a) the anticipatory postural preparation aspects of the activities a person must perform and
(b) one other motor control characteristic that is an important part of the action preparation process.

Attention as a Limited Capacity Resource

Concept: Preparation for and performance of motor skills are influenced by our limited capacity to select and attend to information.

After completing this chapter, you will be able to

■ Define the term *attention* as it relates to the performance of motor skills

■ Discuss the concept of *attention capacity,* and identify the similarities and differences between fixed and flexible central-resource theories of attention capacity

■ Describe *Kahneman's model of attention* as it relates to a motor skill performance situation

■ Describe the differences between central- and multiple-resource theories of attention capacity

■ Discuss *dual-task techniques* that researchers use to assess the attention demands of performing a motor skill

■ Explain the different types of *attentional focus* a person can employ when performing a motor skill

■ Define *visual selective attention* and describe how it relates to attention capacity limits and to the performance of a motor skill

■ Discuss how skilled performers engage in visual search as they perform open and closed motor skills

APPLICATION

When you are driving your car on an open highway that has little traffic, it is relatively easy for you to carry on a conversation with a passenger in the car or on a cell phone at the same time. But what happens when the highway you are driving on becomes congested with other traffic? Isn't it difficult to carry on a conversation with your passenger or on your phone while driving under these conditions?

Consider some other examples in which doing more than one activity at a time may or may not be a problem. A skilled typist can easily carry on a conversation with someone while continuing to type— but a beginner cannot. A child learning to dribble a

ball has difficulty dribbling and running at the same time, whereas a skilled basketball player does these two activities and more at the same time. A physical therapy patient tells the therapist not to talk to her while she is trying to walk down a set of stairs.

These examples raise an important human performance and learning question: Why is it easy to do more than one thing at the same time in one situation, but difficult to do these same things simultaneously in another situation? The answer to this question comes from the study of *attention* as it relates to the performance of multiple activities at the same time.

Another aspect of attention occurs when you need to visually select and attend to specific features of the environmental context before actually

Attention and Memory

carrying out an action. For example, when you reach for a cup to drink the coffee in it, you visually note where the cup is and how full it is before you reach to pick it up. When you put your door key into the keyhole, you first look to see exactly where it is. When you need to maneuver around people and objects as you walk along a corridor, you look to see where they are, what direction they are moving in, and how fast they are going. To drive your car, you also must visually select information from the environment so that you can get safely to your destination.

In sports activities, visual attention to environmental context information is also essential. For example, visually selecting and attending to ball- and server-based cues allows the player to prepare to hit a return shot in tennis or racquetball. Skills such as determining where to direct a pass in soccer or hockey, or deciding which type of move to put on a defender in basketball or football, are all dependent on a player's successful attention to the appropriate visual cues prior to initiating action.

In the following discussion, you will be introduced to the concept of attention as it relates to the types of motor skill performance situations we have just considered. As you will see here, and in the remaining chapters in this book, the concept of attention is involved in important ways in the learning and performance of motor skills. Although the specific definition of this concept is difficult to identify, there is general agreement that it refers to our limited capability to engage in multiple cognitive and motor activities simultaneously (commonly referred to as "multitasking") and our need to selectively focus on specific environmental context features when we perform motor skills.

DISCUSSION

When the term is used in the context of human performance, **attention** refers to several characteristics associated with perceptual, cognitive, and motor activities that establish limits to our performance of motor skills. A common view of attention is that it relates to consciousness or awareness. When used in this way, attention refers to what we are thinking about (or not thinking about), or what we are aware of (or not aware of), when we perform activities. A related view extends the notion of attention to the amount of cognitive effort we put into performing activities. We will use both meanings of *attention* in this chapter as they relate to the types of situations described in the introduction.

For example, detecting performance-related information in the environment as we perform a skill can be an attention-demanding activity. We observe and attend to the environment in which we move to detect features that help us determine what skill to perform and how to perform it. Although this observation and detection activity demands our attention, it does not always require that we are consciously aware of what we observe and detect that directs our actions.

Since the earliest days of investigating human behavior, scholars have had a keen interest in the study of attention. For example, as early as 1859, Sir William Hamilton conducted studies in Britain dealing with attention. Around the same time, William Wundt, generally acknowledged as the "father of experimental psychology," investigated the concept of attention at the University of Leipzig in Germany. In America, William James provided

---

Application Problem to Solve   Describe a motor skill that you perform that requires you to do more than one thing at the same time. Describe how you can simultaneously perform these multiple activities by identifying what you think about, what you do not think about, and what you visually focus on as you perform these activities.

---

attention   in human performance, characteristics associated with consciousness, awareness, and cognitive effort as they relate to the performance of skills with particular reference to the limitations associated with these characteristics on the simultaneous performance of multiple skills and the detection of relevant information in the performance environment.

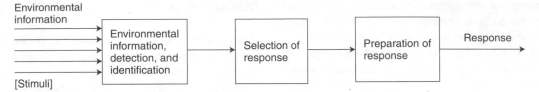

FIGURE 9.1   A generic information-processing model on which filter theories of attention were based. The figure illustrates the several stages of information processing and the serial order in which information is processed. Filter theories varied in terms of the stage at which the filter occured. Prior to the filter, the system could process several stimuli at the same time. In the model illustrated in this figure, the filter is located in the detection and identification stage.

one of the earliest definitions of attention in 1890, describing it as the "focalization, concentration, of consciousness."

Unfortunately, this late-nineteenth- and early-twentieth-century emphasis on attention soon waned, as those under the influence of behaviorism deemed the study of attention no longer relevant to the understanding of human behavior. A renaissance in attention research occurred, however, when the practical requirements of World War II included the need to understand human performance in a variety of military skills. Researchers were interested in several attention-related areas, such as the performance of more than one skill at the same time; the selection of, and attention to, relevant information from the performance environment; the performance of tasks where people had to make rapid decisions when there were several response choices; and the performance of tasks where people had to maintain attention over long periods of time. The discussion in this chapter will address two of these issues: the simultaneous performance of multiple activities, and the detection of, and attention to, relevant information in the performance environment.

ATTENTION AND MULTIPLE TASK PERFORMANCE

Scientists have known for many years that we have attention limits that influence performance when we do more than one activity at the same time.

In fact, in the late nineteenth century, a French physiologist named Jacques Loeb (1890) showed that the maximum amount of pressure that a person can exert on a hand dynamometer actually decreases when the person is engaged in mental work. Other researchers in that era also pointed out this multiple-task performance limitation (e.g., Solomons & Stein, 1896). Unfortunately, it was not until the 1950s that researchers began to try to provide a theoretical basis for this type of behavioral evidence.

Attention Theories

The most prominent among the first theories addressing attention limitations[1] was the *filter theory* of attention, sometimes referred to as the *bottleneck theory*. This theory, which evolved into many variations, proposed that a person has difficulty doing several things at one time because the human information-processing system performs each of its functions in serial order, and some of these functions can process only one piece of information at a time. This means that somewhere along the stages of information processing, the system has a *bottleneck*, where it filters out information not selected for further processing (see figure 9.1). Variations of this theory were based on the processing stage in which the bottleneck occurred. Some contended it existed very early, at the stage of detection of environmental information (e.g., Welford, 1952, 1967; Broadbent, 1958), whereas others argued that it

[1]For an excellent review and discussion of the history and evolution of attention theories, see Neumann (1996).

occurred later, after information was perceived or after it had been processed cognitively (e.g., Norman, 1968).

This type of theoretical viewpoint remained popular for many years, until it became evident that the filter theories of attention did not adequately explain all performance situations. The most influential alternative proposed that information-processing functions could be carried out in parallel rather than serially, but attention limits were the result of the *limited availability of resources* needed to carry out those functions. Just as you have limited economic resources to pay for your activities, we all have limited attention resources to do all the activities that we may attempt at one time.

Theories emphasizing attentional resource limits propose that we can perform several tasks simultaneously, as long as the resource capacity limits of the system are not exceeded. However, if these limits are exceeded, we experience difficulty performing one or more of these tasks. Theorists who adhere to this viewpoint differ in their views of *where the resource limit exists.* Some propose that there is one central resource pool from which all attention resources are allocated, whereas others propose multiple sources for resources.

Finally, more recent attention theories have moved away from the concept of a central capacity limit to one that emphasizes the selection and integration of information and activities associated with the various functional aspects of human performance, such as those depicted in figure 9.1. The primary focus of these theories has been in the area of visual selective attention, which will be discussed later in this chapter.

Central-Resource Capacity Theories

According to some attention theories, there is a central reservoir of resources for which all activities compete. Following the analogy of your economic resources, these **central-resource theories** compare human attention capacity to a single source from which all activities must be funded. To illustrate this view, consider a rather simplistic analogy in which the available attention resources exist within one large circle, like the one depicted

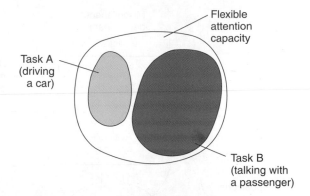

FIGURE 9.2   Diagram showing that two tasks (A and B) can be performed simultaneously (e.g., driving a car while talking with a passenger) if the attention demanded by the tasks does not exceed the available attention capacity. Note that the amount of available capacity and the amount of attention demanded by each task to be performed may increase or decrease, a change that would be represented in this diagram by changing the sizes of the appropriate circles.

in figure 9.2. Next, consider as smaller circles the specific tasks that require these resources, such as driving a car (task A) and talking with a friend (task B). Each circle by itself fits inside the larger circle. But for a person to successfully perform both tasks simultaneously, both small circles must fit into the large circle. Problems arise when we try to fit into the large circle more small circles than will fit.

Kahneman's attention theory. A good example of a central resource theory is one proposed by Nobel laureate Daniel Kahneman (1973). Although this theory was originally presented many years ago, it continues to influence our present views about attention (e.g., Tombu & Jolicoeur, 2005). And although some researchers (e.g., Neumann, 1996) have pointed out shortcomings in Kahneman's theory in terms of accounting for all aspects of attention and human performance, it continues to serve as a useful guide

central-resource theories of attention   attention-capacity theories that propose one central source of attention resources for which all activities requiring attention compete.

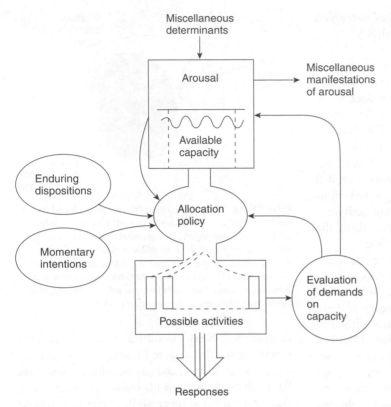

FIGURE 9.3   Kahneman's model of attention. [From Kahneman, D. (1973). *Attention and effort,* © 1973, p. 10. Reprinted by permission of Prentice Hall, Inc., Englewood Cliffs, NJ]

to direct our understanding of some basic characteristics of attention-related limits on the simultaneous performance of multiple activities.

Kahneman views attention as *cognitive effort,* which he relates to the mental resources needed to carry out specific activities. The location of the source of these resources is central, which means the CNS; furthermore, there is a limited amount of these resources available for use at any given time. In Kahneman's model (see figure 9.3), the single source of our mental resources from which we derive cognitive effort is presented as a "central pool" of resources (i.e., available capacity) that has a *flexible capacity*. This means that the amount of available attention can vary depending on certain conditions related to the individual, the tasks being performed, and the situation. According to the illustration in figure 9.2, this flexible central-capacity theory states that the size of the large

circle can change according to certain personal, task, and situation characteristics.

Kahneman views the *available* attention that a person can give to an activity or activities as a general *pool of effort*. The person can subdivide this pool so that he or she can allocate attention to several activities at the same time. Allocation of attention resources is determined by characteristics of the activities and the allocation policy of the individual, which in turn is influenced by situations internal and external to the individual.

Figure 9.3 depicts the various conditions that influence the amount of available resource (i.e., attention capacity) and how a person will allocate these resources. First, notice that the central pool of available resources (i.e., available capacity) is represented as a box at the top of the model. The wavy line indicates that the capacity limit for the amount of attention available is flexible. Notice also that

A CLOSER LOOK

An Attention-Capacity Explanation of the Arousal-Performance Relationship

A widely held view of the relationship between arousal and performance is that it takes the form of an inverted U. This means that when we graph this relationship, placing on the vertical axis the performance level ranging from poor to high, and placing on the horizontal axis the arousal level ranging from very low to very high, the plot of the relationship resembles an inverted U. This type of relationship indicates that arousal levels that are either too low or too high will result in poor performance. However, between these extremes is a range of arousal levels that should yield high performance levels.

If, as Kahneman's model indicates, arousal levels influence available attention capacity in a similar way, we can attribute some of the arousal level-performance relationship to available attention capacity. This means that arousal levels that are too low or too high lead to poor performance, because the person does not have the attentional resources needed to perform the activity. When the arousal level is optimal, sufficient attention resources are available for the person to achieve a high level of performance.

within this box is the word "Arousal." Kahneman included this word to indicate that the arousal level of the person significantly influences that person's available attention capacity at any given time. More specifically, a person's attention capacity will increase or decrease according to his or her *arousal level*. **Arousal** is the general state of excitability of a person, reflected in the activation levels of the person's emotional, mental, and physiological systems. If the person's arousal level is too low or too high, he or she has a smaller available attention capacity than he or she would if the arousal level were in an optimal range. This means that for a person to have available the maximum attention resources, the person must be at an optimal arousal level.

Second, another critical factor determining whether the amount of available attention capacity is sufficient for performing the multiple tasks is the *attention demands, or requirements, of the tasks to be performed*. This factor is represented in Kahneman's model in figure 9.3 as the *evaluation of demands on capacity*. The important point here is that tasks differ in the amount of attention they demand. As a result, the person must evaluate these demands to determine if he or she can do them all simultaneously or if he or she will not be able to perform some of them.

Finally, *three general rules influence how people allocate attentional resources*. One is that we

allocate attention to ensure that we can complete one activity. A second rule is that we allocate attentional resources according to our *enduring dispositions*. These are the basic rules of "involuntary" attention, which concern those things that seem to naturally attract our attention (i.e., distract us). We typically will "involuntarily" direct our attention to (or be distracted by) at least *two types of characteristics of events* in our environment, even though we may be attending to something else at the time.

A third rule is that the event is *novel* for the situation in which it occurs. These events can be visual or auditory. In terms of novel visual events, think about why fans at a basketball game who sit behind the basket like to stand and wave objects in the air while a player is attempting to shoot free throws. Or, consider why you become distracted while driving your car when a ball rolls onto the street in front of you. That we spontaneously and involuntary allocate our visual attention to novel events such as these is well supported by research evidence (see Cole, Gellatly, & Blurton, 2001; and Pashler & Harris, 2001, for excellent reviews of this evidence).

---

arousal   the general state of excitability of a person, involving physiological, emotional, and mental systems.

This bicycle rider, who can drink water, steer the bike, pedal the bike, maintain balance, see ahead to determine where to go and how to avoid road hazards, etc., demonstrates the simultaneous performance of multiple activities.

Unexpected noise also presents a novel event that spontaneously and involuntarily attracts our attention. For example, how many times have you directed your attention away from the person teaching your class to one of your classmates when he or she sneezes very loudly or drops a book on the floor? Consider a different type of example. Why is a professional golfer who is preparing to putt distracted by a spectator talking, when a basketball player who is preparing to shoot a free throw is not distracted by thousands of spectators yelling and screaming? The most likely reason is that the golfer does not expect to hear someone talking while preparing to putt, but for the basketball player, the noise is a common part of the game. As

a result, the noise is novel in one situation but not in the other.

The second characteristic of events that will involuntarily direct our attention is the *meaningfulness* of the event to us personally. A classic example of this characteristic is known as the *cocktail party phenomenon,* which was first described in the 1950s (Cherry, 1953). Undoubtedly, you have experienced this phenomenon yourself. Suppose you are at a party in a room filled with people. You are attending to your conversation with another person. Suddenly you hear someone near you mention your name in a conversation that person is having with other people. What do you do? You probably redirect your attention away from your own conversation to the person who said your name. Why did you do this? The reason relates to the meaningfulness of your name to you. Even though you were attending to your own conversation, this meaningful event caused you to spontaneously shift your attention. In sports, it is not uncommon to hear athletes say that while they are performing, the only person they hear saying something to them is the coach. Why? In this competitive situation, the person's coach is very meaningful to the athlete.

The third rule concerning our allocation of attention relates to a person's *momentary intentions*. This phrase means that a person allocates attention in a situation according to his or her specific intentions. Sometimes, these intentions are self-directed, which means the person has personally decided to direct attention to a certain aspect of the situation. At other times, momentary intentions result from instructions given to the person about how or where to direct his or her attentional resources. For example, if a physical therapist tells a patient to "pay close attention to where you place your foot on the stair step," the patient has the "momentary intention" to allocate his or her attention according to the therapist's instruction.

Multiple-Resource Theories

Multiple-resource theories provide an alternative to theories proposing a central resource pool of attention resources. Multiple-resource theories contend that we have several attention mechanisms,

A CLOSER LOOK

Attention and Cell Phone Use while Driving

A common concern throughout the world is the use of cell phones by people who are driving motor vehicles. Many countries, and some cities and states in the United States, have passed laws that prohibit cell phone use while driving. In some instances, the laws prohibit the use of both handheld and hands-free cell phones, while in other cases, laws allow hands-free cell phone use. The following information, taken from an article by Strayer and Johnston (2001), provides some basis for concern.

- A study by the United States Department of Transportation indicated that as many as half of the motor vehicle accidents in the United States can be related to driver inattention and other human error.
- A survey of cell phone owners reported that approximately 85 percent use their phones while driving, and 27 percent of those use the phones on half of their trips (Goodman et al., 1999; a summary of their report is available online at www.nhtsa.dot.gov).
- A study of cell phone records of 699 people who had been involved in motor-vehicle accidents reported that 24 percent were using their cell phones within the 10 min period before the accident (Redelmeier & Tibshirani, 1997).

Although research evidence supports a relationship between cell phone use and motor vehicle accidents, the issue of cell phone use as the cause of accidents remains unsolved. However, researchers who have investigated this issue, in either car simulators or simulated driving situations in laboratories, report evidence that indicates an attention-related basis for driving accidents. In their article, Strayer and Johnson reported a series of experiments in which participants engaged in a simulated driving task in a laboratory. The results indicated these things:

- Participants missed two times more simulated traffic signals when they were engaged in cell phone conversations; and, when they responded correctly to the signals (i.e., red lights), their reaction time (RT) was significantly slower than when they were not using the cell phone.
- No significant differences were found between handheld and hands-free cell phone use for the number of missed traffic signals and RT (a result that is problematic for a multiple-resource theory of attention). (It is worth noting that a study by Treffner and Barrett [2004] found critical problems with movement coordination characteristics when people were using a hands-free mobile phone while driving.)
- The generation of phone conversations influenced the number of missed traffic signals and RT more than did listening to the radio or to a section of a book on audiotape.

Comparisons of conversations on cell phones and conversations with car passengers have consistently found that cell phone conversations are related to more driving errors than are passenger conversations. For example, in a comparison of driving performance while conversing on a cell phone, conversing with a passenger, and having no conversation, researchers at the University of Utah found that when drivers engaged in cell phone conversations, they increased their driving errors (Drews, Pasupathi, & Strayer, 2008). The conversation characteristics were distinctly different, which the researchers contended influenced the results. The primary difference was that passenger conversations would change as traffic situations changed, which led to a shared awareness of traffic characteristics. Cell phone conversations did not reflect this shared awareness.

each having limited resources. Each resource pool is specific to a component of performing skills. Using a government analogy, the resources are available in various government agencies, and competition for the resources occurs only among those activities related to the specific agencies.

multiple-resource theories   theories of attention proposing that there are several attention resource mechanisms, each of which is related to a specific information-processing activity and is limited in how much information it can process simultaneously.

LAB LINKS

Lab 9 in the Online Learning Center Lab Manual provides an opportunity for you to experience the dual task procedure to assess attention capacity demands of two tasks performed simultaneously.

The most prevalent of the multiple-resource theories was proposed by Navon and Gopher (1979), Allport (1980), and Wickens (1980, 1992).

Wickens proposed what has become the most popular of these theories. He stated that resources for processing information are available from three different sources. These are the *input and output modalities* (e.g., vision, limbs, and speech system), the *stages of information processing* (e.g., perception, memory encoding, response output), and the *codes of processing information* (e.g., verbal codes, spatial codes). Our success in performing two or more tasks simultaneously depends on whether those tasks demand our attention from a common resource or from different resources. When two tasks must be performed simultaneously and share a common resource, they will be performed less well than when the two tasks compete for different resources.

For example, the multiple-resource view would explain variations in the situation involving driving a car while talking with a passenger in the following way. When there is little traffic, driving does not demand many resources from any of the three different sources. But when traffic gets heavy, resource demand increases from these two sources: input-output modalities and stages of information processing. These are the same two sources involved in providing attention resources for carrying on a conversation with a friend. As a result, to maintain safe driving, the person must reduce the resource demand of the conversation activity.

An advantage of multiple-resource theories is their focus on the types of demands placed on various information-processing and response outcome structures, rather than on a nonspecific resource capacity. The resource-specific attention view provides a practical guide to help us determine when task demands may be too great to be performed simultaneously. For example, if one task requires a hand response and one requires a vocal response, a person should have little difficulty performing them simultaneously, because they do not demand attention from the same resource structure. Conversely, people have difficulty performing two different hand responses simultaneously because they both demand resources from the same structure. (For a more in-depth discussion of the multiple-resource view of attention, and its practical applications in the field of human factors, see Hancock, Oron-Gilad, & Szalma, 2007.)

THE DUAL-TASK PROCEDURE FOR ASSESSING ATTENTION DEMANDS

A common experimental procedure used to investigate attention-limit issues is the **dual-task procedure.** The general purpose of experiments using this technique is to determine the attention demands and characteristics of the simultaneous performance of two different tasks. Researchers typically determine the attention demands of one of the two tasks by noting the degree of interference caused on that task while it is performed simultaneously with another task, called the *secondary task.*

The *primary task* in the dual-task procedure is typically the task of interest, whose performance experimenters are observing in order to assess its attention demands. Depending on the purpose of the experiment, the performer may or may not need to maintain consistent primary-task performance, whether performing that task alone or simultaneously with the secondary task.

If instructions in the experiment require the participant to pay attention to the primary task so that it is performed as well alone as with the secondary task, then secondary-task performance is the basis researchers use to make inferences about the attention demands of the primary task. On the other hand, if the experiment does not direct the person to attend primarily to either task, performance on both tasks is compared to performance when each task is performed alone.

A CLOSER LOOK

Dual-Task Techniques Used to Assess Attention Demands of Motor Skill Performance

Researchers typically have used one of two dual-task techniques in their investigations of the attention demands associated with the preparation and performance of motor skills. Each technique relates to a specific attention-demand issue.

Continuous Secondary-Task Technique

Purpose. To determine if attention capacity is required *throughout* the performance of a motor skill.

Procedure. A person performs the primary and secondary tasks separately and simultaneously. When the person performs both tasks simultaneously, he or she is instructed to concentrate on the performance of the primary task while continuously performing the secondary task.

Rationale. If the primary task demands full attention capacity, performance will be poorer on a secondary task while performing it together with the primary task than when performing only the secondary task. If attention capacity can be shared by both tasks, simultaneous performance should be similar to that of each task alone.

Example. As a person walks from one end of a hallway to the other, he or she must listen to words spoken through earphones; when the person hears each word, he or she must repeat the word that was spoken just prior to that word (i.e., the secondary task is a short-term memory task that involves interference during the retention interval).

Secondary-Task Probe Technique

Purpose. To determine the attention demands required by the *preparation* of a skill, by the performance of *specific components* of a skill, or at *specific times* during the performance of a skill.

Procedure. A person performs the primary and secondary tasks separately and simultaneously. The secondary task (a discrete task) is performed at predetermined times before or during primary-task performance (i.e., the secondary task "probes" the primary task).

Rationale. If a probed site of the primary task demands full attention capacity, performance will be poorer on a secondary task while performing it together with the primary task than when performing only the secondary task. If attention capacity can be shared by both tasks at the probed site, simultaneous performance should be similar to that of each task alone.

Example. As a person reaches for and grasps a cup of water to drink from it, he or she must listen through earphones for a "beep" sound at any time just before or during the performance of the activity. As soon as the person hears the "beep" he or she says "bop" into a microphone (i.e., the secondary task is a simple auditory-reaction time task that requires a vocal response).

FOCUSING ATTENTION

In addition to having to allocate attention among several activities, people also direct attention to specific features of the environment and to action preparation activities. This attention-directing process is known as **attentional focus.** As opposed to attentional demands, which concern the allocation of attentional resources to various tasks that need to be performed simultaneously, attentional focus concerns the marshaling of available resources in

dual-task procedure   an experimental procedure used in the study of attention to determine the amount of attention required to perform an action, or a part of an action; the procedure involves assessing the degree of interference caused by one task when a person is simultaneously performing another task.

attentional focus   the directing of attention to specific characteristics in a performance environment, or to action-preparation activities.

A CLOSER LOOK

Dual-Task Interference during Gait in People with Parkinson's Disease

A study by O'Shea, Morris, and Iansek (2002) provides a good example of the use of the dual-task procedure to study attention demands of activities, and an opportunity to consider the relationship between movement disorders and attention demands as it relates to multiple-task performance.

Participants: 15 people (mean age = 68.3 yrs) with Parkinson's disease (PD) and 15 comparison people (mean age = 67.7 yrs) without PD. The people with PD were in a self-determined "on" phase of their medication cycle.

Walking tasks:
1. Walk 14 m at a self-selected speed (single task: free walking)
2. Walk while transferring as many coins as possible from one pocket to another on their opposite side (motor secondary task: manual object manipulation)
3. Walk while counting backward aloud by threes from a three-digit number (cognitive secondary task: subtraction)

Standing tasks: Perform the coin transfer task and the digit subtraction task while standing.

Results:

Walking tasks change from walking only to walking while performing a secondary task:

	Walking Speed		Stride Length	
	PD Group	No–PD Group	PD Group	No–PD group
With Coin Task:	−18.5%	−7.4%	−15.4%	−7.4%
With Subtraction Task:	−18.7%	−6.9%	−18.7%	−6.9%

Secondary tasks change from performing it while standing to performing it while walking:

	PD Group	No–PD Group
Coin task (coins/min rate)	−17.4%	0.0%
Subtraction task (responses/min rate)	−4.7%	+13.1%

Conclusions: People with PD showed
- a greater amount of deterioration in their walking gait characteristics when they had to simultaneously perform a manual object-manipulation task and cognitive task involving subtraction than comparably aged people who did not have PD
- a slower rate of performing a manual object-manipulation task and a cognitive task involving subtraction when they had to perform these tasks while walking than when they performed them while standing

order to direct them to specific aspects of our performance or performance environment.

We can consider attentional focus in terms of both width and direction of focus. *Width* indicates that our attention can have a *broad or narrow* focus on environmental information and mental activities. *Direction* indicates that our attention focus can

be *external or internal:* attention may be focused on cues in the environment or on internal thoughts, plans, or problem-solving activities. Nideffer (1993) showed that the broad and narrow focus widths and the external and internal focus directions interact to establish four types of attention-focus situations that relate to performance.

Individuals in performance situations require specific types of attention focus to achieve successful performance. For example, a person needs a broad/external focus to walk successfully through a crowded hallway, but a narrow/external focus to catch a ball. Sometimes, situations require us to shift the type of attention focus and the object of that attention. We do this by engaging in what is referred to as *attention switching*. It is an advantage to switch attention focus rapidly among environmental and situational pieces of information when we must use a variety of sources of information for rapid decision making. For example, a football quarterback may look to decide if the primary receiver is open; if not, he must find an alternate receiver. In the meantime, the quarterback must make decisions related to whether or not he is about to be tackled or kept from delivering a pass. Each of these activities requires attention and must be carried out in the course of a few seconds. To do this, the player must rapidly switch attention between external and internal sources of information.

However, certain kinds of attention switching can be a disadvantage in the performance of some activities. For example, a person performing a skill that requires a rapid, accurate series of movements, such as typing, piano playing, or dancing, will be more successful if he or she focuses attention on a primary source of information for extended periods of time. Problems can arise if the person's attention is switched too frequently between appropriate and inappropriate sources of information. For example, if a pianist is constantly switching visual attention from the written music to the hands and keys, he or she will have difficulty maintaining the precise timing structure required by the piece being played.

Focusing Attention on Movements versus Movement Effects

If, as we just discussed, it is best for people to narrow their attention focus while performing certain skills, a relevant question concerns the specific location of the attention focus. Although Nideffer presented the direction options of internal and external to represent the location, there is an alternative way to use these terms when referring to the

performance of a specific skill. Is it preferable to focus attention on one's own movements (*internal focus*) or on the effects of one's own movements (*external focus*)? This question has intrigued scientists for many years, which we can see if we look at the classic and influential work of William James (1890). He raised this same question more than a century ago and offered as an answer that the directing of attention to the "remote effects" (i.e., outcome of a movement, or movement effects) would lead to better performance than attention to the "close effects" (i.e., the movements). He presented an example of a reaching/aiming movement to illustrate his point: "Keep your eye at the place aimed at, and your hand will fetch [the target]; think of your hand, and you will likely miss your aim" (p. 520).

The German scholar Wolfgang Prinz (1997) formalized this view by proposing the **action effect hypothesis** (Prinz, 1997), which proposes that actions are best planned and controlled by their intended effects. The theory basis for this hypothesis relates to how we code sensory and motor information in memory. Prinz contends that we represent both in memory in a common code, which argues against the separation of perception and action as unique and distinct events. Without going further into the theory issues involved, the common coding view predicts that actions will be more effective when they are planned in terms of their intended outcomes rather than in terms of the movement patterns required by the skill.

An interesting application of this hypothesis was reported in an article in *The New Yorker* magazine (Acocella, 2003) about the great ballerina Suzanne Farrell. Although retired from performing, she teaches ballet to experienced students and

---

action effect hypothesis   the proposition that actions are best planned and controlled by their intended effects. When related to attention focus, this hypothesis proposes that the learning and performance of skills are optimized when the performer's attention is directed to the intended outcome of the action rather than on the movements themselves.

professional dancers. In her teaching, she emphasizes that the dancers concentrate on the effect they want to create with movements rather than on the movements themselves.

When researchers have investigated the action effect hypothesis, they have reported strong support with evidence based on a variety of laboratory and sports skills (e.g., Wulf, McNevin, & Shea, 2001; Wulf & Prinz, 2001). The results of this research have been remarkably consistent in showing that when performers direct their attention focus to the movement effects, they perform the skill at a higher level than when their attention focus is on their own movements. It is important to note here that research has shown that the focus of attention is also relevant for the learning of motor skills. We will discuss the influence of focus of attention on the learning of skills in more detail in chapter 14 when we discuss verbal instructions and their effects on skill learning.

The reason an external focus of attention results in better skill performance has been the subject of some debate (see Wulf & Prinz, 2001, for a discussion of the various issues in this debate). However, the most commonly accepted reason is the *constrained action hypothesis,* which was proposed by Wulf and her colleagues (e.g., McNevin, Shea, & Wulf, 2003; Wulf, McNevin, & Shea, 2001). According to this hypothesis an internal focus "constrains" the motor system because the performer consciously attempts to control it, which results in a disruption of the automatic motor control processes that should control performance of the skill. But when the performer engages in an external focus of attention, the automatic (i.e., Nonconscious) processes control performance. Research support for this view has come from several studies that involved a variety of techniques, including dual-task probe reaction times and EMG assessment (see Zachry, Wulf, Mercer, & Bezodis, 2005 for a brief review of these studies).

ATTENTION AND AUTOMATICITY

Automaticity is an important concept in our understanding of attention and motor skill performance. The term **automaticity** is commonly used to indicate that a person performs a skill or engages in an information-processing activity without demands on attention capacity. We briefly considered the attention capacity demands of a skill in the discussion of the evaluation of the task demands component of Kahneman's model of attention. Information-processing activities include the visual search of the environment that occurs as a person assesses the environmental context regulatory characteristics associated with performing a skill; the use of *tau* when moving toward an object to make or avoid contact with it, or when an object is moving toward a person who needs to catch or strike it; the storing of information in memory and the retrieval of information from memory; the selection of an action to perform and the movement characteristics that must be applied to carry out the action; and the actual production of an action. From an attention point of view, the question of interest with regard to these activities concerns the attention capacity demand of each activity.

Logan (1985, 1988, 1998), who has produced some of the most important research and thinking about the concept of automaticity and motor skill performance, views automaticity as an acquired skill that should be viewed as a continuum of varying degrees of automaticity. This means that rather than considering the attention capacity demand of an information-processing activity in terms of "yes, it demands capacity," or "no, it doesn't demand capacity," the continuum view considers automaticity as related to demanding varying amounts of attention capacity. Logan proposes that, as with skill, people acquire automaticity with practice. As a result, the degree of automaticity for a skill or information-processing activity may be only partially automatic when the attention demand of the activity is assessed.

Researchers have also provided evidence for neural components associated with automaticity as it relates to motor skill performance. For example, research by Poldrack and his associates (Poldrack et al. 2005) used fMRI procedures to show that different brain areas are active when performance of both tasks in a dual-task situation demand attention compared to when one of the tasks does not demand attention when performed in the same situation. (This latter characteristic of no attention demanded by a task indicates automaticity for its performance.) Their results indicated that the supplementary motor area (SMA) and putamen/globus pallidus regions are more involved with automaticity than when each of the two tasks demand attention, when the prefrontal regions are more active.

VISUAL SELECTIVE ATTENTION

In addition to the capacity limits of attention, the selection of performance-related information in the environment is also important to the study of attention as it relates to the learning and performance of motor skills. This area of study is commonly referred to as **selective attention.** Of particular interest to researchers has been *visual selective attention,* which concerns the role of vision in motor skill performance in directing visual attention to environmental information (sometimes referred to as "cues") that influences the preparation and/or the performance of an action. Because the use of vision in this way is primarily an attention issue, it is included here rather than in chapter 7 where we discussed the roles vision plays in the motor control of several motor skills. (For a discussion of the neural basis of selective attention, see Yantis, 2008.)

Researchers have disputed since the end of the nineteenth century about whether visual selective attention is active or passive (sometimes phrased as "top-down or bottom-up," or "goal directed or stimulus driven"). In terms of the information-processing model in figure 9.1, the basis for this dispute concerns how we select information from the environmental context to process in the first stage. Do we visually select relevant environmental cues according to our action intentions and goals, or do we visually attend to environmental cues because of their distinctiveness or meaningfulness in the situation? In their review of the visual attention research literature, Egeth and Yantis (1997) concluded that these two types of visual attention control "almost invariably interact" (p. 270). This means that in most performance situations, our intentions and goals as well as certain characteristics

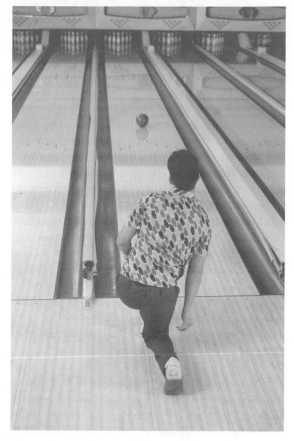

Visual selective attention plays an important role in bowling.

in the environment influence our visual attention. In other words, although we may actively seek environmental cues based on our action intentions and goals, we may also attend to certain cues

automaticity   the term used to indicate that a person performs a skill, or engages in certain information-processing activities, without requiring attention resources.

selective attention   in the study of attention as it relates to human learning and performance, the term used to refer to the detection and selection of performance-related information in the performance environment.

because of their distinct characteristics. You will see evidence of this active-passive visual attention throughout this discussion.

The term **visual search** is used to describe the process of directing visual attention to locate relevant environmental cues. During the preparation process for performing many skills, people carry out visual search to select from the environment those cues that are relevant for the performance of a skill in a specific situation. In the following sections, we consider the actual process of selecting appropriate information from the environment, and give examples from various sport and everyday skills to illustrate how visual search is an important component of the performance of both open and closed motor skills.

As you read the following sections, you may find it helpful to refer back to chapter 6, where we discussed various procedures researchers have used to investigate the role of vision in motor control. You will find that researchers who study visual selective attention have used these same procedures.

Eye Movements and Visual Selective Attention

As you read in chapter 6, eye movement recordings track the location of central vision while people observe a scene. However, an important question arises concerning how well this procedure assesses visual selective attention. The rationale for the use of the procedure is that what a person is looking at (i.e., the point of gaze) should give researchers insight into what information in the environment the person is attending to. But there is an important research question here: Is this a valid assumption? Can we validly relate eye movements to visual attention?

Two characteristics of the use of eye movement recordings provide an answer. First, research evidence has shown consistently that it is possible to give attention to a feature in the environment without moving the eyes to focus on that feature (see Henderson, 1996; Zelinsky et al., 1997; and Brisson & Jolicoeur, 2007, for reviews of this evidence). This would mean that peripheral vision was the source of picking up the relevant information. However, it is *not* possible to make an eye

movement without a corresponding shift in attention. Second, because eye movement recordings are limited to the assessment of central vision, they do not assess peripheral vision. Research evidence has shown that peripheral vision is involved in visual attention in motor skill performance (see Bard, Fleury, & Goulet, 1994 for a brief review of this research). As a result of these two factors, eye movement recordings cannot provide a complete picture of the environmental features to which the person is directing visual attention. Therefore, eye movement recordings typically *underestimate* what a person is visually attending to. However, even with these limitations, the recording of eye movements is a useful technique to provide reasonable estimates of those features in the environment that a person directs visual attention to as he or she prepares and performs a motor skill.

How We Select Visual Cues

Theories concerning how we select certain cues in the environment address the selection of cues for nonmoving as well as moving objects. Both situations are important for the performance of motor skills. For example, visual search for regulatory conditions associated with stationary objects is critical for successful prehension actions. Without detection of these conditions a person would not have the information needed to prepare and initiate movement to reach for and grasp a cup, or any stationary object.

Visual search and intended actions. The visual search for regulatory conditions in the performance environment is an active search that a person engages in according to the action he or she intends to perform. This means that the performer looks for specific cues in the performance environment that will enable him or her to achieve a specific action goal. For example, if a person intends to pick up a cup to drink from it, he or she will visually search for features of the cup and environment that will indicate the movement characteristics to implement. This search could include looking to see how full the cup is, what type of liquid is in it, the location of the cup in terms of distance from the

A CLOSER LOOK

Visual Search and Attention Allocation Rules

If the key to successful selection of environmental information when performing motor skills is the distinctiveness of the relevant features, an important question is this:

What Makes Certain Features More Distinctive than Others?

Insight into answering this question comes from the attention allocation rules in Kahneman's theory of attention (1973), which we discussed earlier in this chapter:

- **Unexpected features attract our attention.** You can see this in your own daily experience. While concentrating on your professor during a lecture, haven't you been distracted when a classmate has dropped some books on the floor? Undoubtedly, you switched your visual attention from the professor

to search for the source of the noise. When the environment includes features that typically are not there, their distinctiveness increases. The result is that people have a tendency to direct visual attention to them.

- **We allocate attention to the most meaningful features.** In the performance environment, the most meaningful cues "pop out" and become very evident to the performer. Meaningfulness is a product of experience and instruction. As a person experiences performing in certain environments, critical cues for successful performance are invariant and increase in their meaningfulness, often without the person's conscious awareness. Instruction also plays a part in the way certain features of cues become more meaningful than others.

---

person, and whether or not there may be obstacles between the person and the cup. By actively looking for these features, the person can prepare the movement characteristics to reach for, pick up, and drink from the cup. This view of a visual search process fits well with the research evidence you saw in chapter 7 that showed the influence of various object and environment features on prehension movement kinematics.

Research evidence also supports the view that we actively visually search the performance environment according to action intentions. For example, Bekkering and Neggers (2002) demonstrated that the focus of initial eye movements differed when participants in their experiment were told to point to or grasp an object. The intention to grasp an object directed participants' visual search to the spatial orientation of an object, whereas the intention to point to the object did not. The authors concluded that a specific action intention enhances the visual detection of those regulatory conditions that are relevant to the intended action.

The feature integration theory. Although researchers have proposed several theories to account

for the characteristics of how we select certain cues in the environment and ignore others (see Neumann, 1996, for a review of these theories), one of the more popular theories is the *feature integration theory* proposed by Treisman in the 1980s (e.g., Treisman & Gelade 1980; Treisman 1988; see also Chan & Hayward, 2009). This theory indicates that during visual search, we initially group stimuli together according to their unique features, such as color or shape. This grouping occurs automatically. These groups of features form "maps" related to the various values of various features. For example, a color map would identify the various colors in the observed scene, whereas a shape map would indicate which shapes are observed. These maps become the basis for further search processes when the task demands that the person identify specific cues. For further processing, we

---

visual search   the process of directing visual attention to locate relevant information in the environment that will enable a person to determine how to prepare and perform a skill in a specific situation.

must use attention, and must direct it to selecting specific features of interest.

The selection of features of interest occurs when a person focuses the *attentional spotlight* on the master map of all features. People can direct attention over a wide or a narrow area, and it appears that the spotlight can be split to cover different map areas. If the person's task is to search for a target having a certain distinct feature, then the target will "pop out" as a result of this search process, because the feature is distinct among the groupings of features. Thus, the more distinctive the feature is that identifies the target of the visual search, the more quickly the person can identify and locate the target. If the distinctive feature is a part of several cues, the search slows as the person assesses each cue in terms of how its characteristics match those of the target. (See Hershler & Hochstein, 2005, for an extended discussion of feature integration theory and factors that influence the "pop out" effect.)

For movement situations, McLeod, Driver, Dienes, and Crisp (1991) proposed a *movement filter* in the visual system that would allow visual attention to be directed at just the moving items in the person's environment. They suggested that this movement filter mechanism can be related to Treisman's feature integration theory's emphasis on the importance of grouping in visual search by operating as a subsystem to a group's common movement characteristics. In light of this view it is interesting to note that Abernethy (1993) described research evidence to demonstrate that in sports involving fast ball action, such as racquet sports, skilled players visually search the playing environment for the *minimal essential information* necessary to determine an action to perform. This information is the invariant perceptual feature of a performance context. We described one of these invariant features in chapter 7 when we discussed the importance of the use of time-to-contact information to catch a ball, contact or avoid an object while walking or running, and strike a moving ball.

Abernethy adds to this example of minimal essential information the detection of the coordination kinematics of an opponent's action, which involves the grouping of displacement characteristics of the joints involved in a coordinated movement pattern. As a person becomes more skillful, his or her visual attention becomes increasingly more attuned to detecting the important kinematic features, which provides the skilled player an advantage over the less-skilled player in anticipating the opponent's action in a situation. In effect then, this minimal essential information "pops out" for the skilled player and directs the player's visual attention as he or she prepares an appropriate action to respond to his or her opponent's action.

VISUAL SEARCH AND MOTOR SKILL PERFORMANCE

Visual search picks up critical cues that influence three parts of the action control process: *action selection, constraining of the selected action* (i.e., determining the specific movement features for performing the action), and *timing of action initiation.* By influencing these processes, the visual system enables a person to prepare, initiate, and execute the movements of an action that conform to the specific requirements of the performance context.

Research investigating visual search in performance situations has produced evidence about what is involved in these important preparation and performance processes. The following research examples illustrate how researchers have investigated a variety of sports and everyday skills, and provide a sense of what we currently know about the characteristics of visual search processes related to the performance of open and closed motor skills.

Visual Search in Open Motor Skills

Returning a badminton serve. The experiments by Abernethy and Russell (1987) described earlier in chapter 6 provide the best example of research investigations of visual search by expert badminton players. They found that the time between the initiation of the badminton server's backswing and the shuttle's hitting the floor in the receiver's court is approximately 400 msec (0.4 sec). Within that time period, there appears to be a critical time window for visually picking up critical cues predicting

A CLOSER LOOK

Two Examples of Severe Time Constraints on Visual Search

There are some situations in sport in which researchers can determine the actual amount of time a person has to engage in visual search and to prepare an action. Two of these are returning a serve in tennis and hitting a baseball. In each of these situations, it is clearly to the player's advantage to detect the information needed as early as possible in order to prepare and initiate the appropriate action.

Preparing to Return a Tennis Serve

A serve traveling at 90 to 100 mi/hr (145 to 161 km/hr) allows the receiver only 0.5 to 0.6 sec to hit the ball. This means that the person must search as soon as possible for the cues that will provide information about the direction, speed, landing point, and bounce characteristics of the ball so that he or she can select, organize, and execute an appropriate return stroke.

Preparing to Hit a Baseball

When a pitcher throws a ball at a speed of 90 mi/hr, it will arrive at home plate in approximately 0.45 sec. Suppose that it takes 0.1 sec for the batter to get his or her bat to the desired point of ball contact. This means that the batter has less than 0.35 sec after the ball leaves the pitcher's hand to make a decision and to initiate the swing. If the pitcher releases the ball 10 to 15 ft in front of the rubber, the batter has less than 0.3 sec of decision and swing initiation time.

where the shuttle will land. This window, which lasts from about 83 msec before until 83 msec after racquet-shuttle contact, provides information about racquet movement and shuttle flight that seems to resolve uncertainty about where the served shuttle will land. Experts use the 83 msec period prior to racquet-shuttle contact more effectively than novices. As a result, experts have more time to prepare their returns. The racquet and the arm are the primary sources to visually search for the anticipatory cues needed to prepare the return.

Returning a tennis serve. Results from two experiments by Goulet, Bard, and Fleury (1989) demonstrate how critical visual search strategies are to preparing to return tennis serves. Expert and novice tennis players watched a film showing a person serving and were asked to identify the type of serve as quickly as possible. The authors recorded the participants' eye movements as they watched the film. Three phases of the serve were of particular interest: the "ritual phase" (the 3.5 sec preceding the initiation of the serve); the "preparatory phase" (the time between the elevation of the arm for the ball toss and the ball's reaching the top of the toss); and the "execution phase" (from the ball toss to racquet-ball contact).

As illustrated in figure 9.4, during the ritual phase, the expert players focused mainly on the head and the shoulder/trunk complex, where general body position cues could be found. During the preparatory phase, they directed visual search primarily around the racquet and ball, where it remained until ball contact. An interesting note was that the experts also looked at the server's feet and knees during the preparatory phase. The important difference between experts and novices was that the visual search patterns of the expert players allowed them to correctly identify the serve sooner than novices could.

More recent research has supported the results of the Goulet et al. (1989) study in which the ball and the server's arm and racquet are the visual focus of attention for skilled tennis players preparing to return a serve. For example, Jackson and Morgan (2007) used an event occlusion procedure similar to the one described in chapter 6. Their results showed that when skilled tennis players could not see the server's arm and racquet or the ball prior to ball-racquet contact, their predictions of the service court in which the ball would land were much worse than when they could see these components.

In an effort to investigate the visual search characteristics of expert players in a more realistic

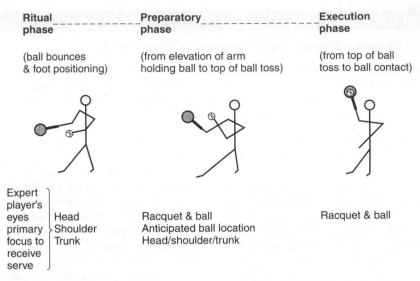

Ritual phase	Preparatory phase	Execution phase
(ball bounces & foot positioning)	(from elevation of arm holding ball to top of ball toss)	(from top of ball toss to ball contact)

Expert player's eyes primary focus to receive serve

| Head Shoulder Trunk | Racquet & ball Anticipated ball location Head/shoulder/trunk | Racquet & ball |

FIGURE 9.4   Illustration showing where expert tennis players in the Goulet, Bard, and Fleury experiment were looking during the three phases of a tennis serve. [*Source:* Based on discussion in Goulet, C., et al. (1989). Expertise differences in preparing to return a tennis serve: A visual information processing approach. *Journal of Sport and Exercise Psychology, 11,* 382–398.]

setting, Singer et al. (1998) assessed the eye movement behaviors of five nationally ranked university male and female tennis players as they returned ten serves on a tennis court. Interestingly, all five players did not use the same visual search strategies. During the phases of the serve that Goulet et al. (1989) called the ritual and preparatory phases, the two highest-ranked players fixated primarily on the arm-racquet-shoulder region of the server, whereas two fixated on the racquet and expected ball toss area. All the players included head fixations during these phases. The players demonstrated more individual variation during the ball toss phase of the serve. Two players visually tracked the ball from the server's hand to the highest point of the toss, one player made a visual jump from the server's hand to the highest point of the toss, one player fixated only on the predicted highest point of the toss, and one player did not fixate on the ball toss but only on the racquet. Differences again were found for the visual search strategies used by the players after the server hit the ball. The two highest-ranked players visually tracked the ball to its landing location,

two players did not track the ball after contact but visually jumped to the predicted landing location, and one player used a combination of these two strategies to return serves.

Baseball batting.   An example of research describing characteristics of the visual search processes involved in baseball batting is a study by Shank and Haywood (1987). They recorded eye movements for college and novice players as they watched a videotape of a right-handed pitcher as if they were right-handed batters. For each of twenty pitches, the players indicated whether the pitch was a fastball or a curve. The expert players correctly identified almost every pitch, whereas the novices were correct only about 60 percent of the time. Participants in both groups did not begin to track the ball until about 150 msec after the ball had left the pitcher's hand. During the windup, experts fixated on the release point, whereas novices tended to shift fixations from the release point to the pitcher's head.

More recently, Kato and Fukuda (2002) investigated the eye movements of nine expert baseball batters as they viewed the pitcher's motion during different types of pitches. The distribution of eye movement fixations indicated that the batters looked primarily at the pitcher's elbow, shoulder, and head, with the primary focus on the elbow. In results similar to those of Shank and Haywood, the batters' visual attention involved the release point. But a difference from the Shank and Haywood results was the batters' direction of their foveal vision on the elbow as a type of "pivot" point from which they could include and evaluate the release point, as well as the entire arm motion and initial ball trajectory, in their peripheral vision.

Soccer actions. To determine whether to shoot, pass, or dribble in soccer, the player must use visual search that is different from that involved in the situations described above. The soccer situation involves many players in the visual scene that must be searched for relevant cues. An experiment by Helsen and Pauwels (1990) provides a good demonstration of visual search patterns used by experienced and inexperienced male players to determine these actions. Participants acted as ball handlers as they viewed slides of typical attacking situations. For each, the person indicated as quickly as possible whether he would shoot at the goal, dribble around the goal-keeper or opponent, or pass to a teammate. The experts took less time to make the decision. Eye movement recordings showed that the experts gained this time advantage because they fixated on fewer features of the scene and spent less time at each fixation.

Another visual search situation in soccer involves anticipating where a pass will go. Williams, Davids, Burwitz, and Williams (1994) showed that experienced players and inexperienced players look at different environmental features to make this determination. Results based on subjects' eye-movement characteristics while watching an actual soccer game showed that the experienced players fixated more on the positions and movements of other players, in addition to the ball and the ball handler. In contrast, inexperienced players typically fixated only on the ball and the ball handler.

Finally, Williams and Davids (1998) reported a comprehensive investigation of visual selective attention and search strategies of experienced and less experienced soccer players in three-on-three and one-on-one situations. Among the many results in this study, two are especially noteworthy. One is that in the one-on-one situations, the experienced players visually fixated longer on the opponent's hip region more than the less experienced players, which indicated their knowledge of the relevant information to be acquired from the specific environmental feature. The other is that in the three-on-three situations, the experienced players used peripheral vision to select relevant information more than the less experienced players. Evidence for the use of peripheral vision came from the results of the spatial occlusion procedure, in which the masking of areas of the video scene surrounding the ball and the player with the ball had a more negative effect on the performance of the experienced players.

Shooting a basketball. When a basketball player shoots a jump shot, when does the player visually search for and detect the relevant information needed to determine when and how to make the shot? To address this question, researchers used the temporal occlusion procedure to investigate expert basketball players shooting a jump shot (Oudejans, van de Langenberg, & Hunter, 2002). The researchers established a simulated game situation in which the players watched a scene on a video project in front of them. The players performed jump shots at a basket on the basis of the actions of the defensive players in the video. The players saw all, none, or only parts of the video. The results indicated that the players' shooting performance was less successful when they could not observe the scene just before they released the ball. The researchers concluded that to successfully shoot a jump shot, players determine their final shooting movement characteristics by visually searching for and using information detected until they release the ball.

Driving a car. Driving a car is a nonsport performance situation in which vision provides information to select and constrain action. In a study that was done many years ago, but continues to be preferred as a demonstration of this role for vision, Mourant and Rockwell (1972) had novice and experienced drivers drive a 2.1 mile neighborhood route and a 4.3 mile freeway route. The novices were students in a driver education class. The results of the eye movement recordings showed that novice drivers concentrated their eye fixations in a small area more immediately in front of the car. More experienced drivers visually searched a wider area that was further from the front of the car. This broader scanning range increases the probability for the detection of important cues in the environment. On the freeway, the novices made pursuit eye movements, whereas the experienced drivers made specific eye fixations that jumped from location to location. That is, the experienced drivers knew which cues were important and specifically searched for those cues. The experienced drivers looked into the rear- and side-view mirrors more frequently than the novices, whereas the novices looked at the speedometer more than the experienced drivers did.

More recently, Chapman and Underwood (1998) extended these findings. They monitored eye movements of novice and experienced drivers as they watched various driving-related scenes that included at least one dangerous situation. In these situations, both types of drivers narrowed their visual search and increased the durations of their eye movement fixations. But the more experienced drivers tended to fixate for shorter amounts of time on specific parts of the scene than the novice drivers. This result indicates that more experienced drivers require less time to detect and process the information obtained from a fixation, which gives them an advantage in determining the appropriate driving action to take in the situation. In addition, the experienced drivers tended to be less variable in where they fixated their eye movements while watching the driving scenes, which, in agreement with the findings of Mourant and Rockwell (1972), indicates their greater knowledge of which environmental cues to look at to obtain the most relevant information. The results of these two studies have been replicated in several other studies (see Falkmer & Gregerson, 2005 for a review of this research).

Prehension while walking. When a person must walk to a table to pick up an object, such as a pen or book, visual search plays an important role in setting into motion the appropriate action coordination. An experiment by Cockrell, Carnahan, and McFayden (1995) demonstrated this role for visual search. Participants were required to walk 3.75 m to a table and pick up an aluminum can or a pencil as they walked by. Results showed that before they began any prehensive action, their eyes moved to fixate on the target. Head movement also preceded the initiation of reaching movements. Thus, the eyes' searching of the environment to determine the location and characteristics of the object started a chain of events to allow the participants to grasp the object successfully.

Locomoting through a cluttered environment. Walking and running through a cluttered environment can occur in everyday situations—we walk around furniture in the house or walk through a crowded mall—and in sport situations: a player runs with a football or dribbles a basketball during a game. People's ability to maneuver through environments like these indicates that they have detected relevant cues and used them in advance to avoid collisions. Visual search is an important part of this process.

According to research by Cutting, Vishton, and Braren (1995), the most important cues involved in avoiding collision in these situations come from the relative location or motion of objects around the object the person needs to avoid. When visually fixating on the object he or she needs to avoid, the person uses relative-displacement and/or velocity information about both the object to be avoided and other objects in front of or behind the object. It is important to note that this decision making is done automatically by the visual system and provides the basis for appropriate action by the motor control system. The key practical point here is that the person needs to visually fixate on the object or objects that he or she wishes to avoid. (See Hollands, Patla, & Vickers, 2002, for a more extensive discussion of this point and related research.)

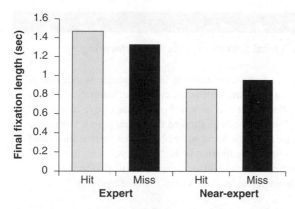

FIGURE 9.5   Results from Vickers (1996) showing expert and near-expert basketball players' mean duration of their final eye movement fixations just prior to releasing the ball during basketball free throws for shots they hit and missed. These final fixations were on the backboard or hoop. [Modified figure 6 (p. 348) in Vickers, J. (1996). *Visual control when aiming at a far target. Psychology: Human Perception and Performance, 22,* 342–354. Copyright © 1996 the American Psychological Association. Adapted with permission.]

Visual Search in Closed Motor Skills

Basketball free throw. Vickers (1996) reported an experiment in which she recorded the eye movements of elite Canadian women basketball players as they prepared to shoot, and then shot, free throws. Two results are especially noteworthy. First, the "experts" (they had made an average of 75 percent of their free throws during the just-completed season) looked directly at the backboard or hoop for a longer period of time just prior to shooting the ball than did the "near experts" (they had made an average of 42 percent of their free throws during the just-completed season). This was especially the case for the final eye movement fixation just prior to the release of the ball which Vickers referred to as the "quiet eye." Second, as can be seen in figure 9.5, the amount of time devoted to the final fixation prior to releasing the ball was related to the shooting success of the experts. They fixated on the backboard or hoop for just over 1.4 sec for shots they made, but almost 0.2 sec less for shots they missed. It is interesting to note that the final fixation duration for the near experts was just the opposite, with a longer fixation

time on shots they missed than on shots they made. Vickers interpreted this finding as evidence that the near experts did not fixate long enough just prior to the release of the ball for the shots they made or missed to allow them to attain the shooting percentage of the expert.

Putting a golf ball. In another experiment by Vickers (1992), she reported eye movement data for lower-handicap golfers (0 to 8 handicaps) and higher-handicap golfers (10 to 16 handicaps). In golf, the lower-handicap golfers are more skilled than those with higher handicaps. Vickers reported that during a series of putts, several differences were found between these two groups during the interval of time just after the golfer completed positioning the ball and just before the initiation of the backswing of the putter (i.e., the preparation phase). First, this time interval was shorter for the low-handicap golfers (approximately 3.7 sec) than for the high-handicap golfers (approximately 4.8 sec). Second, the low-handicap golfers directed more eye movement fixations to the ball during this phase than the high-handicap golfers, who directed more fixations to the putter. Third, there was a relationship between the eye movement fixation during the preparation phase and the success of a putt. Fixations on the club led to more missed putts, whereas fixations on the ball led to more successful putts.

Vickers also described an interesting point that is relevant to our discussion on visual attention. She noted that golfers generally are not consciously aware of eye movements during putting. Golfers tend to associate visual attention with head position, which means they consider a change in visual attention to be related to a change in head movement. However, their head movement to shift visual attention from one location to another is generally initiated by eye movement.

TRAINING VISUAL SEARCH STRATEGIES

Each of the motor skill performance examples discussed in the preceding section had in common the characteristic that people with more experience

The "Quiet Eye"—A Strategic Part of the Visual Search Process for Performing Motor Skills

Research by Joan Vickers and her colleagues discovered an important characteristic of visual search that is associated with successful motor skill performance. This characteristic, which they called the "quiet eye," occurs for both closed and open skills. The research evidence for the "quiet eye" is based on the use of eye-movement recording technology, which was discussed in chapter 6. These recordings showed that when people search the performance environment, they typically fixate their gaze on a specific location or object for a certain amount of time *just before* initiating performance of the activity. This final gaze fixation is the "quiet eye" (i.e., the "quiet" portion of the visual search process). In terms of attention processes involved in motor skill performance, the "quiet eye" characteristic of visual search demonstrates the importance of the visual focus of attention.*

Four Common Characteristics of the "Quiet Eye" (*see McPherson & Vickers, 2004*):
• It is directed to a critical location or object in the performance context
• It is a stable fixation of the performer's gaze
• Its onset occurs just before the first movement common to all performers of the skill
• Its duration tends to be longer for elite performers

These four characteristics indicate the "need for an optimal focus on one location or object prior to the final execution of the skill." (McPherson & Vickers, 2004, p. 279)

The "Quiet Eye" for Closed Skills
For the successful performance of a closed skill the final gaze fixation, just prior to performing the skill, is typically located on the goal object in the performance environment. For example, golfers fixate on the ball, free-throw shooters in basketball fixate on the rim of the basket, walkers fixate on stepping stones along a pathway, etc.
• *Specific closed skills demonstrations of the "quiet eye."* Research has shown the relationship between the "quiet eye" and performance for: golf putting; basketball free-throw shooting; walking on stepping stones; rifle target shooting; dart throwing.

The "Quiet Eye" for Open Skills
Open skills involve moving objects that must be visually tracked, which makes the visual search process different from that used for closed skills. The final gaze fixation (i.e., the "quiet eye") during the performance of open skills is on the moving object, which the eye then tracks for as long as possible before initiating the required movement. For example, batters in baseball or receivers of serves in tennis, table tennis, and volleyball fixate on the oncoming ball and track it to a specific location in space just prior to initiating movement to respond to the oncoming ball.
• *Specific open skills demonstrations of the "quiet eye."* Research has shown the relationship between the "quiet eye" and performance for: batters in baseball; receivers of serves in tennis, table tennis, and volleyball; ice hockey goal tenders; and soccer goal keepers attempting saves.

*For specific references and summaries of the research demonstrating the "quiet eye" for these skills, see Vickers (2007).

in an activity visually searched their environment and located essential information more effectively and efficiently than people with little experience. Therefore, we know that as people become more experienced and skilled in an activity, they acquire better visual search skills. How do people acquire this capability? In many cases, experience alone is the key factor in the acquisition of effective visual search strategies. These strategies are often acquired without specific training and without the person's conscious awareness of the strategies they use. But is it possible to facilitate the acquisition of effective search strategies by teaching novices to use strategies that experts use? A positive answer to this question would provide teachers, coaches, and physical rehabilitation therapists with guidance about how to more effectively design practice and intervention strategies.

Researchers have demonstrated the benefits of providing novices with instructions concerning what to look for and attend to, along with giving them a sufficient amount of practice implementing these instructions. A result of this type of intervention strategy is an increase in the probability that important environmental cues will "pop out" when the person is in the performance situation (see Czerwinski, Lightfoot, & Shiffrin, 1992).

However, Abernethy, Wood, and Parks (1999) emphasized that it is essential for this type of training to be specific to an activity. They pointed out that research evidence has demonstrated the lack of benefit derived from generalized visual training programs, such as those often promoted by sports optometrists (e.g., Wood & Abernethy, 1997). The problem with a generalized training approach to the improvement of visual attention is that it ignores the general finding that experts recognize specific patterns in their activity more readily than do novices.

Several examples of effective visual search training programs have been reported (e.g., Abernethy, Wood, & Parks, 1999; Farrow et al., 1998; Haskins, 1965; Singer et al., 1994; Vera et al., 2008; Vickers, 2007). Most of these programs have been sport specific and have shown that video-based simulations can serve as the basis for effective self-paced training of athletes outside of their organized practice time. However, one caution is that many of the studies that have reported the effectiveness of these programs have not tested their efficacy in actual performance situations or in competition environments (see Williams, Ward, Smeeton, & Allen, 2004, for an extensive review and critique of these studies).

It is interesting to note, however, that studies by Green and Bavelier (2003, 2006) found that highly experienced players of action video games exhibited better visual selective attention capabilities than nonplayers. And, after training nonplayers on an action-video game, the trained nonplayers demonstrated distinct improvement in their visual attention skills.

SUMMARY

We have considered the concept of attention as it relates to human motor skill performance in two ways: the simultaneous performance of multiple activities, and the visual selection of performance-relevant information from the environment.

In the discussion of attention and the simultaneous performance of multiple activities, we discussed the following:

- People have a limited availability of mental resources, which was described as a *limited attention capacity* for performing more than one activity at the same time.

- *Kahneman's attention theory* is an example of a centrally located, flexible limited capacity view of attention. His theory proposes that our attention capacity is a single pool of mental resources that influences the cognitive effort that can be allocated to activities to be performed. The amount of available resources (i.e., attention capacity) can increase or decrease according to the general arousal level of the performer. The allocation of resources is influenced by several factors related to the person and the activities.

- *Multiple-resource theories* provide an alternative view of a limited capacity view of attention by proposing that several different resource pools exist from which attention can be allocated. The resources are specific to a component of performing a skill. Wickens' model describes these components.

- The most common experimental procedure used to investigate the attention demands of motor skill performance is called the *dual-task procedure.*

- *Attentional focus,* which refers to where a person directs his or her attention in a performance situation, can be considered in terms of its width (i.e., broad or narrow) and direction (i.e., internal or external) or in terms of whether attention is focused on the movements or the movement effect.

- *Automaticity* is an important attention-related concept that relates primarily to skilled performance in which the performer can implement knowledge and procedures with little or no demand on attention capacity.

In the discussion of attention and the visual selection of performance-relevant information from the environment, we dicussed the following:

- *Visual selective attention* to performance-relevant information in the environment is an important part of preparing to perform a motor skill.

- The performer usually engages in an active *visual search* of the performance environment according to the information needed to prepare and perform an intended action, although sometimes the environmental information attended to provides the basis for selecting an appropriate action.

- The *feature integration theory* of visual selective attention is one of the more popular explanations of how people visually select and attend to certain cues in the performance environment and ignore others.

- We looked at research related to the visual search involved in the performance of several different open and closed motor skills. Each skill provided evidence that effective visual search strategies are distinctly specific to the requirements of the action and to the skill level of the performer.

- Activity-specific training programs facilitate the use of effective visual search strategies more successfully than general-vision training programs.

POINTS FOR THE PRACTITIONER

- The capability to do more than one activity simultaneously when performing a motor skill can be situation-specific. This means that a person may have more success in some situations than in others. Note these differences and use them as the basis for designing further instruction and practice.

- People will be more likely to be distracted while preparing to perform, or performing, a motor skill when events occur in the performance environment that are not usually present in this environment.

- Skilled individuals will be more likely to perform at their best when their arousal or anxiety levels are optimal for performing the skill in the situation they will experience.

- People will perform motor skills better when they focus their conscious attention (i.e., what they "think about") on the intended outcome of the movement rather than on their own movements.

- You can enhance a person's visual selective attention in performance situations by providing many opportunities to perform a skill in a variety of situations in which the most relevant visual cues remain the same in each situation.

- Provide training for people to visually focus on the most relevant cue in the performance environment and then maintain visual contact with that cue just prior to initiating movement.

RELATED READINGS

Beilock, S. L., Wierenga, S. A., & Carr, T. H. (2002). Expertise, attention, and memory in sensorimotor skill execution: Impact of novel task constraints on dual-task performance and episodic memory. *Quarterly Journal of Experimental Psychology, 55A,* 1211–1240.

Bourdin, C., Teasdale, N., & Nougier, V. (1998). Attentional demands and the organization of reaching movements in rock climbing. *Research Quarterly for Exercise and Sport, 69,* 406–410.

Brauer, S. G., Broome, A., Stone, C., Clewett, S., & Herzig, P. (2004). Simplest tasks have greatest dual task interference with balance in brain injured adults. *Human Movement Science, 23,* 489–502.

Fenske, M. J., & Raymond, J. E. (2006). Affective influences of selective attention. *Current Directions in Psychological Science, 15,* 312–316.

Forster, S., & Lavie, N. (2008). Failures to ignore entirely irrelevant distractors: The role of load. *Journal of Experimental Psychology: Applied, 14,* 73–83.

Fu, S., Greenwood, P. M., & Parasuraman, R. (2005). Brain mechanisms of involuntary visuospatial attention: An event-related potential study. *Human Brain Mapping, 25,* 378–390.

Hiraga, C. Y., Summers, J. J., & Temprado, J. J. (2004). Attentional costs of coordinating homologous and non-homologous limbs. *Human Movement Science, 23,* 415–430.

Moreno, F. J., Ona, A., & Martinez, M. (2002). Computerized simulation as a means of improving anticipation strategies and training in the use of the return in tennis. *Journal of Human Movement Studies, 42,* 31–41.

Radlo, S. J., Steinberg, G. M., Singer, R. N., Barba, D. A., & Melnikov, A. (2002). The influence of an attentional focus strategy on alpha brain wave activity, heart rate, and dart-throwing performance. *International Journal of Sport Psychology, 33,* 205–217.

Shipp, S. (2004). The brain circuitry of attention. *TRENDS in Cognitive Sciences, 8,* 223–230.

Spikman, J. M., Timmerman, M. E., van Zomeren, A. H., & Deelman, B. G. (1999). Recovery versus retest effects in attention after closed head injury. *Journal of Clinical Experimental Neuropsychology, 21,* 585–605.

Strayer, D. L., & Drews, F. A. (2007). Cell-phone–induced driver distraction. *Current Directions in Psychological Science, 16,* 128–131.

van Gemmert, A. W. A., Teulings, H. L., & Stelmach, G. E. (1998). The influence of mental and motor load on handwriting movements in Parkinsonian patients. *Acta Psychologica, 100,* 161–175.

Vickers, J. N., & Williams, A. M. (2007). Performing under pressure: The effects of physiological arousal, cognitive anxiety, and gaze control in biathlon. *Journal of Motor Behavior, 39,* 381–394.

INTERNET RESOURCES

- To visit a website dedicated to the study, understanding, application, and training of the "quiet eye" go to http://quieteyesolutions.com. Included on the Web site are PDF copies of many publications related to research that present evidence of the "quiet eye" for a variety of motor skill performance situations.

- To visit the laboratory at the University of Rochester where the research on the effect of video games on visual attention (Green & Bavelier, 2003) was conducted, and to experience the tasks involved in their three experiments, go to http://www.bcs.rochester.edu/people/Daphne/visual.html#video.

- To read a ScienceDaily.com story "Driving distractions: Why cell phones and driving don't mix," go to http://www.sciencedaily.com/releases/2008/05/080531084958.htm; the story is based on an interview with a university professor who has been researching multi-tasking issues as they relate to attention and human performance.

- To read the autobiography of Daniel Kahneman (who developed the attention theory discussed in this chapter) as written for the Nobel Prize ceremony in 2002, go to http://nobelprize.org/. Click on the Search link, then type "Kahneman" in the Keyword box to locate the autobiography and other features related to his Nobel Prize.

STUDY QUESTIONS

1. (a) Discuss the similarities and differences between fixed and flexible central-resource theories of attention capacity. (b) Discuss the differences between central- and multiple-resource theories of attention capacity.

2. Describe a motor skill situation in which two or more actions must be performed simultaneously, and then discuss how Kahneman's model of attention could be applied to the situation to explain conditions in which all the actions could be performed simultaneously and when they could not be.

3. Discuss two different dual-task techniques that researchers use to assess the attention demands of performing a motor skill. Give an example of each.

4. (a) Describe the width and direction of attention focus options a person has when performing a motor skill. (b) For each type, describe a motor skill situation in which that focus option would be preferred.

5. Discuss whether a person should focus attention on his or her own movements or on the movement effects. Give an example.

6. What is the meaning of the term *automaticity* as it relates to attention and the performance of motor skills? Give an example.

7. (a) What is the meaning of the term *visual selective attention,* and how does it relate to the study of attention? (b) Describe how researchers study visual selective attention as it relates to the performance of motor skills. Give an example.

8. Discuss how skilled performers engage in visual search in the performance of four different types of motor skills.

Specific Application Problem:
You are working in your chosen profession. Describe a situation in which you are helping people learn a skill that involves performing more than one activity at a time (e.g., dribbling a basketball while running and looking for a teammate to pass to). Describe how you would help people acquire the capability to perform this multiple-activity skill beginning with their not being able to do all the activities simultaneously. Indicate how you would take the concept of attention capacity into account in designing this instructional strategy.

Memory Components, Forgetting, and Strategies

Concept: Memory storage and retrieval influence motor skill learning and performance.

After completing this chapter, you will be able to

- Compare and contrast *working memory* and *long-term memory* in terms of duration and capacity of information as well as processing activities in each
- Distinguish *procedural, episodic,* and *semantic* memory as components of long-term memory
- Define *declarative* and *procedural* knowledge
- Give examples of *explicit* and *implicit* memory tests and describe how each relates to assessing, remembering, and forgetting
- Discuss several causes of forgetting for working memory and long-term memory
- Discuss effective strategies to help remember a movement or sequence of movements that must be performed
- Define the *encoding specificity principle* as it relates to practice and test contexts associated with the performance of motor skills

APPLICATION

Have you ever had the experience of calling an information operator to ask for a telephone number and then finding out that you didn't have a pen? Hurriedly, you dialed the number as quickly as possible after the operator gave it to you. Why did you do this? "Obviously," you say, "because I would have forgotten it if I hadn't dialed right away." Do you need to do this with your home telephone number? You can quite readily recall your home number at almost any time, without any assistance.

Consider a few other memory situations. When you are at a party and you are introduced to someone, you often find it very difficult to recall that person's name, even a very short time later. Compare that to remembering a teacher's name from

your elementary school. You can probably name most of your teachers with little difficulty. The situations described so far relate to our use of memory for cognitive or verbal information. Now let's consider a situation involving a motor skill. If you took tennis classes as a beginner (if you haven't taken tennis classes, substitute any physical activity or sport skill you have experienced as a beginner), think about the time when you were shown how to serve a tennis ball for the first time. When you tried it, you found that you had some difficulty remembering all the things that you were supposed to do to perform a successful serve. Think about how remembering in that situation differs quite drastically from how well you can hop onto a bicycle, even after you have not been on one for many years, and ride it down the street.

Application Problem to Solve   Describe a motor skill that you might help people learn. When you give them instructions about how to perform the skill, or specific parts of the skill, how will you give those instructions so that the people will remember what they are supposed to do when they practice the skill?

DISCUSSION

Memory plays an important role in virtually all our daily activities. Whether in conversation with a friend, working mathematical problems, or playing tennis, we are confronted by situations that require the use of memory to produce action.

What is memory? We often think of memory as being synonymous with the words *retention* or *remembering*. As such, most people consider that the word *memory* indicates a capacity to remember. Endel Tulving (1985), a leading contemporary memory researcher and theorist, has stated that *memory* is the "capacity that permits organisms to benefit from their past experiences" (p. 385).

In the discussion that follows, we will consider various issues and questions concerning human memory as it applies to the learning and performance of motor skills. First, we will discuss the different storage systems included in memory. We will then build on this foundation by considering the issue of the causes of forgetting and finally will address how these causes can be overcome by the use of strategies that can help develop a more durable and accessible memory for the skills being learned.

MEMORY STRUCTURE

Views about the structure of memory have gone through many different phases throughout the history of the study of memory, which can be traced back to the early Greek philosophers. However, one characteristic of memory structure that is now commonly accepted is that a part of memory is oriented toward events that have just occurred, while a part is related to events in the past. This is not a new idea. In fact, in 1890, William James wrote of an "elementary" or "primary" memory that makes us aware of the "just past." He distinguished this from a "secondary memory" that is for "properly recollected objects." To primary memory, James allocated items that are lost and never brought back into consciousness, whereas to secondary memory, he allocated ideas or data that are never lost. Although they may be "absent from consciousness," they are capable of being recalled.

The debate about the structure of memory has centered on how this distinction between memory for immediate things and memory for things in a more distant past fits into a structural arrangement. At present, the bulk of the evidence supports the view that there are two components of memory.[1] The evidence for this comes from two different but complementary research approaches to the study of human memory. One of these is taken from the study of cognitive psychology, where inferences about the structure and function of memory are based on observing the behavior of individuals in memory situations. The other approach is that of the neuropsychologist or neurophysiologist, who is interested in explaining the structure of memory in terms of what is occurring in the nervous system during behavioral changes related to memory. Research evidence from both of these approaches provides convincing evidence that the memory system comprises at least two components that are definable by their distinct functions. Also, it is important to note that after reviewing and evaluating the relevant research literature, Healy and McNamara (1996) concluded that although some elaboration of various aspects of the component model of memory is needed, the model remains a useful means of understanding human memory.

---

[1]Although some models and discussions of memory include "sensory memory" as a third component, its role in motor skill learning and performance has not been well established. As a result, it is not included in this discussion.

A Two-Component Memory Model

Several different models of human memory have been developed to represent its component structure. One of the most enduring and influential was presented by Atkinson and Shiffrin in 1968. Using a computer analogy, they conjectured that memory structure should be thought of as similar to computer hardware. They considered that the software that allows the computer to function constitutes the "control processes," which involve memory processes such as storage and retrieval of information and are under the control of the person. The structural components, they concluded, comprise a sensory register, short-term store, and long-term store.

Since the time of Atkinson and Shiffrin's presentation of theory of memory structures, the primary theoretical problem has been to determine the exact nature of these structures. While debate continues about memory structure, there is general agreement that this structure of memory should include different memory storage components in addition to serving a functional role for what the person does with the information in each component. (To read a brief overview of the neuroscience debate about memory structure, see Nee, Berman, Moore, & Jonides, 2008.)

An excellent example of a memory structure model that accommodates these characteristics was proposed by Baddeley (1986, 1995, 2003). According to this view, memory is seen as comprising two functional systems, *working memory* and *long-term memory* (see figure 10.1). Each memory system is defined in terms of its functions. Although a number of different functions have been proposed, we will focus primarily on three: putting information in memory (referred to as storage processes), getting information out of memory (referred to as retrieval processes), and specific functions in each component.

WORKING MEMORY

The **working memory** should be thought of as a system that incorporates characteristics and functions traditionally associated with sensory, perceptual, attentional, and short-term memory processes. Working memory operates in all situations requir-

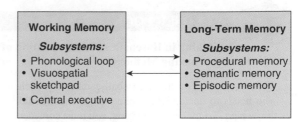

FIGURE 10.1   A schematic diagram of the working memory and long-term memory systems with the subsystems identified for each. The arrows represent the interactive nature of the two systems.

ing the temporary use and storage of information and the execution of memory and response production processes (see Baddeley, 1995). Baddeley (2003) stated that the working memory is a limited capacity system, which temporarily maintains and stores information and provides "an interface between perception, long-term memory, and action." (p. 829). As such, working memory includes memory functions traditionally ascribed to *short-term memory,* as well as other functions typically associated with the attention-related processes we discussed in chapter 9 (Engle, 2002).[2]

Working Memory Functions

Working memory is both a place where information is stored for a short time and a functionally active structure. These two characteristics of working memory enable people to respond according to the demands of a "right now" situation. To do this, *working memory plays a critical role in decision making, problem solving, movement production and*

[2]For a brief review of evidence that identifies neural mechanisms associated with working memory, see Smith (2000).

---

working memory   a functional system in the structure of memory that operates to temporarily store and use recently presented information; it also serves as a temporary workspace to integrate recently presented information with information retrieved from long-term memory to carry out problem-solving, decision-making, and action-preparation activities.

A CLOSER LOOK

Pitching in Baseball: A Demonstration of the Interactive Work Space Function of Working Memory

The situation. You are a baseball catcher or coach who needs to decide which pitch the pitcher should throw next. To make this decision, you must consider information about both the present situation and past experiences. In terms of the present situation you need to consider *who the batter is, the score, who and where the runners on base are, the number of outs, the locations of defensive players in the infield and outfield, the ball and strike count,* and so on. In terms of past experiences you need to consider *the batter's batting history in similar situations, the opposing team's tendencies in this situation—especially if they have runners on base—the pitcher's history of pitching in similar situations,* and so on.

Working memory involvement. The working memory serves as a temporary workspace to enable you to integrate the information about the present situation and past experiences so that you can select the best pitch for right now. After receiving your pitch choice, the pitcher will involve the working memory to retrieve from long-term memory the invariant characteristics of the type of pitch required and then use the temporary workspace to apply specific movement-related features to the pitch, such as speed and location. After the pitch is delivered, the information in working memory is deleted to provide space for new information to allow the pitcher to respond to what the batter does or to throw the next pitch you select.

evaluation, and long-term memory function. With regard to influencing long-term memory function, working memory provides essential processing activity needed for the adequate transfer of information into long-term memory. Finally, it is important to note that an important working memory function is to serve as an *interactive workspace* where various memory processing activities can occur, such as integrating the information in working memory with information that has been retrieved from the more permanent, long-term memory.

According to Baddeley's conception of working memory, its functions are related to three subsystems. The first two reflect the storage function of working memory by storing different types of information. One is the *phonological loop,* which is responsible for the short-term storage of verbal information. Second is the *visuospatial sketchpad* in which visually detected spatial information is stored for short periods of time. The third subsystem, the *central executive,* coordinates the information in working memory, which includes information retrieved from long-term memory. Neurologically, these components of working memory are localized in various brain regions, including the parietal cortex, Broca's area, premotor cortex, occipital cortex, and the frontal cortex. (Baddeley, 2003).

Because working memory involves both storing and processing information, it is important to consider each function separately. In terms of storing information, two characteristics of working memory are essential to understand: the length of time information will remain in working memory, which is called *duration,* and the amount of information that will reside in working memory at any one time, which is called *capacity.*

Duration

Our understanding of the duration of information in working memory comes from research that investigated short-term memory. In terms of the history of science, this research is relatively recent. Peterson and Peterson (1959) were the earliest to report research related to the remembering of words presented one time each. They showed that we tend to lose information (i.e., forget) from working memory after about only 20 to 30 sec. The first experiment published relating working memory storage duration to motor skills was by Adams and Dijkstra in 1966. Results of their experiment indicated that arm positions in space that are experienced one time each are lost from working memory at a rate comparable to that of words.

The results of many other studies that followed the Adams and Dijkstra investigation generally

A CLOSER LOOK

Experimental Procedures to Assess the Duration of Movement Information in Working Memory

The classic experiment by Adams and Dijkstra (1966) set the standard for the procedural protocol researchers have used to investigate the question concerning the duration of movement information in working memory. Because the researchers were interested in movement information, their procedures were designed to require participants to use only proprioceptive information to perform the task.

- **Apparatus.** An arm-positioning apparatus consisted of an almost friction-free handle that could be moved left or right along a metal trackway. This apparatus sat on a table facing the participant in the experiment.
- **Task.** To begin a trial, a blindfolded participant moved the handle of the apparatus along the trackway to a location specified by a physical block (the criterion arm position to be remembered). After returning the handle to the starting point and waiting for a certain amount of time (the retention interval), the participant performed a recall test by moving the handle to his or her estimate of the arm position just experienced (the physical block had been removed). The experimenter recorded the location and the participant returned the handle to begin a new trial, which involved moving to a new position along the trackway.
- **Determining duration.** To determine the length of time movement location information stayed in working memory, the researchers compared various durations of the retention interval. They determined the accuracy of the participants' recall movements for each retention interval length. Duration of the memory for the arm position was assumed to be related to the degree of accuracy of the recall movement. As you can see in figure 10.2 below, arm-positioning recall accuracy decreased (i.e., error increased) very sharply for retention intervals up to 20 sec, and continued to decrease for longer interval lengths.

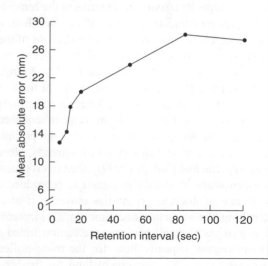

FIGURE 10.2 Results from the experiment by Adams and Dijkstra showing the mean absolute error for the recall of an arm-positioning task following different lengths of retention intervals. [From Adams, J. A., & Dijkstra, S. (1966). Short-term memory for motor responses. *Journal of Experimental Psychology, 71,* 314–318. Copyright © 1966 by the American Psychological Association, Reprinted with permission.]

supported the conclusion that the duration of movement information in working memory is about 20 to 30 sec. Information that is not processed further or rehearsed is lost.

Capacity

We are concerned with not only *how long* information will remain in short-term storage, but also *how much* information we can accommodate. The issue of capacity in working memory was originally presented by George Miller in 1956, in an article that has become a classic in the memory literature. Miller provided evidence to indicate that we have the capacity to hold about *seven items (plus or minus two items),* such as words or digits, in short-term storage. To increase the "size" of an item in memory involves a control process termed *organization,* which we will consider later in this discussion. The newly created larger item, or "chunk" as Miller called it, enables people to recall far more than five to nine individual items at a time. However, research has shown that although the size of a chunk may increase, working memory's capacity for storing them remains constant at about seven (Cowan, Chen, & Rouder, 2004). Thus in terms of storage capacity, items maintained in working memory can vary in size. One of the problems researchers have experienced in investigating the capacity limit of working memory is determining how to objectively define and measure an "item" or chunk.

The definition and measurement problem has been especially problematic for researchers interested in motor skills who are interested in testing Miller's capacity hypothesis in terms of the remembering of movements. In spite of this problem, a few researchers have reported investigations of the capacity limits of working memory for movements. In general, their results agree with the 7 ± 2 range proposed by Miller. For example, in one of the first investigations of this issue, Wilberg and Salmela (1973) reported that an eight-movement sequence of arm-positioning movements was the upper limit of working memory capacity for movements. More recently, Ille and Cadopi (1999) asked twelve- and thirteen-year-old female gymnasts to reproduce a sequence of discrete gymnastics movements after watching the sequence one time on a videotape. The gymnasts' recall performance demonstrated a six-movement capacity limit for the more-skilled gymnasts and a five-movement limit for the less-skilled gymnasts. The results for these young gymnasts are in line with those reported by Starkes, Deakin, Lindley, and Crisp (1987) for young skilled ballet dancers, who showed evidence that an eight-movement sequence was their capacity limit.

To account for research evidence that has shown that highly skilled individuals (i.e., experts) seem to have a working memory capacity that is greater than that of the general population, Ericsson and Kintsch (1995) proposed a memory mechanism they called *long-term working memory.* In addition to having a larger working memory storage capacity, experts also show evidence that performing certain secondary tasks does not interfere with their performance of the activity at which they are skilled. Experts in an activity use long-term working memory when they must have access to a large amount of relevant knowledge at their disposal to use while performing the activity. In addition, the experts use long-term working memory to integrate new information with previously acquired knowledge. It is important to note that as is commonly characteristic of expertise (which we will discuss more fully in chapter 12), long-term working memory is skill specific, which means that it develops as expertise in a skill rather than being a common component of working memory.

Processing Activities

Information that is active in working memory is processed (or manipulated) in such a way that it can be used to accomplish the goal of the problem at hand. The goal may be to remember what you have just been told or shown to do so that you can do the task. Or you may need to use this information to solve a specific movement problem. And in both cases, you would like to remember what you did in each performance situation so that you can use your experience as a reference to help you in some future performance situation. In each case, you will involve working memory processing activities to enable you to achieve different goals.

Consider some examples of motor skill performance situations in which these different working memory processing activities could occur. Suppose your golf instructor has just given you a specific instruction to concentrate on your hand position as you swing a golf club. You must not only remember this instruction as you swing, but also retrieve from long-term memory the correct hand position and evaluate your present hand swing compared with the ideal. Of course, how successfully you

An Alternative View of Long-Term Memory Capacity: "When the Brain's Mailbox Is Full"

An article titled "When the Brain's Mailbox Is Full" appeared in *The New York Times* on July 27, 1999 (Jackson, 1999). The article described an experiment by Dr. H. Lee Swanson, from the University of California at Riverside, that takes issue with the commonly held view that long-term memory has a limitless capacity. Swanson's study, which was reported in the July 1999 issue of the research journal *Developmental Psychology,* found evidence he interpreted as indicating that "As we get older, we run out of places to store information. We have a limited amount of space in our memory system." The decrease in memory capacity, he said, begins around age forty-five for most people, although "not all 'mailboxes' are the same size and people organize them differently. We have different abilities in what we store and some of us are more efficient in what we can store." From an aging perspective, Swanson's view would indicate that when older people have memory lapses, it may not be due to a failure on the brain's part to adequately process information, but "may signal that a mailbox of memory is full."

Because Swanson's study is unique in finding evidence for such a memory capacity limitation, other scholars were quoted in the article as being skeptical about the reliability of the evidence. Dr. Timothy Salthouse, a highly regarded cognitive psychologist at Georgia Tech who investigates age-related memory and human performance, commented that one problem researchers face in the investigation of this issue is, "We don't know how to measure storage capacity." Dr. Robert L. Kahn, a retired psychology professor who coauthored the book *Successful Aging,* which was based on the study of aging by the MacArthur Foundation, rejected Swanson's "mechanistic notion that treats the brain as a bunch of shelves and pigeonholes which run out of space." Instead, he preferred the concept of "the lifelong elasticity of the human brain" and thought that training and mnemonic devices can sharpen memory skills.

make this comparison on your own depends on your stage of learning. But carrying out this verbal instruction invokes the working memory.

Suppose you have just watched a dancer perform a sequence of dance movements and you must now perform that sequence. Working memory processing activity would be involved because you must keep in memory the visually presented sequence of movements and translate that visual information into motor performance. Involved in this translation process would be retrieving from long-term memory the movement information required to carry out the sequence.

Consider also the following example. You are a patient in an occupational therapy session and are given a complex puzzle to put together. You study the pieces and try to determine how the specific pieces fit together. You continually try to match pieces as in the completed puzzle. And you try to determine an appropriate movement strategy that would allow you to put the pieces together quickly

and with little error. Working memory would be actively involved in this problem-solving situation because you carried out several activities requiring several different perception, remembering, and performance characteristics that must be done virtually simultaneously.

LONG-TERM MEMORY

The second component system in the memory structure is **long-term memory,** which is a more permanent storage repository of information. It is what we typically think of when the term *memory* is mentioned. William James (1890) considered long-term memory as "memory proper." This is the

---

long-term memory   a component system in the structure of memory that serves as a relatively permanent storage repository for information.

component of memory that contains information about specific past events as well as our general knowledge about the world.

In terms of the *duration* of information in long-term memory, it is generally accepted that the information resides in a relatively permanent state in long-term memory. Usually, "forgotten" information that is stored in long-term memory is there, but the person is having difficulty locating it. Thus, measuring forgetting and remembering in long-term memory situations can be a tricky problem. We will come back to this important point later in this chapter.

With regard to the *capacity* of long-term memory, it is generally agreed that there is a relatively unlimited capacity for information in long-term memory (e.g., Chase & Ericsson, 1982). In fact, we know neither how much information a person can store in memory nor how to measure the capacity of long-term memory. An unlimited capacity leads to unique problems, however. For example, organization of information in memory becomes much more critical in an unlimited capacity system than in one of a limited capacity. Thus, there is a need to understand how people organize the information stored in long-term memory. This and other related issues unique to long-term memory will be discussed throughout this chapter.

In terms of information duration and capacity characteristics, it becomes obvious that long-term memory is distinct from working memory. Another distinct characteristic of long-term memory is the type of information that is stored there. In the following sections, three types of information stored in long-term memory will be discussed.

Procedural, Episodic, and Semantic Memory

In a commonly referred-to model of long-term memory, Tulving (1985) proposed that there are at least three "systems" in long-term memory: *procedural, episodic,* and *semantic* memories. Each of these systems differs in terms of how information is acquired, what information is included, how information is represented, how knowledge is expressed, and the kind of conscious awareness that characterizes the operations of the system. We will briefly consider each of these systems and how they function and differ.

Procedural memory. This memory system may have the most direct relevance to our discussion of long-term memory because it relates specifically to storing and retrieving information about motor skills. Procedural memory is best described as the memory system that enables us to know "how to do" something, as opposed to enabling us to know "what to do." This distinction is readily seen in situations where you can perform a skill very well (i.e., "how to do it"), but you are not able to verbally describe very well what you did (i.e., "what to do").

The procedural memory system enables us to respond adaptively to our environment by carrying out learned procedures so that we can achieve specific action goals. For the performance of motor skills, procedural memory is critical, because motor skill is evaluated on the basis of producing an appropriate action, rather than simply verbalizing what to do. According to Tulving, an important characteristic of procedural memory is that procedural knowledge can be acquired only through "overt behavioral responses," which, for motor skills, means physical practice.

Semantic memory. According to Tulving (1985), semantic memory can be characterized by "representing states of the world that are not perceptually present" (p. 387) to us right now. This means that we store in this memory system our *general knowledge* about the world that has developed from our many experiences. This includes specific factual knowledge, such as when Columbus reached America or the name of the tallest building in America, as well as conceptual knowledge, such as our concepts of "dog" and "love." How information is represented in semantic memory is currently the source of much debate. The debate ranges from suggestions that all experiences are represented in some fashion in memory to suggestions that individual experiences are not represented in semantic memory, but rather, only abstractions, such as prototypes or schemas, are represented.

Episodic memory. We store in episodic memory our knowledge about personally experienced events, along with their temporal associations, in subjective time. It is this memory system that enables us to "mentally 'travel back' in time" (Tulving, 1985, p. 387).

Hitting a forehand groundstroke during a rally in tennis requires the player to know what to do in the situation and how to execute the stroke.

Tulving views episodic memory as "oriented to the past in a way in which no other kind of memory, or memory system, is" and as "the only memory system that allows people to consciously reexperience past experiences" (Tulving, 2002, p. 6). An example here would be your memory of an important life event. You are very likely to recall this event in terms of both time and space. For example, if you were asked, "Do you remember the first time you drove a car by yourself?" you would retrieve that information from episodic memory. Episodic memory is usually expressed in terms of remembering some experience, or episode. When a person recalls an experience from episodic memory, it is a personal recollection of the event. Tulving (2002) also described episodic memory as a memory system that deteriorates easily and is more vulnerable than other memory systems to neural dysfunction. For performing motor skills, episodic memory can be the source for information that prepares you for an upcoming performance or helps you determine what you are now doing wrong that at one time you did correctly.

Distinguishing between Knowing "What To Do" and Doing It

An important part of relating the three memory systems of long-term memory with the learning and performance of motor skills is the distinction between knowing "what to do" and being able to successfully perform the skill, which is often referred to as knowing "how to do" the skill. Some learning theorists have argued that the information in the episodic and semantic memory systems should be considered **declarative knowledge** (e.g., Anderson, 1987). This knowledge is specified as what we are able to describe (i.e., declare) if we are asked to do so. Thus, declarative knowledge is specific to knowing "what to do" in a situation. This type of knowledge is distinct from *procedural knowledge,* which typically cannot be verbalized or is difficult to verbalize. As described earlier, **procedural knowledge** enables the person to actually perform a skill. This distinction is a useful one and will be referred to in various parts of this chapter.

---

declarative knowledge knowledge about "what to do" in a situation; this knowledge typically is verbalizable.

procedural knowledge knowledge that enables a person to know "how to do" a skill; this knowledge typically is difficult to verbalize or is not verbalizable.

One of the few experiments that has directly distinguished these two types of knowledge as they relate to motor skill performance provides an excellent example of the difference between declarative and procedural knowledge. McPherson and Thomas (1989) classified nine- to twelve-year-old boys as "expert" or "novice" tennis players based on length of playing experience and tournament play. Novices had only three to six months playing experience. The "experts," who had at least two years of experience and had played in junior tournaments, were in an elite group for their age. The players were interviewed after each point (something that the researchers had previously established did not disrupt the quality of performance). Players were asked to state what they had attempted to do on the previous point. When this information was later compared with what they had actually done (which was analyzed from a videotape recording), some interesting results were obtained. First, in terms of having an effective strategy or action goal, the experts knew what to do nearly all the time, whereas the novices generally never knew what to do. Second, although the experts were quite capable of demonstrating that they knew what action goal to establish in a specific situation, they were not always able to accomplish it in their performance of the action. This suggests that the appropriate goal was established but there were problems in the physical execution of the intended action.

A different approach to demonstrating the distinction between declarative and procedural memory is to show that people with memory impairment due to amnesia can learn to perform a motor skill despite evidence of impaired declarative memory related to the task. An example of this type of experiment was reported by Cavaco, Anderson, Allen, Castro-Caldas, and Damasio (2004); chronic amnesic patients were compared to matching normal participants in learning to perform five tasks that were based on real-world experiences, such as weaving fabric, tracing geometric figures, and pouring water into cylinders. The results showed that the amnesic patients improved performance on all five tasks during practice trials and maintained improved performance levels 24 hours and 2 weeks

later. In fact, their performance levels were comparable to the normal control participants. However, when the amnesic patients were given declarative memory tests as part of the 24-hour retention test, they performed much worse than the normal participants and showed no explicit recall of characteristics of any of the five tasks they had practiced.

REMEMBERING AND FORGETTING

A variety of reasons exist to explain forgetting. But before getting into discussing some of those reasons, there are some terms that need to be identified and defined. **Encoding** is the transformation of information to be remembered into a form that can be stored in memory. *Storage* refers to the process of placing information in long-term memory. *Rehearsal* is a process that enables the individual to transfer information from the working memory to long-term memory. **Retrieval** involves the search through long-term memory for information that must be accessed and used in order to perform the task at hand.

ASSESSING REMEMBERING AND FORGETTING

Researchers generally determine what or how much has been remembered or forgotten by using one or both of two categories of memory tests.

Explicit Memory Tests

When we ask people to remember something, we are asking them to consciously call something to mind. Tests of memory that do this same type of thing are known as *explicit* memory tests. These tests assess what a person can *consciously remember.* Two types of explicit memory tests that have been popular in memory research are known as recall tests and recognition tests.

A **recall test** requires a person to produce a required response with few, if any, available cues or aids. This test asks the person to "recall" information that has been presented. In the verbal domain, these tests typically take the form of essay or fill-in-the-blank tests. For example, a recall

A CLOSER LOOK

Typical Explicit Memory Test Paradigms Used in Experiments to Assess Remembering and Forgetting

Researchers who investigate the causes of forgetting and remembering typically use procedures that follow three basic paradigms, depending on whether they are interested in the effects of time or activity. These paradigms are illustrated below from the participant's point of view in terms of the events that take place at specific times during the experiment.

Paradigm to Test the Effect of TIME

Perform movement(s)/skill to be remembered   Perform the memory test

- - -Rest/No activity- - -
[RETENTION INTERVAL]

Time

Paradigm to Test the Effect of PROACTIVE INTERFERENCE

Perform movement(s)/skill to be remembered   Perform the memory test

- - -Perform activity- - -   [RETENTION INTERVAL]

Time

Paradigm to Test the Effect of RETROACTIVE INTERFERENCE

Perform movement(s)/skill to be remembered   Perform the memory test

- - -Perform activity- - -
[RETENTION INTERVAL]

Time

test could ask, "Name the bones of the hand." For motor skills, a recall test requires the person to perform an action on command, such as "Perform the skill I just demonstrated to you" or "Show me how you tie your shoe."

A **recognition test,** on the other hand, provides some cues or information on which to base a response. In this type of test, a person's task is to recognize the correct response by distinguishing it from several alternatives. In the verbal domain, multiple-choice or matching tests are examples of recognition tests. For example, you could be asked, "Which of these is a bone of the hand?" You are then given four alternative answers from which to choose, where only one is correct. To answer the question, you need only to recognize which is the

encoding   a memory process involving the transformation of information to be remembered into a form that can be stored in memory.

retrieval   a memory process involving the search through long-term memory for information needed to perform the task at hand.

recall test   an explicit memory test that requires a person to produce a required response with few, if any, available cues or aids.

recognition test   an explicit memory test that requires a person to select a correct response from several alternative responses.

correct alternative, or which are the incorrect alternatives. For motor skills, an example for a *movement recognition test* would involve having a person produce several different movements and then asking which of these is the one just demonstrated or most appropriate for a specific situation.

In terms of learning and performing motor skills, we are often confronted with both recall and recognition "tests," sometimes in the same situation. For example, if a person must climb a ladder, he or she must *recall* what to do and how it should be done in order to safely and effectively climb the rungs to the desired height. When the person then climbs the ladder, he or she must recognize that the movements performed are the same as those he or she recalled. In a sport context, when a baseball or softball batter must decide whether or not to swing at a pitch, he or she engages in a recognition test when determining if the ball is in the strike zone or not. Then, to produce the appropriate swing, the batter must recall what to do to carry out this action and then be able to recognize if the swing that has been initiated is appropriate for hitting the pitch where it is thrown.

An important benefit of recall and recognition tests is that each provides different information about what has been remembered or forgotten. It is possible for a person to fail to produce a correct response on a recall test, but be able to produce that response when it is one among several alternatives in a recognition test. A value of the recognition test, then, is that it enables the researcher to determine if information is actually stored in memory, even though retrieval cues or aids are needed by the person in order to gain access to that information.

Implicit Memory Tests

Many times people have information stored in memory, but it is stored in such a way that they have difficulty accessing that information so that they can respond correctly on explicit memory tests. This type of situation is especially relevant for procedural memory, which we discussed earlier as one of the long-term memory systems. For example, suppose you were asked to describe the

grammatical rules of a sentence you had just said. Although you may not have been able to identify these rules, you confirmed your knowledge of them by the sentence you articulated. As a result, you demonstrated that you had knowledge about grammar rules stored in memory, but in a form that could not be brought to conscious level so you could verbalize the rules.

For motor skills, we can assess implicit memory by asking a person to verbally describe how to perform a skill and then asking him or her to perform it. As is often the case, especially with highly skilled people, the person can successfully perform a skill but cannot verbally describe what he or she did. For example, if you were asked to verbally describe how you tie your shoes without using your hands, you might not be able to do it, or you might experience some difficulty doing it. Does this mean you don't know how to tie your shoes or that you have forgotten how to tie your shoes? No; in terms of our earlier distinction between procedural and declarative knowledge, it means that you do not have access to, or immediate access to, your declarative knowledge about tying shoes. How would you provide evidence that you know how to tie your shoes? You would physically demonstrate tying your shoes, which would indicate that you had the procedural knowledge necessary to perform this skill.

On the other hand, it is possible to know what to do (i.e., have declarative knowledge), but not be able to actually do what you know you should do (i.e., have poor procedural knowledge). This phenomenon was demonstrated very nicely in the experiment by McPherson and Thomas (1989) that was discussed earlier. They gave young male basketball players an explicit paper-and-pencil test and asked them to indicate what they would do in a given basketball game situation. This information indicated declarative knowledge about what to do. An implicit test was also administered by observing what the players actually did in a situation to determine if they had the procedural knowledge necessary to do what they indicated should be done. The results showed that many of the players knew what to do in each situation, but couldn't actually do it in a game.

THE CAUSES OF FORGETTING

Trace Decay

When forgetting occurs with the passing of time, the cause is generally termed *trace decay* in the memory literature. It should be noted that the term "trace" is not commonly used in contemporary memory research literature. However, it can be thought of as synonymous with what is referred to in this discussion as the memory representation of an action.

An important point about trace decay is that it can be effectively tested as a cause of forgetting only in working memory. However, for long-term memory, a major problem is the practical impossibility of maintaining a no-interference test situation. For example, if you try to recall how to hit a slice serve in tennis after several years of not having performed it, you will have some initial difficulty remembering how to do it. Although time is a factor, you undoubtedly experienced the potentially interfering influences of the many cognitive and motor activities you have performed since you last performed this type of serve. Hence, we observe the interaction of interference and time in the long-term memory situation. As a result, we know very little about the influence of time on forgetting information stored in long-term memory.

Although time undoubtedly influences forgetting of information stored in long-term memory, it is more likely that forgetting involves the misplacing of information or interference from other activity rather than its decay or deterioration. One reason for this is the relative permanence characteristic for information stored in long-term memory. Thus, forgetting typically refers to a retrieval problem rather than to information no longer in memory.

Proactive Interference

Activity that occurs *prior to* the presentation of information that is to be remembered and negatively affects the remembering of that information is known as **proactive interference.**

Proactive interference in working memory. Relatively convincing research evidence suggests that proactive interference is a reason for forgetting movement information held in working memory. One of the best examples of this was provided in an experiment by Stelmach (1969) many years ago. Participants moved to either zero, two, or four locations on an arm-positioning task *before* moving to the location to be recalled. Following a retention interval of 5, 15, or 50 sec, they moved in reverse order to their estimates of each of the locations they had moved to. Thus, the first location recalled was the criterion location. Results showed proactive interference effects as four prior movements and a retention interval of at least 15 sec yielded the largest amount of recall performance error, compared to the other time and activity conditions.

Several attempts have been made to explain why proactive interference affects remembering movement information. One plausible suggestion is that when the proactive interference takes the form of other movements, especially those that are similar to the criterion activity, *confusion* occurs. The individual is unable to make the criterion movement precisely because of the influence of the prior activities on the distinctiveness of the criterion movement.

Proactive interference seems to occur primarily when there is similarity between what is to be remembered and the interfering activity. This similarity seems to relate to "attribute" similarity. That is, if the information to be remembered and the interfering activity relate to the same movement attribute or characteristic, then proactive interference will build up as the number of similar movements preceding the movements to be remembered increases. For example, several studies by Ste.-Marie and her colleagues in Canada have shown that gymnastics judges demonstrate proactive interference effects by exhibiting a judging bias during actual competition based on what they observed a gymnast do during warm-up sessions (Ste.-Marie & Lee, 1991; Ste.-Marie & Valiquette, 1996; Ste.-Marie, Valiquette, & Taylor, 2001).

---

proactive interference a cause of forgetting because of activity that occurs prior to the presentation of information to be remembered.

A CLOSER LOOK

Proactive Interference Influences Gymnastics Judging

A series of studies by Diane Ste.-Marie and her colleagues provide interesting evidence that gymnastic judges' evaluations of a gymnast's performance may be influenced by their having watched the gymnasts during pre-competition warm-up sessions. In each study, the following procedures were used:

Participants: Female gymnastics judges certified by Gymnastics Canada

Study phase: The judges watched videotapes of individual gymnastic elements performed by several gymnasts. The elements were edited parts of actual routines the gymnasts performed. The judges evaluated the performance of each as perfect or with a form error.

Test phase: The judges watched and evaluated the same gymnasts performing elements that were:
1. the same way as in the study phase (SAME);
2. a different way from in the study phase, i.e., with an error if perfect in study phase, or vice versa (DIFFERENT);
3. a new element, which was not in the study phase (NEW)

Results of each study:
• *Ste.-Marie and Lee (1991)* showed the following order of judgment accuracy percentages for the three test-phase conditions:

Highest: SAME; 2nd highest: NEW;
Lowest: DIFFERENT

This order of test accuracy demonstrates that observing and evaluating the performance of previously seen elements biased the judges' evaluations when the elements were performed differently from the previous observation. This bias is seen in the results that show lower judgment accuracy for elements the judges had seen previously, but that were performed differently, than for elements they had not seen previously. Interestingly, the bias occurred even though the judges were not consciously aware that they had seen the elements they evaluated in the same/different test conditions performed in the study phase.

• *Ste.-Marie and Valiquette (1996)* showed the same order of accuracy as the Ste.-Marie and Lee study when the test phase occurred immediately, one day, or one week after the study phases. These results indicate that the bias effects of previous observations persisted for at least one week.

• *Ste.-Marie, Valiquette, and Taylor (2001)* showed the same order of test accuracy as the previous two studies when the study phase involved judging the performance of each element, naming the element performed, or naming the apparatus involved. These results indicate that the test accuracy results in the previous studies were due to watching the gymnasts perform during the study phase and not to the judges being involved in evaluating the performance of each element.

These studies provide excellent demonstrations of the influence of proactive interference on human memory, especially when the previous experiences involve characteristics that are similar to those involved in the test situation.

Proactive interference in long-term memory. For movement information in long-term memory, the role of proactive interfering activities is not well known. It appears that we can quite readily overcome proactive interference effects by actively rehearsing the information. For motor skills rehearsal occurs as we practice. This means that when we actively practice a skill, we strengthen its representation in memory and thus notice few, if any, effects of proactive interference (see Panzer & Shea, 2008; Panzer, Wilde, & Shea, 2006).

Retroactive Interference

If an interfering activity occurs after we perform a movement we need to remember (i.e., *during* the retention interval) and results in poorer retention performance than if no activity had occurred, the forgetting is said to be due to **retroactive interference.**

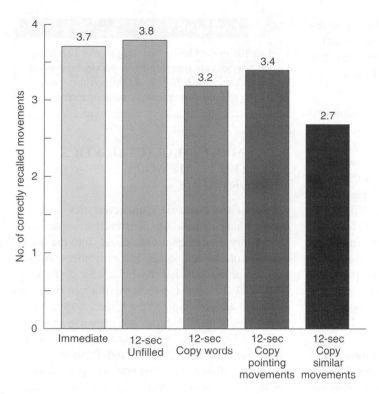

FIGURE 10.3   Free recall results of the experiment by Smyth and Pendleton showing the retroactive interference effects of performance of similar movements to those that had to be remembered. [From Smyth, M. M., & Pendleton, L. R. (1990). Space and movement in working memory. *Quarterly Journal of Experimental Psychology, 42A,* 291–304. Reprinted by permission of the Experimental Psychology Society.]

Retroactive interference in working memory. In working memory, it seems that rather than just any activity causing interference to the extent that retention performance is negatively affected, the *degree of similarity* between the interfering activity and the movement that must be remembered is an important factor. For example, participants in experiments by Smyth and Pendleton (1990) were shown a sequence of four movements, such as a forward bend of the head, both arms raised to shoulder level in front of the body, a bend of the knees, and left leg raised to the side. Following a retention interval, they had to perform these movements, either in sequence (serial recall) or in any order (free recall).

The influence of five different retention interval time and activity conditions on recall performance can be seen in figure 10.3. As you can see, these results showed that only when the retention interval involved subjects in recalling movements that were similar to those they had to remember did

recall performance significantly suffer from activity in the retention interval.

Another characteristic of retroactive interference effects in working memory is one that we discussed for proactive interference. That is, activity during the retention interval causes interference that *increases recall performance error only when there is a certain amount of activity*. As long as the amount of information stays within this limit, remembering is not affected. However, when that limit is exceeded, forgetting occurs, which results in recall performance error increase.

Thus, the available research evidence indicates that retroactive interference for remembering just-presented movements occurs in two specific circumstances. These are situations when the activity

retroactive interference   a cause of forgetting because of activity occurring during the retention interval.

during the retention interval is similar to the movements that must be remembered and when this activity and the movements to be remembered exceed working memory or attention-capacity limits.

Retroactive interference and long-term memory.
It appears that retention interval length and/or activity does not have the same forgetting effects for all types of motor skills stored in *long-term memory*. Research evidence indicates that *certain types of motor skills are remembered better over long periods than are other types.* Your own experiences may provide some support for this. You probably had very little trouble remembering how to ride a bicycle, even after not having been on one for several years. However, you probably did experience some difficulty in putting together the pieces of a puzzle that you had assembled quickly around the same time you learned to ride a bicycle.

The characteristic of skills that distinguishes these two situations relates to one of the classification systems discussed in chapter 1. That is, *continuous motor skills* are typically more resistant to long-term forgetting than are discrete skills, especially when the skill involves producing a series of discrete movements in what is sometimes referred to as a serial discrete skill.

Several reasons have been suggested to explain why this retention difference occurs. One is the difference in the *size of the verbal component* of the two types of skills. Serial discrete skills have a large verbal component, whereas this is small for continuous skills. This characteristic is significant because the verbal component of skills seems to deteriorate over time more readily than motor components. Another reason is that continuous skills are *practiced more* than are discrete skills. This is evident if you consider what a "trial" is for these two types of skills. One trial for a discrete skill is usually one performance of the skill, whereas one trial for a continuous skill is several repetitions of the skill over a much longer period of time. Thus, fifty trials of a continuous skill yield many more practice repetitions of the skill than do fifty trials of a discrete skill.

LAB LINKS

Lab 10a in the Online Learning Center Lab Manual provides an opportunity for you to experience the influence of time and activity on the remembering of limb movements in working memory.

MOVEMENT CHARACTERISTICS RELATED TO MEMORY PERFORMANCE

Location and Distance Characteristics

Actions have many characteristics that we can store in memory. For example, we could store the spatial position of various points of a movement, such as the beginning and the end point of a golf swing. We could also store the distance of a movement, its velocity, its force, and/or the direction of a movement. Two of these, *location* and *distance,* have been extensively examined with regard to how easily they can be stored in and retrieved from memory.

Investigation of the issue was very popular in the 1970s and focused primarily on working memory. Of particular interest were the short-term storage characteristics of spatial positioning movements of the arm. The initial research studies found that movement end-point location is remembered better than movement distance (e.g., Diewert, 1975; Hagman, 1978; Laabs, 1973). An important finding showed that when movement end-point location information is a relatively reliable recall cue, people will use a location-type strategy to recall the movement (Diewert & Roy 1978). However, when location information is totally unreliable and only distance information will aid recall, people will use some nonkinesthetic strategy, such as counting, to help remember the distance of the criterion movement.

Another characteristic of remembering location information is that an arm-movement end location is more easily remembered when it is within the person's own body space (e.g., Chieffi, Allport, & Woodfin, 1999; Larish & Stelmach 1982). For limb-positioning movements, people typically associate the end location of a movement with a body part and use that as a cue to aid their recall performance. Other research, which will be considered later, suggests that people will also spontaneously associate the end location of limb positions with well-known objects, such as a clock face, to aid recall.

What does all this mean for teaching motor skills? One implication is that if limb positions are important for successful performance of the skill, the instructor can emphasize these positions in ways that will facilitate learning the skill. For example, if you are teaching a beginner a golf swing, the important phases of the swing that he or she should concentrate on are critical location points in the swing. The keys could be the beginning point of the backswing or the location point of the top of the backswing. Or if a therapist or athletic trainer is working with a patient who needs to work on flexing or extending his or her knee, emphasizing the position of the lower leg can help the patient remember where the last movement was or to establish a goal for future flexion attempts. If a dancer or Pilates student is having difficulty remembering where her arm should be during a particular movement sequence, a body-part cue about the location of the arm can help her remember the position more effectively.

A note of caution is important here. Instructors of motor skills should not direct people to visually look to the location where the limb should move. Research has consistently shown that visually remembered locations for limb movements will be different from those remembered kinesthetically (see Simmering, Peterson, Darling, & Spencer, 2008, for a review of this research). This means that rather than enhancing the remembering of limb movement positions, the addition of visual information negatively influences how the positions are remembered.

The Meaningfulness of the Movement

Another characteristic that influences remembering movements is the *meaningfulness* of the movement. A movement or sequence of movements can be considered meaningful to an individual if that person can readily relate the movement to something he or she knows. For example, a movement that forms the shape of a triangle is considered more meaningful than one that makes an unfamiliar, abstract pattern. Or, if a movement is similar to one the person can do, then the new movement being learned takes on increased meaningfulness to the person.

The results of an experiment by Laugier and Cadopi (1996) illustrate the influence movement meaningfulness has on remembering movements. Adult novice dancers watched a video of a skilled dancer perform a four-element sequence of dance movements, each of which involved two to four head, body, and/or limb movements. One sequence, which the researchers labeled as a "concrete" sequence, was a sequence commonly performed in dance. Another sequence, labeled as an "abstract" sequence, involved elements that did not belong to any particular style of dance. After fifteen viewings of the dancer performing the sequences, the participants performed the sequence one time. Analysis of the participants' performance indicated that the observation of the concrete sequence led to better form and quality than the observation of the abstract sequence (see figure 10.4).

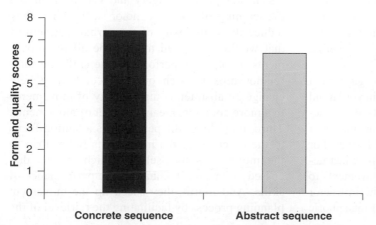

FIGURE 10.4 Results from the experiment by Laugier and Cadopi showing the influence of movement meaningfulness on remembering a four-element dance sequence. Scores reflect form and quality measures of novice dancers' one-time performance of the sequence after fifteen viewings of a skilled dancer performing the sequence. [Modified figure 2, p. 98, in Laugier, C., & Cadopi, M. (1996). Representational guidance of dance performance in adult novices: Effect of concrete vs. abstract movement. *International Journal of Sport Psychology, 27,* 91–108. Adapted with permission of the International Society of Sport Psychology.]

Interviews of the participants indicated that the concrete sequence had a higher degree of meaningfulness to them, which helped them remember the sequence when they performed it.

STRATEGIES THAT ENHANCE MEMORY PERFORMANCE

There are several different strategies people can use to help them remember important movement characteristics of a skill, which in turn facilitate learning the skill. Note that some of these strategies take advantage of the movement characteristics we just discussed that are more easily remembered than others. We will consider three general strategies that research evidence has shown to influence how well a movement is remembered.

Increasing a Movement's Meaningfulness

When people first practice a new skill, it is very likely that the skill will require that they coordinate their body and limbs in a new way. This characteristic makes it also likely that the new coordination pattern of movements will be more abstract than it is concrete. That is, the skill typically has little inherent "meaningfulness" to the learner in terms of spatial and temporal characteristics of the limb coordination needed to perform the skill. As you saw earlier in this discussion, movements that are higher in their meaningfulness will be remembered better than those low in meaningfulness. The instructor can take advantage of this characteristic by presenting to the learner a strategy that will increase the meaningfulness of the movements required to perform the skill. Two strategies are especially effective: visual imagery and verbal labels.

The use of *visual metaphoric imagery* as a memory strategy involves developing in your mind a picture of what a movement is like. As an instructor, it is best to use a metaphor for an image of something that is very familiar to the learner. For example, rather than provide the complex instructions for how to coordinate the arm movements to perform a sidestroke in swimming, the instructor can provide the learners with a useful metaphoric image to use while practicing the stroke. One such image is of themselves picking an apple from a tree with one hand, bringing the apple down, and putting the apple in a basket. Also, research by Nordin and Cumming (2005, 2007) has shown the beneficial use of metaphoric imagery by dancers to help them perform and remember how to perform complex dance skills.

Another effective strategy that increases the meaningfulness of a movement is to attach a meaningful *verbal label* to the movement. One of the earliest demonstrations of the beneficial influence of attaching verbal labels to movements was by John Shea (1977), who had participants move a lever to a stop on a semicircular arm-positioning apparatus. When they arrived at the criterion location, those in one group were provided with a number that corresponded to the clockface location of the criterion location; another group received an irrelevant verbal label such as a nonsensical three-letter syllable; another group received no verbal label about the criterion location. Results, as seen in figure 10.5, indicated that the group given a clockface label showed no increase in error over a 60 sec unfilled retention interval, whereas the other two groups showed a large increase in recall error. In a related experiment, Winther and Thomas (1981) showed that when useful verbal labels are attached to positioning movements, retention performance of young children (age seven) can become equivalent to that of adults.

There are at least four reasons why the use of visual metaphoric imagery and verbal labels aid the learning of complex motor skills. First, they reduce the complexity of the verbal instructions that would be needed to describe all the movements involved in performing the skill and their relationships to each other. Second, they help change an abstract, complex array of movements to a more concrete, meaningful set of movements. Third, they direct the performer's attention focus to the outcome of the movements rather than to the movements themselves, which, as we discussed in chapter 9, enhances the performance of skills. And fourth, they speed up the movement planning process by facilitating the retrieval of the

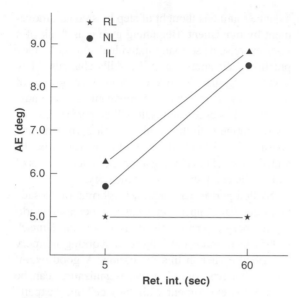

FIGURE 10.5 Mean absolute error computed across positions for the 5 sec and 60 sec retention intervals (ret. int.) in Experiment 1 by Shea. (RL = relevant label, NL = no label, IL = irrelevant label.) [From Shea, J. B. (1997). Effects of labeling on motor short-term memory. *Journal of Experimental Psychology: Human Learning and Memory, 3,* 92–99. Copyright © 1977 by the American Psychological Association. Reprinted with permission.]

appropriate memory representation of the action (Johnson, 1998).

The Intention to Remember

In all the memory experiments considered so far, participants have always known in advance that the movements they were presented or had to practice would be later subject to a recall test. But suppose they were not given this information in advance? Suppose they were told that the goal of the experiment was to see how well they could move their arms to a specified location. If an unexpected recall test was given later, how well would they recall the movements made earlier?

Intentional and incidental memory. The two situations just described are known in the memory research literature as *intentional* and *incidental* memory situations, respectively. In addition to investigating the influence of intention to remember

as an effective remembering strategy, the comparison of these two situations provides insight into the encoding of movement information processes. That is, do we store only information to which we give conscious attention, as in the case of the intentional memory situation, or do we store more information, as would be shown by good memory performance, in the incidental memory situation?

This question has received little research interest in the study of memory for movements. However, the research that has been done indicates that, in general, intention to remember leads to better remembering than no intention to remember. (See Crocker & Dickinson, 1984 for a review of this research.) Yet retention test performance in the incidental situation is typically better than if no previous experience with the test movements had occurred. In fact, some reports show incidental memory test performance to be as good as it was for the intentional situation.

The investigation of intentional and incidental memory strategies is an important one to increase our understanding of memory processes related to encoding and storing information. Research indicates that we encode and store much more information than we are consciously aware of (see, for example, Perruchet, Chambaron, & Fervel-Chapus, 2003).

One implication that the intentional and incidental memory research provides for instructional situations is that memory performance and skill learning can be enhanced by telling students when they begin to practice a skill that they will be tested on the skill later. The effect of this advance knowledge about a test is that students will undoubtedly increase the amount of effort given in practice, a characteristic that you will repeatedly see in this text as beneficial for memory and learning. Also, when there are specific characteristics of a skill performance situation that must be remembered for a later test, a better test performance will result from telling people what these characteristics are.

Subjective Organization

A strategy frequently used by learners of large amounts of information is grouping or organizing the information into units. This strategy, which is known as *subjective organization,* involves the organizing of information that must be remembered in a way that is meaningful to the individual. Other terms that researchers have used to describe this strategy are chunking, clustering, and grouping, among others. An example of implementing this strategy is commonly seen when people need to learn a long monologue for a play, or a list of terms for a test. They often will organize the monologue or list by dividing it into shorter, more manageable chunks to begin memorizing the information. You would likely use a similar strategy if you had to play from memory a long piece of music on an instrument, or had to learn a dance or gymnastics routine. In each of these situations, continued practice typically leads to increasing the size of the chunks.

Although the role of subjective organization in motor skill learning has not been the subject of a large amount of research, there is evidence indicating that when given the opportunity to subjectively organize a sequence of movements, some people will spontaneously create an organized structure. And this subjectively determined organizational structure imposed on the sequence benefits recall performance (e.g., Magill & Lee, 1987). In addition, it is interesting to note that memory performance deficits often seen following a stroke (i.e., cerebrovascular accident) have been found to be due in part to a lack of ability to implement effective organizational strategies (e.g., Lange, Waked, Kirshblum, & DeLuca, 2000). Similarly, people with Parkinson's disease have been shown to have problems with implementing a subjective organization strategy without external guidance (Berger et al., 1999).

One way to apply the benefit of subjective organization to motor skill learning situations is to consider the way a novice approaches the learning of a complex skill. He or she tends to consider complex motor skills as comprising many parts. As the beginner develops his or her ability to execute the skill, the number of components of the skill seems to decrease. This does not mean the structure of the skill itself has changed. Rather, the learner's view of the skill has changed. A good example is a dance or gymnastic floor exercise routine, where each of the routines is made up of many individual parts. To the beginner, a dance routine is thought of step by step and movement by movement. Beginning gymnasts think of a floor exercise as so many individual stunts. As they practice, their approach to the skills changes. They begin to organize the routines into units or groups of movements. Three or four component parts are now considered as one. The result will be performing the entire routine with the requisite timing, rhythm, and coordination. With that result, moreover, will be the added effect of developing a more efficient means of storing the complex routine in memory.

Skilled performers organize information to such an extent that it appears they have an increased working memory capacity; this led Ericsson and Kintsch (1995) to propose the long-term working memory described earlier in this discussion. A good example of this type of subjective organization can be seen in the experiment with "novice" and "expert" eleven-year-old dancers by Starkes et al. (1987) that was mentioned earlier in the discussion of working memory capacity. When these dancers were presented sequences of eight elements that were organized as in a ballet routine, the expert dancers recalled the routine almost perfectly, whereas the novices recalled about half of the sequence correctly. However, when the same number of elements was presented in an unstructured sequence, there was no difference between the skilled and novice dancers in terms of the number of elements they correctly recalled. This result indicates that the organizational structure of the sequence of dance movements was an important factor in the experts' recall performance. In an interesting anecdote, the researchers reported observing an adult principal national-level ballet dancer being able to perform a sequence of ninety-six steps after having seen the sequence demonstrated one time. Thus, organization was apparently a strategy used to reduce the working memory load of this sequence and to increase the memorability of the sequence.

Similar organization effects were reported by Millslagle (2002) for experienced basketball players. Both male and female players were shown slides of structured and unstructured plays that could occur in game situations. On a recognition test given after the players viewed the slides, they more accurately

A CLOSER LOOK

Active and Passive Limb Movements: Evidence for the Application of the Encoding Specificity Principle to Motor Skills

An excellent example of research evidence supporting the application of the encoding specificity principle to the remembering of movements is an experiment done many years ago by Lee and Hirota (1980).

- **Apparatus.** An arm-positioning apparatus on a table facing the participant.
- **Task and experimental conditions.** On some trials, blindfolded participants actively moved the handle of the apparatus along the trackway to a criterion arm position that was specified by a physical block. On other trials, they were passively moved by the experimenter to a criterion arm position. For the recall test on each trial, participants were told to actively move to the arm position just experienced or were passively moved by the experimenter until the participant told the experimenter to stop. This procedure continued until all participants had actively and passively experienced the presentation of each criterion arm position and had performed recall tests in either the same way they had experienced the presentation of the criterion position or the opposite way.
- **Encoding specificity principle predictions.**
  - ▶ Active movements to the criterion arm movements should be recalled better when the movements are actively recalled than passively recalled.
  - ▶ Passive movements to the criterion arm movements should be recalled better when the movements are passively recalled than when they are actively recalled.
- **Results.** As you can see in figure 10.6 below, the results supported the encoding specificity principle. When the movement during the recall test was performed in the same way as it was during the presentation of the criterion arm position (i.e., active–active, passive–passive), recall performance was more accurate than when the recall test was performed differently from the way it was during the presentation of the criterion arm position (i.e., active–passive, passive–active).
  - ▶ Note that there was no advantage to active over passive movements. The difference in recall accuracy related to the relationship between the presentation and recall conditions.

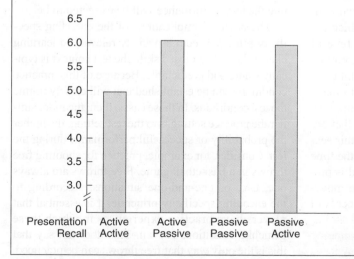

FIGURE 10.6 Results of the experiment by Lee and Hirota showing absolute error for recalling arm-position movements presented as either active or passive and recalled in either the same or opposite conditions. [From data in Lee, T. D., & Hirota, T. T. (1980). Encoding specificity principle in motor short-term memory. *Journal of Motor Behaviour, 12,* 63–67.]

LAB LINKS

Lab 10b in the Online Learning Center Lab Manual provides an opportunity for you to experience practice and test conditions that demonstrate the effects of the encoding specificity principle on remembering movements.

remembered having seen slides that included the structured plays. Interestingly, when results were compared for the players who were guards, forwards, and centers, the guards' recognition accuracy was higher than it was for the forwards and centers. Because guards have more experience determining and implementing plays than the other two positions, the results of this experiment further emphasize the influence of expertise on the organizational structure of the information we store in memory.

PRACTICE-TEST CONTEXT EFFECTS

An important influence on the retention of motor skills is the relationship between the context of practice and the context at the time of the test. The context of a movement relates to both the environmental conditions in which the movement is performed and characteristics related to the person performing the movement. For example, if a memory experiment is performed in a laboratory, the environmental context includes such things as the room in which the experiment is done, the experimenter, the time of day, the noise the participant can hear, the lighting, and so on. Personal context involves such things as the mood of the individual, the limb used to make the movement, the sitting or standing position of the subject, and the sensory feedback sources that are available to the subject. As you will see in this section, differences in these conditions during the time the movement to be remembered or learned is presented or practiced and during the time the movement must be recalled can influence the success of the recall performance.

The Encoding Specificity Principle
An important point to consider regarding the influence of movement context on remembering or learning a motor skill is the relationship between the practice and test contexts. In some situations, especially for closed skills, the test goal is essentially the same as the practice goal. That is, to shoot a free throw, you must stand in essentially the same place and shoot the ball through a hoop that is the same distance from you as it was when you practiced it. In such closed-skill situations, what is known as the **encoding specificity principle** applies.

The encoding specificity principle was introduced by Tulving and Thomson (1973). According to this principle, the more the test context resembles the practice context, the better the retention performance will be. Evidence that this principle applies to motor skills has come primarily from laboratory-based experiments (e.g., Lee & Hirota, 1980; Magill & Lee, 1987). However, as you will see in the discussion in chapter 13 concerning the transfer of learning, ample evidence exists to have confidence in generalizing this principle to the learning and performance of motor skills.

The encoding specificity principle is based on research findings that indicate that the memory representation for an action has stored with it important sensory and motor feedback information that is specific to the context conditions in which the action was practiced. Thus, the more the test conditions match the practice conditions, the more accurate the test performance will be expected to be.

The practical implications of the encoding specificity principle seem especially relevant to learning closed skills. In a closed skill, the test context is typically stable and predictable. Because of this, practice conditions can be established that will closely mimic the test conditions. In these cases, then, the more similar the practice setting is to the test setting, the higher the probability or successful performance during the test. Consider, for example, practice for shooting free throws in a basketball game. Free throws are always one, two, or one-and-one situations. According to the encoding specificity principle, it is essential that players have practice experiences in which these gamelike conditions prevail. This does not say that this is the only way that free throws can be practiced. However, if game performance is the test of interest, it is essential that gamelike practice be provided.

Consider also a physical therapy example where a knee joint replacement patient is working on knee joint flexion and extension. Based on the encoding specificity principle, because test conditions involve active limb movement, practice conditions should emphasize active rather than passive limb movement. Similar practice-test relationships can be established for a variety of skill practice situations.

> **encoding specificity principle**   a memory principle that indicates the close relationship between encoding and retrieval memory processes; it states that memory test performance is directly related to the amount of similarity between the practice and the test contexts; i.e., the more similarity, the better the test performance will be.

SUMMARY

• Memory is best viewed as consisting of two functional component systems: working memory and long-term memory, with each having three subsystems.

• Working memory:
  ► Consists of three subsystems:
    ■ phonological loop
    ■ visuospatial sketchpad
    ■ central executive
  ► Serves two functions:
    ■ short-term storage system for information recently presented or retrieved from long-term memory
    ■ temporary interactive workspace for manipulating information
  ► Has a limited capacity for information storage and the information remains for a short amount of time

• Long-term memory:
  ► Consists of three subsystems:
    ■ Procedural memory

    ■ Semantic memory
    ■ Episodic memory
  ► Stores the different types of knowledge in each subsystem on a more permanent basis
  ► Seems to have no limits in terms of storage capacity

• Forgetting is a term used to describe the loss of memory or the inability to retrieve information from memory. Forgetting is usually measured by determining the amount of information that a person can recall or recognize following a retention interval.

• Both time and activity influence forgetting in both working memory and long-term memory. The causes of forgetting associated with these factors are referred to as trace decay, which means the memory representation deteriorates over time, and interference, which can occur before (proactive interference) or after (retroactive interference) the presentation of the movement to be remembered.

• Movement-related characteristics that influence the remembering of a movement are the movement distance, movement end-location, and the meaningfulness of the movement.

• Strategies that increase how well movements are remembered include the use of visual imagery and verbal labels; the subjective organization of a complex sequence of movements into meaningful units; and the intention to remember.

• The relationship between the practice and test context characteristics influences the remembering of movements according to the encoding specificity principle, which states that increasing the similarity between these context characteristics increases performance on a memory test.

POINTS FOR THE PRACTITIONER

• After giving instructions or a demonstration about how to perform a skill, keep the amount of time until people can physically practice the skill as short and free of other activity as possible.

- Do not describe or demonstrate "what not to do" before or after giving instructions or a demonstration about how to do a skill. If information about "what not to do" is needed, present the information after the people have had opportunities to practice the skill several times.

- If people ask questions about how to perform the skill after you give instructions or a demonstration, repeat the instructions or demonstration before allowing the people to begin physically practicing the skill.

- Instructions that provide specific movement endpoint location information in a metaphoric image or verbal label form, such as analog clockface locations, when appropriate for the movement being learned, will facilitate learning the skill.

- Whenever possible, provide visual metaphoric images and meaningful verbal labels to facilitate skill learning; either is preferable to movement-specific verbal instructions.

- To facilitate the learning of sequential skills, first demonstrate the entire sequence rather than the individual parts to help learners gain a sense of how the parts in the sequence relate to each other spatially and temporally.

- When active movement function is the desired outcome of instruction, active limb movement leads to better learning than passive limb movement.

- To enhance retention test performance, develop practice conditions that are as similar as possible to the test conditions.

RELATED READINGS

Awh, E., Jonides, J., Smith, E. E., Buxton, R. B., Frank, L. R., Love, T., Wong, E. C., & Gmeindl, L. (1999). Rehearsal in spatial working memory: Evidence from neuroimaging. *Psychological Science, 10,* 433–437.

de Fockert, J. W., Rees, G., Frith, C. D., & Lavie, N. (2001). The role of working memory in visual selective attention. *Science, 291,* 1803–1806.

Jonides, J., Lacey, S. C., & Nee, D. E. (2005). Processes of working memory in mind and brain. *Current Directions in Psychological Science, 14,* 2–5.

Kimbrough, S. K., Wright, D. L., & Shea, C. H. (2001). Reducing the saliency of intentional stimuli results in greater contextual-dependent performance. *Memory, 9,* 133–143.

Lawrence, B. M., Myerson, J., & Abrams, R. A. (2004). Interference with spatial working memory: An eye movement is more than a shift of attention. *Psychonomic Bulletin & Review, 11,* 488–494.

Maxwell, J. P., Masters, R. S. W., & Eves, F. F. (2003). The role of working memory in motor learning and performance. *Consciousness and Cognition, 12,* 376–402.

McCullick, B., Schempp, P., Hsu, S. H., Jung, J H., Vickers, B., & Schuknecht, G. (2006). An analysis of the working memories of expert sport instructors. *Journal of Teaching in Physical Education, 25,* 149–165.

McIsaac, H. K., & Eich, E. (2002). Vantage point in episodic memory. *Psychonomic Bulletin & Review, 9,* 146–150.

Palmer, C. (2005). Sequence memory in music performance. *Current Directions in Psychological Science, 14,* 247–250.

Sakai, K., Kitaguchi, K., & Hikosaka, O. (2003). Chunking during human visuomotor sequence learning. *Experimental Brain Research, 152,* 229–242.

Sheeringa, R., Petersson, K. M., Oostenveld, R., Norris, D. G., Hagoort, P., & Bastiaansen, M. C. M. (2009). Trial by trial coupling between EEG and BOLD identifies networks related to alpha and theta EEG power increases during working memory maintenance. *NeuroImage, 44,* 1224–1238.

Sohn, Y. W., & Doane, S. M. (2003). Roles of working memory capacity and long-term working memory skill in complex task performance. *Memory & Cognition, 31,* 458–466.

INTERNET RESOURCES

- To see a tutorial that contains several animated chapters, including one on "Memory," in which various topics related to human memory are animated and discussed, go to http://www.physpharm.fmd.uwo.ca/undergrad/sensesweb/L12Memory/L12 Memory.SWF Type memory in the search box then click on "Memory" Link

- To visit a Web site developed to provide information about memory and memory improvement, go to http://www.memory-key.com/.

- To learn about the brain physiology of memory, go to http://neuro.psyc.memphis.edu/NeuroPsyc/np-gen-ov.htm. This is a Web site developed by the University of Memphis for people who want to increase their knowledge in physiological psychology. The specific section on Memory can be found by clicking on the Memory link under Physiology in the list of Contents.

- To read a brief discussion about "procedural memory failures" go to http://www.memory-key .com/EverydayMemory/procfailures.htm.

- To view a video about a person living a life without the capability of making new memories go to http:// www.youtube.com/watch?v=OmkiMlvLKto. The video also contains several discussions about the neural basis of memory.

STUDY QUESTIONS

1. Discuss how working memory and long-term memory differ in terms of the duration and capacity of information in each.

2. Describe the functions of each of the subsystems for working memory and long-term memory.

3. Describe the meaning of the terms *declarative* and *procedural* knowledge. Give a motor skill example of each.

4. Discuss the primary causes of forgetting in working memory and in long-term memory.

5. Discuss two effective strategies a person can use to help him or her remember a movement or sequence of movements that he or she must perform. Give an example of the use of each strategy in a motor skill performance situation.

6. What is the *encoding specificity principle,* and how does it relate to the performance of motor skills?

Specific Application Problem:
You are working in your chosen profession. Describe how you would develop practice conditions as similar as possible to the test conditions in which the people with whom you work want to achieve success.

UNIT FOUR

Introduction to Motor Skill Learning

CHAPTER 11

Defining and Assessing Learning

Concept: People who assess learning must make inferences from observing performance during practice and tests.

After completing this chapter, you will be able to

- Define and distinguish between the terms *performance* and *learning*
- Identify five general performance characteristics typically observable as motor skill learning occurs
- Describe several different methods to assess motor skill learning
- Discuss two reasons performance during the practice of a motor skill may misrepresent the amount of learning that occurred during practice

APPLICATION

Any practitioner involved in motor skills instruction typically has to provide some type of assessment to determine whether or not the student, athlete, or patient has learned what the practitioner has taught. The following two situations, common in physical education and rehabilitation settings, provide examples of the importance of assessing learning.

Suppose you are a physical educator teaching a tennis unit. If you are teaching your students to serve, how do you determine whether they are actually learning what you are teaching them? What will you look for to assess their progress in learning to serve? How can you be certain that what you are observing is the result of learning and not just luck?

Or suppose you are a physical therapist helping a stroke patient to relearn how to walk without support. What evidence will tell you that this patient is learning to do what you have taught him or her to do? What characteristics of the patient's performance will make you confident that the patient has learned this skill and will be able to walk without assistance at home as well as in the clinic?

Application Problem to Solve Select a motor skill that you might teach to someone in your future profession. What would you expect the person to learn as a result of this experience with you? How would you provide evidence to that person or a supervisor to demonstrate that the skill had been learned? How could you be confident that this evidence meets the criteria established by a definition of learning as it relates to motor skills?

DISCUSSION

In any discussion about the assessment of learning, we need to keep two important terms distinct: *performance* and *learning*. This distinction helps us establish an appropriate definition for the term *learning;* it also helps us consider appropriate conditions under which we should observe performance so that we can make valid inferences about learning.

The Terms "Performance" and "Learning"

Performance	Learning
• Observable behavior	• Inferred from performance
• Temporary	• Relatively permanent
• May not be due to practice	• Due to practice
• May be influenced by performance variables	• *Not* influenced by performance variables

PERFORMANCE DISTINGUISHED FROM LEARNING

Simply put, **performance** is *observable behavior.* If you observe a person walking down a corridor, you are observing him or her perform the skill of walking. Similarly, if you observe a person hitting a baseball, you are observing a performance of the skill of hitting a ball. When used in this way, the term *performance* refers to the execution of a skill at a specific time and in a specific situation. *Learning,* on the other hand, cannot be observed directly, but can only be inferred from characteristics of a person's performance.

Before considering a more formal definition for learning, think about how often we make inferences about people's internal states based on what we observe them doing. For example, when someone smiles (an observable behavior), we infer that he or she is happy. When someone cries, we infer that he or she is sad, or perhaps very happy. When a person yawns, we assume that the person is tired. In each of these situations, certain characteristics about the individual's behavior are the basis for our making a particular inference about some internal state we cannot observe directly. However, because we must base our inference on observed behavior, it is possible that our inference is incorrect. For example, if a student sitting beside you in class yawns during the lecture, you might infer from that behavior that the person is tired because of lack of sleep the night before. However, it may be that he or she is bored.

Learning Defined

We will use the following general definition for the term **learning:** *a change in the capability of a person to perform a skill that must be inferred from a relatively permanent improvement in performance as a result of practice or experience.* It is important to note from this definition that the person has increased his or her *capability, or potential,* to perform that skill. Whether or not the person actually performs the skill in a way that is consistent with this potential will depend on the presence of what are known as *performance variables.* These include factors that can affect a person's performance but not the degree of learning the person has achieved. Some examples include the alertness of the person, the anxiety created by the situation, the uniqueness of the setting, fatigue, and so on. As a result, it is critical that methods used to assess learning take factors such as these into account to allow accurate inferences about learning.

GENERAL PERFORMANCE CHARACTERISTICS OF SKILL LEARNING

We generally observe five performance characteristics as skill learning takes place.

---

performance   the behavioral act of executing a skill at a specific time and in a specific situation.

learning   change in the capability of a person to perform a skill; it must be inferred from a relatively permanent improvement in performance as a result of practice or experience.

Improvement

First, *performance of the skill shows improvement over a period of time.* This means that the person performs at a higher level of skill at some later time than at some previous time. It is important to note that learning is not necessarily limited to performance improvement. There are cases in which practice results in bad habits, which in turn result in the observed performance's failure to show improvement. In fact, performance actually may become worse as practice continues. But because this text is concerned with skill acquisition, we will focus on learning as it involves improvement in performance.

Consistency

Second, as learning progresses, *performance becomes increasingly more consistent.* This means that from one performance attempt to another, a person's performance characteristics should become more similar. Early in learning, performance is typically quite variable from one attempt to another. Eventually, however, it becomes more consistent.

Stability

Although related to the term *variability,* **stability** refers to the influence on skill performance of perturbations, which are internal or external conditions that can disrupt performance. A common internal perturbation is stress, such as is commonly experienced when a person performs a skill under pressure. External perturbations involve environmental conditions that can disrupt performance, such as an obstacle in a person's pathway, the wind, or inclement weather. As learning progresses, performance stability increases. This means that external and internal perturbations have less of an influence on performance. With learning, a person increases the capability to perform the skill despite the perturbations that exist. There are however, limits to the amount of perturbation that can be overcome.

Persistence

The fourth general performance characteristic we observe during learning is this: *the improved performance capability is marked by an increasing amount of persistence.* This means that as the person progresses in learning the skill, the improved performance capability lasts over increasing periods of time. A person who has learned a skill should be able to demonstrate the improved level of performance today, tomorrow, next week, and so on. However, because of some forgetting or other factors, the person may not achieve the same performance level on each of these occasions as he or she did at the end of the practice time devoted to the skill. The persistence characteristic relates to the emphasis in our definition of learning on a *relatively permanent improvement in performance.*

Adaptability

Finally, although not explicitly stated in our definition, an important general characteristic of performance associated with skill learning is that *the improved performance is adaptable to a variety of performance context characteristics.* Some researchers refer to this characteristic as *generalizability,* or how *generalizable* the performance of a skill is. We never really perform a skill when everything in the performance context is exactly the same each time. Something is different every time we perform a skill. The difference may be our own emotional state, the characteristics of the skill itself, an environmental difference such as a change in weather conditions, the place where we perform the skill, and so on. Thus, successful skill performance requires adaptability to changes in personal, task, and/or environmental characteristics. The degree of adaptability required depends on the skill and the performance situation. As a person progresses in learning a skill, his or her capability to perform the skill successfully in these changed circumstances also increases. Later in this book, we will explore some instruction and practice condition characteristics that can influence how well a person adapts to these various situations.

ASSESSING LEARNING BY OBSERVING PRACTICE PERFORMANCE

One way we can assess learning is to record levels of a performance measure during the period of time a person practices a skill. A common way to

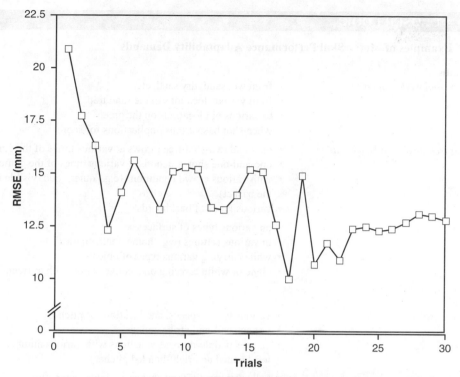

FIGURE 11.1   Performance curve for one person learning a pursuit tracking task. The performance measure is the root mean-squared error (RMSE) for each trial. Notice that because the performance measure is error, lower values represent better performance than higher values.

do this is to illustrate performance graphically in the form of a **performance curve.** This is a plot of the level achieved on the performance measure for each time period, which may be time in seconds or minutes, a trial, a series of trials, a day, etc. For any performance curve, the levels of the performance measure are always on the Y-axis (vertical axis), and the time over which the performance is measured is on the X-axis (horizontal axis).

Performance Curves for Outcome Measures
We can graphically describe performance by developing a performance curve for an outcome measure of performance. An example is shown in figure 11.1, which depicts one person's practice of a complex pursuit tracking task. The task required the person to track, or follow the movement of, a cursor on a computer monitor by moving the mouse on a tabletop. The goal was

to track the cursor as closely as possible in both time and space. Each trial lasted about 15 sec. The outcome measure of performance was the root mean-squared error (RMSE), which was described in chapter 2.

stability   the influence on skill performance of perturbations, which are internal or external conditions that can disrupt performance.

performance curve   line graph describing performance in which the level of achievement of a performance measure is plotted for a specific sequence of time (e.g., sec, min, days) or trials; the units of the performance measure are on the Y-axis (vertical axis) and the time units or trials are on the X-axis (horizontal axis).

A CLOSER LOOK

Examples of Motor Skill Performance Adaptability Demands

Closed Skills

- *Hitting a sand wedge in golf*
  - from wet sand, dry sand, etc.
  - from various locations in the sand trap
  - to various pin locations on the green
  - when shot has various implications for score

- *Shooting free throws in basketball*
  - one- and two-shot free throws at various times of the game
  - one-and-one shot situations at various times of the game
  - with various crowd conditions (e.g., quiet, loud, visible behind the basket)
  - various types of backboards

- *Walking*
  - on various types of surfaces
  - in various settings (e.g., home, mall, sidewalk)
  - while carrying various types of objects
  - alone or while carrying on a conversation with a friend

Open Skills

- *Hitting a baseball/softball*
  - various types, speeds, and locations of pitches
  - various ball-and-strike counts
  - various people-on-base situations with various numbers of outs
  - left-handed and right-handed pitchers

- *Catching a ball*
  - balls that are different shapes, weights, sizes, etc.
  - various speeds and directions
  - in the air, on the ground
  - with one or two hands

- *Driving a car*
  - various sizes of cars
  - various street and highway conditions
  - with or without passengers
  - various weather conditions

Notice that in this graph you can readily observe two of the four behavioral characteristics associated with learning. First, *improvement* is evident by the general direction of the curve. From the first to the last trial, the curve follows a general downward trend (note that because the performance measure is error, improvement involves decreasing error). Second, we can also see *increased performance consistency* in this graph. The indicator of this performance characteristic is performance on adjacent trials. According to figure 11.1, this person showed a high degree of inconsistency early in practice but became slightly more consistent from one trial to the next toward the end of practice. The expectation would be that the person would increase this consistency with additional practice trials.

General types of performance curves. When a person is learning a new skill, the performance curve for an outcome measure typically follows one of *four general trends* from the beginning to the end of the practice period for a skill. This period of time may be represented as a certain number of trials, hours, days, and so on. The trends are represented by the four different shapes of curves in figure 11.2. Note that in contrast to figure 11.1, the curves in this figure show better performance when they slope upward. Curve *a* is a *linear*

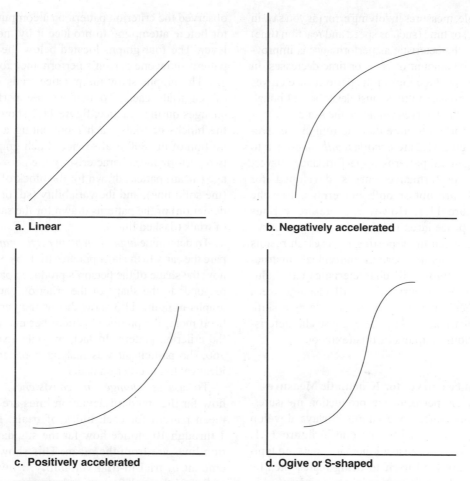

a. Linear

b. Negatively accelerated

c. Positively accelerated

d. Ogive or S-shaped

FIGURE 11.2   Four general types of performance curves. Each curve is based on higher performance scores (which would be on the *y*- or vertical axis) representing better performance than lower scores.

curve, or a straight line. This indicates proportional performance increases over time; that is, each unit of increase on the horizontal axis (e.g., one trial) results in a proportional increase on the vertical axis (e.g., one second). Curve *b* is a *negatively accelerated curve,* which indicates that a large amount of improvement occurs early in practice, with smaller amounts of improvement later. This curve is the most prominent type of performance curve for motor skill learning. It represents the classic power law of skill learning, which we will discuss in some detail in chapter 12. Curve *c* is the inverse of curve

b and is called a *positively accelerated curve.* This curve indicates slight performance gain early in practice, but a substantial increase later in practice. Curve *d* is a combination of all three curves and is called an *ogive* or *S-shaped curve.*

Each curve in figure 11.2 shows better performance as the curve slopes upward. However, as we noted earlier, there are instances in which the slope of the curve is in a downward direction to indicate performance improvement. This occurs when the performance measure is one for which a decrease in the performance level means better performance.

For example, measures involving error (as you saw in figure 11.1) or time (such as speed and reaction time) follow this characteristic as performance is improving when the amount of error or time decreases. In such cases, the directions of the performance curves would be opposite to those just described, although the shapes of the curves would be the same.

It is important to note that the four curves presented in figure 11.2 are *hypothetically smoothed* to illustrate general patterns of performance curves. Typically, performance curves developed for individuals are not smooth but erratic, like the one in figure 11.1. However, there are various statistical procedures that can be used for curve smoothing when the reporting of research results warrants it. Finally, various individual, instructional, and motor skill characteristics can influence the type of curve that will characterize a person's performance as he or she learns a skill. You will learn about several of these characteristics in various chapters of this textbook.

Performance Curves for Kinematic Measures
When we use performance production measures, such as kinematics, we cannot always develop performance curves like the one in figure 11.1. This is the case because a kinematic measure typically does not lend itself to being represented by one number value for each trial. As you learned in chapter 2, kinematic measures involve performance for a period of time *within* a trial. It is important to include this time component in the graphic representation of a kinematic measure.

To assess improvement and consistency in performance for a series of practice trials, researchers commonly show one performance curve graph for each trial or a group (i.e., block) of trials. To show improvement and consistency changes, they depict a representative sample of trials from different stages of practice.

You can see an example of this approach to kinematic measures in figure 11.3. The task required participants to move a lever on a tabletop to produce the criterion movement displacement pattern shown at the top of this figure. Each participant

observed the criterion pattern on a computer monitor before attempting to produce it by moving the lever. The four graphs located below the criterion pattern show one person's performance for 800 trials. The graphs show the practice trials in blocks of ten trials each. To demonstrate performance changes during practice, figure 11.3 shows four of the blocks of trials, each representing a different portion of the 800 trial session. Each graph shows two performance characteristics: the person's average (mean) pattern drawn for the block of ten trials (the solid line); and the variability (sd, or standard deviation) of the patterns drawn for the same block of trials (dashed lines).

To determine *improvement in performance,* compare the early to the later practice trials by examining how the shape of the person's produced pattern corresponds to the shape of the criterion pattern. The graphs in figure 11.3 show that as the person practiced more, the produced pattern became more like the criterion pattern. In fact, in trials 751 through 760, the participant was making a pattern almost identical to the criterion pattern.

To assess *changes in consistency,* compare how far the standard deviation lines are from the mean pattern for each block of trials. For trials 1 through 10, notice how far the standard deviation lines are from the mean. This shows a large amount of trial-to-trial variability. However, for trials 751 through 760, these lines are much closer to the mean, indicating that the person more consistently produced the same pattern on each trial of that block of trials.

ASSESSING LEARNING BY RETENTION TESTS

Another means of inferring learning from performance examines *the persistence characteristic of improved performance* due to practicing a skill. A common means of assessing this characteristic is to administer a retention test. You have been experiencing this approach to assessing learning since you began school. Teachers regularly give tests that cover units of instruction. They use these **retention tests** to determine how much you know, or have

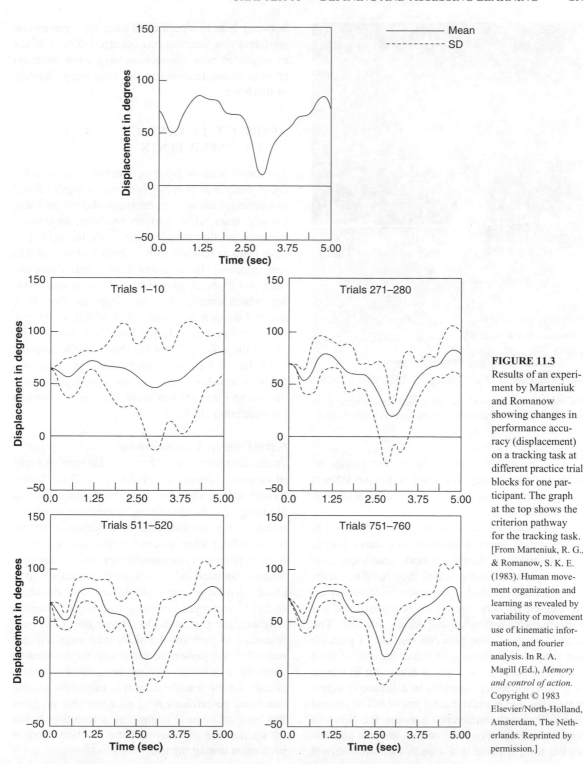

FIGURE 11.3
Results of an experiment by Marteniuk and Romanow showing changes in performance accuracy (displacement) on a tracking task at different practice trial blocks for one participant. The graph at the top shows the criterion pathway for the tracking task. [From Marteniuk, R. G., & Romanow, S. K. E. (1983). Human movement organization and learning as revealed by variability of movement, use of kinematic information, and fourier analysis. In R. A. Magill (Ed.), *Memory and control of action.* Copyright © 1983 Elsevier/North-Holland, Amsterdam, The Netherlands. Reprinted by permission.]

One way to assess how well a person learns a serve in tennis is to use a transfer test, such as performing the serve in a tennis match.

retained from your study. The teacher makes an inference concerning how much you have learned about a particular unit of study on the basis of your test performance.

The typical way to administer a retention test in a motor-skill learning situation is to have people perform the skill they have been practicing after a period of time during which they have not actually practiced the skill. The purpose is to determine the degree of *permanence or persistence* of the performance level achieved during practice. The actual length of time between the end of practice and the test is arbitrary. But the amount of time should be sufficiently long to allow the influence of any performance variables to dissipate to determine what was learned during practice. The critical assessment is the difference between the person's performance level on the first practice day and that on the test. If there is a significant improvement

between these two periods of time, then you can be confident that learning has occurred. You will see examples of how researchers have used retention tests to assess learning in the remaining chapters of this book.

ASSESSING LEARNING BY TRANSFER TESTS

The third means of inferring learning examines the *adaptability aspect of performance changes* related to learning. This assessment method involves using **transfer tests,** which are tests involving some novel situation, so that people must adapt the skill they have been practicing to the characteristics of this new situation. Researchers have most commonly used two types of novel situations to assess learning, which practitioners can adapt for their own needs. One is a new context in which the people must perform the skill; the other is a novel variation of the skill itself. Rather than consider specific examples of how researchers have used various types of transfer tests to assess learning, we will discuss research studies involving transfer tests in the remaining chapters of this book.

Novel Context Characteristics

Practitioners and researchers can use various kinds of context changes in transfer tests. One characteristic that researchers have commonly used is to change the *availability of augmented feedback,* which is the performance information a person receives from some external source. For example, in many practice situations, the person receives augmented feedback in the form of verbal information about what he or she is doing correctly or incorrectly. If you were assessing learning to discover how well the person could rely on his or her own resources to perform the skill, then your requirement that the person perform without augmented feedback availability would be a useful context change for the transfer test. It is important to note that some researchers refer to a test that involves this type of context change as a retention rather than a transfer test, because the practiced skill is performed during the test.

Another context characteristic a test administrator can change is the *physical environment* in which a person performs. This is especially effective for a learning situation in which the goal is to enable a person to perform in locations and situations other than those in which he or she has practiced. For example, if you are working in a clinic with a patient with a gait problem, you want that patient to be able to adapt to the environmental demands of his or her everyday world. Although performing well in the clinic is important, it is less important than performing well in the world in which the patient must function on a daily basis. Because of this need, the transfer test in which the physical environment resembles one in the everyday world is a valuable assessment instrument.

The third aspect of context that can be changed for a transfer test is the *personal characteristics* of the test taker as they relate to skill performance. Here, the focus is on how well a person can perform the skill while adapting to characteristics of himself or herself that were not present during practice. For example, suppose you know that the person will have to perform the skill in a stressful situation. A test requiring the person to perform the skill while emotionally stressed would provide a useful assessment of his or her capability to adapt to this situation.

Changes in the environmental context and personal characteristics provide not only opportunities to assess a person's capability to adapt what has been learned, but also opportunities to *assess the stability* of what has been learned. Environmental context changes, such as the introduction of other people walking in a hallway or an obstacle in the pathway, can serve as perturbations that might alter the performance of a skill. Requiring a person to perform a skill while emotionally stressed can do the same. The degree to which the person's performance is disrupted by these external and internal perturbations provides evidence of the amount of performance stability a person has acquired as a result of practice.

Novel Skill Variations

Another aspect of adaptability related to skill learning is a person's capability to successfully perform a novel variation of a skill he or she has learned.

This capability is common in our everyday experience. For example, no one has walked at all speeds at which it is possible to walk. Yet, we can speed up or slow down our walking gait with little difficulty. Similarly, we have not grasped and drunk from every type of cup or glass that exists in the world. Yet when we are confronted with some new cup, we adapt our movements quite well to the cup characteristics and successfully drink from it. These examples illustrate the importance to people of producing novel variations of skills. One of the ways to assess how well a person can do this is to use a transfer test that incorporates this movement adaptation characteristic.

Note that one of the ways to get people to produce a novel skill variation is to alter the performance context in some way so that they must adapt their movements to it. In this way, the transfer test designed to assess capability to produce novel skill variations resembles a transfer test designed to assess capability to adapt to novel performance context features. The difference is the learning assessment focus.

ASSESSING LEARNING FROM COORDINATION DYNAMICS

Another method of assessing learning involves the observation of the stabilities and transitions of the dynamics of movement coordination related to performing a skill. According to this approach, when a person begins to learn a new skill, he or she is not really learning something new, but is evolving a new spatial and temporal coordination pattern from an old one. When viewed from this perspective,

retention test   test of a practiced skill that a learner performs following an interval of time after practice has ceased.

transfer test   test in which a person performs a skill that is different from the skill he or she practiced or performs the practiced skill in a context or situation different from the practice context or situation.

learning involves the transition *from the initial movement coordination pattern (i.e., the intrinsic dynamics), represented by a preferred coordination pattern the person exhibits when first attempting the new skill, to the establishment of the new coordination pattern* (see Zanone & Kelso, 1994, for a detailed discussion). *Stability and consistency* of the coordination pattern are important criteria for determining which coordination state (initial, transition, or new) characterizes the person's performance.

For example, a person who is learning handwriting experiences an initial state represented by the coordination characteristics of the upper arm, forearm, and hand while engaged in handwriting at the beginning of practice. These characteristics make up the preferred spatial and temporal structure the person and the task itself impose on the limb, so the limb can produce movement approximating what is required. This initial stable state must be changed to a new stable state in which the person can produce fluent handwriting. Learning is the process that occurs during the transition between these two states and during the development of the consistency and stability of the new state.

An example of this approach to assessing skill learning is an experiment by Lee, Swinnen, and Verschueren (1995). The task (see figure 11.4) required participants to learn a new asymmetric bimanual coordination pattern. (We briefly considered in chapter 7 the motor control difficulties associated with these types of tasks.) To perform the task, they simultaneously moved two levers on a tabletop toward and away from the body at the same rate (15 times in 15 sec). Their goal was to produce ellipses on the computer monitor. To accomplish this, they had to coordinate the movement of their arms so that the right arm on each cycle was always 90 degrees out-of-phase with the left arm. Recall from the discussion of relative phase in chapter 2 that this means that the position of the right arm's lever at any point in time had to be 90 degrees different from the position of the left arm's lever. For example when the left arm's lever was at 0 degrees, the right arm's lever had to be at 90 degrees. This 90-degree

LAB LINKS

Lab 11 in the Online Learning Center Lab Manual provides an opportunity for you to experience the influence of a performance variable during practice as you learn a new motor skill.

difference had to be maintained throughout the 15 sec of movement.

The initial coordination pattern for the two arms for one participant is shown in figure 11.4 as the arm-to-arm displacement relationship performed on the pretest. The diagonal lines seen in the day 1 (pretest) graph were the result of the person moving the arms in-phase, in a motion resembling that of windshield wipers. The consistency of this coordination pattern is indicated by the amount of overlap of the fifteen diagonal lines produced during the pretest. Notice the person's tendency to produce that same diagonal pattern on the pretest trial on day 2, after having performed sixty practice trials of the ellipse pattern on day 1.

By the end of day 3, this person had learned to produce the ellipse pattern. Evidence for this is the consistent production of fifteen ellipses in both the pretest and the posttest trials on day 3. However, notice the instability of the performance in the many trials between the old and the new stable patterns (exhibited on the day 1 pretest and the day 3 posttest). This instability occurs during the transition between two stable states and characterizes the process of learning a new skill.

PRACTICE PERFORMANCE MAY MISREPRESENT LEARNING

It may be misleading to base an inference about learning solely on observed performance during practice. There are at least two reasons for this. One is that the practice situation may involve a performance variable, which was described earlier in this discussion as having the potential to artificially inflate or depress performance. The second reason is that practice performance may be misleading if it involves performance plateaus.

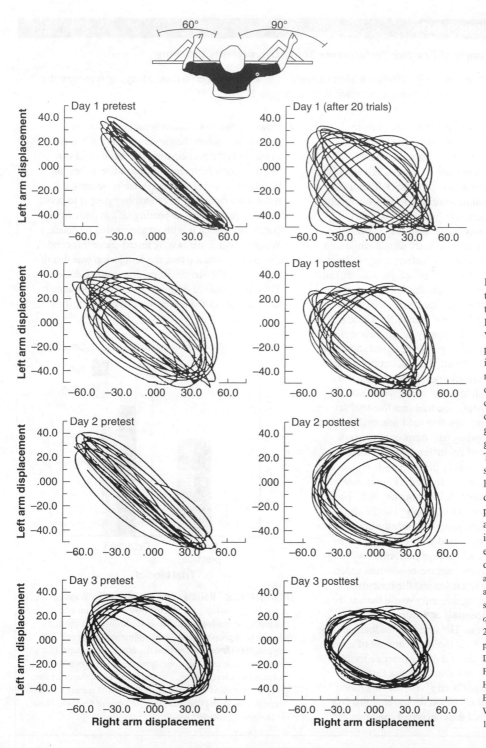

FIGURE 11.4 The task and results from the experiment by Lee, Swinnen, and Verschueren. The top panel shows the task, in which participants moved two levers to draw ellipses on the computer monitor (the dotted lines on each graph represent the goal ellipse pattern). The series of graphs shows the results as the left-arm × right-arm displacements of one person for the pretest and posttest (and some intermediate) trials for each of three practice days. [From Lee, T. D. et al. (1995). Relative phase alterations during bimanual skill acquisition. *Journal of Motor Behavior, 27,* 263–274. Reprinted with permission of the Helen Dwight Reid Educational Foundation. Published by Heldref Publications, 1319 Eighteenth Street NW, Washington, DC 20036–1802. Copyright © 1995].

A CLOSER LOOK

An Example of Practice Performance That Misrepresents Learning

An experiment by Winstein et al. (1996) is a good example of how practice performance may not represent the influence of a variable on the learning of a motor skill (see figure 11.5).

- **Purpose of the experiment:** Which of three different knowledge of results (KR) conditions would be best as an aid to help people learn a partial-weight-bearing task? This task is a skill often taught by physical therapists. (KR refers to performance-outcome information a person receives from a source external to himself or herself.)
- **The task:** The participants' goal was to learn to support 30 percent of their body weight while stepping on a floor scale with a preferred leg while on crutches. The target amount of weight was marked on the scale for each person. Participants in one group could see the scale needle move as they were stepping on the scale (concurrent KR). These participants were able to correctly adjust their weight on each trial. Two other groups received augmented feedback after performing the task (terminal KR). Participants in these groups could not see the scale needle during each trial, but saw a red line on the scale after completing one trial or a five-trial set (the five-trial group saw five red lines, each marked with the corresponding trial number of the set).
- **Practice trials and retention test:** All three groups performed eighty practice trials on one day. Two days later, they performed a retention test that consisted of twenty trials without any KR about the amount of weight they applied to the scale.
- **Results:** *During the practice trials* the concurrent KR group performed with very little error. The two terminal KR groups performed with significantly more error than the concurrent group. However, *on the retention test* the concurrent group performed significantly worse than at the end of the practice trials and worse than both of the terminal groups. The terminal feedback groups performed with about the same amount of error as they produced at the end of the practice trials.
- **Conclusion:** It is important to notice that if the retention test had not been given, the conclusion about the best KR condition for learning this task would have favored the concurrent condition.

However, this conclusion would be based on performance when the various types of KR were available to the participants. The more valid way to determine which feedback condition is best for learning is when no KR is available, because it reflects the therapy goal of enabling people to perform the partial-weight-bearing task in daily living conditions, which is with no augmented feedback. When the participants were tested under this condition on the retention test, the conclusion was that the *concurrent KR was the worst learning condition.* Thus, performance during practice misrepresented the influence of the KR conditions on learning.

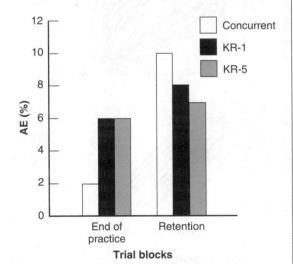

FIGURE 11.5   Results of the experiment by Winstein et al. (1996) showing that performance during practice can misrepresent learning. The graph shows that during practice the group who received augmented feedback concurrently performed better than the other two groups. But on the retention test, this concurrent feedback group's error increased to a level that was worse than that of the other two groups. [Data from Winstein, C. J., et al. (1996). Learning a partial-weight-bearing skill: Effectiveness of two forms of feedback. *Physical Therapy, 76,* 985–993.]

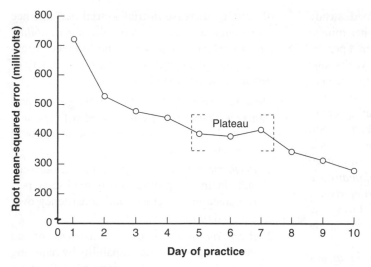

FIGURE 11.6   Results from the experiment by Franks and Wilberg showing the results from one participant performing the complex tracking task for ten days, with 105 trials per day. Notice the performance plateau for three days (days 5, 6, and 7) where performance leveled off before the subject showed improvement again. [From Franks, I. M., & Wilberg, R. B. (1982). The generation of movement patterns during the acquisition of a pursuit tracking task. *Human Movement Science, 1,* 251–272. Copyright © 1982 Elsevier/North-Holland, Amsterdam, The Netherlands. Reprinted by permission.]

Practice Performance May Overestimate or Underestimate Learning

In this textbook, you will see examples of variables whose presence during practice influences performance in such a way that performance overestimates or underestimates learning. One way to overcome these problems is to use retention or transfer tests to assess learning. If a person's practice performance does represent learning, then that person's performance on a retention test should demonstrate the persistence characteristic and not deviate too much from his or her performance at the end of practice. Similarly, transfer test performance should demonstrate the person's increased capability to adapt to novel conditions.

Performance Plateaus

Over the course of learning a skill, it is not uncommon for a person to experience a period of time during which improvement seems to have stopped. But for some reason, at some later time, improvement starts to occur again. This period of time during which there appears to be no further performance improvement is known as a **performance plateau.**

Examples of performance plateaus are difficult to find in the motor learning research literature because most of this research presents performance curves that represent the average for a group of participants. To find evidence of a performance plateau, individual participants' results are needed. An experiment reported by Franks and Wilberg (1982) is an example of this latter case, and it provides a good illustration of a performance plateau (figure 11.6). This graph shows one individual's performance on a complex tracking task for ten days, with 105 trials each day. Notice that this person showed consistent improvement for the first four days. Then, on days 5 through 7, performance improvement stopped. However, this was a temporary characteristic; performance began to improve again on day 8 and the improvement continued for the next two days. The steady-state performance on days 5 through 7 is a good example of a performance plateau.

The concept of a performance plateau has a historical place in motor learning research. The first evidence of a plateau during skill learning is attributed to the work of Bryan and Harter (1897), who published their observations of new telegraphers

---

performance plateau   while learning a skill, a period of time in which the learner experiences no improvement after having experienced consistent improvement; typically, the learner then experiences further improvement with continued practice.

learning Morse code. The authors noted steady improvement in the telegraphers' letters-per-minute speed for the first twenty weeks. But then a performance plateau occurred that lasted six weeks; this was followed by further performance improvement for the final twelve weeks. Since this early demonstration, researchers have been debating about whether a plateau is a real learning phenomenon or merely a temporary performance artifact (see Adams, 1987, for the most recent review of plateau research). At present, most agree that *plateaus are performance rather than learning characteristics.* This means that plateaus may appear during the course of practice, but learning continues during these times.

There are several *reasons performance plateaus* occur. One is that the plateau represents a period of transition between two phases of acquiring certain aspects of a skill. During this transition, the person is developing a new strategy that the task requires to increase the level of performance already achieved. Consequently, no performance improvement occurs until the new strategy is successfully implemented. Other possible explanations for a performance plateau may be that it represents a period of poor motivation, a time of fatigue, or a lack of attention directed to an important aspect of a skill. Finally, it is possible the plateau may be due not to these performance characteristics but to limitations imposed by the performance measure. This is the case when the performance measure involves what are known as *ceiling* or *floor effects.* These effects occur when the performance measure will not permit the score to go above or below a certain point.

SUMMARY

- To effectively study concepts and issues related to the learning of motor skills, it is important to distinguish the terms *performance,* which is an observable behavior, and *learning,* which is inferred from the observation of performance.

- People typically demonstrate five general performance characteristics as they learn a motor skill: performance *improvement* over a period of time, an increase in trial-to-trial performance *consistency,* an increase in performance *stability,* a *persistence* of an improved performance capability, and the capability to *adapt* to a variety of performance context characteristics.

- The assessment of one or more of the general performance characteristics associated with learning forms the basis for four methods commonly used to assess motor skill learning:

  1. *Performance curves* of performance outcome and kinematics provide a way to observe performance improvement and consistency over a period of time.

  2. *Retention tests* assess persistence of an improved performance capability by requiring the performance of the practiced skill after a period of time during which the skill was not practiced.

  3. *Transfer tests* assess the acquired capability to adapt to performance situations and contexts that were not experienced during practice.

  4. Graphical representations of *movement coordination patterns* during practice and tests provide a means of assessing the consistency and stability of coordination characteristics associated with performing a motor skill.

- The assessment of learning on the basis of practice performance only can sometimes lead to incorrect inferences about learning, because

  1. Certain *performance variables* can artificially inflate or depress practice performance so that the observed performance during practice over- or underestimates the amount a person has learned during practice. Retention and transfer tests provide ways to determine the extent to which performance during practice represents learning.

  2. *Performance plateaus,* which appear on performance cues as periods of time during which performance does not improve, give the appearance that learning has stopped even though it has not. Providing additional practice trials can establish a means of determining whether learning continued during a performance plateau.

- As people learn motor skills they not only show improvement in their performance of the skill, but also become more consistent in their performance from one attempt to another, perform the skill at close to their improved level after periods of not performing the skill, and successfully perform the skill in new situations.

- To provide evidence of motor skill performance improvement and consistency, use performance curves of outcome and kinematic measures as well as diagrams that show the movement displacement relationship between two joints or limbs.

- Although performance improvement is an important feature of learning a motor skill, the amount of improvement during practice or therapy sessions may be artificially influenced by characteristics of the practice sessions, such as the availability of augmented feedback. To determine the degree to which practice characteristics influence skill learning, evaluate performance during retention or transfer tests.

- To observe how well people can apply what they learn during practice to how they will actually use the skill, administer transfer tests that require them to perform the skill in conditions that are similar to those they will experience when they need to perform the skill.

- People who are learning a skill often experience performance plateaus. It is important to provide encouragement to continue to practice to improve performance and offer possible movement strategy alternatives.

RELATED READINGS

Christina, R. W. (1997). Concerns and issues in studying and assessing motor learning. *Measurement in Physical Education and Exercise Science, 1,* 19–38.

Kelso, J. A. S., & Zanone, P. G. (2002). Coordination dynamics of learning and transfer across different effector systems. *Journal of Experimental Psychology: Human Perception and Performance, 28,* 776–797.

Langley, D. J. (1997). Exploring student skill learning. A case for investigating subjective experience. *Quest, 49,* 142–160.

Lee, T. D., & Swinnen, S. P. (1993). Three legacies of Bryan and Harter: Automaticity, variability, and change in skilled performance. In J. L. Starkes & F. Allard (Eds.), *Cognitive issues in motor expertise* (pp. 295–315). Amsterdam: Elsevier.

Magnuson, C. E., Shea, J. B., & Fairbrother, J. T. (2004). Effects of repeated retention tests on learning a single timing task. *Research Quarterly for Exercise and Sport, 75,* 39–45.

Memmert, D., Raab, A., & Bauer, P. (2006). Laws of practice and performance plateaus concerning complex motor skills. *Journal of Human Movement Studies, 51,* 239–255.

Russell, D. M., & Newell, K. M. (2007). On no-KR tests in motor learning, retention, and transfer. *Human Movement Science, 26,* 155–173.

Tallet, J., Kostrubiec, V., & Zanone, P. G. (2008). The role of stability in the dynamics of learning, memorizing, and forgetting new coordination patterns. *Journal of Motor Behavior, 40,* 103–116.

INTERNET RESOURCES

- A good resource for information about the assessment of learning in physical education is on the Web site of the National Association of Sport and Physical Education (NASPE), which is an association of the American Alliance of Health, Physical Education, Recreation, and Dance (AAHPERD). You can find materials to download as well as purchase at http://www.aahperd.org/naspe/.

- Tips for getting through what we referred to in this chapter as a "performance plateau" in learning to dance or learning a new dance are presented in a "Dance Tips" segment titled "Plateaus in Learning." To read these tips go to http://www.twosteptidewater.com/dance-tips-menu-two-step-tidewater_virginia.htm. Scroll down the menu and click on number 20: Plateaus in Learning.

STUDY QUESTIONS

1. Explain how the terms *performance* and *learning* differ and why we must *infer* learning from performance situations.

2. What five performance characteristics typically characterize the learning of a skill? Give an example of each for a motor skill learning situation.

3. What is an advantage of using transfer tests in making a valid assessment of learning? Give an example of a real-world situation that illustrates this advantage.

4. What is a performance plateau? What seems to be the most likely reason a performance plateau occurs in motor skill learning?

5. Describe a motor skill learning situation in which it may be possible to under- or over-estimate the amount of learning during practice. Indicate how you would demonstrate this misrepresentation.

Specific Application Problem:
You are working in your chosen profession. Your supervisor asks you to provide evidence that the people you have been working with have learned the skill or skills you wanted them to learn or that they wanted to learn. Describe the evidence you would provide in response to this request; discuss why this evidence should satisfy your supervisor's request.

The Stages of Learning

Concept: Distinct performance and performer characteristics change during skill learning.

After completing this chapter, you will be able to

■ Describe characteristics of learners as they progress through the stages of learning as proposed by Fitts and Posner and by Gentile

■ Describe several performer- and performance-related changes that occur as a person progresses through the stages of learning a motor skill

■ Discuss several characteristics that distinguish an expert motor skill performer from a nonexpert

APPLICATION

Have you ever noticed that people who are skilled at performing an activity often have difficulty teaching that activity to a beginner? This difficulty is due in part to the expert's failure to understand how the beginner approaches performing the skill each time he or she tries it. In other words, the expert has difficulty behaving or thinking like a beginner. To facilitate successful skill acquisition, the teacher, coach, or therapist must consider the point of view of the student or patient and ensure that instructions, feedback, and practice conditions are in harmony with the person's needs.

Think for a moment about a skill you are proficient in. Remember how you approached performing that skill when you first tried it as a beginner. For example, suppose you were learning the tennis serve. Undoubtedly you thought about a lot of things, such as how you held the racquet, how high you were tossing the ball, whether you were transferring your weight properly at contact, and so on. Now, recall what you thought about after you had lots of practice and had become reasonably proficient at serving. You probably did not continue to think about all the specific elements each time you served.

In the rehabilitation clinic, imagine that you are a physical therapist working with a stroke patient and helping him or her regain locomotion function. Like the tennis pro, you are a skilled performer (here, of locomotion skills); the patient is like a beginner. Although there may be some differences between the sport and the rehab situations because the patient was skilled prior to the stroke, in both cases you must approach skill acquisition from the perspective of the beginner.

Application Problem to Solve Select a motor skill that you perform well for recreational or sports purposes. Think back to when you first learned to perform this skill. Try to remember how successful you were and what you had the most difficulty doing, as well as characteristics of your performance of that skill and what you thought about when you performed it. Then recall how your performance and your approach to performing the skill changed as you had more experience performing it and became more skillful. How many specific performance-related characteristics that changed can you identify, and how did they change?

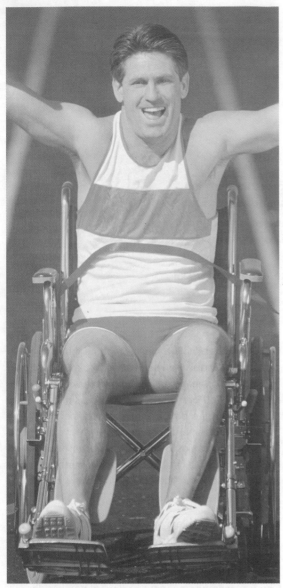

Learning to compete in wheelchair racing involves distinct stages of learning while progressing from being a beginner to being a highly skilled performer.

DISCUSSION

An important characteristic of learning motor skills is that all people seem to go through distinct stages as they acquire skills. Several models have been proposed to identify and describe these stages. We discuss two of the more influential of these next. It is important to note that each of these models presents performer and performance characteristics associated with each stage of learning that we will refer to throughout the chapters that follow.

THE FITTS AND POSNER THREE-STAGE MODEL

Paul Fitts, to whom you were introduced in chapter 7, and Michael Posner presented the acknowledged classic learning stages model in 1967. Their model continues to be referred to in textbooks and by researchers today. They proposed that learning a motor skill involves three stages. During the *first stage,* called the **cognitive stage** of learning, the beginner[1] focuses on cognitively oriented problems. For example, beginners typically try to answer questions such as these: What is my objective? How far should I move this arm? What is the best way to hold this implement? Where should this arm be when my right leg is here? Additionally, the learner must engage in cognitive activity as he or she listens to instructions and receives feedback from the instructor.

Performance during this first stage is marked by a large number of errors, and the errors tend to be large ones. Performance during this stage also is highly variable, showing a lack of consistency from one attempt to the next. And although beginners may be aware that they are doing something wrong, they generally do not know what they need to do to improve.

The *second stage* of learning in the Fitts and Posner model is called the **associative stage** of learning. The transition into this stage occurs after an unspecified amount of practice and performance improvement. The cognitive activity that characterized the cognitive stage changes at this stage, because the person has learned to *associate*

---

[1]The term "beginner" is used here and throughout the following chapters to refer to a person who is beginning to learn, or relearn, a skill.

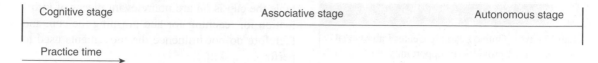

FIGURE 12.1   The stages of learning from the Fitts and Posner model placed on a time continuum.

specific environmental cues with the movements required to achieve the goal of the skill. The person makes fewer and less gross errors since he or she has acquired the basic fundamentals or mechanics of the skill, although they need to be improved. Because this type of improvement still is required, Fitts and Posner referred to this stage as a *refining* stage, in which the person focuses on performing the skill successfully and being more consistent from one attempt to the next. During this refining process, performance variability begins to decrease. In addition, people acquire the capability to detect and identify some of their own performance errors.

After much practice and experience, which can take many years, some people move into the **autonomous stage** of learning, which is the *final stage* of learning. Here the skill has become almost *automatic,* or habitual. People in this stage do not consciously think about the specific movement characteristics of what they are doing while performing the skill, because they can perform it without conscious thought. They often can do another task at the same time; for example, they can carry on a conversation while typing or walking. Performance variability during this stage is very small: skilled people perform the skill consistently well from one attempt to the next. Additionally, these skilled performers can detect their own errors and make the proper adjustments to correct them. Fitts and Posner pointed out the likelihood that not every person learning a skill will reach this autonomous stage. The quality of instruction and practice as well as the amount of practice are important factors determining achievement of this final stage.

It is important to think of the three stages of the Fitts and Posner model as parts of a continuum of practice time, as figure 12.1 depicts. The amount of time a person will be in each stage depends on the

skill being learned and the practice conditions, as well as the characteristics of the person. Individual differences can influence one person to spend more time in a specific stage than another person. Similarly, the same person could spend more time in one stage for one type of skill than for another type of skill. It is also important to note that people who are learning a skill do not make abrupt shifts from one stage to the next. There is a gradual transition or change of the learner's characteristics from stage to stage. Because of this, it is often difficult to detect which stage an individual is in at a particular moment. However, as we will consider in more detail later in this discussion, the beginner and the skilled performer have distinct characteristics that we can observe and need to understand.

GENTILE'S TWO-STAGE MODEL

Another model that motor learning researchers commonly refer to was proposed by Gentile (1972, 1987, 2000). In contrast to Fitts and Posner, she viewed motor skill learning as progressing through

---

cognitive stage   the first stage of learning in the Fitts and Posner model; the beginning or initial stage on the learning stages continuum.

associative stage   the second stage of learning in the Fitts and Posner model; an intermediate stage on the learning stages continuum.

autonomous stage   the third stage of learning in the Fitts and Posner model; the final stage on the learning stages continuum, also called the *automatic stage.*

LAB LINKS

Lab 12a in the Online Learning Center Lab Manual for chapter 12 provides an opportunity for you to learn a new motor skill and experience a progression through some learning stages.

at least two stages and presented these stages from the perspective of the goal of the learner in each stage.

Initial Stage of Learning

In the *initial stage,* the term Gentile used for the first stage, the beginner has *two important goals* to achieve. One is to acquire a *movement coordination pattern* that will allow some degree of success at achieving the action goal of the skill. This means that the beginner must develop movement characteristics that match the regulatory conditions of the environmental context in which the skill is performed. Recall from the discussion of Gentile's taxonomy of motor skills in chapter 1 of this text that the term *regulatory conditions* refers to those characteristics of the environmental context that determine the movement characteristics the person must use to achieve an action goal. For example, if a person is beginning to rehabilitate his or her prehension skills, he or she must focus on developing the arm and hand movement characteristics that match the physical characteristics associated with the object to be grasped. If, in the prehension example, the person must reach and grasp a cup that is on a table, the regulatory conditions include the size and shape of the cup, location of the cup, amount and type of liquid in the cup, and so on.

The second goal of the beginner is to learn to *discriminate between regulatory and nonregulatory conditions* in the environmental context in which he or she performs the skill. Unlike regulatory conditions, the **nonregulatory conditions** are those characteristics of the performance environment that do *not* influence the movement characteristics required to achieve an action goal. To continue with the example of reaching and grasping a cup, the color of the cup or the shape of the

table the cup is on are nonrelevant pieces of information for reaching for and grasping the cup, and therefore do not influence the movements used to perform the skill.

To achieve these two important goals, the beginner explores a variety of movement possibilities. Through trial and error, he or she experiences movement characteristics that match and do not match requirements of the regulatory conditions. As a result, these experiences are successful as well as unsuccessful. In addition, because the learner must solve numerous problems to determine how to achieve the action goal, he or she engages in a large amount of cognitive problem-solving activity. When the learner reaches the end of this stage, he or she has developed a movement coordination pattern that allows some action goal achievement, but this achievement is neither consistent nor efficient. As Gentile (2000) described it, "Although the learner now has a general concept of an effective approach, he or she is not skilled. The action-goal is not achieved consistently and the movement lacks efficiency" (p. 149).

Later Stages of Learning

In the second stage, which Gentile called the *later stages,* which suggests the possibility of more than one stage, the learner needs to *acquire three general characteristics.* First, the person must develop the capability of *adapting* the movement pattern he or she has acquired in the first stage to the specific demands of any performance situation requiring that skill. Second, the person must increase his or her *consistency* in achieving the goal of the skill. Third, the person must learn to perform the skill with an *economy of effort.*

Fixation and diversification as learning goals. A unique feature of the second stage in Gentile's model is that the *learner's goals depend on the type of skill.* More specifically, the open skill and closed skill classifications specify these goals. *Closed skills require* **fixation** of the basic movement coordination pattern acquired during the first stage of learning. This means that the learner must refine this pattern so that he or she can consistently

A CLOSER LOOK

Gentile's Learning Stages Model Applied to Instruction and Rehabilitation Environments

During the Initial Stage
- Have the learner focus on achieving the action goal, which will allow the development of the basic movement coordination pattern of the skill.
- Establish practice situations that provide opportunities to discriminate regulatory from nonregulatory characteristics.

During the Later Stage
Closed skills. In practice situations, include characteristics as similar as possible to those the learner will experience in his or her everyday world or in the environment in which he or she will perform the skill.
Examples:
- reaching, grasping, and drinking from a variety of sizes and shapes of containers

- writing with the same type of implement on the same type of surface
- shooting basketball free throws as they would occur in a game
- shooting arrows under match conditions

Open skills. In practice, systematically vary the controllable regulatory conditions of actual performance situations, while allowing naturally varying characteristics to occur as they normally would.
Examples:
- walking from one end of a hallway to the other while various numbers of people are walking in different directions and at various speeds (systematically vary the numbers of people; allow the people to walk at any speed or in any direction they wish)

---

achieve the action goal. The learner works toward developing the capability to perform the movement pattern with little, if any, conscious effort (i.e., automatically) and a minimum of physical energy. Thus, practice of a closed skill during this stage must give the learner the opportunity to "fixate" the required movement coordination pattern in such a way that he or she is capable of performing it consistently.

On the other hand, *open skills require* **diversification** of the basic movement pattern acquired during the first stage of learning. An important characteristic of open skills, which differ from closed skills in this way, is the requirement for the performer to quickly adapt to the continuously changing spatial and temporal regulatory conditions of the skill. These conditions change within a performance trial as well as between trials. This means that the learner must become attuned to the regulatory conditions and acquire the capability to modify movements to meet their constantly changing demands on the performer. As a result,

the learner must acquire the capability to automatically monitor the environmental context and modify the movements accordingly. Thus, practice of an open skill during this stage must provide

nonregulatory conditions characteristics of the performance environment that do *not* influence the movement characteristics required to achieve an action goal.

fixation the learner's goal in the second stage of learning in Gentile's model for learning closed skills in which learners refine movement patterns so that they can produce them correctly, consistently, and efficiently from trial to trial.

diversification the learner's goal in the second stage of learning in Gentile's model for learning open skills in which learners acquire the capability to modify the movement pattern according to environmental context characteristics.

The Initial Stage of Learning to Bowl

A study by Langley (1995) provides a good illustration of the performer and performance characteristics described for the initial stage of learning in both the Fitts and Posner and the Gentile learning stages models. Langley assessed student thought processes during a beginning bowling class that met for ten weeks. He had each student complete a questionnaire at the end of each class; he also took extensive observational and interpretive notes, and he interviewed the students at the beginning, middle, and end of the ten-week session.

The results of this study indicated that student thoughts focused primarily on errors in task performance. In the first week, the primary errors of concern related to lack of control of the ball, which related to inconsistency of throws and aiming problems. In the middle week, students began to describe the movement characteristics and outcomes of their throws as keys to what they needed to focus on to improve. By the end of the course, students indicated problems with consistency and accuracy of the hook ball. Consistent with expectations of learning stages models, these beginning bowlers showed evidence of an initial lack of an appropriate movement pattern to achieve the action goal, inconsistent performance, a lack of knowledge about specific components of the skill (e.g., aiming), and the development of error detection capabilities.

the learner with experiences that will require these types of movement modifications.

Movement modification requirements. One aspect of the second stage of learning in Gentile's model that requires further consideration concerns the features of the acquired movement pattern that the performer must change to meet performance situation demands. Although Gentile's model indicates that fixation of the pattern is the goal of the second stage for closed skills, the performer may need to make movement modifications. But closed skill modifications differ from those required for open skills. You saw some examples of these differences in the discussion of the adaptability component of our definition of learning in chapter 11. You can relate these differences to the distinction between invariant features and parameters of a coordination pattern, which were discussed in chapter 5.

For *closed skills,* movement modifications typically involve movement parameter changes rather than changes of the invariant features of the movement coordination pattern itself. For example, when bowling the second ball of a frame, the bowler is confronted with a different pattern of pins than he or she experienced with the first ball. But rather than change the movement coordination pattern used to bowl the ball, the bowler modifies specific movement characteristics such as location of ball release or ball speed. In golf, a ball in different types of grass or sand may require the golfer to modify his or her stance or the trajectory of the downswing, but not the invariant coordination features of the swing itself. Similarly, situations requiring prehension may require various widths of grasp apertures or amounts of grasp force, but the basic invariant features of the reach-and-grasp action will remain consistent.

However, for *open skills,* the performer may be required to change either the invariant features or the parameters of the movement pattern. For example, if the action goal for a tennis player is to return a serve, he or she may prepare to hit a forehand groundstroke but have to change to a backhand when the serve is hit. Or if the action goal of a pedestrian is to cross a street at an intersection, he or she may begin to walk but have to change to a run partway across, because the traffic signal has changed.

Finally, it is important to note that the types of movement changes required by closed and open skills involve different action planning and preparation demands for the performer. Closed skills allow the learner to plan and prepare either without any or with a minimum of time constraints. However, time constraints severely limit the amount of time the performer has to plan and prepare the performance of an open skill. This difference indicates that during practice of open skills, the performer must acquire the capability to quickly attend to the environmental regulatory conditions as well as to anticipate changes before they actually occur.

PERFORMER AND PERFORMANCE CHANGES ACROSS THE STAGES OF LEARNING

Stages-of-learning models indicate that in each learning stage, both the person and the skill performance show distinct characteristics. In this section, we will look at a few of these characteristics. This overview has two benefits: first, it provides a closer look at the skill learning process, and second, it helps explain why instruction or training strategies need to be developed for people in different learning stages.

Changes in Rate of Improvement

As a person progresses along the skill learning continuum from the beginner stage to the highly skilled stage, the *rate* at which the performance improves changes. Although, as you saw in figure 11.2 in chapter 11, there are four different types of performance curves representing different rates of improvement during skill learning, the *negatively accelerated pattern is more typical of motor skill learning* than the others. This means that early in practice, a learner usually experiences a large amount of improvement relatively quickly. But as practice continues, the amount of improvement decreases.

This change in the rate of improvement during skill learning has a long and consistent history in motor learning. In fact, in 1926 Snoddy mathematically formalized a law known as the **power law of practice.** According to this law, early practice is characterized by large amounts of improvement. However, after this seemingly rapid improvement, further practice yields improvement rates that are much smaller. Exactly how long the change in rates takes to occur depends on the skill.

LAB LINKS

Lab 12b in the Online Learning Center Lab Manual for chapter 12 provides an opportunity for you to compare characteristics of novices and experts performing the same skill.

Crossman (1959) reported what is today considered the classic experiment demonstrating the power law of practice. He examined the amount of time it took cigar makers to produce one cigar as a function of how many cigars each worker had made since beginning work at the factory. Some workers had made 10,000 cigars, whereas others had made over 10 million. The skill itself was a relatively simple one that could be done very quickly. The first notable finding was the relationship between performance improvement and the amount of experience. Workers still showed some performance improvement after seven years of experience, during which time they had made over 10 million cigars (see figure 12.2). In addition to this remarkable result, he found evidence of the power law of practice for these workers. As you can see in figure 12.2, the majority of all the improvement occurred during the first two years. After that, performance improvement increments were notably smaller.

In a more recent demonstration of the power law of practice, Chen, Liu, Mayer-Kress, and Newell (2005) had experiment participants learn to perform a pedalo locomotion task. The pedalo is a commercially available device that has two plastic pedals, on which a person stands; these are connected to four wheels by two iron rods that act like cranks

power law of practice   mathematical law describing the negatively accelerating change in rate of performance improvement during skill learning; large amounts of improvement occur during early practice, but smaller improvement rates characterize further practice.

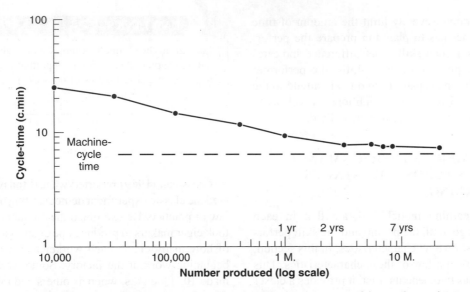

FIGURE 12.2   The results from the study by Crossman showing the amount of time workers took to make a cigar as a function of the number of cigars made across seven years of experience. Note that both axes are log scales. [From Crossman, E. R. F. W. (1959). A theory of the acquisition of speed skill. *Ergonomics, 2,* 153–166. Copyright © 1959 Taylor and Francis, London.]

and go through the pedals. The task is to stand on the plastic pedals and move them with the feet so that the wheels move forward or backward. The task involves dynamic balance and requires coordination of the torso and limbs to keep the pedalo moving. For the experiment, the participants' goal was to achieve the fastest movement time (MT) they could while moving as smoothly as possible for a specified distance. They practiced the task for fifty trials a day for seven days. The results showed that MT decreased during practice in a pattern that was consistent with the power law of practice. This means that MT decreased rapidly on the first two days, but then decreased very little for the remaining practice trials.

The difference in rate of improvement between early and later practice is due partly to the amount of improvement possible at a given time. Initially, there is room for a large amount of improvement. The errors people make during early practice trials are large and lead to many unsuccessful attempts at performing the skill. Because many of these errors are easy to correct, the learner can experience a large

amount of improvement quickly. However, as practice continues, the amount of improvement possible decreases. The errors people make later in practice are much smaller. As a result, their correction of these errors yields less improvement than they experienced earlier in practice. And certainly from the learner's perspective, attaining notable improvement seems to take longer than it did before.

Changes in Movement Coordination

In the discussion in chapter 5, you saw that to perform a complex motor skill (i.e., one that involves several limbs or limb segments), the motor control system must solve the *degrees of freedom problem.* Recall that when we relate this problem to the muscles and joints, it concerns the need to constrain the many degrees of freedom of movement associated with the muscles and joints involved in performing the skill. For the beginning learner, solving this problem is a critical part of the learning process. In fact, solving this problem underlies the achievement of an important goal for the learner in Gentile's initial stage of learning, which is to acquire a movement coordination pattern that would allow some success at achieving the action goal.

Bernstein, whom we noted in chapter 5 first identified this problem, described a strategy beginners typically use to gain initial control of the many degrees of freedom associated with performing a complex motor skill (Bernstein, 1967; Whiting, 1984). This strategy, which researchers now refer to as **freezing the degrees of freedom,** involves holding some joints rigid (i.e., "freezing" them) while performing the skill. For example, suppose a beginner must perform a skill such as a racquetball forehand shot, which, at the joint level, involves the coordination of three degrees of freedom for the arm used to hit the ball: the wrist, elbow, and shoulder joints. The common strategy the beginner uses to control these joints so that he or she can hit the ball is to keep the wrist and elbow joints "locked" (i.e., "frozen"). This strategy makes the arm and hand move as if they were a stick, with the arm and hand segments acting as one segment.

As the person practices the skill, a freeing of the degrees of freedom emerges as the "frozen" joints begin to become "unfrozen" and operate in a way that allows the arm and hand segments to function as a multisegment unit. This new unit eventually demonstrates characteristics of a *functional synergy,* which means that the individual arm and hand segments work together in a cooperative way to enable optimal performance of the skill. It is interesting to note that Southard and Higgins (1987) reported evidence demonstrating this kind of strategy and coordination development for the arm movement of the racquetball forehand shot. They showed that a primary benefit of the development of the functional synergy of the arm segments was an increase in racquet velocity at ball impact.

Researchers have demonstrated similar coordination development characteristics for several other skills. For example, Anderson and Sidaway (1994) showed that when beginning soccer players initially tried to kick a ball properly, they limited the movements of their hip and knee joints. The problem with this strategy is that it limits the velocity that can be generated by the hip joint, because the player cannot use the knee joint effectively.

With practice, however, players' kicking velocity increased, as their hip and knee joints acquired greater freedom of movement and increased functional synergy. Figure 5.2, which was presented in chapter 5 as an example of a graphic representation of coordination patterns, portrayed the pre- and post-practice knee-and-hip relationship results from this study.

These kinds of coordination changes are not limited to sports skills or to people acquiring new skills. Stroke patients going through physical therapy to help them move from sitting to standing and then to sitting again, show coordination development characteristics similar to those of people acquiring a new skill (Ada, O'Dwyer, & Neilson, 1993). In this experiment, recovering stroke patients progressed from being able to sit-stand-sit without assistance one time to being able to perform this sequence three times in a row in 10 sec. As the patients progressed, the coordination between the hip and the knee joints showed marked improvement changes which demonstrated the development of the functional synergy required for these joints to allow unaided standing.

An important feature of coordination changes during learning is their relationship to observed performance. Recall that according to Gentile's stages of learning model the beginner works on achieving action goal success, which is typically seen in performance outcome measures (e.g., increasing the number of free-throws made with a basketball). As the person improves his or her performance in terms of action goal achievement, there are underlying coordination changes occurring. During the initial stage of learning these coordination changes establish an "in-the-ballpark" but unstable movement pattern. It is during the

---

freezing the degrees of freedom   common initial strategy of beginning learners to control the many degrees of freedom associated with the coordination demands of a motor skill in order to achieve the action goal; the person holds some joints rigid (i.e., "freezes" them) while performing the skill.

Controlling Degrees of Freedom as a Training Strategy in Occupational Therapy

A case study of a thirty-four-year-old hemiplegic woman who had suffered a stroke demonstrates how a thera-pist can use an understanding of the degrees-of-freedom problem to develop an occupational therapy strategy (Flinn, 1995). To increase impaired left-arm strength and function during the first two months of outpatient therapy, the therapist engaged the patient in *using the impaired arm* to perform several functional tasks for which the degrees of freedom were restricted.

- Initially, the therapist decreased the number of joints involved by restricting the movement of certain joints and decreasing the amount of movement required of the limb against gravity.

  Example: The patient used the impaired arm to apply her wheelchair brakes, dust tables, and provide postural stability as she brushed her teeth using her non-impaired arm.

- During the next two months, as the patient's use of her left arm improved, the therapist increased the

  degrees of freedom by requiring the use of more joints to perform tasks.

  Example: In the initial therapy period, the patient simply pushed silverware from the counter into the drawer; now she grasped each object from the counter, lifted it, and placed it in the drawer.

- Finally (a couple of months later), the therapist again increased the degrees of freedom demands by focusing treatment specifically on the every-day multiple degrees-of-freedom tasks the patient would have to perform at her regular workplace.

later stages of learning that the movement pattern stabilization process occurs to allow consistent and efficient performance of the skill. (See Teulier, Nourrit, & Delignières, 2006, for a more in-depth discussion of the relationship between changes in performance outcome characteristics and associ-ated coordination characteristics during the learn-ing of a complex motor skill).

Changes in Altering an Old or Preferred Coordination Pattern

Because we have learned to perform a variety of motor skills throughout our lives, we have devel-oped preferred ways of moving. In fact, each of us has developed a rather large repertoire of movement patterns that we prefer to use. When confronted with learning a new skill, we often determine that it resembles a skill we already know how to per-form. As a result, we typically begin practicing the new skill using movement characteristics similar to those of the skill we already know. For example, it is common for an experienced baseball player to use a swing resembling baseball batting when he

or she first practices hitting a golf ball. Similarly, experienced tennis players use their well-learned tennis groundstrokes when first learning to hit a racquetball or badminton shuttlecock.

When a person is learning a new skill that requires altering an established coordination pat-tern, an interesting transition from old to new pat-tern occurs. The experiment by Lee, Swinnen, and Verschueren (1995) that we discussed in chapter 11 provides a good example of this change. Recall that participants had to learn to bimanually move two levers simultaneously in a 90-degree out-of-phase arm movement relationship in order to draw ellipses on the computer monitor. In chapter 11, figure 11.4 showed that when they first were confronted with this task, the participants' preferred way of coor-dinating their arms was to move both arms at the same time, producing diagonal patterns. The influ-ence of this preferred movement pattern remained for more than sixty practice trials. Participants did not consistently produce the new coordination pat-tern until they had performed 180 practice trials. Instability characterized the coordination patterns they produced on trials between these two demonstrations of stable patterns.

The experiment by Lee and colleagues demonstrates several things. First, it shows that people approach skill learning situations with distinct movement pattern biases that they may need to overcome to achieve the goal of the skill to be learned. Second, it is possible for people to overcome these biases, but often this takes a lot of practice (the actual amount varies among people). Finally, as illustrated in figure 11,4, an observable pattern of stability-instability-stability characterizes the transition between production of the preferred movement pattern and production of the goal pattern. The initially preferred and the newly acquired goal movement patterns are distinguished by unique but stable kinematic characteristics over repeated performances. However, during the transition period between these stable patterns, the limb kinematics are very irregular or unstable.

People who provide skill instruction should note that this transition period can be a difficult and frustrating time for the learner. The instructor or therapist who is aware of this can be influential in helping the person work through this transition stage. One helpful strategy is providing extra motivational encouragements to keep the person effectively engaged in practice.

Changes in Muscles Used to Perform the Skill

If practicing a skill results in coordination changes, we should expect a related change in the muscles a person uses while performing the skill. EMG patterns produced while people practiced skills have shown that early in practice a person uses his or her muscles inappropriately. Two characteristics are particularly noteworthy. First, more muscles than are needed commonly are involved. Second, the timing of the activation of the involved muscle groups is incorrect. As a person continues to practice, the number of muscles involved decreases so that eventually a minimal number of muscles needed to produce the action are activated, and the timing of when the involved muscles are activated becomes appropriate.

Researchers have provided evidence showing these types of change during practice for a variety of physical activities. For example, muscle activation changes have been demonstrated for sport skills such as the single-knee circle mount on the horizontal bar in gymnastics (Kamon & Gormley, 1968), ball throwing to a target (Vorro, Wilson, & Dainis, 1978), dart throwing (Jaegers et al., 1989), the smash stroke in badminton (Sakuari & Ohtsuki, 2000), rowing (Lay, Sparrow, Hughes, & O'Dwyer, 2002), and the lunge in fencing (Williams & Walmsley, 2000). Also, researchers have shown muscle activation differences resulting from practice in laboratory tasks, such as complex, rapid arm movement and manual aiming tasks (Schneider et al., 1989), as well as simple, rapid elbow flexion tasks (Gabriel & Boucher, 1998) and arm-extension tasks (Moore & Marteniuk, 1986).

The change in muscle use that occurs while a person learns a skill reflects a *reorganization of the motor control system* as that skill is acquired. As Bernstein (1967) first proposed, this reorganization results from the need for the motor control system to solve the degrees-of-freedom problem it confronts when the person first attempts the skill. By structuring muscle activation appropriately, the motor control system can take advantage of physical properties of the environment, such as gravity or other basic physical laws. By doing this, the motor control system reduces the amount of work it has to do and establishes a base for successful skill performance.

Changes in Energy Cost

Because the performer and performance changes we have described in the preceding sections occur as a result of practicing a skill, we can reasonably expect that the learner would become a more economical (i.e., efficient) user of energy. This change, then, would be consistent with a proposal in Gentile's stages of learning model that the development of an economy of effort is an important goal of the later stages. Economy of movement refers to minimizing the energy cost of performing a skill. Beginners expend a large amount of energy (i.e., have a high energy cost), whereas skilled

A CLOSER LOOK

Muscle Activation Changes during Dart-Throwing Practice

An experiment by Jaegers et al. (1989) provides an easy to follow illustration of how the sequence and timing of muscle activation reorganizes as a person practices a skill. Individuals who were inexperienced in dart throwing made forty-five throws at a target on each of three successive days. Several arm and shoulder muscles were monitored by EMG.

The *three muscles primarily involved in stabilizing the arm and upper body* were the anterior deltoid, latissimus dorsi, and clavicular pectoralis.

- *On the first day of practice:* The three muscles erratically initiated activation both before and after the dart release.
- *At the end of the last day of practice:* The three muscles initiated activation according to a specific sequence.
  —The clavicular pectoralis and anterior deltoid became active approximately 40 to 80 msec prior to dart release; they turned off at dart release.
  —The latissimus dorsi became active just before dart release and remained active for 40 msec

after dart release. Then, the anterior deltoid again initiated activation.

The primary muscle involved in producing the forearm-extension–based throwing action was the lateral triceps.

- *During the initial practice trials:* The lateral triceps initiated activation erratically, both before and after dart release.
- *At the end of the last day of practice:* The lateral triceps consistently initiated activation approximately 60 msec prior to dart release and remained active until just after dart release.

---

performers perform more efficiently, with minimum expenditure of energy.[2]

Several energy sources have been associated with performing skills. One is the *physiological energy* (also referred to as *metabolic energy*) involved in skilled performance; researchers identify this by measuring the amount of oxygen a person uses while performing a skill. They also determine physiological energy use by measuring the caloric cost of performing the skill. People also expend *mechanical energy* while performing; scientists determine this by dividing the work rate by the metabolic rate of the individual. As we learn a skill, changes in the amount of energy we use occur for each of these sources. The result is that we perform with greater efficiency; in other words, our energy cost decreases as our movements become more economical.

Researchers have been accumulating evidence only recently to support the prediction that energy cost decreases as a result of practicing a skill. For

example, *oxygen use* decreased for people learning to perform on a complex slalom ski simulator in practice sessions over a period of several days (Durand et al., 1994; Almasbakk, Whiting, & Helgerud, 2001). Similar decreases in oxygen use were reported by Lay, Sparrow, Hughes, and O'Dwyer (2002) for people learning to row on a rowing ergometer, which is commonly used by crew team members as a training device. Sparrow (Sparrow & Irizarry-Lopez, 1987; Sparrow & Newell, 1994) demonstrated that oxygen use, heart rate, and *caloric costs* decrease with practice of a motor skill for persons learning to walk on his or her hands and feet (creeping) on a treadmill moving at a constant speed. And Heise (1995; Heise & Cornwell, 1997) showed *mechanical efficiency* to increase as a function of practice for people learning to perform a ball-throwing task. (For a more in-depth discussion of energy expenditure as it relates to the learning of motor skills, see Sparrow, Lay, & O'Dwyer, 2007).

Students learning to scuba dive provide an interesting example of the decrease in physiological

---

[2]Note that many prefer the term *economy* to *efficiency;* see Sparrow and Newell (1994).

energy cost as measured by oxygen use. People first learning to dive typically use much more oxygen than they do when they become more experienced. The easy demonstration of this change is a comparison of the levels of oxygen used in the tanks of beginning and experienced divers. The beginners typically use more oxygen for the same length of dive.

In addition to demonstrating a reduction in energy cost, learners also experience a decrease in their rate of perceived exertion (RPE). RPE, which is a measurable subjective perception, refers to the amount of effort (i.e., exertion, or energy) a person feels that he or she is expending while performing a skill. A nice demonstration of changes in both energy use economy and RPE was reported in an experiment by Sparrow, Hughes, Russell, and Le Rossingnol (1999). Novice rowers performed on a rowing ergometer for one practice session each day for six days. The results showed that when the rowers performed at their preferred stroke rates, metabolic energy expenditure economy increased, while heart rate, oxygen consumption, and RPE significantly decreased during the six days of practice.

Changes in Visual Selective Attention

Because vision plays a key role in the learning and control of skills, it is interesting to note how the use of vision changes as a function of practicing a skill. Because we discussed most of these characteristics and changes at length in chapters 6, 7, and 9, we will mention them only briefly here. Beginners typically look at too many things, which often leads them to direct their visual attention to inappropriate environmental cues. As a person practices a skill, he or she directs visual attention toward sources of information that are more appropriate for guiding his or her performance. In other words, the person gains an increased capability to direct his or her vision to the regulatory features in the environment that will provide the most useful information for performing the skill. Also, people get better at appropriately directing their visual attention earlier during the time course of performing a skill. This timing aspect of directing visual attention is important because it increases the time

available in which the person can select and produce an action required by the situation.

A good example of research evidence that demonstrates the change in visual selective attention across the stages of learning is an experiment by Savelsbergh, Williams, van der Kamp, and Ward (2002). They recorded the eye-movement characteristics of novice and expert soccer goalkeepers in a simulated penalty kick situation. The goalkeepers observed life-size video clips of professional players taking penalty kicks that were directed to six areas of the goal. The goalkeepers moved a joystick to intercept the ball; if they positioned it in the correct location at the moment the ball crossed the goal line, a save was recorded. As expected, the expert goalkeepers performed better than the novices, especially in terms of making more saves and better predictions of ball height and direction. In addition, the experts initiated their joystick response closer to the time of foot-ball contact, and made fewer joystick position corrections. The visual search characteristics were identified in terms of time periods before and after foot-ball contact by the kicker. Overall, the experts made fewer eye-movement fixations of longer duration to fewer areas of the scene involving the kicker. These results indicated that the experts reduced the amount of visual information they needed to attend to, and they extracted more information from the most relevant parts of the scene. As the kicker began the approach to the ball and eventually made ball contact, the experts progressively moved their fixations from the kicker's head to the nonkicking foot, the kicking foot, and the ball. They made very few fixations on other areas of the kicker's body. In contrast, the novices spent more time fixating on the kicker's trunk, arms, and hip areas and less time on the head, nonkicking foot, and ball. Interestingly, at foot-ball contact, the expert goalkeepers fixated on the ball more than two times longer than the novices.

Changes in Conscious Attention Demands When Performing a Skill

According to the Fitts and Posner learning stages model, early in practice the learner consciously thinks about almost every part of performing the

Soccer goalkeepers will develop more effective and efficient visual search strategies as their stage of learning progresses and they become more skillful.

skill. But as the person practices the skill and becomes more proficient, the amount of conscious attention he or she directs to performing the skill itself diminishes to the point at which he or she performs it almost automatically.

We see an everyday example of this change in the process of learning to shift gears in a standard shift car. If you have learned to drive a standard shift car, you undoubtedly remember how you approached shifting gears when you first learned to do so. Each part of the maneuver required your conscious attention. You thought about each part of the entire sequence of movements: when to lift off the accelerator, when to push in the clutch, how to coordinate your leg movements to carry out these clutch and accelerator actions, when and where to move the gear shift, when to let out the clutch, and finally, when to depress the accelerator again. But what happened as you became a more experienced driver? Eventually, you performed all these movements without conscious attention. In fact, you undoubtedly found that you were able to do something else at the same time, such

as carry on a conversation or sing along with the radio. You would have had great difficulty doing any of these things while shifting when you were first learning to drive. Evidence that this type of attention-demand change occurs with experience was provided by Shinar, Meir, and Ben-Shoham (1998) in a study that compared experienced and novice licensed car drivers in Israel. Results showed that while shifting gears, the novice drivers tended to miss traffic signs that the experienced drivers did not miss.

An experiment that compared novice and skilled baseball batters also demonstrates the change in conscious attention demands that occurs across the learning stages continuum. Gray (2004) had "skilled" university and "novice" recreational baseball players hit simulated baseball pitches that varied in speed and height. On some trials the players only swung at the pitches. On other trials, they had to perform a secondary task in response to an audible tone. One type of secondary task, which was extraneous to the hitting skill, required the players to verbally identify the tone as high or

A CLOSER LOOK

Driving Experience and Attention Demands of Driving a Standard Shift Car

Shinar, Meir, and Ben-Shoham (1998) used a dual-task procedure to determine the influence of years of driving experience on the attention demands for driving a standard shift car. They asked forty licensed drivers (ages eighteen to sixty-six years) to drive their own manual or automatic transmission cars along a 5 km route through downtown Tel Aviv. The route involved streets with multiple lanes, many intersections, many traffic signs, heavy traffic, and many pedestrians and pedestrian crossings. The secondary task involved the drivers observing traffic signs and verbally reporting each sign that indicated "Slow—Children on the Road" and "No Stopping."

The results showed that the experienced drivers (median = eight years of experience) of either the manual or automatic transmission cars detected similar percentages of the two signs. However, the novice drivers (median = one and one-quarter years of experience) of manual transmission cars detected lower percentages of the signs than those who drove automatic transmission cars. Thus, driving experience led to a reduction in the attention demanded by the action of gear shifting to such an extent that driving a manual transmission car in heavy traffic became similar to the attention demanded when driving an automatic transmission car.

---

low. The other type of secondary task, which was related to the hitting skill, required the players to verbally identify whether the bat was moving up or down at the time of the tone. The tone occurred at any time after the ball appeared to the batter. The results showed that the extraneous secondary task led to an increase in swing errors for novice players but not for skilled players. But, for the skill-related secondary task, just the opposite occurred as swing errors increased for skilled but not for novice players. Thus skilled players had reduced the conscious attention demanded by swinging the bat and could respond to the tone without disrupting their swing. Evidence for this attention demand change was shown by the disruption in the swing when they had to attend to a specific movement characteristic of their bat swing, something they did not normally do. On the other hand, the novice players were not disrupted by the skill-related secondary task because it required them to respond to something they typically gave attention to when swinging at a pitch.

Finally, consider some experiences that you or your friends have had with learning motor skills. If you learned to type on a computer keyboard, on your first attempts to type a word or sentence you undoubtedly directed your conscious attention

to each finger hitting the correct key for every letter. You probably could not carry on a conversation with a friend while you were typing because the typing task demanded all your attention. But, as you practiced and became more skilled, you no longer needed to direct your attention to your fingers and the keys for each letter, and you could talk with a friend while you typed. Similarly, when athletic trainers first learn to tape an ankle, they direct their conscious attention to the application of each strip of tape to make sure it is located properly and applied smoothly. But after a lot of practice taping ankles, trainers no longer need to direct all their attention to these aspects of taping. You can probably think of additional situations that resemble these. The examples demonstrate that a common characteristic of learning a motor skill is that the amount of conscious attention demanded by the movements of the skill itself decreases as the learner progresses along the stages of a learning continuum and becomes more skillful.

Changes in Error Detection and Correction Capability

Another performance characteristic that improves during practice is the capability to identify and correct one's own movement errors. An individual can use this capability either during or after the performance of the skill, depending on the time constraints involved. If the movements are slow enough, a person can correct or modify an ongoing movement while the action is occurring. For example, if a person grasps a cup and brings it to the mouth to drink from it, he or she can make some adjustments along the way that will allow him or her to accomplish each phase of this action successfully. However, for rapid movements, such as initiating and carrying out a swing at a baseball, a person often cannot make the correction in time during the execution of the swing because the ball has moved past a hittable location by the time the person makes the correction. For both types of skills, performers can use errors they detect during their performance to guide future attempts.

An excellent example of research evidence that demonstrates the change in error detection and correction capability is a study involving gymnasts at different stages of learning (Robertson, Collins, Elliott, & Starkes, 1994). Novice and skilled gymnasts walked across a balance beam as quickly as possible with either full or no vision of the beam as they walked. Results showed that with no vision, both groups made significantly more form errors (unintentional deviations from a relaxed upright standing position) than with vision, but the novices made many more than the skilled gymnasts (see figure 12.3). In addition, with no vision available, the skilled gymnasts maintained the amount of time they took to traverse the beam with full vision, while the novices took almost two times longer. The skilled gymnasts maintained their movement time in the no-vision condition by taking more steps and making more form errors. The authors concluded that the results indicate that "part of becoming skilled involves developing the ability to rapidly and efficiently correct movement errors" (p. 338). It is important to add to this comment that these corrections indicate the capability to detect the errors. And, as we discussed in chapter 6, vision is an essential source for detecting and correcting these movement errors while traversing the beam.

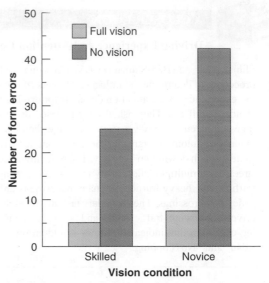

FIGURE 12.3   The results of the experiment by Robertson et al. showing the number of form errors made by novice and skilled gymnasts as they walked across a balance beam with full vision or no vision as they walked. [Source: Modified Figure 4, p. 337 in Robertson, S., Collins, J., Elliott, D., & Starkes, J. (1994). The influence of skill and intermittent vision on dynamic balance. *Journal of Motor Behavior, 26,* 333–339.]

Changes in Brain Activity: Plasticity

You read in chapter 4 that the behavior others can observe when we perform a motor skill has an underlying neural structure. This structure, which typically comprises several brain areas that are active at the same time, changes as beginners become more skilled at performing a skill. This activity change exemplifies the **plasticity** of the brain, which is one of its most important characteristics. (For an in-depth discussion of the history and evolution of the use of the term plasticity as it relates to the nervous system, see Berlucchi & Buchtel, 2009).

With the advent of brain imaging technology, an impressive number of researchers have been actively investigating the changes in brain activity associated with the learning of motor skills. A common finding is that the brain areas active during the early stage of learning are not always the same areas active during later stages of learning.

A CLOSER LOOK

Changes in Brain Activity as a Function of Learning a New Motor Skill

The availability of brain scanning technology has allowed researchers to investigate the brain activity associated with learning and performing a motor skill. A group of Belgian researchers used fMRI to observe the brain activity of people learning a new motor skill (Puttermans, Wenderoth, & Swinnen, 2005).

- **Participants:** Eleven right-handed adults (five women, six men; avg. age = 23.9 yrs)
- **Motor skill to be learned:** Because the study involved the use of an MRI scanner, the motor skill that participants were required to learn had to be one that could be performed while lying supine within the space limitations of the scanner. The goal of the skill was to flex and extend the right and left wrists simultaneously and continuously for 28.5 sec. The unique characteristic of the skill was that the right wrist had to move twice as fast as the left wrist during each 2 sec movement cycle. This means that the participants had to learn to flex and extend the left wrist once in 2 sec while they flexed and extended the right wrist twice in the same time period (i.e., a 1:2 frequency ratio). Each trial was 28.5 sec and included a metronome to pace the movements.

- **Practice:** Participants practiced the skill for eight consecutive days during which they performed 40 trials with visual feedback provided about the results at the end of each trial.
- **fMRI scanning:** Scanning runs occurred before training began (pretraining), in the middle of training (after day 4), and after training was completed on the eighth day (posttraining).
- **Behavioral results:** Kinematic analyses of wrist movements indicated that all participants were able to perform the skill as specified by the final day of training.
- **Brain activity results:** fMRI scans indicated the following from pre- to posttraining:
  Brain activity decreased: bilateral opercular areas, bilateral ventrolateral prefrontal cortex, right ventral premotor and supramarginal gyrus, anterior cingulated sulcus, and supplementary motor area.
  Brain activity increased: primary motor cortex, posterior cingulate, putamen, and right anterior cerebellum.
- **Conclusions:** In general, the brain activity changes revealed a learning-related shift from prefrontal-parietal control during initial practice to subcortical control during skilled performance.

Because of the physical limitations of the scanning devices used for fMRI and PET, the typical motor skill studied in this type of research is sequence learning. The task typically requires participants to learn to associate stimuli on a computer monitor with finger, hand, or foot movements and then practice a specified sequence of these movements.

Doyon and Ungerleider (2002; see also Doyon, Penhune, & Ungerleider, 2003) proposed a model to describe the neuroanatomy and the associated brain plasticity of motor skill learning, especially as it relates to the learning of movement sequences. They proposed that the brain structures most commonly associated with skill acquisition are the striatum (the caudate and putamen of the basal

ganglia), cerebellum, and motor cortex regions of the frontal lobe—namely the SMA (supplementary motor area), premotor cortex, and motor cortex, among others. The model indicates that these brain areas form "two distinct cortical-subcortical circuits: a cortico-basal ganglia-thalamo-cortical loop, and a cortico-cerebello-thalamo-cortical loop" (Doyon et al., 2003, p. 253). Note that the primary difference between the two loops is that

plasticity   changes in neuronal activity in the brain that are associated with shifts in brain region activation; these changes are commonly associated with behavioral changes or modification.

one involves the basal ganglia, the other the cerebellum. Early in learning, the cortico-cerebello-thalamo-cortical loop is more involved, even though the striatum and cerebellum are typically activated together with specific motor cortex regions as the learner engages in the cognitive and motor activity that characterizes initial learning of a skill. Well-learned skills, on the other hand, involve more activity in the basal ganglia, especially the putamen and globus pallidus and the inferior parietal lobe of the cerebral cortex.

In general, then, as a motor skill becomes more "automatic," which would occur when a person is in the Fitts and Posner autonomous stage of learning, "a distributed neural system composed of the striatum and related motor cortical regions, but not the cerebellum, may be sufficient to express and retain the learned behavior" (Doyon et al. 2003, p. 256). The model proposes that the early involvement of the cerebellum in learning a motor skill seems to be related to adjusting movement kinematics according to sensory input in order to produce an appropriate movement. Results of several fMRI and PET studies have shown general support for the Doyon and Ungerleider model, although specific brain areas active at the various stages of learning may differ depending on the skill that was learned in the experiment (see, for example, Grafton, Hazeltine, & Ivry, 2002; Lafleur et al. 2002; Parsons, Harrington, & Rao, 2005).

A PERFORMER CHARACTERISTIC THAT DOES NOT CHANGE ACROSS THE STAGES OF LEARNING

Researchers who have investigated the use of sensory feedback across the stages of learning have consistently shown that *learning is specific to the sources of sensory feedback available during practice.* This means that if we use visual feedback during practice in the first stage of learning, we continue to need to use it in the same way as we become more skillful in later stages. Proteau and Marteniuk (1993) presented a good example of research evidence of this feedback dependency.

They allowed participants to see their movements as they practiced to learn to perform a 90 cm aiming movement in 550 msec. Then, after 200 or 2,000 practice trials, the visual feedback was removed. We would expect that if the participants had learned to rely on sensory feedback sources other than vision as they practiced, increasing the amount of practice with vision would decrease the need for vision to perform the skill. However, the results showed just the opposite effects. Participants who had visual feedback removed after 2,000 trials performed less accurately than those who had it removed after 200 trials. Rather than decreasing their dependency on visual feedback, the participants increased dependency. Similar results were reported for participants learning the same type of manual aiming task with visual feedback but then having it removed after 100, 1,300, and 2,100 trials (Khan, Franks, & Goodman, 1998). Other types of motor skills have also shown this effect, such as walking across a balance beam (which you saw in the preceding section), walking a specific distance on a narrow line on the floor (Proteau, Tremblay, & DeJaeger, 1998), a serial arm-movement skill (Ivens & Marteniuk, 1997), one-handed catching of a thrown ball (Whiting, Savelsbergh, & Pijpers, 1995), and a weightlifting skill (Tremblay & Proteau, 1998).

Why does dependency increase for sensory feedback sources available during practice as a person advances through the stages of learning? Proteau and his colleagues hypothesize that the dependency develops because the sensory feedback becomes part of an integrated sensory component of the memory representation of the skill. As a result, if the person must perform without the same sensory feedback available, retrieval of the representation from memory is less than optimal, because the sensory information available in the performance context is not compatible with the sensory information stored in the memory representation of the skill. Consequently, performance is less accurate than it would have been with all the stored sensory information available in the performance context.

A CLOSER LOOK

Mirrors in Dance Studios and Weight Training Rooms: Are They Necessary?

If you walk into most dance studios and weight training rooms, you will see full-length mirrors on at least one wall, if not more. The most common reason given for their presence is that they provide an added source of visual feedback that will help the dancers and lifters improve their technique. But according to the evidence discussed in this chapter about practicing with this type of visual feedback when the performance context does not include mirrors, the mirrors may hinder learning more than they help it.

According to several studies by Luc Proteau and others, the longer people practice in the presence of this type of visual feedback, the more dependent on that feedback they become. This means that when an individual must perform without the mirror, that person will not perform as well as if he or she had practiced without the mirror all along or, at least, for enough time to not depend on the mirror.

Powerlifters: Tremblay and Proteau (1998) provided evidence that this view applies to powerlifters learning to "perfect" their form for the squat lift. When

the lifters who practiced with a mirror for 100 trials were asked to perform the lift without the mirror, they increased the amount of error of their knee joint angle by 50 percent. Rather than the mirror helping them perfect their form, it led to poorer form when the mirror wasn't available.

Dancers: Although we don't have research evidence based on dancers, we have evidence that some professional dance teachers do not use mirrors during classes and rehearsals. Two examples were described in the magazine *The New Yorker* (January 6, 2003) in an article by Joan Acocella. After the author observed a dance class taught by the great ballerina Suzanne Farrell, she stated, "Again and again, she tells dancers to stop looking in the studio mirror" (p. 53). The other example involves George Balanchine, the originator of the New York City Ballet Company, considered by many to have been one of the world's best choreographers. Balanchine forbade his dancers to look in the mirror. He told them, "I'm the mirror" (p. 53).

EXPERTISE

If a person practices a skill long enough and has the right kind of instruction, he or she eventually may become skilled enough to be an *expert.* On the learning stages continuum we presented earlier in this discussion (figure 12.1), the expert is a person who is located at the extreme right end. This person is in an elite group of people who are exceptional and outstanding performers. Although motor skill expertise is a relatively new area of study in motor learning research, we know that experts have distinct characteristics. Most of our knowledge about experts in the motor skills domain relates to athletes, dancers, and musicians. Although they are in seemingly diverse fields, experts in these skill performance areas have some similar characteristics. Some of these will be examined next.

Amount and Type of Practice Leading to Expertise

In the first extensive study of experts from a diverse number of fields, Ericsson, Krampe, and Tesch-Romer (1993) reported that expertise in all fields is the result of *intense practice for a minimum of ten years.* The critical point in this statement is "intense practice." Although the length of time is relevant, more important for the attainment of expertise is the type of practice in which a person engages. According to Ericsson and his colleagues, the specific type of intense practice a person needs to achieve expertise in any field is *deliberate practice,* which refers to "individualized training activities especially designed by a coach or teacher to improve specific aspects of an individuals' performance through repetition and successive refinement" (Ericsson & Lehmann, 1996, p. 278f). During this type of practice, the

Experts Compared to Novices: Vision

Bruce Abernethy, one of the world's leading researchers on the issue of expertise as it relates to the use of vision in the performance of motor skills, summarized some primary research findings in an article published in 1999 in the *Journal of Applied Sport Psychology*. The following are some of his key points about the comparison between experts and novices in their use of vision in performance situations in which there is a very brief window of time to detect and use visual information, such as hitting a pitched baseball or returning a racquetball serve.

No Differences
- General vision measures (e.g., visual acuity) and nerve function measures (e.g., nerve conduction velocity) show no differences. *Experts' superior performance relates more to the superior use of visual information.*
- Visual search patterns may or may not differ. *Experts exhibit superior use of visual information even when search patterns are similar.*

Differences
- Experts are faster and more accurate in recognizing patterns in their own skill domain. *"Patterns" refer to coordination patterns related to an action and to patterns involving several people.*
- Experts detect and use important action-directing cues faster. *The result is better anticipation and faster implementation of a required action.*

person receives optimal instruction, as well as engaging in intense, worklike practice for hours each day. As the person develops toward expertise, he or she begins to need personalized training or supervision of the practice regime. Research investigating the deliberate practice hypothesis has consistently found support for the influence of this type of practice on the development of expertise in many different performance domains, such as sports, ballet, music, painting, surgery, etc. (see Ericsson, 2008; Ericsson & Williams, 2007, for reviews of this research).

A characteristic of expertise that emerges from the length and intensity of practice required to achieve expertise in a field is this: *expertise is domain specific* (see Ericsson & Smith, 1991). This means that characteristics of experts are specific to the field in which they have attained this level of success. There is little transfer of the capabilities in the field of expertise to another field in which the person has no experience. (For evidence supporting the sport-specific nature of expertise, see a study of elite triathletes and swimmers by Hodges, Kerr, Starkes, Weir, & Nananidou, 2004).

Experts' Knowledge Structure
A notable characteristic common to expert skill performers is that they know more about an activity than nonexperts do. More important, this expert knowledge is structured quite differently as well. Research investigating experts in a number of diverse skills, such as chess, computer programming, bridge, and basketball, has shown that the expert has developed his or her knowledge about the activity into more organized concepts and is better able to interrelate the concepts. The expert's knowledge structure also is characterized by more decision rules, which he or she uses in deciding how to perform in specific situations. Additionally, because of the way the knowledge is structured, the expert can remember more information from one observation or presentation.

Problem solving, decision making, and anticipation. The benefit of these knowledge structure characteristics is that they enable the expert to solve problems and make decisions faster and more accurately than a nonexpert can and to adapt to novel environments more easily. For example, an expert basketball player bringing the ball down the floor can look at one or two players on the other team and know which type of defense the team is using; anticipate what the defenders and his or her teammates will do; then make decisions about whether to pass, dribble, or shoot. The beginner would need to take more time to make these same decisions because he or she would need to look at more players to obtain the same information.

Experts' Use of Vision

When experts perform an activity, they use vision in more advantageous ways than nonexperts do. We discussed many of these characteristics in chapters 7 and 9. For example, experts search their environment faster, give more attention to this search, and select more meaningful information in less time. Also, experts do not need as much environmental information for decision making, primarily because they "see" more when they look somewhere. Undoubtedly due in part to their superior visual search and decision-making capabilities, experts can use visual information better than nonexperts to anticipate the actions of others. And experts recognize patterns in the environment sooner than nonexperts do. Experts achieve these vision characteristics after many years of experience performing a skill; studies have shown the characteristics to be a function more of experience than of better visual acuity or eyesight.

SUMMARY

- When people begin to practice a new motor skill, and continue to practice the skill, they typically progress through distinct, although continuous, stages of learning. We discussed two models that describe these stages.

- The *Fitts and Posner model* proposes that the learner progresses through three stages:
  - ▶ *Cognitive stage*—The beginner engages in much cognitive activity such as problem solving, directing attention to the movements, and so on.

  - ▶ *Associative stage*—In this intermediate stage the learner reduces the amount of cognitive activity involved in performing the skill and works to refine the skill to increase performance success and consistency.

  - ▶ *Autonomous stage*—The learner performs skillfully, almost automatically, with little conscious attention directed to the movements.

- *Gentile's model* proposes that the learner progresses through two stages:
  - ▶ *Initial stage*—The goals of the beginner are to develop a movement coordination pattern that will allow some degree of successful performance and to learn to discriminate regulatory and nonregulatory conditions.

  - ▶ *Later stages*—The learner's goals are to acquire the capability of adapting the movement pattern acquired in the initial stage to specific demands of any performance situation; to increase performance success consistency; and to perform the skill with an economy of effort. Movement goals are skill specific in this stage, as closed skills require a *fixation* of the movement pattern; open skills require a *diversification* of the movement pattern.

- Several distinct performer and performance changes occur as the learner progresses through the learning stages. We discussed the following changes:
  - ▶ *Rate of improvement:* The amount of improvement decreases (*power law of practice*).

  - ▶ *Movement coordination:* To control the many degrees of freedom required by a skill, the beginner initially "freezes" certain joints of limbs but eventually allows the limb segments involved to work together as a functional synergy.

  - ▶ *Altering an old or preferred coordination pattern:* The use of preferred coordination patterns typify initial performance when learning a skill; with practice these patterns become increasingly less stable and eventually become stable new coordination patterns.

▶ *Muscles involved:* The number of muscles activated by a beginner decreases with practice; the timing pattern of muscle activation becomes optimal for successful performance.

▶ *Energy cost/movement efficiency:* The amount of energy beginners use decreases; movement efficiency increases.

▶ *Visual selective attention:* Visual attention increasingly becomes directed specifically to appropriate sources of information.

▶ *Conscious attention:* The amount of conscious attention given to the movement characteristics of a skill is reduced.

▶ *Error detection and attention:* The capability to detect and correct one's own performance errors increases.

▶ *Brain activity:* Specific brain regions activated during the initial stage of learning are not always the same areas activated during later stages.

• A performer characteristic that *does not change* across the stages of learning is the reliance on sensory information that was available during the early practice stage.

• *Expertise* refers to a high level of skill performance that characterizes a person at the extreme opposite end of the learning continuum from the beginner.

▶ Expertise is typically the result of *deliberate practice* for a minimum of ten years.

▶ Experts have a *knowledge structure* that is organized into more concepts related to performing the activity, and they are better able to interrelate the concepts. However, the knowledge structure is activity specific.

▶ Experts who perform in activities that involve severe time constraints for decision making and anticipation visually search the performance environment in a way that allows them to select more meaningful information in a short amount of time.

POINTS FOR THE PRACTITIONER

• When working with people who are at the initial stage of learning, the emphasis of instruction should be on achieving the action goal. Allow beginners the opportunity to explore various movement options to determine which movement characteristics provide them the greatest likelihood of success.

• Expect beginners to make many movement errors and be inconsistent in how they perform the skill from one attempt to another.

• After beginners have demonstrated that they can perform a skill with some degree of success, the emphasis of instruction should be on increasing the likelihood of their achieving success each time they try the skill, and performing the skill more efficiently.

• Instruction for closed and open skills should be similar for beginners, with an emphasis on their developing movement characteristics that enable them to experience some degree of success at achieving the action goal of the skill. But after they have achieved this level of success, instruction for closed and open skills should differ. For closed skills the emphasis should be on the repetition of successful movements in situations that would occur in the environmental context in which the skill would be performed; for open skills the emphasis should be on successful adaptation to a variety of regulatory conditions that would typify the open skill being learned.

• Expect beginners to show large amounts of improvement relatively quickly, but lesser amounts of improvement as more skill is developed. It may be necessary to remind the person or people you are working with of this characteristic to motivate them to continue to practice when they experience less improvement than previously.

• Expect beginners to perform a skill with movement strategies that resemble those they used for a skill they have previously learned and experienced.

These strategies may help them initially experience success achieving the action goal of the skill but will eventually not allow them to achieve levels of success that would characterize a skillful performer—that is, an expert.

RELATED READINGS

Bebko, J. M., Demark, J. L., Osborn, P. A., Majumder, S., Ricciuti, C. J., & Rhee, T. (2003). Acquisition and automatization of a complex task: An examination of three-ball cascade juggling. *Journal of Motor Behavior, 35,* 109–118.

Carey, J. R., Bhatt, E., & Nagpal, A. (2005). Neuroplasticity promoted by task complexity. *Exercise and Sport Sciences Reviews, 33,* 24–31.

Duffy, L. J., Baruch, B., & Ericsson, K. A. (2004). Dart performance as a function of facets of practice amongst professional and amateur men and women players. *International Journal of Sport Psychology, 35,* 232–245.

Furuya, S., & Kinoshita, H. (2007). Proximal-to-distal sequential organization of the upper limb segments in striking the keys by expert pianists. *Neuroscience Letters, 421,* 264–269.

Haibach, P. S., Daniels, G. L., & Newell, K. M. (2004). Coordination changes in the early stages of learning to cascade juggle. *Human Movement Science, 23,* 185–206.

Hoffman, L. R., & Field-Fote, E. C. (2007). Cortical reorganization following bimanual training and somatosensory stimulation in cervical spinal cord injury: A case report. *Physical Therapy, 87,* 208–223.

Keith, N., & Ericsson, K. A. (2007). A deliberate practice account of typing proficiency in everyday typists. *Journal of Experimental Psychology: Applied, 13,* 135–145.

LeRunigo, C., Benguigui, N., & Bardy, B. G. (2005). Perception–action coupling and expertise in interceptive actions. *Human Movement Science, 24,* 429–445.

Schraw, G. (2005). An interview with K. Anders Ericsson. *Educational Psychology Review, 17,* 389–412.

Sparrow, W. A., & Newell, K. A. (1998). Metabolic energy expenditure and the regulation of movement economy. *Psychonomic Bulletin & Review, 5,* 173–196.

Starkes, J. L., & Ericsson, K. A. (Eds.) (2003). *Expert performance in sports: Advances in research on sport expertise.* Champaign, IL: Human Kinetics. [Contains 15 chapters written by leading researchers in the area of sport expertise.]

Steenbergen, B., Marteniuk, R. G., & Kalbfleisch, L. E. (1995). Achieving coordination in prehension: Joint freezing and postural contributions. *Journal of Motor Behavior, 27,* 333–348.

Ward, P., Hodges, N. J., Williams, A. M., & Starkes, J. L. (2004). Deliberate practice and expert performance: Defining the path to excellence. In A. M. Williams & N. J. Hodges (Eds.). *Skill acquisition in sport: Research, theory, and practice* (pp. 231–258). London: Routledge.

INTERNET RESOURCES

- To read an article and view graphic presentations about the process of developing coordinated movement in robots, go to http://robotics.snu.ac.kr/. Click on the link "Research" to go to a page presenting a discussion of "movement coordination and learning" as it relates to robotics.

- To learn to juggle 3 balls, watch an instructional video "Learn How to Juggle 3 Balls" at http://www.youtube.com/watch?v=T16_BVIFFPQ.

- To learn to tie a tie, watch an instructional video "How to Tie a Tie—Expert Instruction on How to Tie a Tie" at http://www.youtube.com/watch?v=MbXzI-IAdSc.

- To read a research study that compared experts (astronauts) and novices (pilots of transport planes) on their visual scanning of the instrument panel of a space-shuttle cockpit simulator during situations involving malfunctions that needed to be corrected, go to http://isis.arc.nasa.gov/. Click on Publications link and find reference for Huemer, V., Hayashi, M., Renema, F., Elkins, S., McCandless, J. W., & McCann, R. S. (2005).

- To see how a coaches information service at the University of Edinburgh (Scotland) applies the Fitts and Posner stages of learning model to teaching swimming, go to http://www.coachesinfo.com/. Under "Sports to Choose From…" click on Swimming and go to "Learn to Swim" and find the link for the Nature of Practice.

STUDY QUESTIONS

1. Describe some characteristics of learners as they progress through the three stages of learning proposed by Fitts and Posner.

2. How does Gentile's learning stages model differ from the Fitts and Posner model? How does her model relate specifically to learning open and closed skills?

3. Describe four performer or performance changes that research has shown to occur as a person progresses through the stages of learning a motor skill.

4. Describe a performer characteristic that does *not* change across the stages of learning. Describe an example.

5. Describe what an expert is and how a person can become an expert motor skill performer. What are some characteristics that distinguish an expert from a nonexpert?

Specific Application Problem:

(a) You are working in your chosen profession. Describe a motor skill that a person you are working with is trying to learn, relearn, or improve performance of. Specify which stage of learning this person is in.

(b) Describe the performer and performance characteristics you would expect to see for this person.

(c) Describe how the characteristics you described in part b should change as the person learns the skill.

Transfer of Learning

Concept: Transfer of learning from one performance situation to another is an integral part of skill learning and performance.

After completing this chapter, you will be able to

- Define *transfer of learning* as it applies to the learning of motor skills
- Discuss why transfer of learning is an important concept for motor learning
- Discuss two reasons proposed to explain why transfer occurs
- Define *negative transfer* and relate it to motor skill learning situations
- Discuss the difference between *symmetric* and *asymmetric* bilateral transfer
- Discuss hypotheses that attempt to explain why bilateral transfer occurs

APPLICATION

Why do we practice a skill? One reason is to increase our capability of performing the skill in a situation requiring it. We want to be able to accomplish specific action goals when we need to, whether we perform everyday skills, work skills, or sport skills. For example, if you were a physical therapist who was working with the gait problems of a stroke patient, you would want that person to be able to walk in environments outside the clinic. The patient should be able to walk at home, in the workplace, at the grocery store, in the mall, etc. Similarly, if you were an athletic trainer, it would be essential for you to prepare the injured athlete you are rehabilitating to perform his or her sport's skills in competition. And if you were a basketball coach, you would want your players to play well in games as well as in practice. Each of these examples involves the concept of transfer of learning, because of the need to transfer learned capabilities in one environment or situation to a different environment or situation. In fact, one of the goals of practicing a skill is developing the

capability to transfer performance of the skill from the practice environment to some other environment in which the individual must perform the skill so that he or she can achieve the same action goal.

Application Problem to Solve   Select a motor skill that you perform for recreational or sports purposes. When you began learning this skill, what kinds of practice activities did you experience? How well did they prepare you to learn the more complex aspects of this skill? How well did they prepare you to perform this skill in the kinds of situations and contexts in which you eventually had to perform it, such as in competition or in everyday experiences?

DISCUSSION

Transfer of learning is one of the most universally applied principles of learning in education, sports, and rehabilitation. In educational systems, this principle is an important part of curriculum and instruction development, because it provides the basis for arranging the sequence in which the students will learn skills. In sports, the transfer principle provides the basis for the sequencing of skills that must be learned, the development of drills to perform, and the types of practice experiences athletes need prior to engaging in a game or match. In the rehabilitation clinic, this principle forms the basis for the systematic development of protocols that therapists implement with patients. Because of the widespread importance of transfer of learning, you need to have an understanding of this learning phenomenon as part of your conceptual foundation for studying motor learning.

In chapter 11, we used the concept of transfer of learning when we discussed transfer tests as a method of assessing learning. Those tests are based on the transfer of learning principle. That discussion provided you with a good basis for the present discussion, which will provide you with an understanding of the transfer of learning principle itself.

WHAT IS TRANSFER OF LEARNING?

Learning researchers generally define **transfer of learning** as the influence of previous experiences on performing a skill in a new context or on learning a new skill. This influence may be positive, negative, or neutral (zero). **Positive transfer** occurs when previous experience facilitates performance of a skill in a new context or the learning of a new skill. Each of the examples presented in the Application section at the beginning of this chapter involved positive transfer. **Negative transfer** occurs when previous experience hinders or interferes with performance of a skill in a new context or the learning of a new skill. For example, a person who has learned the forehand in tennis before learning the forehand in badminton often experiences some initial negative transfer for learning the mechanics of the stroke. The badminton forehand is a wrist snap, whereas the tennis forehand requires a relatively firm wrist. The third type

of transfer of learning effect is *zero transfer*, which occurs when previous experience has no influence on performance of a skill in a new context or learning of a new skill. Obviously, there is no transfer from learning to swim to learning to drive a car. Nor can we assume that experience with some motor skills will always have an influence on learning new motor skills.

WHY IS TRANSFER OF LEARNING IMPORTANT?

We pointed out earlier that the principle of transfer of learning is an important part of educational curriculum development and instructional methodology, the development of pre-competition practices in sports, and as the development and implementation of systematic approaches to rehabilitation protocols. Thus, from a practical point of view, the transfer principle is very significant for establishing effective motor skills learning environments. But the transfer principle also has theoretical significance, because it helps us understand processes underlying the learning and control of motor skills.

Sequencing Skills to Be Learned

The sequencing of mathematics skills provides a very useful practical example of the transfer principle as it relates to curriculum development in schools. The curriculum from grades K through 12 is based on a simple-to-complex sequence. Teachers present numeral identification, numeral writing, numeral value identification, addition, subtraction, multiplication, and division in this specific sequence, because each concept is based on the concepts that preceded it. A person presented with a division problem needs to know how to add, subtract, and multiply in order to solve the problem. We do not teach algebra before basic arithmetic. We do not teach trigonometry before geometry.

We can make the same point about skills taught in a physical education program, a sports program, or a rehabilitation clinic. Those who develop a curriculum, program, or protocol should incorporate the transfer of learning principle when they sequence skills. Learners should acquire basic or foundational skills *before* more complex skills that require mastery of these basic skills. In other words, there should be a logical progression of skill experiences. An instructor should decide when to introduce a skill by determining how the learning of that skill will benefit the learning of other skills. If the instructor does not use this approach, time is wasted while people "go back" to learn prerequisite basic skills.

Gentile's taxonomy of motor skills (discussed in chapter 1) provides a good example of how the transfer principle can be implemented in any skill training situation. That taxonomy presents sixteen categories of skills, systematically sequenced from less to more complex according to specific skill characteristics (see table 1.1). One use that we discussed for this taxonomy is as a guide to help the therapist select functionally appropriate activities for a rehabilitation patient after making a clinical evaluation of the patient's motor function problems. Gentile based this taxonomy on the principle of positive transfer. She organized the sequence of activities by listing first the activities that a person must perform before performing more complex or difficult ones. The therapist can select appropriate functional activities for a rehabilitation regime by starting with activities related to the taxonomy category in which the therapist identified the skill performance deficit. Then the therapist can increase activity complexity by progressing through the taxonomy from that point, as described in chapter 1.

Instructional and Training Methods

The second important practical application of the transfer of learning principle to motor skill instruction is in the area of instructional methods. For example, a swimming instructor might use dry land drills when teaching students the basic swimming strokes, before letting them try the strokes in the water. The instructor assumes that there will be positive transfer from the dry land drills to the performance of the strokes in water.

There are numerous other examples of incorporating the transfer principle in instructional settings. It is common, for example, to practice a part of a skill before practicing the entire skill (we will discuss this practice method in chapter 18).

Sometimes an instructor simplifies an activity for a person before requiring the person to perform the skill in its actual context; for example, the coach has a person hit a baseball from a batting tee before hitting a moving ball. If the skill being acquired involves an element of danger, the instructor often allows the person to perform the skill with some type of aid so that the danger is removed. For example, a therapist may initially use a body-weight support system to assist a patient who is relearning to walk but cannot support his or her own body weight while standing. Surgeons commonly train on simulators before engaging in surgery with actual patients. And virtual reality training is increasing in its popularity as a training procedure that relies on the principle of transfer. (Note that these and other examples of training methods in which the goal activity is simplified during training will be discussed in chapter 18.)

Assessing the Effectiveness of Practice Conditions

For any instructor, coach, or therapist who wants to determine the effectiveness of a practice routine or instructional method, the rule of thumb should be that *transfer test performance will provide the best assessment.* As you saw in our discussion in chapter 11 concerning the assessment of motor skill learning, a person's performance during practice can over- or underestimate what the person is actually learning. This same principle applies

---

transfer of learning   the influence of having previously practiced or performed a skill or skills on the learning of a new skill.

positive transfer   the beneficial effect of previous experience on the learning or performance of a new skill, or on the performance of a skill in a new context.

negative transfer   the negative effect of prior experience on the performance of a skill, so that a person performs the skill less well than he or she would have without prior experience.

A CLOSER LOOK

Assessing Positive Transfer of Learning

Researchers commonly use a simple experimental design to determine whether positive transfer has occurred from either, (1) experience with one skill to learning another skill or, (2) performing a skill in one situation to performing it in another context. The design is as follows:

Experimental group	(1) Practice skill A	Perform skill B
	(2) Perform a skill in context A	Perform the same skill in context B
Control group	No practice	Perform skill B
	No practice	Perform the same skill in context B

The performance score of interest to the researcher is for skill B (1), or context B (2). If positive transfer is evident, then the performance of the experimental group should be better than that of the control group. Thus, prior experience is better than no prior experience for the skill or practice situation of interest.

To quantify the amount of positive transfer, researchers commonly calculate the *percentage of transfer,* which is the percentage of difference between the experimental and control groups' performance scores on skill B or in context B:

$$Percentage\ of\ transfer = \frac{Experimental\ group\ -\ Control\ group}{Experimental\ group\ +\ Control\ group} \times 100$$

It is important to be aware that a positive percentage will result for all performance measures except those for which a lower value indicates better performance (e.g., error, speed).

to the assessment of practice routines or instructional methods. We can know their effectiveness only by determining their impact on performance in the situation for which the practice or instruction was designed to prepare the student, athlete, or patient. For coaches of sports teams, the transfer test is usually the competition the athlete or team was preparing for. For instructors and therapists, the transfer test is not so easily determined. The instructor or therapist must identify the situations or environments in which the student or patient will need to perform. For the physical education instructor, the test may be performance on a skills test or in a tournament; for a dance instructor the test may be performance in a recital or concert; and for the physical or occupational therapist, the test may be performance of daily living activities at home or work activities in the workplace.

As support for the importance of the transfer test to assess practice conditions and instructional methods, one of the predominant theoretical viewpoints of why transfer of learning occurs emphasizes the importance of the transfer basis for this assessment. The *transfer-appropriate processing theory of transfer,* which will be presented later in this discussion, asserts that *the effectiveness of any practice condition should be determined only on the basis of how the practiced skill is performed in a "test" context.* This means that if we are deciding whether one instructional or practice strategy is superior to another to facilitate skill learning, we should not reach a conclusion until we have observed the person performing the practiced skill in its appropriate test performance situation.

WHY DOES POSITIVE TRANSFER OF LEARNING OCCUR?

The theoretical significance of the concept of transfer of learning becomes evident as we attempt to determine why transfer occurs. For example, if we know

If a person's goal for learning to ride a bicycle is to deliver newspapers, then the greatest amount of transfer between practice and test will occur when the practice experience includes opportunities for throwing a newspaper while riding a bicycle.

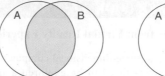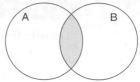

FIGURE 13.1 The two circles (A and B) in this figure can represent two skills or two performance contexts. For either theory proposed to explain why transfer of learning occurs, consider the amount of overlap between the two circles (the shaded area) as representing the degree of similarity between the two skills or performance contexts. More transfer should occur between the two skills or contexts in the set of circles on the left than in the one on the right.

Similarity of Skill and Context Components

The more traditional view of why positive transfer occurs contends that transfer is due to the similarity between the components of two skills or of two performance situations. In this view, the more similar the component parts of two skills or two performance contexts are, the greater will be the amount of positive transfer between them.

An important question concerning the similarity of skill components is this: What constitutes a "component part"? There are two answers to this question. One is any observable movement part of a skill, such as an overarm movement or a ball striking movement. However, it is important to note that the similarity of movement parts can also be considered in terms of their kinematic characteristics. Although we would expect positive transfer between two skills when compared at either level of similarity, different amounts of positive transfer would be expected when the similarities were compared at these two levels. For example, both baseball pitching and football passing include overarm throwing movements that are somewhat similar when compared in terms of observable movement, but become decidedly less similar when compared on the basis of their kinematics. The kinematic difference between these skills was nicely demonstrated in a study of high school and college baseball pitchers and football quarterbacks (Fleisig et al., 1996). However, students in a physical education course showed that practicing fundamental overarm throwing for several classes yielded

why transfer occurs, we have a better understanding of what a person learns about a skill that enables the person to adapt to the performance requirements of a new situation or to learn a new skill.

Although researchers have proposed several reasons over the years to explain why transfer of learning occurs, we will discuss only two of the more prominent hypotheses here. Both consider the *similarities* between the two situations to be critical for explaining transfer. However, they differ in their explanations of which similarities account for transfer. One hypothesis proposes that transfer of learning occurs because the components of the skills and/or the context in which skills are performed are similar. The other proposes that transfer occurs primarily because of similarities between the amounts and types of learning processes required (see figure 13.1).

Transfer from Virtual Reality Experience to a Real Environment

Virtual reality refers to three-dimensional computer-generated environments that can be explored and experienced in real time. Although there appear to be many potential applications of the use of virtual reality as a training strategy for motor skills, this potential remains to be determined. However, an interesting experiment by Wilson, Foreman, and Tlauka (1997) in England offers a look into one use of virtual reality in motor skills training contexts.

The focus of this study was on the training of people to be familiar with the spatial layout of a building, especially in terms of locating specific objects on three floors. Participants were in three groups: the real group, which experienced training in the real environment by being guided through the building floors; the computer group, which experienced being guided through a three-dimensional virtual reality version of the floors; and the control group, which did not experience training. Following training, participants performed several tests to assess their spatial knowledge

of the location of the objects pointed out during training. The results showed that the real and computer training groups performed better on the tests than the control group and were not different from each other for two of the three floors. Interestingly, further investigation showed that the simulation of the floor for which the real group performed better was not as detailed as for the other two floors.

In addition to demonstrating both the identical elements and transfer-appropriate processing explanations for transfer, this study also suggests potential applications for motor skills training. For example, in rehabilitation contexts, virtual reality training could provide preparatory motor and cognitive experiences for patients who need to experience locomoting in a variety of environmental contexts. Similar applications can be made for sports skills training where participation in new contexts will have an impact on the athletes' performance.

---

positive transfer benefits for learning both an overhead clear in badminton and the javelin throw (O'Keefe, Harrison, & Smyth, 2007).

The second answer is that a component part can relate to task-specific coordination dynamics, such as those we discussed in chapter 5. For example, from a dynamic pattern view of motor control, coordination tendencies and phase relationships that are common between tasks promote positive transfer (e.g., Kelso & Zanone, 2002; Wenderoth, Bock, & Krohn, 2002).

This similarity of components view has its roots in some of the earliest motor learning research which was carried out by E. L. Thorndike at Teachers College, Columbia University, in the early part of the 1900s. To account for transfer effects, Thorndike (1914) proposed the **identical elements theory.** In this theory, "elements" are general characteristics of a skill or performance context—such as the purpose of the skill or the attitude of the person performing the skill—or specific characteristics of the skill, such

as components of the skill being performed. Additionally, Thorndike considered identical elements to include mental processes that shared the same brain cell activity as the physical action.

According to a *similarity of skill components* comparison, we would expect the amount of transfer between the tennis serve and the volleyball serve to be greater than that between the tennis serve and the racquetball serve. And for a comparison on the basis of the *similarity of context components,* we would expect a higher degree of transfer to occur when practice conditions included transfer test context characteristics than when they do not. In a clinical situation, for example, physical therapy protocols that include walking in the patient's everyday living environment will yield more positive transfer than those that involve experiences only in the clinic.

Similarity of Processing Requirements
The second hypothesis explaining why positive transfer occurs proposes that it results from the

The Relationship between Practice and Test Contexts Applied to Golf Performance

Golfers and golf teachers often wonder why golfers don't always transfer their performance on the practice range to their play on the golf course. Robert Christina, a motor learning researcher, and Eric Alpenfels, a PGA teaching professional at Pinehurst Country Club in North Carolina, presented an answer to this question in a paper they presented at the World Scientific Congress of Golf in Scotland and published in the proceedings of that meeting (Christina & Alpenfels, 2002). They prefaced their recommendations with the following statement:

> With traditional training (a) students are given immediate feedback or instruction after each swing, (b) they hit balls repeatedly the same distance with the same club from good and level lies, (c) they stroke putts repeatedly from the same distance (d) they do not rehearse their pre-shot routine, and (e) they do not simulate competitive conditions to practice like they play. We argue that such conditions are likely to produce a level of learning that will enhance performance on the practice range or putting green, but not a level of learning that will enhance its transfer from the practice range to the golf course. Indeed, if the latter prediction is correct, future research also may find that traditional training conditions promote a false sense of confidence in golfers by deceiving them into thinking that the enhanced performance experienced on the practice range will transfer to the golf course when they play the game. (p. 234)

Their answer to the problem that golfers experience as a result of traditional training was based on the transfer of learning principle that maximizing the similarity between conditions during practice and test optimizes test performance. It's important to note that they did not propose that golfers stop practicing on the practice range. Rather, they stated that golfers should add to their practice the types of situations they would expect to experience during an actual round of golf, which they referred to as "transfer training." The following are some of their suggestions for implementing effective transfer training to enhance golf performance on the course.

- Practice all of the golf technique and cognitive skills that are needed during play on the course; practice these skills in the same way as they will be used during play on the course.
- Instruction and practice of golf skills should take place in a context that simulates the playing context as much as possible. If practice cannot take place on the course itself, which would be the optimal simulation of the playing context, the golfer can simulate shots and conditions by imagining them on individual shots on the practice range. The great golf professionals had in common that when they practiced they approached each shot with a specific purpose that included how the ball should be hit and where it should go.
- Instructors should provide feedback to golf students less frequently than after every shot, which will encourage the golfer to be more cognitively engaged in the learning process and will more closely simulate the feedback conditions that exist during play on the course, where there is no instructor feedback available.
- Practice with the different clubs that would be used during play on the course. Rather than hitting many shots in a row with just one club, hit practice shots one at a time sequentially with each club and rotate through the sequence of clubs several times.
- Practice around a green just as if playing on the course. Include situations that will require different types of shots, such as chips, pitches, lobs, and sand shots. Follow these shots up with what would occur next based on each shot's result. When the ball gets on the green, putt until it is holed out.
- Practice the competitive pressure that will occur during play on the course by simulating it as closely as possible. This can be done by imagining the pressure situations or by actually competing with another player on the practice range, sand trap, or green.

similarity of the cognitive processes required by the two skills or two performance situations. This hypothesis finds its clearest expression in the view that explains transfer effects in terms of transfer-appropriate processing (see Lee, 1988). This view maintains that although similarity in skill and context components explains some transfer effects, it cannot explain all transfer effects. A key point of the **transfer-appropriate processing theory** is the similarity between the learning or performance cognitive processes required by the two performance situations. In this view, two components of positive transfer are critical: the cognitive processing activity a person must do to be successful in performing the transfer task and the similarity between that activity and the activity required during the training experience.

Some examples of transfer-appropriate processing include situations where the transfer task requires a person to engage in problem-solving activity, rapid decision making, application of rules, attention control, and the simultaneous performance of two or more tasks. For positive transfer to occur between the training and transfer tasks, the training task also must involve these same types of activities. What is especially important to note here is that the training and transfer tasks do not need to have similar movement components. The critical characteristic is the similarity between the cognitive processing demands of the training task and those of the transfer task.

Merit in Both Hypotheses

Although much remains unknown about the cause of transfer of learning, evidence points to the value of both hypotheses in accounting for transfer effect. As indicated by figure 13.1, we can expect the amount of positive transfer to be related to the amount of similarity between skills and performance contexts. It appears that the similarity-of-processing view is actually an extension of the components view that comes into play when skill components and context similarities are minimal, but cognitive processing activities are similar. However, as Schmidt and Young (1987) concluded in their extensive review of transfer in motor skills,

we do not know very much about what accounts for the transfer phenomenon. Unfortunately, research investigating this question has been minimal during recent years, despite the fact that much more research is needed if we are to answer the question of *why* transfer occurs.

NEGATIVE TRANSFER

Although negative transfer effects appear to be rare and temporary in motor skill learning, people involved in motor skill instruction and rehabilitation need to be aware of conditions that may contribute to negative transfer. Because negative transfer effects can occur, it is important to know how to avoid such effects and to deal with them when they occur.

Negative Transfer Situations

Simply stated, negative transfer effects occur when an old stimulus requires a new but similar response. This means that the *environmental context characteristics of two performance situations are similar, but the movement characteristics are different.* Two situations that are especially susceptible to negative transfer effects involve a *change in the spatial locations of a movement* and a *change in the timing structure of the movement.*

An example of the *spatial location change* occurs when you must drive a car different from your own. If both cars are five-speed stick shifts, what happens when reverse is in a different location from the one you are accustomed to in your own car? Typically, you find yourself trying to shift to the location of reverse for your own car. This happens especially when you are not paying close attention to shifting. This example demonstrates that when we learn a specific spatially oriented movement to accomplish an action goal, we require attention and

---

transfer-appropriate processing theory   an explanation of positive transfer proposing that transfer is due to the similarity in the cognitive processing characteristics required by the two skills or two performance situations.

time to learn a similar movement that is in a new direction or end-location because of the negative transfer effect of the previous learning experience.

The second situation that leads to negative transfer effects involves a *change in the timing structure* of a sequence of movements from a previously learned sequence. Two different types of timing structure conditions are involved here. One is the *rhythmic pattern, or relative time structure,* learned for a sequence of movements. When people learn a specific relative time structure for a sequence of movements, such as when they learn a piece of music, a dance sequence, and the like, and then are asked to perform the sequence and ignore the rhythmic structure they learned, they typically produce the learned rhythmic structure for a number of trials (e.g., Summers, 1975). The second timing structure condition involves what appear to be *intrinsic bimanual coordination timing relationships.* An example of this situation can be seen in the results of the experiment by Lee, Swinnen, and Verschueren (1995) that was described in chapter 11. Participants were asked to produce a bimanual coordination pattern that is difficult to perform and varied markedly from their natural coordination pattern tendency, which was to move the arms in temporal synchrony. Recall that after achieving a small amount of progress in performing the new pattern by the end of the first day of practice (refer to figure 11.4), the participants reverted back to producing their natural symmetrical bimanual pattern. Thus the intrinsic coordination tendency to move the arms in temporal and spatial symmetry interfered with the participants' learning of a new asymmetrical movement pattern for the arms.

We often see either of the conditions that induce negative transfer effects when a person tries to "unlearn" a way of performing a skill and learn a new way to perform it. This type of situation occurs in many skill learning contexts. For example, athletes who go from high school to college commonly have to learn to perform a skill in a way that is different from how they performed it in high school. Even though the way they performed it in high school was successful, the college coach knows that to achieve success at the college level, the athlete

needs to learn to perform the skill differently. In the rehab clinic, physical and occupational therapists often interact with patients who have learned to perform a skill in a certain way because of a disability. However, the therapist knows that continued performance in this manner will lead to additional physical problems, which means the patient must acquire a different manner of performing the skill. In these types of situations, people typically show a decrement in performance when they begin practicing the skill in a new way. But with continued practice, performance begins to improve and eventually exceeds the level achieved previously.

Negative Transfer Effects Are Temporary
In each of the negative transfer situations described in this discussion, a common characteristic has been that the negative effects do not continue through all stages of learning. This is because negative transfer effects are temporary in nature and typically influence skill learning only in the early learning stage. However, it is important for the practitioner to be aware of this characteristic, because the negative transfer effects a person experiences early in practice may discourage a person's interest in pursuing the learning of the new skill or a new way to perform a well-learned skill. In addition, it is important that the practitioner be aware of the aspects of a skill that will be most affected by negative transfer effects and give particular instructional attention to these aspects to help the person overcome these effects.

Why Do Negative Transfer Effects Occur?
There are at least two likely reasons why negative transfer occurs. The first relates to the *memory representation* developed as a result of learning a skill.

---

identical elements theory   an explanation of positive transfer proposing that transfer is due to the degree of similarity between the component parts or characteristics of two skills or two performance contexts.

As a result of much practice performing a skill in one specific way, a specific perception-action coupling has developed between the perceptual characteristics of the task and the motor system. This coupling becomes a part of the memory representation for the action. When a person sees familiar perceptual characteristics in a performance environment, the motor system organizes itself in a preferred way to respond to those characteristics. Although this perception-action coupling allows for fast and accurate performing, it can become problematic when the familiar perceptual situation requires a movement that is different from what was learned. As you have seen in several discussions in this book, to change from the preferred state (i.e., the learned movement for the perceptual event) to a new state is difficult and takes practice.

Another possibility is that negative transfer results from *cognitive confusion.* In the car shift example, the requirements for shifting into reverse in the new car undoubtedly lead to some confusion in the driver about what to do. Undoubtedly you have had a similar experience when you have had to type on keyboards that differ in the locations of certain keys, such as the backspace or delete key. When you first begin typing on the new keyboard, you have difficulty striking the keys that are in different locations. What is notable here is that the problem is not with your limb control; you know how to strike keys in a sequence. Rather, the problem is related to the confusion created by the unfamiliar locations of the keys.

Fortunately, negative transfer effects can be overcome with practice. You probably have experienced this for either gear shifting or typing, or for both. Just how much practice is required depends on the person and the task itself.

BILATERAL TRANSFER

When transfer of learning relates to learning of the same task but with the contralateral limb, it is known as **bilateral transfer,** although it is sometimes referred to as *intermanual transfer, cross-transfer,* or *cross-education.* This well-documented phenomenon demonstrates our ability to learn a particular skill more easily with one hand or foot

LAB LINKS

Lab 13 in the Online Learning Center Lab Manual provides an opportunity for you to experience the bilateral transfer phenomenon.

after we already have learned the skill with the contralateral hand or foot.

Experimental Evidence of Bilateral Transfer
Experiments designed to determine whether bilateral transfer does indeed occur have followed similar experimental designs. The most typical design has been the following:

	Pretest	Practice Trials	Posttest
Preferred limb	X	X	X
Nonpreferred limb	X		X

This design allows the experimenter to determine if bilateral transfer to the nonpracticed limb occurred because of practice with the other limb. In the sample experimental design, note that the practice limb is the preferred limb. However, this does not need to be the case; the preferred limb/nonpreferred limb arrangement could be reversed. In either case, the researcher compares pretest-to-posttest improvements for each limb. Although the practiced limb should show the greater amount of improvement, a significant amount of improvement should occur for the nonpracticed limb, indicating that bilateral transfer has occurred.

Investigation of the bilateral transfer phenomenon was popular from the 1930s through the 1950s. In fact, the bulk of the evidence demonstrating bilateral transfer in motor skills can be found in the psychology journals of that period. One of the more prominent investigators of the bilateral transfer phenomenon during the early part of that era was T. W. Cook. Between 1933 and 1936, Cook published a series of five articles relating to various concerns of bilateral transfer, which they called cross-education. Cook

A CLOSER LOOK

An Example of Bilateral Transfer for Mirror Writing

Mark Latash (1999) reported a study in which students in his undergraduate class at Penn State University were required to learn a new skill as part of their class experience. The new skill was mirror writing, which involved handwriting a sentence on a piece of paper while looking in a mirror so that it would read correctly in the mirror, not on the paper. During a pretest the students wrote the sentence, "I can write while looking in the mirror," five times with one hand and then the other hand. For each trial, they timed how long it took to write the sentence and counted the errors they made. The students then practiced writing

the sentence fifteen times a day, five days a week, for three weeks using the dominant hand only. At the end of the practice period, they did a posttest that required them to perform the task as in the pretest. By comparing the writing performance of the nondominant hand during the pre- and posttests, the students could determine if bilateral transfer resulted from the 225 practice trials with the dominant hand. The results showed that on the posttest for the nondominant hand, they wrote the sentence 40 percent faster than on the pretest, and their errors decreased by 43 percent.

terminated this work by asserting that the evidence was sufficiently conclusive to support the notion that bilateral transfer does indeed occur for motor skills.

Given such a foundation of evidence, very few experiments published since those by Cook have investigated only the question of the occurrence of the bilateral transfer phenomenon (e.g., Latash, 1999; Nagel & Rice, 2001; Rice, 1998; Weeks, Wallace, & Anderson, 2003). The bulk of the research literature since the 1930s has addressed several issues related to bilateral transfer. Among these are the direction of the greater amount of transfer and the reason bilateral transfer occurs, both of which will be discussed next.

Symmetry versus Asymmetry of Bilateral Transfer

One of the more intriguing questions about the bilateral transfer effect concerns the direction of the transfer. The question is this: Does a greater amount of bilateral transfer occur when a person learns a skill using one limb before learning it with the contralateral limb **(asymmetric transfer),** or is the amount of transfer similar when either limb is used first **(symmetric transfer)**?

Reasons for investigating this question are theoretical as well as practical. From a theoretical perspective, knowing whether bilateral transfer is symmetric or asymmetric would provide insight,

for example, into the role of the two cerebral hemispheres in controlling movement. That is, do the two hemispheres play similar or different roles in movement control?

A more practical reason for investigating this question is that its answer can help professionals design practice to facilitate optimal skill performance with either limb. If asymmetric transfer predominated, the therapist, instructor, or coach would decide to have a person always train with one limb before training with the other; however, if symmetric transfer predominated, it would not make any difference which limb the person trained with first.

The generally accepted conclusion about the direction of bilateral transfer is that it is *asymmetric.* But there is some controversy about whether

---

bilateral transfer transfer of learning that occurs between two limbs.

asymmetric transfer bilateral transfer in which there is a greater amount of transfer from one limb than from the other limb.

symmetric transfer bilateral transfer in which the amount of transfer is similar from one limb to another, no matter which limb is used first.

Using Bilateral Transfer in Occupational Therapy Treatment Strategies

Occupational therapists use various treatment strategies to help clients with impairments to one arm. One approach is to use a compensation strategy that will teach the client to compensate for the loss of the use of one arm either by using the nonimpaired arm in new ways or modifying an environment to allow more opportunity to use the nonimpaired arm. However, another approach is to help the person improve the use of the impaired arm. When this type of therapy approach is used, the bilateral transfer phenomenon can provide a basis for the development of a specific therapy strategy. Nagel and Rice (2001) carried out the following experiment to determine whether they could demonstrate bilateral transfer for a meaningful and purposeful activity that involved a fine motor skill.

- *Participants:* Graduate and undergraduate students who were right-hand dominant and without any neurological or orthopedic problems that would affect their task performance.
- *Task:* Participants performed a small maze-type game that required them to use one hand to move a metal ball through a maze. They moved the ball by holding a stem added to the maze with the thumb

and index finger and moving it to control the ball movement.

- *Experimental conditions and procedures:* A training group practiced the task with the left hand three times a day for seven days (i.e., 21 trials). A control group did not practice the task. Both groups performed a pretest and posttest with the right and left hands.
- *Results:* Bilateral transfer effects between the trained and untrained arms for the training group were found for movement time (the amount of time needed to complete the maze task on a trial) and the number of force oscillations (an index of movement efficiency). No statistically significant between-arm differences were found for the control group.

Although the participants in this experiment did not have unilateral limb impairments, the authors concluded that the results have implications for occupational therapy treatments. They suggested that occupational training with the unimpaired limb could be used as initial training, especially during the first few days after surgery or accident.

---

this asymmetry favors transfer from preferred to nonpreferred limb, or vice versa. The traditional view has been that there is a greater amount of transfer when a person practices initially with the preferred limb.

Although some controversy continues about this question, there is sufficient evidence to recommend that for most skill training and rehabilitation situations, the greater amount of transfer occurs *from the preferred to the nonpreferred limb.* This approach not only is consistent with the bulk of the research literature concerned with bilateral transfer, but also is supported by other factors that need to be taken into account, such as motivation. Initial preferred-limb practice has a greater likelihood of yielding the types of success that will encourage the person to continue pursuing the goal of becoming proficient at performing the skill with either limb.

Why Does Bilateral Transfer Occur?

As we saw for explanations proposed to account for positive and negative transfer effects, cognitive and motor control explanations have been offered to answer the question of why bilateral transfer occurs.

The cognitive explanation of bilateral transfer.

The *cognitive explanation* states that the basis for the positive transfer from a practiced to a nonpracticed limb is the important cognitive information related to what to do to achieve the goal of the skill. This information is relevant to performing the skill regardless of the limb involved and is critical information acquired during the initial stage of skill learning. As a result of practice with one limb, the relevant cognitive information is acquired, which makes it available when the skill is performed with the other limb.

A CLOSER LOOK

Bilateral Transfer Training for Using an Upper-Extremity Prosthesis

For physical therapists who work with patients who will be fitted for, or who recently began wearing, a prosthetic limb on an amputated arm, an important goal is to facilitate the daily functional use of the prosthesis. Research by Weeks, Wallace, and Anderson (2003) provides a training option that is based on bilateral transfer. The training engages patients in the use of a prosthetic simulator with the intact limb. The researchers provided evidence of the effectiveness of this type of training by having non-amputees wear the prosthetic simulator shown in figure 13.2 and practice using it to perform three tasks.

The simulator: It included a figure-8 harness that was fitted around the shoulder contralateral to the prosthesis. It was attached to a cable that ran across the back and upper arm of the limb with the prosthesis. The cable inserted into the proximal end of the simulator and ran the length of the simulator to interface with a split-hook device that was identical to that of a regular prosthesis. The simulator split-hook device was a voluntary-opening device, which means that the wearer opened it by adjusting the tension of the cable with motions of the torso, shoulders, and arm.

The three tasks: Each task began from a common starting point, which was a microswitch button located at the person's midline and 20 cm from the table at which they sat. The tasks required the manipulation of various objects at different locations.
1. *Toggle-switch task:* The participant moved the prosthesis 25 cm forward and 20 cm upward to grasp and flip the paddle of a small toggle switch upward. Important in the performance of this task was to grasp the switch, not just flip it without grasping it first.
2. *Fine-aiming task:* The participant was given a stylus (10 cm long, 0.7 cm diameter) and had to place it in a hole directly in front of the start location to activate a microswitch located 2 cm under the task board.

FIGURE 13.2   Upper-limb prosthetic simulator. Courtesy of Stephen A. Wallace.

3. *Prehension task:* The participant reached 20 cm laterally and 10 cm forward to grasp a 200 g metallic cylinder (4.2 cm high, 2.8 cm diameter, covered in fine-grain sandpaper) and transport it to the opposite side of the task board and place it in a 3.5 cm diameter target well with a lip 1.5 cm high.

Training: Before being seated at the task table, participants were helped with putting on the simulator. They then watched a video of a model wearing the simulator and demonstrating how to control it. During a second viewing of the video, participants imitated

(*Continued*)

A CLOSER LOOK (*Continued*)

Bilateral Transfer Training for Using an Upper-Extremity Prosthesis

the control motions with the model. They then sat at the task table to begin the testing protocol, which was

Pretest: Participants performed five trials of each task with the prosthesis on the transfer arm (i.e., nonpractice arm).

Practice: Participants practiced each task thirty times with the prosthesis on the arm not used for the pretest.

Posttest: Participants performed five trials of each task with the prosthesis on the arm used for the pretest.

Results: Practice benefited bilateral transfer. This was shown in the results by comparing the pretest and post-test performances (movement initial time and movement time) for the control group (performed the pretest and posttest but not the practice trials) with the two bilateral transfer groups (one practiced with the preferred arm, the other with the nonpreferred arm). The bilateral transfer groups showed a greater amount of performance improvement on the posttest with the nonpracticed arm, which demonstrated bilateral transfer from the practiced to the nonpracticed arm.

We can relate the cognitive explanation of bilateral transfer to the "identical elements" theory Thorndike proposed, which we discussed earlier. This explanation gives strong consideration to those elements of a skill related to the performer's knowing "what to do." For example, we can consider the performance of a skill with one limb and then the other to be essentially two distinct skills. Throwing a ball at a target using the right arm is a different task from throwing a ball with the left arm. However, elements of these skills are common to both, regardless of the hand the thrower is using. Examples would be the arm-leg opposition principle, the need to keep the eyes focused on the target, and the need to follow through. Each of these elements represents what to do to successfully throw the ball at a target and does not specifically relate to either arm.

Proponents of this view predict that if a person achieves proficiency at a skill using the right arm, the person does not need to relearn the common cognitive "what to do" elements when he or she begins practicing with the left arm. The person should begin with the left arm at a higher level of proficiency than he or she would have had if he or she had never practiced with the right arm.

The motor control explanation of bilateral transfer. The *motor control explanation* for bilateral transfer incorporates the generalized motor program and the dynamic pattern theories of motor control as well as

our understanding of motor efference in the nervous system. According to the *generalized motor program (GMP) theory,* which we discussed in chapter 5, the muscles involved in the performance of a skill are *not* an invariant characteristic of the GMP. Rather, muscles are a parameter that the person adds to the GMP to allow the achievement of an action goal in a specific situation. As we discussed in chapter 1, action goal achievement can be attained for many motor skills by using a variety of movements. Thus the GMP does not develop as a muscle-specific program to control motor skill performance. Based on this characteristic of the GMP, the theory predicts that because practicing a skill with one limb establishes the development of a GMP with its invariant characteristics, the skill could be performed with the contralateral limb by applying to the GMP the muscles parameter for that limb.

The *dynamic pattern theory* of motor control also provides a basis for bilateral transfer. This theory of motor control also states that what is learned is not specific to the limb used to practice the skill. The dynamic pattern theory refers to skill learning as "effector independent," which means that when a motor skill is learned, coordination dynamics are learned without reference to the limb, or limbs, involved in practicing the skill. For example, Kelso and Zanone (2002) showed that participants in an experiment who learned a novel relative phase (similar to the bimanual coordination task described in chapter 11) with their arms or legs transferred the relative phase characteristics to the nonpracticed pair of limbs. Similar results were reported more recently by Camachon, Buekers, and Montagne (2004) for the transfer between walking and arm movements. Note that these experiments do not involve bilateral transfer as we have considered it. However, they demonstrate the effector independence of skill learning and the ease with which people can transfer what is learned to a different set of effectors, which supports the motor control explanation for bilateral transfer.

A second argument proponents of a motor control explanation offer is based on evidence showing that at least some bilateral transfer of skill is mediated in the brain by interhemispheric transfer of the motor components of the task (Hicks, Gualtieri, & Schroeder, 1983). One way researchers have demonstrated this mediation is by measuring the EMG activity in all four limbs when one limb performs a movement. When EMG activity occurs, it tells researchers that the central nervous system has forwarded commands to those muscles. In fact, research conducted as long ago as 1942 showed that the greatest amount of EMG activity occurs for the contralateral limbs (i.e., the two arms), a lesser amount occurs for the ipsilateral limbs (i.e., arm and leg on the same side), and the least amount occurs for the diagonal limbs (Davis, 1942).

Functional magnetic resonance imaging (fMRI) has also established a neural basis for bilateral transfer. For example, a series of experiments involving the learning of a 12 item finger sequence with the right hand found that the supplemental motor area (SMA) of the cortex had more activity when the skill was performed well with the left hand than when it was performed poorly (Perez, Tanaka, Wise, et al., 2007). In fact, in one of these experiments when SMA activation was blocked by the use of transcranial magnetic stimulation (TMS), no bilateral transfer occurred.

Which of the two explanations of bilateral transfer is correct? Research evidence indicates that *both cognitive and motor factors are involved in bilateral transfer.* There is no doubt that cognitive components related to "what to do" account for much of the transfer that results from practicing a skill with one limb. This is quite consistent with what we have discussed thus far in this book. For example, both the Fitts and Posner and the Gentile models of the stages of skill learning described in chapter 12 propose that determining "what to do" is a critical part of what a learner acquires in the first stage of learning. There is likewise no doubt that bilateral transfer involves a motor control basis as well. This is consistent with our discussion in chapter 5 of the control of coordinated action. It is also consistent with research evidence that there is some motor outflow to other limbs when one limb performs a skill.

SUMMARY

Transfer of learning concerns the influence of previous experiences on the performance of a skill in a new context or on learning a new skill.

- The influence of the previous experience may facilitate, hinder, or have no effect on the performance of a skill in a new context or on the learning of the new skill.

- The importance of the transfer of learning concept can be seen in its integral role in curriculum development in education, practice conditions in sports contexts, and treatment protocol development in rehabilitation programs.

- The transfer of learning concept is basic to the process of making inferences about the influence on motor skill learning of practice conditions and instructional methods.

- These are two of the hypotheses proposed to account for why positive transfer occurs:

  1. Positive transfer is a function of the similarity of the components of the skills performed and of the environmental contexts in which the skills are performed.

  2. Positive transfer is a function of the similarity of the cognitive processing activities involved in the two situations.

- Negative transfer effects, which are typically temporary and overcome with practice, occur primarily when a new movement is required for a familiar environmental context.

- Two hypotheses proposed to account for why negative transfer effects occur are the following:
  1. The difficulty inherent in altering a preferred perception-action coupling that has been developed for moving in a specific environmental context.
  2. The initial cognitive confusion that results when a person is not certain about how to move in a familiar environmental context.

- Bilateral transfer is a phenomenon in which improvement in the performance of a nonpracticed limb results from practice with the contralateral limb.

- Bilateral transfer is typically asymmetric, with the preferred-to-nonpreferred transfer direction yielding greater transfer than vice versa.

- Two hypotheses have been proposed to account for why bilateral transfer occurs:
  1. A cognitive hypothesis proposes that a person applies the knowledge acquired with practice of one limb about what to do to perform the skill to the initial performance of the skill with the contralateral limb.
  2. A motor control hypothesis proposes that the motor control system learns to perform a skill in a non–limb-specific way, which provides the basis for the system specifying a nonpracticed limb to perform the skill at some future time, and the expectation that performance with the nonpracticed limb will be higher than if there had been no practice with the other limb.

POINTS FOR THE PRACTITIONER

- The sequencing of skills or activities should be based on the concept of transfer of learning. This means that each skill or activity benefits from previous skills or activities and will benefit those that follow. Follow the simple-to-complex rule of sequencing skills and activities.

- When teaching motor skills, include practice opportunities in contexts and situations that are, or simulate, the contexts and situations in which people will use the skills in their everyday life, work, or recreation.

- Before developing a program of instruction or rehabilitation, consider the previous motor skill performance experiences the person or people have had. Take advantage of opportunities to allow them to benefit from experiences that promote positive transfer; prepare to help them overcome negative transfer experiences.

- Take advantage of bilateral transfer when working with people who have an injured or impaired limb.

- When teaching a skill that a person should learn to perform equally well with either limb, take advantage of bilateral transfer by beginning practice with the person's preferred limb. After the person has developed a reasonable degree of proficiency performing the skill with that limb, have the person practice with the other limb. Shortly thereafter, have the person alternate practice with each limb.

RELATED READINGS

Betker, A. L., Desai, A., Nett, C., Kapadia, N., & Szturm, T. (2007). Game-based exercises for dynamic short-sitting balance rehabilitation of people with chronic spinal cord and traumatic brain injury. *Physical Therapy, 87,* 1389–1398.

Driskell, J. E., Johnston, J. H., & Salas, E. (2001). Does stress training generalize to novel settings? *Human Factors, 43,* 99–110.

Ferguson, M. C., & Rice, M. S. (2001). The effect of contextual relevance on motor skill transfer. *American Journal of Occupational Therapy, 55,* 558–565.

Gautier, G., Thouvarecq, R., & Larue, J. (2008). Influence of experience on postural control: Effect of expertise in gymnastics. *Journal of Motor Behavior, 40,* 400–408.

Lam, T., & Dietz, V. (2004). Transfer of motor performance in an obstacle avoidance task to different walking conditions. *Journal of Neurophysiology, 92,* 2010–2016.

Meyer, R. K, & Palmer, C. (2003). Temporal and motor transfer in music performance. *Music Perception, 21,* 81–104.

Obayshi, S. (2004). Possible mechanism for transfer of motor learning: Implication of the cerebellum. *Cerebellum, 3,* 204–211.

Park, J. H., & Shea, C.H. (2002). Effector independence. *Journal of Motor Behavior, 34,* 253–270.

Sanders, R., Li, S., & Hamill, J. (2009). Adjustment to change in familiar and unfamiliar task constraints. *Journal of Sports Sciences, 27,* 651–659.

Shields, R. K., Leo, K. C., Messaros, A. J., & Somers, V. K. (1999). Effects of repetitive handgrip training on endurance, specificity, and cross-education. *Physical Therapy, 79,* 467–475.

INTERNET RESOURCES

- For information about the life and work of E. L. Thorndike, who was one of the earliest scholars to develop a theory about why transfer of learning occurs, go to http://www.indiana.edu/~intell/ethorndike.shtml.

- To view a Web site dedicated to presenting a database of practice drills from various sports that have been submitted by anyone (typically by coaches and athletes who have used them), go to http://www.sportspracticedrills.com/. To apply the content of this chapter, use your knowledge about transfer of learning to assess the effectiveness of each practice drill you watch.

- For an overview of virtual reality training, with links to specific applications of it, go to http://www.5dt.com/virtualinfo.html.

- To watch a video describing the development of an electronic robotic prosthetic arm, called the "Luke" arm (by Dean Kamen, the developer of the Segway) go to http://www.youtube.com/watch?v=R0_mLumx-6Y.

- To read about the application of transfer of learning principles to teaching, with particular reference to art teachers but applicable to any teaching area, go to http://www.bartelart.com/arted/transfer.html.

STUDY QUESTIONS

1. Define the term *transfer of learning*. Describe and give an example of the three types of transfer of learning that can occur based on the type of influence of previous experiences.

2. Discuss two reasons why transfer of learning is an important concept in our understanding of motor learning and control.

3. What are two reasons proposed to explain why positive transfer occurs? For each of these, give a motor skill example.

4. What situation characteristics predict negative transfer? Give two motor skill performance examples of these characteristics and indicate why negative transfer would occur in each.

5. What is bilateral transfer? What is the issue underlying the question of whether bilateral transfer is symmetric or asymmetric?

6. Discuss two hypotheses that explain why bilateral transfer occurs.

Specific Application Problem:
Select a motor skill that you might teach in your future profession. Describe two activities or drills that you would use as two sequential preliminary activities before teaching the motor skill. Indicate why you would use each activity or drill and why you would expect positive transfer from each.

Instruction and Augmented Feedback

CHAPTER 14

Demonstration and Verbal Instructions

Concept: Effective methods of providing instructions for helping a person to learn motor skills depend on the skills and the instructional goals.

After completing this chapter, you will be able to

- Describe what an observer perceives from a skilled demonstration of a motor skill and procedures researchers have used to arrive at this conclusion
- Discuss the influence of beginners observing other beginners as they practice a skill
- Identify the main features of the two predominant theories about how observing a demonstration helps a person learn a motor skill
- Give examples of how instructions can influence where a person directs his or her attention when performing a motor skill
- Define *verbal cues* and give examples of how they can be used in skill learning or relearning situations

APPLICATION

If you wanted to instruct someone about how to perform a skill, how would you do it? Probably, you would demonstrate the skill, verbally describe what to do, or use some combination of both approaches. But do you know enough about the effectiveness of these different means of communication to know which one to prefer or when to use each one or both?

Demonstrating skills is undoubtedly the most common means of communicating how to perform them. We find demonstrations in a wide range of skill acquisition situations. For example, a physical education teacher may demonstrate to a large class how to putt in golf. An aerobics teacher may demonstrate to a class how to perform a particular sequence of skills. A baseball coach may show a player the correct form for bunting a ball. In a rehabilitation context, an occupational therapist may

demonstrate to a patient how to button a shirt, or a physical therapist may demonstrate to a wheelchair patient how to get from a bed into the chair. Consider also some examples of how practitioners in other professions use demonstration as an instructional strategy. Aerobics and fitness instructors often demonstrate to their clients how to perform specific activities. Pilates and yoga instructors show their clients how to perform specific movements. And athletic trainers commonly demonstrate taping techniques to student trainers.

The practitioner demonstrates a skill because he or she believes that in this way the learner receives the most helpful, as well as the most amount of, information in the least amount of time. But, we should know when demonstration is effective and when it may be less effective than some other means of communicating how to perform a skill.

Similarly, the instructor should know when verbal instructions are an effective means of communicating how to perform a skill. And if verbal instructions are given, what characterizes the most effective instructions?

> **Application Problem to Solve**   Describe a motor skill that you might help people learn. Describe how you would provide them with information about how to perform the skill before they begin practicing the skill. Indicate why you would present this information in this way and not in some other way.

DISCUSSION

It is ironic that although demonstration is a very common method of providing information about how to perform a skill, there is not as much research related to it as we might expect. However, in recent years researchers have shown an increased interest in the role of demonstration in motor skill learning.

There seem to be at least two reasons for the increased interest in demonstration and skill learning. One reason is the phenomenal growth of interest in the role of vision in skill learning. Because demonstrating how to do a skill typically involves visual observation on the part of the learner, researchers have been able to use the study of demonstration and skill learning to assess how the visual system is involved in skill acquisition and performance. Another reason for the current interest is that we know so little about how to effectively implement this very common instructional strategy. As a result, researchers have been making an increased effort to improve our understanding of the role of demonstration in skill instruction and learning.

In a comprehensive review of research investigating the role of demonstration in motor skill acquisition, McCullagh and Weiss (2001) discussed evidence that indicates demonstration is more effective under certain circumstances than under others. And in an article that reviewed research concerning instruction of sports skills, Williams and Hodges (2005) questioned many popular beliefs that influenced practice and instruction in the coaching of soccer. One of the beliefs they questioned, which the researchers listed as "myths," was "Myth 1: Demonstrations are always effective in conveying information to the learner" (p. 640). Thus both reviews of research related to the effectiveness of demonstrations as an instructional strategy concluded that the practitioner should use demonstration only after determining that the instructional situation indeed warrants the use of demonstration, rather than some other form of providing information about skill performance. In the following sections, we consider some of the concerns that practitioners need to take into account before making this instructional decision.

What the Observer Perceives from a Demonstration

The decision about the situations in which demonstration would be preferred should be based on our knowledge of what a person actually "sees" when a skill is demonstrated. Note the use of the word "sees" rather than "looks at." What we see and what we look at can be very different. What we "see" is what we *perceive* from what we look at. This distinction is particularly relevant to the discussion of demonstration, because what a person perceives from a skill demonstration is not necessarily something that he or she specifically

DEMONSTRATION

The terms **modeling** and **observational learning** often are used interchangeably with the term *demonstration*. Because *demonstration* is more specific to the context of instruction about how to perform a skill, we will use this term in this text.

> **modeling**   the use of demonstration as a means of conveying information about how to perform a skill.
>
> **observational learning**   learning a skill by observing a person perform the skill; also known as *modeling*.

A CLOSER LOOK

Perceiving a Throwing Action from Observing a Point-Light Display

An experiment by Williams (1988) provides an example of the use of the point-light technique. Eighty adults (ages eighteen to twenty-five years) and eighty children (ages fourteen to fifteen years) observed a video point-light display of a side view of the arm of a seated person throwing a small plastic ball at a target (see figure 14.1). The video showed only dots of light at the shoulder, elbow, and wrist joints of the person throwing the ball. The author showed participants the video three times and then asked them what they had seen. Results showed that 66 percent of the children and 65 percent of the adults responded that they had seen a throwing motion. An additional 25 percent of the adults and 23 percent of the children made this response after seeing the video one additional time.

a.

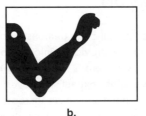

b.

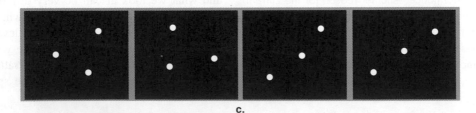

c.

FIGURE 14.1   An example of use of the point-light technique in motor learning research. (a) The model demonstrating the throwing of a small ball at a target. (b) A static image of the point-light display of the model's arm with lights at the shoulder, elbow, and wrist joints. (c) Four still frames of the video shown to subjects. From left to right, these depict the arm at the start of the throw, at maximal flexion, at release of the small ball, and at completion of the throw. [Reproduced with permission of author and publisher from Williams, J. G. (1989). Visual demonstration and movement production: Effects of timing variations in a model's action. *Perceptual and Motor Skills, 68,* 891–896. © Perceptual and Motor Skills 1989.]

looks at or looks for. It is also important to keep in mind that what we perceive may be at a conscious or nonconscious level of awareness. For example, when people are asked later to describe verbally what they saw in a demonstration that helped them perform a skill, they do not always give a very accurate accounting.

Research evidence has shown consistently that the observer perceives from the demonstration information about the coordination pattern of the skill (e.g., Ashford, Bennett, & Davids, 2006; Horn & Williams, 2004). More specifically, *the observer perceives and uses invariant features of the coordinated movement pattern* to develop his or her own movement pattern to perform the skill.

Two types of research evidence support this view. One involves the investigation of the visual perception of motion; the other is the investigation of the influence of demonstration on learning a complex skill. Taken together, these two types of research indicate that the visual system automatically detects in a movement pattern invariant information for determining how to produce the observed action. In some manner, which scientists do not fully understand and continue to debate, the person translates the perceived information into movement commands to produce the action.

The Visual Perception of Motion

Research investigating the perception of human motion attempts to answer questions about how people recognize movement patterns they see in their world. An important principle developed from this research is that people rarely use specific characteristics of the individual components of a pattern to make judgments about the pattern. Rather, they use relative information about the relationships among the various components.

Using a procedure known as the **point-light technique,** researchers have identified the relative information involved in the visual perception of human movement. This procedure involves placing lights or light-reflecting markers on the joints of a person who is then filmed or videotaped performing an action or skill. Then the researcher plays the film or video so that the person who watches the film or video sees only bright dots in motion. The first reported use of this procedure (Johansson, 1973) showed that people could accurately label different gait patterns, such as walking and running, by observing the moving dot patterns. Later, Cutting and Kozlowski (1977) showed that from observing moving dot patterns, people actually could identify their friends. Since that time, an impressive amount of research has shown similar results for the perception of human motion based on point-light displays of a variety of movements. (For a review of this research see Blake & Shiffar, 2007). Using a computer simulation, Hoenkamp (1978) showed that the movement characteristic people use to identify different gait patterns is not any one kinematic variable, but the *ratio of the time duration between the forward and return swings of the lower leg.*

This groundbreaking research on the perception of human movement provided two important conclusions that help our understanding of observational learning. First, people can recognize different gait patterns accurately and quickly without seeing the entire body or all the limbs move. Second, the most critical information people perceive in order to distinguish one type of gait pattern from another is not any one characteristic of the gait, such as velocity of the limbs. Instead, people use the invariant relative time relationship between two components of gait. From these conclusions we can hypothesize that the invariant relationships in coordinated movement constitute the critical information involved in observational learning.

---

point-light technique   a research procedure used to determine the relative information people use to perceive and identify coordinated human actions; it involves placing LEDs or light-reflecting material on certain joints of a person, then filming or videotaping the person performing an action; when an observer views the film or video, he or she sees only the points of light of the LEDs or light-reflecting markers, which identify the joints in action.

FIGURE 14.2   A person performing on the slalom ski simulator. Note that the person has attached LED markers for movement analysis purposes.

Investigating What the Observer Perceives from a Skilled Demonstration

The second type of research providing evidence about what an observer uses from a skill demonstration provides more direct evidence that people perceive invariant relationships. An example is an experiment by Schoenfelder-Zohdi (1992) in which subjects practiced the slalom ski simulator task shown in figure 14.2. This simulator consisted of two rigid, convex, parallel tracks on which a movable platform stood. A participant stood on the platform with both feet and was required to move the platform to the right and then to the left as far as possible (55 cm to either side) with rhythmic slalom ski–like movements. The platform was connected on either side to each end of the apparatus by strong, springlike rubber bands, which ensured that the platform always returned to the center (normal) position. Thus, the participant had to learn to control the platform movement by using smooth ski-like movements, just as he or she would if actually

skiing. Participants practiced this skill for several days after they had either observed a skilled model perform the task or received verbal information about the goal of the task. A movement analysis of limb movements showed that participants who had observed the skilled demonstration developed coordinated movement patterns earlier in practice than did those who had not observed the demonstration. Figure 14.3 shows one example of these results.

Similarities between a skilled model's and a novice's coordination characteristics provide important evidence that observers of skilled demonstrations detect and use invariant coordination features to guide their own performance of a skill. However, stronger support of this conclusion comes from evidence showing performance similarities that result from observations of full-body and point-light models. An example of this type of evidence was provided by Horn, Scott, Williams, and Hodges (2005). They found that observers who watched video displays and those who watched point-light displays

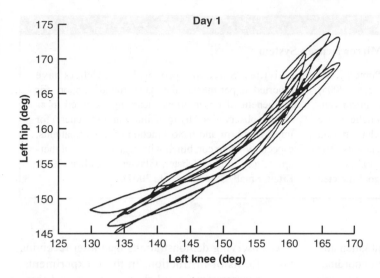

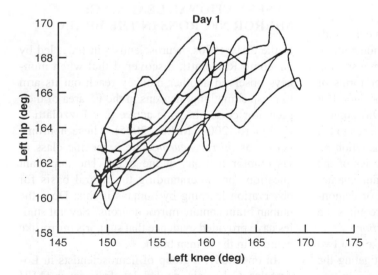

FIGURE 14.3 Angle-angle diagrams of the left knee and left hip for two people practicing on the slalom ski simulator. Both graphs show the relationship of these joints after one day of practice. The top graph is from the person who watched a skilled model demonstrate; the lower graph is from the person who did not watch a demonstration. [From Schoenfelder-Zohdi, B. G. (1992). *Investigating the informational nature of a modeled visual demonstration,* Ph. D. dissertation, Louisiana State University. Reprinted by permission.]

of a soccer-chipping skill showed no differences in their imitation of the model's relative motion characteristics. Additionally, a study by Abernethy and Zawi (2007) showed that expert badminton players predicted the direction of an opponent's strokes

in advance of racquet–shuttlecock contact just as well when they viewed full-body film and point-light displays. Although this study did not investigate modeling, it demonstrates that, through years of observing opponents in action, skilled athletes

A CLOSER LOOK

Clinical Implications of a Mirror Neuron System

In a review of mirror neuron research, Pomeroy and colleagues in London, England (Pomeroy et al., 2005) concluded that the existence of a human mirror neuron system in the brain suggests the beneficial use of observation-based therapy for the rehabilitation of upper arm movement in poststroke patients. The therapy would involve stroke patients observing a healthy person's arm movements during goal-directed activities. Since that proposal, researchers have reported experiments that have found support for the benefit of observational learning (referred to as "action observation" by rehabilitation researchers) for improving arm and hand function of stroke patients, especially when combined with regular physical therapy (e.g., Celnik, Webster, Glasser, & Cohen, 2008; Ertelt, Small, Solodkin et al., 2007).

---

learned to visually detect and use invariant kinematic information related to specific movement coordination patterns. (For an in-depth review of research addressing the question of what is learned during observational learning, see Hodges, Williams, Hayes, & Breslin, 2007).

The Influence of Skill Characteristics

Research investigating the influence on learning of demonstration has produced equivocal findings about the effectiveness of skill demonstration. Some researchers have found that demonstration leads to better skill learning than other forms of instruction; others have found that it does not. But as Magill and Schoenfelder-Zohdi (1996) pointed out, a closer inspection of that research leads to the conclusion that the influence of demonstration on skill acquisition depends on characteristics of the skill being learned. The most important characteristic leading to the beneficial effect of demonstration is that the skill being learned requires the *acquisition of a new pattern of coordination.*

We see this clearly when we organize into two categories the results of research investigating the effect of demonstration on skill learning. In one category are those experiments in which participants learned more quickly after demonstration than after other forms of instruction. In experiments in this category, participants typically learned skills requiring them to acquire new patterns of limb coordination. In the other category are experiments in which participants usually learned skills no better

after observing demonstrations than after receiving other forms of instruction. In these experiments, the participants practiced skills that required them to acquire new parameter characteristics for well-learned patterns of limb coordination.

THE NEURAL BASIS FOR OBSERVATIONAL LEARNING: MIRROR NEURONS IN THE BRAIN

In the early 1990s, neuroscientists in Italy, led by Giacomo Rizzolatti, discovered that when monkeys observed another monkey reach out its arm to grasp something, neurons in the F5 area of their premotor cortex became active (see Rizzolatti & Craighero, 2004; Miller, 2005). These neurons, known as *mirror neurons*, are a specific class of visuomotor neurons in the brain. The important question for understanding the neural basis for observation learning by humans is this: Does the human brain contain mirror neurons? Several studies have provided evidence that supports mirrorlike neurons in the human brain.

In one study, a group of neuroscientists in Los Angeles, California, pooled data from seven fMRI studies in which people observed and imitated simple finger movements (Molnar-Szakacs, Iacoboni, Koski, & Mazziotta, 2005). The researchers noted that during observation, specific areas activated in the *inferior frontal gyrus (IFG),* which is in the inferior frontal lobe of the cerebral cortex. Two sections of the IFG activated during observation

A CLOSER LOOK

Beginners Learn by Observing Other Beginners: Learning the Tennis Volley

An experiment by Hebert and Landin (1994) nicely illustrates how practitioners can facilitate skill acquisition for beginners by having them observe other beginners.

Participants: Female university students who had no previous formal training or regular participation in tennis

Task: Tennis forehand volley with the nondominant hand

Practice procedures: All participants first saw a brief instructional videotape that emphasized the basic elements of the volley

- *Learning model group:* Participants practiced the volley for fifty trials; the instructor provided verbal feedback after each trial. Each student in this group had a student, who was not in this group, observe and listen to a videotape of her practice trials.
- *Observer groups:* After observing the learning models, participants were divided into two groups and began their own fifty trials of practice.

　—*Observer group with verbal feedback:* Participants in this group received verbal feedback from the instructor after each practice trial.
　—*Observer group without verbal feedback:* Participants in this group did not receive verbal feedback from the instructor after each practice trial.
- *Control group:* Participants in this group practiced fifty trials of the volley without having observed the learning model participants or receiving verbal feedback from the instructor.

Results: On a posttest of the volley given after the practice trials, both observer groups performed better than the control group.

Conclusion: Having beginning tennis players observe other beginners practice a skill before they begin to practice will facilitate their learning of the skill.

(the pars triangularis and the dorsal section of the pars opercularis) but not during the movement imitation. Interestingly, the IFG includes the region of the brain known as Broca's area, which is important in speech production.

Researchers in Germany (Zentgraf et al., 2005) used fMRI to assess brain activity during the observation of whole-body gymnastics movements. Their results showed that when participants were asked to observe with the intent to imagine themselves imitating the movements, activation was recorded in the *supplementary motor area (SMA)* of the cortex. Interestingly, when the participants were asked to observe the movements with the intent to judge their accuracy and consistency, the pre-SMA area activated. Other fMRI research has found mirrorlike neuron activity in the *parietal cortex,* which is involved in interhemispheric visuomotor integration (Iacoboni & Zaidel, 2004), and *lateral temporal cortex,* which is involved in

processing complex visual motion (Beauchamp, Lee, Haxby, & Martin, 2003). In addition to using fMRI, researchers have also used EEG recordings to provide evidence of the involvement of a mirror neuron system during action observation (e.g., Calmels, Hars, Holmes, Jarry, & Stam, 2008).

Taken together, these brain activity recording methods indicate the existence of a mirror neuron system, although many questions remain unresolved concerning its specific characteristics and functions. (For a more complete review of research on the mirror neuron system and its implications for physical rehabilitation, see Iacoboni & Mazziotta, 2007).

Observing Skilled Demonstrations

A common guiding principle for demonstrating a skill is that the demonstrator should perform the skill correctly. Why would more accurate demonstration lead to better learning? Two reasons are evident from the research literature. The first reason follows our discussion of perception of information in the preceding section. If the observer perceives and uses information related to invariant movement patterns, it is logical to expect the quality of performance resulting from observing a demonstration to be related to the quality of the demonstration. Another reason is that in addition to picking up coordination information, an observer also perceives information about the strategy used by the model to solve the movement problem. Typically, the observer then tries to imitate that strategy on his or her initial attempts at performing the skill.

Novices Observing Other Novices Practice

Although the theoretical predictions and the empirical evidence indicate that it is preferable for beginners to observe skilled demonstrators, evidence indicates that beginners can derive learning benefits even from observing unskilled demonstrators, especially if both the observers and the models are beginners. What this means is that the models are "demonstrators" only in that the observers are watching them practice.

One proposed benefit of this use of demonstration is that it discourages imitation of a skilled model's performance of the skill and encourages the observer to engage in more active problem solving. We can trace evidence for the benefit of this approach to the 1930s (e.g., Twitmeyer, 1931), although widespread interest in this approach did not develop until Adams (1986) published some experiments. Since then, others have pursued the investigation of the use and benefit of observing an unskilled model (e.g., McCullagh & Meyer, 1997; Pollock & Lee, 1992; Weir & Leavitt, 1990). Results of this research have consistently shown that beginners who observe other beginners practicing a skill will perform at a higher level when they begin to perform than the beginners they observed.

One way to effectively implement this use of demonstration is by pairing students, athletes, or patients in situations where one of the pair performs the skill while the other observes. After a certain number of trials or amount of time, the pair switches roles. On the basis of what we know

from the research literature, learning of the skill can be facilitated for both the performer and the observer by having the teacher, coach, therapist, or some other knowledgeable person provide verbal feedback to the performer. Another effective strategy is to provide the observer of the pair with a checklist of key aspects of the skill. The observer should look for each aspect, check it on the list, and then provide some feedback to the performer. Under these conditions, the observer actively engages in problem-solving activity that is beneficial for learning. The learner observes what the unskilled model does, what the "expert" tells him or her is wrong with the attempt, what the model does to correct errors, and how successful he or she is on the succeeding attempts.

The Timing and Frequency of Demonstrating a Skill

One of the reasons for demonstrating a skill is to communicate how to perform the skill. For the beginner, demonstration provides an effective means of communicating the general movement pattern of the action or skill. As we discussed in chapter 12, Gentile considered this to be the goal of the first stage of learning. When applied to the use of demonstration, Gentile's view suggests two things. The first is that it is beneficial to demonstrate a skill *before the person begins practicing it.* The second is that the instructor should *continue demonstrating during practice as frequently as necessary.*

Earlier, we pointed out that a skilled demonstration communicates the invariant characteristics of a movement pattern. If this is the case, then we would expect that the more frequently a beginner observes a skilled demonstration, the more opportunity the beginner will have to acquire the movement pattern.

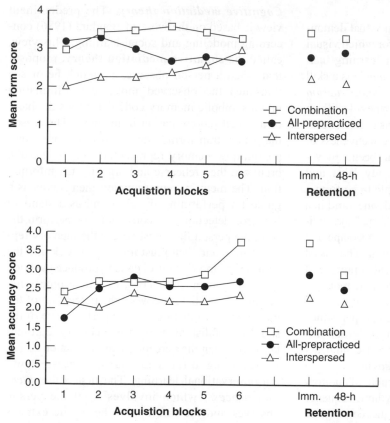

FIGURE 14.4   The results of the experiment by Weeks and Anderson showing form and accuracy scores for practice trials and retention tests for an overhand volleyball serve for three groups that observed ten skilled demonstrations in different amounts and at different times before and during practice. The form scores represent the mean of ten aspects of form, each rated on a scale of 0 to 5, with 0 indicating a complete absence of the aspect, and 5 indicating the aspect was performed as recommended. [Source: Figures 1 (p. 266) and 2 (p. 267) in Weeks, D. L., & Anderson, L. P. (2002). The interaction of observational learning with overt practice: Effects on motor learning. *Acta Psychologica, 104*, 259–271.]

At least two research studies support this latter point. One, by Carroll and Bandura (1990), involves the learning of complex movement patterns of a computer joystick; the other, by Hand and Sidaway (1993), involves the learning of a golf skill. Both experiments provided evidence that more frequent observations of the model yielded better skill learning.

An experiment by Weeks and Anderson (2000), which investigated the issue of the timing of demonstrations, provides some additional insight into both the timing and frequency questions. The demonstrated skill involved a skilled volleyball player hitting an overhand serve. Participants, who had no previous experience hitting this serve, observed a video of ten demonstrations and performed thirty serves. The all-prepractice group watched all ten before performing the thirty serves; the interspersed group observed one demonstration and then performed

three serves, in series throughout the practice period, and the combination group viewed five demonstrations before performing fifteen serves, then viewed five demonstrations before performing the final fifteen serves. All participants performed in two retention tests, which were 5 min and 48 hr respectively after the practice session. The results (figure 14.4) showed the benefit of the combination and all-prepractice conditions, as both led to better form and accuracy scores than the interspersed condition. In terms of the timing and frequency of demonstrations, these results indicate that several demonstrations should precede practice. Although it would be interesting to see how these demonstration schedules would have influenced learning had they been implemented in several days of practice, the results for one practice session reveal the importance of prepractice demonstrations.

Auditory Modeling

Our discussion so far has focused on visual demonstration. However, there are skills for which visual demonstration is less effective for learning than other forms of demonstration. An example is a skill for which the *goal is to move in a certain criterion movement time or rhythm*. For these types of skill, an auditory form of demonstration seems to work best.

A good research example of the effectiveness of auditory modeling when the goal is a specific movement time is an experiment by Doody, Bird, and Ross (1985). The task required people to perform a complex sequential movement with one hand in a criterion movement time of 2.1 sec. Visual and auditory demonstration groups observed a videotape of a skilled model before each practice trial. The visual demonstration group saw only the video portion of the tape and heard no sound. The auditory demonstration group heard only the audio portion of the modeled performance and did not see the task performed by the model. Results indicated that the group that heard the audio portion of the performance did better than the visual demonstration–only group.

Two research examples of the benefit of auditory modeling to aid the learning of a rhythmic sequence involve a laboratory task and a sequence of dance steps. In an experiment by Wuyts and Buekers (1995), people who had no prior dance or music experience learned a sequence of thirty-two choreographed steps. For acquiring the rhythmic timing of this sequence, participants who heard only the timing structure learned it as well as those who both saw and heard the sequence performed by a model. The second example is an experiment by Lai, Shea, Bruechert, and Little (2002) in which they found that auditory modeling enhanced the learning of a sequence of five time intervals when two keyboard keys were alternately depressed. Before each practice trial, participants heard a sequence of tones that represented the timing sequence they were to learn.

How the Observing of Demonstrations Influences Learning

In terms of learning theory, an important question is this: Why does observing demonstrations benefit motor skill learning? Two different views propose answers to this question.

Cognitive mediation theory. The predominant view is based on the work of Bandura (1986) concerning modeling and social learning. This view, called the **cognitive mediation theory,** proposes that when a person observes a model, he or she translates the observed movement information into a symbolic memory code that forms the basis of a stored representation in memory. The reason the person transforms movement information into a cognitive memory representation is so that the brain can then rehearse and organize the information. The memory representation then serves as a guide for performing the skill and as a standard for error detection and correction. To perform the skill, the person first must access the memory representation and then must translate it back into the appropriate motor control code to produce the body and limb movements. Thus, cognitive processing serves as a mediator between the perception of the movement information and the performance of the skill by establishing a cognitive memory representation between the perception and the action.

According to Bandura, four subprocesses govern observational learning. The first is the *attention process,* which involves what the person observes and the information he or she extracts from the model's actions. Because of the importance of the attention process for learning, directing full attention to the demonstration rather than the mere observation of it is important for optimal learning. The second is the *retention process,* in which the person transforms and restructures what he or she observes into symbolic codes that the person stores in memory. Certain cognitive activities, such as rehearsal, labeling, and organization are involved in the retention process and benefit the development of this representation. The *behavior reproduction process* is the third subprocess; during it, the person translates the memory representation of the modeled action and turns it into physical action. Successful accomplishment of this process requires that the individual possess the physical capability to perform the modeled action. Finally, the *motivation process* involves the incentive or motivation to perform the modeled action. This process, then, focuses on all those factors that influence a person's motivation to perform.

Unless this process is completed, the person will not perform the action.

Several research studies have provided support for the cognitive mediation theory by demonstrating evidence that is in line with predictions of the theory. For example, Ste.-Marie (2000) provided support for the prediction that *attention* is an important process in observational learning. In a series of four experiments, participants who had to divide their attention between performing a cognitive secondary task (counting backwards by threes) and observing a model did not learn the skill as well as those who did not perform a secondary task. In an experiment discussed in chapter 10, Smyth and Pendleton (1990) showed that the prevention of the *rehearsal* process hindered learning a skill. In their experiment, some participants engaged in movement activity during the interval of time between the demonstration of a sequence of movements and their attempts to reproduce those movements. These participants recalled fewer movements than those who did not engage in activity during this time interval. And Blandin and Proteau (2000) provided evidence that observational learning involves the development of effective *error detection and correction,* which the cognitive mediation theory describes as an important function of the memory representation that develops during observational learning. In two experiments, participants' estimations of their performance error and their use of that estimation on the next practice trials were similar for an observational learning situation and one in which participants did not observe a model.

Dynamic view of modeling. The second view is based on the direct perception view of vision proposed many years ago by J. J. Gibson (1966, 1979). Scully and Newell (1985) adapted Gibson's view to the visual observation of a skilled demonstration and proposed the **dynamic view of modeling** as an alternative to Bandura's theory. The dynamic view questions the need for a symbolic coding step (the memory representation step) between the observation of the modeled action and the physical performance of that action. Instead, it maintains, the visual system is capable of automatically processing visual information in such a way that it constrains the

motor control system to act according to what the vision detects. The visual system "picks up" from the model salient information that effectively constrains the body and limbs to act in specific ways. The person does not need to transform the information received via the visual system into a cognitive code and store it in memory. This is the case because the visual information directly provides the basis for coordination and control of the various body parts required to produce the action. Thus, the critical need for the observer in the early stage of learning is to observe demonstrations that enable him or her to perceive the important invariant coordination relationships between body parts. Additional observations of the model will benefit the learner by helping the person learn to parameterize the action.

In addition to the type of research evidence provided in the experiment by Schoenfelder-Zohdi (1992), which we considered earlier, evidence based on the use of the point-light display as the model has supported the prediction that the observer of a skilled demonstration perceives invariant coordination characteristics. An experiment by Horn, Williams, and Scott (2002) is a good example of this type of evidence. Female novice soccer players viewed a video of a skilled performer, a point-light display of a skilled performer, or no model. The skill involved chipping a soccer ball a distance of 5 m over a barrier (0.35 m height) onto a target area located 2.5 m from the barrier. The point-light

---

cognitive mediation theory   a theory for explaining the benefit of a demonstration proposing that when a person observes a skilled model, the person translates the observed movement information into a cognitive code that the person stores in memory and uses when the observer performs the skill.

dynamic view of modeling   a theoretical view explaining the benefit of observing a skilled model demonstrate a skill; it proposes that the visual system is capable of automatically processing the observed movement in a way that constrains the motor control system to act accordingly, so that the person does not need to engage in cognitive mediation.

display, which was made from the video of the model performing the skill, showed eighteen light-reflecting markers attached to the models major joints. The video and point-light display were shown life-size to the participants on a screen at three different times during the practice session. The results showed that during practice and on a retention test, target accuracy was similar for the video and point-light display groups, with both groups more accurate than the no-model group. And the kinematic characteristics were similar for participants in the video and point-light display groups. As a result, the evidence provides support for the dynamic view's contention that the observer detects and uses coordination information based on the movement of limb segments, which is the only information the point-light display provided.

Which view is correct? Unfortunately, there is no conclusive evidence in the research literature that shows one of these two views of the modeling effect to be the more valid one. As you saw in the discussions of each view, both have research support for some specific assertions. As a result, until we have research evidence that one view cannot explain, we must consider which view is a possible explanation of why modeling benefits skill acquisition. The cognitive mediation theory has been the more prominent of the two, receiving more attention in motor skills research. However, the dynamic view is growing in popularity.

VERBAL INSTRUCTIONS AND CUES

Verbal instructions rank with demonstration as a commonly used means of communicating to people how to perform motor skills. Evidence supports the value of verbal instructions for facilitating skill acquisition. Several factors are particularly important for developing effective verbal instruction.

Verbal Instructions and Attention

An important performer characteristic we discussed in chapter 9 that relates to giving verbal instructions is that the person has a limited capacity to attend to information. Because of this limitation,

To teach goalkeeping skills, the instructor must decide when to use demonstrations and when to provide verbal instructions.

the practitioner must take into account several characteristics about the instructions they give. We will consider some of these in the following sections.

The quantity of instructions. It is easy to overwhelm the person with instructions about what to do to perform a skill. We can reasonably expect that a beginner will have difficulty paying attention to more than one or two instructions about what to do. Because the beginner will need to divide attention between remembering the instructions and actually performing the skill, a minimal amount of verbal information can exceed the person's attention-capacity limits. In addition to concerns about attention capacity, the instructor should include other important attention-related considerations when giving verbal instructions. Several of these are discussed in the following sections.

Verbal instructions to focus attention on movement outcomes. An important function of instructions is to direct learners' attention to focus on the features of the skill or environmental context that will enhance their performance of the skill. A key point with regard to the content of these instructions relates to our discussion of attention and consciousness in chapter 9. Recall that attention can be either conscious or nonconscious, with the person either aware or not aware of what is being attended to. When we relate this point to attention focus during the performance of a motor skill, we need to review the research evidence we briefly discussed in chapter 9, which showed that a key part of skill learning is *where* a person directs his or her conscious attention when performing a skill. That research evidence was based on investigations of the *action effect hypothesis* (Prinz, 1997), which proposes that actions are best planned and controlled by their intended effects. The hypothesis predicts that actions will be more effective when a person focuses his or her attention on the intended outcomes of an action, rather than on the movements required by the skill. To test the action effect hypothesis in motor skill learning situations, researchers have designed experiments in which instructions that direct participants' attention to their own movements (i.e., internal focus of attention) are compared to those that direct attention to the movement outcome (i.e., external focus of attention) (see Wulf & Prinz, 2001, for a review of this research).

The following research examples illustrate two types of experiments that have tested and supported the action effect hypothesis. And they demonstrate *two different ways to give verbal instructions to direct attention to movement outcomes*. The first involves instructions presented in a way that establishes a *discovery learning* situation. This means that the instructions focus the learner's attention on the action goal of the skill. Then, as the learner practices the skill, he or she "discovers" how to move to achieve that goal. The second example involves the *use of metaphoric imagery* in instructions, which directs the learner's attention to move according to the image, which is the intended movement outcome of the skill. Recall that we discussed the use of metaphoric images in chapter 10 as a strategy for enhancing memory.

In a study reported by Wulf and Weigelt (1997) participants practiced the slalom-ski simulator task (described earlier in this chapter and pictured in figure 14.2). Everyone was told that the goal of the task was to continuously move the platform for 90 sec as far as possible to the left and right at a rate of one complete cycle every 2 sec. Participants in one group were also told to try

to exert force on the platform after it passed the center of the ski simulator, based on a movement characteristic of people who demonstrated high performance levels on the ski simulator. Another group was not given this additional instruction, which means the only instructions they received concerned the action goal (i.e., the desired effect of their movements). Because they were told only about the action goal, this group experienced a discovery learning situation.

As figure 14.5 shows, the additional movement attention-directing instructions led to poorer performance during practice trials and on a transfer test in which participants performed under stress (they were told they were being observed and evaluated by a skiing expert). Interestingly, in a follow-up experiment, which was based on the assumption that more experience with the task would allow participants to direct more attention to the specific information in the instructions, the attention-directing instructions were given after three days of practice. But, once again, rather than aid learning, the instructions had a negative effect.

Numerous other research investigations have found that instructions that promote an external focus of attention lead to better learning than an internal focus. These studies are especially noteworthy because they have found this benefit for a variety of motor skills, such as swinging a golf club, shooting a basketball, serving a volleyball, passing in soccer, and throwing a dart. In addition, instructions to focus attention externally have been shown to benefit the learning of balance skills by healthy adults as well as those who have Parkinson's disease or who have had a stroke. (For brief reviews of the research showing these results, see Emanuel, Jarus, & Bart, 2008; Wulf, Landers, Lewthwaite, & Töllner, 2009; Wulf & Su, 2007).

An experiment in which instructions used *metaphoric imagery* to direct attention to the movement outcome was reported by Wulf, Lauterbach, and Toole (1999). Participants, who were university students with no previous experience playing golf, practiced hitting golf pitch shots into a circular target from a distance of 15 m. Everyone was given the same demonstration and instructions about the

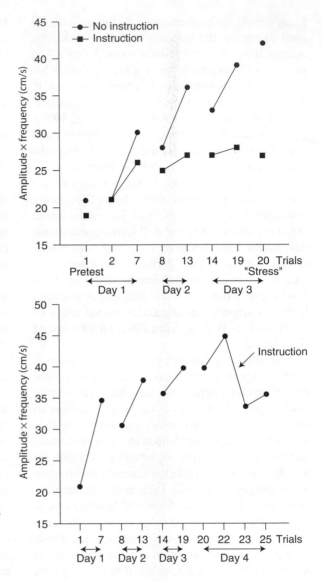

FIGURE 14.5 The top graph shows the results of the first experiment by Wulf and Weigelt which compared a group that received instructions about a movement component of the slalom ski simulator task and a group that did not receive the instructions. The bottom graph shows the results of their second experiment in which one group received the movement component instructions on the fourth day of practice.

[Reprinted with permission from *Research Quarterly for Exercise and Sport, Vol. 1, No. 4,* 262–367. Copyright © 1997 by the American Alliance for Health, Physical Education, Recreation and Dance, 1900 Association Drive, Reston, VA 20191.]

stance and how to grip the club. But one group was told to focus their attention on the swinging motion of the arms during each swing. These participants also received specific instructions about the various movements involved in the swing and practiced several swings without holding a club before they practiced hitting a ball. A second group was told to focus their attention on the club head's pathway during the back- and down-swing (i.e., the "action effect"). They received specific instructions that emphasized the metaphor of the pendulum-like motion of the club. The results showed that the participants who directed their attention to the club movement consistently produced higher target accuracy scores during practice trials and on a 24 hr retention test.

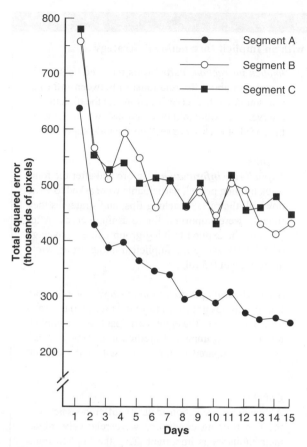

FIGURE 14.6 The results of the experiment by Magill, Schoenfelder-Zohdi, and Hall (1990) showing the superior performance on the repeated segment A compared to the random segments B and C for a complex tracking task. [Source: R. A. Magill et al., "Further Evidence for Implicit Learning in a Complex Tracking Task" paper presented at the annual meeting of the Psychonomics Society, November, 1990, New Orleans, LA.]

Verbal instructions to focus attention on invariant environmental context regulatory conditions. Another issue associated with attention and the content of instructions relates to the selective attention problem of what in the environment to look for that will help perform a skill. The importance of this issue relates to a critical goal of the initial stage of learning, accordingly to Gentile's learning stages model. As we discussed in chapter 12, this goal is to learn the regulatory conditions that direct the movements required to achieve the action goal of the skill.

Sometimes we ask people to tell us what they were looking for or looking at when they performed a skill, so that we can help them correct their visual attention focus. However, research investigating the need for conscious awareness of environmental cues when learning skills reveals that people can learn to select relevant cues from the environment without being consciously aware of what those cues are.

A good example of research demonstrating this result is an experiment reported by Magill (1998). Participants watched a target cursor move in a complex waveform pattern across a computer screen for 60 sec. The participants' task involved pursuit tracking of the target cursor by moving a lever on a tabletop to make their own cursor stay as close as possible to the target cursor. The unique feature was that the target cursor moved randomly for the second and third 20 sec segments on every trial, but it made the same movements on every trial during the first 20 sec segment. The participants practiced this pursuit-tracking task for approximately twenty-four trials on each of fifteen days. The results, shown in figure 14.6, indicated that as they practiced,

A CLOSER LOOK

Training Anticipatory Skills in Tennis with an Implicit Instructional Strategy

An objective of tennis instruction is to enhance players' capabilities to anticipate as early as possible the direction of a ball hit by an opponent. This objective was at the heart of an experiment by Farrow and Abernethy (2002) in which they compared two training techniques designed to increase junior tennis players' anticipation skills for returning serves. Both techniques were based on the hypothesis that the sources of information used by the skilled players to anticipate serve direction could be used to train less skilled players. All participants experienced the following sequence of tests and training: *Pretest— Training (4 wks, 3 days/wk)—Posttest—Retention Test (32 days later)*

Tests and Training

Participants watched videotapes of skilled players' serves, which were from the receiver's view. During the tests, their task was to indicate as quickly as possible whether the serve direction was to their forehand or backhand. On some trials they verbally indicated the direction, while on others they moved with their racquets in the direction. Tapes were edited and programmed to stop at one of five time periods before and after racquetball contact (i.e., temporal occlusion): T1—900 msec before ball contact (start of ball toss); T2—600 msec before ball contact (ball toss almost at zenith); T3—300 msec before ball contact (racquet at top of backswing); T4—at ball contact; T5—after follow-through. Each training session consisted of watching temporally occluded videotapes of various professional tennis players hitting serves and then physically practicing the return of 50 serves.

Training Techniques

Explicit instruction: Participants received specific instruction about the relationship between information sources in the server's action and the direction of a serve. These sources were highlighted in instructional videos, verbal and written information, and verbal feedback provided during the physical practice trials.

Implicit instruction: Participants received no specific instruction about the relationship between information sources in the server's action and the direction of a serve. They were told that their task was to estimate the speed of each serve seen on the videotape.

Results

Explicit rule information: Before and after the four-week training period, participants were asked to write down all the rules, coaching tips, and strategies they thought were important for returning serves. After training, the explicit training group wrote an average of 2.5 rules, while the implicit training group wrote an average of 0.5 rules.

Serve direction prediction accuracy: Overall, both training groups improved from the pretest to the posttest. But seven of the eight participants in the implicit training group improved prediction accuracy *at ball contact,* compared to three of eight in the explicit group.

Conclusion

Although the prediction accuracy differences between the two training conditions were relatively minor, their similarity is important. That the implicit training led to test performance that was similar to that of explicit training indicates that the anticipatory information required to predict serve direction can be learned without being consciously aware of the specific sources for the information. However, it is important to note two important characteristics of the implicit training condition:

1. The participants directed attention to the server and the serve on each videotape, because they had to estimate the speed of the serve.
2. The training period involved a large number of trials of observing a variety of servers and serves that were temporally occluded at various times before and after each serve.

they performed better on the first segment than on the other two segments. But what is more important is that when interviewed, none of the participants indicated that they knew that the target cursor made the same pattern during the first segment on every trial. Thus the participants attended to and used the regularity of the cursor movement during the first segment, even though they were not consciously aware of that characteristic. This lack of conscious awareness of the invariant movement pattern of the target cursor indicates that the participants *implicitly* learned the regulatory environmental context features that directed their movements as they tracked the target cursor.

Although the research just described indicates that people can learn to use relevant environmental context features without being instructed to look for them, there is a common assumption that we can facilitate skill learning by giving instructions that would make people aware of these features. For example, a tennis teacher may tell a student that a certain racquet-head angle at ball contact during a serve indicates a specific type of serve, which the student should try to look for to predict that type of serve. However, what is not so commonly known is that this type of instruction could actually hinder rather than facilitate learning, especially when the specific features looked for occur infrequently in a series of trials.

Green and Flowers (1991) reported an experiment that serves as a good example of the research evidence demonstrating this negative effect. Participants played a computer game in which they manipulated a joystick to move a paddle horizontally across the bottom of the monitor to try to catch a "ball," which was a dot of light, that moved for 2.5 sec from the top to the bottom of the screen. The ball moved according to one of eight pathways. On 75 percent of the trials, the ball made deviations from the normal pathway that predicted the specific final position of the ball. Thus, participants' detection of these pathway-deviations characteristics could help them increase their catching accuracy. One group of participants received explicit instructions about these characteristics and their probability of occurring; the other group did not. Participants practiced for five days for a total of 800 trials. The results showed that both groups improved. However, the explicit-instruction group made more errors than the group that had had no instruction. The authors concluded that the instructed participants directed so much of their attentional resources to trying to remember the rule and looking for its occurrence that their performance was disrupted, because they did not have sufficient attention to devote to the catching task itself.

Research has also shown the negative influence of explicit information on the implicit learning of an open motor skill by stroke patients. In an experiment by Boyd and Winstein (2004), patients who had experienced a basal ganglia stroke practiced a pursuit tracking task similar to the one described earlier in the Magill (1998) study, except that a trial was only 30 sec. One group of patients was told about the repeating portion of the pathway. Rather than helping the patients to perform the task better than those who were not given this information, the awareness of this task characteristic led to poorer learning.

Verbal Instructions Influence Goal Achievement Strategies: Speed-Accuracy Skill Instructions

Another factor that we need to consider is that verbal instructions direct the person's attention to certain performance goals of the skill. A good example of this is the way verbal instructions can bias the strategy a person uses to learn speed-accuracy skills which we discussed in chapter 7. An experiment by Blais (1991) illustrates this type of strategy bias. The task was a serial pursuit tracking task in which participants controlled a steering wheel to align a pointer as quickly and accurately as possible to target positions on a screen. Three groups of participants received verbal instructions that emphasized being accurate, being fast, or being both accurate and fast. The instruction emphasis was especially evident during the first of the five days of practice. On this day, the "speed instruction" group recorded the fastest movement times, whereas the "accuracy group" produced the most accurate performance. The group told to emphasize both speed and accuracy adopted a strategy that led to fast movement times—but at the expense of performance accuracy. And although the "accuracy instruction" group performed the most accurately, its participants did so in a manner that eventually gave them the fastest average overall response time, which included reaction time, movement time, and

Considerations for Experts When Giving Verbal Instructions to Novices

We generally assume that beginners should be taught by people who are highly skilled in the activity to be learned. However, highly skilled performers (i.e., experts) can have problems when they give verbal instructions to beginners. We might expect certain types of problems because of some of the differences between experts and novices that we considered in chapter 12. Two differences that are especially relevant are these:

- *Their knowledge structures about the skill.* Compared to those of novices, experts' knowledge structures tend to be more conceptual and organized, with more interrelationship among the concepts. Novices, on the other hand, tend to have knowledge structures that involve more concrete and specific pieces of information, with few concepts and interrelationships among them.

- *The attention demands required to perform the skill.* Novices need to direct conscious attention to more, and different, aspects of the performance of a skill than experts.

An experiment by Hinds, Patterson, and Pfeffer (2001) provides some evidence and insight about the problems experts can have providing instructions to novices. In this experiment, experts in the domain of electronics instructed novices about how to build an electronic circuit, which involved connecting wires in specific ways to make the electronic components for several different devices, such as a radio or motion detector. Results showed that the experts provided instruction that was too conceptual and included too few concrete details to guide the novices. Interestingly, the experts' self-reported assessment of their teaching skill did not correlate well with the type of instructions they provided.

---

movement-correction time for errors. Thus, for this task, where both speed and accuracy were equally important for overall performance, instructions that initially emphasize accuracy led to the best achievement of the two-component goal.

The results of the Blais (1991) experiment are consistent with predictions of both the motor program and dynamic pattern theories we discussed in chapter 5. To apply the speed-accuracy skill to those theories, the movement accuracy component refers to the movement pattern used to perform the skill. In both theories the movement pattern consists of invariant characteristics that remain the same when the skill is performed at different speeds. For these motor control theories, movement speed can be readily changed according to the demands of the performance situation or intention of the performer. As a result, these theories predict that initial practice for a speed-accuracy skill should emphasize movement accuracy and a later emphasis on the speed component.

Verbal Cues

One of the potential problems associated with verbal instructions is that they can contain too little or too much information and not provide

the learner with what he or she needs to know to achieve the goal of the skill. To overcome this problem, instructors can use verbal cues to direct people to know what to do to perform skills (Landin, 1994). **Verbal cues** are short, concise phrases that serve to (1) direct the performer's attention to regulatory conditions in the environmental context or (2) prompt key movement components of skills. For example, the cue "Look at the ball" directs visual attention, whereas the cue "Bend your knee" prompts an essential movement component. Research has shown these short, simple statements to be very effective as verbal instructions to facilitate learning new skills, as well as performing well-learned skills. Teachers, coaches, or therapists can implement verbal cues in several different ways in skill learning settings.

Verbal cues and demonstrations. One way is to *give verbal cues along with a demonstration* to supplement the visual information (e.g., McCullagh, Stiehl, & Weiss, 1990; Zetou, Tzetzis, Vernadakis, & Kioumourtzoglou, 2002). When used this way, verbal cues aid in directing attention, and can guide rehearsal of the skill a person is learning. An example of a study showing the benefit of this use of

A CLOSER LOOK

Guidelines for Using Verbal Cues for Skill Instruction and Rehabilitation

- Cues should be short statements of one, two, or three words.
- Cues should relate logically to the aspects of the skill to be prompted by the cues.
- Cues can prompt a sequence of several movements.
- Cues should be limited in number. Cue only the most critical elements of performing the skill.

- Cues can be especially helpful for directing shifts of attention.
- Cues are effective for prompting a distinct rhythmic structure for a sequence of movements.
- Cues must be carefully timed so that they serve as prompts and do not interfere with performance.
- Cues should initially be spoken by the performer.

verbal cues was reported by Janelle, Champenoy, Coombes, and Mousseau, (2003) for learning a soccer accuracy pass. Non–soccer players who observed a skilled model video demonstration with accompanying verbal and visual cues learned the pass with more appropriate form and outcome accuracy than in five other practice conditions. The verbal cues, which were presented by audiotape along with the video, were short descriptions of the specific movement characteristics of the critical areas of the kick. The visual cues were arrows on the video that pointed to the critical areas of the kick. The comparison practice conditions involved discovery learning (i.e., they were told the accuracy goal of the skill but had to "discover" the best way to pass the ball to achieve the goal), verbal instructions only, a skilled model video demonstration with the visual cues, a skilled model video demonstration with the verbal cues, and a skilled model video demonstration only. Note that in this study the addition of visual cues enhanced the benefit of the verbal cues. Together, the visual arrows and the verbal cues focused the participants' attention to the parts of the skill that were critical to successful performance.

Verbal cues that focus attention while performing. Another way to use verbal cues is to *give cues to help learners focus on critical parts of skills.* For example, in an experiment by Masser (1993), first-grade classes were taught to do headstands. In one class, before students made each attempt to swing their legs up into the headstands, the instructor said, "Shoulders over your knuckles," to emphasize

the body position critical to performing this skill. The cued students maintained their acquired skill three months after practice, whereas the students who had not received this verbal cue performed the headstand poorly three months later. A similar result occurred in an experiment using verbal cues to emphasize critical parts of the forward roll.

Verbal cues as prompts. Performers also can *use verbal cues while performing* to prompt themselves to attend to or perform key aspects of skills. Cutton and Landin (1994) provided a research example demonstrating the effectiveness of this technique for nonskilled individuals. Instructors taught university students in a beginning tennis class five verbal cues to say out loud each time they were required to hit a ball. These were as follows: "ready," to prompt preparation for the oncoming ball; "ball," to focus attention on the ball itself; "turn," to prompt proper body position to hit the ball, which included turning the hips and shoulders to be perpendicular with the net and pointing the racquet toward the back fence; "hit," to focus attention on contacting the ball; and "head down," to prompt the stationary position of the head after ball contact. The students who used

---

verbal cues   short, concise phrases that direct a performer's attention to important environmental regulatory characteristics, or that prompt the person to perform key movement pattern components of skills.

verbal cues learned tennis groundstrokes better than those who did not, including a group that received verbal feedback during practice.

Verbal cues aid skilled performance. Verbal cues have also been used to *improve the performance of skilled athletes.* For example, Landin and Hebert (1999) had university female varsity tennis players use self-cueing to help them improve their volleying skills. Players learned to say the word "split," to cue them to hop to a balanced two-foot stop that would allow them to move in any direction. Then, they said, "turn," to cue them to turn their shoulders and hips to the ball. Finally, they said, "hit," to direct their attention to tracking the ball to the point of contact on the racquet and to cue themselves to keep the head still and hit the ball solidly. After practicing this cueing strategy for five weeks, the players showed marked improvements in both performance and technique.

The purposes of verbal cues. The various uses of verbal cues just described indicate that verbal cues can be used for two different purposes. Sometimes the cue *directs attention* to a specific environmental event or to specific sources of regulatory information (in our example, "ready," "ball," and "hit" are such cues). In other cases, the cue *prompts action,* for either a specific movement ("head down") or a sequence of movements ("turn"). The key to the effectiveness of verbal cues is that as the person practices and continues to use the cues, an association develops between the cue and the act it prompts. The benefit is that the person does not need to give attention to a large number of verbal instructions and can focus attention on the important perceptual and movement components of the skill.

SUMMARY

In this chapter, we discussed demonstration and verbal instructions and cues as effective means of communicating information about how to perform motor skills.

Demonstration

- A benefit of observing a skilled demonstration is that the observer detects the invariant characteristics of the movement pattern involved in the performance of the skill.

- The point-light technique and research about what an observer perceives from a skilled demonstration shows that demonstration tends to be a more effective means of instruction when the skill being learned requires a new movement coordination than when it involves a new parameter of a well-learned coordination pattern.

- Observation by a beginner of another beginner practicing a skill can facilitate skill learning.

- Skills should be demonstrated several times before a beginner practices a skill, with additional demonstrations during practice as needed.

- Auditory forms of demonstration are effective for the learning of motor skills that have a specific overall movement time goal or require a specific rhythmic sequence or beat.

- Two prominent theoretical views that propose explanations for the benefit of demonstration on skill learning are

  ► The *cognitive mediation theory,* which proposes that observation of a demonstration leads to the development of a memory representation of the observed skill that the performer must access prior to performing the skill.

  ► The *dynamic view* which proposes that people do not need cognitive mediation because the visual system can constrain the motor control system to act according to what has been observed.

Verbal Instructions and Cues

- Several attention-related factors are important to consider when using verbal instructions to communicate how to perform a motor skill:

  ► The amount of information included in verbal instructions should take into account learners' attention-capacity limitations.

- ► According to the action effect hypothesis, verbal instructions should direct the learner's focus of attention to movement outcomes rather than to the movements themselves.

- ► Novice learners can learn invariant environmental context regulatory conditions without conscious awareness of them (i.e., implicit learning), although attention focus on the environmental context is important.

- ► Instructions influence the novice learner to direct attention to certain performance goals, which influences the strategies the learner uses to begin practicing a skill.

- Verbal cues are short concise phrases that serve to
  - ► Direct the performer's attention to regulatory conditions in the environmental context.
  - ► Prompt key movement components of skills.

- Verbal cues can be given by an instructor or the performer to
  - ► Direct an observer's attention during a demonstration of a skill.
  - ► Direct a performer's attention to critical parts of skills.
  - ► Prompt movements while performing a skill.

POINTS FOR THE PRACTITIONER

- Demonstrations by a skilled model have their greatest influence on skill learning when the skill requires the learning of a new movement coordination pattern.

- People who are in the initial stage of learning a skill can benefit from observing others who are also novices. Consider using this strategy with large groups by having the people work in pairs where one practices the skill for several trials while the other observes, and then they switch roles.

- A demonstration by a skilled model can be done by the practitioner, a person in the group who can perform the skill well, or a skilled model on a video.

- Frequent demonstrations result in better learning than less frequent demonstrations, especially in the initial stage of learning.

- Be certain that the people observing a demonstration can see the critical features of the skill being demonstrated.

- If visual and/or verbal cues are used with a demonstration, keep them simple and focused on the critical features of the skill that need to be emphasized. Avoid providing a running verbal commentary along with a demonstration.

- Use auditory cues to demonstrate timing and rhythm characteristics of skills.

- Verbal instructions should present the minimum amount of information necessary to communicate what a person needs to do to perform a skill. Providing too much information in verbal instructions can be like providing no verbal instructions at all.

- Provide verbal instructions that focus attention on the outcome of a movement rather than on the movement itself.

- When teaching open skills, provide verbal instructions that focus attention on areas in the environmental context where critical invariant regulatory conditions can be observed. Expect that the detection and perception of much of this critical information will occur without the person's conscious awareness of what he or she perceives.

- To ensure the detection and perception of critical invariant regulatory conditions, allow the person to perform the skill in a variety of environmental contexts and situations.

- Emphasize movement form rather than speed for a person's initial practice attempts when teaching a speed-accuracy skill.

RELATED READINGS

Almeida, Q. J., Wishart, L. R., & Lee, T. D. (2002). Bimanual coordination deficits with Parkinson's disease: The influence of movement speed and external cueing. *Movement Disorders, 17,* 30–37.

Buchanan, J. J., Ryu, Y. U., Zihlman, K., & Wright, D. L. (2008). Observational practice of relative but not absolute motion features in a single-limb multi-joint coordination task. *Experimental Brain Research, 191*, 157–169.

Calvo-Merino, B., Glaser, D. E., Grèzes, J., Passingham, R. E., & Haggard, P. (2005). Action observation and acquired motor skills: An fMRI study with expert dancers. *Cerebral Cortex, 15*, 1243–1249.

Deakin, J. M., & Proteau, L. (2002). The role of scheduling in learning through observation. *Journal of Motor Behavior, 32*, 268–276.

Gray, J. T., Neisser, U., Shapiro, B. A., & Kouns, S. (1991). Observational learning of ballet sequences: The role of kinematic information. *Ecological Psychology, 3*, 121–134.

Gray, R. (2004). Attending to the execution of a complex sensorimotor skill: Expertise differences, choking, and slumps. *Journal of Experimental Psychology: Applied, 10*, 42–54.

Hodges, N. J., Hayes, S. J., Breslin, G., & Williams, A. M. (2005). An evaluation of the minimal constraining information during observation for movement reproduction. *Acta Psychologica, 119*, 264–282.

Hodges, N. J., & Williams, A. M. (2007). Current status of observational learning research and the role of demonstrations in sport. *Journal of Sports Sciences, 25*, 495–496. [*Note: this article is an "editorial" that introduces a series of research articles in this issue of the journal.*]

Jacobs, A., Pinto, J., & Shiffrar, M. (2004). Experience, context, and visual perception of human movement. *Journal of Experimental Psychology: Human Perception and Performance, 30*, 822–835.

Laguna, P. L. (2008). Task complexity and sources of task-related information during the observational learning process. *Journal of Sports Sciences, 26*, 1097–1113.

Laugier, C., & Cadopi, M. (1996). Representational guidance of dance performance in adult novices: Effect of concrete vs. abstract movements. *International Journal of Sport Psychology, 27*, 91–108.

McNevin, N. H., Wulf, G., & Carlson, C. (2000). Effects of attentional focus, self-control, and dyad training on motor learning: Implications for physical rehabilitation. *Physical Therapy, 80*, 373–385.

Steel, K. A., Adams, R. D., & Canning, C. G. (2006). Identifying runners as football teammates from 400 msec. video clips. *Perceptual and Motor Skills, 103*, 901–911.

Sweeting, T., & Rink, J. E. (1999). Effects of direct instruction and environmentally designed instruction on the process and product characteristics of a fundamental skill. *Journal of Teaching Physical Education, 18*, 216–233.

Vogt, S., & Thomaschke, R. (2007). From visuomotor interactions to imitation learning: Behavioural and brain imaging studies. *Journal of Sports Sciences, 25*, 497–517.

Wulf, G., Shea, C., & Park, J. H. (2001). Attention and motor performance: Preferences for and advantages of an external focus. *Research Quarterly for Exercise & Sport, 72*, 335–344.

INTERNET RESOURCES

- To experience the speed-accuracy trade-off phenomenon and how you can influence it by emphasizing speed or accuracy, as well as improve your keyboarding skills, go to http://www.typingmaster. com/support/intra/user_manual.html.

- To read about the point-light technique and to see some examples, go to http://astro.temple. edu/~tshipley/. Under Current Research Projects, click on Biological Motion. To view examples of a variety of movements in point-light displays, go to the Point-Light Archive part of this Web site.

- To watch a video about the discovery, characteristics, and importance of mirror neurons, go to http://www.pbs.org/wgbh/nova/sciencenow/ video/3204/q01-220.html.

- To read about the availability of video demonstrations for
  - strength training and fitness activities, go to http://www.global-fitness.com/strength/ s_video.html.
  - a wide variety of sports skills, go to http:// www.sportsnationvideo.com/.
  - athletic trainers, go to http://www.athletic trainer.com/.

STUDY QUESTIONS

1. (a) What are two types of research evidence that show that observing a skilled demonstration of a motor skill influences the acquisition of the coordination characteristics of the skill? (b) Discuss what this research evidence tells us that we can apply to the use of demonstrations when teaching motor skills.

2. (a) Describe how observing an unskilled person learning a skill could help a beginner learn that skill. (b) Discuss why a learning benefit should result from a beginner observing another beginner learning a skill.

3. What are the main features of the two predominant theories about how observing a

demonstration helps a person to learn that skill? How do these theories differ?

4. What is the action-effect hypothesis and how does it relate to instructions influencing *where* a person directs his or her attention when performing closed and open skills.

5. Describe two purposes for using verbal cues. Give an example for each.

Specific Application Problem:
Select a motor skill that you might teach in your future profession. Your supervisor has asked you to develop and defend a plan for providing information to the people you will work with about how to perform the skill. In your plan, describe the skill you will teach and relevant characteristics of the people you will teach, whether you will use demonstrations, verbal instructions, or both, and some specific characteristics of your choice. In your defense of this plan, emphasize why the information you will present and how you will deliver it would be preferable to other ways of providing these people with information about how to perform this skill.

CHAPTER 15

Augmented Feedback

Concept: Augmented feedback provides information that can facilitate skill learning.

After completing this chapter, you will be able to

- Distinguish between task-intrinsic feedback and augmented feedback as they relate to performing a motor skill
- Define *KR* and *KP* and give examples of each
- Describe skill learning conditions in which augmented feedback would or would not influence learning
- Compare and contrast quantitative and qualitative augmented feedback
- Describe situations in which various types of augmented feedback, such as videotape replay, movement kinematics, and biofeedback would be effective for facilitating skill learning
- Identify situations in which concurrent augmented feedback would be beneficial or detrimental to skill learning
- Describe two time intervals associated with the giving of terminal augmented feedback during practice and how their lengths and the activity during each influence skill learning
- Describe various ways to reduce the frequency of giving augmented feedback as ways to facilitate skill learning

APPLICATION

Think about a time when you were beginning to learn a new physical activity. How much success did you experience on your first few attempts? Most likely, you were not very successful. As you practiced, you probably had many questions that you needed someone to answer to help you better understand what you were doing wrong and what you needed to do to improve. Although you may have been able to answer many of your questions on your own as you continued to try different things while you practiced, you found that getting an answer from the instructor saved you time and energy.

This situation is an example of what we discussed in chapter 12 as typical in the early stage of learning a skill, or relearning a skill following an injury or illness. The significance of this example is that it points out that an important role played by the practitioner is to give augmented feedback to the learner to facilitate the skill acquisition process.

Consider the following situations. Suppose that you are teaching a golf swing or fitness activity to a class, helping a new student athletic trainer to tape an ankle, or working in a clinic with a patient learning to walk with an artificial limb. In each situation, the people practicing these skills can make lots of mistakes and will benefit from receiving augmented feedback.

When they make mistakes, which they do in abundance when they are beginners, how do you know which mistakes to tell them to correct on subsequent attempts? If you had a video camera available, would you videotape them and then let them watch their own performances? Or would it be even more beneficial to take the videotapes and have them analyzed so that you could show them what their movements looked like kinematically? There are many ways to provide augmented feedback. But before you use any one of these, you should know how to implement that method most effectively and when to use it to facilitate learning.

Application Problem to Solve Describe a motor skill that you might help people learn. Describe how you would give them feedback as they practice the skill and indicate why you would give feedback in this way and not in some other way.

DISCUSSION

When people perform a motor skill, they can have available to them *two general types of performance-related information (i.e., feedback)* that will "tell" them something about the outcome of the performance or about what caused that outcome. One is **task-intrinsic feedback,** which is the sensory-perceptual information that is a natural part of performing a skill. Each of the sensory systems can provide this type of feedback. We discussed three of these in chapter 6: touch, proprioception, and vision. For example, if a person throws a dart at a target on the wall, he or she receives *visual* task-intrinsic feedback from seeing the flight of the dart and where it lands on the target. In addition, the person receives *tactile and proprioceptive* task-intrinsic feedback movement of his or her body posture along with arm and hand movement as the person prepares to throw the dart and as the dart is thrown. Other sensory systems can also provide task-intrinsic feedback, as does the *auditory* system when the person hears the dart hit, or not hit, the target.

The second general type of performance-related information is *in addition to* task-intrinsic feedback.

Although various terms have been used to identify this type of feedback, (*e.g., external feedback, task-extrinsic feedback*) the term that will be used in this book is **augmented feedback.** The adjective "augmented" refers to adding to or enhancing something, which in this case involves *adding to or enhancing task-intrinsic feedback.* It *enhances* the task-intrinsic feedback when augmented feedback provides information the person's sensory system can readily detect on its own. For example, a teacher or coach might tell a golfer where his or her hands were positioned at the top of the swing, even though proprioceptive feedback would allow the person to feel for himself or herself where they were. In a clinical environment, a therapist might show an amputee patient EMG traces on a computer monitor to enhance the patient's own proprioceptive feedback to help the patient activate appropriate muscles when learning to operate a prosthetic device.

In other situations, augmented feedback *adds* information that the person cannot detect using his or her sensory system. For example, the golf teacher or coach might tell the golfer where the ball went because the golfer was concentrating so much on keeping his or her head down during the swing that he or she did not see it after it was hit. Likewise, a therapist might tell a patient how much his or her body swayed because vestibular problems prevent the patient from being able to detect this information. In each of these situations, augmented feedback provides performance information that otherwise would not be available to the person.

---

task-intrinsic feedback   the sensory feedback that is naturally available while performing a skill.

augmented feedback   a generic term used to describe information about performing a skill that is added to sensory feedback and comes from a source external to the person performing the skill; it is sometimes referred to as extrinsic or external feedback.

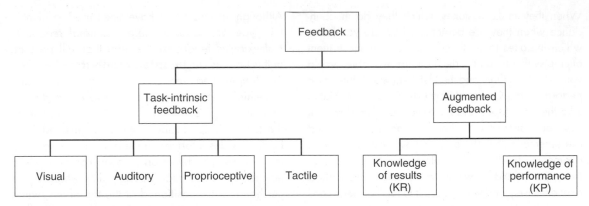

FIGURE 15.1   Illustration of the different types of feedback in the feedback family that are related to learning and performing motor skills.

THE FEEDBACK FAMILY

Note that the term *feedback* is common to both categories of performance-related information described in the preceding paragraphs. As a result, it is important to consider the term "feedback" as a generic term that describes information people receive about their performance of a motor skill during or after the performance. To help conceptualize the relationship between the two general types of performance-related feedback, consider these two types of feedback as related members of the same family. Figure 15.1 graphically describes the feedback family relationships for task-intrinsic feedback and augmented feedback, as well as for the related specific types of each.

TYPES OF AUGMENTED FEEDBACK

In Figure 15.1, note that there are *two categories of types of augmented feedback: knowledge of results* and *knowledge of performance.* Each category can involve a variety of ways of presenting augmented feedback; this will be the topic of discussion later in this chapter.

Knowledge of Results (KR)

The category of augmented feedback known as **knowledge of results** (commonly referred to as **KR**) consists of *externally presented information about the outcome of performing a skill or about achieving the goal of the performance.* In some situations, KR describes something about the performance outcome (i.e., result). For example, if a teacher tells a student in an archery class, "The shot was in the blue at 9 o'clock," the teacher is providing performance outcome information. Similarly, if a therapist shows a patient a computer-generated graph indicating that this leg extension was 3 degrees more than the last one, the therapist is giving KR to the patient about the outcome of his or her leg extension movement.

Sometimes, KR does not describe the performance outcome, but simply tells the performer whether he or she has achieved the performance goal. This is the case when some external device gives a "yes" or "no" signal indicating whether or not the performance goal was achieved. For example, to augment proprioceptive and visual feedback for a patient working on achieving a specific amount of leg extension, the therapist could set a buzzer to be activated when the patient achieved the goal number of degrees of movement. Although the buzzer would provide no information about how close to the goal or how far from it the movement was if it had not been achieved, the patient would know that he or she had not achieved the goal unless the buzzer sounded. There are some additional examples of KR in table 15.1.

It is important to point out that we are using the term KR to refer to a type of augmented feedback. Although a person can obtain knowledge about the results of an action from his or her own

TABLE 15.1   Examples of Augmented Feedback

• **A golf instructor tells a student:**	KR ➔ "Your shot went into the right rough."
	KP ➔ "You did not take your backswing back far enough before you began your downswing."
• **A physical therapist tells a patient:**	KR ➔ "You walked 10 feet more today than you did yesterday."
	KP ➔ "You should bend your knees more as you walk."
• **A student driver in a simulator**	KR ➔ sees the number of errors he or she made after completing a session.
	KP ➔ sees a light flash each time he or she makes an error while driving in a session.
• **A sprinter in track**	KR ➔ sees a posting on the scoreboard of the amount of time to run the race.
	KP ➔ sees a videotape replay of his or her race.
• **A gymnast**	KR ➔ sees the judges' scores after completing a routine.
	KP ➔ looks at a computer monitor to see a stick figure representation of his or her body, limb, and head displacement when he or she performed the routine.
• **A knee rehabilitation patient**	KR ➔ reads a display on an exercise machine that indicates the number of degrees of leg extension he or she had on that leg extension exercise repetition.
	KP ➔ hears a buzzer when a target muscle is active during a leg extension exercise.

sensory system, such as seeing whether the basketball missed the basket or went in, this type of performance-related information is task-intrinsic. It does not refer to the specific type of performance-related information the term KR refers to in this text. The importance of this distinction is that it allows us to distinguish the specific influences of task-intrinsic and augmented feedback on skill learning.

Knowledge of Performance (KP)

The second category of augmented feedback is **knowledge of performance** (known as **KP**). This is information about the *movement characteristics that led to the performance outcome.* The important point here is that KP differs from KR in terms of which aspect of performance the information refers to. For example, in the archery situation described above, the teacher would provide KP by telling the student that he or she pulled the bow to the left at the release of the arrow. Here, the teacher

augments the task-intrinsic feedback by telling the student what he or she did that caused the arrow to hit the target where it did.

In addition to giving KP verbally, there are various nonverbal means of providing KP. For example, video replay is a popular method of showing a person what he or she did while performing a skill. Video replay allows the person to see what he or she actually did that led to the outcome of that performance. Although video replay can show

---

knowledge of results (KR)   category of augmented feedback that gives information about the outcome of performing a skill or about achieving the goal of the performance.

knowledge of performance (KP)   category of augmented feedback that gives information about the movement characteristics that led to a performance outcome.

Augmented Feedback as Motivation

An instructor can use augmented feedback to influence a person's perception of his or her own ability in a skill. This is an effective way to influence the person's motivation to continue pursuing a task goal or performing a skill. The verbal statement "You're doing a lot better" can indicate to a person that he or she is being successful at an activity. Evidence supporting the motivational effectiveness of this type of verbal feedback comes from research relating to self-efficacy and performance of skills.

For example, Solmon and Boone (1993) showed that in a physical education class environment, students with high ability perceptions demonstrated longer persistence at performing a skill and had higher performance expectations than those with low ability perceptions. In her reviews of self-efficacy research as it relates to skill performance, Feltz (1992; Feltz & Payment, 2005) concluded that the success or failure

of past performance is a key mediator of a person's self-perceptions regarding ability.

Visual augmented feedback has also been shown to have motivational benefits for learning motor skills. An interesting example comes from its use in a physical therapy context. People with neurological gait disorders reported that the addition of visual augmented feedback about their performance on a Lokomat driven gait orthosis (a robotic-assisted gait training device) made them more motivated to train on the device than when this additional feedback was not provided (Banz, Bollinger, Colombo, Dietz, & Lünenburger, 2008).

An important implication of these findings is that the practitioner can present augmented feedback in a way that influences a person's feelings of success or failure which, in turn, influence a person to continue or to stop his or her involvement in participating in a physical activity.

---

a performance outcome, it is commonly used as KP. Another means of providing KP that is increasing in popularity as computer software becomes more accessible is showing the person computer-generated kinematic characteristics of the just-completed performance. In clinical environments, therapists also use biofeedback devices to give KP. For example, a therapist can attach a buzzer to an EMG recording device so that the person hears the buzzer sound when he or she activates the appropriate muscle during the performance of an action. In each of these situations, sensory feedback is augmented in a way that informs the person about the movement characteristics associated with the outcome of an action.

THE ROLES OF AUGMENTED FEEDBACK IN SKILL ACQUISITION

Augmented feedback plays two roles in the skill learning process. One is to *facilitate achievement of the action goal of the skill.* Because augmented feedback provides information about the success of

the skill in progress or just completed, the learner can determine whether what he or she is doing is appropriate for performing the skill correctly. Thus, the augmented feedback can help the person achieve the skill goal more quickly or more easily than he or she could without this external information.

The second role played by augmented feedback is to *motivate the learner to continue striving toward a goal.* In this role, the person uses augmented feedback to compare his or her own performance to a performance goal. The person then must decide to continue trying to achieve that goal, to change goals, or to stop performing the activity. This motivational role of augmented feedback is not the focus of our discussion here. Others, however, have discussed it in the motor learning literature (e.g., Little & McCullagh, 1989). Scholars interested in the pedagogical aspects of physical education teaching (e.g., Solmon & Lee, 1996; Silverman, Woods, & Subramaniam, 1998) increasingly are studying the effects of augmented feedback on people's motivation to engage in, or continue to engage in, physical activities. In addition, augmented feedback functions as an important factor in influencing students' perceptions of ability (e.g., Fredenberg, Lee, & Solmon, 2001). And exercise psychologists have shown that augmented feedback is influential in motivating people to adhere to exercise and rehabilitation programs (e.g., Annesi, 1998; Dishman, 1993).

HOW ESSENTIAL IS AUGMENTED FEEDBACK FOR SKILL ACQUISITION?

When a researcher or practitioner considers the use of augmented feedback to facilitate skill acquisition, an important theoretical and practical question arises: *Is augmented feedback necessary for a person to learn motor skills?* The answer to this question has theoretical implications for the understanding of the nature of skill learning itself. The need, or lack of need, for augmented feedback to acquire motor skills tells us much about what characterizes the human learning system and how it functions to acquire new skills. From a practical perspective, determining the necessity for augmented feedback for skill learning can serve to guide the development and implementation of effective instructional strategies. As you will see, the answer to this question is not a simple yes or no. Instead, there are *four different answers.* Which one is appropriate depends on certain characteristics of the skill being learned and of the person learning the skill.

Augmented Feedback Can Be Essential for Skill Acquisition

In some skill learning situations, people, for various reasons, cannot use the task-intrinsic feedback to determine what they need to do to improve performance. As a result, augmented feedback is essential for learning. There are at least three types of situations in which a person may *not* be able to use important task-intrinsic feedback effectively.

First, some skill performance contexts do not make critical sensory feedback available to the person. For example, when a performer cannot see a target that he or she must hit, the performer does not have important visual feedback available. In this case, augmented feedback adds critical information that is not available from the task performance environment itself.

Second, because of injury, disease, and the like, the person does not have available the sensory pathways needed to detect critical task-intrinsic feedback for the skill he or she is learning. For these people, augmented feedback serves as a substitute for this missing information.

Third, in some situations the appropriate task-intrinsic feedback provides the necessary information and the person's sensory system is capable of detecting it, but the person cannot use the feedback. For example, a person learning to extend a knee a certain distance or to throw a ball at a certain rate of speed may not be able to determine the distance moved or the rate of speed of the throw because of lack of experience. In these situations, augmented feedback helps to make the available task-intrinsic feedback more meaningful to the performer.

Augmented Feedback May Not Be Needed for Skill Acquisition

Some motor skills *inherently provide sufficient task-intrinsic feedback,* so augmented feedback is redundant. For these types of skills, learners can use their own sensory feedback systems to determine the appropriateness of their movements and make adjustments on future attempts. An experiment by Magill, Chamberlin, and Hall (1991) provides a laboratory example of this type of situation. Participants learned a coincidence-anticipation skill in which they simulated striking a moving object, which was a series of LEDs sequentially lighting along a 281 cm long trackway. As they faced the trackway, they had to use a handheld bat to knock down a small wooden barrier directly under a target LED coincident with the lighting of the target. KR was the number of msec that they contacted the barrier before or after the target lighted. Four experiments showed that participants learned this task regardless of the number of trials on which they received KR during practice. In fact, receiving KR during practice did not lead to better learning than practice without KR.

A CLOSER LOOK

Teacher Feedback Relationships in Physical Education Classes

Silverman, Woods, and Subramaniam (1999) examined the relationship between teacher feedback and several different practice and performance characteristics for eight classes of middle school physical education. Although each teacher taught one activity, the eight classes involved a variety of activities: volleyball, soccer, badminton, basketball, and ultimate. The teachers were videotaped for two classes in a row in which motor skill was the focus of instruction. The researchers observed the videotapes and recorded characteristics of several different teacher behavior categories, including teacher feedback. Among the various results of the analysis of the data from this study was the finding that *the amount of teacher feedback given to students was significantly correlated with the amount of appropriate practice in which students engaged,* regardless of skill level. These results indicate that even though research has shown that teacher feedback and skill achievement are not highly correlated, teacher feedback has a positive impact on the students' participation in class by influencing them to engage in activity that is appropriate for helping them learn the skills that are the focus of the class instruction.

A motor skill that does not require augmented feedback to learn it has an important characteristic: *a detectable external referent* in the environment that the person can use to determine the appropriateness of an action. For the anticipation timing task in the Magill et al. experiment, the target and other LEDs were the external referents. The learner could see when the bat made contact with the barrier in comparison to when the target lighted; this enabled him or her to see the relationship between his or her own movements and the goal of those movements. It is important to note here that the learner may *not* be consciously aware of this relationship. The sensory system and the motor control system operate in these situations in a way that does not demand the person's conscious awareness of the environmental characteristics (see Magill, 1998). Thus, the enhancement of these characteristics by providing augmented feedback does not increase or speed up learning of the skill.

Practice condition characteristics also influence the need for augmented feedback. One of these characteristics is the existence of an observational learning situation, which we discussed in chapter 14. Two different types of observational learning situations can be influential. In one, the learner observes a skilled model perform the skill. For example, in an experiment by Magill and Schoenfelder-Zohdi (1996), people who observed a skilled demonstration learned a rhythmic gymnastics rope skill as well as those who received verbal KP after each trial. In the other situation, the learner observes other beginners practice. For example, Hebert and Landin (1994) showed that beginning tennis players who watched other beginners practice learned the tennis forehand volley as well as or better than beginning players who received verbal KP. In both of these situations, beginners were able to practice and improve without augmented feedback.

There is an interesting parallel between skill learning situations in which learners do not need augmented feedback and results of studies investigating the use of teacher feedback in physical education class settings. These studies consistently have shown low correlations for the relationship between teacher feedback and student achievement (e.g., Lee, Keh, & Magill, 1993; Silverman, Tyson, & Krampitz, 1991). This finding suggests that the amount and quality of teacher feedback is influential for improving the skills of beginners in sport skills class settings, but we should not see it as the most important variable. Other variables, such as observational learning, appear to be capable of precluding the need for augmented feedback. Our understanding of the extent of this influence awaits further research.

Augmented Feedback Can Enhance Skill Acquisition

There are some types of motor skills that people can learn without augmented feedback, but they will *learn them more quickly or perform them at a higher level* if they receive augmented feedback during practice. For these skills, augmented feedback is neither essential nor redundant. Instead, it *enhances the learning of these skills beyond what could be achieved without augmented feedback.*

Skills in this category include those for which improvement does occur through task-intrinsic feedback alone, but because of certain skill or learner characteristics, performance improvement reaches only a certain level. One type of skill that fits this description consists of relatively simple skills for which achievement of the performance goal is initially easy to attain. An example is a movement goal of moving as quickly as possible. Initially, a person can assess if a particular attempt was faster than a previous one. However, improvement seems to stop at a certain level of performance usually because the learner's lack of experience results in his or her decreased capability to discriminate small movement-speed differences. To improve beyond this level of performance, the person requires augmented feedback.

Another type of skill for which augmented feedback enhances learning is any complex skill that requires a person to acquire an appropriate multilimb pattern of coordination. For such skills, learners can attain a certain degree of success simply by making repeated attempts to achieve the performance goal. But this goal achievement process can be speeded up with the addition of KP. More specifically, the KP that works best is information about critical components of the coordination pattern.

The best research example of this type of skill is an experiment by Wallace and Hagler (1979). Participants learned a one-hand basketball set shot with the nondominant hand, from a distance of 3.03 m from the basket, and 45 degrees to the left side of the basket. After each shot, one group received verbal KP about errors in their stance and limb movements during the shot. Another group received only verbal encouragement after each shot. Both groups could see the outcome of each shot. Figure 15.2 depicts the results. Note that KP provided an initial boost in performance for the first fifteen trials. Then, the verbal encouragement group caught up. However, similarity in performance between the two groups lasted only about ten trials; after this point, the verbal encouragement group showed no further improvement, whereas the group receiving KP continued to improve.

Augmented Feedback Can Hinder Skill Learning

An effect of augmented feedback on skill learning that many might not expect is that it can hinder the learning process and, in some cases, actually make learning worse than it would have been otherwise. This effect is especially evident when a beginning learner becomes dependent on augmented feedback that will not be available in a test situation. Typically, the performance improvement the learner experienced during practice deteriorates in the test situation. In fact, in some situations, not only does performance deteriorate when augmented feedback is withdrawn, but the test performance is no better than if augmented feedback had not been given at all.

The characteristic of tasks that is the most likely to lead to a dependency on augmented feedback is task-intrinsic feedback that is minimal or difficult to interpret. When performing these types of tasks, people typically substitute augmented feedback for task-intrinsic feedback, because it gives them an easy-to-use guide for performing correctly.

Several types of situations can lead a person to become dependent on augmented feedback. We will discuss three later in this chapter. One concern is the presentation of erroneous augmented feedback. Another situation involves the presentation of concurrent augmented feedback, which refers to giving augmented feedback while a person performs a skill. The third occurs when augmented feedback is given too frequently during practice.

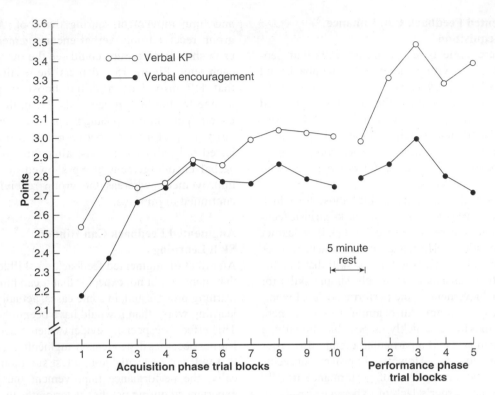

FIGURE 15.2   Results of the experiment by Wallace and Hagler showing the benefit of verbal KP for learning a basketball shooting skill. [Reprinted with permission from *Research Quarterly for Exercise and Sport, Vol. 50, No. 2,* 265–271. Copyright © 1979 by the American Alliance for Health, Physical Education, Recreation and Dance, 1900 Association Drive, Reston, VA 20191.]

THE CONTENT OF AUGMENTED FEEDBACK

In this section, we will focus on important issues concerning the content of augmented feedback, and then examine several types of augmented feedback that practitioners can use. We will consider five issues related to the content of augmented feedback. Each of these concerns some of the kinds of information augmented feedback may contain.

Information about Errors versus Correct Aspects of Performance

An often debated issue about augmented feedback content is whether the information the instructor conveys to the learner should refer to the mistakes he or she has made or those aspects of the performance

that are correct. Research evidence consistently has shown that *error information is more effective for facilitating skill learning,* especially in terms of durability and transfer capability. This evidence supports an important hypothesis, that focusing on what is done correctly while learning a skill, especially in the early stage of learning, is not sufficient by itself to produce optimal learning. Rather, the experience the person has in correcting errors by operating on error-based augmented feedback is especially important during skill acquisition to enhance performance of the skill in different environments and situations, as well as to enhance the capability to self-correct errors while performing the skill.

Another way of looking at this issue is to consider the different roles augmented feedback plays. Error information directs a person to change certain

A CLOSER LOOK

KP about Certain Features of a Skill Helps Correct Other Features

Participants in an experiment by den Brinker, Stabler, Whiting, and van Wieringen (1986) learned to perform on the slalom ski simulator, like the one illustrated in the preceding chapter in figure 14.2. Their three-part goal was to move the platform from left to right as far as possible at a specific high frequency, and with a motion that was as fluid as possible. On the basis of these performance goals, three groups received different types of information as KP after each trial: the *distance* they had moved the platform, how close they were to performing at the criterion platform movement *frequency,* and how fluid their movements were (i.e., *fluency*). All three groups practiced for four days, performing six 1.5 min trials each day, with a test trial before and after each day's practice trials.

Early in practice, the type of KP an individual received influenced only the performance measure specifically related to that feature of performing the skill. However, on the last two days of practice, KP about *distance caused people to improve all three performance features*. Thus, giving KP about one performance feature led to improvement not only of that one, but also of the two other performance features.

performance characteristics; this in turn facilitates skill acquisition. On the other hand, information indicating that the person performed certain characteristics correctly tells the person that he or she is on track in learning the skill and encourages the person to keep trying. When we consider augmented feedback from this perspective, we see that whether this feedback should be about errors or about correct aspects of performance depends on the goal of the information. Error-related information works better to facilitate skill acquisition, whereas information about correct performance serves better to motivate the person to continue.

KR versus KP

Two relevant questions concerning the comparison of the use of KR and KP in skill learning situations are these: Do practitioners use one of these forms of augmented feedback more than the other? Do they influence skill learning in similar or different ways?

Most of the evidence addressing the first question comes from the study of physical education teachers in actual class situations. The best example is a study by Fishman and Tobey (1978). Although their study was conducted many years ago, it is representative of more recent studies, and it involves the most extensive sampling of teachers and classes of any study that has investigated this question. Fishman and Tobey observed teachers in eighty-one classes

teaching a variety of physical activities. The results showed that the teachers overwhelmingly gave KP (94 percent of the time) more than KR.

An answer to the second question, concerning the relative effectiveness of KR and KP, is more difficult to provide because of the lack of sufficient and conclusive evidence from research investigating this question. The following examples of experiments provide some insight into a reasonable answer.

Two of the experiments suggest that KP is better than KR to facilitate motor skill learning. Kernodle and Carlton (1992) compared KR with videotape replays and verbally presented technique statements as KP in an experiment in which participants practiced throwing a soft, spongy ball as far as possible with the nondominant arm. KR was presented as the distance of the throw for each practice trial. The results showed that KP led to better throwing technique and distance than KR. Zubiaur, Oña, and Delgado (1999) made a similar conclusion in a study in which university students with no previous volleyball experience practiced the overhead serve in volleyball. KP was specific information about the most important error to correct as it related to action either before hitting or in hitting the ball. KR referred to the outcome of the hit in terms of the ball's spatial precision, rotation, and flight. The results indicated that KP was more influential for learning the serve.

However, a study by Silverman, Woods, and Subramaniam (1999) provided evidence for the benefit of both KR and KP in terms of how each related to how often students in physical education classes would engage in successful and unsuccessful practice trials during a class. They observed eight middle school teachers teaching two classes each in various sport-related activities. The results indicated that teacher feedback as KR and as KP showed relatively high correlations with the frequency of students engaging in successful practice trials (.64 and .67, respectively).

These studies indicate that *both KR and KP can be valuable* for skill learning. With this in mind, consider the following hypotheses about conditions in which each of these forms of augmented feedback would be beneficial. *KR will be beneficial for skill learning* for at least four reasons: (1) Learners often use KR to confirm their own assessments of the task-intrinsic feedback, even though it may be redundant with task-intrinsic feedback. (2) Learners may need KR because they cannot determine the outcome of performing a skill on the basis of the available task-intrinsic feedback. (3) Learners often use KR to motivate themselves to continue practicing the skill. (4) Practitioners may want to provide only KR in order to establish a discovery learning practice environment in which learners are encouraged to engage in problem-solving activity by making trial and error as the primary means of solving the problem of how to perform a skill to achieve its action goal.

On the other hand, *KP can be especially beneficial* when (1) skills must be performed according to specified movement characteristics, such as gymnastics stunts or springboard dives; (2) specific movement components of skills that require complex coordination must be improved or corrected; (3) the goal of the action is a kinematic, kinetic, or specific muscle activity; (4) KR is redundant with the task-intrinsic feedback.

Qualitative versus Quantitative Information

Augmented feedback can be qualitative, quantitative, or both. If the augmented feedback involves a numerical value related to the magnitude of some

When giving verbal KP, it is important to provide information that is meaningful to the person to whom it is given.

performance characteristic, it is called **quantitative augmented feedback.** In contrast, **qualitative augmented feedback** is information referring to the quality of the performance characteristic without regard for the numerical values associated with it.

For *verbal augmented feedback,* it is easy to distinguish these types of information in performance situations. For example, a therapist helping a patient to increase gait speed could give that patient qualitative information about the latest attempt in statements such as these: "That was faster than the last time"; "That was much better"; or "You need to bend your knee more." A physical education teacher teaching a student a tennis serve could tell the student that a particular serve was "good," or "long," or could say something like this: "You made contact with the ball too far in front of you." On the other hand, the therapist could give the patient quantitative verbal augmented feedback using these words: "That time you walked 3 seconds faster than the last time," or, "You need to bend your knee 5 more degrees." The teacher could give quantitative feedback to the tennis student like this: "The serve was 6 centimeters too long," or "You made contact with the ball 10 centimeters too far in front of you."

Practitioners also can give quantitative and qualitative information in *nonverbal forms of augmented feedback.* For example, the therapist could give qualitative information to the patient we have described by letting him or her hear a tone when the walking speed exceeded that of the previous attempt or when the knee flexion achieved a target amount. The teacher could give the tennis student qualitative information in the form of a computer display that used a moving stick figure to show the kinematic characteristics of his or her serving motion. Those teaching motor skills often give nonverbally presented quantitative information in combination with qualitative forms. For example, the therapist could show a patient a computer-based graphic representation of his or her leg movement while walking along, displaying numerical values of the walking speeds associated with each attempt or the degree of knee flexion observed on each attempt. We could describe similar examples for the tennis student.

How do these two types of augmented feedback information influence skill learning? Although the traditional view is that quantitative augmented feedback is preferred, results from an experiment by Magill and Wood (1986) suggest a different conclusion. Each participant practiced moving his or her arm through a series of wooden barriers to produce a specific six-segment movement pattern. Each segment had its own criterion movement time, which participants had to learn. Performance for the first sixty trials showed no difference between qualitative and quantitative forms of KR. However, during the final sixty trials and on the twenty no-KR retention trials, quantitative KR resulted in better performance than qualitative.

These results suggest that people in the early stage of learning give attention primarily to the qualitative information, even when they have quantitative information available. The advantage of this attention focus is that the qualitative information provides an easier way to make a first approximation of the required movement. Put another way, this information allows learners to perform an action that is "in the ballpark" of what they need to do, which, as we discussed in chapter 12, is an important goal for the first stage of learning. After they achieve this "ballpark" capability, quantitative information becomes more valuable to them,

because it enables them to refine characteristics of performing the skill that lead to more consistent and efficient achievement of the action goal.

Augmented Feedback Based on Error Size

A question that has distinct practical appeal is this: How large an error should a performer make before the instructor or therapist gives augmented feedback? To many, it seems reasonable to provide feedback only when errors are large enough to warrant attention. This approach suggests that in many skill learning situations, practitioners develop **performance bandwidths** that establish performance error tolerance limits specifying when they will or will not give augmented feedback. When a person's performance is acceptable (i.e., within the tolerance limits of the bandwidth) the practitioner does not give feedback. But if the performance is not acceptable (i.e., the amount or type of error is outside the bandwidth) the practitioner gives feedback.

Research supports the effectiveness of the performance bandwidth approach. For example, in the first reported experiment investigating this procedure, Sherwood (1988) had participants practice a rapid elbow-flexion task with a movement-time goal of 200 msec. One group received KR about their movement-time error after every trial, regardless of the amount of error (i.e., 0 percent bandwidth). Two other groups received KR only when

---

quantitative augmented feedback   augmented feedback that includes a numerical value related to the magnitude of a performance characteristic (e.g., the speed of a pitched baseball).

qualitative augmented feedback   augmented feedback that is descriptive in nature (e.g., using such terms as *good, long*), and indicates the quality of performance.

performance bandwidth   in the context of providing augmented feedback, a range of acceptable performance error; augmented feedback is given only when the amount of error is greater than this range.

A CLOSER LOOK

Quantitative versus Qualitative Augmented Feedback and the Performance Bandwidth Technique

Cauraugh, Chen, and Radlo (1993) had subjects practice a timing task in which they had to press a sequence of three keys in 500 msec. Participants in one group received quantitative KR about their movement times (MT) when MT was *outside* a 10 percent performance bandwidth. A second group, in the reverse of that condition, received quantitative KR only when MT was *inside* the 10 percent performance bandwidth. Two additional groups had participants "yoked" to individual participants in the outside and inside bandwidth conditions. Members of these two groups received KR on the same trials their "yoked" counterparts did. This procedure provided a way to have two conditions with the same frequency of augmented feedback, while allowing a comparison between bandwidth and no-bandwidth conditions.

In terms of KR frequency, those in the outside bandwidth condition received quantitative KR on 25 percent of the sixty practice trials; those in the inside condition received KR on 65 percent of the trials. The interesting feature of this difference is that the remaining trials for both groups were implicitly qualitative KR trials, because when they received no KR, the participants knew that their performance was "good" or "not good." The retention test performance results showed that the two bandwidth conditions did not differ, but both yielded better learning than the no-bandwidth conditions. These results show that establishing performance bandwidths as the basis for providing quantitative KR yields an interplay between quantitative and qualitative KR that facilitates skill learning.

---

their error exceeded bandwidths of 5 percent and 10 percent of the goal movement time. The results of a no-KR retention test showed that the 10 percent bandwidth condition resulted in the least amount of movement time variability (i.e., variable error), whereas the 0 percent condition resulted in the most variable error. Other researchers have replicated these results (e.g., Lee, White, & Carnahan, 1990; Cauraugh, Chen, & Radlo, 1993).

A practical issue concerning the use of the bandwidth technique relates to the instructions provided about the bandwidth procedure. This issue is relevant because when the learners receive no augmented feedback about their performance, the implicit message is that it was "correct." There is an instruction-related question here: Is it important that the learner explicitly be told this information, or will the learner implicitly learn this information during practice? According to the results of an experiment by Butler, Reeve, and Fischman (1996), the bandwidth technique leads to better learning when the participants know in advance that not receiving KR means they are essentially "correct."

Erroneous Augmented Feedback

One of the ways augmented feedback hinders learning is by providing people with erroneous information. While this statement may seem unnecessary because it makes such common sense, the statement gains importance when it is considered in the context of practicing a skill that can be learned *without* augmented feedback. In this skill learning situation, augmented feedback is redundant with the information available from task-intrinsic feedback. As a result, most people would expect that to provide augmented feedback would be a waste of time because it would not influence the learner. But research evidence shows that this is not the case, because even when augmented feedback is redundant information, beginners will use it rather than ignore it.

The first evidence of this type of effect was reported by Buekers, Magill, and Hall (1992). Participants practiced an anticipation timing task similar to the one used by Magill, Chamberlin, and Hall (1991), which was described earlier in this chapter as a task for which KR is not needed to learn the task.

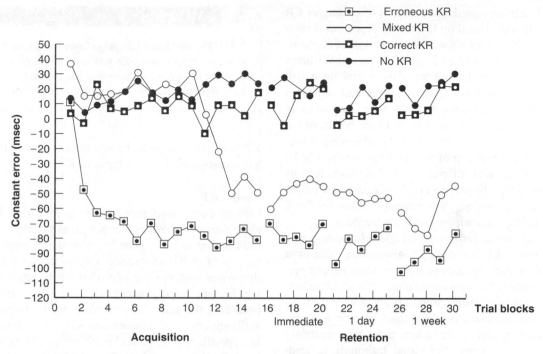

FIGURE 15.3 Results of the experiment by Buekers et al., showing the effects of erroneous KR compared to no KR and correct KR for learning an anticipation timing skill. Note that participants in the mixed-KR group received correct KR for their first fifty trials and then received erroneous KR for their last twenty-five practice trials. [From Buekers, M. J., Magill, R. A., & Hall, K. G. (1992). The effect of erroneous knowledge of results on skill acquisition when augmented information is redundant. *Quarterly Journal of Experimental Psychology, 44 (A),* 105–117. Reprinted by permission of The Experimental Psychology Society.]

In the Buekers et al. experiment, three of four groups received KR after every trial. The KR was displayed on a computer monitor and indicated to the participants the direction and amount of their timing error. For one of these groups, KR was always correct. But for another group, KR was always erroneous by indicating that performance on a trial was 100 msec later than it actually was. The third KR group received correct KR for the first fifty trials, but then received the erroneous KR for the last twenty-five trials. A fourth group did not receive KR during practice.

The results (figure 15.3) showed two important findings. First, the correct-KR and the no-KR groups did not differ during the practice or the retention trials, which confirmed previous findings that augmented feedback is not needed to learn this skill. Second, the erroneous KR information led participants to learn to perform according to the KR

rather than according to the task-intrinsic feedback. This latter result suggested that the *participants used KR, even though it was erroneous information.* Even more impressive was that the erroneous KR influenced the group that had received correct KR for fifty trials and then was switched to the erroneous KR. After the switch, this group began to perform similarly to the group that had received the incorrect KR for all the practice trials. In addition, the erroneous information not only influenced performance when it was available but also influenced retention performance one day and one week later on no-KR. A subsequent experiment (McNevin, Magill, & Buekers, 1994) demonstrated that the erroneous KR also influenced performance on a no-KR transfer test in which participants were required to respond to a faster or slower speed than they practiced.

The preceding demonstrations of erroneous KR effects were based on laboratory tasks, but similar results have been shown for sports skills. For example, an experiment by Ford, Hodges, and Williams (2007) had skilled soccer players kicking a ball to a target, which required that the ball achieve a specific height during its flight. One group of players received erroneous KR about the height of the ball's flight during each kick by observing a prerecorded video clip of a kicked ball that reached a height that was different from their own. Results showed that the players eventually based the height of their kicks on the erroneous video feedback rather than on their own sensory feedback.

Why would erroneous KR affect learning a skill for which KR is redundant information? The most likely reason appears to be that when people perform skills, they rely on augmented feedback to help them deal with their uncertainty about what the task-intrinsic feedback is telling them. For the anticipation timing and soccer kicking tasks, the uncertainty may exist because the visual task-intrinsic feedback is difficult to consciously observe, interpret, and use. Evidence for an uncertainty-based explanation has been demonstrated in experiments by Buekers, Magill, and Sneyers (1994), and Buekers and Magill (1995).

The important message for practitioners here is that people, especially those who are in the early stage of skill learning, will use augmented feedback when it is available, whether it is correct or not. Because of their uncertainty about how to use or interpret task-intrinsic feedback, beginners rely on augmented feedback as a critical source of information on which to base how they will move corrections on future trials. As a result, instructors need to be certain that they provide correct augmented feedback.

TYPES OF KNOWLEDGE OF PERFORMANCE

Most of the research on which we base our knowledge of augmented feedback and skill learning comes from laboratory experiments in which researchers gave KR to participants. Although most of the conclusions from that research also apply to

LAB LINKS

Lab 15a in the Online Learning Center Lab Manual provides an opportunity for you to develop a priority list of KP statements that you might give as feedback to people learning or relearning a motor skill.

KP, it is useful to look at some of the research that has investigated different types of KP.

Verbal KP

One of the reasons practitioners give verbal KP more than verbal KR is that KP gives people more information to help them improve the movement aspects of skill performance. One of the problems that arises with the use of verbal KP is determining the appropriate content: what to tell the person practicing the skill. This problem occurs because skills are typically complex and KP usually relates to a specific feature of skill performance. The challenge for the instructor or therapist, then, is selecting the appropriate features of the performance on which to base KP.

Selecting the skill component for KP. The first thing the practitioner must do is perform a *skill analysis* of the skill being practiced. This means identifying the various component parts of the skill. Then, he or she should prioritize each part in terms of how critical that part is for performing the skill. Prioritize by listing the most critical part first, then the second most critical, and so on. To determine which part is most critical, decide which part of the skill absolutely must be done properly for the person to achieve the skills action goal. For example, for the skill of throwing a dart at a target, the most critical component is looking at the target. This part is the most critical because even if a beginner did all other parts of the skill correctly (which would be unlikely), there is a very low chance that he or she would throw the dart accurately without looking at the target. In this case, then, looking at the target would be first on the skill analysis priority list, and would be the first part of the skill assessed in determining what to give KP about. (For two examples

A CLOSER LOOK

An Example of Basing Verbal KP on a Skill Analysis

In an experiment by Weeks and Kordus (1998), twelve-year-old boys who had no previous experience in soccer practiced a soccer throw-in. The participants' goal was to perform throw-ins as accurately as possible to a target on the floor. The distance to the target was 75 percent of each participant's maximum throwing distance. They received verbal KP on one of eight aspects of technique, which the researchers referred to as "form." Which aspect of form each participant received was based on the primary form problem identified for a throw-in. The researchers constructed a list of eight "form cues" on the basis of a skill analysis of the throw-in and used this list to give verbal KP. The eight form cues were these:

1. The feet, hips, knees, and shoulders should be aimed at the target, feet shoulder width apart.
2. The back should be arched at the beginning of the throw.
3. The grip should look like a "W" with the thumbs together on the back of the ball.
4. The ball should start behind the head at the beginning of the throw.
5. The arms should go over the head during the throw and finish by being aimed at the target.
6. There should be no spin on the ball during its flight.
7. The ball should be released in front of the head.
8. Feet should remain on the ground.

---

of research reporting the use and benefit of a skill analysis approach to selecting skill components as the basis for verbal KP, see Magill & Schoenfelder-Zohdi, 1996; Weeks & Kordus, 1998).

Descriptive and prescriptive KP.   After determining which aspect of the skill about which to give KP, the practitioner needs to decide the content of the statement to make to the learner. There are *two types of verbal KP statements*. A **descriptive KP** statement simply describes the error the performer has made. The other type, **prescriptive KP,** not only identifies the error, but also tells the person what to do to correct it. For example, if you tell a person, "You moved your right foot too soon," you describe only the problem. However, if you say, "You need to move your right foot at the same time as you move your right arm," you also give prescriptive information about what the person needs to do to correct the problem.

Which type of verbal KP better facilitates learning? The answer is that it varies with the stage of learning of the person practicing the skill. For example, the descriptive KP statement, "You moved your right foot too soon," would help a beginner only if he or she knew the actual time at which the right foot was supposed to move. Thus, descriptive

KP statements are useful to help people improve performance only after they have learned what they need to do to make a correction. This suggests that *prescriptive KP statements are more helpful for beginners. For the more advanced performer, a descriptive KP statement often will suffice.*

Video Recordings as Augmented Feedback

The availability and use of video recordings as augmented feedback argues for the need for practitioners to know about how to use them effectively. It is common to find Internet sites and articles in professional journals that offer guidelines and suggestions for the use of video replays as feedback (e.g., Bertram, Marteniuk, & Guadagnoli, 2007; Franks &

---

descriptive KP   a verbal knowledge of performance (KP) statement that describes only the error a person has made during the performance of a skill.

prescriptive KP   a verbal knowledge of performance (KP) statement that describes errors made during the performance of a skill and states (i.e., prescribes) what needs to be done to correct them.

A CLOSER LOOK

Skilled Athletes Progress through Distinct Stages As They Learn to Use Video Replays

A study by Hebert, Landin, and Menickelli (1998) investigated the use of video replays as a part of the practice sessions for skilled female tennis players who needed to improve their attacking shots. Although the players who watched the video replays improved more than the players who did not, the athletes required a period of time to learn to use the replays effectively. According to the researchers' field notes and recordings of the athletes while they watched the videotapes, this period of time involved a progression through four stages in their use of the replays:

1. Players familiarized themselves with observing themselves on video. They made general comments about how they personally looked on videotape as well as about their playing techniques.

2. Players began to recognize specific technical errors in their attack shots.

3. Players became more analytical as they made direct connections between their technique and the outcome of that technique.

4. Players began to use their observations of replays to indicate corrections they should make to their technique errors. They indicated awareness of the key aspects of their performance that related to successfully hitting the attack shot.

Maile, 1991; Jambor & Weekes, 1995; Trinity & Annesi, 1996). However, very little empirical research exists that establishes the effectiveness of video replays as an aid for skill acquisition. In fact, the most recent extensive review of the research literature related to the use of video recordings as a source of augmented feedback in skill learning situations was published many years ago (Rothstein & Arnold, 1976). One likely reason why more recent reviews have not been published is that the research reported since that review has supported its general conclusions rather than establish different ones.

The most significant conclusion from that review was that the critical factor for determining the effectiveness of video replays as an instructional aid was the *skill level of the learner rather than the type of activity*. For beginners to benefit from video replays, they require the assistance of an instructor to point out critical information. Advanced performers do not appear to need instructor aid as frequently, although discussions with skilled athletes suggest they often receive greater benefit from observing replays when they receive some form of attention-directing instructions, such as verbal cues and checklists.

A good example of research that demonstrated the benefit of having an instructor point out what the observer of the video replay should look for was reported in an experiment that compared video replay as KP to verbal KP and no KP for teaching moderately skilled golfers to hit a golf ball for distance and accuracy (Guadagnoli, Holcomb, & Davis 2002). Three groups engaged in 90 min training sessions on each of four days: a control group, which the researchers called the "self-guided" group, practiced without any KP but could hit as many golf balls as they wanted; a verbal KP group received feedback from a PGA teaching professional throughout each session. The video KP group saw video replays of their swings throughout the sessions as well as getting the verbal KP from the teaching professional. The goal was to hit golf balls with a 7-iron as far as possible along a straight line. Performance was assessed by several distance and accuracy measures. Figure 15.4 shows the results for the "accuracy distance" measure, which was calculated by subtracting the distance a ball was off the straight target line from the total distance. This result, which is representative of the other measures, indicates the effectiveness of the video replay added to the verbal KP group for learning the golf swing: the video KP group performed better than the other two groups on a retention test given two weeks after the end of the training sessions (i.e., two-week

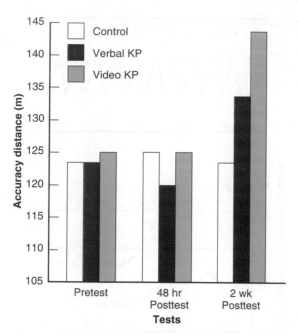

FIGURE 15.4 Results of the experiment by Guadagnoli et al. (2002) showing that video replays with verbal KP (video KP) led to better long-term retention performance than no KP (control) and verbal KP for learning to hit a golf ball for distance and accuracy. The performance measure "accuracy distance" is the total distance a ball traveled minus the distance from the target straight line. [Data from figure 2 (p. 990) in Guadagnoli, M., Holcomb, W., and Davis, M. (2002). The efficacy of video feedback for learning the golf swing. *Journal of Sports Sciences, 20,* 615–622.]

posttest). An interesting characteristic of this study demonstrates the importance of augmented feedback in relation to the amount of practice for learning of a skill. Because the golfers were not limited to hitting a specified number of balls during each training session, the three groups differed in the number of balls hit during training. Interestingly, the control group hit the most practice balls, but performed worse than the other two groups. The video KP group hit the fewest practice balls but learned the skill better than the other two groups.

Research evidence also establishes that video replays *transmit certain types of performance-related information more effectively than other types.* One of the best examples of an experiment that supports this conclusion was one conducted

many years ago by Selder and Del Rolan (1979). They compared videotape replays and verbal augmented feedback (in the form of KP) in a study in which twelve-to-thirteen-year-old girls were learning to perform a balance beam routine. All the girls used a checklist to critically analyze their own performance after each trial. One group used verbal KP to complete the checklist; another group completed the checklist after viewing videotape replays of each trial. At the end of six weeks of practice, the videotape group scored significantly higher on the routine than the verbal KP group. More important, when each factor of the total routine score was evaluated, the videotape group scored significantly higher on only four of the eight factors: precision, execution, amplitude, and orientation and direction. The two groups did not differ on the other four: rhythm, elegance, coordination, and lightness of jumping and tumbling.

The results of this study suggest that video replay facilitates the learning of those performance features that performers can readily observe and determine how to correct on the basis of what they see on the video replay. However, for performance features that are difficult to visually discern, video replay is no more effective than verbal KP.

Movement Kinematics as Augmented Feedback

With the widespread availability of computer software capable of providing sophisticated kinematic analysis of movement, it has become increasingly common to find sport skill instruction and physical rehabilitation situations in which people can view graphically presented kinematic representations of their performances as a form of feedback. Unfortunately, as was the case with the use of video replays, there is little research evidence that provides definitive answers to questions concerning the effectiveness of this means of providing augmented feedback. However, the few studies that have been reported provide some insight into the use of this form of augmented feedback.

One of the first studies to investigate the use of movement kinematics did not involve a computer and was carried out many years ago. This study is important because it illustrates the historical interest in this type of feedback, it involved a real-world training situation, and it exemplifies the positive effect that kinematic information can have on skill learning. Lindahl (1945) investigated the methods used to train industrial machine operator trainees to precisely and quickly cut thin disks of tungsten with a machine that required fast, accurate, and rhythmic coordination of the hands and feet. The traditional approach to training for this job was a trial-and-error method. To assess an alternative method, Lindahl created a mechanism that would make a paper tracing of the machine operator's foot movement pattern during the cutting of each disk. During training, the trainers showed the trainees charts illustrating the correct foot action (see the top portion of figure 15.5), and periodically showed them tracings of their own foot action. The results (see the bottom portion of figure 15.5) indicated that this training method based on movement kinematic information as augmented feedback enabled the trainees to achieve production performance levels in eleven weeks, compared to the five months required by trainees who used the traditional trial-and-error method. In addition, the trainees reduced their percentage of broken cutting wheels to almost zero in twelve weeks, a level not achieved by those trained with the traditional method in less than nine months.

A comprehensive series of experiments reported by Swinnen and his colleagues serve as good examples of more recent laboratory research (Swinnen et al., 1990; Swinnen, Walter, Lee, & Serrien, 1993). Participants in these experiments practiced a bimanual coordination task that required them to simultaneously move two levers, but with each lever requiring a different spatial-temporal movement pattern. Kinematic information was presented as augmented feedback in the form of the angular displacement for each arm superimposed over criterion displacements. In several experiments, the kinematic augmented feedback was compared with various other forms of augmented feedback. The results consistently demonstrated the effectiveness of the use of the displacement information.

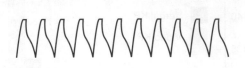

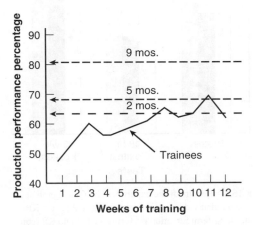

FIGURE 15.5 The upper panel illustrates the foot action required by the machine operator to produce an acceptable disk cut in the experiment by Lindahl. The graph at the bottom indicates the production performance achieved by the trainees using graphic information during twelve weeks of training. The dashed lines indicate the levels of performance achieved by other workers after two, five, and nine months of experience. [From Lindahl, L. G. (1945). Movement analysis as an industrial training method. *Journal of Applied Psychology, 29,* 420–436, American Psychological Association.]

An experiment by Wood, Gallagher, Martino, and Ross (1992) provides a good example of the use of graphically displayed movement kinematics for learning a sports skill. Participants practiced hitting a golf shot with a 5-iron. A commercially marketed golf computer monitored the velocity, displacement, and trajectory path of each swing as the head of the club passed over light sensors on the platform from which the ball was hit. This information was then displayed on a monitor. One group saw a template of an optimum pattern along with the kinematics; a second group did not see this template. A third group received the same kinematic information

A CLOSER LOOK

A Case Study of the Use of Center of Gravity as Augmented Feedback for Balance Training for Stroke Patients

A form of augmented feedback that has been used for balance training in physical therapy contexts is the visual presentation on a computer monitor of a person's center of gravity. A case study reported by Simmons and associates (1998) is an interesting example of the effectiveness of this type of augmented feedback in a clinical setting.

The patient: A seventy-four-year-old poststroke, hemiparetic male with whom therapists were working to help him regain balance control while standing.

Balance training therapy: Following a pretest, the patient engaged in three balance training therapy sessions a week for four weeks. During each therapy session the patient stood on two force plates while looking at a computer monitor placed at eye level. On the monitor, he could see a small white dot superimposed on a white cross, which indicated an appropriate center of gravity while standing. During each

therapy session, a clear plastic template marked with a circular pattern of eight alphabetic letters was placed on the monitor. A verbal command to the patient indicated that he should initiate a weight shift that would cause the white dot to move from the center and hit the target letter and then return the dot back to the center cross. The patient did this for six 1 min intervals with a 45 sec rest between intervals. A posttest followed at the end of the 4 wk training period, and a retention test was given two weeks later.

Results: One of the tests simulated a sudden loss of balance, which involved a quick (400 msec) 5.7 cm forward and backward movement of the force plates on which the patient was standing. The patient's performance on this motor control test during the 2 wk retention test showed a 60 percent improvement for response strength of the affected leg, and a marked shift in balance onto the affected leg in the patient's attempts to regain balance.

---

verbally in the form of numbers. A fourth group received no augmented feedback. On a retention test given one week later without augmented feedback, the group that had observed the graphic presentation of the swing kinematics along with the optimum pattern template performed best.

Another type of kinematic related information that has been effectively used as augmented feedback is a person's *center of pressure (COP)*. This biomechanical type of information is most commonly used as a type of augmented feedback for people learning or improving static and dynamic balance skills. For example, a study by Taube, Leukel, and Gollhofer (2008) investigated the use of a handheld laser pointed at a target on a wall to provide augmented visual feedback of each participant's COP to assist them in maintaining upright standing balance on both rigid and unstable surfaces. Results showed that participants maintained better balance stability when they used the laser pointer device than when they did not.

Biofeedback as Augmented Feedback

The term **biofeedback** refers to an augmented form of task-intrinsic feedback related to the activity of physiological processes, such as heart rate, blood pressure, muscle activity, and the like. Several forms of biofeedback have been used in motor skill learning situations. The most common is *electromyographic (EMG) biofeedback,* which provides information about muscle activity.

EMG biofeedback has been commonly used in physical rehabilitation settings and research. Although researchers continue to debate its effectiveness there is general agreement that it can benefit motor skill learning. (For a review and critical

---

biofeedback   a type of augmented feedback that provides information about physiological processes through the use of instrumentation (e.g., EMG biofeedback).

analysis of the use of EMG biofeedback in physical therapy see Huang, Wolf, & He, 2006). The following two research examples illustrate some of the positive results researchers have reported for the use of EMG as a source of augmented feedback. An experiment by Brucker and Bulaeva (1996) used EMG biofeedback with long-term cervical spinal cord–injured people to determine if it would help them increase their voluntary EMG responses from the triceps during elbow extension. Results indicated that participants who experienced only one 45 min treatment session significantly increased their triceps EMG activity; and those who experienced additional treatment sessions demonstrated even further increases.

The purpose of a study by Intiso and colleagues (1994) was to determine the effectiveness of EMG biofeedback to help poststroke patients overcome foot drop of the paretic limb during the swing phase of walking. Some patients received EMG biofeedback during their physical therapy, whereas others did not. A unique characteristic of this study was the use of gait analysis to assess foot drop during the gait cycle. Results of this analysis demonstrated that the EMG biofeedback intervention led to better recovery than physical therapy without the biofeedback.

A unique type of biofeedback was used by Chollet, Micallef, and Rabischong (1988) for swimmers. The researchers developed swimming paddles that would provide information to enable highly skilled swimmers to maintain their optimal velocity and number of arm cycles in a training session. The swimming paddles contained force sensors and sound generators that transmitted an audible signal to transmitters in a swimmer's cap. The sensors were set at a desired water-propulsion-force threshold; when the swimmer reached this threshold, the paddles produced a sound audible to the swimmer. The results showed that this device helped swimmers maintain their stroke count and swimming speed when they otherwise would have found it decreasing through the course of a long-distance practice session.

Finally, another type of biofeedback has been applied in the training of competitive rifle shooters (Daniels & Landers, 1981). Heartbeat biofeedback was presented audibly to help these athletes learn to squeeze the rifle trigger between heartbeats, which is a characteristic of elite shooters.

In general, research evidence has supported the effectiveness of biofeedback as a means of facilitating motor skill learning. However, debate continues concerning the specific situations in which the use of biofeedback is an effective and preferred form of augmented feedback, especially in physical rehabilitation situations (e.g., Moreland & Thomson, 1994; Moreland, Thomson, & Fuoco, 1998).

An additional concern about the use of biofeedback as augmented feedback is the tendency for people to become dependent on it to help them perform the skill. The result of this dependency is that when they must perform the skill without biofeedback, their performance level decreases. This concern is not unique to the use of biofeedback but to all types of augmented feedback. We will address this issue, along with strategies to overcome the problem, in the last section of this chapter in which the frequency of presenting augmented feedback will be discussed.

TIMING ISSUES RELATED TO AUGMENTED FEEDBACK

Finally, three important questions arise about the timing of giving augmented feedback. To continue with the example in which you are teaching a person to play golf, one question is this: Should you give augmented feedback while the person swings, after he or she has hit the ball, or both times? If you give feedback after the person hits the ball, the second question arises: How soon after the person's hitting of the ball should you give augmented feedback? The third question concerns whether you should give augmented feedback every time the person hits the ball, or only a few times during the practice session.

Concurrent and Terminal Augmented Feedback

Is it better to give augmented feedback while a person is performing a skill, in what is known as **concurrent augmented feedback** or at the end of a practice attempt, in what we call **terminal augmented feedback?** Unfortunately, a search through the motor learning research literature suggests that

A CLOSER LOOK

Concurrent Augmented Feedback Can Take Various Forms

When augmented feedback is given concurrently, it typically enhances task-intrinsic feedback while a person is performing a skill. The following examples illustrate the various forms that this enhancement can take.

Activity Characteristic	Activity Example	Concurrent Augmented Feedback
Continuous movement accuracy	Steering in a car simulator through a narrow, winding street	Continuous visible or audible signal when vehicle is inside or outside the street boundaries
Move a specific amount of distance for a period of time	Knee-extension device that measures range of motion	Continuous curve on computer monitor showing knee angle
Activate specific muscle	Walking	Continuous audible signal when the target muscle is activated

there is no unequivocal answer to this question. However, a guideline emerges from that literature that can help us answer the question. Terminal augmented feedback can be effective in almost any skill learning situation, although the teacher or therapist must consider the nature of its effect in light of our discussion earlier in this chapter of the four different effects augmented feedback can have on skill learning. Concurrent augmented feedback, as you will see in the following sections of this discussion, seems to be most effective when the task-intrinsic feedback is difficult to use to determine how to perform the skill or improve performance. Because most of the discussion thus far in this chapter has involved terminal augmented feedback, the focus of this section will be on concurrent augmented feedback.

Effects of concurrent augmented feedback on learning. Research evidence has shown two general types of effects for the use of concurrent augmented feedback in skill learning situations. The more common is *a negative learning effect.* Although performance improves very well during practice when the feedback is available, it declines on retention or transfer trials during which the augmented feedback is removed. In these situations, the concurrent augmented feedback influences learners to direct their

attention away from the critical task-intrinsic feedback and toward the augmented feedback. The result is that they substitute the information derived from augmented feedback for the important information they should acquire from task-intrinsic feedback. The result is that the augmented feedback becomes an integral part of what is learned, and therefore necessary for future performance.

Two experiments, one involving a continuous skill and the other involving a discrete skill, provide examples of research that has demonstrated this negative learning effect. Verschueren, Swinnen, Dom, and DeWeerdt (1997) had elderly healthy adults and Parkinson's patients practice the continuous bimanual coordination task described in chapters 11 and 12 (see figure 11.4). The task required that they learn to move two levers simultaneously for 20 sec in such a way that they would draw ellipses

concurrent augmented feedback   augmented feedback that is provided while a person is performing a skill or making a movement.

terminal augmented feedback   augmented feedback that is provided after a person has completed the performance of a skill or a movement.

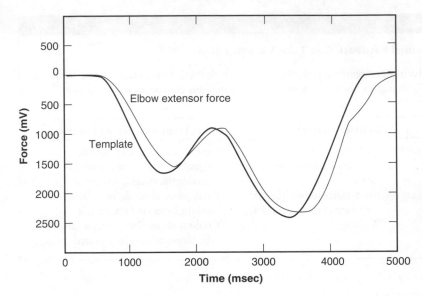

FIGURE 15.6 An example from the Vander Linden et al. experiment of what a participant saw during and/or after a trial on which they attempted to produce a 5 sec elbow-extension force trace that replicated as closely as possible the template trace. [Reprinted from Vander Linden, D. W. et al. (1993). "The effect of frequency of kinetic feedback on learning an isometric force production task in nondisabled subjects," *Physical Therapy, 73,* 79–87 with permission of the American Physical Therapy Association.]

on the computer monitor. During the practice trials, participants saw on the monitor the drawings produced as they moved their arms. The results showed that participants in both groups made considerable improvement during practice when the concurrent visual augmented feedback was available. But their performance dropped dramatically on retention test trials without the augmented feedback.

The negative learning effect has also been demonstrated for the learning of a discrete task. Vander Linden, Cauraugh, and Greene (1993) compared concurrent and terminal augmented feedback for learning a 5 sec isometric elbow-extension force production task, which is illustrated in figure 15.6. Participants received augmented feedback by seeing the force produced during the performance of the task on each trial. One group received this feedback concurrently. Two other groups received this feedback after they completed performing the task. One of these two groups saw this information after every trial; the other saw it after every other trial. During the practice trials, the concurrent augmented feedback group performed the task better than the two terminal groups. However, forty-eight hours later on a retention test with no augmented feedback, the concurrent group's performance declined to a level that was the poorest of the three groups.

The second general effect is that concurrent augmented feedback *enhances skill learning.* A variety of situations have produced this effect. Some of these are the training of flight skills for airplane pilots (e.g., Lintern, 1991), the rehabilitation of motor skills in physical therapy (e.g., Intiso et al., 1994), the activation of specific muscles or muscle groups (e.g., Brucker & Bulaeva, 1996), and the learning of certain types of bimanual coordination laboratory tasks (e.g., Swinnen et al., 1993). In these experiments, concurrent augmented feedback enhanced relevant features of the task-intrinsic feedback that were difficult to discern without the enhancement. Because most of these experiments are described elsewhere in this book, there is no need to describe them here.

Predicting learning effects of concurrent augmented feedback. Two related hypotheses have been proposed to help us better understand how to predict when concurrent augmented feedback will have a positive or negative effect on learning. First, Annett (1959, 1969, 1970) stated that augmented feedback should be considered in terms of its information value, which he related to the "informativeness" of the task-intrinsic feedback and the augmented feedback. When the information value

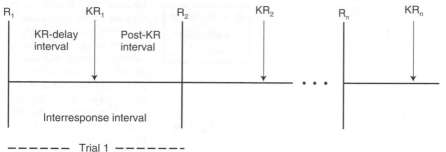

FIGURE 15.7 Intervals of time related to KR during the acquisition of a skill.

of task-intrinsic feedback is low, but the information value of the augmented feedback is high, concurrent augmented feedback will most likely lead to a dependency on the augmented feedback.

Lintern and his colleagues (Lintern, 1991; Lintern, Roscoe, & Sivier, 1990) added another dimension to Annett's hypothesis by proposing that practicing with augmented feedback will benefit learning to the extent that the feedback sensitizes the learner to properties or relationships in the task that specify how the system being learned can be controlled. This means that *for concurrent augmented feedback to be effective, it must facilitate the learning of the critical characteristics or relationships in the task as specified by the task-intrinsic feedback.* Negative learning effects will result when the augmented feedback distracts attention away from these features. But positive learning effects will result when the augmented feedback directs attention to these features.

THE KR-DELAY AND POST-KR INTERVALS

The second timing issue related to augmented feedback concerns when the feedback is given terminally. Two intervals of time are created between two trials: the **KR-delay interval** and the **post-KR interval.**[1] These intervals are depicted graphically

in figure 15.7. To understand the relationship between these intervals and skill learning, we must understand the influence of two variables: *time,* or the length of the interval, and *activity,* or the cognitive and/or motor activity during the interval.

The Length of the KR-Delay Interval
It is not uncommon to see statements in textbooks indicating that a learner should receive augmented feedback as soon as possible after performing a skill, because delaying it beyond a certain amount of time would lead to poorer learning. A significant problem with this viewpoint is that it has little research evidence to support it. Such a view comes from research based predominantly on animal learning (see Adams, 1987). Research has established that humans use augmented feedback as more than a reward: augmented feedback has informational value that humans use to solve problems associated with learning a skill. Whereas animal learning studies have shown that delaying reward leads to decreased learning, human skill learning studies have shown that delaying augmented feedback does not have this negative effect.

KR-delay interval   the interval of time between the completion of a movement and the presentation of augmented feedback.

post-KR interval   the interval of time between the presentation of augmented feedback and the beginning of the next trial.

---

[1]Note that the terminology used to describe these two intervals follows the traditional labels used in the majority of the research literature, even though we have been using the term KR in a more specific way than these interval labels imply. It is important to see these intervals as relevant to *all* forms of augmented feedback.

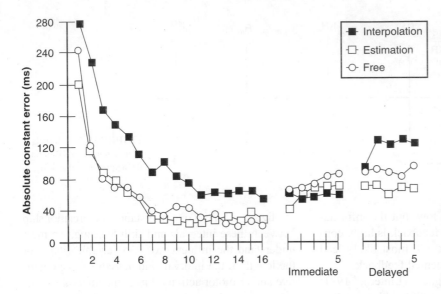

FIGURE 15.8 Results from the experiment by Swinnen showing the influence of estimating the experimenter's movement error (interpolation group) and the influence of estimating the participant's own error (estimation group) during the KR-delay interval, compared with no activity during the interval (free group). [From Swinnen, S. P. (1990). Interpolated activities during the knowledge of results delay and post-knowledge of results interval: Effects on performance and learning. *Journal of Experimental Psychology: Learning, Memory, and Cognition, 16,* 692–705. Copyright © 1990 by the American Psychological Association. Reprinted with permission.]

Activity During the KR-Delay Interval

Researchers investigating the effects of activity during the KR-delay interval have found *three types of outcomes*. The most common effect of activity during the KR-delay interval on skill learning is that it has *no influence on learning*. Experiments have demonstrated this result since the 1960s (e.g., Bilodeau, 1969; Boulter, 1964; Marteniuk, 1986).

The second type of effect is much less common. There is some evidence, although it is sparse, that activity during the KR-delay interval *hinders learning*. Two specific types of activities have shown this negative effect. One type includes activities that involve the same learning processes required by the primary task being learned. For example, Marteniuk (1986) showed that when another motor or cognitive skill had to be learned during the KR-delay interval, these activities interfered with learning of the primary skill. The other type of activity that research has shown to hinder skill learning involved estimating the movement-time error of another person's movement, which the second person performed during the interval. In an experiment by Swinnen (1990), people learned to move a lever a specified distance, involving two reversals of direction, in a criterion movement time. Participants who engaged in the error estimation activity during the KR-delay interval showed worse performance on a retention test than those who did nothing or who performed a non-learning task during the interval.

Subjective performance evaluation. The third type of effect is that certain activities during the KR-delay interval actually can *benefit learning*. One type of activity that has consistently demonstrated this effect requires the person to evaluate his or her own performance. We will refer to this activity as the *subjective performance evaluation strategy.* Research has established the effectiveness of two approaches to the use of this strategy. One requires the estimation of the outcome of the performance, the other requires the estimation of the movement-related characteristics of the performance of the skill. Swinnen (1990), in the experiment described above, compared the strategies of the participant estimating his or her own performance outcome error with estimating performance outcome error of another person's movement. Figure 15.8 shows that subjective performance estimation led to a learning benefit, but estimating another person's performance hindered learning. More recently, Sherwood (2008) further established the learning benefit of the subjective performance error strategy in an experiment

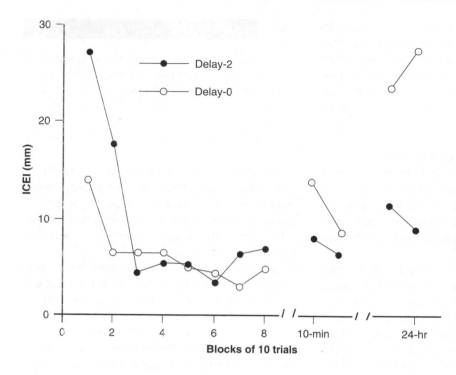

FIGURE 15.9 Results of the Anderson et al. experiment showing the beneficial effects of delaying a trial's KR for two trials (delay-2) compared to presenting KR after each trial (delay-0) for learning a manual aiming task. [Reprinted with permission from *Research Quarterly for Exercise and Sport, Vol. 65, No. 3,* 286–290. Copyright © 1994 by the American Association for Health, Physical Education, Recreation, and Dance, 1900 Association Drive, Reston, VA 20191.]

involving four different laboratory learning tasks, in which participants estimated their own error on each trial prior to receiving KR.

The second type of beneficial subjective performance estimation involves the estimation of specific characteristics of some of the movement-related components of an action. In an experiment by Liu and Wrisberg (1997) participants practiced throwing a ball at a target as accurately as possible with the nonpreferred arm and without vision of the target. Participants received KR by seeing where on the target the ball had landed on each trial. During the KR-delay interval, some of the participants rated on 5-point scales the appropriateness of the force, angle of ball release, and ball trajectory of the throw, and then estimated the throw's point value on the target. The results indicated that these participants performed more accurately on a retention than those who had not used the estimation strategy.

We find an interesting parallel to the subjective performance evaluation strategy in what researchers call the *trials-delay procedure.* Here, experiment participants receive KR for a trial after they complete performance on a later trial. Anderson, Magill, and Sekiya (1994) reported one of the most recent experiments providing evidence for the effectiveness of this effect. Participants practiced making a blindfolded aiming movement. One group received KR about distance error after every trial (delay–0). A second group received KR two trials later (delay–2), which meant that they were told their error for trial 1 after completing trial 3. Results (figure 15.9) were that while the delay condition hindered performance during practice, it led to better performance on a twenty-four-hour retention test.

Learning processes. What do these different effects of activity reveal about learning processes that occur during the KR-delay interval? During this time interval, the learner is actively engaged in learning processes involving activities such as developing an understanding of the task-instrinsic feedback and establishing essential error detection capabilities.

For instructional purposes, the most significant implication of the effects of activity during the

KR-delay interval is that people who are practicing a skill can use a beneficial strategy after they complete the performance of a skill and before they receive augmented feedback. That is, they could verbally describe what they think they did wrong that led to a less than desired performance outcome.

The Length of the Post-KR Interval

The significance of the post-KR interval is that it is during this period of time that the learner develops a plan of action for the next trial. This planning occurs during this interval because the learner now has available both task-intrinsic feedback and augmented feedback.

If the learner processes critical skill learning information during the post-KR interval, we would expect there to be a minimum length for this interval. Although there is not an abundance of research that has investigated this issue, there is empirical evidence from many years ago that provided evidence that indeed, this interval can be too short (e.g., Weinberg, Guy, & Tupper, 1964; Rogers, 1974; Gallagher & Thomas, 1980). For optimal learning, a minimum amount of time is needed for the learner to engage in the learning processes required. Conversely, there is no evidence indicating an optimal length for the post-KR interval. Research consistently has shown no apparent upper limit for the length of this interval.

Activity during the Post-KR Interval

The effect of engaging in activity is similar for the post-KR interval to that for the KR-delay interval. Depending on the type of activity, activity can have no effect on learning, interfere with learning, or benefit learning.

The most common finding has been that activity during the post-KR interval *has no effect on skill learning.* The best example is in an experiment by Lee and Magill (1983) in which participants practiced making an arm movement in 1,050 msec. During each post-KR interval, one group attempted the same movement in 1,350 msec, one group engaged in a cognitive activity involving number

LAB LINKS

Lab 15b in the Online Learning Center Lab Manual provides an opportunity for you to experience the effects on motor skill learning of estimating your own error during the KR-delay interval during practice.

guessing, and a third group did no activity. At the end of the practice trials, the two activity groups showed poorer performance than the no-activity group. However, this was a temporary performance effect rather than a learning effect: on a no-KR retention test, the three groups did not differ.

Several researchers have reported results indicating that activity during the post-KR interval *hinders learning.* Of these, only those by Benedetti and McCullagh (1987) and Swinnen (1990, experiment 3) included appropriate tests for learning. In both of these experiments, the interfering activity was a cognitive activity. Participants in the experiment by Benedetti and McCullagh engaged in a mathematics problem-solving task, whereas those in the experiment by Swinnen guessed the movement-time error of a lever movement the experimenter made during the post-KR interval.

Only one experiment (Magill, 1988) has demonstrated that *beneficial learning effects* can result from activity in the post-KR interval. Participants learned a two-component arm movement in which each component had its own criterion movement time. During the post-KR interval, one group had to learn two additional two-component movements, one group had to learn a mirror-tracing task, and a third group did not engage in activity. Results showed that the two groups that engaged in activity during the post-KR interval performed better than the no-activity group on a transfer test in which they learned a new two-component movement.

What do these different effects of activity tell us about learning processes that occur during the post-KR interval? They support the view we discussed earlier that learners engage in important planning activities during this time period. They use this planning time to take into account the discrepancy between the task-intrinsic and the augmented feedback, to determine how to execute the next attempt at performing the skill. Much of this planning seems to require cognitive activity; we see this in the experiments showing that engaging in attention-demanding cognitive problem-solving activity during this interval hinders learning.

FREQUENCY OF PRESENTING AUGMENTED FEEDBACK

For many years, the view was that augmented feedback should be given during or after every practice trial (i.e., 100 percent frequency), because no learning occurred on trials without augmented feedback. However, beginning with the influential review and evaluation of the KR literature by Salmoni, Schmidt, and Walter (1984) and continuing to the present time, this traditional view has been revised as researchers have provided evidence that is contrary to predictions of that viewpoint.

The Reduced Frequency Benefit

Sufficient research evidence has now accumulated for us to say confidently that the *optimal frequency for giving augmented feedback is not 100 percent*. The most influential evidence to support this conclusion was an experiment by Winstein and Schmidt (1990). They had participants practice producing the complex movement pattern shown in the top panel of figure 15.10 by moving a lever on a tabletop to manipulate a cursor on a computer monitor. During the two days of practice, participants received KR after either 100 percent or 50 percent of the trials. For the 50 percent condition, the experimenters used a *fading technique* in which they systematically reduced the KR frequency; they provided KR after each of the first twenty-two trials of each day, then had participants perform eight trials with no KR, then systematically reduced the frequency from eight to two trials for the remaining eight-trial blocks each day. The results of this experiment are presented in the bottom panel of figure 15.10. In a no-KR retention test given one

LAB LINKS

Lab 15c in the Online Learning Center Lab Manual provides an opportunity for you to compare the effects on motor skill learning of different frequencies of receiving KR during practice

day later, the faded 50 percent frequency condition led to better retention performance than the 100 percent condition produced. In fact, people who had received KR after every practice trial showed retention test performance at a level resembling that of their first day of practice.

The Winstein and Schmidt (1990) study has generated a great deal of research since it was published. The research has focused on two predominant themes: providing additional empirical support for the reduced frequency benefit, and determining whether or not an optimal frequency exists to enhance skill learning. Two interesting conclusions have resulted from these research efforts. First, although a reduced frequency of augmented feedback can benefit motor skill learning, it may *not* benefit the learning of all motor skills. Second, an optimal relative frequency appears to be specific to the skill being learned.

Theoretical Implications of the Frequency Effect

The challenge for those interested in developing motor learning theory is to establish why giving augmented feedback less than 100 percent of the time during practice is better for skill learning. One possible reason is that when people receive augmented feedback after every trial, they eventually experience an attention-capacity "overload." After several trials, the cumulative effect is that there is more information available than the person can handle.

A more likely possibility is that giving augmented feedback on every trial leads to engaging the learner in a fundamentally different type of learning processing than he or she would experience if it were not given on every trial. Schmidt and his colleagues (e.g., Salmoni, Schmidt, & Walter, 1984; Winstein & Schmidt, 1990) proposed

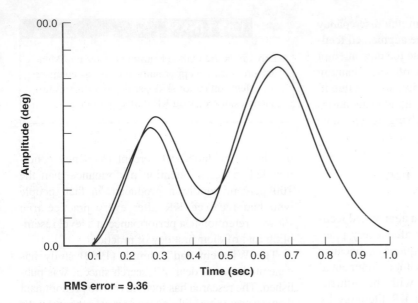

RMS error = 9.36

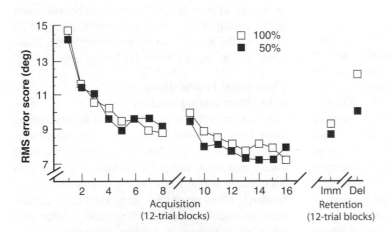

FIGURE 15.10   The top panel shows the goal movement pattern in the Winstein and Schmidt experiment. A sample of one participant's attempt to produce this pattern is superimposed. The RMS error score is shown as the subject saw it. Note that the goal pattern lasted for 0.8 sec while the participant produced a 1.0 sec pattern. The bottom panel shows the results of this experiment for the 100 percent KR frequency and 50 percent KR frequency groups, where the 50 percent group had KR frequency "faded" from 100 percent to 0 percent. [From Winstein, C. J., & Schmidt, R. A. (1990). Reduced frequency of knowledge of results enhances motor skill learning. *Journal of Experimental Psychology: Learning, Memory and Cognition, 16,* 677–691. Copyright © 1990 American Psychological Association. Reprinted by permission.]

this view, which they called the **guidance hypothesis.** According to this hypothesis, if the learner receives augmented feedback on every trial (i.e., at 100 percent frequency), then it will effectively "guide" the learner to perform the movement correctly. However, there is a negative aspect to this guidance process. By using augmented feedback as the guidance source, the learner develops a dependency on the availability of augmented feedback so that when he or she must perform the skill without it, performance will be poorer than if augmented feedback were provided. In effect, augmented feedback becomes a crutch for the learner that is essential for performing the skill.

The hypothesis further proposes that receiving augmented feedback less frequently during practice

A CLOSER LOOK

When Reduced Frequency of KR is Not Beneficial: Learning with Proprioception Deficits

Parkinson's disease (PD) is characterized by basal ganglia dysfunction. As a result, people with PD have a compromised proprioceptive feedback system that often leads to their having difficulty with the timing control of movements and integrating sensory and motor information. Because of this deficit, it would be expected that people with PD would benefit from KR as an external source of performance information to make the types of movement corrections needed to learn a motor skill that requires precise timing of an arm movement. An experiment reported by Guadagnogli, Leis, Van Gemmert, and Stelmach (2002) tested this hypothesis by comparing PD patients with normal age-matched individuals on the effect of different frequencies of KR for learning a motor skill.

Participants: Twenty PD patients (avg. age = 65.2 years); Twenty normal age-matched adults

Task: Make an arm-pointing movement as close as possible to a goal movement time (based on 65 percent of a participant's maximum speed). The movement began at a home position on a tabletop in front of the participant and moved to a target located behind a barrier that required the arm to initially move to the right to avoid the barrier and then to the left to the target. The minimum distance possible was 39 cm.

Practice and test: Sixty practice trials followed by 10 min of general conversation (i.e., a "filled" retention interval) followed by a fifteen-trial no-KR retention test.

KR conditions: KR was displayed on a computer monitor as the percentage too fast or too slow of the goal movement time (presented on a computer monitor); for example, if goal movement time was 2,000 msec, and movement was 2,400 msec, KR was displayed as "20% too fast."

One-half of PD patients and control participants received KR on
• 100 percent of the practice trials
• 20 percent of the practice trials

Results:
End of practice: Absolute error (AE) and variable error (VE) scores did not differ between the two KR frequencies, although the PD patients had higher amounts of error than the controls.

No-KR retention test: The PD patients with 20 percent KR frequency during practice had higher AE and VE scores than those with 100 percent KR frequency. The control participants with 100 percent KR frequency during practice had higher AE and VE scores than those with 20 percent KR frequency.

Conclusion: Consistent with research with healthy adults, KR presented on 100 percent of the practice trials led to poorer learning of the arm movement skill than when KR was presented on only 20 percent of the practice. However, the opposite result was found for the PD patients. As hypothesized, to learn the movement timing skill, the PD patients depended on KR during practice as an external source of information to provide movement time feedback that they could not interpret through their own proprioceptive feedback system or integrate with the motor system

---

individualizing the systematic reduction of the frequency of augmented feedback in practice situations. The bandwidth technique gives the practitioner a specific guideline for when to provide augmented feedback that encourages the learner to engage in important learning strategies. And because the bandwidth is related to individual performance, the learner can engage in these strategies at his or her own rate.

Self-Selected Fr

Another tec'
mented feea
learner *receiv.*
or she asks for i.
this approach apj
ticipating more ac
tics of the practice c
presentation of augm

encourages the learner to engage in more beneficial learning strategies during practice. For example, active cognitive and movement problem-solving activities increase during trials with no augmented feedback. The learner does not become dependent on the availability of augmented feedback and therefore can perform the skill well, even in its absence. (For an extensive review of research investigating the guidance hypothesis and an experiment that provides support for it, see Maslovat, Brunke, Chua, & Franks, 2009).

TECHNIQUES THAT REDUCE AUGMENTED FEEDBACK FREQUENCY

Now that we have established that it is generally more effective to provide augmented feedback less frequently than on every practice trial, a question that remains concerns how to implement ways that reduce frequency. The fading technique, described in the previous section, is one useful approach to reducing frequency. But several other techniques are effective as well.

Performance-Based Bandwidths
Earlier in this chapter we discussed a strategy for presenting augmented feedback that involved providing it only when a person's performance error was larger than a predetermined amount. We referred to this strategy as giving augmented feedback according to *performance-based bandwidths*. If we relate this bandwidth technique to the augmented feedback frequency issue, we can see how the bandwidth technique influences the frequency of presenting augmented feedback.

Lee, White, and Carnahan (1990) were the first to investigate this relationship. In their experiment they paired individual participants so that one of ch pair received KR only on the trials on which ther of the pair received KR in 5 percent and cent bandwidth conditions. The reason for ing of participants (a procedure known as was to control for the possibility that the -based bandwidth benefit for learning educed KR frequency. Thus, KR fresame for each pair of participants,

but the KR frequency for the participant i width condition depended on the 5 and criteria. Results showed that the bandwi KR conditions led to better retention perf The researchers concluded that the perfe based bandwidth technique reduces au feedback frequency, which is an importan why the technique enhances learning.

Two additional experiments will serve as ples of research that provide support for the le benefit derived from the relationship betwee performance-based bandwidth technique and mented feedback frequency. Goodwin and Meeu (1995) compared 0 percent and 10 percent bandwidth conditions with those that were sys atically expanded (0-5-10-15-20 percent) and c tracted (20-15-10-5-0 percent) for learning to a golf ball a criterion distance. The two conditi that resulted in the best retention test performan showed interesting KR frequencies. The frequencie for the 10 percent bandwidth condition reduced from 62 percent during the first twenty trials, to betweer 47 percent and 50 percent on the remaining trials. For the expanding bandwidth condition, KR frequencies began at 99 percent for the first twenty trials when the bandwidth was 0 percent, but then eventually reduced to 19 percent by the end of the practice trials, as the bandwidths increased in size. Lai and Shea (1999) reported similar findings for the learning of a complex spatial-temporal movement pattern. These results indicate that for the performance-based bandwidth technique it is the reduction of KR frequency during practice that is important to improved learning.

From an instructional perspective, the bandwidth technique provides a useful means of

---

guidance hypothesis   a hypothesis indicating that the role of augmented feedback in learning is to guide performance to be correct during practice; however, if it is provided too frequently, it can cause the learner to develop a dependency on its availability and therefore to perform poorly when it is not available.

by Janelle, Kim, and Singer (1995) provided initial evidence that this strategy can enhance the learning of motor skills. College students practiced an underhand golf ball toss to a target on the ground. The students received KP about ball force, ball loft, and arm swing during practice. Compared to groups that received KP according to experimenter-determined frequencies (all of which received it less frequently than on every trial), the participants who controlled KP frequency themselves performed more accurately on the retention test.

Janelle substantiated and extended these results in a later study in which videotape replay was a source of augmented feedback in addition to verbal KP (Janelle, Barba, Frehlich, Tennant, & Cauraugh, 1997). Participants in the self-regulated group controlled the augmented feedback schedule by requesting KP at will during 200 practice trials. An important characteristic of this experiment was that individual participants in another group were paired (i.e., yoked) to participants in the self-regulated condition to receive KP on the same trials, but without requesting it. The importance of this yoked condition was to control for the possibility that the effect of self-regulation of augmented feedback is due only to reduced frequency. Results showed that participants in the self-regulated condition learned the throwing accuracy task with more accuracy and better throwing technique than participants in the other KP and yoked conditions.

In terms of augmented feedback frequency, it is interesting to note that participants in the self-controlled condition requested KP on only 7 percent of the practice trials in the Janelle et al. (1995) experiment, and on only 11 percent in the Janelle et al. (1997) experiment. These low frequencies indicate that there is some relationship between the self-controlled procedure and the reduced relative frequency of augmented feedback. However, because people in the self-controlled conditions in both experiments performed better on retention tests than those in the frequency-yoked conditions, the benefit of the self-controlled situation is more than a simple frequency effect.

Why do beginners ask for feedback from an instructor? An experiment by Chiviakowsky and Wulf (2002) asked this question to participants in an experiment involving the learning of a sequential timing task. Each participant was asked on a questionnaire, "When/why did you ask for feedback?" Two-thirds of the participants answered that it was after what they considered to be a good trial (i.e., a trial during which they thought their performance was relatively successful). None indicated they asked for feedback after what they thought was a bad trial. Similar findings have been reported by these researchers in two additional experiments (Chiviakowsky & Wulf, 2005, 2007).

Research showing that learning is enhanced when learners can select when they want augmented feedback, and the fact that this selection typically occurs after trials that are thought to be relatively successful, provides interesting insight into the role of augmented feedback in skill learning. In general these results indicate the importance of augmented feedback as a source of information to confirm a learner's subjective evaluation of his or her performance. Two points are especially relevant from these findings. *First*, the use of augmented feedback in this way allows beginners to engage in their own problem-solving strategies as they learn the skill. *Second*, these results provide excellent evidence that learners use augmented feedback as a source of motivation to continue to practice. When they perform a relatively successful trial they ask for augmented feedback to reinforce their own subjective evaluation of their performance, which encourages them to continue to practice the skill. (For a more in-depth discussion of why receiving augmented feedback after good trials benefits learning, see Chiviakowsky & Wulf, 2007).

Summary and Averaged Augmented Feedback
Another way to reduce the frequency of augmented feedback presentations is to give a listing of performance-related information after a certain number of practice trials. This technique, which is known as *summary augmented feedback,* reduces the presentation frequency of augmented feedback while providing the same amount of information as if it were given after every trial.

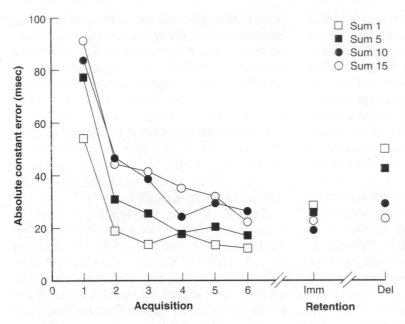

FIGURE 15.11   Results of the experiment by Schmidt et al., showing the effects of learning a timing movement with different summary KR conditions. (Sum 1 = KR after every trial; Sum 5 = KR for five trials presented every five trials, etc.) [From Schmidt, R. A., et al., (1989). Summary knowledge of results for skill acquisition: support for the guidance hypothesis. *Journal of Experimental Psychology: Learning, Memory and Cognition. 15,* 352–359. Copyright © 1989 American Psychological Association. Reprinted by permission.]

The summary technique could be advantageous in several types of skill learning situations. For example, suppose that a therapy patient must do a series of ten leg extensions in relatively rapid succession. To give augmented feedback after every extension may not be possible, if time limits restrict access to performance information after each attempt. A summary of all ten attempts could help overcome this limitation. Or suppose that a person is practicing a shooting skill for which he or she cannot see the target because of the distance involved. Efficiency of practice could be increased if that person did not receive augmented feedback after each shot, but received information about each shot after every ten shots.

The first study to generate a great deal of interest in the summary technique was a laboratory-based experiment by Schmidt, Young, Swinnen, and Shapiro (1989). The task involved moving a lever along a trackway to achieve a goal movement time. During the practice trials, participants received KR after every trial or in summary form after five, ten, or fifteen trials. The results of this experiment (see figure 15.11) showed very little difference between the conditions during practice and on a retention test

given ten minutes after practice. But on a retention test two days later, the group that had received KR after every trial performed the worst, whereas the group that had received summary KR after every fifteen trials performed the best.

In an experiment involving the learning of target shooting with rifles, Boyce (1991) provided one group with KP after every shot, and another group with KP about every shot after each fifth shot. The results showed no difference in eventual shooting performance by these groups. Although the summary method did not yield better performance than the method giving KP after every shot, its effectiveness as an instructional technique was established, because it was just as effective for improving performance as the other method.

Numerous studies have provided evidence supporting the benefit of the summary technique for motor skill learning (e.g., Schmidt, Lange, & Young, 1990; Wright, Snowden, & Willoughby, 1990; Guay, Salmoni, & Lajoie, 1999; Herbert, Heiss, & Basso, 2008). However, a very practical question remains to be answered: What is the optimal number of performance attempts, or practice trials, to include in a summary augmented feedback statement? Although there have been several attempts to determine whether a specific number of trials is optimal, the results have been equivocal. Two answers appear reasonable at the present time on the basis of results of research that has investigated this question.

First, Sidaway, Moore, and Schoenfelder-Zohdi (1991) concluded that the positive effects of the summary technique are not due to the number of trials summarized, and stated that their results argue against the notion of an "optimal summary length." Instead, they argued that the summary effect is related either to the reduced frequency of presenting augmented feedback or to the trials delay involved in presenting augmented feedback using the summary technique (note that the summary technique has characteristics similar to the trials-delay procedure, which we discussed earlier in this chapter).

An alternative answer is one we have seen related to many of the issues discussed in this book. The "optimal" summary length may be specific to the skill being learned. Guadagnoli, Dornier, and Tandy (1996) provided evidence for this possibility by showing that longer summaries are better for the learning of simple skills, whereas shorter summaries lead to better learning of more complex skills.

One of the possible strategies people may use when presented with a listing of augmented feedback is to *estimate an average for the series of trials* that the summary includes. The research literature provides some evidence that this may occur. In experiments in which the learner receives the average score for all the trials in a series, the results have shown that this procedure leads to better learning than presenting augmented feedback after every trial (Young & Schmidt, 1992), and no better or worse than after every trial or after every third trial (Wulf & Schmidt, 1996). But when compared to the summary technique, no differences are found in terms of their influence on skill learning (Guay, Salmoni, & Lajoie, 1999; Weeks & Sherwood, 1994; Yao, Fischman, & Wang, 1994).

Finally, *why are these two feedback presentation methods effective?* Their effectiveness is undoubtedly due to the same factors that lead to the benefit of reducing augmented feedback frequency,

as explained by the guidance hypothesis. During practice trials on which they receive no augmented feedback, people engage in beneficial learning activities that are not characteristic of people who receive augmented feedback after every trial.

SUMMARY

- Augmented feedback is performance-related feedback that is provided by an external source; it adds to or enhances *task-instrinsic feedback,* which is performance-related feedback directly available to the sensory system during the performance of a skill.

- Two types of augmented feedback are distinguished on the basis of the aspect of a skill performance to which the information refers:

  ► *Knowledge of results (KR)* refers to the performance of a skill.

  ► *Knowledge of performance (KP)* refers to the movement-related characteristics associated with the outcome of the performance of a skill.

- Augmented feedback plays two roles in the skill learning process:

  ► To facilitate achievement of the action goal of the skill.

  ► To motivate the learner to continue to strive toward the achievement of a goal.

- The need for augmented feedback for skill learning can be described in four different ways:

  ► It can be essential for skill learning.

  ► It may not be essential for skill learning.

  ► It can enhance skill learning beyond what is possible without it.

  ► It can hinder skill learning.

- Augmented feedback content issues include the following:

  ► Should the information conveyed to the learner refer to the errors made or to those aspects of the performance that were correct?

- ▶ Should the augmented feedback be KR or KP?
- ▶ Should the augmented feedback be quantitative or qualitative?
- ▶ Should the augmented feedback be based on the size of the error(s) and/or number of errors?
- ▶ What is the effect of erroneous augmented feedback on skill learning?

- KP can be presented to the learner in several different forms:
  - ▶ Verbal KP, which can provide either descriptive or prescriptive information.
  - ▶ Video replays of skill performances.
  - ▶ Movement kinematics associated with a performance of a skill.
  - ▶ Biofeedback.

- In addition to giving augmented feedback after a person has completed a trial, or after the performance of a skill (i.e., *terminal augmented feedback*), it can be presented during the performance (i.e., *concurrent augmented feedback*).

- Concurrent augmented feedback can have negative and positive effects on skill learning.

- Two intervals of time associated with terminal augmented feedback are the KR-delay interval and the post-KR interval. Both require a minimum length of time, although a maximum length has not been determined. Engaging in activity during these intervals can hinder, benefit, or have no effect on skill learning.

- Research indicates that the optimal frequency for giving augmented feedback is less than on every practice trial. The guidance hypothesis represents the most commonly held view for explaining the learning benefit of a reduced frequency.

- Several techniques will reduce augmented feedback frequency:
  - ▶ Performance-based bandwidths.
  - ▶ Performer-selected frequency.
  - ▶ Summary and averaged augmented feedback.

POINTS FOR THE PRACTITIONER

- Evaluate the need for KR or KP in any skill instruction situation in terms of the type of augmented feedback that would most effectively facilitate learning the skill.

- More specific or technologically sophisticated augmented feedback is not necessarily better. Beginners need feedback that will help them make a "ballpark" approximation of the movements they need to make to achieve the action goal.

- Augmented feedback that is a combination of error-correction information and information about what was done correctly can be helpful for skill acquisition and motivation to continue to try to achieve the action goal of the skill.

- Determine the verbal KP to give according to the most critical error made during a practice attempt. Identify this error on the basis of an analysis of the skill's component parts and a prioritized list of the importance of each part for achieving the action goal.

- Prescriptive verbal KP is better than descriptive verbal KP for beginners.

- Video replays can be effective as augmented feedback for beginners when you point out errors and provide information about how to correct them. The decision to provide this type of information for more skilled individuals can be based on the individual's choice.

- Computer-generated displays of the kinematics of a skill performance will be more effective for learners who are at a more advanced stage of learning than a beginner.

- Biofeedback can be effective to facilitate skill learning when it provides information people can use to alter movements and when they do not become dependent on its availability.

- Do not feel compelled to give augmented feedback after every practice attempt. When you do not give augmented feedback, you provide opportunities for people to determine what their own sensory feedback tells them about performing the skill they are learning.

- The performance-bandwidth strategy of providing augmented feedback can be especially useful when instructing groups of individuals where it is difficult to interact with each person individually on every performance attempt.

- Allow people you are working with to determine when they would like to receive KR or KP.

- On occasion, ask the people you are working with to tell you what movement errors they made and how they should correct them before you give them this information.

RELATED READINGS

Badets, A., & Blandin, Y. (2005). Observational learning: Effects of bandwidth knowledge of results. *Journal of Motor Behavior, 37,* 211–216.

Becker, A. J., & Wrisberg, C. A. (2008). Effective coaching in action: Observations of legendary collegiate basketball coach Pat Summitt. *Sport Psychologist, 22,* 197–211.

Betker, A. L., Desai, A., Nett, C., Kapadia, N., & Szturm, T. (2007). Game-based exercises for dynamic short-sitting balance rehabilitation of people with chronic spinal cord and traumatic brain injuries. *Physical Therapy, 87,* 1389–1398.

Carnahan, H., Vandervoort, A. A., & Swanson, L. R. (1996). The influence of summary knowledge of results and aging on motor learning. *Research Quarterly for Exercise and Sport, 67,* 280–287.

Chen, D. D., Hendrick, J. L., & Lidor, R. (2002). Enhancing self-controlled learning environments: The use of self-regulated feedback information. *Journal of Human Movements Studies, 43,* 69–86.

Downing, J. H., & Lander, J. E. (2002, Nov./Dec.). Performance errors in weight training and their correction. *Journal of Physical Education, Recreation, and Dance, 73,* 44–52.

Kontinnen, N., Mononen, K., Viitasalo, J., & Mets, T. (2004). The effects of augmented auditory feedback on psychomotor skill learning in precision shooting. *Journal of Sport & Exercise Psychology, 26,* 306–316.

Krause, D., Wünnemann, M, Erlmann, A., Hölzchen, T., Mull, M., Olivier, N., & Jöllenbeck, T. (2007). Biodynamic feedback training to assure learning partial load bearing on forearm crutches. *Archives of Physical Medicine and Rehabilitation, 88,* 901–906.

Magill, R. A. (2001). Augmented feedback and skill acquisition. In R. N. Singer, H. A. Hausenblaus, & C. Janelle (Eds.), *Handbook on research in sport psychology* (2nd ed.), pp. 86–114. New York: Wiley.

Mouratidis, A., Vansteenkiste, M., Lens, W., & Sideridis, G. (2008). The motivating role of positive feedback in sport and physical education: Evidence for a motivational model. *Journal of Sport & Exercise Psychology, 30,* 240–268.

Sanchez, X., & Bampouras, T. M. (2006). Augmented feedback over a short period of time: Does it improve netball goal-shooting performance? *International Journal of Sport Psychology, 37,* 349–358.

Schmidt, R. A., & Wulf, G. (1997). Continuous concurrent feedback degrades skill learning: Implications for training and simulation. *Human Factors, 39,* 509–525.

Smith, S. L., & Ward, P. (2006). Behavioral interventions to improve performance in collegiate football. *Journal of Applied Behavioral Analysis, 39,* 385–391.

Van Vliet, P. M., & Wulf, G. (2006). Extrinsic feedback for motor learning after stroke: What is the evidence? *Disability and Rehabilitation, 28,* 831–840.

Winchester, J. B., Porter, J. M., & McBride, J. M. (2009). Changes in bar path kinematics and kinetics through use of summary feedback in power snatch training. *Journal of Strength and Conditioning Research, 23,* 444–454.

INTERNET RESOURCES

- To read about a popular video-based performance analysis program that can be used to provide augmented feedback in sports, physical education, and physical rehabilitation settings, go to http://www.dartfish.com.

- To read a summary of a study, funded by the National Athletic Trainers Association (NATA) Foundation, which investigated the use of augmented feedback to help people decrease impact forces of a jump landing, go to http://www.natafoundation.org/ refgrants/Onate.pdf. This report was published in the Supplement to the *Journal of Athletic Training,* April–June, 2000, Vol. 38, No. 2, pp. 19–20, and was included in a presentation at the 2003 NATA Annual Meeting in St. Louis, Missouri.

- To read an article for rowing coaches about the use of augmented feedback to change a rower's technique, go to http://www.brianmac.demon. co.uk/articles/scni19a4.htm.

- To read a summary of the development and use of a training system, which involves a virtual environment and augmented feedback, designed to assist in the physical rehabilitation of people with neurological impairments, go to http://web. mit. edu/bcs/bizzilab/members/holden/. Included on this page is a list of articles the researcher has published concerning the training system.

  To read about other projects in this laboratory at M.I.T., go to http://web.mit.edu/bcs/bizzilab/.

STUDY QUESTIONS

1. (a) Describe the two general types of performance-related feedback a person can receive during or after performing a motor skill. In your description, indicate the characteristic that differentiates the two. (b) Discuss why the distinction between these two types of feedback is important.

2. What are the two types of information referred to by the terms KR and KP? Give two examples of each.

3. Describe skill learning conditions where augmented feedback would (a) be necessary for learning, (b) not be necessary for learning, and (c) not be necessary for learning but would enhance learning beyond what would occur without it.

4. (a) How do quantitative and qualitative augmented feedback differ, and how do they influence the learning of motor skills? (b) Describe how you would use these two forms of augmented feedback in a motor skill learning situation.

5. Describe a situation in which you would use video replay as a form of augmented feedback to (a) help a beginner learn a new skill, (b) help a skilled person correct a performance problem. Indicate why the video replay would facilitate learning for each situation.

6. Describe a situation in which you would use kinematic information as augmented feedback to help someone learn a motor skill and explain why you would use it.

7. Describe a skill learning situation in which you would use some form of biofeedback. Indicate how you would use it, and why you would expect it to facilitate the learning of the skill.

8. What is the difference between concurrent and terminal augmented feedback? Give two examples of each.

9. (a) What are two types of activity during the KR-delay interval that have been shown to benefit skill learning? (b) Why does this benefit occur?

10. (a) What seems to be the most appropriate conclusion to draw regarding the frequency with which an instructor should give augmented feedback during learning? (b) How does the guidance hypothesis relate to the issue of augmented feedback frequency?

11. Describe a skill learning situation in which (a) giving summary augmented feedback would be a beneficial technique, (b) using the self-selected frequency strategy would be beneficial.

Specific Application Problem:
Select a motor skill that you might teach in your future profession. Your supervisor has asked you to develop and defend a plan for providing augmented feedback for this skill for the people you will work with. In your plan, describe the skill you will teach and relevant characteristics of the people you will teach. In your defense of this plan, emphasize why the type of augmented feedback you will use and how you will deliver it would be preferable to other types and uses of augmented feedback.

Practice Conditions

CHAPTER 16

Practice Variability and Specificity

Concept: Variability of practice experiences is important for learning motor skills.

After completing this chapter, you will be able to

- Explain the meaning of the term *practice variability* and its relation to predictions of theories of motor skill learning
- Discuss ways to implement practice variability in skill learning or relearning contexts
- Describe how the *contextual interference effect* relates to organizing variable practice
- Discuss the relevance of contextual interference as a basis for scheduling practice for novice learners and skilled performers
- Identify reasons why contextual interference benefits motor skill learning
- Describe the practice specificity hypothesis and contrast it with the practice variability hypothesis

APPLICATION

A primary reason a person practices a skill is to increase his or her capability of performing it in future situations that will require the skill. For example, a basketball player needs to be successful shooting free throws in games. A student in a physical education class who will receive a grade based on performance on skills tests wants to practice those skills in ways that will lead to a high level of performance on the tests. Dancers need to perform in recitals, performances, and competitions. Athletic trainers practice taping an ankle or knee so they can do it effectively and quickly with athletes when needed. And physical rehab patients practice skills so that they can perform them as needed in their everyday environment. Because of this future performance requirement, teachers, coaches, athletic trainers, and therapists must design and establish practice conditions that will lead to the greatest probability of successful performance in situations that will require the practiced skills.

Consider two more specific examples. Suppose you were taking golf lessons, and your instructor told you to go to the practice range and hit a basket of practice balls. You know you need practice hitting your long irons. What would be the best way for you to spend your practice time using your long irons to hit the basket of balls so that you can improve your performance with those irons when you play a round of golf on the golf course? Or suppose you are a physical therapist working with a patient who recently had knee replacement surgery. You want the patient to work on ascending and descending stairs. What would be the most effective way to schedule the practice of these two tasks to facilitate your patient's capability to ascend and descend the stairs in his or her home every day?

One practice characteristic that increases the chances for future performance success is the variability of the learner's experiences while he or she practices. This includes variations of the characteristics of the context in which the learner performs the skill, as well as variations of the skill he or she is practicing. The practitioner must address several important questions to determine how to optimize the types and amount of variation to include in practice experiences. First, what aspects of performing the skill should he or she vary? Second, how much variety of experiences is optimal? Third, how should the variety of experiences be organized in the practice sessions? We consider these questions in the discussion that follows.

> **Application Problem to Solve**   Describe a motor skill that involves the performance of several variations. If you were teaching or helping people rehabilitate their performance of these variations, how would you schedule them to be practiced in the period of time you have available? Why would you consider this practice schedule to be better than any other schedule that could be created?

DISCUSSION

A consistent characteristic of theories of motor skill learning and control is their emphasis on the learning and performance benefits derived from practice variability. In these theories, **practice variability** refers to the variety of movement and context characteristics the learner experiences while practicing a skill. For example, in Schmidt's (1975) schema theory, a key prediction is that successful future performance of a skill depends on the amount of movement variability the learner experiences during practice. Similarly, Gentile's learning stages model (1972, 2000) emphasized the learner's need during practice to experience variations of regulatory and nonregulatory context characteristics. And dynamic pattern views of skill learning stress the learner's need to explore the perceptual motor workspace and to

discover optimal solutions to the degrees-of-freedom problem posed by the skill (e.g., McDonald, Oliver, & Newell, 1995; Vereijken & Whiting, 1990).

THE FUTURE PERFORMANCE BENEFIT OF PRACTICE VARIABILITY

The primary benefit a learner derives from practice experiences that promote movement and context variability is an increased capability to perform the skill in a future test situation. This means that the person has acquired an increased capability not only to perform the practiced skill, but also to adapt to novel conditions that might characterize the test situation. When viewed from the perspective of transfer of learning, the inclusion of movement and context variability in practice can be seen as a means of enhancing positive transfer from the practice to the test contexts.

Variable versus Constant Practice

One way to establish that practice variability benefits future performance is to compare the effects on retention or transfer test performance of practice situations involving one variation of a skill (i.e., *constant practice*) with those involving several variations of the skill (i.e., *variable practice*). This type of comparison has been the standard research strategy for testing Schmidt's (1975) schema theory hypothesis that greater amounts of variable practice lead to better learning than lesser amounts. Although an abundance of published research studies have investigated and generally supported this hypothesis (see van Rossum, 1990, for a review of this research), two examples will illustrate these studies.

In two experiments reported by Shea and Kohl (1990, 1991), the participants' goal was to learn to

> **practice variability**   the variety of movement and context characteristics a person experiences while practicing a skill.

apply 175N of force to press a handle. A constant practice group practiced this skill for 289 trials, while a variable practice group practiced producing four different amounts of force (125N, 150N, 200N, and 225N). Notice that none of the variations practiced by the variable practice group was the 175N goal. When both groups performed a retention/transfer test for the 175N goal (the test was a retention test for the constant group but a transfer test for the variable group), the variable group performed more accurately than the constant group.

An experiment involving a sports skill also showed that variable practice yields better learning than constant practice (Shoenfelt, Snyder, Maue, McDowell, & Woolard, 2002). In this study, participants practiced shooting basketball free throws. The constant practice group, which practiced only from the free-throw line, improved during the three weeks of practice, but two weeks later on a retention test, returned to their pretest level of performance. On the other hand, three variable practice groups, only one of which included shooting from the free-throw line, improved during practice and performed on the retention test at a higher level than they had on the pretest.

Performance errors benefit learning. An apparent irony concerning the benefit of an increased amount of practice variability is that it is usually associated with an *increased amount of performance error during practice.* However, this relationship is consistent with research evidence that shows more performance error can be better than less error for skill learning, when it occurs in the initial learning stage. A good example of this evidence is an experiment by Edwards and Lee (1985). Each participant had to learn to move his or her arm through a specified pattern in 1,200 msec. Participants in the prompted group engaged in practice designed to minimize performance errors. They were told that if they moved according to a "ready and 1, 2, 3, 4, 5" count on a tape, they would complete the movement in the criterion time. Each person practiced until he or she could do three trials in a row correctly at 1,200 msec. Those in the trial-and-error group were told the goal movement time and received knowledge of

results (KR) about their timing error after each trial. The results indicated that the two groups performed similarly on the retention test, but the trial-and-error group performed more accurately on a transfer test when both groups had to move in a different amount of time, which was 1,800 msec.

What is particularly interesting about these results is how much the two groups differed in the amount of error each produced during practice. The prompted group performed with very little error during practice, whereas the trial-and-error group experienced much error, especially during the first fifteen trials. Yet experiencing less error during practice was no more beneficial for retention test performance, and it was detrimental for transfer to a novel variation of the practiced movement.

Similar results have been reported in a physical rehabilitation setting. For example, when acute stroke patients were instructed, by either a trial-and-error or errorless learning method, to put on a sock, those who practiced by trial-and-error performed better on a transfer test that involved a variation of the practiced task (Mount, Pierce, Parker, DiEgidio, Woessner, & Spiegel, 2007). Although the physical rehabilitation research literature presents some evidence that shows the benefits of instructional strategies that minimize the amount of performance errors by people with specific cognitive disorders (see Mount et al., 2007, for a brief review of this research), the effectiveness of "errorless" learning strategies does not carry over to healthy populations.

IMPLEMENTING PRACTICE VARIABILITY

The first step in determining how to provide an appropriate amount of practice variability is to assess the characteristics of the future situations in which the learner will perform a skill. Of particular relevance here are the *characteristics of the physical context* in which he or she will perform the skill and the *skill characteristics* that the performance situation will require. If you again view this situation as a transfer of learning situation, then you will see the value of using the test conditions to

A CLOSER LOOK

Constant and Variable Practice for Learning to Shoot Free Throws in Basketball

The experiment by Shoenfelt, Snyder, Maue, McDowell, and Woolard (2002) involved university students who were not skilled basketball players practicing basketball free throws.

Practice and Test Schedules

Pretest   40 free throws (20 sets of 2 shots)

Practice   40 free throws per day (20 sets of 2 shots) M, T, W, Th, each week for 3 weeks

Weekly tests   Each Monday's session of 40 free throws was a weekly progress test

Retention test   40 free throws (20 sets of 2 shots) two weeks after the last practice session

Practice Variability Conditions

Constant practice (C)   Free-throw shooting from the free-throw line only

Variable practice – Front & Back (VFB)   Free-throw shots from 2 ft in front of and 2 ft behind the free-throw line (randomly assigned in each practice session)

Variable practice – Combination (VC)   Free-throw shots from 2 ft in front of and 2 ft behind the free-throw line (randomly assigned in each practice session)

Variable practice – Random (VR)   Free-throw shots from the "elbow" to the left and to the right of the key, and from the top of the key (randomly assigned in each practice session)

Results

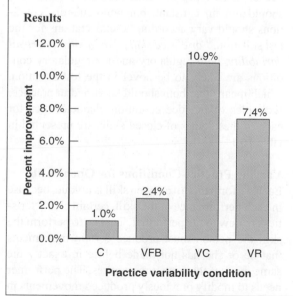

FIGURE 16.1 Results from the experiment by Schoenfelt et al. showing the pre- to posttest percentage of improvement for the four practice variability groups (C = Constant practice; VFB = Variable Front and Back practice; VC = Variable Combination practice; VR = Variable Random practice). [*Source:* Data from Schoenfelt, E. L., Snyder, L. A., Maue, A. E., McDowell, C. P., & Woolard, C. D. (2002). Comparison of constant and variable practice conditions on free-throw shooting. *Perceptual and Motor Skills, 94,* 1113–1123.]

determine what the practice environment should be like. As we discussed in chapter 13 and illustrated in figure 13.1, effective transfer is a function of the similarities between skill, context, and cognitive processing characteristics of the practice and test situations. A high degree of similarity between these characteristics in the two situations enhances transfer between the practice and the test.

LAB LINKS

Lab 16 in the Online Learning Center Lab Manual provides an opportunity for you to experience and compare the effects of constant and variable practice on learning a motor skill.

Varying the regulatory conditions when practicing snowboarding increases the person's capability to snowboard in conditions not previously experienced.

Varying Practice Contexts

It is important to keep in mind that when people perform skills, they do so in contexts that have identifiable characteristics. As we discussed in chapter 1, Gentile (2000) pointed out that some features of the performance context are critical for determining the movement characteristics of an action (which she called regulatory conditions), whereas other features (nonregulatory conditions) have no influence.

Consider some examples of *regulatory conditions* that influence a person's walking behavior. Certain movement characteristics will be different when you walk on a concrete sidewalk than when you walk on ice or on sand. Also, you walk differently on a busy sidewalk that is cluttered with other people than on a sidewalk empty of people. When regulatory conditions like these may vary from one performance context to another, it is important that practice conditions include a variety of similar conditions.

Nonregulatory conditions also play a role in influencing transfer between practice and test. For walking, some nonregulatory conditions would include the physical environment around the walking pathway, such as buildings, trees, and open space. Although these features do not influence the movements directly, we know from our study of incidental memory in chapter 10 that they can influence the degree of success a person may achieve in carrying out the action in a unique context. Again, when nonregulatory conditions will vary from one performance context to another, practice conditions should provide opportunities to experience these characteristics.

Varying Practice Conditions for Closed Skills

The first step in making the decision about what to vary during the practice of a closed skill is to determine whether or not the skill involves intertrial variability for the regulatory conditions in the test situation. *For closed skills that do not involve intertrial variability of regulatory conditions,* nonregulatory conditions may be novel. For the practice of these types of skills, regulatory conditions should remain constant, but nonregulatory conditions should vary according to expectations for the test situation. *For closed skills that involve intertrial variability,* both regulatory and nonregulatory conditions are likely to be novel in the test situation, which means that both should be varied in practice. Examples of practice condition characteristics for each of these types of closed skills are presented in table 16.1.

Varying Practice Conditions for Open Skills

Each performance of an open skill is unique, because in each performance of the skill, certain characteristics are new to the performer. That is, to perform the skill the person must produce certain movements that he or she has not made before in exactly the same manner this situation requires. The performer needs to modify previously produced movements in order to achieve the goal of the skill. For example, if you are preparing to return a serve in tennis, it is likely that certain characteristics of the ball action will be unique to this particular serve. Thus, in addition to variations of nonregulatory conditions, practice of open skills also needs to include a variety of

TABLE 16.1   Examples of Varying Practice Conditions for Two Types of Closed Skills

Intertrial Variability of Regulatory Conditions	No Intertrial Variability of Regulatory Conditions
Golf shot using a 7-iron The goal is to successfully make shots with the 7-iron during a golf match.	**Basketball free throw** The goal is to shoot free throws successfully in basketball games.
Regulatory conditions that remain constant in a match • 7-iron characteristics • golf ball characteristics	**Regulatory conditions that remain constant in games** • basket height • basket distance from free-throw line • basketball characteristics
Regulatory conditions that can vary in a match • goal for the shot • distance of required shot • location of ball	**Nonregulatory conditions that can vary in games** • number of free throws to be taken • importance to game of making the free throws • crowd noise • length of the game
Nonregulatory conditions that can vary in a match • number of hole being played • number of strokes ahead or behind • cloudy or sunny skies • importance of a particular shot	*Practice conditions* should include as many *nonregulatory* conditions as possible to be similar to those that could be experienced in a game.
Practice conditions should simulate as many *regulatory* and *nonregulatory* conditions as possible to be similar to those that could be experienced in a match.	

experiences with regulatory conditions that change from one attempt to another.

ORGANIZING VARIABLE PRACTICE

Having established that practice variability benefits skill learning, we next must consider how the practitioner should organize the variable experiences within a practice session or unit of instruction. The following example illustrates how this practice organization question is involved as the motor skills professional develops practice conditions.

Suppose you are an elementary school physical education teacher organizing a teaching unit on throwing for your classes. You have determined that you will devote six class periods to this unit. You want the students to experience three variations

of the throwing pattern: the overhand, underhand, and sidearm throws. How should you arrange these three different throws for practice during the six class periods? Figure 16.2 shows three possible arrangements. One is to practice each throw in blocks of two days each (blocked practice). Another possibility is to practice each throw in a random arrangement with 5 min blocks devoted to each particular pattern (random practice). Thus, each day students would experience six 5 min blocks, with no specified order of occurrence for the three patterns; the only stipulation would be that they practice all three an equal amount over the course of the unit. The third arrangement, serial practice, also involves a 5 min block for each pattern. However, in this approach students practice each pattern for two sets of five minutes every day in the same order.

		Class day					
		1	2	3	4	5	6
Blocked practice	30 min	All overhand	All overhand	All underhand	All underhand	All sidearm	All sidearm
Random practice	5 min 5 min 5 min 5 min 5 min 5 min	Underhand Overhand Underhand Sidearm Underhand Overhand	Overhand Sidearm Sidearm Underhand Overhand Overhand	Sidearm Overhand Sidearm Underhand Underhand Sidearm	Overhand Sidearm Sidearm Underhand Overhand Overhand	Underhand Overhand Underhand Sidearm Underhand Overhand	Sidearm Overhand Sidearm Underhand Underhand Sidearm
Serial practice	5 min 5 min 5 min 5 min 5 min 5 min	Overhand Underhand Sidearm Overhand Underhand Sidearm	Overhand Underhand Sidearm Overhand Underhand Sidearm	Overhand Underhand Sidearm Overhand Underhand Sidearm	Overhand Underhand Sidearm Overhand Underhand Sidearm	Overhand Underhand Sidearm Overhand Underhand Sidearm	Overhand Underhand Sidearm Overhand Underhand Sidearm

FIGURE 16.2 A six-day unit plan demonstrating three different practice structures (blocked, random, and serial) for teaching three different throwing patterns (overhand, underhand, and sidearm). All classes are 30 min long and all but the blocked practice schedule are divided into 5 min segments. Each practice condition provides an equal amount of practice for each throwing pattern.

This organization question is not unique to physical education. It applies to any situation in which learners must practice and learn several variations of a skill. Consider a few examples. In a therapy situation, a patient may need to practice grasping objects of different sizes, weights, and shapes. A patient who has had a knee joint replacement may need to practice walking on different types of surfaces. In a dance setting, a dancer may need to practice tempo variations in a routine or other variations of particular components of a routine. Each of these situations involves the same organization problem: How should the schedule of practice for these variations be organized within the practice time available?

The Contextual Interference Approach to Organizing Variable Practice

One way to solve the variable practice schedule problem is to apply the learning phenomenon known as the *contextual interference effect*. William Battig (1979), who first demonstrated this effect, introduced the term **contextual interference** to refer to the *interference* that results from performing various tasks or skills within the *context* of practice. You can think of the term "interference" here as referring to memory and performance disruption.

Different amounts of contextual interference can result from the organization of the practice schedule. The blocked, random, and serial practice schedule organization options described earlier can be viewed as located along a continuum of contextual interference (see figure 16.3). A *high amount of contextual interference* occurs at one extreme, when the practice schedule involves a random arrangement of trials so that all the task variations are performed in each practice session. In this schedule, the task variation practiced on each trial would be randomly determined. At the opposite extreme, a *low amount of contextual interference* results from a schedule that organizes the practice of each task variation in its own block, or unit, of time. Other schedules, such as the serial schedule described earlier, fall along the continuum between these two extremes. It is important to note here that the two practice schedules just described are based on trials, but the three schedules in figure 16.3 are based on time intervals. For developing practice schedules associated with

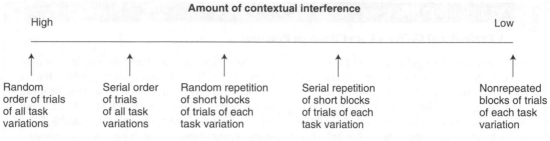

FIGURE 16.3   The amount of contextual interference that is possible in a practice situation is portrayed as a continuum ranging from high to low. Also presented are sample variable practice schedules in terms of how each relates to the amount of contextual interference created by the schedule.

contextual interference either trials or time intervals are appropriate.

The **contextual interference effect** occurs when *a high amount of contextual interference results in better learning* (i.e., retention and transfer performance) of the task variations than a low amount. What is especially noteworthy about this effect is that prior to Battig's initial demonstration of it, researchers traditionally viewed interference as something that hinders learning. According to that view, a low amount of contextual interference during practice should lead to better learning than a high amount. However, Battig's research showed an important exception to the traditional view of interference. It is important to note in this regard that a negative influence of interference is often found for high contextual interference schedules during practice. But this interference turns out to be a learning benefit, because the high contextual interference practice schedules result in better performance on retention and transfer tests than low contextual interference practice schedules.

Research Evidence for the Contextual Interference Effect

The first evidence of the contextual interference effect for motor skill learning was reported by Shea and Morgan (1979). Participants practiced three variations of movement patterns in which the goal was to move one arm through a series of small wooden barriers as rapidly as possible. One group followed a blocked practice schedule (i.e., low contextual interference) in which each movement pattern was practiced in its own unit of trials. A second group practiced according to a random schedule (i.e., high contextual interference) in which the practice of each pattern was randomly distributed throughout the practice trials. An important point here is that both groups practiced for the same number of trials, only the scheduling of trials differed.

Results showed that the random practice schedule led to poorer performance during practice, but better performance on retention and transfer tests. Thus, random practice resulted in better learning of the three pattern variations and allowed for better

---

contextual interference   the memory and performance disruption (i.e., interference) that results from performing multiple skills or variations of a skill within the context of practice.

contextual interference effect   the learning benefit resulting from performing multiple skills in a high contextual interference practice schedule (e.g., random practice), rather than performing the skills in a low contextual interference schedule (e.g., blocked practice).

A CLOSER LOOK

A Professional Golfer's Use of Random Practice

Amy Alcott, a professional golfer on the LPGA tour, described in *Golf Magazine* (December, 1991) a drill she uses to help her make a swing of the correct length and strength for the distance. She practices pitch shots that are 20, 40, 60, and 80 yards from flags marking each distance. Before she hits a ball, her teacher, Walter Keller, calls out the yardage for the shot. She looks at the flag, sets up, and swings. Then, her teacher calls out another yardage for the next shot. She says that "One after another, he'd call out yardages—60, 20, 40, 80, 40, 60." Alcott states that she finds this type of practice "invaluable," and repeats it from time to time throughout the season.

performance for a new pattern. Since the Shea and Morgan experiment, numerous other studies have been reported (see Brady, 1998; Magill & Hall, 1990). The evidence from this research establishes that the contextual interference effect is generalizable to learning motor skills.

One of the striking negative effects of low contextual interference practice is that it inhibits performance of the practiced skills in novel performance contexts. Contextual interference experiments commonly show this. Although blocked practice sometimes leads to blocked retention test performance that is similar to performance following random practice, a large decrement in retention performance is typical when researchers test the skills under random conditions (e.g., Shea, Kohl, & Indermill, 1990). On the other hand, high contextual interference practice does not show the same transfer problem. Thus, low contextual interference practice appears to develop a practice context dependency that decreases a person's capability to adapt to novel test contexts.

The contextual interference effect outside the laboratory. Battig's original demonstration of the contextual interference effect was based on the learning of cognitive skills, such as word lists. Much of the research involving motor skills has been based on the learning of laboratory tasks, such as the barrier-knockdown task used by Shea and Morgan (1979). If we want to have confidence in the application of laboratory-based principles of motor learning to real-world contexts, it is important to establish that learning phenomena demonstrated in the laboratory also exist in real-world settings. We will look at a few examples of research that provide evidence that the contextual interference effect occurs in learning situations outside the laboratory.

One of the first experiments that presented this type of evidence was reported by Goode and Magill (1986). College women with no prior badminton experience practiced the short, long, and drive serves from the right service court. They practiced these serves three days a week for three weeks with 36 trials in each practice session, for a total of 324 trials (108 trials per serve) during the practice period. The low contextual interference condition was a modification of the blocked condition used in previous studies; in this study, the blocked practice group practiced one serve each day of each week. The group on a random practice schedule practiced each serve randomly in every practice session. In this condition, the experimenter told each participant which serve she should perform next.

As you can see in figure 16.4, the results demonstrated the contextual interference effect. The group that practiced with the random schedule outperformed the blocked practice group on the retention and transfer tests. What is especially remarkable is that on the transfer test, which involved serving from the left service court, the random group showed no deterioration in performance. On the other hand, students in the group that had practiced in a blocked schedule were not able to adapt well

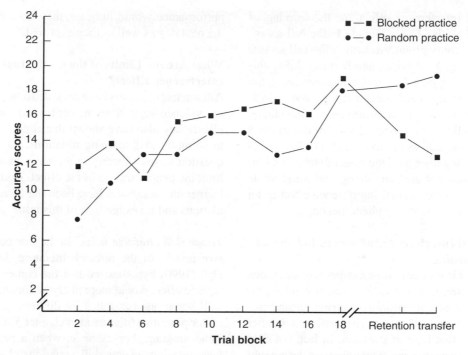

FIGURE 16.4   Results from the experiment by Goode and Magill showing the effects of blocked and random schedules of practice for three types of badminton serves on acquisition, one-day retention, and transfer. [Reprinted with permission from *Research Quarterly for Exercise and Sport, Vol. 57, No. 4,* 308–314. Copyright © 1986 by the American Alliance for Health, Physical Education, Recreation, and Dance, 1900 Association Drive, Reston, VA, 20191.]

to this new performance context. In fact, learners in this group performed in the new context about as well as they had when they had begun practicing the serves from the right court three weeks earlier.

The Goode and Magill study showed the benefit of high contextual interference for *beginners* learning an actual sport skill (the badminton serve). However, although their experiment used a sport skill, the authors carried it out in controlled experimental conditions. Those who seek even more real-world validity should note that Wrisberg and Liu (1991) attained the same results as Goode and Magill, but in an actual class setting. In that study, students learned the serves in a unit of instruction in an actual physical education class.

Another experiment worth noting demonstrates that the contextual interference effect for real-world skills exists not only for beginners, but

also for *skilled individuals.* Hall, Domingues, and Cavazos (1994) had skilled baseball players practice hitting different types of pitches to improve their batting performance. The players engaged in forty-five extra pitches of batting practice three days a week for five weeks. Batters hit fastballs, curves, or change-ups according to a blocked or random schedule. In the blocked schedule, players practiced hitting one of these pitches on each day, whereas in the random schedule, they hit all three types of pitch, randomly presented, each day. The results showed that on a test involving a random sequence of pitches, like one that would occur in a game, players who had experienced the random practice schedule performed better than those who had practiced according to the blocked schedule.

In addition to these few examples, several other studies have found evidence that demonstrates the contextual interference effect for the learning of real-world skills. These include basketball shooting skills, tennis groundstrokes, volleyball serves, rifle shooting, knot tying, handwriting skills, chiropractic spine manipulation, and computer game skills (see Brady, 1998; Enebo & Sherwood, 2005; Ollis, Button, & Fairweather 2005; Ste-Marie, Clark, Findlay, & Latimer, 2004, for discussions of the various studies involving these skills). When considered together with the research based on laboratory tasks, research involving real-world skills establishes the contextual interference effect as an important motor learning phenomenon.

Contextual Interference Influences Judgments about Learning

In chapter 11, you saw some examples of situations in which performance during practice misrepresents the amount of learning occurring during practice. The contextual interference effect is another example of this type of situation. In fact, not only does practice performance misrepresent the amount of learning, but in addition the learners' judgments about how much they are learning are influenced by the practice schedule experienced. Judgment about how much we are learning while we practice is referred to as *metacognition,* which concerns "what we know about what we know." The assessment of this information is typically done by asking people to predict how well they think they will do on a retention test. A study by Simon and Bjork (2001) demonstrated that people who use a blocked schedule for practicing three goal movement times and patterns of a five-key sequence of numbers on a computer number pad consistently overestimated their performance on a test that would occur the next day. In contrast, participants who followed a random practice schedule more accurately estimated their test performance.

Why would this type of overestimation of learning occur for the blocked practice schedule? One reason is that people who are practicing according to this schedule are performing relatively well. They use this level of performance as the basis for predicting how well they will perform the next day. But because they are not learning as much as their

performance would indicate, they do not perform the next day as well as they expected.

What Are the Limits of the Contextual Interference Effect?

Although researchers have provided a large amount of evidence supporting the contextual interference effect, they also have shown that it does not apply to all motor skill learning situations. As a result, a question arises concerning the characteristics that limit the generalization of the effect. Both task and learner characteristics have been the focus of speculations and investigations of this issue.

Motor skill characteristics. In the first comprehensive review of the research literature, Magill and Hall (1990) hypothesized that the contextual interference effect would more likely be found for motor skill variations controlled by different generalized motor programs (discussed in chapter 5) than by the same program. For example, when a person practices learning several skill variations characterized by different relative time patterns, a high contextual interference practice schedule should lead to better learning than a low contextual interference schedule. However, when the skill variations are characterized by the same relative time patterns, but different overall speeds, there should be no advantage to a high over a low contextual interference practice schedule. When removed from the context of the generalized motor program, the Magill and Hall hypothesis proposed that for the learning of skill variations, the contextual interference effect should be found when the characteristics of the variations are more dissimilar than similar.

In his assessment of the research that investigated this hypothesis, Brady (1998) concluded that research involving laboratory tasks tends to support the hypothesis (e.g., Wood & Ging, 1991; Wulf & Lee, 1993). But when research involves applied settings, higher amounts of contextual interference tend to enhance the learning of skill variations that are more similar than different. For example, compared to a low contextual interference practice schedule, moderate and high contextual interference practice schedules produced better learning

A CLOSER LOOK

Judgments about How Much People Are Learning during Practice

An important study by Simon and Bjork (2001) investigated how well people who are practicing multiple variations of a motor skill can assess their own learning during practice, which is commonly referred to as *metacognition.* The significance of their study is twofold. First, it was the first investigation of metacognition as it relates to the learning of motor skills (it has a longer history in the study of verbal-conceptual learning; see Nelson, 1992.) Second, it demonstrated that practicing multiple variations of a motor skill with a low amount of contextual interference influences learners to be overconfident about how well they will perform on an upcoming test.

The Simon and Bjork (2001) Experiment
Participants: Forty-eight undergraduate university students.

Motor skills practiced: The task required participants to learn to press three specified five-key sequences on the number pad of a computer keyboard. The sequences differed in the patterns of numbers to press and overall goal movement times (MT). (*Sequence 1* was the 9-5-1-2-3 keys with a 900 msec MT goal; *Sequence 2* was the 3-6-5-8-4 keys with a 1,200 msec MT goal; *Sequence 3* was the 4-2-5-8-9 keys with a 1,500 msec MT goal.)

Practice conditions: Participants practiced each sequence in a blocked or random order until they performed thirty successful trials for each sequence; that is, they pressed the correct keys (unsuccessful trials were repeated later in the practice session). Knowledge of results (KR) was provided after each trial in terms of (a) whether or not the correct keys had been pressed, (b) the actual MT for the trial, and (c) the number of milliseconds faster or slower the actual MT was than the goal MT.
- *Blocked practice schedule*—All trials of each sequence were practiced as a unique set of trials until the thirty-trial criterion was achieved for the sequence (e.g., 900—900—900 . . . 1,200—1,200—1,200 . . . 1,500—1,500—1,500 . . .).
- *Random practice schedule*—Each of the three sequences was practiced in a random order until the thirty-trial criterion was achieved for each sequence.

Assessment of participants' judgment of learning (JOL): At the end of every fifth successful trial, participants were asked to predict as closely as possible their estimate of how close they would come to the goal MT for that sequence on a test scheduled for the next day (they were told to predict as if they would receive no additional practice trials).

Retention test: One day after completing the practice trials, participants performed a paper-and-pencil test of their recall of the key-press sequences and goal MTs they practiced the previous day and predicted their expected MT performance in terms of how close they would come to each goal MT. They then performed three trials of each sequence in a blocked order and random order. No KR was provided on any of these trials.

Results:
Practice trials:
- *MT Accuracy:* The blocked practice group performed significantly more accurately than the random practice group for the first half of the practice trials (only the thirty successful trials were analyzed). The two groups were not significantly different for the second half.
- *Predictions:* Participants' predictions of their next-day retention test performance indicated that the blocked practice group predicted better performance than the random practice group. This difference was statistically significant across all the practice trials.

Retention test:
- *Keystroke Sequence and MT Accuracy:* The random practice group performed with significantly more accuracy than the blocked practice group for recalling the three sequences practiced the previous day and performing the sequences according to their goal MTs.
- *Predictions:* Participants' predictions of their that-day retention test performance indicated that the blocked practice group continued to predict better performance than the random practice group. However, the blocked practice group performed with significantly less MT accuracy.

A CLOSER LOOK

An Application of the Contextual Interference Effect to the Physical Therapy of Stroke Patients

A study by Hanlon (1996) demonstrated the benefit of a random practice schedule for the physical therapy of unilateral stroke patients who needed to rehabilitate the use of their hemiparetic (i.e., partially paralyzed) arm to perform functional movement sequences.

Participants: Twenty-four adult patients with chronic hemiparesis due to a unilateral cerebrovascular accident (CVA), which is commonly called a stroke.

Movement sequence practiced: Participants used their hemiparetic arm to perform a five-step sequence designed to approximate steps needed to (1) open a cupboard door, (2) grasp a coffee cup by the handle, (3) lift the cup off its shelf, (4) place the cup on the counter, and (5) release the grasp.

Practice conditions:
• *Random practice schedule*—Ten trials in one session per day until participants achieved the performance criterion of three consecutive correct trials. Between each trial of the movement sequence, participants performed three other tasks with the hemiparetic arm: (1) pointing, (2) touching specified objects, (3) touching specified spots on a horizontal surface.
• *Blocked practice schedule*—Ten trials in one session per day until participants achieved the performance criterion of three consecutive correct trials.
• *No practice control condition*—No practice trials.

Retention tests: All participants performed the five-step movement sequence for five trials 2 and 7 days after the end of the practice sessions.

Results:
Practice trials:
• No statistically significant difference between the random and blocked practice groups for the mean number of trials required to achieve the performance criterion.
Retention tests:
• The *random practice group* performed significantly more successful trials on both retention tests than the blocked practice group and the no-practice control group.
• Interestingly, the blocked practice group did not differ from the no-practice control group on the number of correctly performed trials on the first retention test, but performed significantly better on the second retention test.

Conclusion: The experiment demonstrated that it is possible to create the contextual interference effect in a clinical setting by interposing other activities between trials, or repetitions, of the skill or activity being rehabilitated. The functional benefit is a longer-lasting performance improvement than would result from repeating repetitions without the intervening activities.

---

of one-hand basketball set shots from different distances and angles (Landin & Hebert, 1997), but not better learning of three different volleyball skills (French, Rink, & Werner, 1990).

Two reasons may account for this discrepancy between the laboratory and applied settings. First, the learning of sport skills requires more practice than has been included in those studies that have not found the effect. Because sport skills tend to be more complex and difficult than the typical laboratory skills used in contextual interference research, much more practice would be required to learn the sport skills. The second reason is that the learning of sport skills may require a progression of low to high amounts of contextual interference rather than only a high amount (see Porter, 2008). Unfortunately, these two possibilities remain speculative until we have a sufficient amount of research evidence that either supports or does not support them.

Learner characteristics. Researchers have also proposed that several *learner characteristics* may limit the effect of contextual interference on skill learning. Of the characteristics suggested, *age and skill level* appear to be the most likely limiting factors. When participants in studies have been children, the highest amounts of contextual interference typically do not enhance learning. In fact, Brady's (1998) review points out that for children, practice schedules that produce lower amounts of contextual interference tend to produce better learning. In terms of skill level, Hebert, Landin, and Solmon (1996) found that low-skilled students in university tennis classes performed forehand and backhand strokes better on a retention test following blocked practice, whereas high-skilled students performed no differently following blocked or alternating-trials practice schedules.

In summary, we know that certain factors limit the extent of the generalization of the contextual interference effect in motor skill learning situations. Unfortunately, we do not have a definitive account of the specific characteristics that establish those limits. Although there is general agreement that both task- and learner-related characteristics influence the degree to which contextual interference influences the learning of motor skill variations, we must wait for much more research evidence to allow us to confidently identify the specific characteristics.

An encouraging perspective on this issue was presented by Guadagnoli and Lee (2004) in their proposal of a *challenge point hypothesis* for determining effective practice conditions based on difficulty characteristics of the tasks and the skill level of the person. The "challenge point" refers to the implementation of specific practice conditions that will optimally challenge the person in a way that will enhance skill learning. Determining the challenge point involves a consideration of both the difficulty level of the skill being learned and the skill level of the learner. The hypothesis makes two predictions concerning the implementation of levels of contextual interference in practice schedules. First, random practice will be optimal for learning skills with the lowest levels of difficulty, but less optimal for skills with the highest levels of difficulty.

Second, for beginners, or those with low skill levels, lower levels of contextual interference will be optimal; while higher levels of contextual interference will be more effective for more skilled individuals. Although these predictions fit the model the authors created, we need empirical evidence to determine how well they apply to specific motor skill learning situations.

Implications for the Practitioner

Given the inconclusive nature of our present knowledge about the specific factors that limit the generalization of the effect of contextual interference on skill learning, what should the practitioner do? To answer this, refer to figure 16.3. It is important to keep in mind that our present knowledge is different for the top and bottom portions of the continuum in this figure. In terms of the top half, we know that moderate and high amounts of contextual interference generally produce better learning of skill variations than low amounts. However, the bottom half of the figure remains unresolved in terms of the amount of contextual interference specific practice schedules produce when they arc used for the learning of specific skill variations. As a result, view the continuum in figure 16.3 as representing a generic relationship between the various practice schedules and the amount of contextual interference each produces.

For the practitioner, when several variations of a skill must be learned, the best course of action would be to select a practice schedule that should produce a moderate to high amount of contextual interference (according to figure 16.3). But he or she should be prepared to modify the schedule after practice begins in order to accommodate individuals who do not respond well to the practice schedule. For example, some individuals may require a practice schedule that produces a lower amount of contextual interference, such as a blocked schedule, until they acquire the basic movement patterns of the skill variations. However, it is important that the practitioner base any practice schedule modification on performance difficulties evident from retention or transfer tests rather than on those from practice sessions.

The Effectiveness of a Moderate Contextual Interference Practice Schedule

It may be preferable to learn some motor skill variations by practicing according to a schedule that involves a moderate rather than a high amount of contextual interference. A study by Landin and Hebert (1997) provides a good example of this type of practice situation.

Participants were university undergraduate students who had very little experience playing basketball. They practiced the one-hand set shot from six positions on the basketball court that varied in angle and distance from the basket. The *low contextual interference* group practiced according to a blocked schedule by shooting six consecutive shots from each position on each of three practice days. The *moderate contextual interference* group followed a blocked-serial schedule by shooting three shots from each position in sequence and then repeating the sequence. The *high contextual interference* group followed a serial

schedule by taking one shot from each position in sequence and then repeating the sequence six times.

On the day after the end of practice, each group performed three transfer tests: a twelve-trial blocked schedule for three of the practice positions; a twelve-trial serial schedule for the same three positions; and a ten-trial free-throw test (the free-throw line was one of the six practiced positions). All three groups improved their shooting performance during practice, but they did not differ from each other at the end of practice. However, the blocked-serial practice schedule group performed better than the other two groups on all three tests. In addition, low amounts of contextual interference during practice led to poor adaptation to change. The blocked practice group maintained their end-of-practice performance level for the blocked and free-throw tests, but their performance on the serial test decreased to the level of their first day of practice.

ACCOUNTING FOR THE CONTEXTUAL INTERFERENCE EFFECT

An important question that remains unanswered is this: Why does the contextual interference effect occur? Two hypotheses predominate the several accounts for this effect. One is the *elaboration hypothesis;* the other is known as the *action plan reconstruction hypothesis.* Although we will not debate these two hypotheses at length, we will consider each briefly.

The Elaboration Hypothesis
In their experiment that first showed the contextual interference effect for learning motor skills, Shea and Morgan (1979) proposed that the effect is related to the elaboration of the memory representation of the skill variations that a learner is practicing.[1] During random practice, a person engages in more strategies, as well as more different strategies, than an individual who practices according to a

blocked schedule. Also, because in a random practice schedule the person retains in working memory all the skill variations he or she is practicing, the person can compare and contrast the variations so that each becomes distinct from the other. The result of engaging in these cognitive activities during practice is that the learner develops a more elaborate memory representation for the skills that he or she then can access more readily during a test.

The Action Plan Reconstruction Hypothesis
An alternative hypothesis, by Lee and Magill (1985), stated that high amounts of contextual interference benefit learning because the interference requires a person to reconstruct an action plan on the next practice trial for a particular skill variation. This is necessary because the person has partially or completely forgotten the action plan he or she developed on the previous practice trial for that skill variation, because of the interference of the intervening practice trials of the other skill variations. In contrast, the person following a blocked practice schedule can use the

[1]Shea and Zimny (1983) developed a more formal version of the elaboration hypothesis.

same action plan he or she used on the previous trial, or a slightly modified one.

Consider the following illustration of how these different practice schedules would require different types of action plan activity. If you must add a long set of numbers and then you are immediately asked to do the same problem again, you probably will not re-add the numbers, but will remember and repeat only the answer. In contrast, if you are required to add several additional lists of numbers and then are given the first list again, you probably will have forgotten the solution to that problem and therefore will have to add the same numbers again. The intervening problem-solving activity requires you to re-solve a problem you have solved already.

Lee and Magill hypothesized that the high contextual interference practice condition is like the addition situation in which there are several other problems to solve before you see the first problem again. When a learner practices a motor skill, the interference created by the practice trials between two trials of the same skill variation causes the person to forget much of the action plan he or she developed for the first trial. As a result, the learner must reconstruct and modify that plan to attempt the skill on the next trial. On the other hand, the blocked practice schedule is like the addition problem in which the next trial follows immediately, and it is easy to remember the solution and therefore be successful on the next trial.

In the motor learning context, high contextual interference conditions require learners to engage more actively in problem-solving activity during practice. Although this activity typically leads learners to perform more poorly during practice than they would with a low contextual interference schedule, this short-term performance deficit becomes a long-term benefit, because it leads to better retention and transfer test performance.

Research Supports Both Hypotheses
Much research is needed to determine which of the two hypotheses best accounts for the contextual interference effect. In his review of the research literature, Brady (1998) discussed several studies that provide support for each hypothesis. Since the publication of that review, Immink and Wright (2001) presented empirical evidence supporting roles for both explanations. Based on the results of two experiments, they concluded that random practice not only promotes a refinement of motor programming processes (i.e., the action plan reconstruction hypothesis), it also enhances the strength and quality of the memory representation of the movement variations learned during practice (i.e., the elaboration hypothesis). Results such as these indicate that rather than being competing explanations for the contextual interference effect, the elaboration and reconstruction hypotheses are complementary.

Regardless of which hypothesis, or combination of hypotheses, accounts for the contextual interference effect, two important learner-related characteristics are associated with the effect. One is that *higher levels of contextual interference involve greater attention demands during practice* than lower levels, which is predicted by both the elaboration and reconstruction hypotheses. Li and Wright (2000) provided evidence of the greater attention demands for random compared to blocked practice by requiring participants to perform a secondary choice reaction-time task between practice trials and just before initiating their movements for a practice trial. These results help explain earlier results that showed higher physiological activation associated with higher levels of contextual interference (e.g., Husak, Cohen, & Schandler, 1991). The second characteristic, which we discussed earlier, was identified by Simon and Bjork (2001): *people who practice according to a blocked schedule tend to overestimate how well they are learning during practice.*

PRACTICE SPECIFICITY

In chapter 13, you learned that the amount of transfer of learning is a function of the degree of similarity between practice and test characteristics, which means that the best learning will occur when practice characteristics are the same as those of the test. However, this conclusion appears to be at odds with the discussion so far in the present chapter in which practice variability is presented as an important practice characteristic that is critical for successful future test performance. How, then, can both of these seemingly contradictory principles be correct?

The **specificity of practice hypothesis** is one of the oldest principles of human learning. Its origins can be traced back to the early 1900s when Thorndike (1914; Thorndike & Woodworth, 1901) presented the *identical elements theory* to explain why positive transfer occurs between two skills or skill learning situations. Briefly, this theory, which was discussed in chapter 13, proposed that the more "elements" (i.e., physical and mental characteristics) two skills or situations have in common, the greater the amount of transfer of learning or performance. The practice specificity hypothesis can also be linked to our discussion in chapter 3 about motor abilities where we considered the specificity of motor abilities hypothesis, which was attributed to Franklin Henry in the 1960s (e.g., Henry, 1961a, 1961b). Henry's hypothesis proposed that motor abilities are independent and task specific and that individuals have varying levels of many motor abilities. In addition, the relationship between performances by a person on two different skills would depend on the degree of common abilities between the skills. Finally, in chapter 12 in the discussion of various performer and performance characteristics that change during the course of learning a skill, you read about the influence of practice specificity in skill learning for a performer-related characteristic that does not change.

Researchers generally agree that sufficient research evidence exists to support the practice specificity hypothesis for at least three characteristics of motor skill learning and performance. We have discussed each of these in previous chapters, but we will consider them here as they apply to the practice specificity hypothesis. After discussing each characteristic, we will address the question of how this hypothesis relates to the practice variability hypothesis and contextual interference effect.

Practice Specificity for Sensory/Perceptual Characteristics

As you read in chapter 12, research by Proteau and his colleagues in Canada (e.g., Proteau, 1992) has demonstrated that motor skill learning is *specific to the sources of sensory/perceptual information*

available during practice. The specific focus of their research has been on the role of visual and proprioceptive information available during the performance of a skill. That focus was motivated by views on motor learning and control that emphasized visual sensory feedback as important in the early stage of learning but as diminished in importance with practice and eventually being replaced by proprioceptive feedback (e.g., Fleishman's view on the relationship of motor abilities to skill learning, which was discussed in chapter 3, and the Schmidt schema theory's hypothesized changes over the course of skill learning, which was discussed in chapter 12).

In contrast to views such as these, Proteau's research consistently showed that if a person has vision available during practice, vision remains an essential source of sensory information throughout the stages of learning. In fact, performance decreases when vision is not available during a retention or transfer test. Several examples of this research were presented in chapter 12 in which researchers showed support for Proteau's hypothesis for the learning of a variety of motor skills, such as manual aiming, power lifting, and walking. An especially notable finding in these examples is that as the amount of practice with vision increases, the need for vision on a subsequent retention or transfer test also increases (Proteau, Tremblay, & DeJaeger, 1998). More recent research has shown that this increased need for vision is not because the availability of vision during practice prevented the processing of proprioceptive information, but because practice with vision influences people to prefer to use the same motor plan to perform the practiced skill without vision available (on transfer tests) as they used during practice with vision (Mackrous & Proteau, 2007).

A different approach to the practice specificity effect of vision during learning involved the use of observational learning (Osman, Bird, & Heyes, 2005). The experiment involved participants learning an eight-item sequence in a serial reaction time task on a computer keyboard. After observing a skilled model demonstrate the sequence with the right hand, participants then practiced the task with their right hand and then their left hand. Results showed that the observation of the model influenced performance only with the right hand.

Neurophysiological evidence also demonstrates the practice specificity effect for sensory characteristics. For example, in a study in which researchers used fMRI to observe the brain activity associated with learning a timing skill (Jantzen, Steinberg, & Kelso, 2005), participants practiced tapping their thumb with the index finger to a specific rhythm that was paced by either a visual or auditory metronome. Eventually the metronome stopped but the participants continued to tap the rhythm. The brain areas active during practice with the visual metronome remained active during the tapping without the visual metronome. These brain areas were those in the visual dorsal stream, which we discussed in chapter 6 as the vision-for-action visual system.

Practice Specificity for Performance Context Characteristics

In chapter 10, you read that the encoding specificity principle is a well-established characteristic of memory. This principle identifies the strong association between encoding and retrieval contexts for memory performance by stating that the more a memory test (i.e., retrieval) context resembles the practice (i.e., encoding) context, the better will be the retention performance. Recall that in chapter 10 we discussed that an important part of the performance context issue is the distinction between intentional and incidental remembering. *Intentional* remembering refers to when you must remember specified characteristics of an environmental context, whereas *incidental* remembering refers to the remembering of related but nonessential parts of the context. For example, you are practicing the return of a serve in tennis, and you are told to estimate and report the ball speed for a serve. If you are then asked to report not only the ball speed but also the location in the service court where the ball landed, you will undoubtedly be able to report both, even though you were not instructed to give attention to or remember the ball's landing location. In this example, reporting the ball speed represents intentional remembering; reporting the ball's landing location represents incidental remembering.

Research by David Wright and his colleagues extended the performance context aspect of the encoding specificity principle to motor skill learning

situations. Their research has consistently shown that characteristics of a practice environmental context that are not part of the skill to be learned become part of what gets learned (e.g., Wright & Shea, 1991, 1994). In these experiments participants typically learned three- or four-digit sequences of key presses on a computer keyboard. Participants saw specific sequences of the numeral keys displayed on the computer monitor as the intentional items they needed to learn. In addition, each sequence was color coded, which created an association between a number sequence and its color. Because participants were not told about the color-coding feature, color was an incidental part of the performance context; it was not a part of what was to be learned. However, when participants were shown the number sequence and color combinations on transfer tests, their performance was better than when they were shown the same number sequences that were different colors. Thus they learned not only the number sequences that they were told to learn, but also the colors associated with the sequences. Interestingly, in interviews after the experiment, participants indicated that they were unaware of the number-color relationship.

What is evident from the research investigating performance contexts is that people *learn more about the context than they are explicitly instructed to learn*. Parts of the environmental context in which a skill is practiced get included in what people learn. When these incidental parts of the context are available during a test, they serve as cues, or aids, to help retrieve the memory representation of the learned skill. Conversely, when these incidental environmental context features are not available during the test environment, performance is diminished. Examples of this effect include the use of mirrors in dance studios and weight training rooms. Because the mirrors are part of the practice environment, the

---

specificity of practice hypothesis   the view that motor skill learning by practice condition characteristics, especially the sensory/perceptual information available, performance context characteristics, and cognitive processes involved.

A CLOSER LOOK

Brain Region Activity Shows Context Specificity for Learning Rhythmic Timing

A study by Jantzen, Steinberg, and Kelso (2005) investigated brain areas involved in the learning and performance of a rhythmic timing task. Their results demonstrated practice specificity effects by showing a context-dependent network of brain regions activated according to whether a visual or auditory signal guided the practice of a timing task that required movements that were synchronized (in music terms, this means move with the beat) or syncopated (move off the beat) with the signal.

The rhythmic timing task: A visual or auditory metronome paced participants to coordinate index finger and thumb opposition (i.e., moving the index finger to touch the thumb) at a continuous rate of 1.25 movements per second.

Visual metronome: A red dot appeared on a computer monitor

Auditory metronome: A tone heard through headphones

Synchronized movement trials: Touch the thumb at the same time the signal occurred (continue movement at same rhythm after signal stopped; i.e., transfer test)

Syncopated movement trials: Touch the thumb midway between the signals (continue movement at same rhythm after signal stopped; i.e., transfer test)

Brain activity assessment: Each participant was placed in a supine position in an MRI scanner, the head fixed with a vacuum pillow. The scanner had fMRI capabilities.

Results:
Timing performance with and without pacing signal: Participants achieved the required movement rates for both the synchronized and syncopated coordination modes.

Brain activity: When the visual signal paced performance, brain activity involved areas typically involved in the integration of visual and motor information and the translation of visual sensory information into motor output. These areas were the middle temporal lobe, bilateral superior parietal lobe, and ventral premotor cortex. What is more interesting is that these regions remained active when the participants performed the movements without the visual pacing signal present. Activity in these areas was absent when the auditory signal paced performance.

Conclusion: The brain activity results support the practice specificity hypothesis proposed by Proteau (e.g., Proteau, 1992) that motor skill learning is specific to the sources of sensory/perceptual information available during practice. Practice with the visual signal activated brain areas specific to visually guided coordination even when the visual signal did not appear during the transfer trials.

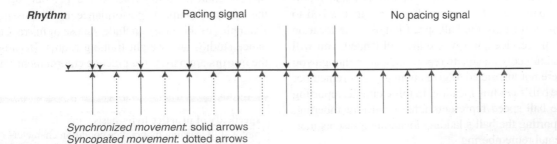

Synchronized movement: solid arrows
Syncopated movement: dotted arrows

visual feedback received from them becomes part of what is learned. When the mirrors are not available, performance of these activities will be at a lower level than it would be with the mirrors present.

According to Shea and Wright (1995), the selection of a skill to perform in a situation and the speed of its selection depend on the strength of the relationship between intentional and incidental features in the performance environment. The implication for skill training is to include as many features of a test environmental context as possible in the practice environmental context. For example, if a goal of gait training in physical therapy is for the patient to be able to walk in a crowded mall as part of his or her daily living activities, then therapy sessions should include supervised walking in a crowded mall when the therapist determines that the patient can engage in this type of activity. In terms of its application to sports situations, the learning of the incidental parts of players' environmental context during practice and competitions leads to the "home field advantage" that is commonly observed in sports competitions.

Practice Specificity for Cognitive Processing Characteristics

In chapter 13, one of the explanations of positive transfer considered the similarity of the cognitive processes required by the skills or learning situations. According to the transfer-appropriate processing theory, the type of practice that is best when a person is learning a skill is practice that requires the same type of cognitive processing activity that will be required in a transfer test, regardless of the physical similarity between the practice and test skills and situations. For example, if the test situation will require rapid decision making, practice should consist of activities that require rapid decision making. One of the reasons for this relationship is that the cognitive processing that occurs during practice becomes a part of what is learned. As a result, the cognitive processing demands of a practice situation are a practice-specific aspect of skill learning.

An experiment by Pellecchia (2005) provides a good example of the practice specificity of cognitive demands during skill learning. Participants practiced

standing still for 30 sec on a balance platform on which the surface was covered with a foam pad to reduce somatosensory feedback and increase reliance on vestibular and visual feedback. Two groups of participants practiced only the balance skill (single-task training) or that together with a cognitive secondary task (dual-task training), which was counting backwards by threes from a three-digit number that was randomly presented on each trial. Results showed that when both groups performed a transfer test one week later with the dual-task condition, the single-task training group showed an increase in postural sway, while the dual-task training group did not, which demonstrated that the cognitive processing demands imposed by the dual-task training became a part of what was learned. The similarity between the cognitive processing demands during practice and the test resulted in successful performance on the dual-task transfer test one week later.

Relating the Practice Variability and Specificity Hypotheses

Although the practice specificity hypothesis may appear to be at odds with the practice variability hypothesis, research indicates that each hypothesis is relevant to our understanding of factors influencing motor skill learning by relating to different practice and test characteristics. The *practice variability hypothesis* relates primarily to movement characteristics of the skill performed in practice and test situations; performance context characteristics can be involved, especially when the context requires the performance of several variations of a skill (e.g., Schmidt, 1975, 2003). On the other hand, the *practice specificity hypothesis* relates primarily to certain characteristics associated with practice and test contexts: (a) the sensory-perceptual information available, (b) the environmental context in which the skill is performed, and (c) the cognitive processing requirements.

In addition, when we apply the practice specificity hypothesis to learning movement characteristics associated with a skill, the typical result can show a benefit for performing that skill with those movement characteristics, but poor adaptability to situations that require modification of the practiced movement characteristics. The research we considered earlier in this chapter in which constant and variable practice conditions were compared provides good evidence for the poor transfer test adaptability of a skill when only one variation was practiced. A different perspective on this issue was presented in an experiment in which skilled basketball players, all of whom were university team members, performed shots at various distances from the basket (Keetch, Schmidt, Lee, & Young, 2005). The results showed that they consistently shot more accurately from the foul line than would be predicted from the Schmidt schema theory's practice variability hypothesis. The effect occurred even when the lines of the court were covered, to control for the possible effects of the incidental learning the players had experienced throughout their careers to that point. The researchers attributed the results to a practice specificity effect that had built up over many years of shooting more shots from the foul line than from any other place on the court.

SUMMARY

Variations of movement and context experiences are important ingredients for practice conditions that increase a person's capability to perform the practiced skill successfully and to adapt to conditions he or she has not experienced previously.

- Research evidence shows that *variable practice* leads to superior retention and transfer test performance when compared to *constant practice.*

- To determine the characteristics of a test context that should be varied in practice, identify the regulatory and nonregulatory conditions of the test context. Which of these conditions should be varied in practice depends on whether the skill is a closed or open skill.

- An important practice condition concern is how to organize the variety of experiences for a practice session unit of instruction, or therapy protocol. The *contextual interference effect* provides a basis for scheduling these experiences during practice.

- The contextual interference effect occurs when practice schedules that include higher amounts of contextual interference (e.g., random practice schedules) lead to better learning than those that include low amounts (e.g., blocked practice schedules).

- Research evidence indicates that the contextual interference effect applies to beginners as well as to skilled performers and to laboratory skills and a wide range of sports and everyday skills; however, the effect is not applicable to the learning of all motor skills or to all learning situations. Researchers have not identified the specific factors that limit the generalization of the contextual interference effect.

- Two hypotheses predominate as explanations for why the contextual interference effect occurs: the *elaboration hypothesis* and the *action plan reconstruction hypothesis.*

- The practice specificity hypothesis differs from the practice variability hypothesis and contextual interference effect by proposing that the best transfer test performance will result from practice situations in which characteristics are the most similar to those of the transfer test. Research has shown that the following three characteristics of motor skill learning and performance support this hypothesis:

  ► The sources of sensory/perceptual information available during practice

  ► Performance context characteristics

  ► Cognitive processing characteristics

- Although the practice specificity hypothesis appears to contradict the predictions of the practice variability hypothesis, research indicates that each hypothesis relates to different practice and test characteristics. The practice specificity hypothesis relates primarily to certain characteristics of the practice and test context, whereas the practice variability hypothesis relates specifically to the movement characteristics of the skill that is learned.

POINTS FOR THE PRACTITIONER

- The goal of practice sessions should be to provide opportunities for people to develop the capability to perform activities that will require the use of the skills being practiced and to achieve the action goals of those activities wherever they occur.

- Practice conditions that encourage people to make errors are beneficial for helping people to learn skills in a way that maximizes their capability to perform the skills in a variety of contexts and situations.

- When teaching a motor skill that will require the person to adapt to environmental context conditions or situations that the person hasn't experienced before, design practice conditions that will require the person to perform the skills in as many different environmental context conditions and situations as can be created.

- When teaching a motor skill that will require performance in environmental contexts in which the regulatory conditions will not change, such as shooting free throws in basketball or ascending or descending a set of stairs at home, design practice conditions that will require the person to perform the skills in the specific environmental context in which he or she will be required to perform the skill, but provide experiences with as many nonregulatory conditions and situations as possible.

- When organizing practice sessions for learning multiple skills or variations of a skill, provide opportunities to practice all the skills or variations in each session. When possible, arrange to have the skills in each session practiced in a random arrangement.

- If the test conditions for a skill that a person is learning will not allow visual feedback, develop practice conditions that do not provide visual feedback, such as the use of mirrors, especially for practice sessions that immediately precede the test situation.

RELATED READINGS

Albaret, J. M., & Thon, B. (1998). Differential effects of task complexity on contextual interference in a drawing task. *Acta Psychologica, 100,* 9–24.

Best, K. L., Kirby, R. L., Smith, C., & MacLeod, D. A. (2005). Wheelchair skills training for community-based manual wheelchair users: A randomized controlled trial. *Archives of Physical Medicine and Rehabilitation, 86,* 2316–2323.

Cross, E. S., Schmitt, P. J., & Grafton, S. T. (2007). Neural substrates of contextual interference in motor learning support a model of active preparation. *Journal of Cognitive Neuroscience, 19,* 1854–1871.

Fairbrother, J. T., Shea, J. B., & Marzilli, T. S. (2007). Repeated retention testing effects do not generalize to a contextual interference protocol. *Research Quarterly for Exercise and Sport, 78,* 465–475.

Hall, K. G. (1998, November/December). Using randomized drills to facilitate motor skill learning. *Strategies,* pp. 27–28, 35.

Harbourne, R. T., & Stergiou, N. (2009). Movement variability and the use of nonlinear tools: Principles to guide physical therapist practice. *Physical Therapy, 89,* 267–282.

Lee, T. D., Swanson, L. R., & Hall, A. L. (1991). What is repeated in a repetition? Effects of practice conditions on motor skill acquisition. *Physical Therapy, 71,* 150–156.

Lin, C. H., Fisher, B., Winstein, C. J., Wu, A. D., & Gordon, J. (2008). Contextual interference effect: Elaborative processing or forgetting-reconstruction? A post hoc analysis of transcranial magnetic stimulation-induced effects on motor learning. *Journal of Motor Behavior, 40,* 578–586.

Porter, J. M., Landin, D., Hebert, E. P., & Baum, B. (2007). The effects of three levels of contextual interference on performance outcomes and movement patterns in golf skills. *International Journal of Sports Science & Coaching, 2,* 243–254.

Prtichard, T., Hawkins, A., Wiegand, R., & Metzler, J. N. (2008). Effects of two instructional approaches on skill development, knowledge, and game performance. *Measurement in Physical Education and Exercise Science, 12,* 219–236.

Russell, D. M., & Newell, K. M. (2007). How persistent and general is the contextual interference effect? *Research Quarterly for Exercise and Sport, 78,* 318–327.

Sullivan, K. J., Brown, D. A., Klassen, T., Mulroy, S., Ge, T., Azen, S. P., & Winstein, C. J. (2007). Effects of task-specific locomotor and strength training in adults who were ambulatory after stroke: Results of the STEPS randomized clinical trial. *Physical Therapy, 87,* 1580–1602.

Weeks, D. I., Anderson, D. I., & Wallace, S. A. (2003). The role of variability in practice structure when learning to use an upper-extremity prosthesis. *Journal of Prosthetics and Orthotics, 15,* 84–92.

Williams, A. M., & Hodges, N. J. (2005). Practice, instruction, and skill acquisition in soccer: Challenging tradition. *Journal of Sports Sciences, 23,* 637–650.

INTERNET RESOURCES

- To read how to apply the concepts of practice variability and contextual interference to practicing putting in golf, go to http://golf.about.com/cs/2003seniortour/ht/puttingdrills.htm.

- To see slides that were handouts at a clinic for coaches of the high jump in track and field, go to http://www.usatf.org/groups/Coaches/library/2008/High%20Jump/6DrWillWu.pdf.

- To choose from a variety of sports application topics related to implementing effective practice conditions, go to http://coachesinfo.com.

- To watch a video demonstrating and discussing the application of blocked, serial, and random practice to learning and improving tennis skills, go to http://www.5min.com/Video/Blocked-Serial-and-Random-Practice-28027833.

STUDY QUESTIONS

1. What is meant by the term *practice variability* and why is it important for skill learning?

2. Give an example of how you would implement practice variability for (a) a closed skill without intertrial variability, (b) a closed skill with intertrial variability, (c) an open skill.

3. Define the terms *contextual interference* and the *contextual interference effect* as they relate to the learning and performance of multiple skills or multiple variations of a skill. (b) Discuss how the amount of contextual interference relates to the types of practice schedules that could be developed for situations in which people must learn multiple skills or multiple variations of a skill.

4. Describe four practice schedules that involve different amounts of contextual interference and locate each on a continuum that ranges from low to high amounts of contextual interference.

5. Describe an example that illustrates how you would implement an appropriate amount of contextual interference into the practice schedule for (a) a novice learning a skill and (b) a skilled person.

6. What are two reasons researchers have proposed for the benefits of contextual interference for motor skill learning?

7. Discuss (a) the practice specificity hypothesis in terms of its application to motor skill learning; and (b) how it relates to the practice variability hypothesis.

Specific Application Problem:
In your place of employment in your future profession, your supervisor has asked you to develop a schedule of activities for the people for whom you are responsible (e.g., students, athletes, patients) to help them improve their capability to perform at least three variations of a motor skill. You have a specified number of sessions in which you can work with these people. Describe the specific characteristics of this situation and specify the skills to be learned and the schedule you would design. Justify your plan to your supervisor in terms of why you would expect it to yield the best possible results.

The Amount and Distribution of Practice

Concept: The amount of practice and the spacing or distribution of that practice can affect both practice performance and the learning of motor skills.

After completing this chapter, you will be able to

■ Define *overlearning* in terms of how it relates to the decision about the amount of practice time needed to learn motor skills

■ Describe how an overlearning practice strategy influences the learning of procedural skills and dynamic balance skills

■ Discuss the relationship between overlearning and other practice condition variables

■ Describe how the concept of practice distribution is related to the intertrial interval and to the length and distribution of practice sessions

■ Discuss evidence supporting the benefit for distributed practice of the distribution of practice sessions and possible reasons for this benefit

■ Compare and contrast massed and distributed intertrial interval schedules for discrete and continuous motor skills

■ Describe how to implement knowledge of massed and distributed practice in various skill learning situations

APPLICATION

Teachers, coaches, and therapists must make important decisions about the amount of practice people should engage in, as well as how much time to devote to various activities within and across practice sessions within the total amount of practice time available. In terms of the amount of practice needed to learn a skill, the conventional wisdom seems to be that the more practice a person has, the better his or her performance will be in some future situation. Consider some examples. It seems likely that a dance teacher would encourage a dancer who was a bit tentative in certain parts of a routine to spend as much time as possible going over the routine repeatedly in practice. A golf instructor would probably try to help a person be more successful when putting by

encouraging the person to spend as much time as possible on the practice putting green. And a therapist would typically encourage a rehabilitation patient to practice the skill he or she was relearning as often as possible. Our experiences in situations like these lead us to accept the "more practice is better" approach. But ironically, although this approach seems logical, research evidence indicates that it is not always the best alternative. For example, as you saw in chapter 16 the same amount of practice can yield different learning results when practice follows different schedules. You will see another example of this type of effect in the Discussion section that follows.

After having determined the amount of practice time people need to learn a motor skill, the practitioner needs to determine how much time to devote to various activities within and across practice sessions. He or she must determine the amount of time to devote to each activity in a session, the amount of rest between activities within a session, the length of each session, and the amount of time between sessions.

If you are a physical education teacher organizing a volleyball unit, you need to determine how much time you should devote in each class period to working on the various skills, drills, and other activities that you plan to include. If you have determined the total amount of practice time you want to devote to a given activity in the unit, and you know how many class periods you will have in the unit, you will know how much time you need to spend in each class period on that activity.

Similarly, if you are an athletic trainer or a physical or occupational therapist, you need to determine how much time an athlete or a patient will spend on each activity within a session, how much rest time

Application Problem to Solve   Select a motor skill that you perform well for recreational or sports purposes and for which you received professional instruction. Think back to your early experiences when you practiced the skill with your instructor. Describe as best as you can remember how much practice you engaged in until you performed the skill at a proficient level. And describe the characteristics of the practice sessions in which you were involved with your instructor. How would you do these things in the same way as or differently from your experiences, and why would you keep things the same or change them?

Or recall an experience you had in physical rehabilitation with an athletic trainer or a physical or occupational therapist. Describe as best as you can remember the amount of rehab/therapy you experienced until you could perform the skill at a desired level. And describe the characteristics of the rehab/therapy sessions in which you were involved. How would you do these things similarly to or differently from your experiences, and why would you keep things the same or change them?

you should allow between activities in a session, when the next session should be, and so on. You also may need to instruct the person concerning how to arrange his or her time schedule to do prescribed activities at home.

DISCUSSION

The amount of practice a person devotes to a skill is critical for learning motor skills. This is especially the case when the person has the attaining of expertise as a goal. As we discussed in chapter 12, the impressive work by Ericsson has shown that expertise in any field is the result of intense practice for a minimum of ten years (Ericsson et al., 1993). Clearly, for achieving expertise, more practice is better than less. However, the amount of practice required to attain expertise is not our focus here. Instead, we will focus on the amount of practice a person needs to ensure achieving a specific learning goal associated with a specific period of practice.

There are many situations in which it is important to determine the amount of practice people should experience to achieve specific skill learning goals. Although limitations may exist in many of these situations in terms of the amount of time available for practice, the need to determine the amount of practice required remains. For example, a physical education teacher needs to determine the number of classes within a unit to devote to a specific activity. In sports settings, the amount of practice time available is restricted by a season's schedule or by rules established by professional associations. And, in rehabilitation contexts, the amount of time available for therapy is typically restricted by health care provider agencies.

As we address the issue of optimal amounts of practice, we will limit our discussion to these types of situations and establish some guidelines for the effective and efficient use of available practice time. As suggested by the examples we just considered, this limited focus is particularly relevant to those involved in settings that impose strict practice time limitations on teachers, coaches, and therapists.

OVERLEARNING AND LEARNING MOTOR SKILLS

Researchers historically have investigated the relationship between the amount of practice and the achievement of specific performance goals within the topic of *overlearning*. **Overlearning** is the continuation of practice beyond the amount needed to achieve a certain performance criterion. A teacher, coach, or therapist implements an overlearning strategy by establishing a performance criterion, determining the amount of practice time the learner needs to attain that criterion, and then requiring some percentage of that practice time as extra practice.

When we view it from a theoretical perspective, the idea of assigning extra practice has merit. Those who hold a motor program–based view of motor learning would say that extra practice helps strengthen the generalized motor program and response schema for the skill a person is learning, so that the person can call it into action more readily when necessary. From a dynamic pattern theory perspective, extra practice is a means by which a learner increases the stability of the coordination and control characteristics in the performance of the skill.

Driskell, Willis, and Copper (1992) reviewed and analyzed fifteen research studies that investigated several hypotheses related to overlearning. The first notable point about this review is that the issue of overlearning has not generated a great deal of research over the years. The fifteen studies covered research articles published from 1929 to 1982. However, these studies involved almost 4,000 subjects, which gives us a good basis for discerning the influence of overlearning on skill acquisition and how various factors influence overlearning. The results of this review indicated that for motor skill learning, overlearning has a positive influence on retention performance. And when extra practice of 50 to 200 percent was analyzed, the higher percentages resulted in relatively proportionate higher retention test performance.

Although the Driskell et al. (1992) review provides a comprehensive overview of overlearning

as it relates to skill acquisition, it does not evaluate effects related to specific types of motor skills. Because motor learning research has shown that certain types of skills demonstrate some distinct characteristics with regards to overlearning, we will consider three examples in the following sections.

The Overlearning Strategy for Learning Procedural Skills

Procedural skills constitute one type of motor skill particularly well suited to deriving benefits from an overlearning practice strategy. A procedural skill is an interesting combination of cognitive and motor components. It typically requires a person to perform a series of movements that individually are relatively easy to execute. However, to accomplish the total task, the performer must know which movements to make and in what order. These types of skills are especially common in occupational, industrial, and military settings. For example, people are performing procedural skills when their jobs require them to sort mail into appropriate bins, put together the components of a circuit board for a computer, or type from a written text.

A common problem with procedural skills is that people tend to forget what to do to carry out the entire procedure. This is particularly characteristic of procedural skills that they do not perform routinely every day. For example, several years ago, the U.S. Army was interested in improving the performance of soldiers assembling and disassembling machine guns. This skill was important to study because soldiers typically learned it in a short training period, but did not perform it again until some time after training; it was not a routine part of their daily duties. The problem was that when they performed a later test on this skill, the soldiers typically showed a large decrement in performance, compared to how they had performed at the end of

---

overlearning   practice that continues beyond the amount needed to achieve a certain performance criterion.

training. To overcome this problem, researchers for the U.S. Army Research Institute (Schendel & Hagman, 1982) proposed that an overlearning training strategy (which they referred to as *overtraining*) would be effective for decreasing the amount the soldiers forgot about the procedure.

The researchers compared two forms of overtraining with a no-overtraining situation. An "immediate" overtraining condition required soldiers to perform 100 percent more trials than were necessary to achieve a performance criterion of one correct assembly/disassembly trial. The second overtraining condition also involved an additional 100 percent more practice trials, but these trials were administered as "refresher" training midway through the 8 week retention interval used for all subjects. Results showed that both of these overtraining groups performed better than the no-overtraining control group on the retention test, which required the soldiers to practice until they were again able to assemble and disassemble the gun correctly on a trial. However, the two overtraining groups did not differ from each other in the number of trials it took to retrain to the criterion performance of one correct trial.

Based on the results of this experiment, the authors recommended the immediate overtraining procedure, because it was more cost- and time-effective. Because the trainees were already in the training session, it would take less time and money to have them engage in additional practice there than to bring them back several weeks later for a refresher training session.

The Overlearning Strategy for Learning Dynamic Balance Skills

In an experiment that involved learning a skill that has less of a cognitive component than the gun assembly/disassembly skill, Melnick (1971) investigated the use of overlearning for a dynamic balance skill. Although carried out many years ago, this experiment continues to be the only one reported in the research literature that involves the overlearning of dynamic balance skills. In addition to addressing the question of whether practice beyond what the learner needed to achieve a performance criterion

was beneficial, Melnick asked whether there was an optimal amount of extra practice. In this experiment, people practiced balancing on a stabilometer until they were able to achieve a performance criterion of 28 out of 50 sec. After achieving this criterion, each group was required to perform further trials in one of the following amounts: 0 percent (none), 50 percent, 100 percent, or 200 percent of the initial number of trials of practice. Then, all participants performed a retention test twice, one week and then one month after practice.

The results showed that extra practice was beneficial. All the groups that engaged in practice beyond what they needed to achieve the performance criterion performed better on the retention tests. More interesting, however, was the result that there appeared to be *a point of diminishing returns* for the amount of retention performance benefit in relation to the amount of extra practice. The group that had 50 percent additional practice did as well on the retention tests as the groups that had 100 percent and 200 percent extra practice. So, although additional practice was beneficial, increasing the amount of additional practice beyond a certain amount was not proportionally more beneficial to retention performance.

It's interesting to note here that a similar finding of the lack of benefit for additional practice beyond a certain amount was reported by Kwakkel and Wagenaar (2002) for physical therapy sessions. Although this study did not focus on dynamic balance, it showed that providing additional physical therapy sessions each day during a 5-day-per-week, 20 week period did not result in additional benefits for stroke patients immediately after the onset of their stroke.

The Overlearning Strategy in a Physical Education Class

Researchers also have demonstrated the presence of this phenomenon of "diminishing returns" from increases in the amount of practice for learning skills in physical education classes. A good example of this is an experiment by Goldberger and Gerney (1990). In a unit of instruction, fifth-grade boys and girls practiced several football skills. The goal of this unit was to help students improve their performance of these skills. To simplify matters, we will look only at the two-step football punt. One group practiced these skills according to a teacher-rotated format, in which the teacher divided the class into five subgroups and assigned each to one of five stations where they practiced the skills for 5 min. At the end of every 5 min, students rotated to a new station. Another group of students practiced according to a learner-rotated format: they received index cards describing what they needed to do at each station and then were told to use their 25 min efficiently to practice each skill. Everyone practiced like this for two class periods on two days. The next week, the students performed the skills in a test.

The results showed that the two groups differed in terms of the number of practice trials for this skill, but not in test performance. The teacher-rotated format group actually practiced the skill an average of 7 more trials than the learner-rotated format group. Students in the learner-rotated format group performed from 0 to 67 trials, whereas students in the teacher-rotated group performed from 0 to 87 trials. But there was no difference between the groups in the amount of improvement in their punting performance scores. The additional practice time induced by the teacher-rotated format did not yield an additional skill improvement benefit. Thus, given the time constraints of the unit of instruction, the learner-rotated format was superior, because it provided more efficient use of that time.

THE OVERLEARNING STRATEGY CAN LEAD TO POOR TEST PERFORMANCE

Although the overlearning strategy typically benefits skill learning, some evidence shows that learning deficits may result from providing *too many* extra practice trials. Shea and Kohl (1990) reported an example of this effect in an experiment in which participants learned to push a handle with a specified amount of force (175N). One group practiced this skill for 85 trials. Another group also practiced this skill for 85 trials, but in addition practiced the same skill at four other force goals (125N, 150N,

200N, and 225N) for 51 trials each, for a total of 289 practice trials. A third group practiced the skill with the 175N goal force for 289 trials. One day later, all participants engaged in a retention test in which they performed the skill with the goal force of 175N for 10 trials.

The results showed that the group that practiced the 175N goal force for 289 trials had the poorest performance on the initial 5 trials of the retention test. In contrast, the group that practiced the variable goals performed best. Results for the group that practiced only 85 trials of the 175N goal fell between those of the two other groups. The differences between these groups were most distinct on the first retention trial. However, on the final 5 trials of the retention test, all three groups performed similarly. These results were replicated in another experiment by the same authors (Shea & Kohl, 1991).

Similarly, Travlos (1999) reported that increasing the amount of practice beyond a certain number of trials resulted in poorer transfer test performance. In this experiment, participants attempted to learn the distance of a horizontal line by touching a digitizing tablet with a stylus at locations they estimated to be the beginning and end of the line. Although they could not see their movements, the participants received knowledge of results (KR) about their estimate in terms of the distance it deviated from the 8 in. criterion. Five groups experienced different amounts of practice: 42, 77, 102, 127, and 152 trials. At the end of practice, they performed a transfer test for five trials. This test required them to estimate the horizontal length of a 10 in. line. The results, which you can see in figure 17.1, showed that at the end of practice, all groups performed similarly. However, performance on the transfer test was very much influenced by the amount of practice. Those who practiced the task for 77 and 102 trials performed the transfer test with less error than the other practice groups. Interestingly, 42 practice trials were two few, but 127 and 152 trials were too many; additional practice beyond 102 trials led to decrement in transfer test performance rather than an enhancement of it.

The significance of the results reported in these three experiments is that they run counter to what

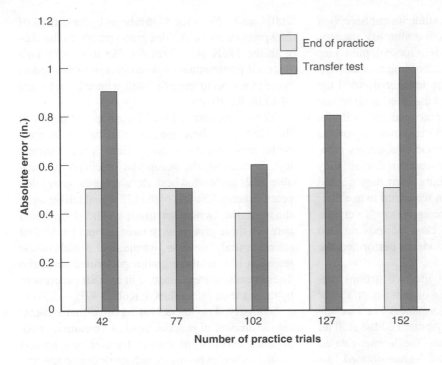

FIGURE 17.1 The results of the experiment by Travlos. Shown here is the amount of absolute error at the end of practice (black bars) and for the transfer test (grey bars) for five amounts of practice. [*Source:* Travlos, A. K. (1999). More practice does not necessarily enhance transfer of learning: Evidence and interpretations. *Perceptual and Motor Skills, 89,* 1161–1175.]

most people would expect. The addition of more practice beyond a certain amount did not improve retention and transfer test performance.

Why would more practice lead to poorer retention and transfer test performance than less practice? One reason could be that because the skills practiced in these experiments were so simple, boredom became a problem after a certain amount of practice. As a result, the learners reduced the amount of attention the task required to improve performance. Or, as Lee, Swinnen, and Serrien (1994) described it, the learners ceased to engage in the amount of *cognitive effort* required to improve task performance.

A second explanation relates to both the motor program–based and the dynamic pattern theories concerning the importance of *practice variability,* which you studied in chapter 16. According to these theories, continued practice of the same movement can result in a decreasing capability to remember the movement as well as to transfer to a movement variation, whereas the practice of variations of the movement results in enhancing the capability to remember and transfer to a related movement. It is interesting to note in this regard

that in the Shea and Kohl experiments, practice of criterion task variations resulted in better retention performance than the same amount of practice of the criterion task only. If these results were extended to performance on a transfer test, we would expect similar results.

OVERLEARNING AND OTHER PRACTICE VARIABLES

It can be useful for a learner to continue to practice a skill even though he or she can perform it correctly; such practice increases the permanence of the person's capability to perform the skill at some future time. However, the research investigating the overlearning strategy has shown rather conclusively that *the amount of practice is not the critical variable influencing motor skill acquisition.* In keeping with the commonly heard expression, "Practice does not make perfect; perfect practice makes perfect," the amount of practice invariably interacts with some other variable to yield optimal skill learning. You have seen this interaction with a number of practice-related variables, such as the type and frequency of augmented feedback and the variability of practice. From this perspective, the amount of practice is beneficial to a point. To establish an optimal learning environment, the instructor and/or learner also must take other practice condition characteristics into account. This does not mean that the amount of practice is unimportant. It does mean that the amount of practice cannot be considered in isolation, but in terms of its interaction with other practice condition variables.

THE DISTRIBUTION OF PRACTICE

Practice distribution (sometimes referred to as the spacing of practice) has been a popular topic for research in motor learning for many years. The most popular era for this study extended from the 1930s through the 1950s, when practice distribution was seen as a way to test learning theories popular at that time. However, researchers have continued to investigate practice distribution issues because of its relevance to applied settings in a variety of contexts.

One of the issues that was the focus of much of the early research concerned the amount of rest people need between practice trials to ensure an optimal learning environment. At issue was the question of whether *massed or distributed* practice trials provided for better learning of motor skills. Some researchers argued that distributed practice was better; others maintained that it did not make much difference which spacing strategy an instructor followed.

Although this early controversy focused on between-trial rest intervals, the study of practice distribution also concerns the amount of practice during each session of practice and the amount of rest between sessions. In this second practice distribution issue, the question of concern is whether it is better to have fewer but longer sessions or more but shorter sessions.

DEFINING MASSED AND DISTRIBUTED PRACTICE

Researchers use the terms **massed practice** and **distributed practice** in a general way to distinguish practice distribution schedules rather than assign specific amounts of time, which would allow for more objective definitions for these terms. The best way to understand these terms is to know that a massed practice schedule involves longer active practice, or work time, and shorter rest periods than a distributed schedule. Although rather vague, these definitions are necessary because of the types of situations to which they apply.

When applied to the *length and distribution of practice sessions,* a *massed schedule* will have fewer practice sessions than a distributed schedule, with each massed practice session requiring more and/or longer practice. A *distributed schedule,* on the other hand, will distribute the same amount of practice time across more sessions, so that each session is shorter than each session in the massed schedule; the distributed practice sessions must be extended over a longer period to achieve the same total amount of practice.

When these terms apply to the *rest intervals between trials,* a *massed schedule* will have either no rest or a very short rest interval between trials. A *distributed schedule* will have much longer rest intervals than a massed schedule. Some researchers have specified that the length of the rest interval for a massed schedule is shorter than the amount of time required to perform the skill, but is as long or longer as the skill performance time for a distributed schedule. Although this conditional approach provides a more objective definition, it does not always describe these schedules as researchers have implemented them, especially for many discrete skills that may require less than one second to perform.

THE LENGTH AND DISTRIBUTION OF PRACTICE SESSIONS

For most instruction and rehabilitation situations, the primary practice distribution concern is how to use an allotted amount of time within and between practice

---

massed practice   a practice schedule in which the amount of rest between practice sessions or trials is very short.

distributed practice   a practice schedule in which the amount of rest between practice sessions or trials is relatively long.

sessions. As with our discussion earlier in this chapter, an important consideration here is that many instruction and rehabilitation situations have specified limits for the amount of time available. For most clinical applications, a patient may receive treatment for only a limited number of sessions because of health care management restrictions. Also, in teaching and coaching situations, there is often little flexibility in the number of days available for classes or practice sessions. For example, if a teacher has only ten days for a unit of instruction, then the practice schedule must fit that limit. Similarly, if a dancer must perform in a concert that is one month away, then the rehearsal schedule must adjust accordingly. Thus, outside limitations may determine how many days a person should devote to practice. However, the instructor, coach, or therapist still decides the number of practice sessions and the length of each one.

The Benefit of More and Shorter Sessions

Although there is not an abundance of research addressing the optimal number and length of practice sessions, the available evidence points to *the benefit of distributed practice.* The general result of experiments comparing a few long practice sessions with more frequent and shorter sessions is that practicing skills during shorter sessions leads to better learning.

The classic example of research supporting this general conclusion is a study published many years ago by Baddely and Longman (1978). They were attempting to determine the best way to schedule training sessions for postal workers on a mail-sorting machine, which required operating a typewriter-like keyboard. The training time limitations were a total of 60 hours and 5 days each week. The researchers distributed this practice time in four different ways. Two groups practiced for 1 hour in each session. One of these groups practiced for only one session each day, which resulted in a total training time of 12 weeks, whereas the second group had two sessions each day, thereby reducing the number of weeks in training to 6. Two other groups practiced for 2 hours in each session. One of these groups had only one session each day, whereas the other had two sessions per day. These latter two groups therefore had 6 weeks and

TABLE 17.1 Results of the Baddeley and Longman Experiment with Practice Distribution Schedules for Training Postal Workers

Practice Schedule	Number of Hours to Type 80 Keystrokes/Minute
1 hr/session–1 session/day (12 weeks training)	55
1 hr/session–2 sessions/day (6 weeks training)	75
2 hrs/session–1 session/day (6 weeks training)	67
2 hrs/session–2 session/day (3 weeks training)	80+

Source: Data from Baddeley, A. D., & Longman, D. J. A. (1978). The influence of length and frequency training session on the rate of learning to type. *Ergonomics, 21,* 627–635.

3 weeks of training, respectively. As this situation demonstrates, there are a variety of ways to distribute 60 hours of practice. The most distributed schedule required workers to train for 12 weeks, whereas the most massed schedule allowed them to complete their training in only 3 weeks. The difference lay in how long each session was and how many sessions occurred each day.

Table 17.1 describes the number of hours the trainees required to achieve a typing speed of 80 keystrokes per minute, which was the motor performance goal for their training. Notice that only those in the most distributed schedule group attained this goal in the allotted training time of 60 hours (they did it in 55 hours). All of the other groups required additional practice time. It is interesting that those in the most massed schedule group, which practiced two 2 hour sessions each day, never achieved this goal. After 80 hours of practice they were still doing only a little better than 70 keystrokes per minute.

Retention tests were given 1, 3, and 9 months after the workers had finished training. After 9 months, the most massed group performed worse on the typing speed test than the other groups, which performed about equally. Finally, the researchers

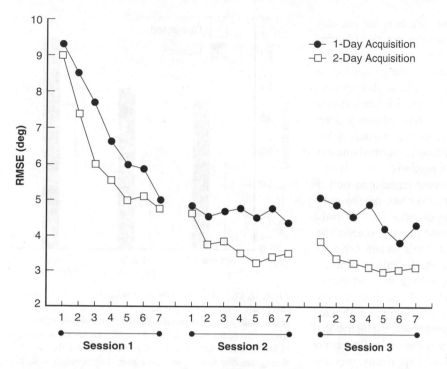

FIGURE 17.2 Results of the experiment by Shea et al. in which one group participated in two practice sessions on one day (circles) and another participated in one session on each of two days (squares). The graph shows the amount of balancing error (RMSE, which was calculated as the amount of deviation, in degrees, from horizontal) for each 90 sec trial on a dynamic balance task. [*Source:* Figure 3, p. 745 in Shea, Lai, Black, & Park. (2000). Spacing practice sessions across days benefit the learning of motor skills. *Human Movement Science, 19,* 737–760.]

obtained a very revealing result from the trainees' own ratings of the training schedules. Although most workers preferred their own schedule, those in the most massed group preferred theirs the most, whereas members of the most distributed liked theirs the least. Interestingly, these preferences were exactly opposite to the performance test results.

The results of this experiment indicate that fitting 60 hours of training into 3 weeks, where there had to be two 2 hour practice sessions each day, was a poor practice schedule. Although those in the most distributed schedule generally attained performance goals in the shortest time, they did not perform any better than two of the other groups on the retention tests. Given all the results, the authors concluded that the 1 hour training sessions were more desirable than the 2 hour sessions, and that one session per day was only slightly more effective than two sessions per day. However, having two 2 hour sessions each day was not a good training schedule.

More recent studies have shown similar learning benefits for distributed practice for a variety of motor skills, as the following examples demonstrate.

Annett and Piech (1985) found that two 5 trial training sessions separated by one day led to better learning of a computer target-shooting game than one 10 trial session. One trial involved shooting at ten singly presented moving targets. On a retention test given one day after the end of the training session, the distributed group not only had more "hits" but also had less error in the shooting attempts.

Bouzid and Crawshaw (1987) reported similar results for the learning of word processing skills. Typists who practiced twelve skills during two sessions of 35 and 25 min each, separated by a 10 min break, required less time to learn the skills and had fewer errors on a test than typists who practiced the skills during one 60 min session.

Shea et al. (2000) showed that distributing practice sessions across days resulted in better learning than massing all the sessions within one day for a continuous dynamic balance task and a discrete key-press timing task. The results for the continuous balance task are shown in figure 17.2. Note that for the first session of trials (each trial involved

90 sec of continuous balancing), both the one-day practice (massed) and the two-day practice (distributed) groups performed similarly. However, during the second practice session the groups began to perform differently. By the end of this session, the distributed group, for whom this session was the next day, had significantly less balancing error. Importantly, this difference continued during the retention test, which each group performed one day after the end of the practice sessions.

Finally, in a study involving learning to putt in golf, Dail and Christina (2004) had novice golfers practice putting a 3.7 m distance for 240 trials. One group followed a massed practice schedule in which they performed all the trials on one day, with short breaks between blocks of 10 trials. In contrast, another group practiced according to a distributed schedule of 60 trials per day for 4 consecutive days. The results, which you can see in figure 17.3, showed that at the end of 240 practice trials, the distributed practice group performed at a higher level than the massed schedule group. More importantly, this difference continued 1 and 7 days later on retention tests of 60 trials. It is also interesting to note that at the end of each block of 10 trials during the practice sessions the experimenters asked the participants to predict their performance on the retention test. For this assessment of their own competence (i.e., metacognition), the participants who experienced the distributed schedule more accurately predicted their retention test performance.

Taken together, the results of these experiments support the learning advantage of distributed over massed practice schedules when the number and length of practice sessions is the concern. And when considered in terms of the types of motor skills involved in the experiments, the benefit of distributed practice extends to a variety of types of skills, which include discrete and continuous skills as well as open and closed skills. Unfortunately, the research does not give us a specific number and length of practice sessions that would be optimal for the learning of all motor skills. However, the conclusion that shorter and more practice sessions lead to better learning than longer and fewer sessions provides an excellent general principle on which

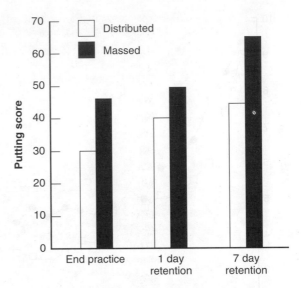

FIGURE 17.3 Results of the experiment by Dail and Christina in which two groups practiced putting a golf ball either in 240 trials in one day (massed practice) or in 4 days of 60 trials each (distributed practice). The graph shows the results (a lower score is better) at the end of the practice trials and during retention tests 1 and 7 days later. [Data from Dail, T. K., & Christina, R. W. (2004). Distribution of practice and metacognition in learning and long-term retention. *Research Quarterly for Exercise and Sport, 75,* 148–155, figure 1.]

to base specific decisions when planning practice, training, or rehabilitation sessions.

Explanations for the Distributed Practice Benefit

There are at least three possible reasons why the distribution of practice sessions across more days leads to better learning than massing the sessions within fewer days. One is that *fatigue* negatively influences learning for massed practice schedules. Although none of the experiments discussed in this section assessed participants' levels of fatigue, it is possible to suspect that fatigue influenced learning because of the task performance requirements. For example, in the Shea et al. (2000) experiment, participants performed a continuous dynamic balance task for 90 sec on each trial. The massed practice schedule required them to perform 14 trials on the same day with only a 20 min break between

A CLOSER LOOK

Relating Practice Distribution and Contextual Interference to Skill Learning Contexts

The concept of contextual interference can be incorporated into practice distribution by organizing practice sessions to include principles related to both. The following are some examples that relate to three different skill learning contexts.

- **Physical education class.** If several drills or other kinds of activity are planned for the day's lesson, use a station-organization approach by assigning each skill or activity to a location in the gym or on the field so that there are several stations. Divide the class into groups and assign each to a station. Let the groups stay in their stations for about 12–15 minutes and then rotate to the next station. Continue this rotation approach for the entire period. If the class period is sufficiently long, allow for two or more rotations.

- **Sports-related practice.** Practices for team and individual sports typically include several activities. Rather than spend an extended amount of time on any one activity, divide in half the amount of time planned for each activity, and do each activity as two sets during practice. The two sets can be randomly or serially scheduled during the practice session.

- **Physical rehabilitation session.** Like sports-related practice sessions, rehab sessions typically involve several activities. If the planned activities allow, apply the approach described for sports-related practice by dividing in half the total amount of time planned for each activity, and do each activity as two randomly or serially scheduled sets during the session.

---

trials 7 and 8. On the other hand, participants in the distributed practice schedule performed the second set of seven trials on the following day. Similarly in the Dail and Christina (2004) experiment, participants who experienced the massed practice schedule performed 240 putts in one session, with short rest breaks only after each set of 10 trials. In contrast, those who practiced according to the distributed schedule performed only 60 trials in each session.

Second, the massing of practice within a day or a few days may reduce the amount of *cognitive effort* used on each trial as practice continues beyond a certain critical amount. We considered this explanation earlier in this chapter when we discussed reasons why more practice beyond a certain amount could lead to diminished learning. The massing of practice trials may institute a practice condition in which performance of the skill on each trial becomes so repetitive that it becomes monotonous or boring. As a result, the learner begins to decrease the amount of cognitive effort involved in each trial, which in turn diminishes the level of learning.

The possibility that either or both fatigue and reduced cognitive effort accounted for the poorer learning that resulted from the massed compared to the distributed practice sessions can be seen in the results of the Shea et al. (2000) and Dail and Christina (2004) experiments. As you can see in figure 17.2, although it is not portrayed in figure 17.3, lower practice performance in both studies did not begin until the last several trials for the massed practice condition. This suggests that as participants continued to practice, the effects of fatigue or reduced cognitive effort eventually began to influence their performance in a negative way. And this influence affected not only their practice performance but also their retention test performance, indicating an influence on their learning the skills.

The third explanation relates to *memory consolidation,* which is a long-term memory storage process. The memory consolidation hypothesis proposes that to store in memory the relevant information we need to learn a skill, certain neurobiochemical processes must occur. These processes, which transform a relatively unstable memory representation into a relatively permanent one, require

LAB LINKS

Lab 17 in the Online Learning Center Lab Manual provides an opportunity for you to experience a comparison of the effects of massed and distributed practice on the learning of a discrete motor skill.

a certain amount of time without additional practice of the same skill. The distribution of practice across several days provides a better opportunity for the memory consolidation process to take place than does the massing of practice within a day or a few days (see Brashers-Krug, Shadmehr, & Bizzi, 1996; Shadmehr & Brashers-Krug, 1997).

THE INTERTRIAL INTERVAL AND PRACTICE DISTRIBUTION

By far the greatest amount of research on the distribution of practice has investigated the length of the intertrial interval, which relates to the amount of rest a person has between practice trials. One of the problems confronted when trying to understand this research relates to the definition problem described earlier in this chapter.

To elaborate on the general definitions presented earlier, we shall define *massed practice* as practice in which the amount of rest between trials is either very short or nonexistent, so that practice is relatively continuous. *Distributed practice* is practice in which the amount of rest between trials or groups of trials is relatively long. Although the terms "very short" and "relatively long" in these definitions are somewhat ambiguous, they allow us to generalize as much as possible from the research literature on massed versus distributed practice to motor skill learning situations.

A History of Controversy

Although a great deal of research literature exists concerning the distribution of practice as it relates to the length of the intertrial interval, it is filled with controversy about which schedule leads to better

To enhance the learning of continuous motor skills, such as jumping rope, practice sessions should follow distributed schedules.

learning. The controversy is evident in reviews of this literature as well as motor learning textbooks; both provide a variety of answers to the practice distribution question.

Two problems underlie the controversy surrounding this issue. The first relates to the issue of practice performance versus learning effects. Many of the experiments on massed versus distributed practice did not include retention or transfer trials. The second problem is that researchers generally have failed to consider that the two practice distribution schedules may have different learning effects on different types of skills.

Two reviews of the distributed practice research literature have helped resolve these problems and the controversy about which practice schedule is better for learning motor skills (Donovan & Radosevich, 1999; Lee & Genovese, 1988). Both reviews involved a statistical analysis, known as meta-analysis, to evaluate the research literature. Their conclusion was that the *type of task* was an important variable in determining practice distribution effects for schedules related to the length of intertrial rest intervals. More specifically, Lee and Genovese (1988, 1989) provided evidence that the type of practice distribution schedule that results in better learning depends on whether the skill is continuous or discrete. We will look at each of these types of skills next.

Continuous skills. Continuous skills have been the most common type of motor skills used to investigate the effects of massed versus distributed practice between trials. And the most popular task has been the rotary pursuit task, in which a person must keep a handheld stylus in contact with a small disk on a rotating turntable for as long as possible. A trial is usually a specified length of time, such as 20 or 30 sec. What makes this type of task useful for investigating the issue of massed versus distributed practice is that it is quite easy to specify massed and distributed intertrial interval lengths. Massed practice schedules typically have few, if any, seconds of rest between trials, whereas the intervals in distributed schedules are as long as or longer than the trials themselves. Because of this, researchers can establish intertrial interval lengths that are readily identifiable as distinctly massed or distributed. The Lee and Genovese (1988) review found that the consistent result has been that *distributed schedules lead to better learning* than massed schedules for learning continuous motor skills.

Discrete skills. When researchers use discrete skills to investigate the issue of intertrial massed versus distributed practice, a problem arises that is directly related to the definition problem we discussed earlier. If a massed schedule allows no rest between trials, whereas a distributed schedule involves a rest interval that is the same length as

the practice trial, then the two contrasted intertrial intervals will be essentially the same length, because a discrete response is typically very short. For example, if people are practicing a rapid-aiming task that has a duration of approximately 150 msec, the distributed practice condition could, by definition, have a 150 msec intertrial interval. But if the massed condition had no rest between trials, only 150 msec would separate the two practice schedules. Thus, the operational definition of the terms "massed" and "distributed" becomes especially important in experiments using discrete tasks. Probably one reason this has not troubled researchers is that discrete tasks seldom have been used for comparing massed to distributed practice. In fact, in their comprehensive review, Lee and Genovese (1988) found only one study in the research literature that used a discrete task (Carron, 1969). The results of that study, and one subsequently reported by Lee and Genovese (1989), provided evidence that *massed practice schedules result in better learning* for discrete motor skills.

A Final Comment about Practice Distribution and Motor Learning

In this discussion of practice distribution effects on the learning of motor skills, an important distinction was made between two specific issues related to practice distribution: the length and frequency of practice sessions, and the length of the intertrial interval for a series of practice trials. These two issues are often overlooked as distinct even though research evidence supports the distinction. A significant reason for the distinction is that two different conclusions concerning how to best distribute practice are associated with each issue. When the length and frequency of practice sessions is the practice distribution concern, distributed practice results in better learning than massed practice, regardless of the type of skill being learned. On the other hand, when the length of the intertrial interval for a series of practice trials is the concern, the type of skill being learned is an important consideration.

SUMMARY

Issues concerning the *amount of practice* needed to achieve specific skill performance goals historically have been discussed and investigated within the topic of *overlearning*.

- Overlearning is the continuation of practice beyond the amount needed to achieve a certain performance criterion.

- Research investigation of overlearning as a practice strategy has shown that the view that "more is better" is not always appropriate for the learning of motor skills, especially in terms of the benefits derived in relation to the amount of practice experienced; that is, there appears to be a *point of diminishing returns* for amount of practice.

- Research has shown that learning deficits can result when too much overlearning is involved in learning of motor skills that are simple and easy to learn; this effect is probably due to a decrease in the amount of cognitive effort applied after a certain amount of practice.

Issues related to the *distribution of available practice time* involve massed and distributed practice schedules. The terms *massed* and *distributed* are generally defined in relation to each other according to the practice schedule characteristics of each.

- One type of practice distribution schedule involves the *length and frequency of practice sessions;* this type typically concerns a massed schedule of longer sessions within a day or a few days compared to a distributed schedule of shorter sessions across more days than the massed schedule.

- Research evidence shows that practice sessions can be too long and too infrequent to lead to optimal learning. Typically, better learning results when people practice skills in larger numbers of shorter practice sessions than when they do so in sessions that are long and fewer in number.

- We discussed three hypotheses proposed to explain why distributed practice sessions lead to better learning than massed sessions: a fatigue hypothesis, a cognitive effort hypothesis, and a memory consolidation hypothesis.

- The second type of practice distribution schedule involves the *length of the intertrial interval,* which is the rest period between practice trials.

- Research evidence shows that the optimum length for the intertrial interval depends on whether the skill is continuous or discrete. For continuous skills, distributed practice schedules are typically better for learning, but massed practice schedules are preferable for discrete skills.

POINTS FOR THE PRACTITIONER

Overlearning:

- The overlearning strategy works best when the practitioner knows how much practice (i.e., number of trials or amount of time) a person needs to achieve a certain performance level.

- The overlearning strategy can be effective for skills that people will practice for a specified amount of time but then not perform for some period of time afterwards (e.g., the disassembling and assembling of the machine gun in the Schendel and Hagman study).

- Practitioners should not base the amount of extra practice to provide on the view that "more is better." There can be a point of diminishing returns where the extra practice does not yield results proportional to the amount of time and effort required by the extra practice, and the extra practice could actually lead to poorer test performance than would no extra practice. One way to determine the amount of extra practice is to require 100 percent more practice than the amount required by the person to achieve the specified performance criterion.

- Practice requiring the performance of variations of skill characteristics can be an effective means of establishing an overlearning situation.

Practice Distribution:

- Practice sessions can be too long. When in doubt about how long a session should be, opt for a shorter rather than a longer amount of time. If people need more practice time, add more sessions rather than lengthen sessions.

- More frequent practice sessions are preferable to fewer sessions.

- Time saved in terms of the number of days of practice can be a false savings because massing sessions too close together can lead to poor long-term results.

- The length and number of sessions desired by students, trainees, athletes, or patients may not represent the best schedule for learning the skills they need to learn. Remember that if the postal trainees in the Baddeley and Longman study had been allowed to choose their own training schedules, they would have chosen the schedule that led to the poorest learning.

- Make practice trials relatively short for skills that last a reasonably long time and require repetitive movements, such as swimming, bicycling, dancing, keyboarding, and piano playing. Shorter but more trials lead to better learning than longer trials that are infrequently repeated.

- For skills that require relatively brief amounts of time to perform (e.g., hitting a golf ball, serving a tennis ball, shooting a basketball, throwing darts, reach-and-grasp activities), make rest intervals between practice trials short.

RELATED READINGS

Ammons, R. B. (1988). Distribution of practice in motor skill acquisition: A few questions and comments. *Research Quarterly for Exercise and Sport, 59,* 288–290.

Croce, R. V., & Jacobson, W. H. (1986). The application of two-point touch cane technique to theories of motor control and learning: Implications for orientation and mobility training. *Journal of Visual Impairment and Blindness, 80,* 790–793.

Garcia, J. A., Moreno, F. J., Reina, R., Menayo, R., & Fuentes, J. P. (2008). Analysis of effects of distribution of practice

in learning and retention of a continuous and a discrete skill presented on a computer. *Perceptual and Motor Skills, 107,* 261–272.

Lee, T. D., & Wishart, L. R. (2005). Motor learning conundrums (and possible solutions). *Quest, 57,* 67–78.

Mackay, S., Morgan, P., Datta, V., Chang, A., & Darzi, A. (2002). Practice distribution in procedural skills training—A randomized controlled trial. *Surgical Endoscopy and Other Interventional Techniques, 16,* 957–961.

Rhodenizer, L., Bowers, C. A., & Bergondy, M. (1998). Team practice schedules: What do we know? *Perceptual and Motor Skills, 87,* 31–34.

Schmidt, R. A., & Bjork, R. A. (1992). New conceptualizations of practice: Common principles in three paradigms suggest new concepts for training. *Psychological Science, 3,* 207–217.

Siengsukon, C. F., & Boyd, L. A. (2009). Does sleep promote motor learning? Implications for physical rehabilitation. *Physical Therapy, 89,* 370–383.

Todd, M., & Barrow, C. (2008). Teaching memory-impaired people to touch type: The acquisition of a useful complex perceptual-motor skill. *Neuropsychological Rehabilitation, 18,* 486–506.

INTERNET RESOURCES

- To read an application of overlearning to the learning and playing of tennis, go to http://www. tennisserver. com/mental-equipment/me_01_10.html.

- To read what a professional baseball coach says to coaches about massed versus distributed practice, go to http://www.baseballtips.com/. In the Search box, type "massed practice." Then click on the links for "Distributed Versus Massed Practice."

STUDY QUESTIONS

1. Discuss two different ways the term *overlearning* can be used to relate to learning motor skills.

2. (a) Define the term "procedural skill" as it is commonly used in the motor learning literature. (b) What was the recommendation from the results of the Schendel and Hagman study for using an overlearning strategy to help people learn a procedural skill? Indicate why they made this recommendation.

3. Discuss the evidence that would support the view that "more is better" may not be the best approach to implementing an overlearning strategy to help people learn a motor skill.

4. Describe how the concept of practice distribution is related to the intertrial interval and to the length and distribution of practice sessions. Describe a motor skill learning situation for each.

5. Describe three research studies that provide evidence that demonstrates the benefit of distributed over massed practice sessions for learning a motor skill.

6. Discuss three possible explanations for the learning benefit that results from distributed practice sessions compared to massed schedules for the length and number of practice sessions scheduled for learning a motor skill.

7. (a) How do massed and distributed intertrial interval schedules differentially influence the learning of discrete and continuous motor skills?

(b) Why do you think there is a difference in how massed and distributed intertrial interval schedules influence the learning of discrete and continuous skills?

8. Describe how you would implement your knowledge about massed and distributed practice in *one* of the following situations: a physical education or dance class; a practice session for a sport; a physical or occupational therapy session.

Specific Application Problem:
Describe a situation in which you are working with people to help them improve their performance of a motor skill. Part of your job is to determine the amount of time the people need to receive your assistance, and then to schedule the length and number of sessions for them to practice the skill with your assistance. Present a plan that would describe how you would respond to both of these scheduling issues. Include in your plan a rationale to justify these decisions.

CHAPTER 18

Whole and Part Practice

Concept: Base decisions about practicing skills as wholes or in parts on the complexity and organization characteristics of the skills.

After completing this chapter, you will be able to

- Define the terms *complexity* and *organization* as they relate to the relationships among the parts or components of a complex motor skill
- Describe ways to apply the part practice methods of *fractionization* and *segmentation* to the practice of motor skills
- Describe several ways to apply *simplification* methods to the practice of motor skills

APPLICATION

An important decision you must make when you teach any motor skill concerns whether it is better to have the learner practice the skill in its entirety or by parts. Consider the following sport skill instruction situation as an example. Suppose you are teaching a beginning tennis class. You are preparing to teach the serve. Most tennis instruction books break down the serve into six or seven parts: the grip, stance, backswing, ball toss, forward swing, ball contact, and follow-through. You must decide whether to have the students practice all of these parts together as a whole or to have them practice each component or group of components separately.

The question of whether to use whole or part practice also confronts professionals in a rehabilitation setting. For example, when a patient needs to learn the task of getting out of bed and getting into a wheelchair, this decision comes into play. Although this task has distinct and identifiable parts, the therapist must determine whether to have the patient practice each part separately or always practice the whole sequence.

There are other situations in which the whole-part practice decision must be made. For example, a person may need to learn to perform a skill that requires the asymmetric use of both hands, which is common for playing many musical instruments, such as the piano, guitar, or drums, or performing many activities of daily living, such as opening or closing the lid of a jar. Other skills involve the use of either hand, or foot, but only one at a time, such as dribbling a basketball and kicking a soccer ball. In these skills, proficiency with either hand or foot is important for highly skilled performance.

In all the skill learning situations, the practitioner will need to decide whether to begin practice sessions with instruction that engages people in practicing the whole skill or parts of the skill. And if the latter option is chosen, a decision must be made about what kind of part practice. In the following discussion, we will consider these issues in a way that should provide a basis for making these decisions.

Application Problem to Solve Think about the various motor skills that you perform daily or for recreational purposes. If you had to teach each of these skills to someone, how would you decide whether it would be best for that person to begin learning each skill by practicing the whole skill or parts of the skill?

DISCUSSION

The issue of whether to use whole or part practice has been a topic of discussion in the motor learning literature since the early 1900s. Unfortunately, that early research often led to more confusion than understanding. One of the reasons was that researchers tended to investigate the issue in terms of whether one or the other type of practice is better for learning specific skills, without concern for determining skill-related characteristics that could help them make useful generalizations about which practice scheme would be preferable for certain skills. For example, the question of whole versus part practice was investigated for learning a maze task (Barton, 1921) or a piano score (Brown, 1928) as well as for learning how to juggle (Knapp & Dixon, 1952) and master gymnastic skills (Wickstrom, 1958), to name a few examples. Although this research provided useful information about teaching these specific skills, it did little to establish a guiding principle for decisions about whether to use whole or part practice.

An important part of teaching balance beam skills and routines is the decision to practice them as a whole skill or routine, or in parts.

SKILL COMPLEXITY AND ORGANIZATION

A breakthrough in understanding the issue of whole versus part practice occurred in the early 1960s, when James Naylor and George Briggs (1963) hypothesized that the organization and complexity characteristics of a skill could provide the basis for a decision to use either whole or part practice. This hypothesis made it possible for instructors to predict for any skill which method of practice would be preferable.

Naylor and Briggs defined **complexity** in a way that is consistent with the term's use in this text. They stated that *complexity* refers to the number of parts or components in a skill, as well as the attention demands of the task. This means that a highly complex skill would have many components and demand much attention, especially from a beginner. Performing a dance routine, serving a

tennis ball, and getting out of bed and into a wheelchair are examples of highly complex skills. Low-complexity skills have few component parts and demand relatively limited attention. For example, the skills of shooting an arrow and picking up a cup are low in complexity. *It is important to keep the term complexity distinct from difficulty.* As you saw in the discussion of Fitts' law in chapter 7, skills of the same complexity can vary in their level of difficulty.

The **organization** of a skill refers to the relationships among the component parts of a skill. A skill has a *high level of organization* when its component parts are spatially and temporally interdependent.

This means that the successive parts of a highly organized skill are like a chain of events in which the spatial-temporal performance characteristics of any one part are dependent on the spatial-temporal performance characteristics of the part performed just before it. Because of this characteristic, it would be difficult to perform only one part of a highly organized skill. The jump shot in basketball is a good example of a highly organized skill, because the manner in which a person performs each part will depend on the manner in which he or she performed the part(s) that preceded it. Although the arm and hand movements involved in the release of the ball could be practiced separately, the spatial location of the arm and hands as well as the timing of the ball release must be related to other parts of the skill, such as the direction and the height of the jump. In contrast, a skill has a *low level of organization* when the spatial-temporal relationships among the component parts of a skill are relatively independent. As a result, it is possible to practice any one component part by itself, because its spatial-temporal performance characteristics do not depend on those of the part that precedes it. Examples here include many dance routines and handwriting certain words.

Skill Characteristics and the Decision to Use Whole or Part Practice

Based on the Naylor and Briggs hypothesis, assessing the levels of complexity and organization of a skill and determining their relationship helps the practitioner decide whether to use whole or part practice. If the skill is *low in complexity and high in organization,* practice of the whole skill is the better choice. This means that people learn relatively simple skills in which the few component parts are highly related most efficiently using the whole practice method. For example, the skills of buttoning a button, throwing a dart, and putting a golf ball have this combination of characteristics. On the other hand, people learn skills that are *high in complexity and low in organization* most efficiently by the part method. For example, the skills of serving a tennis ball; reaching for, grasping, and

drinking from a cup; and shifting gears on a car have these characteristics.

To determine which of these complexity and organization combinations describe a particular skill, it is necessary to first analyze the skill. This analysis needs to focus on identifying the skill's component parts and the extent to which the spatial-temporal performance characteristics of those parts are interdependent. Next, decide which part of the continuum of skill complexity and organization best represents the skill.

By far, most of the motor skills we perform as a part of our daily living activities and sports would be placed closer to the complex than the simple end of a complexity continuum. This means that for most skills, the practitioner must determine the level of organization that characterizes the skill. For skills that we would place on an organization continuum somewhere between the extremes of low and high, an additional task analysis step is required. For these types of skills, it is necessary to determine which component parts are independent of the others and which group together as interdependent. The result of this analysis will determine which parts could be practiced independently. That is, some of the "parts" a person practices would consist of more than one of the component parts that resulted from the initial task analysis. This grouping of parts can be thought of as a "natural unit" within the skill. Because teachers, coaches, and therapists typically work with motor skills that would suggest some sort of practice, we will first consider issues relevant to part practice.

---

complexity   the number of parts or components and the amount of information-processing demands that characterize a skill; more complex skills have more component parts and involve more information processing demands than less complex skills.

organization   when applied to a complex motor skill, the relationships among the components of the skill.

A CLOSER LOOK

An Example of Making the Decision Regarding Use of Whole or Part Practice

Use skill analysis to determine whether to practice juggling three balls as a whole or in parts:

Skill Analysis

Complexity characteristics

1. Hold the three balls in two hands.
2. Toss ball 1 from hand 1.
3. Catch ball 1 in hand 2 while tossing ball 2 with hand 2.
4. Catch ball 2 in hand 1 while tossing ball 3 with hand 2.
5. Catch ball 3 in hand 1 while tossing ball 1 with hand 2.
6. Repeat steps 2 and 5.
7. Between-component timing: critical for performance.

Organization characteristics. Doing any one part without doing the part that precedes or follows it does not allow the learner to experience critical between-component timing aspects.

Conclusion. Three-ball juggling involves several component parts that are highly interdependent. Therefore, juggling three balls is relatively high in complexity and in organization. *Practicing the whole skill* is the predicted appropriate method.

Empirical Evidence Supporting the Whole Practice Prediction

In an experiment that has become a classic, Knapp and Dixon (1952) told university students who had no previous juggling experience to practice until they could make 100 consecutive catches while juggling three paddle-tennis balls. Results showed that students who followed a whole practice approach achieved this goal in sixty-five trials, whereas those who followed a part practice regime needed seventy-seven trials.

Continuous, discrete, and serial skills. Some researchers have used the skill classification system in which skills are classified as continuous, discrete, or serial, which we discussed in chapter 1, as a way to consider the complexity and organization characteristics of a motor skill. According to this approach, continuous and serial skills would be generally high in complexity but would differ in their levels of organization, although most would have a high level of organization because of the spatial-temporal relationships among the parts of these skills. Serial skills, on the other hand, will have levels of organization that vary according to the skill. Discrete skills are low in complexity because they consist of one identifiable part, which would put them at the high end of the organization continuum. Researchers who have investigated the whole-part practice issue on the basis of these skill classification categories have reported results that are generally consistent with the predictions described in the previous section for the relationship

between the complexity-organization characteristics of a skill and whether the skill should be practiced as a whole or in parts (for a review of this research, see Lee, Chamberlin, & Hodges, 2001).

PRACTICING PARTS OF A SKILL

The decision to use a part practice strategy unfortunately solves only part of the problem, because there are several different ways to implement a part practice approach to the practice of a skill. When selecting a part practice strategy, it is important to apply transfer of learning principles, which we discussed in chapter 13. Part practice strategies should involve positive transfer between and among the practiced parts of a task and between the practiced parts and the whole task.

In their important review of the research literature related to skill training methods, Wightman and Lintern (1985) classified three commonly used part-task strategies. One, called **fractionization,** involves practicing individual limbs first for a skill that involves the asymmetric coordination of the arms or legs. A second method, called **segmentation,** involves separating the skill into parts and then practicing the parts so that after the learner practices one part, he or she then practices that part together with the next part, and so on. Researchers also have called this method the *progressive part method* and the chaining method. A third method of part practice is called **simplification.** This method is actually a variation of a whole practice strategy and involves reducing the difficulty of the whole skill or of different parts of the skill.

Fractionization: Practicing Asymmetric Limb Coordination Skills

Many of the motor skills discussed throughout this text require people to simultaneously move their arms or legs to achieve a specific spatial and/or temporal goal. Recall from the discussion of coordination in chapter 5 that the coordination tendency is for the arms or legs to move spatially and temporally together. What this means in terms of part versus whole practice is that because of this coordination tendency, a skill that requires symmetric spatial-temporal coordination of the arms (e.g., the butterfly and breaststroke in swimming) or legs (e.g., the flutter kick for a crawl stroke in swimming or the leg movements for cross-country skiing) would be high in organization. As a result, a whole practice approach would be preferable. However, when the task requires the two arms or legs simultaneously to do *different* spatial and/or temporal movements (i.e., asymmetric coordination), the question of the use of a part practice strategy becomes more of an issue.

Because asymmetric coordination of the arms is more characteristic of motor skills than asymmetric coordination of the legs, we will address skills in this section that we referred to in chapter 7 as asymmetric bimanual coordination skills. Consider, for example, the simultaneous arm movements involved in the playing of many musical instruments, such as the guitar, violin, and accordion. Each requires the person to simultaneously produce distinctly

different movement patterns with each arm and hand. Other instruments, such as the piano and drums, may require this type of movement characteristic but also include simultaneous asymmetric movement of the legs. Sport skills such as the sidestroke in swimming and the tennis serve also involve this type of bimanual coordination. Is a part practice strategy the best approach for learning these types of skills, or would a whole practice approach be preferable? Some controversy exists among researchers, and there is evidence to support either approach (see Walter & Swinnen, 1994). If a part practice approach is used, the most appropriate strategy is *fractionization.*

For asymmetric bimanual skills, the fractionization strategy involves practicing each arm or hand individually before performing the skill bimanually. A relevant question related to the use of this strategy is this: Does it matter which arm or hand practices first? A feature of asymmetric bimanual coordination skills that is important to consider in answering this question is that one arm or hand will sometimes perform a movement, or sequence of movements, that is more difficult or complex than the other. For example, one hand may perform a movement that requires a higher degree of movement accuracy than the other, or one hand may perform a movement that involves more component parts. Research evidence (e.g., Sherwood,

---

fractionization   a part-task training method related to asymmetric coordination skills that involves practicing each arm or leg separately before performing with them together.

segmentation   a part-task training method that involves separating the skill into parts and then practicing the parts so that after one part is practiced, it is then practiced together with the next part, and so on; also known as the progressive part method.

simplification   a part-task training method that involves reducing the difficulty of specific parts or features of a skill.

A CLOSER LOOK

The Whole-Part Practice Decision for an Orthopedic Surgical Task

The training of surgeons involves teaching surgical tasks that require practice. Because these tasks vary in their complexity and organization characteristics, decisions concerning the use of whole or part practice procedures are essential to teaching surgeons to acquire the skills needed to perform these tasks. Researchers in Toronto, Canada (Dumbrowski, Backstein, Abughaduma, Leidl, & Carnahan, 2005), used this point of view to investigate the procedures used to train medical students to perform the surgical task of bone plating, which involves the immobilizing of a fractured bone by attaching a metal plate to it. The researchers addressed two questions: (1) Is it better to initially practice the bone-plating procedure by performing the whole procedure on each practice attempt or by practicing the individual skills that constitute the procedure? (2) If the answer to the first question is that a part practice strategy is preferable, then would a blocked or random practice schedule for the individual parts be better for learning?

The bone-plating surgical task: A task analysis by two orthopedic surgeons showed that the task is a serial task in which the parts are distinct, must be performed in a specific order, and are interrelated because each succeeding part depends on the performance of the preceding parts. The task analysis identified five parts: (1) sizing the plate and clamping it to the bone, (2) drilling six holes of precise depth and dimension in the bone, (3) measuring the depth of each drilled hole, (4) creating threading in the bone for the screws (called "bone tapping"), (5) inserting the screws.

Participants and practice procedures: Twenty-eight first- and second-year medical students who had no experience in the bone-plating procedure practiced the task on artificial ulna bones. They first watched a video of a surgeon performing the entire procedure and then performed one pretest trial of the entire procedure before they began a 60 min practice period.

Whole and part practice conditions: The students were assigned to one of three groups, one for each of the practice conditions: (1) *whole practice*—performed all five parts in sequence on each practice trial; (2) *blocked part practice*—practiced one part of the procedure three times in a 12 min session before practicing the next part; (3) *random part practice*—practiced each part of the procedure in random order in three 20 min sessions. Each student practiced each part three times during the practice session and received augmented feedback as needed from an orthopedic surgeon.

Posttests: The students performed the entire procedure one time immediately after the end of the 60 min practice session and then one more time 30 min later. They received no augmented feedback during the posttests.

Results: Of the several performance measures, a checklist of specific procedures and a final product evaluation (both were determined and evaluated by a panel of three skilled orthopedic surgeons) showed that whole practice led to the most improvement and best final product. Random part practice was next, although not statistically significantly different from whole practice, and blocked practice was third on both performance measures.

Recommendations for bone-plating surgery training: A whole practice strategy is recommended for the training of the bone-plating surgical procedure. However, if a part practice strategy is used, the parts should be practiced in a random order, which could be done by having a station for each part and having students randomly rotate through the stations after performing one trial at each station.

1994) suggests that practice should begin with the hand or arm that must perform the more difficult or complex movement.

An interesting exception to strict use of practicing each limb separately before performing the skill bimanually was an experiment by Kurtz and Lee (2003) in which participants learned an asymmetric bimanual polyrhythm task. The task simulates a situation that occurs in the playing of musical instruments when one hand plays one rhythmic

Whole and Part Practice Conditions That Facilitate the Learning of Bimanual Coordination Skills

Bimanual coordination skills that require each arm to simultaneously perform different movements are difficult to learn because of the tendency for the two arms to spatially and temporally move together. Walter and Swinnen (1994) discussed various training approaches that would facilitate learning to break this "habit" for skills that require different simultaneous arm movements. Their research involved a task that required participants to place each forearm on a lever on a tabletop and to move them simultaneously so that one arm made a one-direction elbow-flexion movement and the other made a two-direction elbow-flexion-extension movement in a criterion amount of time. Their research demonstrated that the following three techniques accomplished this learning goal.

Note that one involved part-task practice and two involved whole-task practice.

• **Fractionization.** The movement patterns were practiced separately for each arm and then with the two arms moving simultaneously.
• **Speed-based simplification.** Initial practice of the bimanual task was at a slower speed than the criterion; subsequent sets of trials involved the progressive increase of the speed until the criterion speed was practiced.
• **Augmented feedback.** Practice involved the two arms simultaneously moving and augmented feedback provided after each trial as KP (the acceleration-time traces for each limb) or KR (correlation values indicating the degree of between-arm relationship).

pattern while the other plays a different pattern, which is not uncommon for playing the piano or drums. Participants practiced a 2:3 polyrhythm for time cycles of 1.8 sec (i.e., 1,800 msec). To perform the polyrhythm correctly, the left hand taps two beats of equal time intervals (i.e., one every 900 msec) while the right hand tapped three beats of equal intervals (i.e., one every 600 msec). This means that the right hand made one tap 600 msec after the beginning of a cycle, then the left hand made one tap 300 msec later (i.e., 900 msec from the beginning), 300 msec later the right hand made its second tap, and 600 msec later, both hands made their final tap simultaneously.

Practice involved tapping according to a metronome sound. A part practice group practiced each hand separately; a whole practice group practiced both hands together every trial, and a part-whole practice group practiced each hand separately while listing to a metronome beat for both hands. Thus, unlike any of the experiments discussed earlier, in which participants practiced an asymmetric bimanual skill, the Kurtz and Lee experiment included a practice condition that involved unimanual part practice but with participants listening to the same

rhythmic pattern with which the whole practice group practiced. Results, which can be seen in figure 18.1, showed that whole and part-whole practice conditions led to the best transfer performance of the bimanual polyrhythm, which was without a metronome. Although these results differ from those of the typical fractionization type of practice, the discrete polyrhythmic characteristic of the skill may account for the difference. However, it is important to note that consistent with the fractionization practice strategy, the part-whole practice strategy used in the Kurtz and Lee experiment involved unimanual practice. The unique characteristic was that their unimanual practice included simultaneously hearing the rhythmic pattern of the bimanual task.

Segmentation: The Progressive Part Method
Although practicing individual parts can be helpful in learning a skill, the learner can experience difficulty later, when he or she has to put the part back together with the whole skill. One way to overcome this problem is to use the *progressive part method*. Rather than practicing all parts separately before putting them together as

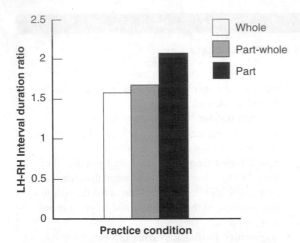

FIGURE 18.1   Results of the experiment by Kurtz and Lee in which three groups practiced a bimanual polyrhythm of two beats for the left hand (LH) and three beats for the right hand (RH) within a 1.8 sec interval. The LH-RH Interval Duration Ratio is the average performance of the left hand as a ratio relative to the right hand. A perfect polyrhythm performance is a 1.5 ratio. The graph shows the bimanual polyrhythm performance on the transfer test for groups that engaged in part-, part- and whole-, and whole-task practice prior to the transfer test. [Data from Kurtz, S., & Lee, T. D. (2003). Part and whole perceptual-motor practice of a polyrhythm. *Neuroscience Letters, 338,* 205–208, figure 3.]

a whole skill, the learner practices the first part as an independent unit, then practices the second part—first separately, and then together with the first part. In this way, each independent part progressively joins a larger part. As practice continues, the learner eventually practices the entire skill as a whole.

A common example of the progressive part method is a frequently used practice scheme for learning the breaststroke in swimming. The breaststroke is easily subdivided into two relatively independent parts, the leg kick and the arm action. Because a difficult aspect of learning the breaststroke is the timing of the coordination of these two parts, it is helpful for the learner to reduce the attention demands of the whole skill by practicing each part independently first. This enables the student to focus his or her attention to just the limb action requirements, because he or she can learn

each part without attending to how to coordinate the two parts as a unit. After practicing each part independently, the swimmer can put them together to practice them as a whole unit, with his or her attention now directed toward the temporal and spatial coordination demands of the arm and leg actions.

Skills that involve learning movement sequences lend themselves particularly well to the progressive part method. Researchers have demonstrated this for both laboratory and real-world skills. For example, Watters (1992) reported that the progressive part method was beneficial for learning to type an eight-key sequence on a computer keyboard. And Ash and Holding (1990) found that people learning a musical score on a piano benefited from a progressive part practice approach. In this experiment, participants learned a musical score of twenty-four quarter notes, grouped into three sets of eight notes. The first two segments were easy and the third segment was difficult. Two types of the progressive part method were better than the whole method for learning to perform this musical score, for which performance was based on errors made, rhythmic accuracy, and rhythmic consistency. Of the two progressive part methods, the one that prescribed an easy-to-difficult progression tended to be better than the one stipulating a difficult-to-easy progression.

A key characteristic of the progressive part method is that it takes advantage of the benefits of both part and whole methods of practice. The part method offers the advantage of reducing the attention demands of performing the whole skill, so that the person can focus attention on specific aspects of a part of the skill. The whole method, on the other hand, has the advantage of requiring important spatial and temporal coordination of the parts to be practiced together. The progressive part method combines both of these qualities. Thus, the attention demands of performing the skill are under control, while the parts are put together progressively so that the learner can practice important spatial and temporal coordination requirements of performing the parts as a whole.

A CLOSER LOOK

The Simplification Method for Learning Three-Ball Juggling

An experiment reported by Hautala (1988) demonstrated that beginning juggling practice by using easier objects is beneficial for learning to juggle three balls.

The participants were boys and girls ten to twelve years old with no previous juggling experience. All of them practiced 5 min per day for 14 days and then were tested for 1 min with the juggling balls.

The experiment compared four practice conditions:

1. Learners began practice using three "juggling balls" of three different colors.
2. Learners began practice using cube-shaped beanbags.
3. Learners followed a progressive simplification scheme:
   a. scarves of different colors
   b. beanbags
   c. juggling balls
4. Learners began practice using weighted scarves and then switched to the balls.

The results of the three-ball juggling test showed this:

• The beanbags practice condition led to the best test performance.

Note: The ball-juggling score for participants in the beanbag practice group was over 50 percent higher than those for the juggling balls group and the progression group, and over 100 percent higher than that of the group that practiced with weighted scarves and then beanbags before using the balls.

Simplification: Reducing Task Difficulty

For a complex skill, simplification can make either the whole skill or certain parts of the skill less difficult for people to perform. There are several ways to implement a simplification approach to skill practice. We will discuss six of these here. Each is specific to learning a certain type of skill. All of them involve practicing the whole skill, but simplify certain parts of the skill in various ways.

Reducing object difficulty. When a person is learning an object manipulation skill, one way to simplify learning the skill is to *reduce the difficulty of the objects.* For example, someone learning to juggle three balls can practice with scarves or bean bags. This reduces the difficulty of the task by involving objects that move more slowly and are therefore easier to catch. Because these objects move more slowly, the person has more time to make the appropriate movements at the right moments. However, the person still must follow the principles of juggling while learning to juggle the easier objects. We would expect early practice using easier objects to enable the person to learn

these juggling principles, and then easily transfer them to juggling with more difficult objects. In fact, research evidence supports this approach to learning to juggle three balls (Hautala, 1988).

Reducing attention demands. Another way to reduce task difficulty is to *reduce the attention demands of the skill without changing the action goal.* This strategy reduces task difficulty by reducing task complexity. One approach to implementing this strategy is to provide physical assistance devices that allow the person to practice the goal of the skill but at the same time reduce the attention demands of the task. For example, Wulf and her colleagues (Wulf, Shea, & Whitacre, 1998; Wulf & Toole, 1999) found that people who used ski poles while they practiced the slalom ski simulator task learned to perform the task without ski poles better than people who practiced without ski poles. The poles allowed the performers to focus more attention on the movement coordination demands of the task. This was possible because of the reduced attention demands for the dynamic balancing component of the task, which resulted from the poles

LAB LINKS

Lab 18 in the Online Learning Center Lab Manual provides an opportunity for you to develop part practice plans for a person who is learning or relearning a motor skill.

enabling better body stability. It is also notable that in these experiments, transfer from performing with poles to doing so without the poles led to no appreciable reduction in performance level.

Physical therapy researchers have reported a method for the rehabilitation of gait that reduces the attention demands of gait while maintaining requisite gait movements. The method involves the use of a *body-weight support (BWS) system,* which is a device that controls the amount of body weight a person needs to support while ambulating either on a treadmill or over ground. As shown in figure 18.2, the patient is placed in a harness device that is attached to pulley systems that lift the patient so that the patient is supporting only a specified amount of his or her own body weight. The BWS reduces the attention demand of gait by providing external control of the patient's posture and balance.

An example of the use and effectiveness of the BWS for gait rehabilitation is a case study of two elderly women who continued to experience chronic gait disabilities as a result of a stroke more than two years earlier (Miller, Quinn, & Seddon, 2002). The BWS was used to systematically increase the amount of body weight controlled by the participants themselves for three sessions a week for 6 to 7 weeks of gait training. During each session, the participants used the BWS for walking on a treadmill and overground. At the beginning of training, the BWS controlled 40 percent of the participants' body weight for each of three 5 min bouts of walking. Over the course of the training, the amount of body weight controlled was reduced to 20 and then 0 percent. In addition, various treadmill speeds were included in the training sessions. Results showed that both women

improved their overground walking in terms of technique and endurance. (To read a brief review of research involving BWS training and an experiment in which the system is successfully used with non-ambulatory stroke patients, see Yagura, Hatakenaka, & Miyai, 2006).

Reducing speed. A third simplification method is useful for the learning of complex skills requiring both speed and accuracy. *Reducing the speed* at which a learner first practices a skill can simplify practice. This approach places emphasis on the relative-time relationships among the skill components and on the spatial characteristics of performing the whole skill. Because a characteristic such as relative time is an invariant feature of a well-established coordination pattern and because people can readily vary overall speed, we would expect that a person could learn a relative-time pattern at a variety of overall speeds. By practicing at a slower speed, the learner would establish the essential relative-time characteristics of a coordination pattern.

It is interesting to note that the training strategy of reducing the speed of a task also benefits the learning of asymmetric bimanual coordination tasks in which each arm performs different spatial-temporal patterns but with the same overall duration of time. What makes this interesting is that in the earlier discussion about the fractionization training strategy, that strategy also facilitated the learning of this type of bimanual task.

Evidence for the beneficial effects of the speed-reduction strategy was provided in an experiment by Walter and Swinnen (1992). Participants practiced an asymmetric bimanual coordination task that required them to use one arm to move a horizontal lever in a one-direction elbow flexion movement while at the same time using the other arm to move a lever in a two-direction elbow flexion-extension movement. One group practiced two sets of twenty trials at reduced speeds before practicing the task at the criterion speed. The other group practiced all trials at the criterion speed. Transfer test results showed that the reduced-speed

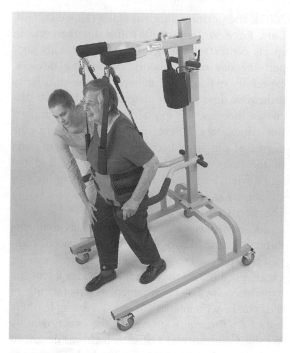

FIGURE 18.2   The Lite Gait body weight support system used in the study by Miller, Quinn, and Seddon. As it is shown here the system is being used for overground locomotion training; it can also be used with a treadmill. [Courtesy of Mobility Research, LLC, Tempe, AZ.]

training group learned to perform the task more accurately than the group that practiced the criterion speed only.

Adding auditory cues. Fourth, for skills having a distinct rhythmic characteristic, *providing auditory cues* that specify the appropriate rhythm works well to reduce task difficulty and facilitate a person's learning of the activity. This approach is especially interesting because it actually simplifies a task by adding an extra component to it. For example, musical accompaniment has been shown to assist Parkinson's disease patients with gait disorders while they practice walking. An example of research support for this simplification procedure was reported by Thaut et al. (1996). The researchers provided patients with Parkinson's disease with

an auditory device that consisted of audiotapes with metronome sounds embedded in instrumental music to designate the rhythmic structure and tempo (i.e., speed) of the music. The patients used the device as part of a three-week home-based gait-training program to pace their steps while walking. Compared to patients who did not use the device, the patients who trained with the auditory accompaniment showed greater improvement in their gait velocity, stride length, and step cadence. In addition, they accurately reproduced the speed of the last training tape without the assistance device. Since that initial study researchers have reported numerous experiments that support the use of auditory cues for gait therapy for Parkinson's disease patients as well as for patients with other movement disorders (e.g., Rochester, Burn, Woods, Godwin, & Nieuwboer, 2009; White, Wagenaar, Ellis, & Tickle-Degnen, 2009), and for therapy for reaching movements with a hemiparetic arm (Malcolm, Massie, & Thaut, 2009).

Sequencing skill progressions. The fifth strategy is related to the progressive part strategy discussed earlier. It involves the *sequencing of skill progressions,* which means that a person practices variations of the skill being learned in a sequence from less to more complex or difficult until the skill itself is practiced. For example, in the discussion in chapter 1 of Gentile's taxonomy of motor skills, we considered the following task sequence to help young baseball players learn to hit pitches thrown by a pitcher: first, hit baseballs off a tee at the same height; next, hit balls off a tee at different heights; then, hit balls thrown by a pitching machine; and finally, hit balls thrown by a pitcher.

The task progression strategy is commonly referred to in the physical education teaching literature (e.g., Rink, 1998). Also included in this strategy is the use of *lead-up games or activities.* Although the task progression strategy has not received strong research support, results of an experiment reported by Hebert, Landin, and Solmon (2000) provided evidence that supported the learning benefit for an easy-to-difficult task progression of four distances from the net to practice the tennis serve, with the first distance at the service line, and then progressing back to serving from the baseline. Interestingly, this study included a progressive part training condition for the tennis serve. Although the progressive part condition yielded positive results, an advantage of the task progression strategy was that it led to high success rates for students of low, middle, and high skill levels.

Simulators and virtual reality. Finally, *simulators and virtual reality (VR) environments* are technical devices that provide ways to simplify certain features of a skill to help people learn skills. These devices have several advantages: people can practice skills without concerns about the cost of accidents or performance errors that would characterize practice in real environments; practitioners can control specific aspects of the performance environments more easily than in real environments; and people can often practice for longer periods of time and with more intensity than they could in a real environment.

Simulators are devices that imitate vehicles, machines, or instruments. For example, automobile and truck simulators are commonly used to train people to drive these vehicles. The military uses a variety of simulators, such as those for airplanes, tanks, and submarines, to train personnel who will operate these vehicles. In sports, simulators include devices such as pitching machines in baseball and softball, ball machines in tennis, and rebounders in basketball. Simulators can be used for training purposes by providing practice experiences before operating the actual device or by providing a practice situation in which certain attention demands are reduced. You read in chapter 13 about an example of the use of a simulator; see the Closer Look box discussion of the study by Weeks et al. (2003) concerning the use of an arm prosthesis simulator to train patients who would be fitted with an actual prosthetic arm.

Research investigations of the effectiveness of simulators have been more common for their use as training devices to help people learn to drive cars (e.g., Fisher et al., 2002), pilot airplanes and helicopters (e.g., Stewart, Dohme, & Nullmeyer,

2002), and perform surgical skills (Howells, Gill, Carr, Price, & Rees, 2008) than for their use in sports contexts. In general, research results support the use of simulators as training devices, especially when they adhere to the similarity principles described in chapter 13 when we discussed theories that explain why transfer occurs. For simulators, these principles concern the degree of similarity between the component parts of the tasks required by the simulator and the real device, between the performance contexts or situations, and between the cognitive processing characteristics.

VR environments simulate real environments through the use of two- and three-dimensional computer graphics. The virtual environments can be experienced in real time, which provides a realistic experience in that environment without being in the actual environment. You saw an example of the use of a VR training strategy in the experiment by Wilson, Foreman, and Tlauka, which was described in chapter 13 in an A Closer Look discussion. In that experiment, VR training was used to familiarize participants with the spatial layout and objects in three floors of a building. Additional examples of VR training reported in the research literature have involved such diverse fields as sports, physical rehabilitation, surgery, and the military. These have included the following:

- Teaching a table tennis stroke (Todoroy, Shadmehr, & Bizzi, 1997)
- Creating individualized treatment exercises to augment dexterity task performance for poststroke patients (Merians et al., 2002)
- Training people to regulate their walking pace so they could walk down a hallway and through doors that were continually opening and closing, at the time the doors were open (Buekers, Montagne, de Rugy, & Laurent, 1999)
- Assessing and training inexperienced powered wheelchair users (Harrison et al., 2002)
- Train reaching behaviors in children with cerebral palsy (Chen, Kang, Chuang et al., 2007)

A CLOSER LOOK

Virtual Reality Training to Step over Obstacles Improves Walking for Poststroke Hemiplegic Patients

Researchers and physical therapists reported a study in which they compared stepping over real or virtual objects on a treadmill as an intervention strategy for poststroke patients with hemiplegia (Jaffe, Brown, Pierson-Carey, Buckley, & Lew, 2004). The intervention was considered an alternative training technique with a goal of improving walking and decreasing the risk for falls and subsequent injuries.

Participants: 20 adults (8 females, 12 males; mean age = 61.5 yr) who had a stroke more than six months earlier (mean = 3.7 yr poststroke); had a diagnosis of hemiplegia; could walk independently; had an asymmetric gait pattern; and a short step-length (lower than 95th percentile of a normal step-length).

Training Interventions: Participants were assigned to either a real or virtual training method. Training for both methods involved stepping over ten stationary objects while walking. Participants wore special "booties" that included contacts and switches for performance analysis purposes and for providing an audio tone to participants when they contacted an object. Each training session included twelve trials, which lasted approximately one hour. There were six sessions over a two-week period.

Real obstacle training: Participants wore a gait-belt and stepped over foam obstacles in a hallway. The obstacles were spaced at intervals of 15–22 in. The

obstacles were 2 × 2 in. square and ranged in height and length based on participants' leg lengths (maximum height = height of inferior border of the patella; maximum length = height of trochanter minus one-half maximum obstacle height).

Virtual obstacle training: Participants, who were held in place by an overhead harness, walked at a self-selected speed on a motorized treadmill while holding onto handrails. They wore a head-mounted display that showed real-time images of the same objects used in the real-obstacle training procedure. The display also provided a lateral view of the participants' legs, which allowed them to observe the position of their feet as they walked, monitor their knee flexion, time their toe-off, and control their stepping height and length.

Results: Performance was assessed by ten outcome measures related to balance, walking velocity, cadence, stride length, endurance, and obstacle clearance. At two weeks posttraining, both groups showed improved performance compared to their pretest performance, but the virtual-reality-trained participants performed better on six of the ten measures.

Conclusion: Virtual reality training can be more effective than real-object training for improving the capability to step over objects as well as various walking characteristics for people with poststroke hemiplegia.

- Training surgeons to perform laparoscopic surgery (Aggarwal, Grantcharov, Eriksen et al.; 2006 Gallagher et al., 1999)
- Training submarine officers to perform various ship-handling tasks (Hays & Vincenzi, 2000)

In each of these situations, the use of a VR environment provided an effective means of practice to either prepare people to perform the skills in a real environment, or augment physical practice in a real environment.

In a review of the "state of the art" for VR applications in physical rehabilitation, Holden (2005) described available equipment, a scientific rationale for the use of VR in physical rehabilitation, and research that has investigated the effectiveness of VR in physical rehabilitation. The areas of study reviewed in physical rehabilitation include stroke rehabilitation, brain injury, Parkinson's disease, orthopedic rehabilitation, balance training, wheelchair mobility, and functional activities of daily living. From this review, Holden concludes that people with disabilities are capable of learning in VR environments and that this learning successfully transfers to real-world environments. In an important extension to these conclusions, You et al. (2005) found evidence that VR training resulted not only in improved locomotor recovery but also in neurological benefits. Their fMRI results showed that the VR training induced a reorganization of brain cortex activation from an abnormal ipsilateral to a normal contralateral activation in the sensory-motor cortex, which they described as playing an important role in the recovery of locomotor function for people with chronic stroke.

A caution against using miming as a simplification method. A common practice in occupational therapy is to have patients mime task performance, or pretend they are performing a task. For example, rather than have a person reach for and grasp a glass of water and drink from it, the therapist asks the person to mime this complete action without the glass present. The problem with this approach is that different patterns of movement characterize the mimed and the real actions.

Mathiowetz and Wade (1995) clearly demonstrated these movement pattern differences for three different tasks for normal adults and adults with multiple sclerosis (MS). The three tasks were eating applesauce from a spoon, drinking from a glass, and turning pages of a book. The authors compared two different types of miming: with and without the object. For both the normal and the MS participants, the kinematic profiles for the three tasks revealed uniquely different characteristics for the real and the mimed situations.

Although this experiment and situation relate specifically to a specific patient population in a physical rehabilitation environment, the results have implications for all skill learning situations. When simplifying the practice of a skill, a therapist, teacher, or coach should have the person perform the natural skill. In each of the simplification methods described in the preceding section, this was always the case.

AN ATTENTION APPROACH TO INVOLVING PART PRACTICE IN WHOLE PRACTICE

Sometimes it is not advisable or practical to separate the parts of a skill physically for practice. This, however, does not mean that a learner cannot practice parts of the whole skill. It is possible to practice the whole skill, but focus attention on specific parts that need work. This approach provides both the advantage of part practice, where emphasis on specific parts of the skill facilitates improvement of these parts, and the advantage of whole practice, in which the emphasis is on how the parts of the skill relate to one another to produce skilled performance.

Both attention theory and research evidence support this attention approach. In Kahneman's model of attention, which was discussed in chapter 9, an important factor in attention allocation policy is called *momentary intentions*. When applied to a performance situation, this factor comes into play when a person focuses his or her attention on a specific aspect of the performance. Because we can manipulate our attention resources in this way, we can direct attention to a specific part of a skill while performing the whole skill.

An example of research evidence supporting the use of this attention-directing strategy for part practice is an experiment by Gopher, Weil, and Siegel (1989). Participants learned a complex computer game, known as the Space Fortress Game, that requires a person to master perceptual, cognitive, and motor skills as well as to acquire specific knowledge of the rules and game strategy. The player must shoot missiles at and destroy a space fortress. He or she fires the missiles from a movable spaceship, controlling spaceship movement and firing using a joystick and a trigger. To destroy the fortress, the player must overcome several obstacles, such as the fortress's rotating to face the spaceship to defend itself, protection of the fortress by mines that appear on the screen periodically and can destroy the spaceship if it runs into them, and so on (see Mané & Donchin, 1989, for a complete description of this computer game).

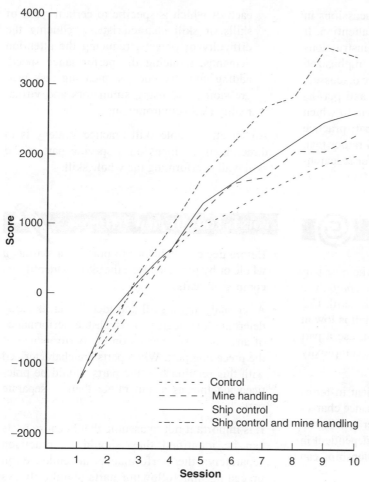

FIGURE 18.3 Results of the experiment by Gopher, Weil, and Siegel showing the change in performance on the computer game Space Fortress for attention-directing instructions related to specific parts of the skill. [Reprinted from Gopher, D. et al. (1989). Practice under changing priorities: An approach to the training of complex skills. *Acta Psychologica, 71,* 147–177, with kind permission of Elsevier Science-NL, Sara Burgerharstraat 25, 1055 KV Amsterdam, The Netherlands.]

In the experiment, three groups received instructions during the first six practice sessions that emphasized a strategy requiring them to direct attention to one specific component of the skill. One group's instructions emphasized focusing attention on controlling the spaceship. The second group's instructions emphasized focusing attention on handling the mines around the fortress. The third group received spaceship control instructions for the first three practice sessions and then mine-handling instructions for the next three sessions. When the researchers compared the performance of these three groups against that of a control group that had not received any strategic instructions, the effectiveness of the attention-directing instructions was evident. As you can see in figure 18.3, the control group improved with practice, but not as much as the three instruction groups did. And the group that received two different strategies outperformed those that received only one.

These results provide evidence that attention-directing instructions can serve to establish a part practice environment while allowing the person to practice the whole skill. And these instructions are more effective than having the person practice the skill without providing such strategies. An important connection needs to be made between the use of attention-directing instructions as a part-practice strategy and our discussions in chapters 9 and 14 about the focus of attention. It is notable that the attention-directing instructions for the computer game just discussed emphasized an external attention focus, which as we discussed, consistently results in better learning and performance than an internal focus. The extent to which attention-directing instructions as a part-practice strategy should emphasize an external rather than an internal focus remains a question for researchers to address.

each of which is specific to certain types of skills or skill characteristics: reducing the difficulty of objects, reducing the attention demands, reducing the performance speed, adding auditory cues, sequencing task progressions, and using simulators and virtual reality (VR) environments.

- An effective whole skill practice strategy is to direct attention focus on a specific part of the skill while performing the whole skill.

SUMMARY

- Make the initial decision to use a whole or part practice strategy on the basis of the *complexity* and *organization* characteristics of the skill. Use a whole practice strategy when the skill is low in complexity and high in organization; use a part practice when the skill is higher in complexity and is lower in organization.

- Parts of a skill that are interdependent in terms of their spatial and temporal performance characteristics should be practiced together as a "natural unit"; parts that are relatively independent in terms of their spatial-temporal relationships can be practiced separately.

- Three methods of part practice were discussed:

  1. *Fractionization* is the practicing of an individual arm or leg of an asymmetric coordination task involving the arms or legs and then practicing them together.

  2. *Segmentation* is a progressive part method that involves practicing parts in sequence such that the first part is practiced until it can be performed at a certain performance level and then the next part is added and practiced, and so on until the skill is practiced as a whole.

  3. *Simplification* involves simplifying parts of the skill, or of the whole skill. We considered several different simplification methods,

POINTS FOR THE PRACTITIONER

- Before deciding whether to practice a skill as a whole or by parts, analyze the skill to identify its component parts.

- After analyzing a skill and identifying its parts, determine the degree to which the performance of any one part depends on the performance of the preceding part. When parts are characterized with this relationship, the parts should be practiced together as a unit rather than as separate parts.

- It is important not to assume that because parts can be identified they should be practiced separately; the performance dependence on preceding and following parts should always direct the decision concerning which parts to practice separately and which parts to practice together.

- When the parts of a skill follow a specific sequence of movements, the preferred way to engage in part practice is the progressive-part method in which parts are practiced in sequence and become increasingly larger until the whole skill can be practiced in its entirety.

- When practicing the parts of a skill is not advisable or possible, consider ways to simplify the whole skill before engaging people in performing the skill as it would be performed in its real-world context.

- When the technology is available, simulator and virtual reality training provide excellent initial means of engaging people in practicing a skill before having them practice the skill as it would be performed in its real-world context.

- Directing attention to a part of a skill while performing the whole skill can be an effective way to correct errors for parts of a skill that should not be practiced as separate parts.

RELATED READINGS

Arias, P., & Cudeiro, J. (2008). Effects of sensory stimulation (auditory, visual) on gait in Parkinson's disease patients. *Experimental Brain Research, 186,* 589–601.

Chang, J. J., Tung, W. L., Wu, W. L., Huang, M. H., & Su, F. C. (2007). Effects of robot-aided bilateral force induced arm training combined with conventional rehabilitation on arm motor function in patients with chronic stroke. *Archives of Physical Medicine and Rehabilitation, 88,* 1332–1338.

Field-Fote, E. C. (2000). Spinal cord control of movement: Implications for locomotor rehabilitation following spinal cord injury. *Physical Therapy, 80,* 477–484.

French, K., Rink, J., Rikard, L., Mays, A., Lynn, S., & Werner, P. (1991). The effects of practice progressions on learning two volleyball skills. *Journal of Teaching in Physical Education, 10,* 261–274.

Gray, R. (2002). Behavior of college baseball players in a virtual batting task. *Journal of Experimental Psychology: Human Perception and Performance, 28,* 1131–1148.

Irwin, G., Hanton, S., & Kerwin, D. G. (2005). The conceptual process of skill progression development in artistic gymnastics. *Journal of Sports Sciences, 23,* 1089–1099.

Lamontagne, A., & Fung, J. (2004). Faster is better: Implications for speed-intensive gait training after stroke. *Stroke, 35,* 2543–2548.

Ng, M. F. W., Tong, R. K. Y., & Li, L. S. W. (2008). A pilot study of randomized clinical controlled trial gait training in subacute stroke patients with partial body-weight support electromechanical gait trainer and functional electrical stimulation: Six-month follow-up. *Stroke, 39,* 154–160.

Nilsen, D. M., Kaminski, T. R., & Gordon, A. M. (2003). The effect of body orientation on a point-to-point movement in healthy elderly persons. *American Journal of Occupational Therapy, 57,* 99–107.

Sveistrup, H., McComas, J., Thornton, M., Marshall, S., Finestone, H., McCormick, A., Babulic, K., & Mayhew, A. (2003). Experimental studies of virtual reality-delivered compared to conventional exercise programs for rehabilitation. *CyberPsychology & Behavior, 6,* 245–249.

INTERNET RESOURCES

- To read about a variety of virtual reality training examples, go to http://www.sciencedaily.com. In the Find box, type "virtual reality training." This will take you to a page on which you can select a large number of news stories about virtual reality as it relates to training a variety of skills.

- For information about juggling, as well as instruction that takes a whole practice approach to learning to juggle, go to http://www.cix.co.uk/~solipsys. Click on the Juggling link. This will take you to a page with several options on the topic of juggling, including a Tutorial link that takes you to a page of juggling instruction.

- To watch a television news story about the use of video games to train medical students go to http://abclocal.go.com/wtvd/story?section=news/health&id=5996041.

STUDY QUESTIONS

1. (a) Define the term "organization" as it relates to the relationship among the parts (or components) of a complex motor skill. (b) Give an example of parts of a skill that demonstrate a high degree of organization. Indicate why you consider these parts to be highly organized.

2. (a) How can you decide whether people would learn a skill best if they practiced it as a whole or in parts? (b) Give a motor skill example to show how to apply these rules.

3. Describe examples of how practitioners can apply the part practice methods of fractionization and segmentation to the practice of skills.

4. Describe three ways practitioners can apply the simplification method to the practice of skills.

5. What is virtual reality (VR) training? Why should it be considered related to the whole-part practice issue for learning motor skills?

6. Describe how you could apply an attention allocation policy factor in Kahneman's model of attention to practicing a motor skill as a means of implementing a type of part practice while practicing a whole skill. Give an example.

Specific Application Problem:
Select a motor skill that in your future profession you might help someone or a group of people learn.
(a) Describe this skill in terms of its component parts.
(b) Describe how each part relates to the part that precedes and/or follows it.
(c) You have been assigned to teach this skill to a group of people who have never performed it. Discuss how and why you would have them begin practicing the skill in parts or as a whole skill.

Mental Practice

Concept: Mental practice can be effective for learning and relearning skills and for preparing to perform learned skills.

After completing this chapter, you will be able to

- Define *mental practice* and describe the several forms it can take
- Describe two roles for mental practice in the learning and performance of motor skills
- Describe how mental practice can be used to aid skill learning and relearning in various settings
- Describe how mental practice can be used to aid performance preparation in various settings
- Discuss three hypotheses proposed to explain why mental practice is effective
- Discuss the meaning of the term *imagery ability* and how it relates to the effectiveness of mental practice

APPLICATION

Situations in which teachers, coaches, and therapists can apply mental practice range from helping a patient employ mental practice to relearn a skill to aiding a world-class athlete perform in a major competitive event. Consider the following three examples.

A gymnast is standing beside the floor exercise mat waiting to begin her routine. Before actually beginning that routine, the gymnast goes through the entire routine mentally, visualizing the performance of each part of the routine, from beginning to end. Following this, the gymnast steps onto the mat and begins the routine.

A stroke patient is having difficulty walking down a flight of stairs. After several failed attempts, the patient is becoming frustrated. The therapist tells the patient to stop practicing and instead to stand on the top step and mentally visualize and feel herself walking down

the stairs perfectly ten times in a row. The patient goes through the entire sequence mentally on each practice attempt. Following this procedure, the therapist has the patient go back to physically practicing this skill.

You are playing golf and have just hit a beautiful drive down the middle of the fairway. You would like to hit a few practice drives to try to reproduce and reinforce the swing that produced such a wonderful result. Although you can't do that, you *can* practice that swing mentally as you walk down the fairway to your next shot.

Notice that each of these three situations had a different goal for mental practice. The gymnast used mental practice to prepare for an immediate performance of a well-learned routine. The rehabilitation patient used mental practice to reacquire a skill. Finally, the golfer used a mental practice procedure to reinforce an appropriate action and thereby aid an upcoming performance of that action.

DISCUSSION

In the motor skill learning and performance literature, the term *mental practice* refers to the cognitive rehearsal of a physical skill in the absence of overt physical movements. We should not confuse this type of mental practice with meditation, which generally connotes an individual's engagement of his or her mind in deep thought in a way that blocks out awareness of what is happening to or around him or her. We can think of meditation as a form of mental practice; in fact, it seems to be a potentially effective means for enhancing physical performance.

In this discussion, we limit the term **mental practice** to mean active cognitive or mental rehearsal of a skill, where a person may think about the cognitive or procedural aspects of a motor skill or engage in visual or kinesthetic imagery of the performance of a skill or part of a skill. When a person engages in mental practice, an observer would notice no movement related to the skill. Mental practice may occur while a person observes another person live, another person on film or video, or himself or herself on film or video. Or it may occur without any visual observation at all.

When mental practice involves visual imagery, it can take the form of either internal or external imagery. In *internal imagery,* the individual approximates the real-life situation in such a way that the person actually "imagines being inside his/her body and experiencing those sensations which might be expected in the actual situation" (Mahoney & Avener, 1977, p. 137). During *external imagery,* on the other hand, the person views himself or herself from the perspective of an observer, as in watching a movie.

Although most discussions of the use of imagery as mental practice involve visual imagery, it is important to note that imagery can take the form of kinesthetic imagery. This form of imagery engages a person in feeling the movements of a skill. Unfortunately, there is very little research that has investigated the use of kinesthetic imagery. But the research available suggests that it can be an effective means of mental practice (e.g., Dickstein & Deutsch, 2007; Féry, 2003; Hall, Buckolz, & Fishburne, 1992). Because of our limited knowledge about kinesthetic imagery, discussions of imagery in this chapter will address visual imagery.

It is also important to note that the type of imagery involved in mental practice differs from the imagery that we discussed in chapter 10 as a memory strategy to enhance performance. The imagery associated with mental practice involves the person imagining himself or herself performing the actual skill, whereas the imagery described as a memory strategy is a metaphoric image in which the skill to be performed is mentally imagined as the movements of something like the skill—such as the mental image often suggested to help beginning swimmers learn the arm coordination pattern for the sidestroke by imagining that one arm reaches to pick an apple off the tree then brings the apple down to put it in a basket held by the other hand at waist level.

TWO ROLES FOR MENTAL PRACTICE

The study of mental practice as it relates to the learning and performance of motor skills follows two distinct research directions. One concerns the role of mental practice in the *acquisition* of motor skills. Here the critical question is how effective mental practice is for a person in the initial stages of learning or relearning a skill. The other research direction addresses how mental practice can aid in the *performance preparation* of a well-learned skill.

People use mental practice as a performance aid in two ways. You saw the first in the gymnast

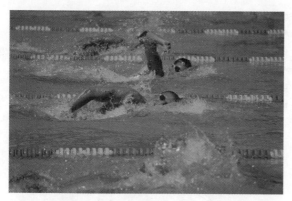

Swimmers often engage in mental practice before they begin a race.

LAB LINKS

Lab 19 on the Online Learning Center Lab Manual provides an opportunity for you to experience the influence of mental practice on motor skill learning and to compare it to physical practice and to a combination of mental and physical practice.

example in the Application section. The gymnast used mental practice to prepare for the immediately upcoming performance. When used this way, mental practice is *a means of action preparation.* You saw the second approach in the example of yourself as a golfer, mentally imaging a successful swing as you walked down the fairway. Here mental practice combines characteristics of both acquisition and performance situations by providing a person with *a means of facilitating the storage and retrieval from memory* of an appropriate action.

Beginning as early as the 1890s, research literature is replete with mental practice studies. Several excellent reviews of this research literature can be consulted for more specific information than will be discussed here (e.g., Dickstein & Deutsch, 2007; Martin, Moritz, & Hall, 1999). These reviews describe the convincing research evidence that supports the concept that mental practice is an effective strategy for aiding both skill acquisition and performance preparation.

MENTAL PRACTICE AIDS SKILL ACQUISITION

Research investigations of the effectiveness of mental practice in motor skill acquisition typically compare mental practice, physical practice, and no practice conditions. In general, results show that physical practice is better than the other conditions. However, mental practice is typically better than no practice. This finding alone is important, because it demonstrates the effectiveness of mental practice in aiding acquisition. Even more impressive is the effect of using *a combination of physical and mental practice.*

One of the more extensive comparisons of combinations of mental and physical practice was an experiment by Hird et al. (1991). The researchers compared six different physical and mental practice conditions. At one extreme was 100 percent physical practice, while at the other extreme was 100 percent mental practice. In between were practice routines requiring 75 percent physical and 25 percent mental practice, 50 percent physical and 50 percent mental practice, and 25 percent physical and 75 percent mental practice. The sixth condition required neither physical nor mental practice, but had participants doing a different type of activity during the practice sessions. Participants practiced two tasks. One required them to place as many round and square pegs in appropriately marked places in the pegboard as they could in 60 sec. The other was a rotary pursuit task in which the target moved in a circular pattern at 45 rpm for 15 sec.

mental practice the cognitive rehearsal of a physical skill in the absence of overt physical movements; it can take the form of thinking about the cognitive or procedural aspects of a motor skill, or of engaging in visual or kinesthetic imagery of the performance of a skill or part of a skill.

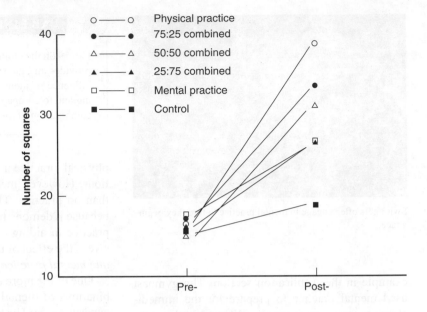

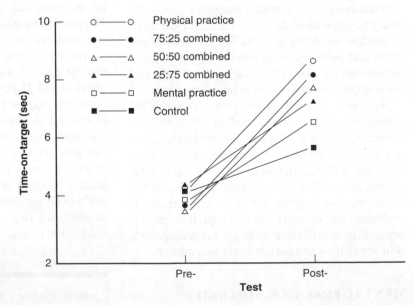

FIGURE 19.1 Results of the experiment by Hird et al. The top graph shows the pre- and posttest results for the different practice conditions for the pegboard task. The bottom graph shows results for the pursuit rotor task. [Reprinted by permission from Hird, J. S., Landers, D. M., Thomas, J. R., & Horan, J. J. (1991). Physical practice is superior to mental practice in enhancing cognitive and motor task performance. *Journal of Sport & Exercise Psychology, 13* (3), p. 288. Human Kinetics, Champaign, IL.]

Results of this experiment (figure 19.1) showed three noteworthy effects. First, consistent with other research findings was the result that mental practice alone was better than no practice for both tasks. Second, as the proportion of physical practice increased for both tasks, the level of posttest performance rose. Third, although physical practice alone was better than combinations of mental and physical practice, the differences were small.

A CLOSER LOOK

Imagery Training as a Posture Development Technique

Two experiments by Fairweather and Sidaway (1993) showed that imagery training can help people diagnosed with postural problems related to abnormal curvature of the spinal column. In one of these experiments, participants were seventeen-year-old males who regularly experienced low back pain and were assessed as having varying degrees of lordosis and kyphosis. The authors compared two different treatments. One involved flexibility and abdominal exercises; the other involved deep muscular relaxation exercises prior to kinesthetic awareness exercises and

visualization practice. The visualization technique consisted of creating images of four different action situations involving trunk, buttocks, pelvis, and thighs. For example, participants were told to visualize their buttocks as unbaked loaves of dough and watch them slide downward toward their heels. Results showed that following a three-week training period during which participants engaged in their respective techniques, both techniques led to improved postural form, as measured by spinal angles, and a reduction in back pain.

The relative similarity in learning effects between physical practice only and combinations of physical and mental practice has been a common finding in research. In fact, an experiment by Allami and colleagues (2008) in France included mental and physical practice combinations like those in the Hird et al. (1991) study and reported similar results. What is especially important to note is that the use of a combination of physical and mental practice often involves only half as many physical practice trials as physical practice only.

Why would a combination of mental and physical practice trials lead to learning effects that are as good as physical practice only? We can derive one answer to this question by considering some points discussed throughout this text about the need to engage in effective practice strategies. An important characteristic of effective strategies for optimizing skill acquisition is cognitive problem-solving activity. Physical practice appears not to be the only means of establishing these beneficial conditions. Mental practice can invoke them as well, although not to the same extent. However, the combination of physical and mental practice appears to establish a learning condition that can optimize these important characteristics.

Mental Practice Benefits
in Rehabilitation Settings

In addition to being beneficial for acquiring new skills, mental practice can be effective in

rehabilitation contexts for the relearning of skills, as well as for the improvement of skill performance. Examples of research concerning physical rehabilitation applications of the use and effectiveness of mental practice include poststroke patients (e.g., Dickstein, Dunsky, & Marcovitz, 2004; Liu, Chan, Wong et al., 2009; Page, Levine, & Leonard, 2005), elderly people with walking balance problems (e.g., Linden, Uhley, Smith, & Bush, 1989), teenagers with abnormal curvatures of the spine (Fairweather & Sidaway, 1993), and injured athletes (Christakou, Zervas, & Lavallee, 2007; Driediger, Hall, & Callow, 2006). The results of this research have consistently supported the functional skill rehabilitation benefit of mental practice, especially in the form of visual and kinesthetic imagery, along with physical practice.

For example, Page et al. (2005) engaged patients who had a stroke for more than one year in mentally practicing activities of daily living (ADLs) in addition to their regular physical performance of those activities during 30 min therapy sessions, two days a week for six weeks. A control group of similar patients practice relaxation techniques in addition to their physical performance of the activities. Results showed that the patients who participated in the mental practice protocol improved their use of their affected limb more than those in the control group.

Another example of research evidence for the effectiveness of mental practice for physical

Using Mental Practice in a Physical Therapy Treatment Program

A case study by Page, Levine, Sisto, and Johnson (2001) showed that when mental practice was combined with physical practice, it effectively complemented a physical therapy program for a 56-year-old male with upper-limb hemiparesis due to a subacute stroke five months earlier. The patient's arm function had not improved since he had been discharged from the hospital, where he had received 30 days of inpatient physical therapy. During the study, the patient received the following protocol:

- **Physical therapy:** Three times per week, in 1 hr segments, for 6 weeks. The exercises in each session involved the arms for 30 min and the legs for 30 min according to the neurodevelopmental treatment (NDT) method.
- **Mental practice:** Two times per week for 10 min in a quiet room 20 min after a physical therapy session; and two times per week at home. Following 2–3 min of relaxation activities, the

patient listened to an audiotape for 5–7 min. The tape included commands for the patient to see himself (external imagery) performing three functional tasks with the affected arm. Each task was mentally practiced for two weeks: reaching for and grasping a cup; turning pages of a large reference book; and reaching for and grasping an item on a high shelf and then bringing the item to himself.

Pretest and posttest comparisons showed the following results:

- Wrist and finger improvements, according to performance on the Fugl-Meyer Scale
- Grip, grasp, and pinch improvements, according to performance on the Action Research Arm Test (ARA)
- Improvements in 6 of the 10 items of the Stroke Rehabilitation Assessment of Movement (STREAM)

---

rehabilitation involved active athletes with grade II ankle sprains (Christakou, Zervas, & Lavallcc, 2007). One group of these athletes received 12 individual mental practices (i.e., imagery rehearsal) plus their regular course of physical therapy, while a second group received only the regular physical therapy treatment. The mental practice involved imagery of the same exercises experienced during the physical therapy treatment on each day. Results showed that the addition of mental practice to the athletes' regular physical therapy during the course of treatment improved muscular endurance more than the physical therapy alone.

Mental Practice Benefits for Power and Speed Training

A characteristic of many motor skills is the need to generate speed over relatively short distances. Sprint events in running, bicycling, and crew are examples of skills involving this characteristic. An experiment by Van Gyn, Wenger, and Gaul (1990) demonstrated that mental practice can be beneficial

for improving power for people learning a 40 m bicycle sprint. After being pretested on a bicycle ergometer (stationary bicycle) to determine peak power for a 40 m sprint, participants began three training sessions each week for six weeks on the bicycle ergometer to improve power performance. Two groups imaged themselves performing the sprint eight times. One of these groups did only the mental practice, whereas the other imagery group did imagery practice while they practiced physically. A third group received only the power training. A fourth group served as a control group by receiving neither the imagery nor the power training. The results showed the benefits of combining mental and physical practice. Only the group that received both the imagery and the power training showed an improvement in sprint times at the end of the six-week training period.

The training of movement speed has also been shown to be influenced by mental practice. For example, in two experiments by Louis and colleagues (2008) in France, participants practiced

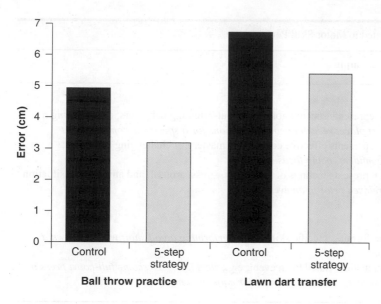

FIGURE 19.2 The results of the experiment by Lidor, Tennant, and Singer that show the comparison of using Singer's five-step strategy and not using the strategy (control) on performance during practice of an overhand ball throw to a target and during a transfer test involving an underhand lawn-dart throw to a target. [*Source:* Modification of figures 3 and 4 in Lidor, Tennant, & Singer (1996). *International Journal of Sport Psychology 27*, 23–36. Modified with permission.]

two tasks, one involving an upper body sequence, the other a lower body sequence. Included in the practice sessions were trials in which participants practiced at self-chosen speeds as well as at speeds that were faster and slower than those speeds. For mental practice, two groups engaged in visual internal imagery of performing the sequences: one group at a faster speed than their self-chosen speeds, the other at a slower speed. One week after the training period of 15 daily 30 trial sessions both groups were asked to perform the two sequences at a self-chosen speed. Interestingly, each group performed faster or slower than their original self-chosen speed, depending on which speed they mentally practiced during the sequences.

Mental Practice as a Part of a General Preparation Strategy That Aids Learning

We see an interesting example of incorporating mental practice into a practice routine in some work from Singer (1986, 1988). He proposed a five-step general learning strategy that involves elements of mental practice in three of the steps. The first step is to get ready physically, mentally, and emotionally. The second step involves mentally imaging performing the action, both visually

and kinesthetically. The third step involves concentrating intensely on only one relevant cue related to the action, such as the seams of a tennis ball. The fourth step is to execute the action. Finally, the fifth step is to evaluate the performance outcome.

Several studies have demonstrated the effectiveness of this general strategy for learning a specific skill. For example, Lidor, Tennant, and Singer (1996) compared people who used this strategy with those who didn't to learn a task involving ball-throwing accuracy. Participants sat on a chair 6 m from a target that was standing on the floor behind a badminton net that was 1.32 m high. The task required them to use an overhand motion to throw a ball over the net at the target. Points for each throw were awarded according to where the ball hit the target. However, for the assessment of performance for research purposes, the actual distance from the center of the target was calculated. The results, which are shown in figure 19.2, indicated that participants who engaged in the five-step general preparation strategy learned to perform the skill more accurately than those who did not use the strategy. It is interesting to note that the transfer test of learning in this study involved the same

TABLE 19.1   Five Types of Imagery Related to Motor Skill Performance

Imagery Type	Description/Example
Motivational	
(a) Specific	Imagery that represents specific goals and goal-orienting behaviors; e.g., *winning a medal for first place; receiving congratulations for a specific accomplishment*
(b) General mastery	Imagery that represents effective coping and mastery of challenging situations; e.g., *being confident; being focused*
(c) General arousal	Imagery that represents feelings of relaxation, stress, arousal, and anxiety in a situation; e.g., *being relaxed prior to an event*
Cognitive	
(a) Specific	Imagery of performing specific skills; e.g., *performing a golf shot; walking down a flight of stairs*
(b) General	Imagery of strategies related to an event; e.g., *strategy to overcome full-court press in basketball; strategy to organize items for cooking a meal*

Adapted from text of Martin, Moritz, & Hall (1999), p. 250.

strategy conditions to perform an underhand throw of a lawn dart from a distance of 3 m from a target mounted on a wall 1.3 m from the floor.

MENTAL PRACTICE AIDS PERFORMANCE PREPARATION

In their review of the research literature related to imagery use in sport, Martin, Moritz, and Hall (1999) described five types of imagery that athletes use for various purposes (see table 19.1). The specific situations in which athletes used imagery were in training periods between competitive events, immediately prior to and during a competitive event, and when they were rehabilitating an injury. Because it would be beyond the scope of this textbook to discuss the three motivational types of imagery, only the two cognitive types will be discussed in this chapter (for a more detailed discussion of motivational types of imagery, see Hall, Rodgers, & Barr, 1990; Murphy, 1994). With regard to the types of imagery described in the Martin et al. study, it is important to point out that although the study specifically addressed the use of imagery by athletes, you should not limit the use of imagery in these situations to athletes. The use of

imagery can benefit anyone engaged in a situation in which he or she must perform a practiced skill for evaluation purposes.

Surveys and anecdotal evidence indicate that athletes use imagery as part of their preparation strategies for a variety of purposes. Among these are arousal-level regulation, attention focus, and the maintenance of positive and confident feelings. This means that prior to competition, athletes tend to use the motivational types of imagery described in table 19.1. Unfortunately, because of the lack of controlled research investigations on the effectiveness of these imagery strategies, empirically based conclusions are not possible. The primary research problem is that in what would seem to be a simple investigation that compares athletes who use an imagery preparation strategy with those who don't, there are no established valid methods for determining if those in the imagery group actually used an imagery strategy, and if they did, what it involved. However, given this limitation, the Martin et al. (1999) review indicates that researchers have reported sufficient evidence to provide "tentative support" (p. 256) for the benefits of the use of imagery as an effective competition preparation strategy.

A CLOSER LOOK

The Relationship between Working Memory and Mental Practice in Stroke Patients

In a study of stroke patients carried out by researchers in Canada (Malouin, Belleville, Richards, Desrosiers, & Doyon, 2004), the verbal, visuomotor, and kinesthetic domains of working memory capabilities were compared to the effectiveness of a combination of physical and mental practice for stroke patients who had motor impairment on one side of their body (hemiparesis). The motor skill practiced was a stand-and-sit task. The motor performance characteristic of interest was the degree of symmetry of vertical forces for each leg, which was assessed by a force plate for each leg.

Working memory tests (standardized tests found in Spreen & Strauss, 1998): The experimenter presented a series of items which each patient had to reproduce immediately in the same order. The items for each type of test were

Verbal: Lists of two and three commonly used and easy to imagine monosyllabic words

Visuomotor: Experimenter tapped on a series of nine blocks randomly

Kinesthetic: Experimenter produced a series of gestures that involved unilateral and bilateral lower-limb movements; movements of the trunk, the intact upper limb, and the affected lower limb (e.g., lift the heel of the unaffected leg with the toes remaining in contact with the floor; flex the trunk forward and touch the affected ankle with the unaffected hand; bring the heel of the affected foot forward and the toes of the unaffected foot backward)

Motor performance task: Patients sat on a chair with each foot on a force plate. They were instructed to stand without using their hands until they heard a tone and then sit down. They were shown on a computer monitor the amount of vertical force that was overloaded on the unaffected leg and told to try to reduce that amount while increasing the amount on the affected leg.

Physical and mental practice: During a familiarization training session, patients performed the motor performance task and were asked to verbalize how they planned and executed the task. Practice involved a series of five-trial blocks of one physical practice trial followed by four mental practice trials, during which they closed their eyes while seated and imagined they were standing and sitting. They indicated to the experimenter when they began and ended each trial.

Results—mental practice effect: The patients improved the amount of force on the affected leg during their standing up and sitting down after just one session of mental practice combined with physical practice. This improvement was maintained one day later on a retention test.

Results—working memory relationship: The amount of improvement on the motor performance task was related to the patients' working memory capabilities. Patients with higher visuomotor working memory scores showed a greater amount of performance improvement. Patients who had impairments on at least two working memory domains had smaller amounts of motor task improvement and demonstrated no lasting improvement on the retention test.

WHY IS MENTAL PRACTICE EFFECTIVE?

At present, there are no comprehensive theories that explain why mental practice in the form of imagery is effective (see Martin et al., 1999, for a discussion of proposed explanations). However, there are three generally accepted hypotheses that propose why mental practice benefits the learning and performance of specific motor skills which we discuss next.

A Neuromuscular Hypothesis

We can trace the notion that mental practice of a motor skill has a neuromuscular basis to the work of Jacobson (1931). When he asked people to visualize bending the right arm, Jacobson observed EMG activity in the ocular muscle, but not in the biceps brachii. However, when he asked them to imagine bending the right arm and lifting a 10-lb weight, he noted EMG activity in the biceps brachii on more than 90 percent of the trials. Since Jacobson's early study, many other researchers have provided evidence for this type of electrical activity in the muscles of people asked to imagine movement (e.g., Bakker, Boschker, & Chung, 1996; Dickstein et al., 2005).

The creation of electrical activity in the musculature involved in a movement as a result of the performer's imaging of an action suggests that the appropriate neuromotor pathways involved in the action are activated during mental practice. This activation aids skill learning by helping establish and reinforce the appropriate coordination patterns that are so essential to develop. For someone performing a well-learned skill, this activation tunes, i.e., primes, the neuromotor pathways that will be activated when the person performs the skill. This tuning process increases the likelihood that the person will perform the action appropriately and reduces the demands on the motor control system as it prepares to perform the skill.

Brain Activity Hypothesis

The results of brain imaging studies have shown that when a person imagines moving a limb, brain activity is similar to when the person physically moves the same limb. Thus, as with the neuromuscular hypothesis, the brain activity hypothesis proposes that mental practice, especially in the form of imagery, is effective because of neurophysiological similarities between the imagined and the actual movements. An example of the research supporting this hypothesis is an experiment by Lafleur et al. (2002) in which PET scans showed changes in brain region activity as a result of mentally practicing a sequence of left-foot movements. At the beginning of training, brain activity associated with the physical execution of the movements was observed bilaterally in the dorsal premotor cortex and cerebellum, as well as in the left inferior parietal lobe. After training, these areas were no longer active but increased activity was observed bilaterally in the frontal cortex and striatum, as well as in the anterior cingulated and a different region of the inferior parietal lobe. The researchers observed similar patterns of brain activity when participants imagined the sequence of foot movements. In addition to these results based on the use of PET scans researchers who have used fMRI to investigate this issue have reported similar findings of the brain region activity relationship between imagined and actual movements (e.g., Ehrsson, Geyer, & Naito, 2003; Hanakawa, Dimyan, & Hallett, 2008; Page, Szaflarski, Eliassen, Pan, & Cramer, 2009).

A Cognitive Hypothesis

As you studied in chapter 12, researchers generally agree that the first stage of learning a motor skill involves a high degree of cognitive activity. Much of this activity is related to questions about "what to do" with this new task. It should not be surprising, then, that mental practice would be an effective strategy for people acquiring a new skill or relearning an old one. Mental practice can help the person answer many performance-related questions without the pressure that accompanies physical performance of the skill. In the later stages of learning, mental practice can be beneficial in assisting the person to consolidate strategies as well as to correct errors.

MENTAL PRACTICE AND IMAGERY ABILITY

Although researchers have proposed both physiological and psychological reasons for the effectiveness of mental practice for learning and performing motor skills, a related factor also might be operating. There is evidence indicating that the effectiveness of the use of imagery as a form of mental practice is related to a person's **imagery ability,** which is the ability to image an action when requested to do so. Some people have great difficulty imaging a described action, whereas others can image with a high degree of vividness and control.

A CLOSER LOOK

Examples of Movement Imagery Questionnaire (MIQ) Items

An Item from the Visual Imagery Subscale

Starting position: Stand with your feet slightly apart and your hands at your sides.

Action: Bend down low and then jump straight up in the air as high as possible with both arms extended above your head. Land with your feet apart and lower your arms to your sides.

Mental task: Assume the starting position. Form as clear and vivid a mental image as possible of the movement just performed. Now rate the ease/difficulty with which you were able to do this mental task.

An Item from the Kinesthetic Imagery Subscale

Starting position: Stand with your feet slightly apart and your arms at your sides.

Action: Jump upwards and rotate your entire body to the left such that you land in the same position in which you started. That is, rotate to the left in a complete (360 degree) circle.

Mental task: Assume the standing position. Attempt to feel yourself making the movement just performed without actually doing it. Now rate the ease/difficulty with which you were able to do this mental task.

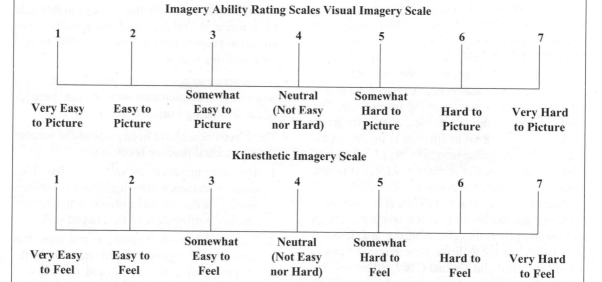

Imagery Ability Rating Scales Visual Imagery Scale

1	2	3	4	5	6	7
Very Easy to Picture	Easy to Picture	Somewhat Easy to Picture	Neutral (Not Easy nor Hard)	Somewhat Hard to Picture	Hard to Picture	Very Hard to Picture

Kinesthetic Imagery Scale

1	2	3	4	5	6	7
Very Easy to Feel	Easy to Feel	Somewhat Easy to Feel	Neutral (Not Easy nor Hard)	Somewhat Hard to Feel	Hard to Feel	Very Hard to Feel

Evidence demonstrating that imagery ability is an individual-difference variable comes from research using tests of movement imagery, such as the Movement Imagery Questionnaire (MIQ), a test of imagery ability designed specifically to apply to motor skill performance (Hall & Pongrac, 1983; Hall & Martin, 1997).[1] The MIQ consists of various action situations that a person is asked to physically perform. Then the person is asked to do one of two mental tasks, to either "form as clear and vivid a mental image as possible of the movement

[1]For a review of movement (motor) imagery ability measurement issues, tests, and relevant research, see McAvinue and Robertson (2008).

---

imagery ability   an individual-difference characteristic that differentiates people who can image an action with a high degree of vividness and control from people who have difficulty imaging an action.

just performed" or "attempt to positively feel yourself making the movement just performed without actually doing it." In this test, the first mental task is called "visual imagery," whereas the second mental task is called "kinesthetic imagery." After performing one of these mental tasks, the person rates how easy or difficult it was to do it. A person may be able to do both visual and kinesthetic imagery easily, do one easily and the other with difficulty, or do both with difficulty.

Because imagery ability is an individual-difference variable, Hall proposed that *imagery ability influences the success of mental practice.* People with a high level of imagery ability will benefit more readily from mental practice of motor skills than those with a low level. To test this hypothesis, Goss et al. (1986) selected people who were categorized from their MIQ scores as high visual/high kinesthetic (HH), high visual/low kinesthetic (HL), or low visual/low kinesthetic (LL). Before each practice trial of four complex arm movement patterns, participants kinesthetically imaged the movement about which they received instructions. The results supported the hypotheses, as the HH group performed the patterns to criterion in the fewest trials, with the HL group next, and the LL group taking the greatest number of trials to achieve criterion. Retention performance showed a similar effect.

Results such as those in the Goss et al. study have led some researchers to question whether the high and low imagery ability effects are due to differences in motivation or the ability to concentrate. An experiment by Lovell and Collins (2002) addressed this question by recording electroencephalograms (EEG) at various brain sites for males who were classified as high or low on movement imagery according to the MIQ. Because of the brainwave activity characteristics recorded during mental imagery across several practice sessions, the authors concluded that their results provided evidence that levels of movement imagery ability are not merely motivation or concentration effects, but relate to distinct neurological processing characteristics associated with the ability to produce mental movement images.

The importance of these experiments is that they support the hypothesis that a relationship exists between imagery ability and the effectiveness of mental practice. In addition, they demonstrate that people with low imagery ability can benefit from mental practice.

SUMMARY

Mental practice involves the cognitive rehearsal of a skill in the absence of overt physical movement.

- Mental practice can take the form of thinking about the cognitive or procedural aspects of a motor skill or seeing or feeling oneself performing a skill or part of a skill.

- Research evidence shows that mental practice can be effective as a practice strategy to facilitate the learning and relearning of motor skills and as an action preparation strategy to prepare to perform well-learned skills.

- As a practice strategy, mental practice works best when used in combination with physical practice of the skill being learned or relearned.

- Three hypotheses have been proposed to account for why mental practice is effective:

  1. The neuromuscular hypothesis is based on research evidence showing EMG recordings in muscles that would be involved in the actual physical performance of the imaged skill.

  2. The brain activity hypothesis proposes that similar brain regions are activated during the imagining of a movement and the physical execution of that movement. Evidence from research involving brain imaging techniques supports this hypothesis.

  3. The cognitive hypothesis points to the benefit of mental practice for answering questions concerning "what to do" that are prevalent during the first stage of motor skill learning.

- The ease or difficulty a person may have in using imagery as a form of mental practice is related to a person's imagery ability. However, regardless of a person's level of imagery ability, he or she can benefit from mental practice.

POINTS FOR THE PRACTITIONER

• Use mental practice as a supplement to physical practice for people who are initially learning a skill.

• Either internal or external imagery can be effective as forms of mental practice.

• To help people learn motor skills, emphasize the use of both visual and kinesthetic forms of imagery as mental practice.

• Expect some people to need training in how to mentally practice.

• When used to prepare to perform a skill just prior to its performance in a specific situation, mental practice can be used as a way to control anxiety levels and to prepare the specific strategies and/or movements required to perform the skill in the upcoming situation.

• Because individual differences exist in how people will engage in mental practice, provide opportunities for people to develop their own ways of implementing mental practice.

RELATED READINGS

Behrmann, M. (2000). The mind's eye mapped onto the brain's matter. *Current Directions in Psychological Science, 9,* 50–54.

Beilock, S. L., & Gonso, S. (2008). Putting in the mind versus putting on the green: Expertise, performance time, and the linking of imagery and action. *Quarterly Journal of Experimental Psychology, 61,* 920–932.

Boschker, M. S. J., Bakker, F. C., & Michaels, C. F. (2002). Effect of mental imagery on realizing affordances. *Quarterly Journal of Experimental Psychology, 55A,* 775–792.

Butler, A. J., & Page, S. J. (2008). Mental practice with motor imagery: Evidence for motor recovery and cortical reorganization after stroke. *Archives of Physical Medicine and Rehabilitation, 87* (12 Supplement 2), S2–11.

Cross, E. S., Hamilton, A. F. de C., & Grafton, S. T. (2006). Building a motor simulation de novo: Observation of dance by dancers. *NeuroImage, 31,* 1257–1267.

Druckman, D. (2004). Be all that you can be: Enhancing human performance. *Journal of Applied Social Psychology, 34,* 2234–2260.

Golomer, E., Bouillette, A., Mertz, C., & Keller, J. (2008). Effects of mental imagery styles on shoulder and hip rotations during preparation of pirouettes. *Journal of Motor Behavior, 40,* 281–290.

Holmes, P., & Calmels, C. (2008). A neuroscientific review of imagery and observation use in sport. *Journal of Motor Behavior, 40,* 433–445.

Jackson, P. L., Lafleur, M. F., Malouin, F., Richards, C., & Doyon, J. (2001). Potential role of mental practice using motor imagery in neurologic rehabilitation. *Archives of Physical Medicine and Rehabilitation, 82,* 1133–1141.

Jedic, B., Hall, N., Munroe-Chandler, K., & Hall, C. (2007). Coaches' encouragement of athletes' imagery use. *Research Quarterly for Exercise and Sport, 78,* 351–363.

Malouin, F., Richards, C. L., Durand, A., Descent, M., Poire, D., Fremont, P., Pelet, S., Gresset, J., & Doyon, J. (2009). Effects of practice, visual loss, limb amputation, and disuse on motor imagery vividness. *Neurorehabilitation and Neural Repair, 23,* 449–463.

Mulder, T., Zijlstra, S., Zijlstra, W., & Hochstenbach, J. (2004). The role of motor imagery in learning a totally novel movement. *Experimental Brain Research, 154,* 211–217.

Nordin, S. M., & Cumming, J. (2007). Where, when, and how: A quantitative account of dance imagery. *Journal of Motor Behavior, 40,* 390–395.

Ouillier, O., Jantzen, K. J., Steinberg, F. L., & Kelso, J. A. S. (2005). Neural substrates of real and imagined sensorimotor coordination. *Cerebral Cortex, 15,* 975–985.

Overdorf, V., Schweighardt, R., Page, S. J., & McGrath, R. E. (2004). Mental and physical practice schedules in acquisition and retention of novel timing skills. *Perceptual and Motor Skills, 99,* 51–62.

Ram, N., Riggs, S. M., Skaling, S., Landers, D. M., & McCullagh, P. (2007). A comparison of modeling and imagery in the acquisition and retention of motor skills. *Journal of Sports Sciences, 25,* 587–597.

Shanks, D. R., & Cameron, A. (2000). The effect of mental practice on performance in a sequential reaction time task. *Journal of Motor Behavior, 32,* 305–313.

Sidaway, B., & Trzaska, A. (2005). Can mental practice increase ankle dorsiflexor torque? *Physical Therapy, 85,* 1053–1060.

Smith, D., & Collins, D. (2004). Mental practice, motor performance, and the late CNV. *Journal of Sport & Exercise Psychology, 26,* 412–426.

INTERNET RESOURCES

• For a discussion about the "Effects of Mental Imagery on Athletic Performance," which includes a discussion on how to implement mental imagery as well as some links to related Web sites, go to a Web site developed by the highly respected Department of Psychology at Vanderbilt University at http://www.vanderbilt.edu/AnS/psychology/ health_psychology/mentalimagery.html.

- To read a sport psychologist's view of the importance of mental practice for preparing for a tennis competition go to http://www.tennisserver .com/mental-equipment/me_98_2.html.

- To learn about a dynamic imagery approach to learning and performing dance, yoga, and Pilates skills (known as the Franklin Method, developed by Eric Franklin), go to http://www.franklin-method.com/.

- To read a research article "Cerebral and cerebellar sensorimotor plasticity following motor imagery-based mental practice of a sequential movement" that reports the use of MRI to investigate brain region activity comparisons for physical and mental practice of a motor skill (the research was reported in 2004 by researchers at the Neuromotor Rehabilitation Research Laboratory and the Neuroimaging Research Laboratory of the Department of Veterans Affairs in Long Beach, California) go to http://www.rehab.research.va.gov/jour/04/41/ 4/absLacourse.html.

STUDY QUESTIONS

1. (a) Define *mental practice*. (b) Describe three ways in which a person can engage in mental practice.

2. Describe an example of how you would implement mental practice procedures to aid the learning of a new skill.

3. Describe an example of how you would implement a mental practice strategy to aid your preparation to perform a well-learned skill.

4. What are three reasons researchers have proposed to explain why mental practice aids motor skill learning and performance?

5. (a) Discuss what is meant by the term "imagery ability." (b) How does imagery ability relate to the effectiveness of mental practice?

Specific Application Problem:
In your place of employment in your future profession, your supervisor has asked you to develop a way for the people you are working with to use mental practice to help them either learn a skill or prepare to perform a skill or skills in a right-now situation. Describe the people you are working with, the skill or skills they are learning or preparing to perform, and the mental practice strategy (or strategies) you would recommend.

Glossary

Ability A general trait or capacity of an individual that is a determinant of a person's achievement potential for the performance of specific skills.

Absolute error (AE) The unsigned deviation from the target or criterion, representing amount of error. A measure of the magnitude of an error without regard to the direction of the deviation.

Acceleration A kinematic measure that describes change in velocity during movement; we derive it from velocity by dividing change in velocity by change in time.

Actions See *motor skills.*

Action effect hypothesis The proposition that actions are best planned and controlled by their intended effects. When related to attention focus, this hypothesis proposes that the learning and performance of skills are optimized when the performer's attention is directed to the intended outcome of the action rather than to the movements themselves.

Action preparation The activity that occurs between the intention to perform an action and the initiation of that action. Sometimes, the term *motor programming* is used to refer to this preparation activity.

Arousal The general state of excitability of a person, involving physiological, emotional, and mental systems.

Ascending tracts Sensory neural pathways in the spinal cord and brainstem that connect with the various sensory areas of the cerebral cortex and cerebellum.

Associative stage The second stage of learning in the Fitts and Posner model. An intermediate stage on the learning stages continuum.

Asymmetric transfer Bilateral transfer in which there is a greater amount of transfer from one limb than from the other limb.

Attention In human performance, characteristics associated with consciousness, awareness, and cognitive effort as they relate to the performance of skills with particular reference to the limitations associated with these characteristics on the simultaneous performance of multiple skills and the detection of relevant information in the performance environment.

Attentional focus The directing of attention to specific characteristics in a performance environment, or to action preparation activities.

Attractors The stable behavioral steady states of systems. In terms of human coordinated movement, attractors characterize preferred behavioral states, such as the in-phase and antiphase states for rhythmic bimanual finger movements.

Augmented feedback A generic term used to describe information about performing a skill that is added to sensory feedback and comes from a source external to the person performing the skill. It is sometimes referred to as extrinsic or external feedback.

Automaticity The term used to indicate that a person performs a skill, or engages in certain information-processing activities, without requiring attention resources.

Autonomous stage The third stage of learning in the Fitts and Posner model. The final stage on the learning continuum. Also called the *automatic stage.*

Axons Extensions from a neuron's cell body that transmit neural impulses to other neurons, structures in the CNS, or muscles; a neuron has only one axon, although most axons branch into many branches. Also called *nerve fibers.*

■

Basal ganglia A subcortical collection of nuclei (caudate nucleus, putamen, and globus pallidus) buried within the cerebral hemispheres; they play an important role in the planning and initiation of movement and the control of antagonist muscles during movement. Also known as the *basal nuclei.*

Bilateral transfer Transfer of learning that occurs between two limbs.

Bimanual coordination A motor skill that requires the simultaneous use of the two arms. The skill may require the two arms to move with the same or different spatial and/or temporal characteristics.

Biofeedback A type of augmented feedback that provides information about physiological processes through the use of instrumentation (e.g., EMG biofeedback).

Brainstem   A brain structure located directly under the cerebral hemispheres and connected to the spinal cord; it contains three areas that are significantly involved in motor control: the pons, medulla, and reticular formation.

∎

Central-resource theories of attention   Attention-capacity theories that propose one central source of attention resources for which all activities requiring attention compete.

Central vision   The middle 2 to 5 degrees of the visual field; it is sometimes called foveal vision.

Cerebellum   A brain structure located behind the cerebral hemispheres and attached to the brainstem; it is covered by the cerebellar cortex and is divided into two hemispheres; it plays a key role in the execution of smooth and accurate movements.

Cerebral cortex   The undulating, wrinkly, gray-colored surface of the cerebrum; it is a thin tissue of nerve cell bodies (about 2 to 5 mm thick) called gray matter.

Cerebrum   A brain structure in the forebrain that consists of two halves, known as the right and left cerebral hemispheres.

Choice RT   The reaction time when the situation involves more than one signal and each signal requires its own specified response.

Closed-loop control system   A system of control in which during the course of an action, feedback is compared against a standard or reference to enable an action to be carried out as planned.

Closed motor skill   A motor skill performed in a stable or predictable environment where the performer determines when to begin the action.

Cognitive mediation theory   A theory for explaining the benefit of a demonstration proposing that when a person observes a skilled model, the person translates the observed movement information into a cognitive code that the person stores in memory and uses when the observer performs the skill.

Cognitive stage   The first stage of learning in the Fitts and Posner model. The beginning or initial stage on the learning continuum.

Complexity   The number of parts or components and the amount of information-processing demands that characterize a skill. More complex skills have more component parts and involve more information processing demands than less complex skills.

Concurrent augmented feedback   Augmented feedback that is provided while a person is performing a skill or making a movement.

Cones   One of two types of photoreceptors in the retina; they detect bright light and play critical roles in central vision, visual acuity, and color vision.

Constant error (CE)   The signed (+/–) deviation from the target or criterion. It represents amount and direction of error and serves as a measure of performance bias.

Contextual interference   The memory and performance disruption (i.e., interference) that results from performing multiple skills or variations of a skill within the context of practice.

Contextual interference effect   The learning benefit resulting from performing multiple skills in a high contextual interference practice schedule (e.g., random practice), rather than practicing the skills in a low contextual interference schedule (e.g., blocked practice).

Continuous motor skill   A motor skill with arbitrary movement beginning and end points. These skills usually involve repetitive movements.

Control parameters   Coordinated movement control variables (e.g., tempo, or speed, and force) that freely change according to the characteristics of an action situation. According to the dynamic pattern view of motor control, when a control parameter is systematically varied (e.g., speed is increased from slow to fast), an order parameter may remain stable or change its stable state characteristic at a certain level of change of the control parameter.

Coordination   The patterning of body and limb motions relative to the patterning of environmental objects and events.

Coordinative structures   Functionally specific collectives of muscles and joints that are constrained by the nervous system to act cooperatively to produce an action.

Cornea   A clear surface that covers the front of the eye; it serves as an important part of the eye's optical system.

Cost-benefit trade-off   The cost (in terms of slower RT) and benefit (in terms of faster RT) that occur as a result of biasing the preparation of an action in favor of one of several possible actions (as opposed to preparing as if each possible action were equally probable).

∎

Deafferentation   A procedure that researchers use to make proprioceptive feedback unavailable (through surgically severing or removing afferent neural pathways involved in the movement). It also can result from injury, surgery, or disease to afferent neural pathways involved in proprioception.

Declarative knowledge   Knowledge about "what to do" in a situation; this knowledge typically is verbalizable.

Degrees of freedom   The number of independent elements or components in a control system and the number of ways each component can act.

Degrees of freedom problem   A control problem that occurs in the designing of a complex system that must produce a specific result. The design problem involves determining how to constrain the system's many degrees of freedom so that it can produce the specific result.

Dendrites   Extensions from a neuron's cell body that receive neural impulses from other neurons; a neuron may have none or as many as thousands of dendrites.

Descending tracts   Motor neural pathways that descend from the brain through the spinal cord.

Descriptive KP   A verbal knowledge of performance (KP) statement that only describes the error a person has made during the performance of a skill.

Diencephalon   A component of the forebrain located between the cerebrum and the brainstem; it contains the thalamus and hypothalamus.

Discrete motor skill   A motor skill with clearly defined movement beginning and end points, usually requiring a simple movement.

Discrimination RT   The reaction time when the situation involves more than one signal but only one response, which is to only one of the signals; the other signals require no response.

Displacement   A kinematic measure describing changes in the spatial positions of a limb or joint during the time course of the movement.

Distributed practice   A practice schedule in which the amount of rest between practice sessions or trials is relatively long.

Diversification   The learner's goal in the second stage of learning in Gentile's model for learning open skills in which learners acquire the capability to modify the movement pattern according to environmental context characteristics.

Dual-task procedure   An experimental procedure used in the study of attention to determine the amount of attention required to perform an action, or a part of an action. The procedure involves assessing the degree of interference caused by one task when a person is simultaneously performing another task.

Dynamic pattern theory   An approach to describing and explaining the control of coordinated movement that emphasizes the role of information in the environment and the dynamic properties of the body and limbs. It is also known as the dynamical systems theory.

Dynamic view of modeling   A theoretical view explaining the benefit of observing a skilled model demonstrate a skill. It proposes that the visual system is capable of automatically processing the observed movement in a way that constrains the motor control system to act accordingly, so that the person does not need to engage in cognitive mediation.

■

Electroencephalography (EEG)   The recording of brain activity by the detection of electrical activity in specific areas on the surface of the cortex by several surface electrodes placed on a person's scalp. Brain activity is recorded as *waves,* which are identified on the basis of the speed of the rhythmic activity.

Electromyography (EMG)   A measurement technique that records the electrical activity of a muscle or group of muscles. It indicates the muscle activity.

Encoding   A memory process involving the transformation of information to be remembered into a form that can be stored in memory.

Encoding specificity principle   A memory principle that indicates the close relationship between encoding and retrieval memory processes. It states that memory test performance is directly related to the amount of similarity between the practice and the test contexts; i.e., the more similarity, the better the test performance will be.

Environmental context   The supporting surface, objects, and/or other people involved in the environment in which a skill is performed.

■

Feedback   Information from the sensory system that indicates the status of a movement to the central nervous system. In a closed-loop system, feedback is used to make corrections to an ongoing movement.

Fine motor skill   A motor skill that requires control of small muscles to achieve the goal of the skill; typically involves eye-hand coordination and requires a high degree of precision of hand and finger movement.

Fitts' law   A human performance law specifying the movement time for an aiming action when the distance to move and the target size are known. It is quantified as $MT = a + b \log_2(2 D/W)$, where a and b are constants and W = target width, and D = distance from the starting point to the target.

Fixation/diversification   The learner's goals in the second stage of learning in Gentile's model. *Fixation* refers to the goal for learning closed skills in which learners refine movement patterns so that they can produce them correctly, consistently, and efficiently from trial to trial. *Diversification* refers to the goal for learning open skills in which learners acquire the capability to modify the movement pattern according to environmental context characteristics.

fMRI (Functional Magnetic Resonance Imaging)   A brain scanning technique that assesses changes in blood flow by detecting blood oxygenation characteristics while a person is performing a skill or activity in the MRI scanner. It provides clear images of active brain areas at a specified time and can provide quantitative information about the levels of brain region activity.

Foreperiod   In a reaction time paradigm, the time interval between a warning signal and the go signal, or stimulus.

Fractionization   A part-task training method related to asymmetric coordination skills that involves practicing each arm or leg separately before performing with them together.

Freezing the degrees of freedom   A common initial strategy of beginning learners to control the many degrees of freedom associated with the coordination demands of a motor skill (e.g., the person holds some arm joints rigid, i.e., "freezes" them, while performing the skill).

■

General motor ability hypothesis   A hypothesis that maintains that the many different motor abilities that exist in an individual are highly related and can be characterized in terms of a singular, global motor ability.

Generalized motor program (GMP)   The memory representation of a class of actions that share common invariant characteristics. It provides the basis for controlling a specific action within the class of actions.

Golgi-tendon organs (GTO)   A type of proprioceptor located in the skeletal muscle near the insertion of the tendons into the muscle; they detect changes in muscle tension, or force.

Gross motor skill   A motor skill that requires the use of large musculature to achieve the goal of the skill.

Guidance hypothesis   A hypothesis indicating that the role of augmented feedback in learning is to guide performance to be correct during practice. However, if it is provided too frequently, it can cause the learner to develop a dependency on its availability and therefore to perform poorly when it is not available.

■

Hick's law   A law of human performance stating that RT will increase logarithmically as the number of stimulus-response choices increases.

■

Identical elements theory   An explanation of positive transfer proposing that transfer is due to the degree of similarity between the component parts or characteristics of two skills or two performance contexts.

Imagery ability   An individual-difference characteristic that differentiates people who can image an action with a high degree of vividness and control from people who have difficulty imaging an action.

Index of difficulty (ID)   According to Fitts' law, a quantitative measure of the difficulty of performing a skill involving both speed and accuracy requirements. It is calculated as the $\log_2 (2 D/W)$, where W = target width, and D = distance from the starting point to the target.

Interneurons   Specialized nerve cells that originate and terminate in the brain or spinal cord; they function between axons descending from the brain and synapse on motor neurons, and between the axons from sensory nerves and the spinal nerves ascending to the brain.

Intertrial variability   An environmental context characteristic in Gentile's taxonomy of motor skills. The term refers to whether the regulatory conditions that exist for the performance of a skill in one situation or for one trial are present or absent in the next situation or trial.

Invariant features   A unique set of characteristics that defines a generalized motor program and does not vary from one performance of the action to another.

Iris   The eye structure that surrounds the pupil and provides the eye its color.

■

Joint receptors   A collection of various types of proprioceptors located in the joint capsule and ligaments; they detect changes in joint movement at the extreme limits of movement and position.

■

Kinematics   The description of motion without regard to force or mass; it includes displacement, velocity, and acceleration.

Kinetics   The study of the role of force as a cause of motion.

Knowledge of performance (KP)   A category of augmented feedback that gives information about the movement characteristics that led to a performance outcome.

Knowledge of results (KR)   A category of augmented feedback that gives information about the outcome of performing a skill or about achieving the goal of the performance.

KR-delay interval   The interval of time between the completion of a movement and the presentation of augmented feedback.

■

Learning   A change in the capability of a person to perform a skill. It must be inferred from a relatively permanent improvement in performance as a result of practice or experience.

Lens   The transparent eye structure that sits just behind the iris; it allows the eye to focus at various distances.

Limbic system   A group of brain structures consisting of parts of the frontal and temporal lobes of the cerebral cortex, the thalamus and hypothalamus, and the nerve fibers that interconnect these parts and other CNS structures; it is involved in the learning of motor skills.

Long-term memory   A component system in the structure of memory that serves as a relatively permanent storage repository for information.

Manual aiming skills   Motor skills that involve arm, hand, and/or finger movements to a target; e.g., putting a key into a keyhole, threading a needle with thread, and typing on a computer keyboard.

Massed practice   A practice schedule in which the amount of rest between practice sessions or trials is very short.

Mental practice   The cognitive rehearsal of a physical skill in the absence of overt physical movements; it can take the form of thinking about the cognitive or procedural aspects of a motor skill, or of engaging in visual or kinesthetic imagery of the performance of a skill or part of a skill.

Modeling   The use of demonstration as a means of conveying information about how to perform a skill.

Motor ability   An ability that is specifically related to the performance of a motor skill.

Motor control   The study of how our neuromuscular system functions to activate and coordinate the muscles and limbs involved in the performance of a motor skill. Researchers may investigate this question while a person is learning a new skill or performing a well-learned or highly experienced skill.

Motor development   The study of human development from infancy to old age with specific interest in issues related to either motor learning or motor control.

Motor equivalence   The capability of the motor control system to enable a person to achieve an action goal in a variety of situations and conditions (e.g., writing your signature with either hand).

Motor learning   the study of the acquisition of motor skills, the performance enhancement of learned or highly experienced motor skills, or the reacquisition of skills that are difficult to perform or cannot be performed because of injury, disease, and the like. Of interest are the behavioral and/or neurological changes that occur as a person learns a motor skill and the variables that influence those changes.

Motor neurons   Nerve cells that send neural impulses from the CNS to skeletal muscle fibers. Also called *efferent neurons*.

Motor program   A memory representation that stores information needed to perform an action.

Motor skills   Activities or tasks that require voluntary head, body, and/or limb movement to achieve a goal.

Motor unit   The alpha motor neuron and all the muscle fibers it innervates; it serves as the functional unit of motor control for the innervation of the muscles involved in a movement.

Motor unit recruitment   The process of increasing the number of motor units needed to increase the number of muscle fibers active at any one time and so increase the amount of force the muscle can exert.

Movements   Behavioral characteristics of specific limbs or a combination of limbs that are component parts of an action or motor skill.

Movement time (MT)   The interval of time between the initiation of a movement and the completion of the movement.

Multiple-resource theories   Theories of attention proposing that there are several attention resource mechanisms, each of which is related to a specific information-processing activity and is limited in how much information it can process simultaneously.

Muscle spindles   A type of proprioceptor consisting of specialized muscle fibers that lie within the fibers of most skeletal muscles; they detect changes in muscle length.

Negative transfer   The negative effect of prior experience on performance of a skill, so a person performs the skill less well than he or she would have without prior experience.

Neuron   A nerve cell; the basic component of the nervous system.

Nonlinear behavior   A behavior that changes in abrupt, nonlinear ways in response to systematic linear increases in the value of a specific variable (e.g., the change from smooth to turbulent water flow in a tube at a specific increase in water velocity; the change from a walking to a running gait at a specific increase in gait velocity).

Nonregulatory conditions   Characteristics of the performance environment that do *not* influence the movement characteristics required to achieve an action goal.

Observational learning   Learning a skill by observing a person performing the skill. Also known as *modeling*.

Open-loop control system   A control system in which all the information needed to initiate and carry out an action as planned is contained in the initial instructions to the effectors.

Open motor skill   A motor skill that involves a nonstable unpredictable environment where an object or environmental context is in motion and determines when to begin the action.

Optic chiasm   The place near the base of the brain where the optic nerve fibers meet and either continue to the same side or cross over to the opposite side of the brain.

Optic nerve   Cranial nerve II; it serves as the means of information transmission from the retina to the brain.

Optical flow   The patterns of rays of light that strike the retina of the eye that emanate from and are specific to objects and features in the environment.

Order parameters   Functionally specific variables that define the overall behavior of a system. They enable a coordinated pattern of movement to be reproduced and distinguished from other patterns (e.g., relative phase). Known also as collective variables.

Organization   When applied to a complex motor skill, the relationships among the components of the skill.

Overlearning   Practice that continues beyond the amount needed to achieve a certain performance criterion.

■

Parameters   Features of the generalized motor program that can be varied from one performance of a skill to another. The features of a skill that must be added to the invariant features of a generalized motor program before a person can perform a skill to meet the specific movement demands of a situation.

Parietal lobe   An area of the cerebral cortex that plays an important role in the control of voluntary movement, such as the integration of movement preparation and execution processes, by interacting with the premotor cortex, primary motor cortex, and SMA before and during movement.

Parkinson's disease   A basal ganglia disorder caused by the lack of production of the neurotransmitter dopamine by the substantia nigra; the disease is characterized by slow movements (bradykinesia), a reduced amount of movement (akinesia), tremor, and muscular rigidity.

Perception-action coupling   The spatial and temporal coordination of vision and the hands or feet that enables people to perform eye-hand and eye-foot coordination skills; that is, the coordination of the visual perception of the object and the limb movement required to achieve the action goal.

Performance   The behavioral act of executing a skill at a specific time and in a specific situation.

Performance bandwidth   In the context of providing augmented feedback, a range of acceptable performance error. Augmented feedback is given only when the amount of error is greater than this tolerance limit.

Performance curve   A line graph describing performance in which the level of achievement of a performance measure is plotted for a specific sequence of time (e.g., sec, min, days) or trials. The units of the performance measure are on the Y-axis (vertical axis) and the time units or trials are on the X-axis (horizontal axis).

Performance outcome measures   A category of motor skill performance measures that indicate the outcome or result of performing a motor skill (e.g., how far a person walked, how fast a person ran a certain distance, or how many degrees a person flexed a knee).

Performance plateau   While learning a skill, a period of time in which the learner experiences no improvement after having experienced consistent improvement. Typically, the learner then experiences further improvement with continued practice.

Performance production measures   A category of motor skill performance measures that indicate the performance of specific aspects of the motor control system during the performance of an action (e.g., limb kinematics, force, EEG, EMG, etc.).

Peripheral vision   The visual field outside the 2 to 5 degrees of central vision.

Plasticity   Changes in neuronal activity in the brain that are associated with shifts in brain region activation; these changes are commonly associated with behavioral changes or modification

Point-light technique   A research procedure used to determine the relative information people use to perceive and identify coordinated human actions. It involves placing LEDs or light-reflecting material on certain joints of a person, then filming or videotaping the person performing an action. When an observer views the film or video, he or she sees only the joints in action.

Positive transfer   The beneficial effect of previous experience on the learning or performance of a new skill, or on the performance of a skill in a new context.

Post-KR interval   The interval of time between the presentation of augmented feedback and the beginning of the next trial.

Power law of practice   A mathematical law describing the change in rate of performance improvement during skill learning. Large amounts of improvement occur during early practice, but smaller improvement rates characterize further practice.

Practice variability   The variety of movement and context characteristics a person experiences while practicing a skill.

Prehension   The action of reaching for and grasping an object that may be stationary or moving.

Premotor area   A cerebral cortex area located in the frontal lobe just anterior to the primary motor cortex.

Prescriptive KP   A verbal knowledge of performance (KP) statement that describes errors made during the performance of a skill and states (i.e., prescribes) what needs to be done to correct them.

Primary motor cortex   A cerebral cortex area located in the frontal lobe just anterior to the central sulcus; it contains motor neurons that send axons to specific skeletal muscles throughout the body.

Proactive interference   A cause of forgetting due to activity that occurs prior to the presentation of information to be remembered.

Procedural knowledge   Knowledge that enables a person to know "how to do" a skill; this knowledge typically is difficult to verbalize or is not verbalizable.

Proprioception   The perception of limb, body, and head movement characteristics. Afferent neural pathways send to the central nervous system proprioceptive information about characteristics such as limb movement direction, location in space, and velocity.

Proprioceptors   Sensory neurons located in the muscles, tendons, ligaments, and joints. These neurons pick up information about body and limb position and changes in position.

Psychological refractory period (PRP)   A delay period during which a person seems to put planned action "on hold" while executing a previously initiated action.

Pupil   The opening in the eye that lets in light; its diameter increases and decreases according to the amount of light detected by the eye.

■

Qualitative augmented feedback   Augmented feedback that is descriptive in nature (e.g., using such terms as *good, long*), and indicates the quality of performance.

Quantitative augmented feedback   Augmented feedback that includes a numeric value related to the magnitude of a performance characteristic (e.g., the speed of a pitched baseball).

■

Reaction time (RT)   The interval of time between the onset of a signal (stimulus) and the initiation of a response.

Recall test   An explicit memory test that requires a person to produce a required response with few, if any, available cues or aids.

Recognition test   An explicit memory test that requires a person to select a correct response from several alternative responses.

Regulatory conditions   Characteristics of the environmental context that determine (i.e., "regulate") the required movement characteristics needed to perform an action.

Relative phase   An index of the coordination between two limb segments or limbs during the performance of a cyclic movement. It is based on calculating the phase angles for each limb segment or limb at a specific point in time and then subtracting one phase angle from the other. Relative phase ranges from 0 (or 360 degrees), which indicates an in-phase relationship between the limb segments or limbs, to 180 degrees, which indicates an antiphase (or out-of-phase) relationship.

Relative time   The proportion, or percentage, of the total amount of time required by each component of a skill during the performance of that skill.

Response time   The time interval involving both reaction time and movement time; that is, the time from the onset of a signal (stimulus) to the completion of a response.

Retention test   A test of a practiced skill that a learner performs following an interval of time after practice has ceased.

Retina   The eye structure that lines the back wall of the eye; as an extension of the brain, it contains the neuroreceptors that transmit visual information to the brain.

Retrieval   A memory process involving the search through long-term memory for information needed to perform the task at hand.

Retroactive interference   A cause of forgetting due to activity occurring during the retention interval.

Rods   One of two types of photoreceptors in the retina; they detect low levels of light and are important for peripheral vision.

Root-mean-squared error (RMSE)   An error measure used for continuous skills to indicate the amount of error between the performance curve produced and the criterion performance curve for a specific amount of time during which performance is sampled.

■

Schema   A rule or set of rules that serves to provide the basis for a decision. In Schmidt's schema theory, an abstract representation of rules governing movement.

Sclera   The firm, white capsule of the eye; we commonly call the anterior portion of it the "white" of the eye.

Segmentation   A part-task training method that involves separating the skill into parts and then practicing the parts so that after one part is practiced, it is then practiced together with the next part, and so on. Also known as the progressive part method.

Selective attention   In the study of attention as it relates to human learning and performance, the term used to refer to the detection and selection of performance-related information in the performance environment.

Self-organization   The emergence of a specific stable pattern of behavior due to certain conditions characterizing a situation rather than to a specific control mechanism organizing the behavior; for example, in the physical world hurricanes self-organize when certain wind and water temperature conditions exist.

Sensory cortex   Cerebral cortex area located posterior to the central sulcus; it includes several specific regions that receive sensory information transmitted via the sensory nerves specific to that type of information.

Sensory neurons   Nerve cells that send neural impulses to the CNS. Also called *afferent neurons*.

Serial motor skill   A motor skill involving a series of discrete skills.

Simple RT   The reaction time when the situation involves only one signal (stimulus) that requires only one response.

Simplification   A part-task training method that involves reducing the difficulty of specific parts or features of a skill.

Skill   (a) An activity or task that has a specific purpose or goal to achieve. (b) An indicator of quality of performance.

Specificity of motor abilities hypothesis   A hypothesis that maintains that the many motor abilities in an individual are relatively independent.

Speed-accuracy trade-off   A characteristic of motor skill performance in which the speed at which a skill is performed is influenced by movement accuracy demands. The trade-off is that increasing speed yields decreasing accuracy, and vice versa.

Stability   A behavioral steady state of a system that represents a preferred behavioral state and incorporates the notion of invariance by noting that a stable system will spontaneously return to a stable state after it is slightly perturbed; the influence on skill performance of perturbations, which are internal or external conditions that can disrupt performance.

Stimulus-response compatibility   A characteristic of the spatial arrangement relationship between a stimulus and a response. The degree of compatibility influences the amount of preparation time in a reaction time task involving stimulus and response choices.

Stroop effect   A type of stimulus-response compatibility situation in which a color's name and ink are the same or different. RT for saying the word is faster when both are the same color than if the word is a different ink color.

Supplementary motor area (SMA)   A cerebral cortex area located on the medial surface of the frontal lobe adjacent to portions of the primary motor cortex.

Symmetric transfer   Bilateral transfer in which the amount of transfer is similar from one limb to another, no matter which limb is used first.

■

Task-intrinsic feedback   The sensory feedback that is naturally available while performing a skill.

Taxonomy   A classification system organized according to relationships among the component characteristics of the group of items or objects being classified.

Terminal augmented feedback   Augmented feedback that is provided after a person has completed the performance of a skill or the making of a movement.

Transcranial magnetic stimulation (TMS)   A non-invasive method of assessing brain activity that involves a short burst (referred to as a pulse) of a field of magnetic waves directed at a specific area of the cortex. This pulse of magnetic activity temporarily disrupts the normal activity in that area of the brain, which allows researchers to observe behavior when that area is not fuctioning.

Transfer-appropriate processing theory   An explanation of positive transfer proposing that transfer is due to the similarity in the cognitive processing characteristics required by the two skills or two performance situations.

Transfer of learning   The influence of having previously practiced or performed a skill or skills on the learning of a new skill.

Transfer test   A test in which a person performs a skill that is different from the skill that he or she practiced or performs the practiced skill in a context or situation different from the practice context or situation.

■

Variable error (VE)   An error score representing the variability (or conversely, the consistency) of performance.

Velocity   A kinematic measure describing the rate of change of an object's position with respect to time. It is derived by dividing displacement by time (e.g., m/sec, km/hr).

Verbal cues   Short, concise phrases that direct a performer's attention to important environmental regulatory characteristics or that prompt the person to perform key movement components of skills.

Vigilance   Maintaining attention in a performance situation in which stimuli requiring a response occur infrequently.

Visual field   The image or scene being viewed; it typically extends approximately 200 degrees horizontally and 160 degrees vertically.

Visual search   The process of directing visual attention to locate relevant information in the environment that will enable a person to determine how to perform a skill in a specific situation.

Visual selective attention   The process of engaging vision in directing attention to specific environmental information (i.e., cues) that influence the preparation and/or performance of an action. It is selective because the specific cues attended to must be chosen from among other possible cues in the performance environment. The selective attention process may be active or passive.

■

Working memory   A functional system in the structure of memory that operates to temporarily store and use recently presented information; it also serves as a temporary workspace to integrate recently presented information with information retrieved from long-term memory to carry out problem-solving, decision-making, and action-preparation activities.

References

References can be found at www.mhhe.com/magill9e.

Name Index

Abahnini, K., 128
Abernethy, B., 104, 124, 125, 126, 131, 164, 210, 217, 284, 313, 324
Abughaduma, R., 414
Acocella, J., 205, 283
Ada, L., 273
Adamovich, S. V., 115
Adams, J. A., 224, 225, 262, 316, 355
Aggarwal, R., 421
Albert, F., 113
Alberts, J., 144
Alcott, A., 378
Allami, N., 431
Allard, F., 102, 130
Allen, D., 217
Allen, J. B., 37
Allen, J. S., 230
Allen, T. J., 113
Allport, D. A., 201, 236
Almasbakk, B., 276
Alpenfels, E., 295
Amazeen, E. L., 159
Amazeen, P. G., 104, 159
Amos, B., 189
Anderson, D. I., 85, 273, 299, 301, 357
Anderson, J., 156
Anderson, J. R., 229
Anderson, L. P., 317
Anderson, S. W., 230
Annesi, J. J., 337, 348
Annett, J., 354, 355, 401
Anson, J. G., 176
Archambault, P. S., 109
Arnold, R. K., 348
Aronson, E., 119
Ashford, D., 311
Ascherleben, G., 110
Ash, D. W., 416
Atkinson, R. C., 223

Audiffren, M., 183
Avener, A., 428

Backstein, D., 414
Baddeley, A. D., 223, 224, 400
Bahill, A. T., 162, 163
Baker, K., 156
Bakker, F. C., 436
Balanchine, G. 283
Balkin, T. J., 180
Bandura, A., 317, 318
Banz, R., 336
Barba, D. A., 40, 363
Barbieri, G., 118
Bard, C., 116, 208, 211, 212
Bardy, B., 98, 100, 120, 153
Barr, K. A., 434
Barrett, R., 201
Barrow, H. M., 50
Bart, O., 321
Bartlett, F., 90
Bartlett, R. M., 42
Barton, J. W., 410
Basso, D. M., 364
Battig, W., 376–377
Bavelier, D., 217
Bear, M. F., 40, 121
Beardshall, A., 180
Beatty, J., 74
Berlucchi, G., 280
Beauchamp, M. S., 315
Beek, P. J., 159
Bekkering, H., 209
Belleville, S., 435
Benedetti, C., 358
Bengtsson, S. L., 75
Bennett, S., 42, 159, 160, 311
Ben-Shoham, I., 278, 279

Berg, W. P., 155
Bergenheim, M., 113
Berger, H. J., 240
Berkinblit, M., 115
Berman, A. J., 114, 116
Berman, M. G., 223
Bernstein, N., 86, 87, 146, 273, 276
Bertram, C. P., 347
Bezodis, N., 206
Bilodeau, I. M., 356
Bingham, G. P., 126
Bird, A. M., 318
Bird, G., 386
Bizzi, E., 114, 404, 420
Bjork, R. A., 380, 381, 385
Black, C., 401
Blais, C., 325, 326
Blake, R., 311
Blandin, Y., 319
Bloedel, J. R., 144
Blouin, J., 115
Blum, L., 51
Blurton, B., 199
Bock, O., 172, 294
Bohlhalter, S., 71
Boivin, K., 128
Bollinger, M., 336
Bonnetblanc, F., 183
Boone, J., 336
Bootsma, R. J., 131, 145, 164
Boschker, M. S. J., 436
Botvinick, M., 119
Boucher, J. P., 276
Boulter, L. R., 356
Bouzid, N., 401
Bowen, K. F., 130
Boyadijan, A., 118
Boyce, B. A., 364
Boyd, L. A., 71, 325
Brace, D. K., 50

Subject Index